COMPANY LAW
AND
GOVERNANCE

COMPANY LAW
AND
GOVERNANCE

AN AUSTRALIAN PERSPECTIVE

Sandra Berns
Paula Baron

Melbourne

OXFORD UNIVERSITY PRESS

Oxford   Auckland   New York

OXFORD UNIVERSITY PRESS AUSTRALIA

Oxford New York
Athens Auckland Bangkok Bogota
Bombay Buenos Aires Calcutta
Cape Town Dar es Salaam Delhi
Florence Hong Kong Istanbul Karachi
Kuala Lumpur Madras Madrid Melbourne
Mexico City Nairobi Paris Port Moresby
Singapore Taipei Tokyo Toronto Warsaw

and associated companies in
Berlin Ibadan

OXFORD is a trade mark of Oxford University Press

© Sandra Berns and Paula Baron 1998
First published 1998

National Library of Australia
Cataloguing-in-Publication data:

Berns, S. S. (Sandra Spelman).
  Company law and governance: an Australian perspective.

Includes index.
ISBN 0 19 553795 5.

1. Corporation law — Australia. 2. Corporate
governance — Australia. I. Baron, Paula. II. Title.

346.94066

Edited by Lucy Davison
Indexed by Max McMaster
Text designed by Anitra Blackford
Cover designed by Anitra Blackford
Cover photograph supplied by The Photo Library —
  Sydney/David Noton Photography
Typeset by Desktop Concepts P/L, Melbourne
Printed by McPherson's Printing Group, Australia
Published by Oxford University Press,
253 Normanby Road, South Melbourne, Australia

BRIEF CONTENTS

v

CONTENTS

Part 3: The Corporate State

Part 4: The Corporate (T)rader

Part 5: Problems of Power

PREFACE

Company Law and Governance originated in our fascination with the corporate regulatory regime's continuing inability to influence more than tangentially the entities that it purports to regulate. As we explored—both in our teaching and in our research—the ramifications of corporate law doctrines, we were increasingly struck by the fact that corporate regulators and corporations seemed to occupy parallel universes. In addition to the regulatory regime's inability to resolve problems that had been present since the birth of modern corporate law in the nineteenth century, much corporate law scholarship appears to have failed to come to terms with central doctrines such as the nature of corporate personality and the notion of the 'interests of the company'.

Two further complications compounded these threshold conceptual difficulties. First, company law is at best an untidy beast. It has been cobbled together from bits of partnership, trust, and contract law, and has been given a statutory overlay in recurring efforts to 'catch up' at the tail end of economic cycles. Thus, by its very nature, it does not lend itself to any straightforward conceptualisation, nor does it yield a simple set of 'rules'.

Second, the matter is further complicated by a substantial 'mismatch' between law and reality. The 'legal company', for want of a better term, is a very different beast from the company as portrayed by management literature on the nature of the firm. Over the years, this 'mismatch' has had a number of significant regulatory consequences. While these consequences can sometimes be glimpsed within that body of doctrine conventionally identified as 'company law' (especially in the doctrinal category known as 'lifting the corporate veil'), they are most strikingly apparent when the company is viewed as a legal subject.

We hope that this book will go some way towards remedying this situation. We have tried to relate the doctrinal framework of company law to the social and economic context in which companies operate. We have also paid more attention than is usual in expositions of corporate law to the company's response to the regulatory regimes impacting upon it. We believe that this is appropriate given the provisions of the *Corporations Law 1990*, s. 161, which states that the company enjoys all of the rights *and duties* of a natural person. This provision has profound implications for our legal system, in that regulatory regimes designed for 'natural persons' are unable to deal effectively with corporate persons.

This perspective is particularly apparent in the chapters on corporate responsibility, on women, and on the problems associated with the regulation of corporate groups. While examination of some of these areas is not conventional in corporate law, we believe that it is essential that the company–community interface be explored. The issues that arise in these areas highlight the problematical nature of a number of the conventional legal doctrines associated with corporate law. In this way, they provide valuable pointers for reform and for redirection.

Because the approach we have taken to corporate law is unconventional, some brief remarks about our own frame of reference and the paradigms within which we work are in order. Both Paula Baron and I have backgrounds in philosophy and political theory as well as in law. As a consequence, and because we believe that it is a matter of profound social importance, we are intensely interested in the way in which corporations are both like and unlike other members of society and other collective entities. An overall concern with social justice issues animates our work, intensifying our concern about the legal system's apparent inability to devise an effective regulatory regime. From within the feminist post-structuralist frame of reference within which we are most at home, it is natural for us to view the corporation as simultaneously a product of the liberal political order and an actor within that order. We hope that our readers find our work provocative as well as useful in providing an overall understanding of the relationship between the legal system and the corporate citizens among us.

While this has been an essentially collaborative work, responsibility for particular chapters can be allocated as follows. I have maintained overall editorial responsibility and responsibility for ensuring that the book came together as a whole. Paula was primarily responsible for chapters 1–4, 9–10, and 13–15. I was primarily responsible for chapters 5–8, 11–12, and 16–17. I would like to extend my thanks to my co-author, Paula Baron. As always, collaborating with Paula has been a joy. We would both also like to extend particular thanks to Tom Kennedy for his research assistance and for the insights into management literature that he provided, and to Carol-Ann Bois for editorial assistance. Last, but by no means least, we thank our partners, children, and pets (not necessarily in that order) for their patience as we struggled to finish this work.

We hope that our readers will be encouraged to think about how we can best live with the companies among us. Much important work remains to be done in this area.

Sandra Berns
Brisbane
August 1997

ABBREVIATIONS

A 2d	*Atlantic Reporter*
A & E	Adolfus and Ellis
AAS	Australian Accounting Standards
AASB	Australian Accounting Standards Board
AAT	Administrative Appeals Tribunal
ABLR	*Australian Business Law Review*
AC	Appeal Cases
ACLC	Australian Company Law Cases
ACLR	Australian Company Law Reports
ACN	Australian company number (or *Australian Corporate News*)
ACSR	*Australian Companies and Securities Reporter*
AD	*Australian Digest*
A Fem LJ	*Australian Feminist Law Journal*
AJCL	*Australian Journal of Company Law*
ALB	*Aboriginal Law Bulletin*
ALJ	*Australian Law Journal*
ALJR	Australian Law Journal Reports
All ER	All England Reports
ALR	Australian Law Reports
ALRC	Australian Law Reform Commission
Am Ec R	*American Economics Review*
AMPL	Asbestos Mines Pty Ltd
ARBN	Australian registered body number
ASX	Australian Stock Exchange
ASC	Australian Securities Commission
ASCR	Australian Securities Commission Reports
ATC	Australian Tax Cases
Atk	Atkyns

ATPR	Australian Trade Practices Reports
Aus Bar Rev	*Australian Bar Review*
Aus Con Rep	Australian Constitutional Reports
BCC	British Company Cases
BCLB	Butterworths Company Law Bulletin
BCLC	British Company Law Cases
BNZ	Bank of New Zealand
Bro CC	Brown's Reports of Cases in Chancery
Bus and Prof Ethics J	*Business and Professional Ethics Journal*
Bus Law	*Business Law*
Calif LR	*California Law Review*
Campb	Campbell's Reports
Carth	Carthew
CEO	chief executive officer
Ch	Chancery
Ch Cas	Chancery Cases
Ch D	Chancery Division
Ch P	Chancery Practice
Chi L Rev	*Chicago Law Review*
CLC	Australian Company Law Cases
CLJ	*Cambridge Law Journal*
CLR	Commonwealth Law Reports
Co Director	*Company Director*
Co Rep	Coke's Reports
Col LR	*Columbia Law Review*
Corp & Bus LJ	*Corporation and Business Law Journal*
CPD	Law Reports Common Pleas Division 1875–80
CSLJ	*Company and Securities Law Journal*
CSLRC	Companies and Securities Law Review Committee
Dalhousie LJ	*Dalhousie Law Journal*
Dick	Dickens
DLR	Dominion Law Reports (Canada)
East	East's Term Reports King's Bench 1800–12
ER	English Reports
Ex D	Exchequer Division
Exch	Exchequer
F	Federal Reports (USA)
F 2d	Federal Reports (USA)
FCR	Federal Court Reports
Finch Rep Temp	Finch's Reports Temporary
FLR	Federal Law Reports
Geo L Rev	*Georgia Law Review*
Geo LJ	*Georgia Law Journal*

Geo Washington LR	*George Washington Law Review*
GNP	gross national product
Griffith LR	*Griffith Law Review*
H & M	Hemming's and Miller's Reports Exchequer 1856–62
Hare	Hare's Chancery Reports
Harv LR	*Harvard Law Review*
Hastings LJ	*Hastings Law Journal*
HLC	Clark's House of Lords Cases
HMSO	Her Majesty's Stationery Office
ICAC	Interstate Corporate Affairs Commission
ICR	Irish Circuit Reports
Illinois LR	*Illinois Law Review*
Insol LJ	*Insolvency Law Journal*
JCLC	*Journal of Criminal Law and Criminology*
J Ec Studies	*Journal of Economic Studies*
J Fin and Ec	*Journal of Finance and Economics*
J Corp Law	*Journal of Corporate Law*
KB	King's Bench
L Ed	*Lawyer's Edition*
LBO	leveraged buyout
Lev	Levinz
LJ Bky	Law Journal Reports Bankruptcy
LJ CH	Law Journal Chancery
LJ (OS)	Law Journal
Lloyd's Rep	Lloyd's Reports
Loyola of Los Angeles LR	*Loyola of Los Angeles Law Review*
LQR	*Law Quarterly Review*
LR Eq	Law Reports Equity
LR QB	Law Reports Queen's Bench
LT	*Law Times*
Macq	Macquarie
Man & G	Manning and Granger
Meg	Megone's Company Cases
Michigan LR	*Michigan Law Review*
Minn L Rev	*Minnesota Law Review*
MLR	*Modern Law Review*
MNC	multinational corporation
Mod	Modern
MULR	*Melbourne University Law Review*
NCSC	National Companies and Securities Commission
Neb	Nebraska
NJ	New Jersey
NSWLR	New South Wales Law Reports

NSWR	New South Wales Reports
NW	Northwestern Reports
NYS	New York State
NZJL	*New Zealand Law Journal*
NZLR	New Zealand Law Reports
NZULR	*New Zealand Universities Law Review*
OHLJ	*Osgoode Hall Law Journal*
OSHA	Occupational Safety and Health Administration
P	Probate
P 2d	Pacific Reports
P Wms	Peere William's Reports Chancery 1695–1735
PCAs	persons in their corporate aspects
Penn L Rev	*Pennsylvania Law Review*
QB	Queen's Bench
QBD	Queen's Bench Division
Qd R	Queensland Reports
QTL	Queensland Television Ltd
QUTLJ	*Queensland University of Technology Law Review*
Russ	Russell and Mylne's Reports 1829–31
S Calif LR	*Southern California Law Review*
SALR	South Australian Law Reports
SASR	South Australian State Reports
SC	Session Cases
Show PC	Shower's Privy Council Reports
Sim	Simmon's and Stuart's PC Reports 1678–95
SJ	*Solicitor's Journal and Reporter*
SR (NSW)	State Reports (New South Wales)
St R Qd	State Reports Queensland
Stan L Rev	*Stanford Law Review*
Syd LR	*Sydney Law Review*
TLR	Times Law Reports
TNC	transnational company
TPA	*Trade Practices Act 1974* (Cth)
TR	Dunlow and East's Term Reports
U Chicago LR	*University of Chicago Law Review*
U Cin LR	*University of Cincinnati Law Review*
U Pitt L Rev	*University of Pittsburgh Law Review*
U Toronto LJ	*University of Toronto Law Journal*
UNSWLJ	*University of New South Wales Law Journal*
US	United States
UTLR	*University of Tasmania Law Review*
UWALR	*University of Western Australia Law Review*
Va LR	*Virginia Law Review*

Vand LR	*Vanderbilt Law Review*
Ves	Vesey Junior's Reports
Ves Sen	Vesey Senior's Reports
Virg L Rev	*Virginia Law Review*
VLR	Victorian Law Reports
VR	Victorian Reports
WALR	Western Australia Law Reports
WAR	Western Australian Reports
Wash LR	*Washington Law Review*
Wheat	Wheaton's Reports
Wisconsin LR	*Wisconsin Law Review*
WLR	Weekly Law Reports
WN	Weekly Notes
WN (NSW)	Weekly Notes (New South Wales)
Y & C Ex	Younge and Collyer (Exchequer, Equity)
Yale LJ	*Yale Law Journal*
YB	Year Books

TABLE OF CASES

Australia

Canada

USA

TABLE OF STATUTES

Commonwealth

ACT

New South Wales

Northern Territory

Queensland

USA

PART 1

BODY AND SOUL

PERSONALITY PLUS?

Introduction

Pick up any company law textbook, and you will probably find that it follows a customary pattern. It will begin by considering the history of the corporate form, or the legal process and consequences of incorporation, and particularly the legal repercussions of personality. These texts will tell you how the contemporary company form came into being, why people choose to conduct their businesses as companies—rather than, say, as partnerships or trusts—and how companies can sue, be sued, and own property. These are important issues both for those involved in commerce and for those who advise them.

But a number of unaddressed questions are hidden beneath this customary narrative. Possibly this is because such questions are assumed to be relatively unproblematic or, at least, irrelevant to the business at hand. How is a corporation to be defined? Does the term 'corporation' mean different things in different contexts, and if so, why? How do our values and beliefs create and re-create our ideas of corporate behaviour and regulation? How can—and, more importantly, why—should a company be equated in law with a living person? How can that proposition be justified?

Perhaps there is another reason that basic company texts rarely explore these issues in any depth. Companies are extraordinarily complex organisations: in their legal conception; in the webs of interests, rights, and obligations that they create; in their social, economic, and political effects; and in the moral and ethical dilemmas that they pose. In a sense, our ability to give a simple definition of what a 'company' is, and to treat limited liability and legal personality as 'givens' (even as controversial 'givens'), allows us to proceed with business. We can think about the problem at hand, whether it be the issue of directors' duties or the rights of shareholders in a takeover, without being drowned in the linguistic and conceptual intricacies of 'companies'.

At the same time, it is our inability, or perhaps our reluctance, to deal with these issues and with this inherent complexity that renders company regulation so susceptible to criticism. The Australian corporate regulatory scheme has been criticised for being inefficient and outdated. Since the inception of legislative regulation of companies, this scheme has essentially changed very little (despite a virtual torrent of legislative reform), while companies themselves have changed a great deal:

> The corporation is a remarkable institution. It has proved functional for the accumulation of financial and material capital, for the organisation both for and of production, and for the marshalling of diverse persons and interests in the pursuit of common purpose(s), purposes that often, if not typically, are worked out or identified through internal corporate processes. Most economic (production and exchange) activity is organised through the corporate form. The corporation is a mode of decision making and of defining reality and values. As a human institution, the corporation manifestly figures in the power structure and belief system of society. It is both a product of and a contributor to power structure and to belief system [*sic*]. The corporation is an evolving phenomenon, a participant in change with regard to both power structure and belief system. As a mode of organizing human activity and focusing the human belief system, the modern corporation, or the modern corporate system, has substantially replaced the church as the principal rival of government in Western society and also augurs eventually to rival the nation state system in what we still refer to, increasingly anachronistically, as international relations. Yet there exists both a symbiotic and a conflictual relationship between the corporation (or the corporate system) and the government.[1]

This chapter seeks to offer some alternative definitions of the company. We want to consider the meaning of legal personality, to identify the reasons for, and implications of, the designation of the company as a legal person, and to identify some of the theoretical approaches to companies, and the implications of these for corporate governance. We will try to focus on the multiplicity of meanings, interests, players, rights, and obligations that are created by corporate forms and by the fact that a company is not a static, but an evolving, phenomenon.[2]

Defining the company

Potentially there are many definitions of the term 'company'. 'Company' is, to a large extent, a 'catch-all' term. In reality, companies differ dramatically in size, function, and purpose. They may be large or small, function in a hierarchical or a democratic way, and pursue primarily one or many business interests. They may be classified according to whether they are public or private, on the basis of their mem-

---

1   W. J. Samuels, 'The Idea of the Corporation as a Person: On the Normative Significance of Judicial Language', in W. J. Samuels & A. S. Miller (eds), *Corporations and Society*, Greenwood Press, New York, 1987, p. 114.

2   Samuels, p. 125.

bers' liability,[3] or in a variety of other ways. To this extent, then, the use of the term 'company' is meaningful only in a very general sense. Although there are some specific provisions that acknowledge diversity (most notably provisions that deal with public, as opposed to private, companies), legislative provisions are, by and large, applicable to all companies, regardless of whether those companies are powerful associations with numerous shareholders, or 'two-dollar' companies. It can be argued, of course, that Parliament has chosen to use a generic term in order to simplify legal regulation. But such simplification can be problematic, as we shall see.

The use of the term 'company' masks not only the diversity of companies but also their very nature. 'Company' is defined as a body of persons combined for a common (especially commercial) object. This is the idea of company that probably first comes to mind. But there are other ideas associated with 'company': the state of being a companion or fellow; a number of persons assembled; to 'consort with', and so on.[4] The modern 'company' derives from the *compania* of ancient Rome. This term in turn derives from the phrase 'cum pane'—literally, 'one with whom one breaks bread'—or 'companion', 'one who accompanies another', 'an associate in', 'a sharer of'. A phrase such as 'a body of persons combined' tends to unify the individuals comprising the company; it assumes that they are working together, unproblematically, in pursuit of a common (especially commercial) object. But the ideas of associating and sharing are closer to the truth. One can associate and there may still be differences of opinion, imbalances of power, or tensions.[5] 'Association' does not necessarily imply unproblematic union. The idea of 'sharing' highlights the distribution of risks and benefits that is inherent in the corporate form.

The linguistic assumption of unity—the masking of difference—is even more pronounced in the definition of 'corporation' as a 'united body of persons, especially one authorized to act as an individual, artificial person created by charter, prescription, or act of the legislature, comprising many persons (corporation aggregate) or one (corporation sole), municipal corporation—civic authorities of borough, town or city'.[6] In this definition, the mask of unity is taken one step further: the united body becomes one body—a single entity that submerges the interests, the rights, and the liabilities of the individuals who compose it. But more importantly than this, with a swift sleight of hand, the single entity (which only exists in the legal imagination) becomes a person: 'A body corporate is an incorporated legal entity created and recognised by the law. It is an artificial legal person as opposed to individuals who are known as natural persons'.[7] Throughout the case law, the 'person'—

---

3   *Corporations Law 1990*, s. 115 allows the formation of five different types of companies according to the liability of their members: companies limited by shares; companies limited by guarantee; companies limited by both shares and guarantee; unlimited companies; and no liability companies.

4   See P. Redmond, *Companies and Securities Law: Commentary and Materials*, Law Book Company, Sydney, 1988, pp. 25–35.

5   In relation to ideas of 'association', see *Smith v. Anderson* (1880) 15 Ch D 247 at 277 per Brett LJ.

6   J. B. Sykes (ed.), *The Concise Oxford Dictionary of Current English*, 6th edn, Clarendon Press, Oxford, 1979.

7   P. Lipton & A. Herzberg, *Understanding Company Law*, Law Book Company, Sydney, 1991, p. 15. See also H. A. J. Ford & R. P. Austin, *Principles of Corporation Law*, 7th edn, Butterworths, Sydney, 1995, p. 5.

this imagined entity—becomes ever more human. Repeatedly, the metaphor of the human body is used to describe the structure, and sometimes the actions, of the company: '[an] artificial body composed of divers constituent members like the human body, and that the ligaments of this body politic or artificial body are the franchises and liberties thereof which bind and unite all its members together, and the whole frame and essence of the corporation consist therein'.[8] This anthropomorphism recurs throughout much of the case law and reflects the liberal conception of the rational being. The emphasis is on will. Reason has priority over action:

> A company may in many ways be likened to a human body. It has a brain and nerve centre which controls what it does. It also has hands which hold the tools and act in accordance with directions from the centre. Some of the people in the company are mere servants and agents who are nothing more than hands to do the work and cannot be said to represent the mind or will. Others are directors and managers who represent the directing mind and will of the company, and control what it does.[9]

Consider an alternative, albeit somewhat cynical, definition of the corporation: 'Corporation, *n*- An ingenious device for obtaining individual profit without individual responsibility'.[10] Despite its mischievous nature, the definition highlights an important point about the anthropomorphisation of the company. If the company is a device, then it is a human artefact, a product of human action. If the company is a person, then it is given a far more significant ontological status. It occurs naturally, has existed, and continues to exist as an intrinsic part of the social landscape.

This anthropomorphisation is conventionally justified in terms of convenience (although it is to be noted that the 'convenience' of this state expands and contracts).[11] Marshall CJ, in *Trustees of Dartmouth College v. Woodward NH Wheat,* said:

> A corporation is an artificial being, invisible, intangible, and existing only in contemplation of law. Being the mere creature of law, it possesses only those properties which the charter of its creation confers upon it, either expressly or as incidental to its very existence. These are such as are supposed best calculated to effect the object for which it was created. Among the most important are immortality, and, if the expression may be allowed, individuality, properties by which a perpetual succession of many persons are considered as the same, and may act as a single individual. They enable a corporation to manage its own affairs, and to hold property without the perplexing intricacies, the hazardous and endless

---

8 *Sir James Smith's Case* (1691) Carth 217.

9 *H. L. Bolton (Engineering) Co. Ltd v. T. L. Graham & Sons Ltd* [1957] 1 QB 159 per Lord Denning. See also *Donato v. Legion Cabs (Trading) Co-operative Soc. Ltd* (1966) 85 WN (Pt 1) (NSW) 242, where the company secretary becomes the 'natural mouthpiece' of the company.

10 A. Bierce, *The Devil's Dictionary*, as quoted by Lim Wen Ts'ai, 'Corporations and the Devil's Dictionary: The Problem of Individual Responsibility for Corporate Crimes' (1990) Syd LR 311.

11 See, for example, *Smorgon v. Australia & New Zealand Banking Group Ltd* (1976) 134 CLR 475, in which the issue was whether the Federal Commissioner of Taxation could compel a company to give evidence under the *Income Tax Assessment Act 1936*, s. 264(1)(b). The High Court held that s. 264(1)(b) only gave the Commissioner the power to compel natural persons to attend and give evidence.

necessity, of perpetual conveyances for the purpose of transmitting it from hand to hand. It is chiefly for the purpose of clothing bodies of men, in succession, with these qualities and capacities, that corporations were invented, and are in use. By these means, a perpetual succession of individuals are capable of acting for the promotion of the particular object, like one immortal being.[12]

The problem with this anthropomorphisation, at least in functional terms, is that it is often inappropriate. How can we consider a highly complex organisation—which is composed of a multiplicity of power relations, interests, and individual perceptions—to be a single (and single-minded) *rational* being? For example, in *Brambles Holdings Ltd v. Carey*,[13] a company engaged in a carrying business was charged with offences relating to the maximum loads of vehicles. Responsibility for ensuring that the company's vehicles complied with relevant legislation was delegated to three employees. The offences occurred when one of these employees was ill and his replacement had not been properly instructed by the operations manager about his responsibilities. The company raised the defence of honest and reasonable mistake, claiming that it had reasonable grounds for believing that its vehicles complied with the legislation. Could the knowledge and belief of the operations manager be attributed to the company? The other relevant employee had no knowledge of the breach. Bray CJ observed that 'very difficult questions' arise where mental states such as knowledge or belief are attributed to the corporation. In his view, it was a 'fallacy' that the views of a particular officer must be the only criterion for determining the knowledge or belief of the company. However, he also conceded that, 'although I think a corporation has in a proper case the combined knowledge or belief possessed by more than one of its officers, that does not mean that it can know or believe two contradictory things at once. It is rational belief, not schizophrenia, which is to be attributed to it'.[14] A schizophrenic corporation? The idea is truly frightening. What other pathological states could be attributed to the company?

In moral terms, this anthropomorphisation—the equating of a company with a person—can be seen as objectionable. Why should an organisation have an equal, sometimes superior, legal status to that of women or indigenous people, to name but a few? This issue will be discussed at greater length later, but the issue that we wish to identify here is that the definition of the corporation helps to form our beliefs about corporations. It creates and re-creates our conception of the corporate form:

Any answer to the question, what is the corporation? is itself functional in the evolution of the corporation. These answers are attractive and contrived because of their anticipated or desired consequences in that evolution. If positions on the question are inevitable, so is

---

12 (1819) 17 US 518; 4 L Ed 629.

13 (1976) 2 ACLR 176.

14 (1976) 2 ACLR 176 at 182.

the functioning of answers to the question. The corporation is an important part of the economic power structure, and power players attempt to manipulate belief system [*sic*] in order to influence power structure and performance. It is true both that ideas have a life of their own and that they are the object of control and manipulation by power players.[15]

One faction of the power players, the legislators, describe a company as a type of 'body corporate'[16] and then go on to define a 'company' in essentially procedural terms. For instance:

114(1) **Proprietary Companies**. One or more persons may form a proprietary company by:
   (a) subscribing their name to a memorandum, and
   (b) complying with the registration requirements for proprietary companies set out in this Division.

114(2) **Public Companies**. Five or more persons may form a public company by:
   (a) subscribing their names to a memorandum, and
   (b) complying with the registration requirements for public companies set out in this Division.[17]

The effect of such a deceptively simple provision is not to be underestimated. In *Salomon v. Salomon & Co. Ltd*, Lord Macnaghten said:

In order to form a company limited by shares, the [*Companies Act 1862*] requires that a memorandum of association should be signed by seven persons, who are each to take one share at least. If those conditions are complied with, what can it matter whether the signatories are relations or strangers? There is nothing in the Act requiring that the subscribers to the memorandum should be independent or unconnected, or that they or any of them should take a substantial interest in the undertaking, or that they should have a mind and will of their own ... or that there should be anything like a balance of power in the constitution of the company. In almost every company that is formed the statutory number is eked out by clerks or friends, who sign their names at the request of the promoter or promoters without intending to take any further part or interest in the matter.

When the memorandum is duly signed and registered, though there be only seven shares taken, the subscribers are a body corporate 'capable forthwith,' to use the words of the enactment, of 'exercising all the functions of an incorporated company'. Those are strong words. The company attains maturity on its birth. There is no period of minority—no interval of incapacity. I cannot understand how a body corporate thus made

---

15 Samuels, p. 115.

16 Corporations Law, s. 9 defines a corporation as a 'body corporate'—that is, a company or specified unincorporated bodies.

17 See also the definition contained in Corporations Law, s. 9: ' "Company" means a company incorporated or taken to be incorporated, under the Corporations Law of this jurisdiction.' Or see the definition of a proprietary company in s. 45A: 'A proprietary company is a company that is registered as a proprietary company ... or converts to a proprietary company under s 168'.

'capable' by statute can lose its individuality by issuing the bulk of its capital to one person, whether he be a subscriber to the memorandum or not. The company is at law a different person altogether from the subscribers to the memorandum, and, though it may be that after incorporation the business is precisely the same as it was before, and the same persons are managers, and the same hands receive the profits, the company is not in law the agent of the subscribers or trustee for them. Nor are the subscribers as members liable, in any shape or form, except to the extent and in the manner provided by the Act.[18]

So, as Warren J. Samuels points out:

Law, including legal writing, is a technique for the shaping of images, and, as with all governance and politics, it is both a system or process of meaning and an arena for efforts to control shared systems of meaning ... This sociological reality typically is defined in terms of rights and rules, but it is also defined in terms of chains of reasoning and by definitions, such as the definition of the corporation as a person. Law thus defines and redefines legal-economic reality, giving effect to countless forces and efforts to use the law for economic and/or other advantage. Legal definitions of reality encapsulate the fundamental tautologies at the basis of the economic system. These tautologies govern the structure of freedom and control (including hierarchy v equality), the processes of continuity v change and the selective perception of interests to be given legal protection as rights. Legal control of the corporation (or anything else) implies, or presumes, legal recognition and protection in other respects of that which is controlled. Legal definitions evidence, affirm and reinforce the corporation at the same time legal treatment presumes the corporation.[19]

In the next section we will consider the idea of the legal person in more detail.

REVIEW QUESTIONS

1 L. C. B. Gower defines a company as 'an association of a number of people for some common object or objects'.[20] H. A. J. Ford and R. P. Austin define the company as a 'device'. Which definition do you believe is more accurate? Can any one definition adequately define all companies?

2 What logical and practical problems can you see in the idea that a single person can become a company?

3 In some of the other areas of law that you have studied (for example, criminal law or torts), what sorts of problems might be posed by dealing with an incorporeal entity with all the rights and obligations of a natural person?

---

18 *Salomon v. Salomon & Co. Ltd* [1897] AC 22 at 50–1.

19 Samuels, p. 119.

20 L. C. B. Gower, *Principles of Modern Company Law*, 4th edn, Stevens & Sons, London, 1979, p. 3.

The emperor's new clothes: Legal personality

In the legal imagination, the company, then, is a person. It has, in law, 'legal personality'. Section 161 of the *Corporations Law 1990* provides that '[a] company has, both within and outside this jurisdiction, the legal capacity of a natural person'.

There are many aspects to the conception of legal personality. In so-called 'black-letter law' texts, you will find that legal personality involves the ability to enjoy certain rights: to own property, to enter contracts, to sue and be sued, to give evidence in court, and to enter into various other types of legal dealings. Those who cannot enter contracts or engage in property transaction and other legal dealings lack some elements of legal personality.

Legal personality is created by law; it is defined by case law and by legislation. It is, therefore, variable. It can contract and expand at the convenience of the Crown. In some ways, the company is not equated with an ordinary person, but receives a superior status. For instance, it has perpetual succession[21] and, perhaps the most fundamental privilege of the corporation, limited liability. As the corporation is a separate legal person, its members are not personally liable for its debts in the absence of any express provision to the contrary. Where a company is limited by shares, members' liability is limited to the unpaid nominal value of their shares (and, in practice, shares are fully paid up, so there is no further liability). In this case, liability of members is limited without restricting their role in management. Limited liability is fundamental to the growth of corporations and to much of the controversy surrounding them. Some commentators have considered that the development of limited liability was directly responsible for the 'birth of the entrepreneur':[22]

> Some seven men form an Association,
> (If possible, all Peers and Baronets)
> They start off with a public declaration
> To what extent they mean to pay their debts.
> That's called their Capital: if they are wary
> They will not quote it in a sum immense.
> The figure's immaterial—it may vary
> From eighteen million down to eighteen pence.
> I should put it rather low,
> The good sense of doing so
> Will be evident at once to any debtor
> When it's left to you to say
> What amount you mean to pay,
> Why, the lower you can put it at, the better.
> They then proceed to trade with all who'll trust 'em,

---

21 Corporations Law, s. 123. Section 161 also provides that the company has a number of powers additional to those of the natural person.

22 G. Goyder, *The Just Enterprise*, André Deutsch, London, 1987, p. ix.

> Quite irrespective of their capital
> (It's shady, but it's sanctified by custom),
> Bank, Railway, Loan, or Panama Canal.[23]

In the first part of this chapter, we suggested that the ready acceptance of the company as a legal person was morally objectionable. Consider that, in our not so distant past, many people, including women and Aboriginal people, either lacked legal personality completely or had it, at most, in a restricted form. In some ways, then, a company had a greater social standing, and was rendered more important and significant, than many of the individuals who make up our society:

> Rights … are the vehicle through which both ordinary and legal language establish and express protected interests and thereby correlative and conflicting unprotected, and exposed interests. [To say that a corporation is a person] is … to make an 'is' statement but effectively and more importantly to make a normative 'ought' statement about the power structure of the economy.[24]

Yet, if the company is a legal person, it is a very odd 'person'. The analogy has considerable limits, as Buckley LJ notes:

> A corporation has neither body, parts or passions. It cannot bear weapons nor serve in war. It can be neither loyal nor disloyal. It cannot compass treason. It can be neither friend nor enemy. Apart from its corporators, it can have neither thoughts, wishes or intentions, for it has no mind other than the minds of its corporators.[25]

A corporation can be a 'resident' but not a 'citizen', even if it is 'born' in Australia.[26] Because corporations are incapable of personal allegiance, it seems unlikely that they would be regarded as 'subjects of the Queen' for the purposes of s. 117 of the Constitution.[27] Indeed, theirs is a strange personhood, even in terms of legal personhood.

So, if a company is allowed to act in our society, if it is the subject of rights and obligations, what are its concomitant duties? If it has 'no soul to damn and no body to kick', how can it perform the obligations of, and fully participate in, citizenship?[28] If its motivations are rightly those of profit, how can it exercise social responsibility, or be capable of moral or immoral conduct? How can it be

---

23   From W. S. Gilbert, *The Savoy Operas*, vol. 2, Macmillan, London, 1963 (1926), pp. 321–2.

24   Samuels, p. 117.

25   *Continental Tyre & Rubber Co. (GB) Ltd v. Daimler Co. Ltd* [1915] 1 KB 893 at 916 per Buckley LJ.

26   *Australian Temperance and General Life Assurance Society Ltd v. Howe* (1922) 31 CLR 290 (the word 'residents' in s. 75(iv) of the Australian Constitution is not applicable to corporations).

27   The Canadian Supreme Court has held that corporations are entitled to 'freedom of religion' under the Charter of Rights and Freedoms.

28   While the term 'citizenship' has varied connotations, we generally understand it to mean equal membership in a participatory democracy in the Rawlsian sense. See J. Rawls, *Political Liberalism*, Columbia University Press, New York, 1993.

punished for its wrongdoings? How, indeed, can it perceive right from wrong? Sir Arthur Bryant argued that

> [a] limited liability company has no conscience. A priesthood of figures cannot consider claims of amorality and justice that conflict with its mathematical formulas: it must live by its own rules. Man, who once tried to model his life on the divine, came to take his orders from the lender of money and the chartered accountant acting in their purely professional capacity. It is not the profit motive which is to blame. Free men have at all times sought profit from their labour. It is its enthronement to the exclusion of other motives far more important [that is to blame].[29]

How could it be that a fictional entity—a device to enable the accumulation of capital—became more important, in terms of rights, than a real person? As we noted earlier, on one level the issue is one of convenience. In order to resolve disputes, certain institutions or organisations are labelled 'bodies corporate', either by a special act of the legislature or by the 'ritual' of registration. The legal person thus created then has standing to sue or to be sued in the courts. Once again, however, the analogy is limited. While a corporation can bring an action for defamation, it cannot recover for injury to its 'feelings'; it has none to injure (as the law recognises). Because it is incapable of personally appearing in court, it must be represented by counsel. On the other hand, a corporation is clearly a 'resident' for the purposes of the taxation laws and the laws pertaining to incorporation, despite its intangibility. Were it not, it would be utterly beyond the reach of the law.

But legal personhood goes well beyond mere standing. It invokes a substantial range of legal rights, protections, and obligations. The ritual significance of the registration process is to affirm the corporation's fundamental role in capitalism.[30] Think for a moment about the selective nature of the conferral of legal personhood. Partnerships, trading trusts, and unions are not 'legal persons' in the way that a company is; their reality does not supersede that of their members.

From this point of view, conferring legal personhood on the corporation also has a very pragmatic effect. It

> affirm[s] that the corporation is neither a collective organisation nor a governing institution, either of which would tend to render it subject to checks on its power and use of power ... Judicial affirmation of the corporation as a person is epistemologically only superficially a positive, descriptive matter. Much more fundamentally, it is a linguistic means of establishing normative premises functional for subsequent legal reasoning and choice and thereby functional in the normative reformation of the economy.[31]

So the courts, as well as the legislature, have played a very significant role in establishing these normative premises. The legislature directed the courts to recognise a

---

29 Sir A. Bryant, as quoted in Goyder, p. xi.
30 Samuels, p. 122.
31 Samuels, pp. 123, 127.

company as a legal person, but the courts then had to define the relationship between those people who were the body corporate and the separate legal person whom they comprised. They also had to determine the relationship between those who managed or worked in the firm represented by the company and the company itself. Consider the potential issues that could arise from the idea of legal personhood:

> [I]f a shareholder was also in a separate and different relationship with the company, would the two relationships coalesce as when a person is both debtor and creditor of the same person, or would the relationships be entirely separate? Could a member take advantage of rights or property owned by the company and was the converse always ruled out by limited liability? Even simple problems of the company's relationships with other legal persons proved extremely difficult; for example, whether the company existed for every possible contract, how it could make binding contracts, how it committed torts and crimes of which intention is an element (if, indeed, it could do so), and whether it existed at all when one person was the only person involved in its legal structure. A particularly poignant example of this type of problem arose in Queensland in 1966 when all the people involved in the company, both shareholders and directors, were killed in a car accident: did the company still exist? The courts developed a strict idea of separate legal personality in most of these cases, although it never worked completely satisfactorily.[32]

The emperor wears no clothes. Companies are not persons. They are often complex organisations with their own hierarchical structures (both formal and informal), which contribute to, and yet complicate, our system of property. They may perform many functions, and may even be the 'objects of quasi-religious attachment by individuals seeking, establishing or reinforcing self-identification'.[33]

REVIEW QUESTIONS

1   Look carefully at Lord Justice Buckley's description of the limitations on corporate personhood in *Continental Tyre & Rubber Co. (GB) Ltd v. Daimler Co. Ltd* (see p. 11). How are the characteristics interrelated? What is the significance of the 'masculinity' of the overall image? Can you rewrite Lord Justice Buckley's account using 'feminine' images? If this was difficult, what do you think it suggests about the way we see 'personhood'?

2   How could you justify the fact that companies enjoy legal privileges and powers that natural persons do not? Do you think that these justifications are valid?

---

32   D. Wishart, *Company Law in Context*, Oxford University Press, Auckland, 1994, p. 57.
33   Samuels, p. 124.

Legal personality, companies, and State regulation

When individuals start up or take over a business, they must decide upon the way in which they want their business to be structured and administered. They could decide to operate
- as a sole trader
- in a partnership (either with limited or unlimited liability)
- as a company
- as a trading trust, with either themselves or (more usually) a proprietary company acting as the trustee
- as an unincorporated association
- as an association incorporated under one of the state Associations Incorporation Acts
- in a joint venture[34]
- as an agent
- as part of a cooperative.

Each choice has different implications for their relationship with the State. Increasingly they are choosing the corporate form, for a variety of reasons. The most frequently cited reason is that it provides the privilege of limited liability, but the corporate form can also be used to raise capital, to hold legal title to property, to hold family assets, to perform the function of trusteeship, to manage funds, to allow property co-ownership, or to run government enterprises. Despite its versatility, the corporate form is essentially no more than a legal device for separating the investment of capital and business management (although we acknowledge that this may not adequately describe the small family company).

The conferral of legal personhood on the corporation, however, has caused considerable problems for the State. First, the company is the central player in capitalism. It is pivotal to the economy. Yet, this creates a tension. The economy itself is based on the ideas we have of 'the good life', but these ideas are not all the same, nor do they remain static. The economy itself is an 'artefact', the product of human action, and the definition of the company as a legal person is both created by, and re-creates, our idea of the economy. Thus, Samuels argues that,

> [t]o an extraordinarily enormous extent, the organization of society (and thereby the economy) is ultimately a matter of the determination of what power structure and what belief system will channel both the operation of existing relations between persons and

---

34 The term 'joint venture' is used to describe a commercial form in which two or more legal persons (natural or corporate) join together, sometimes by way of a deed of partnership, to pursue a venture in which their combined expertise is useful. Joint ventures are extremely variable. For an example of a joint venture akin to a partnership, see *Canny Gabriel Castle Jackson Advertising Pty Ltd v. Volume Sales (Finance) Pty Ltd* (1974) 131 CLR 321. Those wishing to explore this area in greater depth should see W. D. Duncan, *Joint Venture Law in Australia*, Federation Press, Sydney, 1994.

the creation of the future. What ultimately is involved is the creation and recreation of economic (and social) order, either the reproduction of the existing order or the production, typically gradually and incrementally, of a new order. To no small extent, science, religion, common sense, law and so on are fundamentally contributors to our conception of the economy and thereby help form the creation of the future. Operative within each, however, are structural conflicts as to which conception of the economy, and thereby which future, is to be advanced and thereby made operative in the normative artefact-creation process.[35]

Second, the ability to accumulate capital—and the ability to transmit that capital from one generation to the next—fundamentally affects the locus of power within a society. Legal personhood masks the reality that a corporation is not merely one 'person' equal in power to all others, but may be an organisation so powerful that it rivals the State: 'Power relations, not market relations, are at the heart of the corporation and its dealings with other corporations, government and labor, and often also with the consumer. Without a theory of power, no theory of the modern corporation can go beyond the anthropomorphism of the neo-classical view'.[36]

A third problem for the State is that incorporation creates a complex web of relationships between a company and its members, the members and the board, the board and the company, the company and its creditors, the board and the creditors, and so on. Regulation of the company is no easy matter. Companies vary enormously in structure and size. They are pivotal to the economy, and by their presence within it, they simultaneously create and re-create the meaning of that idea. Their power means that they can often resist, or at least modify, regulatory schemes.

Thus, State regulation of companies has been controversial, difficult, and often ineffective. It has swung between tight regulation of corporate activity and more lenient regulation, depending on whether corporations are viewed as vehicles for 'corporate cowboys' or vehicles for economic growth. These views, however, are not mutually exclusive. Often, corporations are both: 'If it had not been for the stock-market crash of October 1987 some of the entrepreneurs recently brought before the courts would have received honours from the Queen instead'.[37]

At any particular time, the State draws the lines between legitimate and illegitimate risk-taking by entrepreneurs in response to its prioritisation of social goods such as economic growth, market confidence, or consumer welfare. The responsibilities of directors and other persons expand and contract in response to this prioritisation and in keeping with the dominant power relations at the time:

The making of laws in relation to companies and the persons who are involved in the formation and management of companies could be described as one of the contemporary growth industries. I think it is fair to say, however, that since the introduction of the

---

35 Samuels, p. 117.
36 Anon., 'Galbraith and the Theory of the Corporation' (1984) 7 *Journal of Post-Keynesian Economics* 43 at 59.
37 N. E. Renton, *Company Directors: Masters or Servants?* Wrightbooks, Melbourne, 1994, p. xv.

concept of limited liability the potential for companies and the dealing in interests in them to be used as a means of defrauding both the gullible and the greedy has been recognised and so it is that over a long period of time as the wit of man has been applied to the pursuit of material gain through the use of companies it has been necessary for the law to become more and more complex to the extent that in these times few if any could honestly claim to have a complete understanding of all the intricacies of the regulatory provisions that now apply. Be that as it may, one theme which prevails throughout the whole complex structure of company law is that those in a position to take advantage of the special position they may exercise in the promotion or management of companies must always act with the utmost care, diligence and honesty so that those who are less well informed are not unfairly taken advantage of.[38]

More pragmatically, as Robert Dugan points out, the overriding concern of regulators has been to prevent the corporate entity from serving as a vehicle for involuntary transfers of wealth. Since the beginnings of the modern company, regulators have sought to protect creditors from the consequences of limited liability,[39] while simultaneously encouraging the risk-taking facilitated by limited liability.

Company law, therefore, has been both complex and inconsistent. Like its predecessors, the Corporations Law is not a code. Rather, it runs parallel to the common law, and as a consequence, company law is a mixture of statutory regulation and general law principles. The constant amendment of Australia's statutory schemes has been a source of considerable concern, criticism, and frustration on the part of business people, lawyers, commentators, and judges alike. Since the introduction of the state companies legislation in the early 1960s, the legislation governing corporations has increased some 450 per cent. The bulk of this increase has occurred since the 1970s.[40] Despite this torrent of legislation, a judge of the New South Wales Supreme Court stated that 'the improvements in the justice system, both legislative and curial, … are so marginal as to be unnoticeable and ineffective'.[41] A practitioner noted that the costs of justice have increased without a corresponding increase in the chances of justice.[42] A legal academic wrote that 'a major regret of corporate law writers, jurists, lawyers and business people is that company law is unnecessarily complex and voluminous. Rules are not always clearly thought out or concisely and clearly expressed'.[43] Even the Australian Securities Commission recognised that 'company law is becoming excessively complicated and there is a risk that people will turn away from companies altogether. We have seen a spectacular

---

38 *Chew v. NCSC (No. 2)* (1985) 3 ACLC 212 per Olney J.

39 R. Dugan, *Company: A Transactional Approach*, Butterworths, Wellington, 1994.

40 John M. Green, ' "Fuzzy Law": A Better Way to Stop "Snouts in the Trough"?' (1991) CSLJ 146. Green notes that this figure does not include legislation affecting the operation of companies, such as the *Trade Practices Act 1974* (Cth).

41 Justice Andrew Rogers, commenting on the 15-year period following the collapse of the Cambridge Credit Corporation, in 'Avalanche Threatens' (1990) *Australian Law News* 16.

42 Green, p. 146.

43 J. F Corkery, *Directors' Powers and Duties*, Longman Cheshire, Melbourne, 1987, p. xxv.

loss of confidence in the capital generation context. There is a real risk of a similar loss of confidence in the utility of company law in the operating business context'.[44] Contrast this with the relatively stable regulation of another significant economic vehicle—the partnership.

In addition to the problems caused by the pendulum swing of regulatory policy, the Corporations Law has been amended because its underlying assumptions—the ideas of legal personality and limited liability—are not questioned:

> When limited liability was first enacted in 1855 and consolidated in the Companies Act of 1862, British industry was controlled by the individual proprietors of a very large number of small family enterprises. Before the Act of 1855, the proprietor of a business stood to lose all he possessed if his business became insolvent and his partner or backer likewise. Only after 1855 did limited liability make it practically possible for a company to grow indefinitely, until we come to the position today, when a small group of men exercise control over commercial empires that are richer than many sovereign states. The size and scale of industrial organization has altered out of recognition since the invention of limited liability one hundred and more years ago. But in that time virtually nothing has been done to bring company law into line with social reality.[45]

The company is not a static, but an evolving, phenomenon.[46] Yet it is not merely a question of bringing company law into line with social reality. It is not that simple. Company law is *part* of that reality; it creates, shapes, alters, and distorts that reality. As the company has continued to evolve, increased efforts have been made to understand the nature of, and reasons for, its existence.

Theories of the corporation

> [T]he legal definition of the corporation will give effect to one set of preconceptions of privateness and publicness or another, to one belief system or another, to one set of policy premises or another. Involved in all this is a language, a system of discourse.[47]

In the ongoing search for a more efficient scheme of corporate regulation, various commentators have proposed theoretical models to explain the nature of the company.

The dissatisfaction with the existing model of the corporation is reflected in the number of alternative models proposed by twentieth-century theorists. The traditional model of the corporation is that of the fictitious legal entity, the sole

---

44 P. Cranswick, Background to the Corporations Law and Australian Securities Commission: The ASC's Philosophy, paper presented at ASC Seminar, Hobart, March 1991.

45 Goyder, p. 4.

46 No single definition is capable of capturing the meaning of the term 'company'. To the extent that it is possible to offer a definition, the authors would simply suggest that the term 'company' may be appropriately used wherever an entity has been granted corporate status by the jurisdiction in which it carries on its primary business.

47 Samuels, p. 121.

purpose of which is ordinarily the pursuit of profit. Attempts have been made to construct a new variant of this traditional economic model that can accommodate such contemporary values as corporate social responsibility and shareholder democracy. One exponent of this model, Melvin Eisenberg,[48] argues that the corporation empirically derives its moral legitimacy from widespread popular acceptance of the desirable economic outcomes that it produces. Corporate legitimacy flows primarily from the efficient utilisation of economic resources, and secondarily from ethical notions regarding the sanctity of private property. As in the traditional economic model, the corporation has a single objective: that of conducting business activities in order to make a profit. However, as the company is also a social institution, the pursuit of this goal 'must be constrained by social imperatives and may be qualified by social needs'.[49]

But 'economic theory', maintains Samuels, 'fails to account adequately for the ontological status of firms, taking them as given, individual economic units'.[50] Nor does the model offer any guidance on the extent to which these other needs and imperatives may qualify the pursuit of profit. Thus, the model has also been criticised in the following terms:

> Professor Eisenberg does not advocate the adoption of a true economic model that would prohibit legal, ethical and humanitarian conduct unrelated to corporate profit and shareholder gain. Instead, he offers a revised 'restatement' complete with anomalies and unexplained limitations. [In this model] the intuitive legitimacy of specific applications overrides the authority of the conceptual paradigms. The paradigms are supposed to decide difficult cases, not give way in difficult areas.[51]

The contractual model is aligned to the traditional economic model. Under this model, the rights and responsibilities within a corporation are considered to be a matter of private contract. Shareholders create the corporate form by free agreement. They collectively own the corporation as private property, and consent to restrict their immediate control of their investment capital in return for certain rights. Among these are the right to elect the board democratically, to make extraordinary business decisions, and to receive properly declared dividends. The board's obligation is to pursue the legitimate commercial expectations of the investors.[52] The emphasis here is clearly upon the internal relations of the corporation. In the USA, however, such a view has constitutional implications in that, if the company is perceived to be nothing more than a private contract, the role of the State in determining rights and obligations is limited. Historically, in the USA, the transition

---

48 M. Eisenberg, 'Corporate Legitimacy, Conduct and Governance: Two Models of the Corporation' (1983) 17 *Creighton Law Review* 1

49 Eisenberg, p. 6.

50 Samuels, p. 125.

51 R. C. Mangrum, 'In Search of a Paradigm of Corporate Responsibility' (1983) 17 *Creighton Law Review* 21 at 26, reprinted by permission.

52 Mangrum at 27.

from incorporation by special legislation to general incorporation is said to confirm the contractual view, and to provide justification for the notion that duties are owed primarily to the shareholders, rather than to the general public.[53]

Some analysts claim that the contractual model is best justified by reference to ethical, rather than historical, analysis. Roger Pilon, for instance, refers to the natural law tradition, according to which 'freedom of contract was rather more highly regarded'.[54] He continues: 'From a normative perspective the corporation is justified under a Nozickian variant of this tradition because it might arise by a process that violates no one's rights'.[55] This contract model makes two claims. The first is that the law recognises the right of shareholders to demand that management be constrained strictly by profit motivation, and the second is that ideas of private property and contract rights should be respected even if they run counter to the public interest.

Either variation of the contract model assumes that the competitive market controls the operations of the company. State regulation is, therefore, largely unnecessary. This view, however, seems questionable today. Nineteenth-century notions of *laissez-faire* and freedom of contract have given way to a more paternalistic view of the role of the State and a greater emphasis on the public interest. This is reflected in the USA by the Tentative Draft No. 1 of the American Law Institute's Principles of Corporate Governance and Structure, s. 2.01, which provides that

> the objective of the business corporation is to conduct business activities with a view to corporate profit and shareholder gain except that, even if corporate profit and shareholder gain are not thereby enhanced, the corporation, in the conduct of its business,
>
> (a)　is obliged, to the same extent as a natural person, to act within the boundaries set by law,
>
> (b)　may properly take into account ethical principles that are generally recognised as relevant to the conduct of business, and
>
> (c)　may devote resources, within reasonable limits, to public welfare, humanitarian, educational and philanthropic purposes.

Similarly, the idea that a corporation is an inherently 'private' entity belies the complexity of the so-called 'public/private distinction':

> [L]egal rights are obviously public in character (they are what they are at least in part because of government action or inaction) but they are also private in character in that they pertain to nominally private parties and they are arguably the result of a matrix of private pressures on government to resolve conflicts of interest in one way or another. In

---

53　R. Hessen, 'A New Concept of Corporations: A Contractual and Private Property Model' (1979) 30 *Hastings Law Journal* 1327; R. Hessen, *In Defense of the Corporation*, Hoover Institution Press, Stanford University, Stanford, Calif., 1979.

54　R. Pilon, 'Corporations and Rights: On Treating Corporate People Justly' (1979) 13 Ga LR 1245, at 1251–2. We are puzzled by Pilon's notion that corporate persons ought to be treated 'justly'.

55　Pilon at 1262.

other words, rights are in some sense both private and public and what is instructive is the selective way in which they are perceived and acted upon as one or the other.[56]

A similar reliance on a static notion of the public/private divide is evidenced by the concessional theory of the corporation. This model is based upon the idea that the corporation was originally a public, rather than a private, institution. In medieval times, royal assent was necessary in order for corporate identity to be granted. Throughout history, many joint stock companies that were granted corporate identity were involved with essentially public operations, such as building and operating railways. As Mary Stokes[57] points out, in the eighteenth and nineteenth centuries, this theory found doctrinal expression in the *ultra vires* rule—that is, the notion that corporate bodies should operate within the narrowly defined powers that were granted to them by the statute or charter that conferred corporate identity upon them. From these origins of the corporate form, it can be argued that the corporation was essentially a public body, rather than a piece of private property. This model, however, can be criticised on the basis that it rests upon a historical, rather than a contemporary, understanding of corporations. Corporate identity is freely available upon compliance with certain basic formalities. The company is born through the ritual of incorporation. As the ritual is relatively freely available, it can hardly be seen as a privilege.

Political models of the corporation are based upon the idea that the company is a real, rather than a fictional, entity, which exists separately from its shareholders. Robert Dahl's conception of this model relies on ideas of democratic pluralism[58]— that is, the conception that, in a rational society, every institution ought to be controlled by those groups affected by it. Consumers, employees, shareholders, and the general public are each affected by corporate power and, therefore, each ought to have some input into the governance of the company. The corporation, in effect, has a moral responsibility to these various constituents, but this responsibility has not traditionally been recognised by the law. For these interests be recognised, the law must be reformed so that the board of a corporation operates on a democratic basis, comprising representatives from each group and owing fiduciary duties to all its affected constituents. This model expressly rejects the traditional corporate model, whereby such duties are owed only to shareholders.[59] There is some concern, however, that a diffusion of management responsibility would result in the disappearance of investment capital and the dilution of any meaningful accountability on the part of management.

An alternative paradigm, and one that seeks to impose greater community responsibility upon the corporation, is offered by the public interest model. This

---

56 Samuels, p. 120.

57 M. Stokes, 'Company Law and Legal Theory', in W. Twining (ed.), *Legal Theory and Common Law*, Basil Blackwell, Oxford, 1986, pp. 135, 162.

58 R. Dahl, *After the Revolution? Authority in a Good Society*, Yale University Press, New Haven, 1970, p. 7.

59 Mangrum at 21.

model originated as early as the 1920s and 1930s, when 'idealised notions of democracy, property and contract rights received continuous haranguing by ... political scientists who insisted that society ought to focus on the public interest rather than legal abstractions'.[60]

The empirical findings of A. A. Berle and G. C. Means in *The Modern Corporation and Private Property*[61] were that the increasing numbers of shareholders resulted in a corresponding diminution of their control over corporate policy. It was suggested, therefore, that administrative elites controlled economic power in corporate America, just as they controlled politics in democratic America.[62] Berle, in searching for a corporate model, retained the contract model, but adjusted it: while individual shareholders had little or no control over the corporation, management was obliged to serve the shareholders' investment interests.[63] E. Merrick Dodd, on the other hand, maintained that, as the public corporation existed as a separate entity from its shareholders, it had social responsibilities of its own. Management 'should concern themselves with the interests of employers, consumers and the general public, as well as of stockholders'.[64]

This public interest view was interpreted in different ways. For instance, some writers, such as John Kenneth Galbraith, argued that management's profit obligation demands only fair or normal return on investment capital. Public interest demands that more emphasis is placed on economic growth than on shareholder profit.[65] Other public interest theorists, such as Ralph Nader, maintained that, as the law creates and protects those rights called 'property' or 'the corporation', the same law can rearrange those bundles of rights if it is in the public interest to do so.[66] Although the public interest view coincides with the changing legislative and judicial view of the corporation, it leaves unanswered the question of how to reconcile the conflict of interests inherent in the internal operation of corporations.

The inherent flaw in these various models is that they tend to confuse corporate structure and corporate purpose, thereby failing to distinguish clearly between the rights and obligations of the State and the rights and obligations of the corporation. The internal structure of the corporation is based upon contractual principles; as an organisation, it most certainly appears to act in its own interests, and those interests are fundamentally based on notions of property and the pursuit of profit. Yet, the

---

60 Mangrum at 33.

61 A. A. Berle & G. C. Means, *The Modern Corporation and Private Property*, revised edn, Harcourt, Brace & World, New York, 1968.

62 Mangrum at 33.

63 A. A. Berle, 'Corporate Powers as Powers in Trust' (1931) 44 Harv LR 1049 at 1052: 'All powers granted to a corporation or to the management of a corporation, or to any group within the corporation, whether derived from statute or charter or both, are necessarily and at all times exercisable only for the rateable benefit of all the shareholders as their interest appears'.

64 E. M. Dodd, 'For Whom are Corporate Managers Trustees?' (1932) 45 Harv LR 1145.

65 J. K. Galbraith, *The New Industrial State*, Hamish Hamilton, London, 1967, pp. 166–78.

66 R. Nader, M. Green, & J. Selizman, *Taming the Giant Corporation*, Norton, New York, 1976, pp. 15, 33–5, 63. See also R. Nader & M. Green, *Corporate Power in America*, Grossman Publishers, New York, 1973.

company must operate within the wider context of the State. Regulators have attempted, then, to prevent the company, in the pursuit of its interests, from functioning above or outside contemporary moral and legal norms to a socially unacceptable degree. Indeed, if a company is truly a person, why should it be allowed to function outside these norms at all?

Conclusion

We might liken a company to a ghost. It is a legal person, without actually being a person. It is a 'citizen' with privileges that, in many ways, surpass those of other, less important citizens. It does not exist, but is of fundamental importance to capitalist economies. It is subject to highly detailed regulation, which has proved to be largely ineffective. The company shapes our perception of what a company should be, just as it relies on that perception for its very existence—a strange, disturbing, and elusive ghost indeed!

REVIEW QUESTIONS

1 Read the following passage and discuss:

> Companies with their inherent desire for uniformity, regulation, control and bureaucracy, combined with the twentieth century image of the 'corporation man', complete with his 'corporation family and home', have probably done far more than they realise to foster the present welfare state with its egalitarian standards. Although company spokesmen speak triumphantly of the advantages of competition and individual initiative, they generally prefer the ordered and well trodden ways of mankind and fiercely eschew signs of eccentricity and unconventionality within their own organisations. It is also worth recording that the growth of freely transferable shares in companies, which first developed under the protection of the courts of Chancery, against the traditional position of the common law, has also helped in the development of the social welfare state. Once a share is freely transferable, there is nothing to prevent the State from acquiring such shares, and in fact one of the first instances of the British Government's intervention in this sphere was when the Conservative administration under the leadership of Disraeli acquired the Khedive's holding of shares in the Suez Canal company of 1881. This was to start something of a fashion for States to acquire holdings in important national and international ventures.[67]

This passage may usefully be compared with n 23 and the accompanying text.

---

67 H. H. Mason, 'The Historical Development of the Corporation as a Legal Unit', in K.E. Lindgren, H. H. Mason, & B. L. J. Gordon, *The Corporation and Australian Society*, Law Book Company, Sydney, 1974, pp. 1, 10–11.

2 Try to write a brief definition of each of the following characteristics of companies, and specify why they are important in the modern commercial world:
  - perpetual succession
  - entity
  - limited liability
  - transferability of interest
  - commercial capacity.

2

RULING THE GHOST:
A SHORT HISTORY OF
CORPORATE REGULATION

Introduction

The history of corporate regulation is characterised by a number of tensions. Significant among these has been the tension between public welfare and private good. Much has been written, particularly in feminist literature, about the shifting boundaries between the public and the private spheres. With regard to corporate regulation, the most hotly debated issue has been where the boundaries should be drawn (if at all) between entrepreneurial risk-taking and protection of the many parties affected by the activities of companies: employees, consumers, creditors, investors, and minority shareholders. Many companies wield enormous economic and political power. As perpetual entities, many have accumulated power over generations. That power necessarily poses the question of responsibility: to what extent can and should governments ensure that corporate activities are carried on responsibly?

To some extent, it is not possible to reconcile risk-taking and the protection of individuals. At any particular point in time, a government must choose its priorities. The history of corporate regulation tends to be characterised by pendulum swings between deregulation, corporate abuse and excess, and a corresponding regulatory response, followed by concerns about a static or declining economy. This inevitably leads to a renewed effort at deregulation, and so the cycle begins again.

The objectives of this chapter are to explore the ways in which specific historical, political, and economic factors have shaped the modern corporate form as we know it, to reveal the tensions inherent in the development of company law, and to consider the problems caused by reactive law reform and the barriers to effective reform. We shall begin by considering the ways in which private and public good (and the company's role in shaping the 'good') have been confused. We shall then consider the historical origins of a number of the modern company's salient features before discussing the Australian experience of corporate regulation.

Public v. private

Over time, the company has become the preferred moneymaking entity. Faceless, without conscience, with 'no soul to damn and no body to kick', it pursues its individual good, often to the detriment of public welfare. Yet, this was certainly not always the case. It can be argued that the associative form was adopted originally to serve a public, rather than a private, purpose. In the twelfth and thirteenth centuries, for instance, the precursors of the commercial company, the guilds and the boroughs, were instituted primarily to serve a collective interest. Boroughs were municipal associations that sought release from feudal control under their particular charters. The merchant guild at this time was often the means by which municipal self-government and municipal charters were gained. A guild was a body of citizens that possessed an exclusive right to trade within the borough free of tolls. The quest for a borough charter was often financed by town trade, and prominent guild members were often the representatives and councillors of the new corporation. Guild members did not form an association that pursued a joint venture, but they did pursue a common purpose, and there were occasional examples of common action.[1] The guild's primary function was to maintain and protect the immunity from tolls that was granted by the borough charters. Importantly, in both borough and guild, considerations of social welfare and social good took precedence over the interests of members of the corporation.

By the late sixteenth century, the guilds had broken down as a means of regulating particular industries, and the chartered corporation had come to be the main form by which trade was regulated. For the next hundred years, however, corporations were still ostensibly formed to serve public purposes such as 'the advantage of the public' or 'the advancement of religion, of learning, and of commerce'.[2] With the rise of the capital fund, however, the tension between public purpose and private interest escalated. This mounting tension is reflected both in the *Bubble Act 1720* and in such cases as *Buck v. Buck*[3] and *The King v. Webb*,[4] which were decided under it.[5] Because of the importance of these developments to our understanding of the regulatory problems posed by the modern company, it is useful to explore these events and the ways in which this tension played itself out within them.

The financial environment preceding the passage of the Bubble Act was a classic embodiment of the 'boom' phase of a 'boom–bust' economic cycle. Highly speculative investment vehicles were dangled before an apparently insatiable and gullible public. After the disastrous collapse of the South Sea Company, the Bubble Act was passed. This Act declared certain acts—such as opening books for

---

1   W. H. Holdsworth, *A History of English Law*, vol. 2, Methuen, London, 1942, p. 385.

2   W. Blackstone, *Commentaries on the Laws of England*, vol. 1, Garland, New York, 1978, pp. xviii, 127.

3   (1808) 1 Campb 547; 170 ER 105.

4   (1811) 14 East 406; 104 ER 658.

5   The Act and the cases decided under it are discussed in some detail in P. Baron, 'Bringing Back the Bubble? Regulation of Corporate Abuse by an Action in Public Nuisance' (1992) 11 UTLR 149.

public subscription, presuming to act as if a corporate body, pretending to make stocks transferable, and pretending to act under an obsolete charter—illegal, with all such acts constituting a public nuisance. Despite evidence of widespread abuse of the corporate form, there were few prosecutions under the Act. One reason for this was that the Act was badly drafted. However, for our present purposes, it is useful to look at some of the prosecutions that did eventuate and, in particular, to consider the relationship between public purpose and private interest, as played out in the judgments.

In *Buck v. Buck*, the plaintiff employed the defendant to purchase shares in the British Ale Brewery on his behalf. The highest premiums on shares in the company were then £5 each, but the defendant charged and received £50 each as the premium upon the shares so purchased. It was alleged that the excess on the original premium was money had and received to the plaintiff's use. The court held that no action was available. The company was a public company, incorporated neither by charter nor by Act of Parliament. Its stock had been raised by public subscription, and its shares were transferable. The plaintiff argued that the company was outside the Act because the 'object of the British Ale Brewery was to carry on a lawful trade in a lawful manner, and to furnish to the public at a cheap rate, and of a good quality, an article of the first necessity'.[6] It was a public benefit, therefore, instead of a public nuisance. The Act did not apply because it was only intended to prohibit companies that tended to the common grievance, prejudice, or inconvenience of the public. While clever, this argument was rejected by the court. It held, therefore, that the company came within the prohibitions of the Bubble Act and that the parties were equally at fault.

In *The King v. Webb*, the defendants were prosecuted for having covenanted by a deed of co-partnership to raise £20 000 by subscriptions of £1 per share for the purpose of making and selling bread. Each member was obliged to buy a weekly quantity of bread not exceeding a shilling in value per share. The jury considered that the company was originally created for altruistic motives, which were beneficial to the townsfolk, but that nonetheless the scheme was 'prejudicial to the bakers and millers of the town and neighbourhood in their trades'.[7] Lord Ellenborough held that the facts did not bring the defendants within the prohibitions of the Act because the purpose for which the capital was raised was not 'manifestly tending to the common grievance, and being in this case expressly found to have been beneficial',[8] it did not fall within the Bubble Act.

The slipperiness of the notions of public and private that are played out in these cases is of considerable interest. In *Buck v. Buck*, the court was persuaded to focus entirely upon the manner in which the shares were marketed and the extent to which those activities fell within the intention of the Act; in the *Webb* case, the court

---

6   *Buck v. Buck* (1808) 1 Campb 547 at 549; 170 ER 1052 at 1053.
7   *The King v. Webb* (1811) 14 East 406 at 413; 104 ER 658 at 661.
8   (1811) 14 East 406 at 421; 104 ER 658 at 664.

sought the relevant 'nuisance' in the trade of the company, rather than in the manner in which its shares had been marketed.

The Bubble Act was repealed in 1825.[9] With the rise of capital and society's increasing faith in ethical egoism, the public interest became confused with, and ultimately subordinated to, the pursuit of private gain. Much of the accepted model of company law is a legacy of this subordination. Virtually all of the doctrinal structure of contemporary company law is a product of the nineteenth century, the heyday of individualism and *laissez-faire* economics. One of the issues that we will examine in this chapter is whether this doctrinal structure ought to remain unquestioned.

REVIEW QUESTION

Think about the kinds of abuses that the Bubble Act was enacted to curb. Which interpretive paradigm (that in *Buck* or that in *Webb*) seems more appropriate, given the nature of the abuses that were prevalent at the time?

The modern company: Its salient features

The most significant developments in modern company law took place between 1844 and 1897, in the heyday of British *laissez-faire* liberalism. C. A. Cooke[10] identifies six pieces of legislation that created the corporate form as we know it. These were the *Railways Regulation Act 1844*, the *Joint Stock Companies Act 1844*, the *Companies' Winding Up Act 1844*, the *Joint Stock Banks Act 1844*, the *Companies Clauses Act 1845*, and the *Joint Stock Companies Act 1847*. The existing law on companies was then largely consolidated by the massive *Companies Act 1862*.[11] The decisions in *Foss v. Harbottle*[12] and *Salomon v. Salomon & Co. Ltd*[13] may be added to these legislative developments.

Briefly, the import of these developments was as follows. The Railways Regulation Act established the principle that railway companies were a class of company formed under special parliamentary sanction to carry on a public undertaking. It was reasoned that, as such companies had special powers, they should be subject to

---

9 See T. Hadden, *Company Law and Capitalism*, Weidenfeld & Nicolson, London, 1972. Hadden maintains that this was probably as a result of the 'official embarrassment caused by a sudden spate of new unincorporated flotations' (p. 13).

10 C. A. Cooke, *Corporation, Trust and Company*, Manchester University Press, Manchester, 1950, p. 135.

11 Hadden notes that these legislative developments resulted from periods of intense activity in company flotation in the periods 1824–25 and 1834–36, which were followed by a large number of failures and consequential losses by investors. A new outbreak of insurance and annuity frauds in the early 1840s led directly to the appointment of the first comprehensive company law reform committee; see Hadden, p. 14.

12 (1843) 2 Hare 461; 67 ER 189.

13 (1897) AC 22.

control by the State in the public interest. The 'State airlines' (such as Qantas), which operate as the flagships of many modern nation states, are latter-day replicas of such entities. The notion that public utilities, such as railroads and electricity companies, had a particular duty to uphold the public interest created a distinction between private and public companies. This distinction focused not on the ownership of shares and their transferability, but upon the purpose for which these companies were formed and the powers that they might exercise. The legacy of this approach remains with us in the vast number of public institutions (including hospitals and universities, as well as more 'commercial' operations) that continue to be incorporated by special Act of Parliament and governed thereafter by their Act of incorporation. Against this background, the present Australian move to privatisation is of particular interest.

The Joint Stock Companies Act 1844 established the framework of later company law and granted the privileges of incorporation to the equitable company. The Companies' Winding Up Act interposed the 'body' of the company between members and company creditors. The Joint Stock Banks Act drew a distinction between unincorporated and incorporated firms by reference to size, and provided that deeds of settlement should be in the form prescribed. The Companies Clauses Act had two effects. First, it provided that the Board of Trade could provide a licence to a company that wished to purchase, hold, take on lease, or hold on mortgage any land beyond that of its business premises. Prior to this legislation, the Mortmain rule[14] provided that a company could only hold without licence enough land for occupation as a place of business. The legislation did not abolish this rule but removed doubts about the extent of the Board of Trade's licensing powers. Second, this legislation relaxed the procedures relating to promoters.[15] The Companies Act was primarily a consolidating Act, but it also transferred jurisdiction over winding-up from the Court of Bankruptcy to the Court of Chancery, replaced the 'creditors' representative' of the earlier winding-up Acts with the 'liquidator', included insurance and banking companies in its provisions, and introduced companies limited by guarantee. *Foss v. Harbottle* established both the 'proper plaintiff' and the 'internal management' rules, and *Salomon v. Salomon & Co. Ltd* entrenched the separate entity doctrine in corporate law.

Together, these legislative and judicial developments established and consolidated the salient features of the modern corporation. These features may be identified as:

- a contractual division of power between management and the general meeting
- the contractual determination of rights and obligations among members themselves
- freely transferable shares

---

14 This was an ancient rule framed by the Crown to preclude the alienation of lands to corporate bodies, by which the benefits of the incidents of tenure were lost. It was directed originally at religious societies.

15 This is discussed at greater length in the next chapter.

- the nature of the share as personal property
- the attachment of voting rights to shares rather than to individual owners
- the separate entity doctrine
- limited liability.

We will discuss each of these features in turn, identifying their origins and discussing their implications for corporate regulation.

Contractual determination of obligation

Both the rights and obligations of the members among themselves, and the division of power between management and the general meeting, are determined by the contract of association. Historically, the contractual resolution of rights and obligations among the members themselves derives from the *Joint Stock Companies Act 1856* and is a reflection of the fact that the company was a statutory version of the earlier company.[16] Prior to this legislation, associative rights and obligations had been established by the deed of settlement, a device that was used extensively from the eighteenth century. The deed of settlement was necessitated because, at common law, an unincorporated group of people could not own property in common. Chancery avoided this rule by holding that property could be held in trust for such an unincorporated group. This was accomplished by mutual covenants between the members of the company and the trustees whom they selected. A deed of settlement was drafted, in which these covenants were set out and every member of the group was deemed to assent to those terms. The trustees covenanted to observe the terms of the deed and to apply the fund settled on them for the purpose specified. This form of association flourished in the period 1825–52. In 1834 this equitable company was given legislative recognition by the *Trading Companies Act 1834*[17] and, subsequently, by the passage of the Joint Stock Companies Act of 1844.

Historically, the contractual division of power between the board and the general meeting derives from late nineteenth-century case law. At the time that *Foss v. Harbottle* was heard, the prevailing view was that directors were merely delegates of the general meeting and were, therefore, subject to its ultimate control. The rationale for this decision was that, as a share bestows a right to a proprietary ownership of the company, the body of corporators in the general meeting are the proprietors of the

---

16 It is worth noting that, in the USA, the identical doctrine has a very different history. The American corporation is a lineal descendant of the chartered corporation (which is partly why the term 'corporation' is more conventional in the USA than the British 'company'). A 'right' to a corporate charter was recognised in the USA in the eighteenth century, and the first general incorporation statute was enacted by the state of New York in 1811. The advantages that this had for American enterprise were a driving force behind British developments, both statutorily and through the ingenuity of the legal profession.

17 This Act began with a recitation that companies were being formed that it would be inexpedient to incorporate at common law, but it was recognised that these companies should be able to claim some of the privileges of incorporation. The Act empowered the Crown to grant to trading and other companies, by Letters Patent, those privileges that could be conferred by charter of incorporation.

company. Hence, they are entitled to control the company, although they may delegate its day-to-day management.[18]

In the 20 years following *Foss v. Harbottle*, delegation theory acquired an increasingly vigorous (and somewhat inconsistent) contractual overlay, and the delegation involved became more or less irrevocable. In *Automatic Self-Cleansing Filter Syndicate Co. Ltd v. Cunninghame*,[19] it was held that the contract in the articles[20] entitled the directors to manage the company. As a consequence, the court would not allow the general meeting to interfere with the board in the exercise of its powers under the contract. The general meeting resolved to sell a company undertaking after the board refused to do so. Collins MR stated:

> I cannot see anything in principle to justify the contention that the directors are bound to comply with the votes or the resolutions of a simple majority at an ordinary meeting of the shareholders. I do not think it true to say that the directors are agents. I think it is more nearly true to say that they are in the position of managing partners appointed to fill that post by a mutual arrangement between all the shareholders.[21]

If this contractual variant of delegation theory is pursued to its logical conclusion, the only effective control that a general meeting can exercise over the board is the threat of removal from office (and even this may be weakened by articles that entrench directors' power).[22] For this reason, delegation theory represents the ultimate step in the separation of management and ownership within the company.

Philosophically, both the contractual determination of rights and obligations among the members themselves and the contractual division of power may be linked to three important ideas: the significance of enforcement of voluntary obligations, the value of individualism, and the idea of the limited State. Although we shall discuss each of these ideas in turn, it is important to note that these assumptions were (and are) interdependent.

---

18 Some of these ideas will be examined in more detail in subsequent chapters, especially chapters 8 and 9. The connection between ownership and control is deeply entrenched in Western culture. While superficially plausible, the proprietary analysis upon which delegation theory rests is complex and inconsistent. It is fundamentally unsatisfactory and the source of a good deal of confusion.

19 [1906] 2 Ch 34.

20 In this case, the articles contained a provision that paralleled art. 66 of table A.

21 [1906] 2 Ch 34 at 45.

22 Delegation theory did not die away completely, however. See, for instance, *Marshall's Valve Co. v. Manning Wardle* [1909] 1 Ch 267; *Dowse v. Marks* (1913) 13 SR (NSW) 332. Delegation theory is discussed in more detail in chapter 14. Here it is worth noting that the operation of delegation theory in the corporate context is fraught with difficulty. Conventional understandings of delegation refer to notions such as 'you can delegate performance but not responsibility'. Underlying such ideas is the insistence that the delegator remains responsible for the way in which his or her delegate performs. In the case of the company, all such ideas are profoundly problematical.

REVIEW QUESTION

What are the implications of the idea that the board is a coordinate, essentially autonomous body in relation to the shareholders in general meeting?

Individualism

Williams notes the extraordinary development of the term 'individual' from its original medieval meaning of 'indivisible'. He writes:

> The emergence of notions of individuality, in the modern sense, can be related to the break-up of the medieval social, economic and religious order. In the general movement against feudalism there was a new stress on a man's personal existence over and above his place or function in a rigid hierarchical society. There was a related stress, in Protestantism, in a man's direct and individual relation to God, as opposed to this relation mediated by the Church. But it was not until C17 and C18 that a new mode of analysis, in logic and mathematics, postulated the individual as the substantial entity … from which other categories and especially collective categories were derived. The political thought of the Enlightenment mainly followed this pattern. Argument began from individuals, who had an initial and primary existence, and laws and forms of society were derived from them.[23]

The idea that political rights and obligations arose from the interest and will of dissociated individuals was fundamental to Thomas Hobbes's theory.[24] He assumed a person's nature to be inherently acquisitive: 'Life itself … can never be without desire' and 'the felicity of this life' is only 'continual success in obtaining those things which a man from time to time desireth'.[25] People desire, but they also reason, and so they are necessarily preoccupied with ways of fulfilling their desires. A person is the rational maximiser of his or her own interests: 'the power of a man … is his present means to obtain some future apparent good'. It follows that society is, by nature, competitive. People inevitably desire and compete for scarce resources, '[a]nd therefore if any two men desire the same thing, which nevertheless they cannot both enjoy, they become enemies'.[26]

While the Hobbesian world view was bleak and ruthless—society plunging, in the absence of strong government, towards the 'war of all against all'—the Lockean vision was, if less brutal, equally acquisitive. John Locke considered that, as people's primary motivation was to protect their 'life, liberty and estate', their main obligation was to protect themselves. Only if this self-preservation was not at risk was there a secondary duty to protect the rest of humanity. It was thus the charge of each individual to act in his or her own interest. Self-preservation was seen as necessary to promote the common good.

---

23 R. Williams, *Keywords*, Fontana, Glasgow, 1976, pp. 135–6.
24 C. B. Macpherson, *The Political Theory of Possessive Individualism*, Clarendon Press, Oxford, 1962, p. 1.
25 T. Hobbes, *Leviathan*, Penguin, Harmondsworth, 1981, part I, p. vii.
26 Hobbes, part I, p. xiii.

Consent

The implications of this belief in individualism were numerous. In particular, Ian Shapiro notes that the view of rights that developed from the ideas of the seventeenth-century contract theorists 'assumes that the individual will is the cause of all actions, individual and collective; it ascribes decisive epistemic and hence moral authority to the individual over his actions, on the grounds that he has privileged access to the contents of his own mind. For this reason individual consent becomes vital to the whole idea of political activity'.[27]

The idea of individual consent led to an increasing emphasis upon contractual theories of obligation. As cottage or farm-based production gave way to factory-based production, there was an attendant growth in urbanisation. The nexus of mutual rights and obligations created and maintained by the feudal structure was progressively destroyed. New guidelines were needed to determine obligations in this bewildering new world. Contractual theories of obligation were especially appropriate. In the nineteenth century, in particular, the performance of one's contracts was an important feature of legal and economic life. Individuals had sole proprietorship of their own persons and thus the right (even the duty) to further their own advantage by means of the contract. In contract law, this belief may be seen in the idea of freedom of contract—that is, the freedom to make, but not to break, contracts.[28] In company law, this idea could be found in the rigid and formalistic interpretation of the company constitution.

Individualism and the enforcement of contractual obligations were to lead courts to uphold the decisions of management, despite frequent opposition from shareholders. Two very different (and mutually inconsistent) ideas contributed to this trend. First, the courts insisted that, by contract, shareholders had delegated their management powers to the directors. Having covenanted with other shareholders and with the company to so delegate, they were not entitled to resile from their covenant (the courts could not, after all, condone a breach of contract). Second, given that, by covenant, management powers were vested in the directors, the courts were profoundly reluctant to question their decisions. Time and time again, the courts expressed their reluctance to second-guess decisions made upon commercial grounds. Here, a number of very different ideas came together. First, it was easy to move from the idea that the managers were the 'guiding will' of the corporation (no other 'will' being available to guide corporate acts) to the idea that they had a unique understanding of the 'corporate good'. The reasoning for corporate persons proceeded, by analogy, from that used in relation to natural persons. The tenets of possessive individualism dictated that individuals were best placed to know and to act upon their own interests. In a similar vein, it seemed easy to argue that, as managers represented the guiding will of the company, they were in a privileged position with

---

27 I. Shapiro, *The Evolution of Rights in Liberal Theory*, Cambridge University Press, Cambridge, 1986, p. 275.

28 See, for instance, the classic formulation of the rule in *Printing and Numerical Registering Co. v. Sampson* (1875) LR 19 Eq 462 at 465.

respect to determining the 'corporate interests'. Thus an uneasy identification between the 'interests of the company' and the policies of management seemed inevitable, courts frequently declining to declare management decisions unacceptable unless the decisions were clearly such that no reasonable manager could have made them. The fundamental flaw with this argument, of course, was that it frequently identified company interests only with management. Coupled with the idea of the limited State, this view condoned, or at least turned a blind eye to, abuses within the corporate structure.

REVIEW QUESTION

What tensions can you see arising from the application of an individualist ethos to the corporate structure? How does the Corporations Law seek to resolve such tensions?

The limited State

The idea of the 'limited State' is that there is a 'public' sphere, in which it is proper for government to intervene, and a 'private' sphere, in which government has no role. This idea has been particularly influential in feminist writing, and is explored in chapter 16. For our present purposes, it is worth noting that, in the nineteenth century, many people believed that government should interfere as little as possible in areas such as the family and the market-place.[29] This idea of non-interference in the market-place was to be of particular importance in the development of corporate regulation.

The limited State was advocated by such influential philosophers as Hobbes and Locke. Shapiro points out that, despite Hobbes's political absolutism, he was nevertheless an advocate of economic minimalism:[30]

> Despite the state's absolute power, its actions are conceived of as indirect and regulative, as revealed in the discussions of unemployment and taxation; it is supportive of the institution of the market, revealed in the account of contract and individual freedom; and it is limited, revealed in the discussion of the limits to public property as well as by the fact that Hobbes does not ascribe any further economic roles to the state.[31]

Locke, too, maintained the importance of the limited State. According to Locke's interpretation of the social contract, government was instituted to protect natural rights and, correspondingly, its power was circumscribed by the individual's natural freedom. Just as no one should harm another in the enjoyment of life, liberty, and estate, government should refrain from interfering with the

---

29 See F. E. Olsen, 'The Family and the Market: A Study of Ideology and Legal Reform' (1983) 96 Harv LR 1497.

30 These ideas are considered at greater length in P. Baron, 'Shells of Steel and Bodies of Pulp: Commercial Man, Commercial Morality' (1993) 11 *Law in Context* 3.

31 Shapiro, p. 34.

individual's enjoyment of these rights. Should government fail to so refrain, its legitimacy could be called into question.[32]

As Raymond Williams suggests, the values of individualism and the limited State, as propounded by Locke and Hobbes, were reinforced and expanded by classical economics, theology, and Darwinism. For instance, in the century after Locke, Adam Smith's *Wealth of Nations* laid the foundations of classical economics: 'it is not from the benevolence of the butcher, the brewer or the baker that we expect our dinner, but from their regard to their own interest. We address ourselves not to their humanity but to their self-love, and never talk to them of our own necessities but of their advantages'.[33] The pursuit of self-interest was, in Smith's view, not only a 'natural' characteristic of man; it was also demanded by the good of all:

> He generally, indeed, neither intends to promote the public interest, nor knows how much he is promoting it … he intends only his own gain, and he is in this, as in many other cases, led by an invisible hand to promote an end which was not part of his intention … By pursuing his own interest he frequently promotes that of the society more effectively than when he really intends to promote it.[34]

The implications of this passage are that the profit motive—each person's pursuit of his or her self-interest—automatically controls prices; that the free market is self-regulating and should not (in fact, cannot) tolerate State interference; and that the individual pursuit of material gain, unhindered by State interference, will thus further the common good.

Utilitarianism, which was introduced by Jeremy Bentham in the late eighteenth century, reinforced the ideal of furthering the common good by pursuing self-interest.[35] Utilitarianism justified egoism on the grounds of the 'greatest good for the greatest number'. This principle was considered to be the only rational guide to private morals and to public policy. The 'felicific calculus' or 'moral arithmetic' determined the greatest good. The assumption that self-interest motivates all human conduct was the basis for this principle.[36]

From a scientific perspective, the principles of Charles Darwin also supported the beliefs of social contract and classical economics. If the struggle for existence within a hostile environment determined who would survive in the natural world, then, by analogy, competition in civil society was 'natural' and 'survival of the fittest'

---

32 The power of government was that of 'making laws with penalties … for the regulating and preserving of property and of employing the force of the community in the execution of such laws … and all this only for the public good'. See J. Locke, 'True End of Civil Government', in E. Barker, *Social Contract: Essays by Locke, Hume and Rousseau*, Oxford University Press, London, 1960, part IX, p. 131.

33 A. Smith, *Wealth of Nations*, Modern Library, New York, 1937 (1776), p. 14.

34 Smith, p. 423.

35 R. D. Altick, *Victorian People and Ideas*, W. W. Norton & Co., New York, 1973, p. 116.

36 However, we should note that these ideas are very complex. For example, what many of us would describe as 'altruistic' conduct—giving to charity or foregoing a benefit so that another might gain—would have been characterised by Bentham as 'self-interested' in the sense that the individual derived pleasure from giving. The self-interest of which classical utilitarians spoke is not to be confused with any form of selfishness.

was a 'natural' law. Indeed, Herbert Spencer used the biological principles of Darwin to promote 'Social Darwinism', which was essentially 'extreme *laissez-faire* endowed with a (supposed) biological sanction'.[37]

While philosophy, economics, and biology justified egoism on ostensibly rational grounds, Calvinism furnished its theological justification. One of the great social phenomena of the nineteenth century was the rise to power of the middle class. Manufacturers, financiers, providers of consumer goods and services, and commodity-brokers gained strength as the economy shifted from land and cottage to the factory. Correspondingly, the influence of the landed gentry declined, and for most of the nineteenth century, wage earners did not attain political self-consciousness or effective organisation.[38] The middle class was mainly Protestant. Protestantism stressed personal salvation through the conduct of one's daily life and the importance of private conscience over theological dogma. The moral code of Protestantism valued frugality, self-denial, dedication to one's calling, and the value of hard work. Its ethics were those of sobriety, thrift, cleanliness of person, tidiness of home, good manners, respect for law, honesty in business affairs, chastity, and seriousness.[39] Self-help and self-reliance were simultaneously the keys to eternal life and to material success: '[prevailing religious thought] was the natural counterpart of a social philosophy which repudiated teleology and which substituted the analogy of a self-regulating mechanism, moved by weights and pulleys of economic motives, for the theory which had regarded society as an organism composed of different classes untied by their common subordination to a spiritual purpose'.[40]

Ideas such as of individualism and the limited State brought about a marked change of thinking about the role of government, the conduct of commercial matters, and the regulation of companies. In the Middle Ages, for instance, a great number of statutes dealt with the conduct of specific trades.[41] These laws were made to ensure not only that a commodity was manufactured honestly, but also that it was fairly and reasonably priced, that an adequate amount of skill went into its manufacture, and that there was fair treatment of labourers.[42] Indeed, W. H. Holdsworth

---

37 Altick, p. 232.

38 Altick, p. 232. The rise in power of the middle class was not, of course, an overnight phenomenon. It had been developing since the Elizabethan era and had been at the core of both the Protestant Reformation and the Puritan Revolution. For a comprehensive discussion of this rise in power, see R. H. Tawney, *Religion and the Rise of Capitalism*, Penguin, Harmondsworth, 1938.

39 G. H. Sabine, *A History of Political Theory*, 3rd edn, George H. Harrap & Co., London, 1954, p. 175. These characteristics were particularly true of that variant of Protestantism known as Calvinism. Calvinism had a significant impact on early social contract theory, in particular the social contract theory of Rousseau, and Calvinist ideology underwrote many of the doctrines of early capitalism. See M. Walzer, *The Revolution of the Saints: A Study in the Origins of Radical Politics*, Atheneum, New York, 1976.

40 Tawney, p. 194.

41 See, for example, the *Victuallers in London Act 1357*; *Victuallers in London Act 1472*; *Fishermen's Act 1361*; *Wool, Silk, Worsted and Broadcloth Manufacturers Act 1455*; *Wax Chandlers Act 1433*; *Shoemakers Act 1464*; *Boyers Act 1472*; *Tilers Act 1477*; *Fullers Act 1482*; *Horners Act 1462*.

42 See, for instance, the Fullers Act, against using fulling mills to make caps, as these threw men out of work and did the work to an inferior standard.

notes that the burden of proof was on those who denied the State's right to interfere.[43] In contrast, Shapiro notes the effect of adopting the idea of the limited State:

> This negative libertarian view of social life in general, and of the production, exchange,
> and consumption of wealth in particular, was also of great importance in the subsequent
> history of the liberal ideology of individual rights. Indispensable as it obviously is to the
> functioning of a capitalist market, it became deeply embedded in the emerging social sys-
> tem. Hobbes did not intend to justify such a system nor had he any very clear idea of
> what it was. His negative libertarianism survived and achieved the preeminent status it
> did in the concomitant ideology because of its affinity with these emerging economic and
> social relations. It provided the conceptual tools for the construction of an ideology that
> could legitimate these relations.[44]

This view is supported by Cooke, who with specific reference to company law, comments on the theoretical direction of the law engendered by the belief in individualism:

> [T]he English law of corporations, trusts and companies has been concerned much more
> with the rules governing the conduct of individuals than with logical classification of
> groups. It has not, perhaps, always been clear that the transactions of groups are the trans-
> actions of individuals and that it is individuals who carry on the affairs of corporations …
> Once within the legal machine the law is concerned with the behaviour of the individu-
> als who compose, act for, or transact business on behalf of the corporation.[45]

The individualistic view had a significant impact upon business ethics. After all, if
one's primary duty is that of self-preservation, then one's ethical duties to others do
not come into play unless self-preservation is not at stake—and one can argue that, in
business, one's self-preservation is always an issue. One's duty to others is thus limited, in essence, to the duty of honesty. Ethically, there was no requirement, for
instance, of fair dealing, or of a duty of care to one's shareholders or one's creditors.

One of the more influential legal expressions of the belief in limited government and individualism in company law is to be found in *Foss v. Harbottle*. In this
case, promoters (also directors of the company) sold the company plots of land at
allegedly exorbitant prices. The court refused to allow two minority shareholders
to maintain an action on behalf of the company. The court held that the company
itself was the proper plaintiff in the action because it was for the company to
determine whether or not proceedings should be entered into. It was not for the
court to interfere with the decision of the company. The doctrine that emerged
from this case came to be known as 'the rule in *Foss v. Harbottle*' and contained
two distinct limbs or rules. These rules were the 'proper plaintiff' rule and the
'internal management' or 'business judgment' rule. Together they contributed to
the separation of management and ownership of the corporation. The internal
management rule, coupled with the contractual division of power within the cor-

---

43 Holdsworth, pp. 467–8.
44 Shapiro, p. 63.
45 Cooke, pp. 188–9.

poration, created a situation in which courts were reluctant to question the management decisions of the board. The proper plaintiff rule restricted the rights of shareholders to rectify improper decisions of the board.[46] Together these rules created considerable problems for corporate regulation. They facilitated, in particular, abuses of power within the company, such as oppression and unfair dealing, which the courts were reluctant to rectify.

REVIEW QUESTION

To what extent is the idea of a 'limited State' an ideological device for justifying State action or inaction?[47]

The share

Modern corporate law is centred around three important ideas relating to the share. These are the idea of the share as personal property, the idea of freely transferable shares, and the idea of voting rights attaching to shares. These ideas have been evolving since around the seventeenth century.

The conception of a share as personal property derived from the distinction between equity capital[48] and the business enterprise itself together with appurtenances pertaining to it. Subscribed capital is a liability, while the land, buildings, stock, cash, goodwill, and balance of profit are assets.[49] From the point of view of the shareholder, the share represents funds advanced to the 'company' in the hope of gain, whether by way of dividends or by way of capital appreciation. In a solvent liquidation, the company will be obliged to return capital to its shareholders. For this reason, development of the idea of shares as personal property[50] is the result of the rise of the capital fund and a development of accounting practice.[51]

---

46 Briefly, these rules operate as follows. According to the 'indoor management' rule, outsiders are entitled to assume that corporate acts that appear to have been authorised by the appropriate corporate organ are so authorised. The 'proper plaintiff' rule, fully stated, insists that where a wrong is done to the company, the company is the proper plaintiff. This second rule has affinities with the notion of privity of contract. In essence, it specifies that only the one who has been wronged is entitled to bring legal action against wrongdoers. In the corporate context, this poses a particular problem. Where the directors have committed wrongful acts against the company (for example, diverting corporate opportunities to themselves), they are unlikely to be willing to initiate legal action against themselves. This makes it very difficult to bring the directors to account for wrongdoing.

47 In considering this question, you may wish to read M. Thornton, 'The Cartography of Public and Private', in M. Thornton (ed.), *Public and Private: Feminist Legal Debates*, Oxford University Press, Melbourne, 1995, pp. 2–16.

48 The term 'equity capital' refers to the funds provided to the company by its shareholders. This concept runs parallel to that of 'debt capital', which refers to the funds provided to the company by its other creditors.

49 On the conception of a share as personal property, see *Bligh v. Brent* (1836) 2 Y & C Ex 281 and *R v. Dock Coy of Hull* (1786) 1 TR 219.

50 Technically, a share is a chose in action—a bundle of rights and obligations that cannot be reduced to physical possession.

51 *Drybutter v. Bartholomew* (1723) 2 P Wms 127; *Townsend v. Ash* (1745) 3 Atk 336; *Stafford v. Buckley* (1750) 2 Ves Sen 171; *Swayne v. Fawkener* (1696) Show PC 207; *Sandys v. Sibthorpe* (1778) Dick 545; but see *Howse v. Chapman* (1799) 4 Ves 542, in which a share in a company (the Bath Navigation) was held to be real estate.

It would appear that a share in a joint stock company was considered to be a saleable asset from the outset of the joint stock system. The transferability of shares on paper seems to have begun with the East India Company, which kept books in which the transfer of stock was recorded.[52] In time, it became common for statutes incorporating joint stock companies to provide that shares could be assigned by entry in the transfer book.[53] It was, of course, possible to transfer shares by using the trust, but L. C. B. Gower notes that

> incorporation, with the resulting separation of the business from its members, greatly facilitates the transfer of the members' interests, although even without formal incorporation much the same end was achieved through the device of the trust coupled with an agreement for transferability in the deed of settlement. But this end could only be approximately attained since the member, even after transfer, would remain liable for the firm's debts incurred during the time when he was a member. Moreover, in the absence of limited liability, his opportunities of transfer would in practice be much restricted.[54]

By the middle of the seventeenth century, the ownership of a share was associated with financial, rather than personal, participation in a company. By the end of that century, there was a market in London for shares in major companies.[55]

Attaching suffrage to shares was a later development. In the early corporation, each individual member had a right to vote in corporate affairs, but the individual had one vote only. This was the case, for instance, in the East India Company. There was no necessary connection between suffrage and the number of shares held. As corporate membership evolved into a system whereby shares in a capital fund accumulated for trading purposes, suffrage became progressively restricted, first to those members who held shares, and then to those members who held shares of a defined value. For instance, in the statute that founded the Greenland Company,[56] it was provided that each subscriber of £500 should have one vote, but that each subscriber of £1000 or more shall have two votes. By the eighteenth century, in the absence of a specific provision, all shareholders had one vote each, but this rule could be avoided by splitting a stock holding and assigning part of it. This practice was condemned in 7 Geo III, c. 48 (1767), which provided that no member of a joint stock company who had held shares for less than 6 months could exercise a vote.[57] During this period votes had to be exercised in person, there being no gen-

---

52 See *Johnson v. East India Co.* (1679) Finch Rep Temp 430.

53 *Greenland Co. Act 1692*, s. 24; *Bank of England Act 1694*, s. 25; *National Land Bank Act 1695*, s. 17. See also *Bank of England v. Moffatt* (1791) 3 Bro CC 260; *Cock v. Goodfellow* (1721) 10 Mod 489 at 498.

54 L. C. B. Gower, *Principles of Modern Company Law*, 4th edn, Stevens & Sons, London, 1979, p. 106. It is also interesting to note that, for a time, freely transferable shares constituted a public nuisance under the Bubble Act. This is discussed below.

55 Hadden, p. 8.

56 Greenland Co. Act.

57 Cooke, pp. 73–4. See also the Companies Act, and *Moffatt v. Farquhar* (1878) 7 Ch D 591 and the cases cited therein.

eral right to vote by proxy.[58] Indeed, proxy voting was prohibited at common law,[59] but the right to issue proxies could be given to a company by special grant.[60]

The implications of these developments were extremely significant. First, by attaching voting rights to the shares themselves, the democratic nature of the corporation declined.[61] The potential for abuse within the company, particularly when coupled with the idea of limited government, increased dramatically. Second, because the transference of shares on paper was increasingly facilitated, the company was more often seen to be an abstract entity, defined not in terms of people, but in terms of numbers (as discussed below).[62] Hadden notes a further development in the disconnection of enterprise and investor: 'Through the joint stock company it was now possible to raise large sums of capital for any profit-making enterprise from persons who could not in any way be regarded as having any direct connection with the enterprise. Capitalism of this kind was the base upon which our modern commercial society has been founded'.[63] The third implication was that the share became an important, and volatile, source of wealth, as the South Sea Bubble incident was to reveal.

The separate entity doctrine

In law, a corporation is a separate legal entity from its members. It can thus enjoy rights and be subject to duties that are distinct from those enjoyed by the members of the association. The obvious applications of this idea occur in areas such as the company's rights to own property or to make contracts; indeed, such legal rights are among the purposes for which the corporate form is sought, and they are essential to the idea of the perpetual existence of the company. The idea of corporate personality has further implications, and it is to some of these ramifications that we shall now turn.

The full implications of the separate entity doctrine became apparent with the seminal decision of *Salomon v. Salomon & Co. Ltd.*[64] In this case, Aron Salomon was

---

58 Proxy voting is a feature of modern corporate life that requires some explanation. With the growth of modern capital markets, personal attendance at general meetings has become the exception rather than the rule for a majority of shareholders. It is usual for shareholders to receive 'proxy forms' together with the statutorily required notice of general meetings and of the business to be transacted at those meetings. Those shareholders who so choose may complete these proxy forms either by specifying the way in which they wish to vote on particular items or by authorising a representative, normally the board, to exercise their votes. Because very few shareholders actually attend meetings or individually exercise the voting rights attached to their shares, those proxies that are submitted can vest substantial power in the board.

59 *Harben v. Phillips* (1882) 23 Ch D 14.

60 Cooke, p. 74. See the *Mines Adventurers Act 1710* and the *Northumberland Fishery Society Act 1789*.

61 The association of participatory rights with an abstract entity, 'the share', rather than with an individual, marked a decisive shift in the understanding of what a company is and paved the way for the rise of the passive investor.

62 It is worth noting that today it is commonplace for shares to be held in 'brokerage' or 'street' names, further distancing the connection between the shareholder and the company.

63 Hadden, p. 8.

64 This case will reappear like a talisman in our explorations of corporate law. It is fundamental, not only to an understanding of the development of corporate law, but also to any intelligent understanding of corporate governance. It will be discussed in depth in our exploration of the doctrine known as the 'corporate veil' in chapter 7.

the owner of a boot business. He formed a company under the Companies Act with capital of £40 000. He sold his business to the company for £30 000. The company paid for the business by issuing Salomon with 20 000 fully paid shares and £10 000 in debentures.[65] Salomon thus owned 20 000 shares in the company. Six other members of his family were also shareholders and owned one share each. The company had a short life. When it went into liquidation, its assets were £6000, and its liabilities were £10 000 owed to Salomon under the debentures and £7000 owed to other unsecured creditors. Salomon claimed all the assets as the sole secured creditor of the company. The liquidator sued Salomon on the basis that the company was effectively Salomon himself and that the issue of debentures by him to himself was a fraud on the company.

At first instance, Vaughan Williams J held that the company was merely an agent for Salomon. As a consequence, he took the view that Aron Salomon was then obliged to indemnify the company by paying the creditors. The Court of Appeal also found against Aron Salomon. Lindley J. suggested that the debentures were nothing more than a device to defraud creditors ('one substantial man and six mere dummies do not make a company'[66]).

The House of Lords, however, found for Aron Salomon. The latter had merely 'availed himself to the full of the advantages offered by the Companies Act'. Lord Macnaghten maintained that he could not 'understand how a body corporate made "capable" by statute can lose its individuality by issuing the bulk of its capital to one person …The company is at law a different person altogether from the subscribers to the memorandum'.[67] As all the members of the company knew the true state of affairs, there could be no fraud on the company and the creditors understood that they were dealing with a limited company and thus had the opportunity to protect themselves. The agency argument was also rejected. If the company were not a legal person, it could not be an agent. If it were a legal person, it acted for itself and not as Aron Salomon's agent.

The case of *Salomon* shows, we believe, the abstraction of the corporate form that took place in the nineteenth century. Two factors, in particular, contributed to this abstraction. The first is the development of accounting practice—in particular, the development of 'double entry' accounting.[68] This led to an abstraction of the share, and ultimately of the company itself. The corporation became a profit and loss account, an agglomeration of capital, rather than a collection of individuals. Cooke notes this development:

[T]he concept of a common stock or a common fund of capital (whether in goods or money) began to be of importance. Losses were lessened to an individual who spread

---

65 A debenture is an instrument acknowledging the existence of a debt. The debt may be either secured (as was the case in *Salomon*) or unsecured.

66 The 'dummies' were, of course, Aron Salomon's wife and children!

67 (1897) AC 22 at 51.

68 Discussed at greater length by Hadden, pp. 65–9.

his risks over a number of ventures and outlets for the investment of profits were multiplied. In this development, the rise of accounting was a necessary factor, promoted mainly by Italian ingenuity in assessing the results of voyages on the great trade routes across the Mediterranean. The importance of the double entry system of keeping books lies not in its arithmetic, but in its metaphysics ... The business men created the financial entity of the business, a fund separate and distinct from its subscribers, linked with them by debits and credits.[69]

Cooke goes on to note that, whether the individual was a member of a chartered corporation operating a joint stock fund or the shareholder of a trust operating a joint stock fund, 'he had a claim or an obligation, a claim to a share of profits or an obligation to subscribe to the fund and to meet the fund's losses. And in either instance he had something which could be sold, whether it was the stock of an incorporated company or the share of and in a trust'.[70]

This faith in numbers may be linked to Hobbes, whose theory was inherently mathematical in the sense that he believed that society could be explained in terms of addition of 'desires' and subtraction of 'aversions':

> These small beginnings of Motion, within the body of Man, before they appear in walking, speaking, striking, and other visible actions, are commonly called ENDEAVOUR.
>
> This Endeavour, when it is toward something which causes it, is called APPETITE, or DESIRE ... and when the Endeavour is fromward something, it is generally called AVERSION.[71]

This mathematical model was taken up in the early nineteenth century by utilitarianism, which was based upon the principle of 'the greatest good for the greatest number'. It did so by determining the greatest 'good' by mathematical calculations of units of pleasure and pain. The 'good' was inherently material in nature: bank deposits, lucrative investments, and the ownership of land. It made no allowances for 'the promptings of conscience' or for such intangibles as 'generosity, mercy, compassion, self-sacrifice or love'.[72] It is easy to see how such a theory would facilitate the abstraction of the company, which was no longer perceived as a group of individuals but as an account.

In addition to this abstraction, the separate entity doctrine was aided by legal positivism. Positivism maintains that 'law is a system of rules which can be identified through their pedigree and that the judge is bound to apply it in some straightforward way'.[73] Thus, the role of the judge is merely to enforce the *existing* rules. What the law *ought* to be is a political question for the legislature. The decision in

---

69 Cooke, p. 185.
70 Cooke, p. 186.
71 Hobbes, part I, p. 6.
72 Altick, pp. 116, 117, 133–4.
73 S. Berns, *Concise Jurisprudence*, Federation Press, Sydney, 1992, p. 21.

Salomon was a rigidly formalistic interpretation of the 1862 legislation and one that was blind to its own consequences.

The decision in *Salomon* was to have important implications for company law. First, it established the legality of the one-person company, a seemingly unusual development given that the legislature had shortly before rejected the legitimacy of the limited partnership form. It also meant that traders could not only limit their liability to the money that they put into the venture, but also avoid serious risk to the major portion of that money by subscribing to secured debentures rather than shares. It opened up the availability of the company as a means of realising taxation advantages and escaping some legal obligations. It allowed entrepreneurs to abuse the corporate form by amassing debts in the company's name, and then escaping unscathed after a company collapse to pursue new ventures.

REVIEW QUESTION

> Recently we have seen the development of one director–one shareholder com-
> panies—that is, a sole trader can incorporate, being the only director and
> shareholder in the company. Is this taking the idea of separate legal identity
> to illogical extremes? What benefits can you see in this development?

Limited liability

The problems of the separate entity doctrine were exacerbated by the development of limited liability. As the corporation is a separate legal person, its members are not personally liable for its debts in the absence of any express provision to the contrary. Where a company is limited by shares, members' liability is limited to the unpaid nominal value of their shares (and in practice, shares are fully paid up, so there is no further liability). In this case, liability of members is limited without restriction on their role in management.

Until the nineteenth century, limited liability was looked upon with some degree of suspicion. The principle was recognised with regard to non-trading corporations as early as the fifteenth century. It was seen primarily, however, as avoiding the risk of the company's property being seized in the payment of the members' separate debts. It was not widely perceived to be a method of enabling members to escape liability for the company's debts. This was because the constitution of a company could expressly or impliedly confer upon the company a power on call on its members for contributions (leviations). Creditors could then claim payment indirectly from members by applying to the court for an order compelling the company to raise a leviation.[74] Consequently, it became common

---

74   This rule was established in *Salmon v. Hamborough Company* (1671) 1 Ch Cas 204. The company, the Merchant Adventurers of England, incorporated by letters patent, had been raising large loans by contract under its common seal. The plaintiff lent the company £2000, but when he sought to recover in 1656, it was objected that the company had no common stock and that those in control refused to levy actions on its members to meet the obligation. The Lords finally agreed to order the company 'to make such a leviation upon every member as shall be sufficient to satisfy the said sum'.

for the liability of shareholders to be limited to the subscribed amount, and large unincorporated companies in the early nineteenth century often petitioned for special rights in this regard. Even in the eighteenth century, limited liability was limited to the legal separation of the corporation from its members. Members could still be indirectly liable for company debts.[75]

As late as 1844, the Joint Stock Companies Act defined the joint stock company as a kind of partnership with more than twenty-five members or with shares transferable by a partner without consent of the co-partners (s. 2). Members were all liable personally, though this personal liability came after the liability of the company itself. There was, however, some separation of members' liability from that of the company in the concession that a company could become bankrupt as a company, and thus the corporate bankruptcy did not imply the bankruptcy of members in their personal capacities (s. 2).

The Companies Winding Up Act provided that the Bankruptcy Court could direct the creditors' assignees in bankruptcy to apply to the Chancery Court for directions 'to compel a just contribution' for all members of the company towards the full payment of all the debts and liabilities of the company, including the costs of winding-up. In 1848 the Winding-Up Act provided that shareholders could wind up the company themselves before the creditors. Shareholders thus had some chance of settling the affairs of the company and so limiting their liability.

At this time, it was possible to establish a joint stock company with limited liability with the express consent of Parliament or the Crown. Existing companies formed under the Joint Stock Companies Act (except insurance companies), or companies formed under private acts, could obtain limited liability subject to certain conditions. In such cases, the Board of Trade would issue the company, in its new name, a certificate of registration with limited liability. However, under such procedures, limited liability was a privilege, granted ordinarily to the rich and powerful. Increasingly, there were calls for the democratisation of limited liability. The response to this call was the *Limited Liability Act 1855*. This limited the extent of a shareholder's liability (after execution against the company) to the amount not paid up on his or her shares. Provided that certain conditions were adhered to, a fully paid-up shareholder was free of further liabilities (ss. 1 and 2).

Within 12 months, however, the Limited Liability Act was repealed. R. R. Formoy notes that, although this did not give much time to observe the workings of the Act, its defects were obvious:

> Limited liability only applied after complete registration, and the promoters, therefore, of a company only provisionally registered were still liable without limit for all expenses incurred previous to complete registration. By section 17 of the Act the provisions of the Winding-up Acts 1848 and 1849 were extended to companies with limited liability, and the effect of limiting the liability of shareholders was to make the winding-up not nearly

75   See, for instance, *Naylor v. Brown* (1673) Rep temp Finch 83; *Edmunds v. Brown* (1668) 1 Lev 237(78).

such a prize as it had been formerly in the days of unlimited liability, when many of the cases of winding-up had been a speculative bid for costs, and the Judges had had to exercise their power of referring unopposed petitions to the master to institute a preliminary enquiry as to whether it was expedient that the company be wound up.[76]

However, in 1856, the Joint Stock Companies Act provided that any company that complied with the terms of the Companies Act by adding the word 'limited' to its formal title as a warning to those who dealt with it was entitled to limit its liability, and that of its members, to the amount of the subscribed capital. In support of this development, it was argued that

[t]he principle we should adopt is this, not to throw the slightest obstacle in the way of limited companies being formed … and when difficulties arise to arm the courts of justice with sufficient powers to check extravagance or roguery … That is the only way the legislature should interfere, with the single exception of giving the greatest publicity to the affairs of such companies that everyone may know on what grounds he is dealing.[77]

The Act provided that incorporation occurred on the registration of the Memorandum and Articles, and that

[t]he Subscribers of the Memorandum of Association, together with such other Persons as may from Time to Time become Shareholders in the Company, shall thereupon be a Body Corporate by the Name prescribed in the Memorandum of Association, having a perpetual Succession and a Common Seal, with Power to hold Lands, but with such pecuniary Liability on the Part of the Shareholders as is herein-after mentioned.[78]

For limited companies, liability extended only to the amount, if any, due on unpaid shares (ss. 61, 63, 66).

Limited liability and a strict interpretation of the separate entity doctrine were to have considerable impact upon corporate regulation. In particular, these features would serve to limit the social responsibilities of companies. Third parties were taken to be put on notice that they were dealing with a limited company, and the liability of shareholders was accordingly restricted. The losses that third parties then experienced were, effectively, 'their own fault'.

REVIEW QUESTION

Generally, in the case of small proprietary companies, creditors attempt to overcome the problems caused by limited liability by requiring the directors to provide them with personal guarantees. Unfortunately, employees of such

---

76 R. R. Formoy, *The Historical Foundations of Modern Company Law*, Sweet & Maxwell, London, 1923, p. 122.

77 R. Lowe, in introducing the Companies Act, Great Britain, *Parliamentary Debates*, 1856, vol. 140, col. 131, as quoted in Hadden, p. 17.

78 *Joint Stock Companies Act 1856.*

companies cannot overcome the problem in the same way (for an example of this, read chapter 16). Can you think of ways to overcome this problem?

The Australian experience

The first company regulations in the Australian colonies were local in character, and generally followed the lead of British law. The same pattern continued in the early years of statehood. During this early period, the states guarded their independence jealously, and the local character of the regulations in force created many difficulties as incorporated entities sought to move from state to state. Before 1844 there were some unincorporated joint stock companies operating under a deed of settlement, and there were also some chartered companies. Public utilities could sue and be sued, but remained unincorporated. The British *Company Act 1862* provided the basic model for colonial legislation, although Victoria was innovative. It introduced the no liability company (for mining) in 1871,[79] and Sir Isaac Isaacs introduced an audit requirement for public companies in 1896.[80] The distinction between public companies and private companies was an early development. Victorian innovations such as the no liability company are uniquely Australian, and even today no parallels exist in other jurisdictions.

By the early 1960s, variation between states had produced a chaotic situation. The first draft Uniform Companies Bill was produced in 1961 and was enacted by the states in 1961 and 1962. The Eggleston Committee was established following a share-market crash in 1967. The Eggleston Committee made substantive recommendations regarding accounts, audit requirements, disclosure of shareholdings, insider trading, takeover requirements, and powers of investigation. Despite this attempt at achieving a consistent form of regulation, uniformity between the states gradually decreased as the recommendations were adopted to varying degrees by state parliaments. A major reason for this inconsistency has been the constitutional limitations on the Commonwealth's power.

Constitutional limitations

The Australian Constitution grants either concurrent or exclusive powers to the Commonwealth in specific areas. The remaining, or 'residual', powers belong to the states. Company law is not a specified Commonwealth head of power, but s. 51(xx) grants the Commonwealth power over foreign, trading, and financial corporations. The constitutional language is imprecise and thus leaves certain questions open. Exactly what is the scope of the Commonwealth's power over corporations? Does it

---

79 *Mining Companies Act 1871.*
80 *Companies Act 1896*, s. 24.

include the power to create corporations? How do we determine what a 'trading' or 'financial' corporation is?

These questions have proved challenging for the courts. The High Court, in *Huddart Parker & Co. v. Moorehead*,[81] adopted a narrow interpretation of the power in s. 51(xx). The Commonwealth had enacted the *Australian Industries Preservation Act 1906* in order to regulate restrictive trade practices. In s. 5, this Act provided that it was an offence for, *inter alia*, any trading corporation to enter into a contract 'with intent to restrain trade or commerce within the Commonwealth to the detriment of the public'. Section 8 of the Act also provided that it was an offence for, *inter alia*, a trading corporation to monopolise any part of trade or commerce 'with intent to control, to the detriment of the public, the supply or price of any service, merchandise or commodity'. If the Comptroller General had reason to believe that an offence under the Act had been committed, he could compel the alleged offender to answer certain questions. Huddart Parker refused to answer these questions and was fined. It then refused to pay the fine on the basis that the Act was unconstitutional.

On appeal of the matter to the High Court, Griffiths CJ and Barton J accepted that, at least in theory, the corporations power extended to the regulation of any corporate conduct within the legal capacity of corporations, but considered that this was subject to the reserved power of the states with respect to intrastate trade.[82] The court based its decision upon a narrow interpretation of the word 'formed', as meaning 'already in existence'.

The regulation of corporations, then, was essentially a state matter.[83] But this was both inefficient and inconvenient. In 1970 the non-Labor states—Victoria, New South Wales, and Queensland—formed the Interstate Corporate Affairs Commission (ICAC). This development was essentially a response to the Labor Party's stated intention to propose Commonwealth legislation. These states were subsequently joined by Western Australia, and the scheme came into force in 1974. It covered a variety of matters, including incorporation, prospectuses, regulation of the securities industry, the approval of trustees and trust deeds for corporate interests, accounts and audit, proclamation of investment companies, exemption powers for takeovers, and fund-raising.

With the election of a Liberal government in 1975, a scheme was developed in which Commonwealth legislation was to be given force by the several states. A Ministerial Council, composed of state and Commonwealth leaders, was established to review and supervise the legislation. The National Companies and Securities Commission (NCSC) was given responsibility for policy and administration. Uniform legislation was enacted. All amendments passed by the Commonwealth Parliament were automatically enacted in the states, but the states could withdraw from the

---

81 (1909) 8 CLR 330.

82 (1909) 8 CLR 330 at 354 per Griffiths CJ.

83 The decision of *Huddart Parker* was not challenged until *Strickland v. Rocla Concrete Pipes Ltd* (1971) 124 CLR 468. In that decision, the narrow interpretation of s. 51(xx) adopted in *Huddart Parker* was overturned, but the High Court did not determine the scope of the Commonwealth's constitutional power in regard to corporations.

scheme on one year's notice. This power to withdraw from the scheme emphasised its consensual nature and guaranteed that measures that were unacceptable to the states could not be introduced.

The *Uniform Act* came into force in July of 1982. In essence, it fine-tuned the 1962 legislation and made no radical changes. Divergence among the states remained possible until January 1991 under legislation such as the Supreme Court Rules, the Criminal Codes, and property laws and business name registration Acts.

The period since 1982 has been characterised by reformist legislation. This has increased the tension between the common-law background of company law and the new statutory reforms, and has led to increasing divergence from British company law. The most notable change during the period before the Corporations Law was the enactment in 1984 of s. 67 of the Uniform Act, giving the corporation the rights and powers of a natural person and abolishing the doctrine of *ultra vires*.[84]

Meanwhile, judicial interpretation of the corporations power proceeded. In particular, the judiciary was faced with the difficulty of determining when a corporation can be considered to be a trading corporation for the purposes of s. 51(xx) of the Constitution. In deciding this question, should we look to the purposes of the corporation and its internal restrictions, or to its activities? In *R v. Trade Practices Tribunal, Ex parte St George County Council*,[85] several municipal councils united to form the St George County Council, which was incorporated under the *Local Government Act 1919–69* (NSW). Section 417 of that Act authorised the corporation to 'establish, acquire and conduct trading undertakings'. One of the trading activities of the council was the supply of electricity and electrical appliances. The council offered a subsidy for the installation of off-peak hot-water cylinders, but only where those cylinders were purchased from the St George County Council retail outlets. The Trade Practices Commission considered that this was a breach of the *Restrictive Trade Practices Act 1971*. The council, however, refuted this on the basis that it was a municipal, rather than a trading, corporation and was therefore not within the scope of Commonwealth power. The council's argument was based on a

---

84 The doctrine of *ultra vires* entered corporate law, both in the USA and in the Anglo-Australian legal system, from the chartered corporation. Because corporations operated under a Charter from the Crown, or as was the case in the USA, from the Commonwealth, they were incorporated for specific purposes, which invariably included some formal provision by which they were obliged to advance the public good. Because they operated under the authority of the Crown (in much the same way as municipal authorities), if they acted outside the objects and powers granted in their charters, they acted *ultra vires*. The consequence, in the public sphere, had simply been to invalidate legislation that was beyond the authority of the municipal corporation. In the commercial sphere, the doctrine of *ultra vires* provided a trap for those dealing with corporate persons. All those dealing with corporate persons were presumed to be fixed with knowledge of the company's objects and powers, those being included in its public documents. As a consequence, where a contract was *ultra vires* the company, that contract was invalid. Even if the other party had contracted with the company in good faith, and had fully performed its part of the contract, the company was not bound by *ultra vires* contracts. The doctrine is identical to that which operates in constitutional law in federations such as Australian, Canada, and the USA. In that setting, it defines the separation of powers between the Commonwealth and the states, and invalidates legislation that is beyond the power of either branch of government. Some would argue that its presence in constitutional law is also a disaster.

85 (1974) 130 CLR 533.

number of factors, including its terms and source of incorporation and the fact that the Local Government Act expressly provided that the goods and services provided by the corporation be supplied 'as cheaply as possible'. This last feature, of course, limited any potential profit that the council may have made out of its activities; and profit is an essential feature of trading.

The majority of the High Court found in favour of the council. In the view of Menzies and Gibbs JJ, the *purpose*, rather than the activities, of the corporation was the deciding factor:

> A trading corporation is one formed for the purpose of trading. However ... the mere fact that a corporation is trading does not mean that it is a trading corporation. It is necessary to determine the true character of the corporation, upon a consideration of all the circumstances that throw light on the purpose for which it was formed. Thus there is no difficulty in holding that the fact that a corporation carries on some trade which is merely incidental or ancillary to the fulfilment of its main purpose does not give it the character of a trading corporation.[86]

Barwick CJ and Stephen J, however, considered that the current activities of the county council were the deciding factor, and as the council was undoubtedly trading, it was a trading corporation.

The issue of whether one looked to the purpose or the activities of a corporation when determining its character came before the court again in *R v. Federal Court of Australia, Ex parte Western Australian National Football League (Inc.) (Adamson's Case)*.[87] In this case, the Western Australian National Football League and the West Perth Football Club were registered under the *Associations Incorporation Act 1987* (WA), which prohibited the incorporation of associations that were created for the purpose of 'trading or securing pecuniary profit for its members' (s. 2). Despite this fact, the league made considerable income from such activities as television and broadcasting rights, gate fees, and money that was paid to the league when a footballer obtained clearance to play elsewhere.

Adamson was a professional footballer. He wanted to transfer from a club in Perth to one in Adelaide. Both the club in South Australia and the South Australian Football League were incorporated under the *Associations Incorporation Act 1985* of South Australia. This Act, like the Western Australian legislation, provided that associations incorporated under its provisions should not have the purpose of trading or securing pecuniary profits. In turn, the South Australian and the Western Australian football leagues were members of the National Football League of Australia, which was a company that was limited by guarantee and was incorporated in Victoria. The rules of the latter corporation prohibited a club from engaging players without clearance. Adamson moved to South Australia. He then sought clearance from the Western Australian League to play with a South Australian club but was refused the clearance.

---

86 (1974) 130 CLR 533 at 562–3.
87 (1979) 143 CLR 190.

Adamson applied to the Federal Court to gain the requisite clearance, relying on s. 45(2) of the *Trade Practices Act 1974* (TPA). The leagues and club argued that the TPA did not apply to them as they were not trading corporations. The majority of the High Court decided that the current activities of the relevant corporation were the deciding factor in determining whether the corporation in question was 'trading':

> [H]aving regard to the diversification of corporate activity and the virtual elimination of ultra vires from the law relating to companies registered under Companies Acts ... the nature of a company may not be discernible from a perusal of its memorandum. The only sure guide to the nature of the company is a purview of its current activities, a judgment as to its nature being made after an overview of all those activities.
>
> ... for constitutional purposes a corporation formed within the limits of Australia will satisfy the description 'trading corporation' if trading is a substantial corporate activity. Its activities rather than the purpose of its incorporation will designate its relevant character. But so to say assumes that such trading activities are within its corporate powers, actual or imputed. It is the corporation which satisfies the description which is the subject matter of the power. Thus its corporate capacity or incapacity cannot be ignored. But once it is found that trading is a substantial and not a merely peripheral activity not forbidden by the organic rules of the corporation, the conclusion that the corporation is a trading corporation is open.[88]

More recently, the Commonwealth attempted to introduce national legislation to regulate corporations. The states reacted to what was perceived to be an intrusion upon their powers. In *NSW v. Commonwealth*,[89] several states challenged the constitutional validity of certain sections of the Commonwealth *Corporations Act 1989*, which provided among other things for the incorporation of trading and financial corporations. By a six-to-one majority, the High Court held that s. 51(xx) of the Constitution did not empower the Commonwealth to make laws with respect to the incorporation of trading and financial corporations. The majority judgment focused on the phrase 'formed within the limits of the Commonwealth'. Following the narrow approach in *Huddart Parker*, this phrase was deemed to be limited to corporations that had already been incorporated in Australia. The process of incorporation itself was excluded. Accordingly, the court held that the provisions of the Corporations Act that dealt with incorporation were invalid.

The current scheme is the result of negotiations between the Commonwealth and the states following the decision in *NSW v. Commonwealth*, and it came into effect, after many delays, at the beginning of January 1991. Under the new regime, the Commonwealth Parliament has enacted legislation for the Australian Capital Territory, which is then applied in each state as a law of that state. The objective of this scheme is to create a 'national' body of legislation, although it depends upon cooperative arrangements between the states and the

---

88 (1979) 143 CLR 190 at 208–9.
89 (1990) 8 ACLC 120.

Commonwealth, and for the law to be applied within each jurisdiction as federal rather than state law. Under this scheme, the Australian Securities Commission (ASC) replaced the NCSC and state corporate affairs commissions as the sole administering authority of the scheme.

REVIEW QUESTION

Which test—that of the company's purpose or that of its activities—do you consider to be more appropriate in determining the company's character? What test should be applied when the corporation has not engaged in any activities whatsoever? See *Fencott v. Muller* (1983) 152 CLR 570.

Conclusion

As the brief outline above has tried to show, legislative regulation of companies has been primarily reactive rather than proactive. The regulation of corporate structures is closely tied to economic considerations. In light of this fact—and of the share-market collapse in 1987, with the concomitant turmoil in the corporate sector—the recent burst of corporate law reform should not come as any surprise:

> The 1980s was a decade of deregulation and debt. Growth in private debt during the decade averaged 17% per annum. It was also a period of pronounced corporate malpractice and significant change in corporate regulation.
>
> It is often argued that the response by Government and regulators to the 1980s corporate malpractice was characterised by a systems failure of regulation rather than a wholesale failure of substantive law. There is much to this argument ...
>
> Although faults in the regulatory framework were the primary impetus for reform, the need to remove inadequacies in certain areas of the substantive law also acted as a catalyst. Substantive law reform has taken place in relation to public fundraising, licensing of investment advisers, insider trading, mandatory accounting standards, directors' duties, related party transactions, insolvency law, the introduction of a mandatory trade plus 5 days settlement regime for the Australian Stock Exchange (ASX) and the legislation for the establishment of a central electronic clearing house for equity transactions.
>
> With a satisfactory regulatory framework already established, future directions for reform will focus on improving and simplifying current corporate law so as to satisfy the twin policy goals of enhancing business performance and providing investor protection ...
>
> Equally important is the recognition that the constant of change which has occurred in corporate regulation in the last number of years is of itself a source of uncertainty for corporate Australia. We must therefore take care when determining whether to proceed with any particular reforms.[90]

---

90 M. Lavarch, 'The Government's Approach to Corporate Law Reform' (1994) 4 AJCL 1.

However, government also seeks to encourage entrepreneurial risk-taking in order to ensure the further economic well-being of the nation. But, as any cursory examination of corporate law regulation shows, the economic well-being of all is not necessarily ensured by the uncontrolled pursuit of profit by corporations. At some point, community pressure to protect third parties affected by the activities of corporations leads government to seek tighter regulation of corporations.

There are, however, significant barriers to a comprehensive reform of Australian corporate regulation. The first is a widespread assumption that corporate activity should be based on the traditional model. This means that reformist legislation tends to 'tinker' at the margins, rather than effecting any widespread and significant reforms.[91] The second is that corporations wield significant political power; indeed, some corporations rival nation states in this regard and thus may work to block comprehensive reform. The third is that companies are extremely diverse, and the webs of interests and relationships they create are complex. It is very difficult for one legislative scheme to cater to the requirements of such a wide variety of corporate forms, functions, and compositions.

It must be acknowledged, of course, that Australia is not alone in its struggle to regulate the corporate form. Since its inception, the unscrupulous have used the corporate form to abuse trust and evade legal obligations. In general, the efforts of the State to control this abuse have had limited success. In the face of these barriers to effective reform, it is worthwhile stopping to assess how effective the recent reforms to the Australian legislative scheme are likely to be.

REVIEW QUESTIONS

1 Why did the previous cooperative scheme pose substantial difficulties for enforcement? What changes have been made to the Corporations Law to eliminate these difficulties?

2 How can understanding the historical background of company law assist in understanding contemporary problems?

3 How significant is the fact that, historically, legislative regimes governing company law developed as a response to external economic and social pressures (for example, the social cost of bankruptcies caused by unwise investment during boom times and the consequential catastrophic losses during economic downturns)?

4 Of what, if any, significance is the fact that present capital requirements are substantially less stringent than those in early regulative regimes?

5 Is it fair to say that the pursuit of private profit should result in the public good?

---

91 Similarly, despite the general approbation of government moves to simplify the Corporations Law, Keturah Whitford expresses concern that the opportunity to rationalise the Corporations Law will be lost if a piecemeal approach to reform is adopted, rather than a focus upon the purpose of provisions. See K. Whitford, 'The Year that was— An Overview of Corporate Law, 1993' (1994) 4 AJCL 35.

6 Can the tension between entrepreneurial risk-taking and protection of individuals be reconciled?

7 Assess the likely effectiveness of the reforms contained in the Second Corporate Law Simplification Bill 1995. To what extent do those reforms challenge the traditional model of the corporation?

3

From Conception to Birth

Introduction

In this chapter, we shall consider the creation of the company and, in particular, the role and the duties of promoters. We have already observed in chapter 1 that, throughout company law, many judges and commentators use human analogies to describe the company. In the formation of the company, you will find references to the 'gestation' of the company, its 'birth', the 'midwives' who attend to its birth, and promoters as standing in '*loci parentis*' to the company.[1] But if the promoter is the 'parent' of the company, then there have been some very bad parents. A classic example of this is to be found in the case of *Gluckstein v. Barnes*.[2] A syndicate was formed to buy a property being sold by a liquidator. The syndicate paid out a debt owing to mortgagees of the property at a discount of £20 000. The syndicate then bought the freehold for £140 000. A company was formed to buy the land, which was sold to it by the syndicate for £180 000, subject to the charge given the syndicate. The profit of £40 000 was disclosed to the shareholders, but not the profit of £20 000 that arose by way of the discount on the mortgage. The company succeeded in bringing an action to recover this sum from the syndicate, all the promoters who shared the secret profit being severally liable for the full amount (with the right of contribution from co-promoters). Lord Halsbury had this to say about the promoters:

> My Lords, we decline to discuss the question of disclosure to the company. It is too absurd to suggest that a disclosure to the parties to this transaction is a disclosure to the company of which these directors were the proper guardians and trustees. They were there by the terms of the agreement to do the work of the syndicate, that is to say, to cheat

---

1   See, for instance, *Re English and Colonial Produce Co.* [1906] 2 Ch 435, in which the court refers to the 'infancy' of the business; *Gluckstein v. Barnes* [1900] AC 240 at 248, in which Lord Macnaghten rather colourfully refers to the company as 'half-fledged and just struggling into life, bound hand and foot while still unborn'.
2   [1900] AC 240.

the shareholders; and this, forsooth, is to be treated as disclosure to the company, when they were really there to hoodwink the shareholders, and so far from protecting them, were to obtain from them the money, the produce of their nefarious plans.[3]

This case is not an isolated instance of a rogue promoter. In fact, there was a spate of nineteenth-century cases in which unscrupulous promoters exploited the idea of corporate separate legal identity for their own pecuniary gain.[4] As we shall see, the regulation of this sort of activity was difficult, as the State was torn between the protection of the investing public, on the one hand, and the encouragement of entrepreneurial activity, on the other.

In this chapter, we shall consider the definition of 'promoter', and the legal duties and liabilities that arise from the creation of the company. First, however, we shall outline the way in which a corporation is created, and describe the different types of companies that can be created under the *Corporations Law 1990*.

It's a company! The birth

As we saw in the first chapter, s. 114 of the Corporations Law provides that a company is formed by the requisite number of persons subscribing their name to a memorandum, and by complying with the registration requirements for proprietary companies set out in this division. There are no specific restrictions on the type of person who can incorporate. Section 85 defines 'person' to include bodies politic and corporate.[5] The creation of the company, then, is simply a matter of formalities. Registration is the act by which the State recognises the separate legal identity of the company.

All companies that intend to operate in Australia must be registered. The requirements of an application for registration are set out in s. 118. Essentially, this section provides that the requisite number of subscribers should lodge an application for registration together with documents specified in s. 118(2) with the Australian Securities Commission (ASC). The state or territory in which a company is to be registered is the company's 'home jurisdiction' for the purposes of registration. Should a company want to carry on business in another state or territory, s. 166A gives it the same rights and powers as it would have if it were a company registered in that jurisdiction.

In addition to the prescribed information, an application must be accompanied by specific documentation. This documentation includes consents to act as a director (s. 222(1)), names of persons who have consented to act as directors (s. 222(4)),

---

3   [1900] AC 240 at 246.

4   See, for instance, *Whaley Bridge Calico Printing Co. v. Green and Smith* (1879) 5 QBD 109; *Twycross v. Grant* (1877) 2 CPD 469; *Emma Silver Mining Co. Ltd v. Grant* (1879) 11 Ch D 918; and *Bagnall v. Carlton* (1877) 6 Ch D 371.

5   Note that trade unions cannot incorporate under the Corporations Law as they are governed by specific legislation, such as the *Industrial Relations Act 1988* (Cth), pt 9.

notice of address of the proposed registered office (s. 218(1)), and the memorandum and articles (if any). Proprietary companies must have at least one director (who ordinarily resides in Australia), while public companies must have three directors, two of whom must ordinarily reside in Australia. There are restrictions on who can be a director—for instance, a body corporate cannot be appointed as a director.[6]

We have already noted the importance of the corporate form in our society. Recently there have been proposals to reform the procedural requirements necessary for the formation of the company in order to make the process simpler and, *inter alia*, more attractive to small business. The Second Corporate Law Simplification Bill 1995 attempts to reduce the complexity of setting up a new company. Lodgment of a completed application form will be the only step required. When the ASC is satisfied that s. 118 has been complied with, it will register the company, allot an Australian company number (ACN) to it,[7] and issue a certificate of registration.[8]

In addition, the Bill proposes that the memorandum and articles of the company will be replaced by the constitution and replaceable rules of the company. These are not mandatory and, if they are not provided, the Corporations Law will govern the situation. If the company chooses to have a constitution, however, this must be lodged with the ASC. Some rules will apply to public companies as mandatory provisions of the Corporations Law. The rules will be found in the body of the Corporations Law and not, as they are now, in a table.

Additional reforms contained within the Second Corporate Law Simplification Bill include the following:
- the common seal will be optional
- the minimum number of members for public companies will be one
- public companies will be required to open their offices at specified times, but proprietary companies will not be required to open their registered offices and will not have to display their names outside their registered offices
- annual returns will be simplified
- new rules for the holding and conduct of meetings will be introduced.

REVIEW QUESTIONS

1 Given the considerable controversy that arose out of the corporate excesses of the 1980s, is the current push towards facilitating the creation of corporations, and the less stringent requirements for so-called 'small' proprietary companies introduced by the Second Corporate Law Reform Bill, justified? What benefits are likely to flow from making the corporate form more attractive to small business?

---

6   Corporations Law, s. 221(3).
7   Corporations Law, s. 120(1).
8   Corporations Law, s. 121(1).

2 Should there be restrictions on the persons entitled to incorporate?
3 Do you think that the principle of limited liability is of economic benefit, or do its disadvantages outweigh its advantages?

Naming baby

Many companies wish to be known by a company name. Where this is the case, a company that seeks registration under s. 118 must reserve that name prior to its application for registration.[9] Company names are available under s. 367, unless they have been reserved, registered, included on the national business names register, or are declared unacceptable.[10] The class of company must also be identifiable from the name adopted (for example, from the use of 'Ltd' or 'NL'), as must its proprietary status. Thus, 'Barker Pty Ltd' denotes a proprietary company in which the liability of members is limited (the classifications of public and private companies, and of those denoting liability, are discussed below).[11]

Companies do not have to use a name as such,[12] but all Australian companies must have a number.[13] The company's application may, according to s. 372, stipulate that the ACN is to be the name of the company. Section 219 provides that a company must state its name and ACN, or alternatively, just its ACN, on negotiable instruments,[14] company seals,[15] and public documents. The purpose of this is to make it clear which corporation is being dealt with.

You may wish to think about what constitutes a 'public document'. In *National Education Advancement Programs Pty Ltd v. Ashton*,[16] Young J found that an examination paper published by an education company did not need to include the company's ACN. The examination paper was intellectual property, rather than being in the nature of trade and business documents that characterised 'public documents'. His Honour noted the difficulties of deciding what constituted a public document, but observed that if the document was one that could possibly be part of a process of business transactions, or of a contract that involved the company, then the ACN should be on the document. There was no need for an ACN if the document was non-contractual.

---

9   Corporations Law, ss. 373 & 120(2).

10 See r. 4.2.01 of the Corporations Regulations.

11 On the general issue of corporate names, see P. Latimer, 'Names' (1987) 3 QITLJ 133.

12 See *F. Goldsmith (Sicklesmere) Ltd v. Baxter* [1970] Ch 85 at 92, in which Stamp J said that a limited company has identifying characteristics, other than its name, by which it can be identified. These characteristics included a particular business, place of business, particular shareholders, and directors.

13 The ASC ascribed numbers to existing companies during 1990, and new companies are given a number upon registration. Registered bodies other than those registered under the Corporations Law (or the earlier companies legislation) are assigned an Australian registered body number (ARBN).

14 *Lindholst & Co. A/S v. Fowler* [1988] BCLC 166.

15 Under the Second Corporate Law Simplification Bill, company seals will no longer be necessary.

16 (1996) 14 ACLC 30.

Although it seems clear from this case that s. 219 is directed to public documents that have a public or business nature, the ACN may not be necessary if the company is readily identifiable by other means. In *Re Scandon Pty Ltd; Scandon Pty Ltd v. Powermate Pty Ltd*,[17] the court refused to set aside a statutory demand that did not include the creditor's ACN. In the demand in question, the creditor had used its full and correct name, so that there was no doubt about its identity. The omission of the ACN from the demand was not of sufficient gravity as to constitute 'some other reason', for the purposes of s. 459J(1)(b), for setting it aside.

Under s. 122, a certificate under the common seal of the ASC stating that a company has been registered is conclusive evidence that the requirements of the Corporations Law have been complied with, that the company has been registered, and that the date of the commencement of the registration is that specified on the certificate.[18] The purpose of this is to absolve third parties dealing with the company from inquiry about whether the requirements for incorporation have been met. Section 122, however, does not bind the Crown,[19] including the ASC.[20]

In addition to these pre-incorporation formalities, certain post-incorporation procedures also need to be followed. These include a meeting of the initial subscribers shortly after incorporation to carry out certain formalities, such as appointing bankers for the company; determining how cheques are to be signed; and appointing directors (if these are not named in the articles).

REVIEW QUESTIONS

1 The fact that registration does not bind the Crown means that registration may be set aside if, for instance, the corporation is formed for an illegal purpose. You may wish to consider what would constitute an 'illegal purpose' and thus justify the setting aside of registration. In particular, think about parallel examples in contract law, such as contracts that are unenforceable because they are against public policy. A good instance of this parallel can be seen in *R v. Registrar of Companies; Ex parte HM Attorney-General*.[21] In this case, Lindi St Claire was advised by a letter from the Inland Revenue Policy Division that the division considered prostitution to be a taxable trade. Ms St Claire was then advised by her accountant to structure her business as a limited liability company. She negotiated with the Registrar of Companies for a company

---

17 (1996) 14 ACLC 124.

18 On the effect of s. 122, see *Cotman v. Brougham* [1918] AC 514 at 523; *H. A. Stephenson & Son Ltd v. Gillanders, Arbuthnot & Co.* (1931) 45 CLR 476 at 500–1; *Jubilee Cotton Mills Ltd v. Lewis* [1924] AC 958.

19 In *Bowman v. Secular Society Ltd* [1917] AC 406 at 439, Lord Parker held that a certificate of corporate registration was not so expressed as to bind the Crown, and the Attorney-General, on the Crown's behalf, could institute proceedings by way of *certiorari* to cancel a registration improperly or erroneously obtained.

20 *ASC v. SIB Resources NL* (1991) 5 ACSR 411. See also s. 461(k), which allows the ASC to wind up a company following investigation on the ground that it is just and equitable to do so.

21 Unreported, 17 December 1980, Divisional Court, Queen's Bench Division.

name. Suggested names, which included 'Prostitute Ltd', 'Hookers Ltd', and 'Lindi St Claire (French Lessons Ltd)', left little doubt about the intended nature of the business. Ultimately the business was incorporated as 'Lindi St Claire (Personal Services) Ltd' and the first object of the company was '[t]o carry on the business of prostitution'. Ackner LJ made an order quashing the registration and incorporation of the company, holding that 'the association is for the purpose of carrying on a trade which involves illegal contracts because the purpose is a sexually immoral purpose and as such against public policy'. Do you consider it fair that Ms St Clair's business was recognised by the State for taxation purposes, but not for the purposes of company registration? What factors would give rise to this inconsistency?

2   Will the misdescription of a company affect the validity of a contract made by the company? See *Moreland Metal Co. Ltd v. Cowlishaw*.[22]

How the form of association is chosen

We have noted above that a company must identify its class within its name. Before we proceed to outline these classes of corporation, it is worth noting that not all corporations are governed by the Corporations Law. Such organisations as, for instance, the Royal College of Surgeons are corporations formed by Royal Charter, and these corporations gain independent status directly from the Crown. Organisations such as universities are often formed by a particular establishing Act. Other corporations are formed by registration under a particular piece of legislation that allows them to exist, such as associations registered under the *Associations Incorporation Act 1981*(Vic.).

Companies that are registered under the *Corporations Law* can be classified in a number of different ways: two important means of classification relate to the type of liability and to the public or private nature of the shareholding. Section 115 of the Corporations Law currently sets out five classes of companies based upon members' liability—companies limited by shares, companies limited by guarantee; companies limited by both shares and guarantee, unlimited companies, and no liability companies—although as we shall see, this system of classification will change when the Second Corporate Law Simplification Bill is enacted.

Company limited by shares

Most of the companies that you examine in a company law course will be companies limited by shares. This type of company is defined in s. 9 as a company formed on the principle of having the liability of a member limited by the memorandum to the amount (if any) unpaid on the shares held by that member. The company must state in its memorandum the amount of its share capital and its division into

---

22   (1919) 19 SR (NSW) 231.

shares of a fixed amount.[23] The important effect of this limited liability is that creditors of the company do not have access to the personal property of the members in order to satisfy debts.[24] Company debts can only be satisfied by recourse to company assets. To put potential creditors on notice of this fact, s. 368(1) provides that a limited company must have the word 'Limited' or its abbreviation, 'Ltd', as part of its name. The creditor is then on notice that he or she should check that the issued capital of the company is sufficiently large and the company has enough assets to cover its debts. In practice, many creditors ensure that they have access to assets other than those of the company by seeking a personal guarantee from the directors. A past member may also be liable to contribute to the company's property on a winding-up in certain circumstances.[25]

A number of changes to this category are proposed by the Second Corporate Law Simplification Bill. Previously, a company that had share capital had to state, at the time at which it was formed, a limit on the amount of share capital it could raise. Corporators also had to divide this amount into shares of a fixed amount of money. So, for instance, a company could have an authorised capital of $100 000 divided into shares of $1 each. Each share then had a nominal (par) value of $1. A company could not lawfully issue a share at less than par value without court permission.

It was common in the nineteenth century for companies to issue shares that had a comparatively high par value, a considerable amount of which was left outstanding. The corporation could then call on this amount when it needed to, particularly in the event of a winding-up. This amount gave creditors a certain degree of security. In more recent times, however, companies have adopted low par values, and their shares have tended to be paid in full. Companies are not required to have any substantial total subscribed share capital (hence the notorious '$2' company), so there is little protection for creditors. Under the Second Corporate Law Simplification Bill, corporators will not have to make a statement of authorised share capital, nor will they have to divide it into shares of par value. The concept of par value, and thus the idea of issuing shares at a discount, will be abolished. Liability of members on winding-up will be limited to the outstanding amount (if any) of what the member agreed to pay the company for the share.

REVIEW QUESTIONS

1 Is your university established by an Act of Parliament? If so, find the establishing Act and an Act establishing a university in another state or territory, and compare them.

2 The practice of getting a guarantee from the directors had proved to be problematic in the case of small family companies in which one director, usually a

---

23 Corporations Law, s. 117(1)(b).

24 P. Lipton & A. Herzberg, *Understanding Company Law*, 5th edn, Law Book Co., 1993, p. 53.

24 Corporations Law, ss. 520–4.

male spouse, has control of the business and his female partner is a 'passive' director, having no control, but incurring all the legal liability of an active director. The *First Corporate Law Simplification Act 1995* aims to overcome the problem of the passive director by requiring only one director in a company:

> the minimum number requirement often leads to women becoming directors of companies controlled by their spouse in which they do not play any meaningful role. This can expose these women to the legal liabilities of a company director, without them having any influence over the operation of the company. As recent cases have shown, people acting as directors without being involved in the company's affairs can be responsible for the company's debts on insolvency. The outcome is similar to the problem which results from 'sexually transmitted debt' when a person acts as a guarantor for the debts of their spouse.
>
> The bill will address these problems.[26]

Do you think that the requirement of only one director will be effective in reducing or eliminating women's debts in those situations in which debts are incurred on the basis of personal guarantees? Give reasons for your answer.

3 What benefits does the abolition of par value have? Can you see any disadvantages flowing from this development?

Company limited by guarantee

Under s. 9 of the Corporations Law, a company limited by guarantee is a company formed on the principle that the liability of its individual members will be limited, by the memorandum, to the amounts that each member undertakes (or 'guarantees') to contribute to the property of the company in the event of its being wound up.[27] Should the company be wound up and not have sufficient assets to meet its liabilities, its members are liable to pay up to the amount specified in the memorandum as the members' guarantees. Most commonly, this type of company is formed by clubs and other non-trading corporate bodies, the capital of which can be met from outside sources, subscriptions, and social activities. This type of company does not raise initial or working capital from its members.[28]

Companies limited by both share and guarantee

This form of company is rare. Under s. 518, a member's liability is limited to the total of any sums unpaid on shares that the member may hold *and* the amount that the member has undertaken to contribute to the company property if the company is wound up. It will no longer be possible to incorporate this type of company under the Second Corporate Law Simplification Bill.[29]

---

26 M. Lavarch, First Corporate Law Simplification Bill 1994, Second Reading Speech, Commonwealth of Australia, *Hansard*, House of Representatives, 8 February 1995, p. 708.

27 See Corporations Law, s. 517.

28 Lipton & Herzberg, p. 54.

29 The First Corporate Law Simplification Act provided that a company limited by share and guarantee could not be registered as a proprietary company (although such companies already in existence could continue to exist).

Unlimited company

According to s. 9, an unlimited company is one that is formed on the basis of having no limit placed upon the liability of its members. Such a company may or may not have share capital. In a winding-up, members are liable for the debts of the company without limit if the company has insufficient assets to meet its debts[30] This sort of company is rarely used for trading, but is often used where a company holds investments. Up until this time, this sort of company has had an advantage over one limited by shares: it could return capital to members without having to comply with the restrictions imposed by s. 195.[31] This was because creditors had access to the personal property of all members to an unlimited extent if the company were to be wound up but were short of funds.

As discussed, however, the Second Corporate Law Simplification Bill includes significant changes to restrictions on reduction of share capital. Shares will not have a par value (although existing arrangements that depend on par value will not be affected), and companies will be able to reduce their capital without obtaining court confirmation if the reduction is fair and reasonable. This ability is not totally unrestricted, however. Shareholder approval will still be required for all reductions, and companies must be solvent and have positive net assets after the reduction.

No liability company

Section 9 defines a no liability company as one that does not have, under its constitution, a contractual right to recover calls made on its shares from a shareholder who defaults in payment of those calls. Thus, the characteristic feature of a no liability company is that shareholders are not liable to pay calls made by the company,[32] although if the shareholders do not pay a call, their shares are forfeited.[33] Only mining companies may be no liability companies.[34] Under ss. 368(2) and 371(g), a no liability company must have the words 'No Liability' or the abbreviation 'NL' at the end of its name. Again, the reason for this is that it constitutes a warning to prospective creditors and shareholders.[35]

It will not be possible to incorporate this type of company after the enactment of the Second Corporate Law Simplification Bill (although existing companies will not be affected). The reason for the abolition of no liability companies is that the removal of par value will make them redundant. The Bill will allow all companies to

---

30 See *Albion Insurance Co. Ltd v. Government Insurance Office of NSW* (1969) 121 CLR 342 for the rights of members in equity to contributions from other members.

31 Lipton & Herzberg, p. 54.

32 Corporations Law, s. 385.

33 Corporations Law, s. 388.

34 Corporations Law, s. 115(2). The no liability company is something of a novelty. It originated in Victoria in the *Mining Companies Act 1871*, ss. 116–20. The *Companies Act 1896* (Vic.), s. 4 provided that the no liability form was available to all ventures, but legislation in 1910 limited the form once again to mining companies. A company will not be a no liability company unless it has an objects clause in its memorandum of association that states 'mining purposes' as the company's sole objects. See *ASC v. SIB Resources NL* for an instance of a company that did not have such an objects clause and was subsequently wound up. The definition of 'mining company' is provided in s. 9 of the Corporations Law.

35 Lipton & Herzberg, p. 55.

do what no liability companies can now do—that is, issue shares without the constraint of par value.

Public and private

In addition to these classifications on the basis of liability, companies may also be classified according to whether they are public companies or proprietary companies. Proprietary companies are created for a small number of individuals who want to retain ownership and control of their company. That is, they do not want to enable the public to subscribe for the company's share capital or to lend money to the company. They usually also wish to restrict the transfer of the company's shares. Proprietary companies are generally formed by small businesses or family-owned businesses. They offer certain advantages: in addition to the fact that it is easier to maintain control of a proprietary company, there is no requirement for an annual general meeting; only one director is required (as opposed to the three necessary for a public company); and a director is not subject to the variety of restrictions that are imposed upon the directors of public companies, such as age limits.

Under the Corporations Law, proprietary companies enjoy certain privileges that public companies do not. Under s. 116(4), they cannot engage in any activity that would require lodgment of a prospectus, but shares can be offered to existing shareholders or employees of the company (or employees of a subsidiary of the company).

Within the category of 'proprietary' companies, there is a further division (introduced by the First Corporate Law Simplification Act) into 'small' and 'large' companies. Originally, the distinction was made between 'exempt' and 'non-exempt' proprietary companies. There were incentives, both in terms of cost and privacy, to fall within the definition of 'exempt'. Section 69 defined an exempt proprietary company as 'a proprietary company no member of which is, and no share in which is owned by, a non-exempt person'. Section 69 went on to define a 'non-exempt' person. A number of advantages were enjoyed by an exempt proprietary company. For example:

- an exempt proprietary company that had appointed an auditor did not need to disclose the financial information in the form of an annual report: s. 335(1)
- if all members agreed, an auditor need not be appointed
- under certain circumstances, an exempt proprietary company could make loans to its directors: s. 234(1) and (3)(a)
- a liquidator of an exempt proprietary company did not need to be registered: s. 532(1), (2), and (4).

Classifying a company as 'exempt', however, was problematic. For instance, the definition tended to be complicated and, as a result, rather inconsistent, so that very large companies could be exempt while small ones might not be. In addition, the financial data that were provided by exempt companies without an auditor were often unreliable.[36]

---

36 L. Griffiths & S. Woodward, *Corporations Law Workbook*, 3rd edn, Law Book Co., Sydney, 1996, p. 33.

The definitions of 'large' and 'small' now found in s. 45A(2)–(6) are based on tests of the size and value of the business. The aim is to ensure that small business operators are not faced with the same regulatory requirements as large businesses: 'Behind this objective is the idea that large companies have an obligation of public accountability that outweighs shareholder confidentiality'.[37]

'Small' proprietary companies will only have to prepare annual financial statements if required to do so by the ASC or by 5 per cent or more of its voting shareholders. 'Large' proprietary companies, on the other hand, must prepare, audit, and lodge accounts with the ASC.

All proprietary companies can pass resolutions without a meeting, by all members signing a minute of the resolution. Single-director or single-shareholder companies can make decisions, provided that these are in writing.

REVIEW QUESTIONS

1 You may wish to consider the effectiveness of these reforms. While the First Corporate Law Simplification Act makes incorporation easier by introducing initiatives addressing the special needs of small business and streamlining the regulation of proprietary companies, small business proprietors should still think carefully about adopting a corporate structure. Many people choose to operate as a company rather than as a partnership or sole-trader business for a variety of reasons: ownership, financing and management flexibility, limited liability, transferability of interests, tax planning, and perpetual existence. Certain factors have traditionally dissuaded people from using the corporate form. These included the paperwork, statutory reporting requirements, and lack of knowledge and experience of company requirements. Are these barriers entirely overcome by the recent reforms?

2 Is the distinction between 'small' and 'large' proprietary companies justified? Is it more effective than the old distinction between 'exempt' and 'non-exempt' companies?

3 What problems can you see arising from the fact that companies can have a single director or shareholder?

4 Is the distinction between 'public' and 'private' companies appropriate? To help you answer this question, you may care to read chapter 5. The idea of the public/private dichotomy is complex and inconsistent.

Promoters

So far, we have considered the procedural requirements of a company's formation and the classification of companies under the *Corporations Law*. We turn now to consider those who create the company: the promoters. As we saw in the factual

---

37 Griffiths & Woodward, p. 34

scenario of *Gluckstein v. Barnes*, outlined at the beginning of this chapter, the separate entity doctrine provides scope for abuse by promoters. After all, it would be relatively simple for an entrepreneurial promoter to sell an asset, such as land, to the company at an inflated price. The law has tried to counter this problem by placing promoters under a fiduciary duty to the company. In particular, promoters must disclose any interest that they may have in a contract with the company. There are, however, a number of problems in this area. The first relates to the definition of 'promoter', the second to the concept of disclosure and, in particular, to whom disclosure should be made, and the third to liability that arises from pre-incorporation contracts. We shall consider each of these problems in turn. First, however, we shall briefly consider the legislative history in this area. As in other areas discussed in this book, this history reveals that there is an inherent tension between the private interests of promoters, protection of the public, and the State's interest in encouraging risk-taking activities.

Regulation of promoters

It became clear at a relatively early stage in the development of modern company law that the private interests of promoters and the interests of the public did not necessarily coincide. This is evident in the evolution of statutory provisions relating to promoters. For instance, the initial legislative attempt to regulate promoters was quite stringent. Under the *Joint Stock Companies Act 1844* (UK), a company was required to file a copy of 'every prospectus or circular addressed to the public' before provisional registration, although the Act did not specify the contents of that prospectus or circular. The *Joint Stock Companies Act 1847* relaxed this provision. It provided that the registration of prospectuses and advertisements with the Registrar of Joint Stock Companies under the 1844 Act 'has been found to be very burdensome to the Promoters of such Companies' and, accordingly, repealed that provision.

The relaxation of the provision in the 1847 Act was a precursor to a shift in government policy that occurred in the period 1856–62. Concern for investor protection gave way, at this time, to a policy of *laissez-faire*. Thus, Robert Lowe, introducing the Joint Stock Companies Bill 1856 into the House of Commons, said:

> We entirely repudiate as the basis of legislation the principle upon which the present *Joint Stock Companies Act* is founded—that it is in the power of the government to prevent the institution of fraudulent companies … [T]he principle we should adopt is this—not to throw the slightest obstacle in the way of limited companies being formed—because the effect of that would be to arrest 99 good schemes in order that the bad 100th might be prevented.[38]

It soon became clear, however, that the policy of encouraging the pursuit of private interests by promoters did not always promote the public good. This was evi-

---

38 Great Britain, *Hansard*, House of Commons, 13 June 1856, pp. 124, 131.

denced by a series of frauds perpetrated by promoters in the years 1860–1920.[39] It was, for instance, common practice for promoters to buy property with the aim of selling the property to a newly promoted public company at an inflated price, paid for either in cash or shares in the new company. The promoter would then sell the company in the market. In the period 1856–65, 36 per cent of the companies formed ceased to exist within 5 years of registration, and after 10 years, some 54 per cent no longer existed. The high incidence of company failures during this period has been attributed to the 'profiteering trio of promoter, lawyer and accountant':

> [M]any companies were deliberately set up in order that after a short fictitious existence they might pass into the winding up process, with birth and burial expenses accruing to their creators. It would be arranged that the first charge on the capital received from investors should be the preliminary promoting and vendor charges, which satisfied the first of the trio, and a preferential charge on the assets in winding up was (and is) the legal expenses, which satisfied the other two. Companies, it must be remembered, were then free from having to state either promoting expenses or vendor contracts or to state the minimum capital on which business could be commenced; therefore, when capital sufficient to pay the above expenses had been collected, the company would pretend to start business, fulfil its promoting agreements—and fail.[40]

These frauds prompted legislative action. In 1867, after a parliamentary committee had noted evidence of abuse in company promotions, the *Companies Act 1867* (UK) provided that details of every contract made by a company, its promoters, directors, or trustees must be disclosed in a prospectus. If such disclosure was not made, then the prospectus was deemed to be fraudulent. This reform, however, was not entirely satisfactory. Because of the high level of abuse, the *Companies Act 1900* (UK) reimposed the requirement of the 1844 Joint Stock Companies Act that prospectuses be registered before issue and that they prescribe their contents in detail.

The redress available to an aggrieved shareholder was also the subject of legislative reform. In *Derry v. Peek*,[41] the directors of a tramway company issued a prospectus, in which they stated that the company had the right to use mechanical motive power instead of horses. The company's special Act of Parliament, however, made that right conditional on the consent of the Board of Trade. The board refused its consent. The plaintiff subscribed for shares in reliance on the prospectus. After the company went into liquidation, he sued the directors for damages for deceit. However, because the directors had honestly but mistakenly believed that the granting of consent was a mere formality, they were held not liable. This decision led to the *Directors Liability Act 1890* (UK). This made promoters and directors liable to

---

39   C. A. Cooke, *Corporation, Trust and Company*, Manchester University Press, Manchester, 1950, p. 145.

40   H. A. Shannon, 'The First Five Thousand Limited Companies and their Duration' (1932) 7 *Economic History* 396 at 418–19.

41   (1889) 14 AC 337.

persons induced to subscribe by false statements in a prospectus, unless the representor had reasonable grounds for believing the statement to be true. The regulators reasoned that, as company securities, unlike goods, do not lend themselves to examination by the buyer without the seller's help, relevant information should be disclosed whenever the public is invited to subscribe for securities:[42]

> It must be generally acknowledged that a person who is invited to subscribe to a new undertaking has practically no opportunity of making any independent inquiry before coming to a decision. Indeed, the time usually allowed between the issue of the prospectus and the making of an application does not permit of any real investigation. The maxim of Caveat Emptor has in the opinion of your committee but a limited application in such cases.[43]

Thus, this approach established minimum standards of disclosure of facts likely to be of relevance to the investor. Such disclosure has remained a fundamental principle of the regulation of the prospectus.

REVIEW QUESTION

Compare the idea that an examination of company securities would not reveal a problem and the rule of the 'latent defect' that developed in the area of product liability. This rule was that, although the law did not impose a general duty of care upon manufacturers towards the general public, a duty of care was owed to the buyer of goods when the goods were intended to reach the consumer in the packaging and form in which they left the manufacturer—that is, the defect was not apparent on an examination by the buyer (or the examination of the goods was not physically possible). See *Grant v. Australian Knitting Mills Ltd*[44] and *Cuckow v. Polyester Reinforced Products Pty Ltd*.[45]

Who is a promoter?

The term 'promoter' does not have a comprehensive legislative or judicial definition.[46] Section 3 of the Joint Stock Companies Act 1844 defined promoters as

---

42 The links between consumerism and the prospectus are to be seen in the adoption of s. 52 of the *Trade Practices Act 1974* (Cth) as the model for liability for the misleading prospectus in the Corporations Law, s. 996. Under this provision, promoters may be liable for loss or damage caused by a prospectus that offers securities for subscription and that contains a false or misleading statement, or omits a material matter.

43 Lord Davey, *Report of the Departmental Committee*, as quoted in P. Redmond, *Companies and Securities Law: Commentary and Materials*, Law Book Company, Sydney, 1988, p. 27.

44 [1936] AC 85.

45 (1970) 19 FLR 122.

46 It should also be noted that the term 'promoter' is not confined to companies: persons who float collective non-corporate investment schemes, such as public unit trusts, are also termed 'promoters'. See *Elders Trustee and Executor Co. Ltd v. E. G. Reeves Pty Ltd* (1987) 157 CLR 1 at 5–6.

'every person acting by whatever name in the forming and establishing of a company at any period prior to the company obtaining a certificate of complete registration'. However, this definition was omitted from subsequent legislation. Section 9 of the Corporations Law provides that

'promoter,' in relation to a prospectus issued by or in connection with a corporation, means a promoter of the corporation who was a party to the preparation of the prospectus or of any relevant portion of the prospectus, but does not include a person by reason only of his acting in the proper performance of the functions attaching to his professional capacity or to his business relationship with a promoter of the corporation.

But, as you will gather from the wording, this definition is relevant only for the purposes of the prospectus provisions.[47] 'Promoter', it has been said, is a business, rather than a legal term.[48] From the cases, it is clear that the term can refer to a wide range of persons: '[a] promoter ... is one who undertakes to form a company with reference to a given project and to set it going, and who takes the necessary steps to accomplish that purpose'.[49] The term thus refers to individuals who take part in such activities as preparation of the memorandum and articles of association; the seeking out of persons who may become subscribers to shares in the company; and the raising of funds from others who may wish to act as creditors to the company.[50] In *Tracey v. Mandalay*, Dixon CJ went a step further and stated:

It is not only the persons who take an active part in the formation of the company and the raising of the necessary share capital to enable it to carry on business who are promoters ... Persons who leave it to others to get up the company upon the understanding that they will profit from the operation may become promoters.[51]

In this case, one promoter was a company, RSC Trading Co. Pty Ltd (RSC), which was inactive because its business had been sold. S and his wife were the only directors and shareholders of this company. They contracted on behalf of RSC to buy some land, with the aim of selling the land at a profit to a new company, which

---

47 See *ASC v. Woods & Johnson Developments Pty Ltd* (1991) 6 ACSR 191 at 194–5.

48 *Whaley Bridge Calico Printing Co. v. Green and Smith* at 111.

49 *Twycross v. Grant* per Cockburn CJ. See also *Wheal Ellen Gold Mining Co. NL v. Read* (1908) 7 CLR 34: 'A promoter is one who brings a company into existence by taking an active role in forming it or in procuring persons to join it as soon as it is technically formed.' In *Tracey v. Mandalay Pty Ltd* (1953) 88 CLR 215 at 241, Dixon CJ, and Williams and Taylor JJ approved the opinion of Cockburn CJ that the term 'promoter' has no precise meaning. However, it 'involves the idea of exertion for the purpose of getting up and starting a company ... and also the idea of some duty towards the company imposed by it or arising from the position which the so-called promoter assumes towards it'. See also *Emma Silver Mining Co. v. Lewis & Son* (1879) 4 CPD 396 at 407; *Lydney and Wigpool Iron Ore Co. v. Bird* (1886) 33 Ch D 85 at 93.

50 *Tracey v. Mandalay Pty Ltd*. Although persons who actively proceed to do what is necessary to incorporate a company are promoters, those acting merely in a professional capacity to incorporate the company on a promoter's behalf are not. This means that solicitors and accountants who only carry out the instructions of the individuals seeking incorporation, and who are not further involved in the company, are excluded. See also *Bagnall v. Carlton* (1877) 6 Ch D 371; *Re Great Wheal Polgooth Co. Ltd* (1883) 53 LJ CH 42; *Jubilee Cotton Mills Ltd. v. Lewis* at 965.

51 (1953) 88 CLR 215 at 242.

was to be formed. This new company would then build a block of units on the land and sell them. The new company was duly incorporated and bought the land. But RSC (and S and his wife) did not disclose the profits that were made in the transaction. The court held that the new company could rescind the transaction.

Now S, Mrs S, and RSC were not the only 'promoters' in this situation. S persuaded G and W to purchase shares in RSC from himself and his wife. This gave G and W a 25 per cent interest in RSC. S told them of the profit that was potentially available from the sale of the land in question. Later, S and Mrs S sold a further 25 per cent to another party, and more shares to T, the company secretary. These parties were also aware of the planned profit. The transaction was held to be voidable against all these parties.

The lack of a comprehensive definition of the term 'promoter' could pose some problems for an aggrieved shareholder. This was raised by Lord Lindley in *Ladywell Mining Company v. Brookes*.[52] In this case, five men leased a mine with the intention of reselling the lease to a company that was yet to be formed. After the purchase, they entered into a provisional contract with a trustee for an intended company for the sale. The company was formed, and its principal object as stated in the company constitution was the purchase of the mine. Four of the five men were company directors. The contract was not disclosed to the company. The five men received £18 000 for the purchase of the mine. Some years later the company was wound up and the facts made known. An action was brought for recovery of secret profits. It was held that there was no evidence that the directors were promoters of the company, nor that they were in a fiduciary relationship to the company. Even if there had been such a duty, it was too late to rescind by the time the action was brought. Lord Lindley said:

> Having considered the whole correspondence, and having examined the evidence with care, we are not surprised at the shareholders being desirous of upsetting this transaction or getting relief if they can. But the evidence is not sufficient to enable them to succeed. It is not proved that when Palin bought … he bought for the company which was ultimately formed nor that when he bought the company was so far formed as to entitle it or its members to claim the benefit of the purchase on any theory of trusteeship; nor is it proved that the new company was buying from the old company. It is plain that the new company did not, in fact, find the money with which the vendors were paid.[53]

The nature of the duty

Much of the case law of promoters was decided in the late nineteenth century,[54] and most of this litigation was concerned with the factual scenario of the sale of a promoter's property to the company at an inflated price. The law sought to over-

52   (1887) 35 Ch D 400.

53   (1887) 35 Ch D 400 at 414.

54   See, for instance, the cases against a professional company promoter, Albert Grant: *Bagnall v. Carlton*; *Twycross v. Grant*; *Emma Silver Mining Co. Ltd v. Grant*.

come the frauds perpetrated by promoters by the application of the doctrine of fiduciary duties:

> The relief afforded by equity to companies against promoters who have sought improperly to make concealed profits out of the promotion, is only an instance of the more general principles upon which equity prevents the abuse of undue influence and of fiduciary relations. The term promoter is a term not of law, but of business, usefully summing up in a single word a number of business operations familiar to the commercial world by which a company is generally brought into existence. In every case the relief granted must depend on the establishment of such relations between the promoter and the birth, formation and floating of the company, as render it contrary to good faith that the promoter should derive a secret profit from the promotion.[55]

This doctrine of fiduciary duties was a recognised exception to the general rule of ethical egoism. In business dealings, in the absence of fraud, duress, or one of the other circumscribed exceptions to the general rule, a person could ruthlessly pursue self-interest in contractual dealings. If, on the other hand, that person made himself or herself another's fiduciary, there was an obligation to act loyally in that other person's interest to the exclusion of self-interest: 'In short, the law in essence condoned selfish behaviour save where it demanded self-less behaviour. Moral action was, in the main, a matter of individual propensity; moral delinquency a matter of social censure'.[56] Lord O'Hagan, in *Erlanger v. New Sombrero Phosphate Co.,* noted that the duties of a fiduciary extended beyond honesty:

> The promoters, who so forgot their duty to the company they formed, as to give it a directorate without independence of position or vigilance and caution in caring for its interest, must take the consequences. And this without the necessary imputation of evil purpose or conscious fraud. The fiduciary obligation may be violated though there may be no intention to do injustice. If the protection, proper and needful for a person standing at disadvantage in relation to his guardian or his solicitor, or to the promoters of a company, be withheld, the guardian, the solicitor or the promoters, cannot sustain a contract equitably invalidated by the want of it, merely because it may be impossible to prove that he is impeachable with indirect or improper motives.[57]

The promoter was under an obligation to disclose all relevant information in regard to his interests and any potential conflicts of interests with the company. He could not compete with the company and he could not receive secret profits.

The distinction between a free agent and a fiduciary was discussed in *Ladywell Mining Co. v. Brookes*, the facts of which are given above. In this case, Cotton LJ, noting that he disliked 'the use of the term promoter', said that

---

55 *Whaley Bridge Calico Printing Co. v. Green* at 111 per Bowen J. In *Gluckstein v. Barnes*, the House of Lords held that disclosure to a board of directors comprising other members of the syndicate formed for the object of making profit was not a sufficient disclosure.

56 P. Finn, 'Commerce, the Common Law and Morality' (1989–90) 17 (1) MULR 87 at 91.

57 *Erlanger v. New Sombrero Phosphate Co.* (1878) 3 AC 1218 at 1257.

the contract was absolute, and not in any way contingent on the company being formed. The money was all paid by Palin and his friends and in my opinion they bought for themselves, and without putting themselves into such a position as to entitle the company when formed to say, 'You were acting for us; you were in a fiduciary position as regards this property, and now, therefore, as you have purported to sell this to us, we are entitled to take it at the price you originally gave for it.' That is an obvious equity. If a man is instructed as agent for another to buy property, whatever price he buys it for he must hand it over at that price to his principal, and he cannot as between himself and his principal, when he has bought at a lower price add to it by pretending to sell to his principal that which he has already bought for his principal.[58]

The reasons for characterisation of a promoter's duties as fiduciary seem clear enough, but the development did pose logical inconsistencies. How could one be a fiduciary for a legal fiction? Lord Cairns explained the duty this way:

[Promoters] stand, in my opinion, undoubtedly in a fiduciary position. They have in their hands the creation and moulding of the company; they have the power of defining how, and when, and in what shape, and under what supervision, it shall start into existence and begin to act as a trading corporation. If they are doing all this in order that the company may, as soon as it starts into life, become, through its managing directors, the purchaser of the property of themselves, the promoters, it is, in my opinion, incumbent upon the promoters to take care that in forming the company they provide it with an executive, that is to say, with a board of directors, who shall both be aware that the property which they are asked to buy is the property of the promoters and who shall be competent and impartial judges as to whether the purchase ought or ought not to be made. We do not say that the owner of property may not promote and form a joint stock company, and then sell his property to it, but we do say that if he does he is bound to take care that he sells it to the company through the medium of a board of directors who can and do exercise an independent and intelligent judgment on the transaction, and who are not left under the belief that the property belongs, not to the promoter, but to some other person.[59]

A further logical problem created by the separate legal entity doctrine is whether, prior to incorporation, a distinction could be made between the interests of the promoter and the interests of the company. At this point, the company exists only in the mind of the promoter. Could the interests of a non-existent entity conflict with the interests of its creator(s)? The case of *Byron Hall Ltd v. Hamilton*[60] suggested not. In this case, three co-venturers arranged to buy land and erect a building upon it. They contributed their services and capital in differing proportions. After commencing this venture, they formed a company, of which two of them were to be the

---

58 (1887) 35 Ch D 400 at 413.

59 *Erlanger v. New Sombrero Phosphate Co.* (1878) 3 AC 1218 at 1236. See also *Tracey v. Mandalay Pty Ltd*; *Wheal Ellen Gold Mining Co. NL v. Read*; *Re Fitzroy Bessemer Steel Co. Ltd* (1884) 50 LT 144; *Gluckstein v. Barnes*.

60 (1930) 45 CLR 37; 4 ALJ 32.

directors. No formalities were observed with regard to this company, and in fact they did not qualify as directors. No express contract to transfer the land to the company was made. However, money was raised in the company's name on overdraft, secured both by personal guarantee and by a mortgage given by them of the land. They used the money to erect a building, and construction proceeded in the company name. The property, however, was never transferred to the company. The court held that there was no obligation to transfer the land to the company. The co-venturers were entitled to deal as they chose in relation to the company, to use the credit of the company, and to use its name for their own purposes. The company was their creature, and they were at liberty to deal with it as they wished.

True confessions: Disclosure

We have seen that promoters are under a duty to disclose the fact that they have an interest in any contract with the company and that they stand to make a profit. The reasoning behind this duty is that, once all the information is available, the individual investor can decide whether to invest or not. Under the idea of self-reliance, the law considers individuals free to make their own bad bargains as long as they are given all necessary information. But given the very different composition of companies, who is it that a promoter should disclose to?

In the first major case on the issue of disclosure, *Erlanger v. New Sombero Phosphate Co.*, the court held that promoters must make full disclosure to an independent board of directors. Consider, however, the potential for abuse here. When can the board be considered truly independent? There is little to stop an unscrupulous promoter from ensuring a cooperative company board. In *Erlanger*, a company was formed to acquire the lease of Sombrero Island, a small island in the West Indies that contained significant phosphate deposits. This company, the Old Sombrero Company, paid £112 400 for the lease. That company was then wound up, and the lease was sold by the liquidator for £55 000 to a syndicate that proposed to form a new company and to sell the lease to it for £110 000. The company was formed, and a cooperative board of directors was established. The sale was set aside on the basis that the promoters had failed to establish an independent board. Lord O'Hagan said:

> The original purchase of the island of Sombrero was perfectly legitimate—and it was not less so because the object of the purchasers was to sell it again, and to sell it by forming a company which might afford them a profit on the transaction. The law permitted them to take that course, and provided the machinery by which the transfer of their interest might be equitably and beneficially effected for themselves and those with whom they meant to deal. But the privilege given them for promoting such a company for such an object involved obligations of a very serious kind. It required, in its exercise, the utmost good faith, the completest truthfulness, and a careful regard to the protection of the future shareholders. The power to nominate a directorate is manifestly capable of great abuse, and may involve, in the misuse of it, very evil consequences to multitudes of

people who have little capacity to guard themselves. Such a power may or may not have been wisely permitted to exist. We venture to have doubts upon the point. It tempts too much to fraudulent contrivance and mischievous deception; and, at least, it should be watched with jealousy and restrained from employment in such a way as to mislead the ignorant and unwary. In all such cases the directorate nominated by the promoters should stand between them and the public, with such independence and intelligence, that they may be expected to deal fairly, impartially, and with adequate knowledge in the affairs submitted to their control. If they have not these qualities, they are unworthy of trust. They are the betrayers and not the guardians of the company they govern, and their acts should not receive the sanction of a Court of justice.[61]

This requirement of an independent board was not always practicable, however. Consider, for example, the case of small proprietary companies. In *Salomon v. Salomon & Co.*, you will remember that a promoter's sale to his company, which was constituted without an independent board, was upheld. All members of the company had agreed to the sale, and no share offering to others was contemplated. Thus, in *Lagunas Nitrate Co. v. Lagunas Syndicate*, Lindley MR said that '[a]fter Salomon's case we think it impossible to hold that it is the duty of the promoters of a company to provide it with an independent board of directors if the real truth is disclosed to those who are induced by the promoters to join the company'.[62]

In this case, company promoters formed a public company to buy their interest in a nitrate mine. They were the initial directors and the sole shareholders of the new company. Two years later, a newly appointed independent board sought to have the contract set aside on the basis that the mines had been overvalued. The judge held, however, that the promoters had made a sufficient disclosure of their interests as promoters to themselves as directors, and the fact that there had not been an independent board from the start was not sufficient to render them liable as promoters. Hence an alternative to making full disclosure to an independent board of directors is to make disclosure to the existing or potential members as a whole. This disclosure can be in the articles, in the prospectus, or in any other way, so long as all those who are or who become members are aware of the effect of the promoters' transactions. In most cases, disclosure is made to shareholders in a prospectus, and this is considered to be satisfactory, provided that the disclosure is full and explicit.

REVIEW QUESTION

Janet owns a building in a retail area of an inner-city suburb, and it has been recently valued at $650 000. She forms a company, Witchwood Pty Ltd, to buy the building for $690 000 and start a wholefood business there. The

---

61   (1878) 3 AC 1218 at 1255.

62   *Lagunas Nitrate Co. v. Lagunas Syndicate* [1899] 2 Ch 392 at 426.

directors of Witchwood are herself and her partner, Margaret. The share-holders are herself, Margaret, Janet's brother Matthew, Matthew's wife, and Janet's mother. Janet comes to you to ask your advice. How should she discharge her burden of disclosure? What facts need to be disclosed in order to discharge the burden? See *Imperial Mercantile Credit Assoc. v. Coleman.*[63]

Remedies for promoters' breaches of duty

Under common law, the main remedy available is rescission—that is, the company gets its money back and the asset is returned to the promoter. However, this remedy has two preconditions. First, the company must not have affirmed the contract. A company affirms a contract if it takes any benefit under the contract. Second, the parties must be able to be restored to their original positions—that is, restitution must be possible[64] (so a bona fide purchaser for value must not have acquired any interest in the property).[65]

If the company elects not to rescind the contract, it cannot recover the secret profit made by the promoter unless the profit arises separately from the contract price.[66] For an instance of this principle, see *Gluckstein v. Barnes* (discussed at the beginning of this chapter), in which an undisclosed £20-000 profit arose by way of discount on the mortgage over the property that was purchased from the vendor by a syndicate. As this profit was independent of that made on the sale of the property itself to the company, the court ordered that it be returned, even though the contract was not rescinded.

Other remedies may also be available to an aggrieved shareholder. For instance, where there has been a fraudulent misrepresentation by the promoter, the contract can be rescinded and damages claimed as well. In other circumstances, the court may order that property acquired by promoters be held in trust on behalf of the company.[67]

Perhaps the doctrine that causes greatest inconvenience in these circumstances is the rule in *Foss v. Harbottle*,[68] which provides that, as the wrong is done to the company, the company is the proper plaintiff. Consequently, shareholders may be forced to take a 'fraud on the minority' action if the promoters are in control of the company.[69] The doctrine was applied in this context in *Re Ambrose Lake Tin and Copper Mining Company.*[70] In this case, shareholders in a mine, T and M, assigned the mine to a trustee, then signed an agreement on behalf of an intended company to buy the

---

63 (1873) LR 6 JL 189.

64 *Lagunas Nitrate Co. v. Lagunas Syndicate.*

65 *Re Leeds and Hanley Theatres of Variety Ltd* [1902] 2 Ch 809.

66 *Tracey v. Mandalay.*

67 See *Tracey v. Mandalay* for examples of alternative orders that can be sought in cases in which *restitutio in integrum* is not possible.

68 (1843) 67 ER 189.

69 This is discussed at greater length in chapter 14, which deals with minority remedies.

70 (1880) 14 Ch D 390.

mine from the trustee for £24 000, to be paid in shares of the new company. The value of the mine at that time was around £6000. Later, the company was wound up and the liquidator called T and M to account for the difference between the nominal value of their shares and the actual value of the mine. It was held that, although the scheme was intended to defraud the public (investors on the stock exchange), there was no fraud to the company because both the shareholders were parties to the arrangement. Brett LJ reasoned that, if anyone had bought shares, their remedy would lie against T and M and not against the company. Therefore, the company suffered no wrong.

Finally, in some situations, promoters of failed companies may also be liable to liquidators.

In addition to the common-law remedies, the Corporations Law, s. 995 provides that promoters can be liable for misrepresentations or non-disclosure in prospectuses. Compensation can be claimed by investors who suffer loss through reliance upon the prospectus (ss. 1005 and 588FH).[71]

REVIEW QUESTIONS

1 Cameron buys an old warehouse in the city with the intention of transferring it to a company, Blueskies Pty Ltd, which he is promoting. When Blueskies is formed, however, he changes his mind and keeps the warehouse. Can the company claim the property?
2 Jill wishes to promote Gaslight Pty Ltd. The proposed business of the company is to retail beeswax candles. During the course of her promotion, she comes across Candlewick Pty Ltd, a candle-manufacturing business that is for sale at a very good price. Jill buys Candlewick and then resells it to Wax Promotions Pty Ltd, a company that manufactures novelty candles. Is she liable to account to Gaslight Pty Ltd?

Pre-incorporation contracts

So far, we have discussed the problem that arises when a promoter can create a company and sell his or her own assets to it at an inflated price, and we have pointed out that the imposition of the doctrine of fiduciary duties, *inter alia*, posed problems of logical inconsistencies. We turn now to a second problem involving promoters: that of pre-incorporation contracts. Again, this is an area in which the doctrine of separate legal identity tends to cloud the logic of the law.

Pre-incorporation contracts are common. Incorporation of a company can take some weeks. During this period, company promoters may wish to bind the proposed company to certain rights or obligations. For instance, individuals establishing a café may not want to wait until the company is incorporated before

---

71   Or s. 567 if the transaction took place before the commencement of pt 5.7B on 24 June 1993.

ordering machinery, office equipment, stock, and so on. The difficulty in these situations is that the company is not yet a separate legal entity. So, if the company is not established, who is liable on the contract? Who is liable if the company is established, but does not wish to proceed with the contract? The common law has developed a number of rules (albeit inconsistent ones) relating to pre-incorporation contracts.

Before discussing these rules, it is important to note that not only have many of these common-law rules been modified by statute, but their practical significance has also been lessened by the use of shelf companies.[72] A shelf company is one that is incorporated in advance by solicitors, accountants, and specialist company formation services, and registered with the ASC. It is then used when a company is needed. The shelf company device can also be used to revive an obsolete company for a new purpose or by new owners. Ordinarily, these companies are acquired by purchasing all the issued shares. Buyers of a shelf company then appoint new directors and arrange for the members to be changed. The use of shelf companies is subject to at least two provisos. First, any contracts must be made in the name that the company has at the time of the contract and second, the constitution must be appropriate for the purposes of the new company. Ordinarily, shelf companies have standard constitutions.

REVIEW QUESTION

In *Re Introductions Ltd*,[73] Introductions Ltd was formed to provide hospitality services for overseas visitors to the Festival of Britain in 1951. It provided deck chairs and amusement machines at a holiday resort for some years. In 1960 new owners wanted to use the company for pig breeding. The new owners neglected to change the company's name or its objects, which were most unsuited to the purpose of breeding pigs! The company's loans from its bank were thus held to be *ultra vires*. Could this happen today? Give reasons for your answer.

Under the common law, the legal position relating to the rights and liabilities arising from pre-incorporation contracts was unclear. In some cases the court held that the promoter was liable;[74] in other cases no one was found to be liable. The company could not be liable as it was not in existence, and the promoters could not be liable because they had purported to act as agents. As there was no company, there was no principal, and so the doctrine of agency could not operate. Thus, there was no contract.[75] Further, under the common law, an incorporated company could

---

72 See *Commonwealth Bank of Australia v. Australian Solar Information Pty Ltd* (1986) 11 ACLR 380; 5 ACLC 124.

73 [1970] Ch 199.

74 *Kelner v. Baxter* (1866) LR 2 CP 174.

75 *Black v. Smallwood* (1966) 117 CLR 52.

not be liable on, or entitled under, a contract purporting to be made prior to incorporation. This is because an entity that did not exist at the time of contracting was incapable of ratification.[76]

But, in the nineteenth century, judges were reluctant to give a decision that would result in there being, in effect, no contract. Courts have placed considerable stress upon the sanctity of contract. To this end, the judicature would, from time to time, interpret the facts and extend the doctrine of agency so as to impose a duty of good faith on promoters,[77] making them liable on the contract, as in the case of *Kelner v. Baxter.*[78] In this case, a wine merchant made a contract with three parties who contracted 'on behalf of the proposed Gravesend Royal Alexandra Hotel Company Ltd'. The company was formed and the wine consumed. The company later failed, and the wine merchant successfully sued the three individuals who had contracted on behalf of the company. The court held that the true construction of the documents in question showed that the individuals intended to be bound personally.

The rule that individuals should be liable for pre-incorporation contracts was not, however, applied consistently. Later cases, such as *Newborne v. Sensolid (Great Britain) Ltd*[79] distinguished *Kelner v. Baxter* on the basis that, where a promoter signs the proposed name of the company, adding his or her own name only to *authenticate* the contract, the promoter is not liable. In *Kelner v. Baxter*, the defendant acted as an agent for a non-existent principal; in *Newborne*, it was held that the promoter did not act as agent. In the latter case, there was a contract for the sale of goods. The contract was purportedly signed by the seller, a company called Leopold Newborne (London) Ltd, and underneath this was written the name of the director of the company, Leopold Newborne. The buyers refused to complete the contract, and a writ was issued in the name of the company. It was then discovered that the company was not registered at the time that the contract was signed. An attempt was made to substitute Leopold Newborne as the plaintiff, but this was unsuccessful. It was held that there was no evidence that the promoter purported to contract either as agent or as principal.

In *Black v. Smallwood*, Black entered into a contract for the sale of land to a company, Western Holding Pty Ltd. The contract was signed by Smallwood and Cooper as directors of Western Holdings. However, the company had not been incorporated at the time of the contract. Smallwood and Cooper refused to proceed with the contract, and Black brought an action to enforce the contract on the basis that Smallwood and Cooper were acting as agents of the company. In deciding the case, the High Court adopted the traditional contractual approach to the

---

76 *Stott Land Development Corp. Ltd v. Dean* [1967] WAR 86; *Summergreene v. Parker* (1950) 80 CLR 304. A company can, however, become party to such a contract by accepting a novation of the rights and obligations of one of its parties, or by the company entering a new contract on similar terms: *Vickery v. Woods* (1952) 85 CLR 336.

77 See *Lydney and Wigpool Iron Ore Co. v. Bird* at 93–4; *Elders Trustee and Executor Co. Ltd v. EG Reeves Pty Ltd* at 233–4.

78 See also *Summergreen v. Parker; Stott Land Development Corp. Ltd v. Dean; Lomax v. Dankel* (1987) 29 SASR 68 at 72–3.

79 [1954] 1 QB 45.

problem, asking 'What was the intention of the parties as ascertained from the terms of the contract?'. The contract in that case was held to be a nullity because, as Windeyer J. stated at 57,

> [t]he document which the respondents signed does not purport to be a contract made by them as agents for the supposed company. They thought that the company existed and that they were in fact directors. It is therefore impossible to regard them as having used the name of the company as a mere pseudonym or firm name or as having intended to incur a personal liability.

The result of this decision was somewhat absurd. The case established a precedent for the proposition that a third party has a remedy where there is no belief that a company has been formed, but no remedy will lie where it is believed in good faith that the company is in existence.

These cases are difficult to reconcile. Obviously, the rule that companies could not contract prior to incorporation, coupled with the principle that promoters could not be liable on such contracts, operated to the prejudice of innocent third parties. This has led to statutory reforms. Yet, the reforms that have taken place in Australia show the danger of merely adapting the existing law in an attempt to overcome abuse without rethinking the principles behind the law.

REVIEW QUESTIONS

1 Is the distinction made in *Black v. Smallwood* between contracts made 'for' and contracts made 'in the name of' another party appropriate? Give reasons for your answer.
2 Could a promoter who contracts on behalf of a company that is never formed, or that is formed but refuses to proceed with the contract, be liable under s. 52 of the *Trade Practices Act 1974* (Cth)? In what circumstances?

Statutory intervention

Under the Corporations Law, legislation has been enacted to facilitate the process of ratifying pre-incorporation contracts. Initial reforms were made in 1981 in response to a report by the Victorian Law Reform Commission,[80] which stated that promoters should bear the greater proportion of the risk that the company would not be incorporated or that the company would not honour its pre-incorporation contractual obligations. Thus, s. 183 aims to enable companies to:

- ratify pre-incorporation contracts
- to impose statutory liability on promoters to compensate third parties where a contract to which s. 183 applies is not ratified

---

80 Victorian Law Reform Commission, 'Pre-incorporation Contracts', Report no. 8, VLRC, Melbourne, 1979. See Companies Code, s. 81.

- and to withhold from promoters, from subsequently formed companies, and from third parties, rights and obligations under pre-incorporation contracts, other than those provided by the section itself.[81]

Effectively, s. 183 states that, where a person either executes a contract in the name of a company where no such company exists, or purports to enter into a contract as agent or trustee for a company that is to be formed, the company may, within a reasonable time after its formation, ratify the contract. For a company to be able to ratify, it must be reasonably identifiable as the company contemplated by the parties when the contract was made.

Once the company ratifies the contract, each party has the normal rights under contract law to sue for breach.[82] If the company is subsequently in breach, the court may order the person who entered into the contract on the company's behalf to pay damages to the other party.[83] In other words, should the company have insufficient or no assets to meet their liabilities under a pre-incorporation contract, promoters might find themselves liable personally for the company's breach.

But this personal liability can be avoided in two ways. First, under s. 183(8) and (9), individuals who have purported to enter into contracts on behalf of non-existent companies can exclude themselves from liability if they obtain the written and signed consent of the other party. And second, liability can be avoided where the company and the other party enter into a new contract in substitution for the pre-incorporation contract (a novation).[84]

Should the company fail to ratify the contract, s. 183(4) provides that the other party can recover from the persons who purported to execute the contract.[85] If the company has been formed, it may have to indemnify the promoter or executor.[86]

Despite the intention of regulators, the status of pre-incorporation contracts is not made certain by this legislation. Section 183(1) of the Corporations Law provides that reference to the formation of a company is to be construed as a reference to the formation of a company that is 'reasonably identifiable' with the company of the name in which the promoter made the contract. What if the original name of the company is scrapped, or the purpose of the company is changed? In such cases a court must look to the name of the company, the identity of the directors, the purpose for which the company is incorporated, and the present activities of the corporation in order to determine whether a company is 'reasonably identifiable'.[87]

---

81 On the general operation of s. 183, see J. P. Hambrook. 'Pre-incorporation Contracts and the National Companies Code: What does Section 81 Really Mean?' (1982) 8 Adel LR 119; C. Gerrard, 'Stamp Duty Implications of Pre-incorporation Contracts' (1984) 12 ABLR 266.

82 Corporations Law, s. 183(3).

83 Corporations Law, s. 183(7).

84 Corporations Law, s. 183(10).

85 See *Bay v. Illawarra Stationery Supplies Pty Ltd* (1986) 4 ACLC 429.

86 Corporations Law, s. 183(5).

87 See *F. Goldsmith (Sicklesmere) Ltd v. Baxter* [1970] 1 Ch 85 at 92; *Oshkosh B'Gosh Inc. v. Don Marbel In Ltd* [1989] BCLC 507.

This is a difficult task. Further, the legislation uses the phrase 'is formed' and may not cover cases in which the company is *assumed* to be formed. So the legislation may not cover the *Kelner v. Baxter* situation, in which a promoter contracts as a principal. Section 183(2) of the Corporations Law provides that ratification must take place within a 'reasonable time'.[88] Again, this gives rise to some uncertainty.

Finally, the Second Corporate Law Simplification Bill has proposed to amend s. 183 so that the section applies to contracts entered into 'for the benefit' of companies yet to be formed, as well as contracts entered into 'on behalf' of non-existent companies. This is to overcome the possibility that the Corporations Law might not cover the situation in which a person purports to enter into a contract as agent of a company, believing it exists when in fact it does not. The new legislation will apply when a person enters into, or *purports* to enter into, a contract on behalf of, or for the benefit of, a company before it is registered.

REVIEW QUESTIONS

1 The report of the Victorian Law Reform Commission of 1979, upon which s. 183 is based, rejected the European solution to the problem of pre-incorporation contracts, which is to substitute the promoter for the company. Under the *European Communities Act 1972* (UK), s. 9(2) (now found in the *Companies Act 1985* (UK), s. 36(4)), a promoter, acting 'for' and 'in the name of' the company, is made personally liable on a contract. The report stated that:

   > It would in most cases be difficult to justify the imposition of contractual obligations on a person wishing to contract with a company in favour of a promoter or 'agent' with whom he had no intention of contracting. This would be particularly so where personal considerations are important, as, for example, where the agreement is one for employment or for the allowing of credit.[89]

   Do you agree? What arguments can be made in favour of a promoter being personally liable on a pre-incorporation contract? Would this solution be simpler?

2 Mark undertakes to incorporate a company, Dogwash Pty Ltd, with a paid-up capital of $15 000. On the basis of this undertaking, Naturepower Pty Ltd enters an agreement to supply Dogwash with shampoos and conditioners at a cost of $1500. Mark signs the contract with Naturepower as agent for Dogwash Pty Ltd. However, a week later, Mark with his partner Robin incorporates as Petclean Pty Ltd, which has a paid-up capital of $2. Can Naturepower enforce the contract?

3 Sharon and Catherine plan to create a recording company, Disk Disk Pty Ltd, to record contemporary, innovative music. Sharon undertakes to approach her solicitor to set up the company and telephones Catherine from the solicitor's

---

88 *Watson v. Davies* [1931] 1 Ch 455; *Dibbins v. Dibbins* [1896] 2 Ch 348.
89 Victorian Law Reform Commission, para. 35.

office to let her know that arrangements for the company are in progress. Catherine then commits the company to leasing a warehouse as a recording studio. She signs the lease in the name of the company, Disk Disk Pty Ltd, Catherine Preston, director. Catherine then discovers that the company has not been incorporated and that the name chosen is not available. Catherine and Sharon choose another name, and the company, on its registration, will be called Contemporary Music Pty Ltd. Advise Catherine, who wishes to know if she is personally liable for the lease.

4 The Second Corporate Law Simplification Bill proposes to change the terminology in this area from 'pre-incorporation contracts' to 'pre-registration contracts'. Which term do you consider more appropriate? Give reasons for your answer.

5 The Second Corporate Law Simplification Bill makes a distinction between 'entering' a contract and 'purporting to enter' a contract. When will someone 'purport' to enter a contract?

Conclusion

In this chapter, we have considered the process of company registration, the classification of companies under the Corporations Law, and the law relating to promoters and pre-incorporation contracts. The law relating to formation of the company reveals the inherent tension between the encouragement of risk-taking by entrepreneurs and the protection of third parties. As a result, much of the law in this area is the result of compromise and, accordingly, less than satisfactory. Even at its inception, the web of interests created by the corporation poses great difficulties for regulators. Let us turn now to consider some of the problems that arise once the company comes into being.

PART 2

THE CORPORATE CITIZEN

4

AN ALIEN IN OUR MIDST?

Introduction

In the chapters that follow, we closely examine the idea of corporate morality. This is not necessarily a typical procedure in a text on company law. Ordinarily, issues of corporate responsibility are relegated to the final chapters or are discussed almost cursorily in the context of liability for crimes and torts. But to a large extent, it is the potential for corporate morality that informs much of the debate currently surrounding corporations, whether that debate is concerned with directors' accountability or with accountability for corporate crime. This may seem an odd thing to say when it is commonly accepted that a corporation has 'no soul to damn and no body to kick'. We have seen that the corporation is merely a legal fiction; it is composed of individuals, and society ordinarily holds individuals fully accountable for their behaviour. As ordinary people, we know that we should act morally, in the sense that we should not kill or steal, and we understand that we will be sanctioned if we do not act morally. We understand that we have ethical responsibilities—to care for the environment, for instance, or to give to the needy. Why, then, do we not expect—indeed, demand—the same sort of behaviour from companies? And why is it that we seem to require different standards of behaviour of individuals acting within corporations, compared with individuals who are not involved in corporations?

The answers to these questions are complex, and we will explore them in depth in the following chapters. But if a company is composed of individuals, and individuals understand (even if they do not always adhere to) their ethical and moral obligations, then a company can potentially be required to act morally and ethically, and importantly, it can be sanctioned if it does not. It also follows that individuals acting within the company can be punished for their wrongdoing. We have seen that judges and commentators are only too eager to ascribe human characteristics to the company: companies have wills, minds, and hands; they have a period of 'infancy'; and they can die. But judges often maintain that companies have 'no soul to damn and no body to kick' and, therefore, cannot act morally, nor can they be effectively sanctioned for their wrongdoings. At the same time, the imposition of the separate legal entity doctrine means that judges are often reluctant to punish the individuals who control or compose the company. In the areas of corporate morality, social responsibility, and accountability, it seems that confusion is endemic. The object of this chapter is to provide an overview of this confusion and to set the scene for the deeper analysis that follows. To this end, the chapter is divided into two parts. The first will explore some of the problems that relate to the idea of corporate social responsibility, in the sense of responsibility to the community at large. The second part will outline the problems that attach to corporate accountability for wrongs—that is, the legal responsibility of companies to the individuals with whom they come into contact.

For the good of us all ...

In chapter 2, we noted that the development of the corporation has been characterised by confusion between private interests and public interests. As you will recall, companies were originally formed on a concessional basis—that is, the privilege of incorporation was granted so that certain public goals might be achieved or public interests served. In time, however, the public good came to be identified with private commercial interests. In the corporate context, this development is reflected in the fact that corporate goals were—and, to a large extent, have continued to be— limited to the single objective of profit-maximisation:

> The market model offers a rigorously consistent and intellectually neat view of the corporation. It views the corporation not simply as an institution but more a set of rules that provides for sufficient exchanges. The corporation serves as an efficient substitute for the more costly and time-consuming means of doing business through multiple contractual arrangements. Of course, this arrangement has a purpose: to transact business efficiently, which under this model, means the maximisation of profits.[1]

This view has limited corporate action, in the main, to the pursuit of profit at the expense of other social considerations. The validity of this limitation is very questionable: pursuit of private interests may, but does not *of necessity*, coincide with the public good. And corporations today may have any number of goals, which are not necessarily restricted to the single-minded pursuit of profit. For instance, with the trend towards so-called 'ethical investment', shareholders may wish to further environmental objectives (the production, for instance, of 'Green' products or the pro-

---

1   D. Schwartz, 'Defining the Corporate Objective: Section 2.01 of the ALI's Principles' (1984) 52 Geo Washington LR 511 at 523.

motion of eco-tourism).[2] On the other hand, management may aspire to model industrial- or consumer-relations policies.[3]

There are, however, a number of problems associated with any theory that advocates increased corporate social responsibility. The first is that of disenfranchisement of shareholders. Provided that the interests of management and shareholding coincide, there is little problem in the company pursuing ethically based common goals. With the schism, however, that generally developed in the early twentieth century between management and ownership, the limitations of the conventional model became readily apparent. Empirically (as we will discuss in the chapter on directors' duties), shareholders who wish to further social goals may have little effective control over management. However, doctrinally, shareholders can restrict management to the pursuit of profit in the exercise of the board's powers. While some companies may be legally constrained from acting in the public good, others will pursue the goal of profit to the detriment of social well-being. Robert Dahl,[4] for example, argues that, in pursuing profit, many companies have ignored social issues, such as environmental degradation, consumer protection, and industrial relations. In effect, some corporations have become 'demi-states' and cannot be made accountable to the people whom they affect. In the next section we will consider these problems—lack of shareholder control, doctrinal limitations, and corporate power—in more detail.

REVIEW QUESTION

Read the following:

> The possibility of abuse of the company form has often been recognized but it is a somewhat narrower idea than the concept of societal harm. It refers to abuse, some wrong dealing, whilst societal harm may conceivably be done by the mere fact of aggregation and accumulation.[5]

What sort of societal harm can result from 'aggregation and accumulation'?

---

2   See also the attempts of groups of American shareholders to force companies to pursue social objectives, often at the expense of profits. One such instance is the *Dow* case, in which shareholders tried to change the company constitution to prevent its sales of napalm. The court in *Medical Committee for Human Rights v. SEC* 432 F 2d 659 (DC Cir 1970) (the *Dow* case) considered that it was proper for shareholders to take such action, even though this had a detrimental effect on profits.

3   This is not to suggest, however, that the definition of corporate goals in terms of profit-maximisation has not been pervasive in modern times. See, for instance, the works of Milton Friedman, such as *Capitalism and Freedom*, University of Chicago Press, Chicago, 1962.

4   R. Dahl, *After the Revolution? Authority in a Good Society*, Yale University Press, New Haven, 1970, pp. 115–40.

5   D. Wishart, *Company Law in Context*, Oxford University Press, Auckland, 1994, p. 169.

Passing the buck: Ownership v. management

Both doctrinally and empirically, the ability for corporations to further socially responsible goals under our received model of regulation has been limited. This situation, at least in part, originates in the separation of ownership and management. This separation results in the disconnection of individual shareholders and the destiny of their savings and, correspondingly, in a lack of political control over management. A considerable body of research has noted that, particularly since the Second World War, patterns of share-ownership have changed dramatically.[6] The status of the shareholder in public companies has shifted from owner to investor, and in turn (as the number of individual investors has declined and there has been a corresponding rise in institutional investors), the status has shifted again from investor to mere beneficiary.[7] Along with this change in the nature of ownership, the development of the contractual division of power between the board and the shareholder[8] has skewed the control of the corporation in favour of management. Shareholders may have little effective control over a board that has no desire to further socially responsible objectives. On the other hand, managers who wish to pursue such objectives against the wishes of shareholders may be legally constrained to pursue only policies concerned with the pursuit of profit.[9]

In a considered discussion of this area, Mary Stokes[10] argues that the corporate barriers to the furtherance of socially responsible objectives result from the threat that managers pose to the liberal conception of political and economic organisation. The doctrinal response to this problem has been twofold. First, regulation by the market has largely been replaced by competition law. Second, legitimacy within the corporation is 'established' by conferring upon directors a broad discretion, supposedly controlled by operational checks. These operational checks are imposed by way of contractual, constitutional, and equitable principles. In the

---

6 This divorce of ownership and control led to the well-known debate, which occurred from 1931 to 1942, between A. Berle and E. M. Dodd on the question 'For whom are corporate managers trustees?'. Although Berle argued at the outset that corporate managers were trustees for the shareholders, he later conceded that Dodd's argument—that management powers were now held in trust for the entire community—was the preferable one. This change in stance was largely the result of the decision in *A. P. Smith Manufacturing Co. v. Barlow* (1953) 13 NJ 145 at 153–4; 98 A 2d 581 at 586, in which the New Jersey Supreme Court justified a corporate charitable contribution on the basis of the corporation's service to charity. See A. Berle, 'Corporate Powers as Powers in Trust' (1931) 44 Harv LR 1049, and 'For Whom *are* Corporate Managers Trustees?' (1932) 45 Harv LR 1365; E. M. Dodd, 'For Whom *are* Corporate Managers Trustees?' (1932) 45 Harv LR 1145, and 'Is Effective Enforcement of the Fiduciary Duties of Corporate Trustees Practicable?' (1934) 2 U Chicago LR 194.

7 J. Nesteruk, 'Corporations, Shareholders and Moral Choice: A New Perspective on Corporate Social Responsibility' (1989) 58 U Cin LR 460.

8 *Automatic Self-Cleansing Filter Syndicate Co. v. Cuninghame* [1906] 2 Ch 34.

9 The next two chapters will elaborate on the social responsibility of companies and allied notions. Interested readers may wish to consult J. E. Parkinson, *Corporate Power and Responsibility: Issues in the Theory of Corporate Law*, Clarendon Press, Oxford, 1993 for an elaboration on some of these matters.

10 M. Stokes, 'Company Law and Legal Theory', in W. Twining (ed.), *Legal Theory and Common Law*, Basil Blackwell, Oxford, 1986, p. 155.

first place, the power of directors is legitimated by the contract of association. On classical contract lines, members of the corporation are supposedly free to contract with whomever they choose and on whatever terms that they choose.[11] In the second place, shareholders, in a manner analogous to that of electors, may appoint or dismiss recalcitrant directors at will. And in the third place, directors are placed under fiduciary duties to the company.

We will explore Stokes's theory at greater length in the next chapter. For the present time, it is important to note that shareholders (paradoxically, it would seem, given this idea of legitimation-through-contract) are often deprived of the ability to pursue socially responsible goals because of the imperfections of this system. Managers, in turn, are restricted in their pursuit of similar goals because these doctrinal checks are imposed in the first place. Few companies draw up a contract of association tailored to the specific needs of the prospective members of the company. This would, in fact, be one way in which shareholders could impose a socially desirable course of action upon management. This is rarely done, however (and would not be of assistance in those situations in which the company already operates). Contractual control is thus largely a fiction. Further, the power of shareholders to appoint or to dismiss directors is only effective where shareholders are both active and have sufficient power (ownership) to exercise control. This is seldom the case. Minority shareholders may also have problems enforcing the fiduciary duties of directors. For instance, Lord Wedderburn states that

> [the] mixed, private and public function [of fiduciaries] is largely at the mercy of private beneficiaries. By ratification after full disclosure they—and only they—may cure the breach of duty where it is ratifiable. The duty to observe a proper business ethic can be largely nullified by a private group of 'owners' or 'members' whom it suits to permit inferior conduct. Questionable business conduct can, this far at least, be made moral by the engine of shareholder democracy.[12]

Because of the dispersion of shareholding in the large public company, shareholders may have no incentive to inform themselves of managerial action or to seek a remedy against such action. In addition, the conventional model is based upon the assumption that the board controls the daily business of the corporation, whereas, in practice (as discussed in chapter 9), much day-to-day management is delegated to the lower levels of management. For all these reasons, effective shareholder control is, in reality, often a fiction.

---

11 See *Corporations Law 1990*, s. 180, which specifies that the memorandum and articles have the effect of a contract under seal.

12 Lord Wedderburn of Charlton, 'The Social Responsibility of Companies' (1985) 15 MULR 1.

No more Mr Nice Guy: Doctrinal restraints

Conversely, the doctrinal controls imposed on directors may restrict pursuit of goals other than profit-maximisation. In law, the corporate interest is identified with the collective interest of the shareholders, and only derivatively with the interests of the community, consumers, or employees. Management is thus limited in the extent to which it can consider the interests of society and of groups within society other than the company's shareholders. David Engel notes that: 'Even the strongest proponents of "more" corporate social responsibility admit that shareholders invariably and overwhelmingly vote down proxy proposals opposed by management—including proposals that purport to seek a greater degree of corporate voluntarism'.[13]

The law imposes limitations upon directors in three main ways. First, where a company has an objects clause, the actions of the directors must always be to further the corporate purpose. Although the doctrine of *ultra vires* no longer operates to affect third parties, it does give a right of action among the members themselves.[14] Second, the board is constrained by the requirement that it acts within the powers conferred upon it by the corporate constitution (although where the articles take the form of article 66, this is unlikely to pose a serious limitation). Finally, and most importantly, the imposition of fiduciary duties may operate to constrain management if it wishes to pursue goals other than profit-maximisation. The law considers the 'best interests of the company' to be served by the pursuit of profit.[15]

The consequence of these limitations is that, even where a company constitution confers an express power to give money to charity, for instance, that power is limited by the requirement that the directors act in the best interests of the company as a whole in making such disposition. A company may thus incur expenses that are reasonably incidental to the execution of its authorised objects, or that contribute generally to the profitability of the business. As Bowen LJ insisted in 1883, '[t]he law does not say that there are to be no cakes and ale, but there are to be no cakes and ale except such as are required for the benefit of the company'.[16] Where, however, the company ceases to have a long-term future, upon which expenditure can be justified, then such expenditure will not be legitimate.[17]

The way in which the law may prevent corporate altruism is illustrated in a number of cases concerning the disposition of corporate assets without tangible return to the company.[18] In *Re Lee Behrens and Co. Ltd*,[19] the issue was that of the validity of a

---

13 D. L. Engel, 'An Approach to Corporate Social Responsibility' (1979–80) 32 Stan L Rev 1 at 7. See, for instance, R. Dahl, 'Governing the Giant Corporation', in R. Nader & M. Green (eds), *Corporate Power in America*, Grossman Publishers, New York, 1973, pp. 10, 15.

14 See Corporations Law, s. 162(7) for the circumstances in which it is proper to rely upon *ultra vires*. For further discussion of the doctrine of *ultra vires*, see chapter 5.

15 See chapter 9.

16 *Hutton v. West Cork Railway Co.* (1883) 23 Ch D 654 at 671.

17 See, for instance, *Hutton v. West Cork Railway*.

18 *Evans v. Brunner Mond and Co. Ltd* [1921] 1 Ch 359; *Re W. and M. Roith Ltd* [1967] 1 WLR 432; [1967] 1 All ER 427; *Charterbridge Corp. Ltd v. Lloyd's Bank Ltd* [1970] 1 Ch D 62.

19 [1932] 2 Ch 46.

deed by which a corporation purported to pay an annuity to the widow of a former managing director. The company constitution contained an express power to provide for the welfare of, *inter alios*, widows and children of former employees. Eve J held[20] that the validity of the corporation's action was to be determined by applying a three-stage test:

1 Is the transaction reasonably incidental to the carrying on of the company's business?
2 Is it a bona fide transaction?
3 Is it done for the benefit of the company and to promote its prosperity?

In *Parke v. Daily News Ltd*,[21] the application of this test struck down the distribution of residual monies arising from the sale of corporate assets to corporation employees, as 'the defendants were prompted by motives which, however laudable, and however enlightened from the point of view of industrial relations, were such as the law does not recognise as a sufficient justification'.

REVIEW QUESTION

Read the following:

> Several hundred years ago, when business enterprises were small affairs involving the activities of men rather than the employment of capital, our law took the position that business is a public profession rather than a purely private matter, and that the business man, far from being free to obtain all the profits which his skill in bargaining might secure for him, owes a legal duty to give adequate service at reasonable rates. Although a growing belief in liberty of contract and in the efficacy of free competition to prevent extortion led to abandonment of this theory for business as a whole, the theory survived as the rule applicable to the carrier and the innkeeper.[22]

To what extent does the *Trade Practices Act 1974* revive the idea that a business person 'owes a legal duty to give adequate service at reasonable rates'?

Powerful competitor or misguided ally?

Some commentators have recognised that this limited view is inappropriate in the modern context. Julia Tolmie points to the symbiosis of the company and the State in order to argue that the traditional public/private dichotomy is otiose. 'The corporation', she claims, 'is a social entity operating in the context of a wider social environment.'[23] At the same time, government may be heavily reliant upon business

---

20 [1932] 2 Ch 46 at 56.
21 [1962] Ch 927 at 962.
22 Dodd, 'For Whom Are Corporate Managers Trustees?' at 1147.
23 J. Tolmie, 'Corporate Social Responsibility' (1992) 15 UNSWLJ 268 at 273. See also H. J. Glasbeek, 'The Corporate Social Responsibility—The Latest in Maginot Lines to Save Capitalism' (1988) 11 Dalhousie LJ 363 at 398.

in its pursuit of economic and social prosperity. This symbiosis has been recognised by some groups. In the United Kingdom, for instance, the Confederation of British Industry has proposed 'a general legislative encouragement [for companies to] recognise duties and obligations ... arising from the company's relationships with creditors, suppliers, customers, employees and society at large; and in doing so to strike a balance between the interests of the aforementioned groups and between the interests of those groups and the interests of the proprietors of the company'.[24] This view is more closely aligned to that of the USA, where there has been greater judicial acceptance of the ability of corporations to act in socially responsible ways. In *People v. Hotchkiss*,[25] a life insurance company was permitted to purchase a hospital for the care and treatment of those of its employees who suffered from tuberculosis. Some shareholders objected to this act, but the court maintained that corporations do

> many humane and praiseworthy acts which formerly might have been questioned as not fairly within the powers or duties of the corporation ... Unless it is shown ... unproductive of beneficial results, the practice may stand as well within the scope of its business. The reasonable care of its employe[e]s, according to the enlightened sentiment of the age and community, is a duty resting upon it, and the proper discharge of that duty is merely transacting the business of the corporation.[26]

Similarly, in *State ex re Sorenson v. Chicago B & O R Co*,[27] the court upheld the right of a railroad corporation to 'donate funds or services to aid in good works', and in *A. P. Smith Manufacturing Co. v. Barlow*,[28] a US$1500 contribution to Princeton University was validated on the basis that the act was responsive to an increased sense of corporate responsibility: 'It seems to us that, just as the conditions prevailing when corporations were originally created required that they serve public as well as private interests, modern conditions require that corporations acknowledge and discharge social as well as private responsibilities as members of the community in which they operate'. A similar view is reflected in the proposal that

> [a] business corporation should have as its objective the conduct of business activities with a view to enhancing corporate profit and shareholder gain, except that, whether or not corporate profits and shareholder gain are thereby enhanced, the corporation, in the conduct of its business:
> • is obliged, to the same extent as a natural person, to act within the boundaries set by law;
> • may take into account ethical considerations that are reasonably regarded as appropriate to the responsible conduct of business; and

---

24 L. C. B. Gower, *Principles of Modern Company Law*, 4th edn, Stevens & Sons, London, 1979, p. 33.
25 (1978) 136 AD 150; 120 NYS 649.
26 (1978) 120 NYS 649 at 651.
27 (1927) 112 Neb 248; 199 NW 535.
28 (1953) 13 NJ 145; 98 A 2d 581.

- may devote a reasonable amount of resources to public welfare, humanitarian, educational and philanthropic purposes.[29]

The interests of employees, creditors, or consumers are not necessarily to be equated with the interests of the company. Employees as a group, for instance, share a common interest (maximising their benefit), and this interest may, or may not, coincide with that of the corporation itself. Similarly, consumers stand outside the corporation, with interests that may be at odds with those of the corporation. This conflict of interests underlies the empirical barrier to greater corporate responsibility identified by Donald Schwartz:

> The voice of the community, expressed in the debate over shareholders' proposals, is relevant, but one must concede that management and shareholders alone make the ultimate decisions. Thus, shareholder proposals, properly viewed, do not seek to reorder basic principles of corporate governance, but only to moderate particular conduct ... Proponents' social advocacy and management's reactions have remained fundamentally faithful to the economic model of the corporation.[30]

Some commentators profess a belief that corporations will, as a result of some sort of historical necessity, develop a social conscience.[31] Wedderburn, for instance, argues that

> none of the philosophies which have predicted an automatic socialisation of corporate life have been justified by the social facts of recent decades. Whereas the internal planning of giant corporations has become 'in effect social planning', the prime exercise of social control has become the task, not of a conscience stricken technocracy, but of government. No new and comprehensive ethic of business seems likely to be born by determined historical forces, springing fully armed like Athena from the head of our ageing economic order.[32]

It must be acknowledged that, to some extent, an expanded corporate social responsibility will inevitably arise because the corporation perceives that it is in its own interests to pursue socially responsible policies. It may believe that such polices will attract favourable publicity and so increase sales—for instance, if it donates money to a worthy cause or adopts more favourable consumer policies. Engel maintains that this motive negates the voluntariness of corporate social responsibility. However, with corporations, as with human individuals, it can be extremely

---

29 American Law Institute, 'Principles of Corporate Governance: Analysis and Recommendations', Tentative Draft no. 2, 1984, cl. 2.01. See also Schwartz; E. Goldstein, 'The Relationship Between the Model Business Corporation Act and the Principles of Corporate Governance: Analysis and Recommendations' (1984) 52 Geo Washington LR 501; and M. A. Eisenberg, 'An Introduction to the American Law's Corporate Governance Project' (1984) 52 Geo Washington LR 495.

30 Schwartz at 526.

31 See, for instance, H. Manne, 'The Limits and Rationale of Corporate Altruism' (1973) 59 Virg L Rev 708; C. Kaysen, 'The Social Significance of the Modern Corporation' (1957) Am Ec R 314.

32 Wedderburn at 17.

difficult, if not impossible, to determine the motive for a particular action.[33] Nor does the motive, of course, affect the beneficial result that may come about from such an act (and surely the result is of primary concern in this context). There will be limits, however, to the extent of this form of social responsibility. In some cases, for instance, a company may fail to implement, say, environmentally sound practices if it cannot perceive that an immediate or long-term profit will result from such an act.[34] Similarly, such action will depend largely on the corporation's visibility to the public and its vulnerability to public criticism. Thus, success will largely depend upon informed and active public opinion. There may be no pressure to engage in such conduct in the case of monopolies or firms that do not sell to the public.[35]

There is, of course, significant resistance to State regulation of corporate conduct. In particular, many representatives of the 'Chicago School' contend that such regulation creates economic inefficiencies. However, Paul Martin argues, first, that this economic viewpoint neglects to recognise the contribution of the law to economic efficiency—that is, by providing a standard of minimal expectations upon which transacting parties might rely—and, second, that the argument makes the implicit assumption that economic efficiency is the collective end of social functions. He remarks that '[t]hese assumptions are incomplete reflections of a more complex social and cultural reality'.[36]

This complexity is reflected in the fact that decisions made in the broader social context require managers to wear a number of hats:

> Managers [engage] in making 'purely business' decisions: by recognizing and properly addressing the broad social implications of such decisions, they can bring out more effective organizational performance. [They also function] as managers whose internal policies turn out to affect outside constituencies[;] as managers who are participants and partners in government (that is, executives themselves are political players when they act as contractors, campaign contributors, and subjects of laws in whose making they have had a voice)[,] as citizens who vote and volunteer in the political process[, and] as individuals who choose to examine their own lives and their potential legacies to society.[37]

Schwartz[38] argues that this could cause paralysis in the corporation. Depriving the corporation of its traditional goal (profit-maximisation) in favour of, for

---

33 A point conceded by Engel at 9, fn. 30.

34 I find it difficult to agree with Engel that a political decision 'to modify the likely longrun consequences to the corporation of some action or inaction that management may be considering—as, for example, by making it illegal, so that management's calculus must include at least the odds and longrun detriment of getting caught—cannot be viewed as a political determination that we want "more" social responsibility'. Surely, this is just the way in which the State expresses its determination that more social responsibility is desired.

35 Tolmie at 280.

36 P. V. Martin, The Law, Ethics, Business and Society: Reconsidering the Relationship, paper presented at the National Corporate Law Teachers Conference, Brisbane, 1993, p. 5.

37 James O'Toole, The Executive's Compass: Business and the Good Society, Oxford University Press, New York, 1993, p. 10.

38 Schwartz at 526.

instance, providing employment or preventing pollution would deprive the corporation of standards on which to base policy choices, and thus, 'any choice is proper'. This, coupled with the extension of decision-making power to those who have no stake in the financial affairs of the corporation, would, he argues, reduce managerial accountability and render shareholders vulnerable to those with no financial interest in the corporation.

REVIEW QUESTIONS

1 David Wishart[39] argues that 'identification of social harm is not amenable to economic analysis'. What does he mean? Do you agree? Give reasons for your answer.
2 For most individuals, the exercise of power carries with it concomitant responsibilities. Is there a connection between power and responsibility in the case of companies? Should there be?

Citizen company?

A barrier to the implementation of State action to enforce social responsibility is that, in many cases, corporations are not perceived as being 'citizens' in the same way that natural individuals perceive themselves to be citizens.[40]

The concept that a corporation ought to act within the boundaries set by law might seem self-evident. Unfortunately, it is not. Some people take the position that a corporation is free to decide whether to obey a given legal rule on the basis of a kind of cost–benefit analysis, in which probable corporate gains are weighed either against probable social costs (measured by the dollar liability imposed for such conduct) or probable corporate losses (measured by dollar liability discounted for likelihood of detection).[41]

This problem is made more pressing by the growth in concentration and power of some corporations. These companies have potential for abuse, with regard both to their internal functions and to their external or social functions. Internally, the objective good of the corporation may be subordinated to the growth of management's power. Externally, giant international commercial enterprises have, in many cases, ceased to owe allegiance to any one state and often have the ability both to shape markets and to frustrate the political policies of the

---

39 Wishart, p. 171.
40 For general discussions of corporate citizenship, see V. Brudney, 'The Independent Director: Heavenly City or Potemkin Village' (1982) 95 Harv LR 597; H. Kripke, 'The SEC, Corporate Governance and the Real Issues' (1981) 36 Bus Law 173; B. Mundheim, 'A Comment on the Social Responsibilities of Life Insurance Companies as Investors' (1975) 61 Va LR 1247.
41 Eisenberg, p. 8.

countries in which they operate. These developments bear out the observations made by A. A. Berle and G. C. Means in 1932:

> The rise of the modern corporation has brought a concentration of economic power which can compete on equal terms with the modern state ... Where its own interests are concerned, it even attempts to dominate the state ... The law of corporations, accordingly, might well be considered as a potential constitutional law for the new economic state, while business practice is increasingly assuming the aspect of economic statesmanship.[42]

Yet, it is widely acknowledged that there are benefits to the nation states in which such corporations operate.[43] These include the introduction of new products, new technology and skills, and new industry. Nation states need, therefore, to ensure that the activities of international corporations bring the maximum net benefits to their residents. States have reacted in varying ways to this need. Many have implemented antitrust laws in an effort to control such companies. The difficulty, however, with many of these provisions is that such attempts are often marred by inconsistencies. On the one hand, nation states seek to regulate the effects of multinationals, but on the other, they condone their activities. Wedderburn argues:

> The final question is set within a paradox. Each of us must find our own way. But none of our societies now *can* stand alone. Each is part of an economic order which is rapidly being internationalized. Each faces transnational enterprises, multinational groups of companies, and world-wide capital markets which easily transcend frontiers and escape the legal jurisdictions of nation states. History threatens to reduce national governments to the status of parish councils in dealing with the large corporations which will span the world ...
>
>   How are we to define, still less enforce, the obligations of transnational corporate management? To whom and for what ends are *they* trustees? How will we—or the global businessmen themselves—identify the 'good citizen' in *international* business?[44]

Similarly, Tom Hadden argues that effective control of multinationals can only come with the development of international legal controls over the operation of these companies and, similarly, with the development of trade union organisation on an international level 'so that the power of the multi-national capital may be met by that of multi-national labour and multi-national government'.[45]

---

42 A. A. Berle & G. C. Means, *The Modern Corporation and Private Property*, revised edn, Harcourt, Brace & World, New York, 1968, p. 357.

43 M. Wilkins, 'The Internationalisation of the Corporation—The Case of Oil', in K. E. Lindgren, H. H. Mason, & B. L. J. Gordon (eds), *The Corporation and Australian Society*, Law Book Company, Sydney, 1974, p. 290. There are, of course, some limits upon the powers of multinationals. Most, for instance, are forced in practice to locate their primary operations in one of the advanced industrial countries. See T. Hadden, *Company Law and Capitalism*, Weidenfeld & Nicolson, London, 1972, p. 450.

44 Wedderburn, p. 29.

45 Hadden, p. 452.

REVIEW QUESTION

Do governments value corporate citizens more highly than individual citizens?

Go directly to gaol? Corporate accountability

To date, we have outlined some of the issues relating to corporate social responsibility. We noted that this area is marked by confusion. We acknowledge the possibility—indeed, desirability—of social responsibility, but have been slow to require companies to act in socially responsible ways. Their social responsibility, it seems, is largely confined to profit-maximisation. We turn now to consider the morality of the relationships between corporations and individuals: the issue of corporate accountability. If society is confused about corporate social responsibility, it would seem to be completely baffled by corporate accountability.

Under the Anglo-Australian law, a corporation may attract liability for legal wrongdoing in two ways: vicariously, for the acts of its agents and employees, or primarily, for corporate deeds. Although vicarious liability for tort is reasonably well developed in Australia, vicarious and primary liability for criminal acts is restricted. A number of commentators have argued for the desirability of an expanded conception of group liability for criminal wrongs. The Western liberal tradition, however, has restricted the imposition of such accountability. Given the significance of individual freedom, it has conventionally been considered unjust or impractical to impose group responsibility. Further, some commentators have argued that the corporation itself cannot commit a legal wrong; only those individuals who compose the corporation can commit such an act.[46] These differences in opinion[47] between individual and group responsibility reflect the theoretical schism between the organic and the contractual or fictional theories of corporations.

Birds of a feather? Group liability

Is it true that corporations have 'no body to kick'? We have seen that companies are merely composed of individuals acting for a common purpose. If, in the

---

46 For early examples of this point of view, see N. C. Collier, 'Impolicy of Modern Decision and Statute Making Corporations Indictable and the Confusion in Morals thus Created' (1910) 71 CLJ 421; J. F. Francis, 'Criminal Responsibility of a Corporation' (1923) 18 Illinois LR 305. For later examples, see L. H. Leigh, *The Criminal Liability of Corporations in English Law*, London School of Economics, London, 1969; J. T. Byam, 'The Economic Inefficiency of Corporate Criminal Liability' (1982) 73 JCLC 582.

47 For a discussion of the contrast between individualism and corporatism, see J. Surber, 'Individual and Corporate Responsibility: Two Alternative Approaches', (1983) 2 Bus and Prof Ethics J 67. Civil law countries have rejected the idea of corporate criminal responsibility because the corporation lacks the requisite *mens rea* to commit the crime. See G. O. W. Mueller, 'Mens Rea and the Corporation' (1957) 19 U Pitt L Rev 21. For further discussion of corporate punishment, see B. Fisse, 'Responsibility, Prevention and Corporate Crime', (1973) 6 NZULR 250l; B. Fisse, 'Reconstructing Corporate Criminal Law: Deterrence, Retribution, Fault and Sanctions' (1982) S Calif LR 1141.

pursuit of that common purpose, an individual is killed or many people suffer serious damage from, say, the escape of hazardous chemicals, can the company as a whole be punished?

Although group accountability has always been possible, the law relating to responsibility for corporate wrongdoing developed along decidedly individualistic lines. Historically, there are examples of collective responsibility in the Western legal tradition. For instance, Lim Wen Ts'ai refers to the collective responsibility that applied to men of the hundred who were fined for murders and robberies taking place in the locality.[48] Samuel Jacob Stoljar, too, records three instances of collective responsibility. First, in early common law, a territorial community might be subject to certain duties, such as paying tallage or repairing the local road, and local residents may have an execution levied upon them if the community did not pay the relevant fine. Second, in medieval Europe, a whole city may be penalised for the offences of a small minority. Finally, until the decretal of Innocent IV in 1245, the Church could excommunicate entire religious houses for the misdemeanours of a few.[49] Notably, however, these examples are from the medieval period, when, as has been discussed previously, there was a stronger conception of community. As the old feudal ties broke down, however, an increasing emphasis was placed upon the individual as the focus of legal rights and obligations.

Even with this rise of individualism, there was some theoretical support for the feasibility of group liability. As a result of the separate entity doctrine, it was possible for liability to attach to a corporation (as opposed to the members of the corporation) for its wrongdoings. In *Salomon v. Salomon*[50] Macnaghten stated:

> The company is at law a different person altogether from the subscribers to the memorandum; and, though it may be that after incorporation the business is precisely the same as it was before, and the same persons are managers, and the same hands receive the profits, the company is not in law the agent of the subscribers or trustee for them. Nor are the subscribers as members liable, in any shape or form, except to the extent and in the manner provided by the Act.

Indeed, this conception of separate personality allowed for a comprehensive development of corporate vicarious liability in tort.[51] Corporations became liable in trover, trespass, and torts involving fraud and malice.[52]

The legal fiction of corporate personality operated, conversely, to restrict corporate responsibility in the criminal law. The criminal law was based upon an individu-

---

48 Lim Wen Ts'ai, 'Corporations and the Devil's Dictionary: The Problem of Individual Responsibility for Corporate Crimes' (1990) 12 Syd LR 311.

49 S. J. Stoljar, *Groups and Entities: An Inquiry into Corporate Theory*, Australian National University, Canberra, 1973, ch 11.

50 [1897] AC 22 at 51.

51 *Citizens' Life Assurance Co. Ltd v. Brown* [1904] AC 423; *Northern Publishing Co. Ltd v. White* [1940] NZLR 75.

52 *Yarborough v. Bank of England* (1812) 16 East 6; *Smith v. Birmingham Gas Co.* (1834) 1 A & E 525; *Maund v. Monmouthshire Canal Co.* (1842) 4 M & G 453; *Eastern Counties Railway Co. v. Broom* (1851) 6 Exch 314.

alistic theoretical and doctrinal basis in the sense that the natural person was the focus of criminal accountability, procedure,[53] and punishment. In order for criminal liability to be attracted, it was necessary to prove that the wrongdoer possessed a certain state of mind. Conceptually, regulators and commentators struggled to reconcile the principle of separate entity with such notions of intrinsically human responsibility. In particular, it was difficult to reconcile ideas of responsibility based upon sin with an entity that lacked a soul. It was claimed that 'the capacity to commit crime presupposes an act of understanding and an exercise of will',[54] but case law held that a corporation was incapable of any act of understanding and had no will to exercise.[55] In the *Mayor of Norwich Case*,[56] for instance, it was declared that a corporation could not be assaulted or imprisoned, and could not commit treason or a felony, 'because these offences belong to the "corporeal law" while the corporation is only a name, which cannot be seen and has no substance'. Behind these statements is the implied rejection of the organic theory of the corporation. The conventional assumption of regulators, both judicial and legislative, was that only individuals, not groups, could be accountable for wrongdoing.[57]

As a consequence of this ethos, many legislative provisions were drafted specifically for natural persons (for instance, legislation in a number of jurisdictions defined homicide as the killing of a human being by another),[58] and corporations could not be convicted of crimes that carried the penalty of imprisonment.[59] Both these difficulties are illustrated in *R v. Cory Bros & Co. Ltd*.[60] During a coal strike, directors of Cory Bros & Co. erected a fence around the company powerhouse to stop pilfering. The fence was electrified, and an unemployed collier was killed when he stumbled accidentally against it. The company was prosecuted for his death, on charges of manslaughter and of building a man trap or other engine calculated to kill or cause grievous bodily harm contrary to the *Offences Against the Persons Act 1861* (UK), s. 31. However, for the reasons given above, Finlay J (albeit with some reluctance) held that a corporation could not be guilty of either offence: 'I am bound by authorities, which show quite clearly that as the law stands an indictment

---

53 Historically, a limited company could not be committed for trial on an indictment, as criminal courts expected the prisoner to stand at the bar and did not permit appearance by attorney. If there was no statutory authority, a company could not be committed by a magistrate in preliminary proceedings for trial of an indictable offence. See Justice Gowans, 'Some Experiences in Criminal Trials in Relation to Company Offences' (1966) 39 ALJ 328. Such legislation as the *Criminal Justice Act 1925* (UK), s. 33 and the *Crimes Act 1900* (NSW), s. 360A overcame this problem by providing that a magistrate could make an order for presentment. Once presented, however, the problem remained of how a company was to plead, given that, at common law, the accused had to appear in person.

54 J. F. Archbold, as quoted in R. S. Welsh, 'The Criminal Liability of Corporations' (1946) 62 LQR 345.

55 *Sutton's Hospital Case* (1613) 10 Co Rep 23a.

56 (1481) YB 21 Edw 4, fol. 13.

57 See, for instance, E. Ledermann, 'Criminal Law, Perpetrator and Corporation: Rethinking a Complex Triangle' (1985) 76 JCLC 285.

58 A company may, however, be convicted of manslaughter if a fine is the authorised penalty and the legislative definition of the crime includes companies: *R v. Murray Wright Ltd* [1970] NZLR 476.

59 *R v. ICR Haulage Ltd* [1944] KB 551.

60 [1927] 1 KB 810.

will not lie against a corporation either for a felony or for a misdemeanour of the nature set out in the second count of this indictment'.[61]

The individualist bias of the law is also illustrated by the priority given to individual rights and obligations over the collective good in issues of punishment and enforcement. In issues of punishment, collective sanctioning was believed to be wrong because of the fear that the innocent, as well as the guilty, would suffer. In questions of enforcement, research has shown that regulators have conventionally preferred civil actions to criminal ones.[62]

REVIEW QUESTION

Read the following:

> The corporation in reality has three elements: the legal entity, the personal shareholder (a natural person directly or indirectly) and the employee. Once the process [of punishment for a crime] is set in motion, the criminal penalty will extend directly or indirectly to all three which is quite unlike the situation of a natural proprietor where only two of these elements are present.[63]

Do you consider this outcome to be fair? If not, do you agree with Eastey J that this is 'a tolerable result for a community where reality dictates corporate criminal accountability'?

A guilty mind?

As a consequence of this individualistic, human bias, the Anglo-Australian legal system restricted corporate liability, particularly in criminal matters. As stated above, corporations could be, and were found to be, vicariously liable in both tortious and criminal matters, although the situations where this could apply in criminal matters were somewhat more restricted than in tort. Under the common law, the general principle was that 'the law does not regard the master as having any such connection with acts done by his servant as will involve him in any criminal liability for them ... unless he has himself actually authorised them or aided or abetted them'.[64] There were, however, three accepted exceptions to this rule: common-law offences of pub-

---

61 *R v. Cory Bros & Co. Ltd* [1927] 1 KB 810 at 818.

62 In Australia, there has been some criticism of the ASC's failure to pursue more criminal prosecutions of offenders. The Commonwealth Director of Public Prosecutions noted that the ASC saw themselves 'as gentleman regulators. They see themselves as protecting the interests of the injured corporation or the disadvantaged shareholder, and they honestly believe that, if they impose a commercial penalty, then that by itself will act as a major deterrent to corporate crime. It will not': as quoted in R. Tomasic, *Corporate Crime and Corporations Law Enforcement Strategies in Australia*, Centre for National Corporate Law Research, University of Canberra, Canberra, 1993, p. 19.

63 *Canadian Dredge & Dock Co. Ltd v. The Queen* (1985) 19 DLR (4th) 314 at 337 per Estey J.

64 Raymond CJ, as quoted in Welsh at 348.

lic nuisance[65] and criminal libel,[66] and certain statutory offences that were interpreted as imposing strict liability upon a company for the acts of its servants, whether authorised or not.[67] These latter offences arose primarily in the domain of social welfare laws, such as pure food and liquor licensing regulations:

> Prima facie, then, a master is not to be made criminally responsible for the acts of his servant to which the master is not a party. But it may be the intention of the Legislature, in order to guard against the happening of the forbidden thing, to impose a liability upon a principal even though he does not know of, and is not party to, the forbidden act done by his servant. Many statutes are passed with this object. Acts done by the servant of the licensed holder of licensed premises render the licensed holder in some instances liable, even though the act was done by his servant without the knowledge of the master … In those cases the Legislature absolutely forbids the act and makes the principal liable without a *mens rea*.[68]

In an offence of strict liability, then, it was unnecessary to impute a state of mind to a corporation in order to attach liability. An illustration of this is to be found in *Moussell Bros Ltd v. London and North-Western Railway Company*. In this case, the *Railway Clauses Consolidation Act 1845*[69] (UK), s. 98 required the owners of goods conveyed by rail to give to the collector of tolls, on demand, an account of the number and quantity of the goods. Under s. 99, a fine would be imposed for the failure to do so 'with intent to avoid the payment of tolls'. The servants of Moussell failed to pay the tolls. The company argued that it was not liable. Atkin J noted that the general common-law rule was that a company was not liable for the wrongs of its servants, but he proceeded to state that legislation may render a company liable if the duty it imposed was absolute. Whether a duty was absolute was a question of 'the object of the statute, the words used, the nature of the duty laid down, the person upon whom it is imposed, the person by whom it would in ordinary circumstances be performed and the person upon whom the penalty is imposed'. After noting that this case was one in which the duty was absolute, His Honour proceeded:

> Once it is decided that this is one of those cases where a principal may be held liable criminally for the act of his servant, there is no difficulty in holding that a corporation may be the principal. No mens rea being necessary to make the principal liable, a corporation is in exactly same position as a principal who is not a corporation.[70]

---

65 *R v. Stephens* (1866) LR 1 QB 702.

66 *R v. Holbrook* (1878) 4 QBD 42; *R v. Kellow* [1912] VLR 162.

67 *Moussell Bros Ltd v. London and North-Western Railway Company* [1917] 2 KB 836; *R v. Australasian Films Ltd* (1921) 29 CLR 195; *Morgan v. Babcock and Wilcox Ltd* (1929) 43 CLR 163; *Schenker and Co. (Aust.) Pty Ltd v. Sheen* (1983) 48 ALR 693.

68 *Moussell Brothers Ltd v. London and North-Western Railway Company* at 840 per Viscount Reading. See also *R v. Australasian Films; Ex parte Colonial Petroleum Oil Pty Ltd* (1944) 44 SR (NSW) 306.

69 8 & 9 Vict, c. 20.

70 [1917] 2 KB 836 at 845.

In addition to this vicarious liability, the common law attached primary liability to the company in certain cases by imputing to it the intention or purpose of its controllers at the relevant time.[71] This became known as the 'identification theory' or 'organic theory' of the corporation: 'A corporation ... must act through living persons ... Then the person who acts is not speaking or acting for the company. He is acting as the company and his mind which directs his acts is the mind of the company ... If it is a guilty mind then that guilt is the guilt of the company'.[72]

Here, then, was a way in which the corporation, an entity without a soul, could be held morally responsible for its wrongs. The corporation was 'reconstructed' as a human individual, with a mind, an ego, and a body. This approach is illustrated by *Lennard's Carrying Co. Ltd v. Asiatic Petroleum Co. Ltd*,[73] in which a ship's cargo was lost because of the vessel's unseaworthy condition. The ship's owners and managing owners were both limited companies. Lennard was the managing director of the latter. He knew (or ought to have known) of the ship's unseaworthiness but took no steps to prevent the vessel putting to sea. When the cargo-owners sued, the ship-owners relied on the *Merchant Shipping Act 1894* (UK), s. 502, which provided that the owner of a British ship would be exempted from liability for 'any loss or damage [to cargo] happening without his actual fault or privity'. The House of Lords held that the company could not rely on the section in the absence of evidence rebutting the presumption of liability:

> [A] corporation is an abstraction. It has no mind of its own any more than it has a body of its own; its active and directing will must consequently be sought in the person of somebody who for some purposes may be called an agent, but who is really the directing mind and will of the corporation, the very ego and centre of the personality of the corporation ...
>
> It must be upon the true construction [of s. 502] ... that the fault or privity is the fault or privity of somebody who is not merely a servant or agent for whom the company is liable upon the footing respondeat superior, but somebody for whom the company is liable because his action is the very action of the company itself.[74]

The identification theory and its limits were considered in *Tesco Supermarkets Ltd v. Nattrass*. In this case, Tesco owned a chain of supermarkets. It reduced a certain washing powder in price as a special offer, and posters in its shops advertised this reduction. A pensioner went to one of Tesco's supermarkets to buy a packet of

---

71 *Federal Commissioner of Taxation v. Whitfords Beach Pty Ltd* (1982) 39 ALR 521; *DPP v. Kent and Sussex Contractors Ltd* [1944] 1 KB 146; *Moore v. I. Bresker Ltd* [1944] 2 All ER 575; *Tesco Supermarkets Ltd v. Nattrass* [1972] AC 153; *Universal Telecasters (Qld) Ltd v. Guthrie* (1977) 15 ALR 439. On the *Tesco* doctrine, see *Collins v. State Rail Authority of NSW* [1986] 5 NSWLR 209; *Nordick Industries Ltd v. Regional Controller of Inland Revenue* [1976] 1 NZLR 194; *Canadian Dredge & Dock Co. Ltd v. The Queen* (1985) 19 CCC (3d) 1; *Kehoe v. Dacol Motors Pty Ltd* [1972] Qd R 59.

72 *Tesco Supermarkets Ltd v. Nattras* at 170 per Lord Reid.

73 [1915] AC 705.

74 [1915] AC 705 at 713–14. The identity doctrine has been applied in a number of merchant-shipping cases. See, for instance, *The Garden City* [1982] 2 Lloyd's Rep 382; *The Lady Gwendolen* [1965] P 294.

the powder but could only find those packets marked at the original price. When he asked the cashier for the reduced price, he was told that only the higher priced items were in stock. He complained to the inspector of weights and measures, who brought a prosecution under the *Trade Practices Act 1968* (UK). A defence to the charge could be established under s. 24(1) if it could be shown that the offence was committed because of 'a mistake or reliance on information supplied to him or through the act or default of "another person ... " ' [or] that he took all reasonable precautions'. In this case, a shop assistant had put out the packs at the regular price and ought to have told the shop manager but did not. The shop manager did not pick up the error. The issue was whether the shop manager was 'another person' in relation to the company; and whether the 'he' in s. 24(1)(b) referred to the shop manager or to the company. In delivering his judgment, Lord Reid quoted from the judgment of Denning LJ in *H. L. Bolton (Engineering) Co. Ltd v. T.J. Graham & Sons Ltd*, which likens a company to the human body (see chapter 1, p. 6).[75] Lord Reid noted that the board, the managing director, and some other superior officers of the company speak and act as the company, but ordinarily subordinates do not. However, in some cases, the board might delegate some of its functions and give the delegate full discretion to act independently of its instructions. He proceeded to note:

> In some cases the phrase alter ego has been used. I think it is misleading. When dealing with a company the word alter is I think misleading. The person who speaks and acts as the company is not alter. He is identified with the company. And when dealing with an individual no other individual can be his alter ego. The other individual can be a servant, agent, delegate or representative but I know of neither principle nor authority which warrants the confusion (in the literal or original sense) of two separate individuals.[76]

These means of attaching liability to the corporation have, however, attracted some criticism. Regarding vicarious liability, it has been acknowledged that the range of crimes that can be committed vicariously is narrow. The application of identification theory is relatively unproblematic where the mental state of the majority shareholder or director is imputed to the corporation,[77] but it becomes more difficult where the corporate officer at fault cannot be said to be the 'alter ego' of the company.[78] Management may restrict its activities to policy-making, however,

---

75   [1957] 1 QB 159 at 171–2.

76   [1957] 1 QB 159 at 172.

77   *Bernard Elsey Pty Ltd v. FCT* (1969) 121 CLR 119.

78   Some legislation provides that, where it is necessary to establish the state of mind of a corporation, it is sufficient to show that a director, servant, or agent of the company had the requisite state of mind, being a director, servant, or agent who engaged in the conduct within the scope of their actual or apparent authority. See, for example, *Proceeds of Crime Act 1987* (Cth); *Fair Trading Act 1985* (Vic.), s. 39(1). The *Tesco* doctrine has also been extended by cases holding that the necessary state of mind need not be of any one individual. Rather, a company may have knowledge comprising different pieces of knowledge possessed by different individuals: *Brambles Holdings Ltd v. Carey* (1976) 2 ACLR 176; 15 SASR 270. By virtue of the application of the separate entity doctrine, it is also possible for a company to aid and abet its manager or vice versa. See *Lewis v. Crafter* [1942] SASR 30; *R v. Goodall* (1975) 11 SASR 94; *Hamilton v. Whitehead* (1989) 7 ACLC 34.

and delegate much of its decision-making power to subordinates. Thus, in appropriate circumstances, those to whom the directors have delegated the company's management must be found to be 'controllers' for the purposes of attaching liability. In *Canadian Dredge & Dock Co. Ltd v. The Queen*,[79] this problem led the court to criticise the *Tesco* doctrine in the following terms:

> The identity doctrine merges the board of directors, the managing director, the superintendent, the manager or anyone else delegated by the board of directors to whom is delegated the governing executive authority of the corporation and the conduct of any of the merged entities is thereby attributed to the corporation ... [A] corporation may, by this means, have more than one directing mind ... The application of the identification rule in *Tesco* may not accord with the realities of life in our country, however appropriate we may find to be the enunciation of the abstract principles of law there made.[80]

A further criticism that has been made of the current means of establishing corporate liability is that, in Australia, there has been some tendency to confuse the two types of liability. For instance, in *Morgan v. Babcock and Wilcox Ltd*, Knox CJ and Dixon J said, '[a]n offence involving corrupt intention can be committed by a corporation only through a servant or agent who, with the necessary mens rea, does or causes to be done, the forbidden act for and on behalf of the corporation acting within the course of his employment or authority'.[81] There are thus two lines of authority: one that holds that there are two distinct forms of liability,[82] and another that holds that a corporation may be criminally liable for the acts of its agents and employees committed in the course of their employment or authority.[83]

REVIEW QUESTIONS

1   What limits are placed on the range of people who can be identified under the 'identification theory' of *Tesco*?

2   If a company can 'know', can a company 'forget'?[84]

---

79   (1985) 19 DLR (4th) 314. In this case, a company was charged with conspiracy to defraud arising out of bid-rigging of dredging contracts. The bid-rigging was performed by the officers of each of the corporations in charge of the dredging operations, and in each case these were the president, vice-presidents, or general managers of the relevant corporations.

80   (1985) 19 DLR (4th) 314 at 336–7. There have been some attempts to make middle managers liable. See *Kehoe v. Dacol Motors Pty Ltd; Ex parte Dacol Motors Pty Ltd* [1972] Qd R 59; *Brambles Holdings Ltd v. Carey*; *Wells v. John R Lewis (Int'l) Pty Ltd*; *Wells v. Spaton* (1975) ATPR 40-007; *Hamilton v. Whitehead*.

81   (1929) 43 CLR 163173–4.

82   *Grain Sorghum Marketing Board v. Supastok Pty Ltd* [1964] Qd R 98; *Ex parte Falstein* (1948) 49 SR (NSW) 133; *Charlesworth v. Penfold Wines Pty Ltd* [1943] VLR 76; *Fraser v. Dryden's Carrying and Agency Co. Pty Ltd* [1941] VLR 103.

83   *Australian Stevedoring Industry Authority v. Oversea and General Stevedoring Co. Pty Ltd* (1959) 1 FLR 298; *Alford v. Riley Newman Ltd* (1934) 34 SR (NSW) 261; *R. v. Police Magistrate at Brisbane* [1924] St R Qd 223.

84   See Lord Wedderburn, 'When Does a Corporation Forget?' (1984) 47 MLR 345 at 347.

Of information and immortality: The possibility of corporate liability

In the modern context, the reality of corporate wrongdoing would appear to be at odds with the individualistic bias of the law:

> When the law was forming, it was individual, identifiable persons who trespassed, created nuisances, engaged in consumer frauds. The law responded with contemporary notions about individuals—what motivated them, terrified them, and constituted justice toward them. Later, as corporations became the dominant vehicle for social action, ... [s]ince a body of law addressed to 'persons' already existed, it was simply transferred to corporations without distinction.
>
> Today's giant corporations, however, are much more than persons who just happen to be especially large and powerful. They are complex sociotechnical organisms—not just men, or even men-and-machines-groups, but men, machines, patterns of reward, ways of doing things, all divided up into loosely coordinated clusters of cells.[85]

Peter Grabosky and Adam Sutton[86] present a series of case studies of corporate crime and harm in Australia, ranging from environmental degradation (lead pollution at Port Pirie) through to health issues (the Dalkon shield and asbestos mining) and commercial fraud (the collapse of Bishopgate Insurance; bottom-of-the-harbour tax-evasion schemes; and medical benefit fund fraud). The prevalence and seriousness of corporate harm stresses the inadequacy of the current regulatory scheme and the necessity of an expanded conception of collective responsibility.

Amoral or immoral?

Some commentators, however, have argued that, far from being incapable of moral action, corporations are paradigm moral agents:

> Not only does the organisation have all the capacities that are standardly taken to ground autonomy—vis. capacities for intelligent agency—but it also has them to a degree no human can. Thus, for example, a large corporation has available, and can make use of, far more information than one individual can. Moreover, the corporation is in principle, 'immortal' and so better able to bear responsibility for its deeds than humans whose sin dies with them.[87]

Increased interest in, and understanding of, corporate organisation has led to an awareness of the feasibility and desirability of collective responsibility. Fisse and Braithwaite, for instance, argue that both persons and corporations are a mix of observable and abstract characteristics. The reductionism inherent in the individualist

85 Christopher Stone, as quoted in Tomasic, p. 5.
86 P. Grabosky & A. Sutton (eds), *Stains on a White Collar*, Hutchinson, Sydney, 1989.
87 M. McDonald, 'The Personless Paradigm' (1987) 37 U Toronto LJ 212 at 219–20.

theory is limited because the whole, they maintain, is always more than the sum of its parts. Thus, regulators should concentrate upon the way in which the parts interact to form wholes.[88] Against the argument that corporations cannot be shown to have the requisite *mens rea* to commit a crime, Brent Fisse and John Braithwaite argue that corporate policy is analogous to human intention.[89] This view may be seen as a logical extension of the organic theory.

Other commentators have argued for corporate responsibility on a variety of different bases. The Chicago School, for instance, favours punishing the corporation on a deterrence basis. If the penalties imposed on the firm are sufficient, it will take internal corrective measures to prevent misconduct by its agents, for which it is legally responsible.[90] From a psychological viewpoint, too, it can be reasoned that a corporation is more than the sum of the individuals belonging to it. John Coffee[91] discusses, the 'risky shift' that occurs in groups—for instance, business people in role plays will make 'riskier' decisions when acting in a small group than when acting alone.[92] This implies that individuals function differently in groups. From a different perspective, Stoljar argues for corporate liability on the basis that the rationale for imposing primary liability is that, in some cases, no single person can be identified as being at fault. If such an argument were enshrined, the corporation as a whole would have to assume liability.[93] In *London Association for Protection of Trade v. Greenlands*[94] and *Campbell v. Thompson*,[95] the associations in question were held liable because of the common interests of their respective members. In the latter case, the judge held only the existing members liable. As Stoljar points out, this is not necessary if the association is held liable:

> Unless persons are acting in concert as joint tortfeasors, or act as principals or accessories in crime, they cannot as a group *commit* a tort or criminal offence, whether the group is incorporated or not … On the other hand, a group of persons may *incur* certain liabilities, of a pecuniary or compensatory kind, where the group engages in an enterprise or activities which are lawful but which in their execution or management may either cause an injury to another or may constitute a statutory (criminal) offence.[96]

Fisse and Braithwaite argue that the corporate ethos should be the standard for corporate criminal responsibility. On this view, a corporation can be convicted

---

88 As an example of this, B. Fisse & J. Braithwaite, *Corporations, Crime, and Accountability*, Cambridge University Press, New York, 1993, p. 480, suggest that 'the corporation', like the term 'the White House', is merely 'shorthand' for a complex organisational process.

89 Fisse & Braithwaite, p. 483.

90 R. Posner, *Economic Analysis of Law*, 2nd edn, Little Brown, Boston, 1977, pp. 165–7.

91 J. C. Coffee, 'No Soul to Damn; No Body to Kick: An Unscandalized Inquiry into the Problem of Corporate Punishment' (1981) 79 Michigan LR 386.

92 See, for instance, M. Shaw, *Group Dynamics: The Psychology of Small Group Behaviour*, 2nd edn, McGraw Hill, New York, 1976.

93 Stoljar, p. 160.

94 [1916] 2 AC 15.

95 [1953] 1 QB 445.

96 Stoljar, p. 172.

where it can be shown that its ethos, or its corporate practices and policies, have encouraged the commission of the criminal act:[97] 'If the reasons given are accepted and acted on within the corporate decision-making process, then we can hold the corporation responsible irrespective of any games played by individual actors among themselves. It is not just that corporate intention … is more than the sum of individual intentions[;] it may have little to do with individual intentions'.[98]

A similar view was also adopted in *Canadian Dredge & Dock Co. Ltd v. The Queen*. It was argued that the identification theory applied in the *Tesco* case could not import into the criminal law a brand of vicarious liability in which the wrongful acts of the directing mind were done, *inter alia*, in fraud on the employer, or for the benefit of the employee. His Honour reasoned that

> the identification doctrine only operates where the Crown demonstrates that the action taken by the directing mind (a) was within the field of operation assigned to him; (b) was not totally in fraud of the corporation, and (c) was by design or result partly for the benefit of the company.
>
> … Where the corporation benefited or was intended to be benefited from the fraudulent and criminal activities of the directing mind, the *rationale* of the identification rule holds. Where the delegate of the corporation has turned against his principal, the *rationale* fades away.[99]

REVIEW QUESTION

What reasons can be given for the phenomenon of 'risky shift'? What are the implications of the phenomenon for corporate regulation?

A slap on the wrists?

A number of judicial and academic commentators, then, have acknowledged the possibility and desirability of corporate liability. There are, however, problems with establishing corporate liability. The first has been canvassed: the individualistic philosophical basis of the law. This problem is well entrenched. Not only does it influence the law substantively and procedurally, but it has also tended to give commercialism and ethical egoism priority over the common welfare. Even in the

---

97 See also Lim Wen Ts'ai & P. H. Bucy, 'Corporate Ethos: A Standard for Imposing Corporate Criminal Liability' (1991) Minn L Rev 1095; A. Foerschler, 'Corporate Criminal Intent: Toward a Better Understanding of Corporate Misconduct' (1990) 78 Calif LR 1287.

98 Fisse & Braithwaite, p. 484. It is to be noted, too, that individuals may act out of loyalty to a small group within the corporation. See Coffee at 396, fn 37.

99 (1985) 19 DLR (4th) 314 at 354–6. See also *Belmont Finance Corp. Ltd v. Williams Furniture Ltd* [1979] Ch 250 at 351, 356.

USA—where it has long been accepted that corporations are vicariously liable for the acts of their employees, whatever grade[100]—the imposition of corporate liability has attracted criticism.[101]

The second difficulty to overcome is that of determining the appropriate penalty for a corporation. As outlined above, punishment has been traditionally considered in individualistic and human terms. Currently, the punishment most frequently imposed upon a corporation is a fine. However, setting the appropriate level of fine is exceedingly difficult: the fine must be sufficient to counter realisable profit, but a fine that is sufficient to deter would in many cases bankrupt the corporation. Thus, in practice, the sanction may bear little relation to the harm inflicted or to the profits made by the breach. There are, however, alternative punishments that are suited to the imposition of collective liability. These include a system of equity fines,[102] the use of adverse publicity orders,[103] corporate probation,[104] and community service orders.

In the Australian corporate context, the regulation of corporate crime has been much criticised. For instance, noting research findings that 'the vast majority of Australian business regulators prefer the gentler means of friendly persuasion', Grabosky and Sutton point to the inadequacy of the law, inadequate penalties, the co-option of the enforcement agency by the industry that it oversees, and inadequate resources available to the agency either because of administrative incompetence or political forces.[105]

The third, and firmly entrenched, difficulty is the acceptability of shareholder passivity. In fact, our current regulatory scheme encourages shareholder passivity in a number of ways, not the least of which is the law's reluctance to punish the company on a collective basis. The traditional view of collective punishment is that the innocent as well as the guilty may be made to suffer. However, if shareholder passivity has allowed a corporation to commit wrongdoing, is it so unjust that the shareholder is punished (albeit indirectly)? In response to the criticism that innocent shareholders will suffer if a corporation is penalised, the court in *Canadian Dredge* said:

---

100   See, for instance, *New York Central and Hudson R v. US* (1909) 212 US 481.

101   See *Canadian Dredge & Dock Co. Ltd v. The Queen* (1985) 19 DLR (4th) 314 at 335.

102   An equity fine is the allocation of a quantity of company shares to a public entity or to those actually or potentially injured by wrongs committed by the company. Coffee, at 420, observes that the advantages of such action are that the overspill of corporate penalties to workers and consumers is reduced; the costs of deterrence are concentrated on the stockholder; higher penalties can be imposed; there is little impact on employees, creditors, and suppliers; and the cost of the fine is less likely to be passed on to the consumers.

103   Coffee, at 425, argues against adverse publicity on the bases that the government tends to be poor at publicity; that such publicity may be drowned out by the great amount of criticism already directed towards corporations; and that corporations can dilute the effect of such publicity by counter-publicity. See also B. Fisse, 'The Use of Publicity as a Criminal Sanction against Business Corporations' (1971) 8 MULR 107.

104   Corporate probation orders involve the idea that a corporation found to be guilty of a significant offence should have one or more outside directors appointed, perhaps from within regulatory authorities. Such directors would have responsibility for reforming communication channels within corporations to ensure that those who delegate authority to lower levels of management are aware of the activities of such delegates. This is to prevent corporate channels of communication from being used to shield decision-makers from knowledge of wrongdoing.

105   Grabosky & Sutton, p. xv.

The corporation which set the directing mind in position to do the wrong will suffer an economic penalty. While it is true that this penalty will feed through to the stockholders, who may well be totally innocent as in the case of a large public company, it may be seen as a risk or cost associated with the privilege of operating through the corporate vehicle ... The corporation in reality has three elements; the legal entity, the personal shareholder ... and the employee. Once the process is set in motion, the criminal penalty will extend directly or indirectly to all three which is quite unlike the situation of a natural proprietor where only two of these elements are present. All this, in my view, while not entirely logical, is a tolerable result for a community where reality dictates corporate criminal accountability in certain circumstances.[106]

Conclusion

I have argued in this chapter that corporate morality and accountability are real possibilities. But demanding morality and accountability from the corporation have not been high priorities on society's list of reforms. This is changing. But we are still bound by ideas that held sway in the nineteenth century: ideas of corporations that no longer hold true, of a lack of regulation that is, perhaps, no longer politically feasible. There can be little doubt that both national and international communities perceive the desirability of a wider conception of corporate responsibility. The division of ownership and management within the corporation that has occurred in the twentieth century, and the empirical evidence of the detrimental results of an untrammelled corporate pursuit of profit, have been influential in the reassessment of corporate social accountability. Specifically, many people have questioned the conventional view that a company's sole or primary aim is necessarily profit-maximisation and that management has little, if any, obligation beyond that owed to shareholders. Consequently, managers are increasingly required to couple their economic, and often political, power with social responsibility.[107] Yet the responsibilities of managers to 'two masters'—the shareholder and the wider community—may well be in conflict: 'Neither public bureaucratic agencies nor private pyramidal organizations were created to cope with the welter of contemporary problems that are global in nature: issues of the environment, international cooperation and competition, and cultural diversity and conflict'.[108] This quotation emphasises the complexity of interests created within and around corporations. It may not be possible for managers to acknowledge all the interests created by the corporation. Schwartz argues:

---

106   *Canadian Dredge Dock Co. Ltd v. The Queen* (1985) 19 DLR (4th) 314 at 337.

107   See, for instance, the corporate reforms suggested by G. P. Brockway in *The End of Economic Man*, W. W. Norton & Co., New York, 1993, pp. 291–5.

108   O'Toole, p. 4.

Corporation law should be able to provide the context in which corporate managers solve problems. The foreseeable short term presents a host of social issues. How far beyond the legal minimum should managers devote resources to protect the environment? To what extent should corporate managers devote corporate resources to create opportunities for disadvantaged minorities beyond those programs required by law? Should corporations decline economic opportunities in foreign countries whose political or social policies are hostile to our own? Must corporations continue their operations in communities that depend upon them and not take advantage of cost-saving opportunities to do business elsewhere? What accommodations should the corporation make to the abandoned communities? To what extent may managers resist takeovers or disaggregations that promise great gains to shareholders in the interest of long-term continuity of the system?

This brief catalogue hardly exhausts the list of social demands and issues that will confront corporate managers, but it may help to articulate some of the issues against which a concept of corporate purpose and powers will apply.[109]

Our received legal model, however, has been slow to impose social responsibility upon corporations, let alone enforce it. Similarly, liberal assumptions regarding obligation, punishment, and enforcement have stood in the way of any expansion of corporate responsibility. To many commentators, the imposition of corporate liability has been inadequate. Tomasic, for instance, notes that 'the historical bases of corporate criminal law have been such that notions of corporate criminal responsibility in the law have failed to come to terms to [*sic*] the nature of the modern complex corporation, whether this involves the corporate group structure or decision making processes within the corporation itself'.[110] In the following chapters, we will explore the idea of corporate morality in more depth.

---

109   Schwartz at 522.
110   Tomasic, p. 12.

5

Morality and the Corporation: A Contradiction in Terms?

Introduction

Questions concerning corporate morality are conventionally submerged in the doctrinal issues of corporate law. Because many lawyers think of companies solely as commercial entities or, more pragmatically, as devices through which business people can limit their exposure to creditors, corporate morality is seldom mentioned, at least in the context of the study of company law or corporations law (although it may figure in a discrete unit covering corporate crime, for example). From the *Bubble Act 1720* onwards, the judiciary has lamented the unregulatable nature of the corporation, proclaiming it, by virtue of its incorporeal—indeed, incorporeal—nature, to be beyond the reach of the law. Yet it is well to note the contradictory subtext of this rationale. Because the corporation has neither the fear of God nor the hope of a reward in heaven, it is firmly located outside the reach of the divine law. Because the corporation has no body, and therefore cannot be imprisoned or even threatened with imprisonment, it is beyond the reach of positive law. While pecuniary penalties can be, and increasingly are, applied, arguments that such penalties 'punish the innocent' remain current: ultimately the shareholders or consumers bear the burden of higher costs.

Despite this, legal discourse is redolent of bodily images, of corporate 'organs', of a corporate 'mind and will'. We regulate corporations 'as if' they were human agents—'as if' they could demonstrate thought, will, action, and purpose. In many ways it is appropriate to suggest that the law itself has endowed the corporation with mind, will, and organs. Why then, does the law persist in providing accounts of the soulless, conscienceless corporation, incapable of loyalty, sacrifice, or even treason?[1] Surely, on the basis of such accounts, terms such as 'corporate morality'

---

1   One such account can be found in *Continental Tyre and Rubber Co. (GB) Ltd v. Daimler Co. Ltd* [1915] 1 KB 893 at 916 per Buckley LJ, as quoted in chapter 1, p. 11.

and 'corporate citizenship' are oxymorons. Relentlessly, however, in different ways in different jurisdictions, the law is stumbling towards a demand for both.[2]

Something very close to a demand for both corporate morality and corporate citizenship is a necessary consequence of s. 161 of the *Corporations Law 1990*,[3] which provides that '[a] company has, both within and outside this jurisdiction, the legal capacity of a natural person'. The ambit of 'the legal capacity of a natural person' necessarily extends beyond the bare power to enter contracts, own and control property, and sue and be sued. While s. 161 was intended *merely* to bury, once and for all, the baggage of *ultra vires* and the mischief that its application[4] had wrought, the natural ambit and consequence of its language are far greater.

Unless a narrow, and fundamentally artificial, reading is adopted, s. 161 endows, and is intended to endow, corporations with all of the legal rights *and obligations* of natural persons. Instead of corporate persons being required to state their objects and purposes in their 'constitutive documents', they are—as is the case with natural persons—free to grow, to adapt, and to change throughout their lives. The only limits upon corporate action are those deriving from their incorporeal character (they cannot marry for example, although it might be instructive to compare mergers to marriage) and those imposed by the general law. While companies may, if they wish, limit their capacity and their freedom of action, just as natural persons may,[5] doing so is a choice made by 'the corporators' and a choice that can, just as readily, be unmade by them. Abolition of the doctrine of *ultra vires* ensures that these 'self-imposed limits' cannot undermine transactions that third parties have entered in good faith. The 'base state' is one in which the corporate person's freedom of action is limited only by the general law. No longer 'enslaved' by its constitutive documents, it is a free agent in a world of free agents. It has been emancipated, bringing a new urgency to the question of whether the corporate 'free agent' has the capacity (and can be compelled) to act as a 'moral agent'. One response to this question, it would seem, is to acquiesce in the views expressed by Lord Denman CJ in *R v. Great North of England Railway Company*[6] in 1843. His Lordship suggested that a company was, by its very nature, incapable of acts of immorality. The reason was simple. According to His Lordship, such acts 'plainly derive their character from the corrupted mind of the person committing them and are violations of the social duties belonging to men and subjects. *A corporation which as such has no social duties cannot be guilty in these cases*'.[7]

---

2   In both the USA and Canada, constitutional recognition of the 'personhood' of corporations has been granted under the Bill of Rights and the Charter of Rights and Freedoms. In Australia this recognition is given by s. 161 of the *Corporations Law 1990*. We will discuss the implications for corporate personhood later.

3   The *Corporations Act 1989* is a Commonwealth statute that enacts the Corporations Law as a law of the Australian Capital Territory. Each of the states and the Northern Territory has applied the Corporations Law through their own Acts. As a result, a single national Corporations Law is enacted throughout Australia.

4   See the discussion of *ultra vires* in chapter 2 on p. 47, fn. 84.

5   In the case of natural persons (just as in the case of corporate persons), this is frequently accomplished by contract. It may also be accomplished by other forms of binding agreement (for example, marriage or religious vows).

6   [1843] *LR QB* 1.

7   [1843] *LR QB* 1 at 315–25 (emphasis added). This view has, we believe, been overtaken by events. Section 161 has, in Australia at least, rendered it untenable.

The unruly corporate body

It is appropriate to begin by looking at the nature of some of these entities called companies[8] and by considering the problems that the law may encounter in dealing with them. Consider the following description of a large multinational based in New York but with operations in nearly a hundred nations:

> Exxon is a typical corporate giant. Like the hundred or so corporations with assets of at least $1 billion and, in combination, the lion's share of America's industrial profits and earnings, Exxon does not really sell the products that produce its mind-boggling revenues. Its oil, chemicals, electronic typewriters, and motors are actually sold by an array of companies that Exxon owns. Business analyst Anthony J. Parisi thus describes Exxon as 'a fabulously wealthy investment club with a limited portfolio.' It invests in thirteen affiliate companies, whose heads, says Parisi, 'oversee their territories like provincial governors, sovereigns in their own lands but with an authority stemming from the power center in New York. The management committee exacts its tribute (the affiliate's profits from current operations) and issues doles (the money needed to sustain and expand those operations).' Most remarkable about Exxon's empire, however, is its scope. It operates in nearly 100 countries. 'Its 195 ocean-going tankers, owned and chartered, constitute a private navy as big as Britain's.'[9]

It is difficult, perhaps impossible, to reconcile this portrait of Exxon with the basic components of corporate law as we know it. In that difficulty lies an initial insight. Given that our existing legal regimes purport to regulate an entity that, in certain respects at least, simply does not exist, perhaps they simultaneously blind us to the need to devise a regulatory regime capable of controlling precisely what Exxon is: a fabulously wealthy investment club with a limited portfolio.

A closer and possibly more disturbing analogy—one that is implicit in Parisi's comments—is between the multinational corporation and an empire such as that of ancient Rome. If Exxon's corporate power centre can be equated to the Roman senate, and its affiliates to the provinces from which tribute is exacted and to which financial support and services are provided, perhaps the corporation—once 'spawned' through the ingenuity of businessmen and barristers, if not legislators[10]—has metamorphosed (at the interface of legal and economic theory) into something

---

8 The natural world provides us with a useful analogy for conceptualising the 'corporate body' in the colonial jellyfish (the best known example of which is the Portuguese Man-of-War). While this type of jellyfish acts as a single entity, it is in fact a colony of single-celled organisms that have lost the capacity to survive and act independently. The entity as a whole has shape, purpose, and, some suggest, the indicia of agency, but we should not forget that it possesses shape and purpose only because of the collective action of numerous smaller organisms of various kinds. Just as the 'forms' of colonial jellyfish vary greatly, corporate forms (or 'corporate jellyfish') are also enormously variable. One of the difficulties that the law encounters is the variability of the corporate person. Corporate persons vary from the enormous multinationals, which will be discussed in this section, to the one-person company. For the most part, the same assumptions are made by corporate law, whether the subject matter of that law is the one-person company or the multinational.

9 W. H. Shaw & V. Barry, *Moral Issues in Business*, 6th edn, Wadsworth Publishing Co., Belmont, Calif, 1995, pp. 199–200.

10 See the discussion of the deed-of-settlement company's evolution in chapter 2.

quite different from the company of the nineteenth century. Just what that something is and how it might be regulated is a very serious question indeed. In this context particularly—where the 'corporate head' is resident in one jurisdiction and various parts of the corporate 'body' are scattered throughout dozens, perhaps hundreds, of other jurisdictions—it is important to recognise the near unintelligibility of ideas such as corporate 'citizenship'. Mary Stokes argues that the features of the modern company pose fundamental problems for the 'political-economic organizations we associate with a liberal democracy'.[11] According to Stokes,

> [w]e make a distinction between public and private power. This distinction reflects the separation of the state from the individual in a liberal society. Liberal democracy has been concerned most explicitly with legitimating the power of the state, or public power. This is because the assumption is made that all important power in society is concentrated in the hands of the state. The arguments used to justify public power are very familiar. They are that the system of representative democracy gives authority to the legislature to make law, and that the power conferred upon all administrative or public bodies is legitimate as it is derived from the legislature. However, in a liberal society a democratic system of government is not considered sufficient by itself to legitimate public power. Liberalism is hostile to the existence of centres of unbridled power, believing that power unless limited and controlled may threaten the liberty and the equality of the individual, which are the two fundamental tenets of liberalism itself. Thus it is sought to subject public power to the Rule of Law. At its broadest the Rule of Law aims to impose limits, controls and checks on the exercise of power. Power must be prevented from being used arbitrarily. Arbitrariness is a difficult concept to define. It will be used to mean the exercise of power for purposes alien to those for which it was conferred.[12]

Stokes goes on to argue that the growth of corporate enterprises—the metamorphosis from the (relatively) small company, in which management could be (and perhaps was) controlled by the shareholders, to the modern multinational—has undermined the classical assumption of economic theory that 'the firm ... behaved identically and was subject to the same constraints whether it took the form of an individual proprietorship, a partnership or a company'.[13] According to Stokes, the 'classical model' has been undermined in three ways. First, the growth in the size of the firm has fundamentally undermined the classical model of a competitive market and has facilitated the growth of monopolistic or oligopolistic power. Second, the separation of management from ownership created an environment that encouraged managers to pursue their own interests rather than those of the company. On this important point, Stokes argues further:

---

11   M. Stokes, 'Company Law and Legal Theory', in W. Twining (ed.), *Legal Theory and Common Law*, Basil Blackwell, London, 1986, pp. 155, 156.

12   Stokes, p. 156.

13   Stokes, p. 158.

In a world of perfect competition it would not be possible for managers to deviate from the profit-maximization form for any length of time even if they were tempted to pursue their own rather than the shareholders' interests. The failure of the market due to imperfect competition to regulate the company as an economic unit is thus indissolubly linked with the increased and potentially unconstrained power of corporate managers.

Stokes describes the third way that the 'classical model' has been undermined as follows:

[O]ne of the cardinal features of the market model of legitimation was that economic power was exercised through exchange transactions in the market. Yet as the company grew in size it was plain that much economic activity was being withdrawn from the sphere of the market and being replaced by a hierarchical, bureaucratic organization within the company. The invisible hand was being replaced by the visible hand.[14]

In Australia, as in the USA and the United Kingdom, the evolution of the corporate raider epitomises the replacement of the invisible hand by the visible hand. The failure of the market to discipline corporate actors is compellingly illustrated both by the evolution of corporate raiders and by the managerial failures that produced asset-rich, but enterprise-poor, take-over targets.

The political and legal response to the failure of the market to discipline corporate actors has been two-fold. The first prong of the attack involved enacting legislation proscribing a variety of business practices that have either led to or enhanced monopoly power. The aim of this legislation was to maintain or restore the market's capacity to discipline individual market actors. During the early part of this century, 'antitrust' legislation, such as the *Sherman Act 1909*, was enacted in the USA. Similar legislation is now in force in most Western jurisdictions, including Australia.[15]

While the apparent inability of the market to discipline corporate actors led to efforts to eliminate 'market imperfections' through anti-trust legislation, another prong of attack has been 'internal'. This prong of attack sought to curb managerial excesses by strengthening minority rights and remedies in the legislative regimes devised for corporate governance. While statutory provisions designed to

---

14 Stokes, pp. 158–9.

15 The *Trade Practices Act 1974* (TPA) represents the current Australian attempt to prevent companies from accumulating enough market power to distort the market. The restrictive trade practices provisions of the TPA (found in part IV of the Act) are designed to promote competition among firms or, in the terms of the legislation, to prohibit conduct that may lessen competition. See P. H. Clarke, 'Trade Practices Policy and the Role of the Trade Practices Commission' (1989) 17 ABLR 231. Despite the TPA's enactment, Australia remains one of the most highly concentrated economies in the world. Very real questions are raised by the oligopolistic character of the Australian market, particularly in the context of the control of the Australian media by a few enormously powerful corporate empires. Michael Stutchbury notes that the oligopolistic character of the Australian market is a significant factor in the inflation-prone nature of the Australian economy. See M. Stutchbury, 'Oligopoly Capitalism a Factor in Australia's "Inflation Proneness"' *Australian Financial Review*, 2 May 1991; A. I. Tonking, 'Concentration in Australian Industry—Has It Gone Too Far?' (1988) 4 QUTLJ 13. A summary of the provisions that apply in the European Union may be found in S. Bronitt, F. R. Burns, & D. Kinley, *Principles of European Community Law: Commentary and Materials*, Law Book Company, Sydney, 1995, pp. 317 ff.

protect minority rights have been a feature of corporate law since the early English provisions, they have been strengthened on a number of occasions this century. The very strengthening of these remedies, however, highlights a further paradox. In the Anglo-Australian context at least, these remedies are (at the risk of some overgeneralisation) most useful and most frequently used in small private companies in which the relationships mimic those of a partnership (or are expected to do so). In other words, they are used because the individuals involved in those companies have expectations that are largely at variance with the corporate form—expectations, in short, akin to those in a partnership. These remedies are largely redundant in a large public company, where proxy voting is the norm and where it is increasingly common for the proxies to be exercised by the chief executive officer (CEO), thereby concentrating power in the CEO and rendering both the board and the general meeting largely redundant, except as 'legal fictions' in a disturbing and paradoxical sense.

The (im)moral corporate body and externalities

A further difficulty has emerged as evidence continues to mount of the social, environmental, and human costs of corporate unwillingness to confront what are called 'externalities' in economic discourse. These so-called 'externalities' range from the 'downstream' effects of smokestack emissions and effluent discharges to the effect of workplace toxins upon employees.[16] The saga of worldwide litigation concerning asbestosis is a classic example of the difficulties that multinational corporations pose for legal institutions and for communities. The dangers posed by the inhalation of asbestos fibres were documented in the United Kingdom as early as 1932, and parallel research was carried out in the USA between 1929 and 1931. However, the primary corporate concern was with 'managing' the release of the information in order to avoid its potential adverse impact upon profitability and to avoid exposing the companies concerned to litigation under workers' compensation law. The deception went further than just the suppression of data concerning the incidence and dangers of asbestos inhalation and the potential danger of mesothelioma; it also involved concealing the condition of affected workers and encouraging them to continue to work in a contaminated environment in which further exposure was inevitable. At a Johns-Manville plant in Canada, the medical director, who had diagnosed seven employees with asbestosis, gave the following explanation for not informing the employees of their diagnosis:

> It must be remembered that although these men have the X-ray evidence of asbestosis, they are working today and definitely are not disabled from asbestosis. They have not been told of this diagnosis, for it is felt that as long as the man feels well, is happy at home and at work, and his physical condition remains good, nothing should be said. When he becomes disabled and sick, then the diagnosis should be made and the claim

---

16   In our view, the concept can properly be extended further to, for example, the social cost of a corporate decision to abandon a factory that has become a part of the social and economic fabric of particular communities.

submitted *by the Company*. The fibrosis of this disease is irreversible and permanent so that eventually compensation will be paid to each of these men. But as long as the man is not disabled, it is felt that he should not be told of his condition so that he can live and work in peace and the Company can benefit by his many years of experience. Should the man be told of his condition today there is a very definite possibility that he would become mentally and physically ill, simply through the knowledge that he has asbestosis.[17]

Today Johns-Manville has capped its liability under a Chapter 11 restructuring,[18] and the majority of victims remain at most, only partially compensated.

In Australia, the interface between corporate law and general law is epitomised by *Briggs v. James Hardie & Co. Pty Ltd*.[19] The plaintiff was a 71-year-old member of the Kumbaingeri people, who contracted asbestosis during his 6-year employment at the asbestos mine at Baryulgil. In order to obtain compensation, the plaintiff sought to name a number of associated companies as co-defendants in negligence litigation, the particular subsidiary that had employed him having been liquidated. For him to succeed in his negligence action, it was necessary for the 'corporate veil' to be lifted to expose the very real financial and managerial connections between fictively separate corporate persons. According to Rogers AJA, there appears to be

> something wrong with the state of the law when, in order to recover compensation for his apparent asbestosis, a person in the position of this plaintiff has to mount a challenge to fundamental principles of company law …
>
> The threshold problem arises from the fact there is no common, unifying principle, which underlies the occasional decision of courts to pierce the corporate veil. Although an ad hoc explanation may be offered by a court which so decides, there is no principled approach to be derived from the authorities …
>
> The rule in *Salomon* was laid down at a time when economic circumstances were vastly different. The principle of laissez faire ruled supreme and the fostering of business enterprise demanded that the principle of limited liability be rigidly maintained. To date, the effect of incorporation has remained the same, notwithstanding the proliferation of conglomerates, holding companies and subsidiaries …
>
> Generally speaking, a person suffering injury as a result of the tortious act of a corporation has no choice in the selection of the tortfeasor … It seems to me reasonable … that different considerations should apply in deciding whether to pierce the corporate veil in actions in tort from the criteria applied in actions in contract, or for that matter, revenue or compensation cases.[20]

---

17 Dr Kenneth Smith, as quoted in Shaw & Barry, pp. 224–5 (emphasis added).

18 'Chapter 11' is the United States *Bankruptcy Code*'s provision for corporate restructuring. On the United States approach, see T. N. Antrobus, 'Bankruptcy and Director's Duties: The US Perspective' (1991) 9 Company and Securities LJ 447. For a comparison with Australian laws, see G. Dal Pont & L. Griggs, 'The Resuscitation of the Corporate Cadaver: An Autopsy of Business Rescue Laws' (1994) 4 AJCL 309.

19 (1989) 7 ACLC 841.

20 (1989) 7 ACLC 841 at 848–63.

The problem is fundamental to the interface between corporate law and general law. Corporate law gives birth to the corporate entity, deeming it to be subject to the general law in the same way as other citizens. Unfortunately, the general law to which it is subject is a law that evolved to deal with individual human beings, not corporate colonies.

We live in a world in which corporate persons, many of them multinational, are the dominant players. Therefore, to dismiss the notion of a corporate conscience as unrealistic (as did Baron Thurlow) seems to acquiesce in very real dilemmas in corporate governance and their implications for corporate regulation, rather than to address them.

Roman Tomasic and his colleagues suggest:

Arguably, the central problem for the modern corporation is the question of legitimacy. Another way of looking at this problem is in terms of the responsibility of the corporation, its directors and members …

Corporation law has for a long time been used as a means of legitimating the actions of the corporation. Sometimes this also seeks to achieve more responsible action (not always successfully) … Ultimately, however, whilst corporation law is far from being a vehicle for corporate social responsibility, it has served as a powerful means of legitimating wider social actions which might be questionable without such laws. Indeed, the cynics might say that the prime role of corporate law is to provide a predictable vehicle for the legitimisation of business malpractice.[21]

Increasingly, concerns about the legitimacy of the corporation encircle the question of social responsibility. The contemporary multinational corporation wields economic and social power, which may well go far beyond the scope of that wielded by any individual government. Corporate decisions have profound social and political impact. A decision to relocate, for example, can mean the economic death of a small mining community or a regional centre. Once a major employer deserts a particular region or town, other businesses are likely to collapse or depart. Sometimes these decisions are necessary, as, for example, where a resource has been exhausted. Sometimes such decisions are made because of the perceived advantages of the shift—for example, because power costs are lower, pollution requirements less stringent, or the taxation regime more favourable. Sometimes such decisions are primarily predicated upon the cost of labour.[22]

---

21 R. Tomasic, J. Jackson, & R. Woellner, *Corporation Law: Principles, Policy and Process*, 2nd edn, Butterworths, Sydney, 1992, p. 4.

22 See Shaw & Barry, pp. 231–3 for a discussion of the factors influencing the closing of the Levi Strauss plant in San Antonio, Texas, and the relocation of operations to Costa Rica and the Dominican Republic: 'it cost $6.70 to make a pair of Dockers at the South Zarzamora plant. Plant management had hoped to reduce that to $6.39 per unit in 1990, but even that would be significantly higher than the per unit cost of $5.88 at the Dockers plant in Powell, Tennessee—not to mention the $3.76 per unit cost Levi could get by using Third World contractors'.

Further questions arise where managerial practices have led to an unacceptably high level of corporate collapses, as has occurred in the recent past. While, in many cases, the directors and managers of failed companies have escaped essentially unscathed, the same cannot be said of many of those associated with those companies. Former employees, creditors, and whole communities have been left to bear the cost. In the case of a Levi Strauss plant closure in San Antonio, almost a year later, only fourteen of the almost a thousand workers shed had secured new employment.[23] Against this background, familiar questions concerning corporate morality and, indeed, corporate citizenship[24] are being raised with renewed vigour.

From a perspective that emphasises the role of the law and of legal institutions in corporate ordering, it is important to recognise that corporate morality (and corporate immorality) is itself, at least in part, a product of the law and of legal institutions. That is, the relationship between corporate morality and legal ordering is not one in which the unruly corporate body has somehow developed independently of, or escaped from, legal regulation, but one in which that body is partly a product of law's recurrent (and not altogether successful) attempts to regulate it. Law legitimates that which it fails to control. Paradoxically, attempted reforms often provide further vehicles by which the unruly corporate body may escape the hands of the regulator. As Tomasic and his colleagues suggest:

> Corporation law may provide a language which serves as the discourse legitimising corporate conduct, a language providing reassuring concepts such as the protection of minority shareholders, directors' fiduciary obligations, the protection of creditors and investor protection. More importantly, however, corporation law provides the owners and managers of capital with a convenient array of legal forms or vehicles for the conduct and organisation of business enterprise. Perhaps the best known of these are the ideas of corporate personality and limited liability, although there is a whole array of other similarly useful conceptual vehicles for more limited economic action. For example, for the purposes of *raising capital* there are the fundamental corporate forms such as the prospectus, shares and debentures; for the purposes of the *management* of corporate life and decision-making there are important legal forms such as general meeting, the board of directors, the memorandum and articles and corporate accounts; for the purposes of *corporate-re-organisation* there are the basic procedures of winding up, mergers and takeovers. There are many other devices in the hands of corporate managers which serve to enhance and legitimise the role of the corporation.[25]

The corporate body is not something outside the law, which the law elects from time to time to act upon. Rather, the corporate body would not exist but for the law,

---

23 Shaw & Barry, pp. 231–3.
24 J. B. White, 'How Should We Talk About Corporations? The Languages of Economics and of Citizenship' (1985) 94 Yale LJ 1416.
25 Tomasic et al., p. 7.

which has participated in its creation and shaping.[26] Its limbs, its organs, its mind, and its soul had their genesis at the interface of law and commerce. If legal institutions and economic theories have collectively engendered, as Baron Thurlow suggested, an entity wholly without conscience, that entity could neither exist nor function 'but for' the law, which endows it with personality, provides it with avenues through which it may receive sustenance, provides vehicles through which its mind and will may be expressed, and facilitates euthanasia when the corporate body is deemed to have at last outlived its usefulness.

REVIEW QUESTIONS

1 What is the gross national product (GNP) of Australia? Exxon's 1992 revenue (the equivalent of the GNP of a nation state) was $103.5 billion. What does this kind of economic clout suggest about the relationship between a company such as Exxon and the nation states within which it and its subsidiaries operate?

2 If a company like Exxon has its corporate 'mind and will' in New York, and its 'organs' distributed both throughout the various states of the USA and through nearly a hundred nations, two very different questions ought to concern us. The first is whether, or if, a company such as Exxon can truly be said to be subject to the rule of law. And, if so, to whose laws and under what circumstances? The second, and more critical, question in the present context concerns the parameters of corporate accountability or moral agency. To what extent can we expect such an entity to comply with the moral standards generally considered acceptable today, and what options are realistically available to any one government where such an entity disregards those standards?

3 A further major issue, and one that you should begin to think about here, is the penalty that the corporation is able to impose for efforts made to regulate it. Corporate migration from jurisdictions with unfavourable taxation regimes, high wages, and stringent testing and liability regimes for defective products and environmental degradation is well known. Very often, the 'favourable regimes' that provide corporate migrants with a new base for their operations are in less developed countries. It is sometimes argued that the loss of corporate residents is too high a price to pay for the protection of employees, consumers, and the environment, and that employment conditions in countries

---

26   Compare Robert Hessen, 'A New Concept of Corporations: A Contractual and Private Property Model' (1979) 30 Hastings LJ 1327. The views we express differ from those put forward by Hessen in at least two respects. First, we do not subscribe to the view that property and contract are 'natural entities'. Rather, they are creatures of the law and of legal institutions. Second, given our view that the enforceability of contracts (and the rules about which contracts are enforced) is itself a political decision, all of the questions that Hessen suggests can be satisfactorily disposed of by this enforceability simply reappear.

such as Australia should be adjusted to more nearly resemble those in our Asian neighbours, for example. Do you agree?

4 The story of the Levi Strauss plant in San Antonio, Texas, is one that has been replayed numerous times in Australia. How should such corporate decisions be treated by corporate regulators? It is worth bearing in mind that inexpensive 'off shore' labour is employed under conditions that, while standard in that jurisdiction, might well be considered illegal and possibly immoral in Australia. How should the legal regime in Australia respond? Is there anything that can be done, particularly against the background of increasing pressure to reduce tariffs and free up the trading environment?

Theoretical perspectives on 'corporate morality'

In this section we will explore a variety of perspectives on corporate morality. Because an understanding of the context in which the corporation evolved, and of its genealogy, is essential to untangling the different theoretical perspectives, we will begin there.

Theories of morality and the firm

Corporate genealogies and their (im)moral consequences

At this point, it is worth spending a few moments on the genealogy of the modern corporation and its pursuit of an ideal that has, perhaps, found ultimate legal expression in s. 161 of the Corporations Law. William Shaw and Vincent Barry suggest that Adam Smith[27] in England and Alexander Hamilton in the USA

challenged the desirability of a direct tie between business enterprise and public policy. Their idea was that business people should be encouraged to explore their own avenues of enterprise. The 'invisible hand' of the market would direct their activities in a socially beneficial direction more effectively than any public official could.

Second, when nineteenth-century reformers argued for changes in incorporation procedures, they talked not only about government favoritism and the advantages of a laissez-faire approach but also about the principle of a corporation's right to exist. Any petitioning body with the minimal qualifications, they asserted, had the right to receive a corporate charter. By contrast, the early Crown-chartered corporations were clearly creations of the state, in accordance with the legal-political doctrine that all corporate status was a privilege bestowed by the state as it saw fit. According to the reformers,

---

27 But see R. C. Solomon, 'Beyond Selfishness: Adam Smith and the Limits of the Market' (1993) 3 *Business Ethics Quarterly* 453 at 457 for a suggestion that Smith's 'invisible hand' 'cannot and should not be construed as "the ultimate governor" of the market nor as anything other than a fanciful description of the benign results of market activity'.

however, incorporation is a by-product of the peoples' right of association, not a gift from the state.[28]

While the genealogies of Australian and United States companies have differed somewhat in their details[29]—the Australian company (as you saw in chapter 1) evolved by way of the deed-of-settlement company in England, whereas the United States corporation is conventionally argued to be a lineal descendent of the chartered corporation—they share a common ancestor in the medieval chartered corporation. The earliest corporate persons were towns, universities, and similar public entities. They were entities that served a profound public purpose, and the 'privilege' of incorporation was granted to help accomplish this 'public purpose'. It was not until the seventeenth century that 'commercial organisations', such as the East India Company, obtained corporate charters. Despite their commercial focus, these early 'commercial corporations' invariably served public purposes as well, most notably, if not always palatably, the extension of Empire.[30] Only when the old mercantilist idea 'that a corporation's activities should advance some public specific purpose' was replaced by the invisible hand of economic theory did the explicit connection between the corporate purpose and the public good finally disintegrate.[31] Once incorporation became freely available, the absence of any connection between corporate status and the public good led to a deeply embedded and continuing concern in the law with the bounds and nature of 'proper corporate purposes', and with the extent to which those purposes might extend beyond the 'narrowly commercial'. Thus in *Hutton v. West Cork Railway Co.*, Bowen LJ said:

> They can only spend money which is not theirs but the company's, if they are spending it for the purposes which are reasonably incidental to the carrying on of the business of the company … the test must be what is reasonably incidental to, and within the reasonable scope of carrying on, the business of the company … The law does not say that there are to be no cakes and ale, but there are to be no cakes and ale except such as are required for the benefit of the company … It is not charity sitting at the board of directors, because as it seems to me charity has no business to sit at boards of directors qua charity. There is, however, a kind of charitable dealing which is for the interest of those who practise it, and to that extent and in that garb (I admit a not very philanthropic garb) charity may sit at the board, but for no other purpose.[32]

Lord Justice Bowen's judgment typifies those of the era, both in its constant reference back to the parameters of 'reasonableness' and in its fundamental ambiguity.

---

28 Shaw & Barry, pp. 201–2. You should think very carefully about the argument that corporate status is a by-product of the people's right to associate. If the State imposes conditions upon incorporation (for example, a minimum level of capital before limited liability is granted) or requires corporate persons to make some contribution to the public good, does that actually infringe upon the people's right to associate?

29 But not, perhaps, in their essentials.

30 See Hessen at 1338–9.

31 P. Baron, 'Shells of Steel and Bodies of Pulp: Commercial Man, Commercial Morality' (1993) 11 *Law in Context* 3.

32 (1883) 23 Ch D 654 at 671.

Many today might suggest that phrases such as 'reasonably incidental' and 'reasonable scope' provide space for policy judgments by the courts, there being no other concrete referent by which they can be given flesh. In 1883, and for many years after, the policy of the law was to read those incidents and that scope narrowly, ultimately tying the interests back to that which was essential to realise a profit for the shareholders (or 'corporators', as they are often called). If the only interests that corporations may properly pursue are 'corporate interests', and those corporate interests are read narrowly, it might well be argued that talk of 'corporate morality' or 'corporate social responsibility' is in fundamental conflict with a law that requires that the corporation concern itself not with morality or questions of social responsibility, but with the pursuit of self-interest (which, in the corporate context, is most usually read as profit).[33] More recently, however, judges have begun to draw connections between the public good and the interests that may properly be seen as corporate interests. One such view of the 'corporate interest' is that provided by the judgment of Berger J in *Teck Corp. Ltd v. Millar*:[34]

> The classical theory is that the director's duty is to the company. The company's shareholders are the company ... and therefore no interests outside those of the shareholders can legitimately be considered by the directors. But even accepting that, what comes within the definition of the interests of the shareholders? By what standards are the shareholders' interests to be measured?
>
> *In defining the fiduciary duties of directors, the law ought to take into account the fact that the corporation provides the legal framework for the development of resources and the generation of wealth in the private sector of the Canadian economy ...*
>
> A classical theory that was once unchallengeable must yield to the facts of modern life. In fact, of course, it has. If today the directors of a company were to consider the interests of its employees no one would argue that in doing so they were not acting *bona fide* in the interests of the company itself. Similarly, if the directors were to consider the consequences to the community of any policy that the company intended to pursue, and were deflected in their commitment to that policy as a result, it could not be said that they had not considered *bona fide* the interests of the shareholders.[35]

---

33 It is useful to compare this understanding of corporate interests (and, by extension, of corporate morality) with the understandings of commerce and of contract that prevailed during the height of *laissez-faire* economics in the nineteenth century. More recently, of course, notions of appropriate conduct in commercial dealings have been radically revised. Literature on the overall area of commercial morality has burgeoned, and notable participants in this discourse are former (and present) members of the judiciary. See P. Finn, 'Unconscionable Conduct' (1994) 8 *Journal of Contract Law* 37; P. Finn, 'Good Faith and Fair Dealing' (parts 1 & 2) (1990) 5 *Australian Insurance Law Bulletin* 101; Sir G. Brennan, 'Commercial Law and Morality' (1989) 17 MULR 100; P. Finn, 'Contract and the Fiduciary Principle' (1989) 12 UNSWLJ 76; P. Finn, 'Commerce, the Common Law and Morality' (1989) 17 MULR 87; M. McHugh, 'Jeopardy of Lawyers and Accountants in Acting on Commercial Transactions' (1988) 22 *Taxation in Australia* 542. For work directly bearing on corporate morality, see P. Finn, 'Simplification and Ethics: A Commentary' (1995) 5 *Australian Journal of Corporate Law* 158.

34 (1973) 33 DLR (3d) 288.

35 (1973) 33 DLR (3d) 288 at 313–14 (emphasis added).

Most notable in the judgment of Berger J is the very explicit reappearance of the conception that corporate interests and the 'public good' are connected. The modernist reinterpretation of this connection is manifested through an explicit link between the legal framework that facilitates corporate activity, on the one hand, and the public interest in the development of resources and generation of wealth within the whole economy, on the other. For Berger J, corporate activity cannot be understood out of context. Rather, it must be explicitly interpreted within the context of the (Canadian) economy as a whole. The current debate is being conducted within the parameters established by these very different texts. The concern with the proper parameters of the 'interests of the company' continues.

The law's schizophrenic approach to corporate morality is exacerbated by the fact that, in both the USA and Canada, corporations have been held by the highest courts in the land to be entitled to basic civil and political rights under the Bill of Rights and the Charter of Rights and Freedoms respectively. In *First National Bank of Boston v. Bellotti* [36] the United States Supreme Court held that corporations were entitled to spend funds to publicise political views that were not materially connected with their property, business, or assets. [37] To disallow such activity constituted a restriction upon their 'freedom of political speech', which the Supreme Court deemed unconstitutional. Similarly, in Canada, corporations have been held to be entitled to freedom of religion under the provisions of the Charter of Rights and Freedoms. Like the wording of s. 161 of the Corporations Law, both of these decisions

> have the effect of blurring the distinction between corporations and individuals. For in deciding that corporations enjoy protection under the First Amendment, the Court laid a basis for claiming that corporations enjoy the same moral and political rights and should therefore bear the same responsibilities as individual human beings. In other words, if corporations have the rights that moral agents have, then like individuals they can and should be held morally responsible for their actions.

> The problem, of course, is that corporations are not individuals but artificial persons created by the law. They are collections of individuals who set goals and policies and perform specific actions. Since corporations are not actual persons, in what sense can they be held morally responsible for their actions? [38]

---

36   (1978) 435 US 765.

37   Perhaps the real message of *Bellotti* is that, if charity cannot sit at the boardroom table, political advertising can. The dissentients in *Bellotti*—White J (with whom Brennan and Marshall JJ concurred) and Rehnquist J—argued forcefully that, while it is easy to understand how a corporation could, reasonably or otherwise, believe that the outcome of an election might well have a material, if indirect, bearing upon its fortunes in the years to come, it is much harder to reconcile that sort of purely self-interested justification with the ethical purposes served by basic civil and political rights. See 805 and 825 respectively. It is hard to reconcile the idea of an entity that has 'no body to kick and no soul to damn' with the values underlying the contemporary faith in rights talk. On the other hand, perhaps what we are witnessing in these decisions extending the protections in national human rights documents to non-natural persons is the ultimate expression of the idea of 'rights as property'. If so, corporate entities can acquire rights in much the same way as they can acquire other assets.

38   Shaw & Barry, p. 202. Noteworthy in the decisions of both paramount courts is their acceptance of the traditional image of the corporate person as a quasi-organic entity. Both judgments are simply incoherent unless the corporation as such is understood to be more than a set of contractual relationships between corporators and managers.

If, as many commentators[39] suggest, corporate Australia, like corporate America, is, for better or for worse, beyond the control of those who would purport to regulate it, then it may be argued that in some ways the law has been more successful than we might wish, not less successful. There is a real, and disconcerting, parallel with the genealogies of the family and family law, which is worth thinking about. The 'liberal' family is substantially a product of the regulatory (and disciplinary) regimes of early liberalism. At the risk of some oversimplification, it developed in a synergistic relationship with the evolution of laws concerning marriage, divorce, family property and income, responsibility for children, and so on during the eighteenth and nineteenth centuries.[40] We are not suggesting that 'family entities' did not exist before the regulatory regimes of early liberal capitalism began to contribute to family discourse. Clearly they did. Nor are we suggesting that corporate entities (in precisely the same sense as quasi-organic entities) did not predate the particular regulatory regimes and corporate forms identified with liberal capitalism. Clearly they did. What we are suggesting is that the contemporary corporation, like the contemporary family, is partly a product of the regulatory regimes that have arisen over the same period. The relationship between the corporation and the law, like that between the family and the law, is both dynamic and synergistic. Many of the developments with which regulators grapple today were made possible by the legal vehicles created by liberal capitalist states. These vehicles—liberated from the need for a Crown or Commonwealth charter, and made available, through market forces, to any wishing to avail themselves of them—were and are entities created upon the model of subordinate political entities. Cut free from these entities, they are both unruled and unrulable.

Exercising judgment: The search for the perfect rule

In general, contemporary Australian debate centres not on conceptual issues such as those addressed in the introduction, but on the more pragmatic issues that are a lingering by-product of the corporate collapses of the 1980s. Here there is a straightforward demand for accountability, coupled with the clear suggestion that there is a direct causal connection between limited liability and these failures of accountability.[41]

---

39 Among them is (now retired) Justice Andrew Rogers of the New South Wales Commercial Division.

40 See, for example, F. E. Olsen, 'The Family and the Market: A Study in Ideology and Legal Reform' (1983) 96 Harv LR 1497; S. S. Berns, 'Regulation of the Family: Whose Interests Does it Serve?' (1992) 1 Griffith LR 152; S. J. Parker, *Informal Marriage, Cohabitation and the Law 1750–1989*, St Martin's Press, New York, 1990.

41 It is, perhaps, disturbing that a symptom is persistently mistaken for the source of the problem. Undoubtedly there are areas where limited liability is wholly inappropriate, and it seems likely that the small private company exemplifies these. In the context of the one- or two-person company, however, limited liability is often fictitious so far as major lending institutions such as banks are concerned. It is only a reality in relation to others with whom the company trades. Limited liability is not inappropriate if one views the public company as a vehicle for passive investment. The difficulty lies in fixing liability upon the actual controllers of the company, be those controllers the CEO, upper levels of employed management, or the board of directors.

Justice Andrew Rogers, formerly Chief Judge of the Commercial Division of the New South Wales Supreme Court, argues that the difficulty is not with those provisions of the Corporations Law that fix liability for misconduct on the part of directors and senior managers. Rather, '[w]hat is needed are two things that are presently lacking. First, a short, sharp clear law supplementing the prohibition against certain behaviour with short, sharp provisions as to the consequences of infringement. Second, procedural laws which will ensure that the action made available is imposed quickly and at relatively little cost to the community'. Justice Rogers continues a little later:

> Let me make the first point by reference to a recent case which did not involve any breach of the criminal law. It did, however, highlight the deficiencies of which I complain. The action involved a foreign bank and a large Australian public company. A former director was called to give evidence and repeatedly declined to give essential evidence on the ground that the answer may tend to incriminate him. The same person had given some of the same evidence that had been sought from him in an examination under the Companies Code, where the privilege to refuse to answer is not available. The answer so given under compulsion, however, cannot be used in other litigation. The farcical situation therefore developed that evidence, which was important in the case before me, could not be required to be given by this witness but could be read by readers of the daily newspapers who were interested in what this person said at the public examination. The rules safeguarding a person against self-incrimination were developed for the protection of the poor and the ignorant against possible oppression. These days the persons claiming protection in relation to the affairs of the company may not only be the most wealthy persons in the court, flanked by a battery of skilled advisers, but possibly also the most intelligent persons in the courtroom.[42]

Where the law makes itself available as a mechanism by which corporate managers can avoid accounting for conduct that they engaged in while stewards of public companies, then, as Justice Rogers suggests, '[t]he time has come to reappraise the whole concept of limited liability and to determine whether the benefits outweigh the obvious detriments'.[43] Justice Rogers suggests further that merely nibbling at the parameters of the insolvent trading provisions will prove both costly and relatively unfruitful. Rather:

> I would suggest legislation to avoid these expensive and possibly inappropriate inquiries. First, prove an infringement of s. 229 [of the Corporations Law]. If that is proved, then every asset which an officer controlled, at the time of the breach of the law, or thereafter, would come under the control of the wronged company to stand as security for the damage the company may recover. The provision would extend to property which was no longer in the name of the officer, unless the new owner could

---

42 Justice A. Rogers, 'A Vision of Corporate Australia' (1991) 1 (1) AJCL 1 at 1–3.
43 Rogers at 5.

demonstrate that he or she or it acquired the asset bona fide for value without notice. This proposal is likely to create screams of protest. But why should it? What it does is to make available, to the creditors and shareholders of the company, assets which the director acquired at some point after the commission of an act of wrongdoing. There should be a presumption that the wrongdoing allowed, or at least facilitated, the acquisition of the assets. Such a measure would avoid, or at least reduce, the delays and the expense involved in the liquidator attempting to prove matters which are largely within the knowledge of the director. It would be up to the officer to show that the profit earnt [*sic*] from the breach or breaches of duty, or the damage or loss suffered by the company, was less than the value of the assets.[44]

In a similar vein, Bryson J suggested in *Lombard Nash International Pty Ltd v. Berentsen*[45] that the senior managers of Australian public corporations owed a duty to account for their stewardship, not only to their creditors and shareholders, but also to the community at large. In another case, Cole J took this argument to its logical conclusion, invoking the public interest and suggesting that it

> requires that those receiving moneys of the public, or administering companies in which the public invest, should be obliged to explain transactions and conduct related to such moneys and business transactions. I see no public interest in such persons being able to escape either civil or criminal responsibility, if such exists, because parties injured by the conduct of such persons, or prosecuting authorities on behalf of the community, are unable to establish factual matters which because of the nature of companies, or the conduct of such persons, is known only to such persons. *The law, at present, protects the interests of the civil and criminal wrong-doers. It should protect the interests of the investing public.* If there be conflict between the private rights of individuals in the conduct of companies in which the public invest, and the rights of members of the investing public, in my view that conflict should be resolved in favour of the members of the public. A person who is responsible for the direction or administration of a company in which the public invest can have little cause for complaint if he be obliged to tell the truth regarding the application of funds received from the public, or management of a business on behalf of shareholders.[46]

The rather narrow focus of this 'duty to account for their stewardship' is largely a product of the environment in which these views were expressed and of the

---

44 Rogers at 6. As noted above, this suggestion is not without merit, provided that the 'actual' as opposed to 'legal' 'controllers are identified and targeted in the way suggested. Sometimes, particularly in Australia, corporate empires are largely controlled by one individual, often through the vehicle of a private family company. It may well be that such structures ought to be prohibited.

45 (1991) 3 ACSR 343 at 346.

46 *Spedley Securities Ltd (in liq.) v. Bond Brewing Investments Pty Ltd* (1991) 4 ACSR 229 at 346. In this context, it is important to note the explicit development of a further tension. Once we begin to envisage corporate stewardship as involving a duty both to the 'investing public' (which surely must encompass, *inter alia*, those who have no current connection with the company) and to the existing shareholders, it seems that little is required to move beyond this and focus upon a duty to the public at large.

background of widespread corporate collapses during the 1980s. It is, however, important to bear in mind that the impact of managerial defalcations, and of the corporate collapses that all too often followed in their wake, extended well beyond the investing public, often involving entire communities.

The American commentator Russell Stevenson has described corporations in these terms: 'Frankensteinian creations of economic necessity, corporate "persons" are deficient in that concatenation of spiritual, social, and political characteristics which in human personalities we call the "soul." Since the individuals who manage corporation do presumably have souls, in this respect, at least, the corporation is very much less than the sum of its parts'.[47] More disturbingly, perhaps, Stevenson identifies a number of features of corporate life that potentially impact to an even greater extent upon the Australian scene:

> The problem of the modern corporation is not size alone … The problem under discussion here is not the existence, but the governance, of large accumulations of physical and human resources. To a seemingly ever-increasing extent the members of society, individual and corporate alike, are awash in an existential sea, out of sight of beacons of external guidance. The individual may make up, in part, for this absence of navigational aids by turning inward for a sense of direction. The corporate personality, however, looks inward into darkness. The corporation has no soul.
>
> Until recently, at least, formal deference has been paid to the theoretical notion that a corporation is controlled by, and is responsible to, its shareholders. That particular myth was dealt a heavy blow by the publication in 1932 of Berle and Means' classic work, *The Modern Corporation and Private Property*, which pointed out for all to see that the emperor had no clothes—that the principal theoretical underpinning of the law of corporations rested on a premise which, at least for the large corporation, was untenable and had probably always been so …
>
> The corporate person is not, the protestations of corporate managers to the contrary notwithstanding, a member of society in the same sense as an individual person. *There is no effective mechanism for socializing a corporation. It cannot be educated. It cannot be shamed. To an increasing extent society is not even capable of punishing it. The result is an institution truly responsible to no one.*
>
> As if to emphasize the institutional non-responsibility of the corporation, even the semblance of 'shareholder democracy' is rapidly being destroyed by recent trends in corporate finance and the securities markets.
>
> The proportion of stock listed on the New York Stock Exchange now controlled by institutional investors has passed one-third and is growing steadily … At its extreme this tendency reaches the point where an institution or small group of institutions owning a controlling interest in a corporation are so closely allied with management that the cor-

---

47 R. B. Stevenson Jr, 'Corporations and Social Responsibility: In Search of the Corporate Soul' (1974) 2 Geo Washington LR 709 at 710.

poration can be realistically said to control itself, and is thus ultimately responsible, even in theory, to no one.[48]

While, in the USA, there have been some (perhaps weak) signs of a resurgence of shareholder democracy during recent years, these are generally sporadic, are focused on highly specific and visible issues, and are less than completely successful. In Australia, the overall picture is bleaker. By and large, share ownership in Australia remains overwhelmingly in the hands of 'institutional investors'. While these 'institutional investors' are often significant players in internecine corporate struggles, there is little, if any, evidence that they serve as an effective external control. Such control should, in principle, moderate corporate conduct and/or act as a force to encourage corporations to be more socially responsible. Indeed, it is hard to see how these 'institutional investors' could be expected to do so. After all, institutional investors are themselves profit-driven corporate persons. Like the companies whose shares they own, as entities they are responsible to no one, as Stevenson suggests. Because their sole, or exclusive, business is that of financial management, one could argue that, unless they are compelled to internalise externalities[49] to a far greater extent than is presently the case, they are even more likely to discount those externalities than the companies they watch over, since their own fortunes depend upon the profitability of those in whom they invest.

While other commentators, such as Gerard Elfstrom,[50] are somewhat less pessimistic, they also acknowledge that corporate moral agency, to the extent that it exists, operates in a different way from that of individual human agents and poses significantly different problems. In the case of multinational corporations, such problems are exacerbated, for a number of reasons. Elfstrom suggests:

> Commercial activity in the international arena does not qualitatively change the nature of corporate moral agency or the conditions of moral sensitivity. However, the present circumstances of multinational commerce are such that moral difficulties are apt to be present in a more intense and less manageable fashion than on the domestic level.

> For one thing, the regulatory agencies and legal strictures that order commercial activity within nations exist in only fragmentary and tenuous fashion on the international level. Indeed, their ability to evade effective governmental control is one of the disgruntling talents multinational corporations possess. One result is that corporations may have a less vivid sense that standards of commercial activity exist. Another is that those who are unscrupulous or irresponsible are more likely to escape unscathed or undetected. Furthermore the size, complexity and geographic dispersal that generally accompany multinational endeavour make it less likely that individuals within these enterprises will have a clear sense of what corporations or their subsidiaries are doing or how they affect

---

48 Stevenson at 712–14 (footnotes omitted and emphasis added).

49 An externality is a hidden cost. For example, polluted water discharged into a river can cause algae blooms and fish kills. The cost of rehabilitating the river is an 'externality'. Typically, firms disregard externalities until regulators compel them to internalise the hidden costs. See discussion of Melvin Anshen's views on pp. 133–4.

50 G. Elfstrom, *Moral Issues and Multinational Corporations*, St Martin's Press, New York, 1991.

human life. Large size and daunting complexity also decrease the probability that any given individual will have explicit responsibility to address moral difficulty. Finally, the cultural, economic and political diversity which attend the operations of multinational corporations increase the likelihood that harm will be caused unknowingly, that enterprises will find themselves in collaboration with unsavory political groups or that their activities will clash with local cultural norms.[51]

According to Elfstrom, while corporations have the two prerequisites for moral agency (in that they are able to control their actions and make rational rather than irrational decisions), this moral agency is less visible because of their size and the complexity of their organisational structure. Further difficulties arise because of the need to apportion responsibility among various individual actors within corporations.

REVIEW QUESTIONS

1 What problems does the replacement of the 'mercantilist' image of public purpose by the invisible hand of economic theory pose for corporate governance and the design of regulatory regimes?
2 In what ways has the legal regime governing corporate persons shaped the entities that it governs?
3 When Stevenson insists that, because corporations cannot be socialised, shamed, or educated, the result is an institution truly responsible to no one, he identifies the critical problem for corporate regulation in the late twentieth century. What are the specific manifestations of the problem he identifies, and how should governments address the problem?

Opposing visions: Two views of corporate morality

Profit-maximisation

The view has been gaining widespread acceptance that corporate officials and labor leaders have a social responsibility that goes beyond serving the interest of their stockholders or their members. This view shows a fundamental misconception of the character and nature of a free economy. In such an economy, there is one and only one social responsibility of business—to use its resources and engage in activities designed to increase its profits so long as it stays within the rules of the game, which is to say, engages in open and free competition, without deception or fraud ... Few trends could so thoroughly undermine the very foundations of our free society as the acceptance by corporate officials of a social responsibility other than to make as much money for their stockholders as possible.[52]

51 Elfstrom, pp. 12–13.
52 M. Friedman, *Capitalism and Freedom*, University of Chicago Press, Chicago, 1962, p. 133.

Those, like Milton Friedman, who believe that the sole obligation of corporate managers lies in profit-maximisation sometimes predicate their arguments upon a presumed 'promissory' relationship between the company and its shareholders. An analogy is drawn between the relationship of the company and its shareholders and the relationship between an investor and a financial adviser. Just as a financial adviser ought to invest a client's money in ways that will maximise the return to that client, so too, according to this line of argument, corporate managers are obliged to maximise profits in the interests of their shareholders. The strongest version of this argument suggests that the manager–shareholder relationship 'imposes an obligation that is inconsistent with any social responsibility other than profit maximization'.[53]

Yet despite a legal environment in which, increasingly, the courts impose fiduciary obligations on, *inter alios*, investment advisers,[54] arguments of this kind are profoundly dissonant in the corporate law context. Courts in the common-law world have been deeply reluctant to suggest that company directors are either fiduciaries for the interests of their shareholders or even, less demandingly, their agents, at least in any uncomplicated sense.[55] While notions such as agency and fiduciary obligations are absolutely central to corporate law, it is clear that, legally, the directors or managers are the agents of 'the company', and that 'the company' is, as a matter of law, specifically and categorically disaggregated from its shareholders. The judges cannot really say just what the company is, but what they can and do say is that the company is not to be confused with its shareholders or even with a majority of those shareholders. 'The company' is, it seems, both more and less than its shareholders at a given time, although, as in *Greenhalgh v. Ardorne Cinemas*,[56] it has sometimes been likened to the 'individual hypothetical shareholder'—a character who may be remarkably similar to the reasonable person (also known as the 'reasonable man').

As a purely legal matter, corporate managers have been held to owe duties to individual shareholders only in cases such as *Coleman & Ors v. Myers & Ors*,[57] in which, by virtue of the family character of the company and the nature of the relationship between the shareholders and the directors, such a duty seemed inevitable. In holding that a fiduciary relationship obtained in the circumstances of that case, Woodhouse J noted that

> it is not the law that anybody holding the office of director of a limited liability company is for that reason alone to be released from what otherwise would be regarded as a

---

53 Shaw & Barry, pp. 210–11.

54 *Hodgekinson v. Simms* (1995) 117 DLR (4d) 161; *Commonwealth Bank v. Smith* (1992) 102 ALR 453; *Dessen Gold Resources v. Royal Bank* [1995] WLR 171.

55 The persistence of the organicist theory of the corporate person is particularly apparent in the efforts of the court to disaggregate the 'interests of the company' from the interests of its members. See, for example, *Ngurli Ltd v. McCann* (1953) 90 CLR 425 at 438–40; *Greenhalgh v. Arderne Cinemas Ltd* [1951] 1 Ch 286 at 291; *Parke v. Daily News Ltd* [1962] Ch 927 at 951–2; *Walker v. Wimborne* (1976) 137 CLR 1.

56 [1951] 1 Ch 286 at 291.

57 [1977] 2 NZLR 225.

fiduciary responsibility owed to those in the position of shareholders of the same company … it is my opinion that the standard of conduct required from a director in relation to dealings with a shareholder will differ depending upon all the surrounding circumstances and the nature of the responsibility which, in a real and practical sense, the director has assumed towards the shareholder … and while it may not be possible to lay down any general test as to when the fiduciary duty will arise for a company director or to prescribe the exact conduct which will always discharge it when it does, there are nevertheless some factors that will usually have an influence upon a decision one way or the other. They include, I think, dependence upon information and advice, the existence of a relationship of confidence, the significance of some particular transaction for the parties and, of course, the extent of any positive action taken by or on behalf of the director or directors to promote it.[58]

Even in this broadly based acceptance of potential for fiduciary obligations in the shareholder–director relationship, however, the emphasis is on the particularity of the relationship: the shareholder's dependence on information and advice, the existence of a relationship of confidence between the director and the particular shareholder, and the significance of a known transaction to the particular parties involved. It is worth remarking upon the incommensurability of this description with the more usual shareholder–director relationship in a large public company. There, as Shaw and Barry note, it is the utter absence of any individual relationship that is noteworthy:

[T]he purchase of stock in a corporation [is] rarely couched in such explicitly promissory terms. Would-be investors pick companies that look profitable or are likely to grow or whose policies appeal to them, and they buy shares in those firms. Or they ask their stockbrokers simply to purchase what 'looks good.' Either way, shares are purchased through a broker from current shareholders, who have acquired their shares the same way. Very few investors put their money directly into a corporation; rather, they buy shares that were initially issued years ago.

Other factors further weaken the analogy between holding stock and entrusting money to a financial manager: (1) Most shareholders aren't even aware who the managers of 'their' corporations are; (2) most shareholders never have direct contact with management; (3) the complexity of management systems in most modern corporations makes it impossible to pinpoint a single manager or group of managers directly responsible.[59]

The prevailing legal position is epitomised by *Percival v. Wright*[60] and *Gething v. Kilner*.[61] In *Percival v. Wright*, Swinfen-Eady J characterised the legal position in these terms:

---

58 [1977] 2 NZLR 225 at 324–5.
59 Shaw & Barry, p. 211.
60 [1902] 2 Ch D 421.
61 [1972] 1 WLR 337.

[A] director purchasing shares need not disclose a large casual profit, the discovery of a new vein, or the prospect of a good dividend in the immediate future, and similarly a director selling shares need not disclose losses, these being merely incidents in the ordinary course of management ... The true rule is that a shareholder is fixed with knowledge of all the directors' powers, and has no more reason to assume that they are not negotiating a sale of the undertaking than to assume that they are not exercising any other power.[62]

In this context, it is worth picking apart the different legal elements that constitute the company's relationship with its 'owners'. First, while it is clear that at common law the general meeting is regarded as the basic organ of power within the company, the powers of both the general meeting and the individual shareholders are strictly circumscribed. While the general meeting theoretically is the fundamental decision-making organ of the company, the responsibility for all day-to-day matters of corporate management is legally vested in the board of directors.[63]

The only sense in which the general meeting may be said to control the board of directors lies in its power to dismiss the board should it see fit, and even this power is, except *in extremis*, largely illusory. In the vast majority of public companies, the board or, even more frequently, the CEO 'controls' the general meeting through the mechanism of proxy voting. As an actual organ of corporate power, the general meeting is effectively redundant. In purely pragmatic terms, the 'deliberations' of the general meeting are a formal mechanism that serves to legitimate, in the eyes of the regulatory authorities, decisions that have largely been made elsewhere. Friedman argues:

The whole justification for permitting the corporate executive to be selected by the shareholders is that the executive is an agent serving the interest of this principal. This justification disappears when the corporate executive imposes taxes and spends the proceeds for 'social' purposes. He becomes in effect a public employee, a civil servant, even though he remains in name an employee of a private enterprise.[64]

This argument is stripped of its skein of rationality by the actual, as opposed to the legal and fictive, processes of corporate governance. Once we accept that, particularly in large companies, the 'real' (rather than 'formal and legal') power lies not with the board of directors but with the multiple levels of management beneath the board, the unreality of the supposed agency relationship is obvious. Largely invisible in legal terms, these managers make the day-to-day decisions that entrench marketing strategies, determine policies, evaluate products, provide costings, and collectively (if generally unconsciously) constitute the 'corporate agent'. Shaw and Barry note:

---

62 [1902] 2 Ch D 421 at 426.

63 Typically the articles of the company include a provision to the effect that 'the business of the company shall be managed by the directors': art. 66(1), table A, schedule 1, Corporations Law ('table A articles'). Essentially such an article vests absolute decision-making power in commercial matters in the board or its delegates.

64 M. Friedman, 'The Social Responsibility of Business is to Increase Its Profits' (13 September 1970) 33 *New York Times Magazine* 122.

Corporate watchdogs like Ralph Nader and Mark Green make the point that, in modern corporate governance, management in fact selects its board of directors by controlling proxy votes. And the board typically rubber-stamps the policies and executive-officer recommendations of management. Furthermore, corporate boards often are ignorant of the activities of chief executive officers. For well over a year after disclosure of multimillion-dollar bribes by Gulf Oil executives, the board of directors claimed it didn't know that the company's chief executive officer and chairman of the board had been personally involved.[65]

On one hand there is a corporate world of formal structures, of increasing legal attempts to build in checks and balances through, for example, enhancing the remedies available to minority shareholders. On the other hand, the centre of gravity of corporate power has shifted away from the 'formal', publicly accountable corporate organs such as the board of directors and the general meeting to legally 'informal' corporate organs such as the CEO and the ranks of professional managers. What this means in practical terms is that legal regulation addresses the formal structures but leaves the informal structures largely unchecked and uncheckable. While these legally informal structures exist outside the regulatory gaze, they wield enormous power. In a legal environment in which the courts have consistently deferred to 'commercial judgment' and in which judicial policy has expressly been to avoid addressing the merits or otherwise of commercial decisions, the law regulates the 'legal fiction' that it has created (successfully or otherwise), while the 'firm' and those associated with it largely escape regulation. To the extent that the 'firm' is regulated at all, the regulatory forces operating upon it come, not from the law and the institutions associated with law, but from Adam Smith's 'invisible hand'. Unfortunately, there is little sign that it has yet succeeded in channelling corporate activity towards anything that could be recognised as the 'common good'.

To complicate matters further, as Christopher Stone and others have noted, corporate roles carry with them their own 'morality'. Firms could not function but for the complex network of roles—and of the obligations and rewards associated with those roles—that defines the internal structure of the firm. We can compare these internal networks to the nervous system of a natural person. Stone puts the problem in these terms: 'Corporate role morality takes as given precisely what classical moral theory wishes to evaluate, the worthiness of the duties assigned by one's role'.[66]

Corporate role morality is, in short, purely descriptive. It lacks the 'critical bite' that moral theory demands, and resolutely refuses to subject the roles themselves to critical moral analysis. If, as seems clear, the modern corporation has, by virtue of its size and complexity, been able to escape the control of the market and is largely

---

65 Shaw & Barry, p. 212.

66 C. Stone, *Where the Law Ends: The Social Context of Corporate Behavior*, Harper & Row, New York, 1975, as quoted in 'Engineering Design: Literature on Social Responsibility versus Legal Liability' Essay 4, Internet <http://ethics/tamu/ethics/essays/design.htm> April 1997.

beyond the reach of the law, perhaps we need to consider very carefully just how public accountability could be embedded in corporate role morality. To do this, we must be prepared to recognise the intimate connections between company and community. These connections go well beyond the narrower goal of profit-maximisation. In the next section, we will look at one form that this recognition has taken.

REVIEW QUESTIONS

1 Many of the difficulties associated with developing an appropriate regulatory regime for corporate persons result from the separation of ownership and management that is fundamental to the limited liability company. What specific difficulties does this separation of ownership and control pose for the law?

2 If corporate directors owe fiduciary duties to 'the company', what, at law, is the company?

3 If, as many commentators on corporate law suggest, the real power in the modern corporation lies not with the board of directors but with middle management, how should the law address this?

A 'social contract' between business and society?

In contrast to the profit-maximisation view, other voices argue that corporations have a range of other obligations. Some suggest that the social power wielded by corporations carries with it (as a more-or-less inevitable consequence) a degree of social responsibility. The corporation can no longer be permitted to conduct its affairs as if those affairs had no consequences or those consequences were immaterial to its overall role. Another way of putting this is to suggest that corporations ought to be held to the same standards of conduct as are ordinary people—that they ought to be held socially accountable in the same way and to the same or greater degree.[67] Melvin Anshen is one of the best known proponents of such views.[68] Shaw and Barry summarise Anshen's arguments for a 'social contract' between business and society thus:

> [T]here is always a kind of 'social contract' between business and society. [S]ociety always structures the guidelines within which business is permitted to operate in order to derive certain benefits from business activity. For instance, in the nineteenth century, society's prime interest was rapid economic growth, which was viewed as the source of all progress, and the engine of economic growth was identified as the drive for profits by unfettered, competitive, private enterprise.

---

67 This accountability can be read narrowly, as in a Hobbesian or Lockean social contract. Here the argument is that the corporation derives benefits from being a member of a community. Because it would not exist without the law, it may be held accountable for the direct and indirect costs it imposes upon the community at large.

68 M. Anshen, 'Changing the Social Contract: A Role for Business' (November–December 1970) *Columbia Journal of World Business* 5.

Today, however, society has concerns and interests other than rapid economic growth … In particular … 'it will no longer be acceptable for corporations to manage their affairs solely in terms of the traditional internal costs of doing business, while thrusting external costs on the public.'

In recent years we have grown more aware of the possible deleterious side effects of business activity, or what economists call *externalities*. Externalities are the unintended negative (or in some cases positive) consequences that an economic transaction between two parties can have on some third party. Industrial pollution provides the clearest illustration. Suppose, for example, that a factory makes widgets and sells them to your firm. A by-product of this economic transaction is the waste that the rains wash from the factory yard into the local river, waste that damages recreational and commercial fishing interests downstream. This damage to third parties is an unintended side effect of the economic transaction between the seller and buyer of widgets.

Defenders of the new social contract, like Anshen, maintain that externalities should no longer be overlooked. In the jargon of economists, externalities must be 'internalized'.[69]

Unless these costs (and perhaps a range of others) are internalised, the price charged for any goods or services will not reflect the 'true social costs' involved in their production.

'Contractarian' theses, such as these, are often accompanied by two further arguments. First, those who advocate holding corporations to higher moral standards point out that corporations are not 'natural phenomena'. Society, through its legal, political, and economic institutions, permits them to exist,[70] extends the benefits of legal personality and limited liability, and affords them access to natural resources, sometimes in a way and to a degree that is contrary to the wishes of other social groups within the community. In return, it is argued, society is entitled to insist not only that the corporation refrain from doing harm, but also that it act in ways that advance certain other social goals. Thus it may be argued that companies must take positive steps, for example, to redress the legacy of discrimination based upon gender or race. Proponents of this and similar positions point out that these are

> responsibilities that each of us, whether individuals or institutions, has simply by virtue of our being members of society. Precisely how far each of us must go to meet these responsibilities depends largely on our capacity to fulfill them, which, of course, varies from person to person, institution to institution. But given their considerable power, corporations seem better able to promote the common good than individuals or small businesses.[71]

Something like this, of course, comes close to being institutionalised government policy in Australia, at least with respect to compliance with laws proscribing discrimination based upon sex or race. Affirmative-action requirements are specifically

---

69 Shaw & Barry, pp. 209–10.
70 Compare Hessen at 1330.
71 Shaw & Barry, p. 216.

targeted at major corporate and Commonwealth employers, and undoubtedly this is a consequence of the view that such employers are likely to have a much greater impact than that of smaller employers.

Much legislation in Australia distinguishes between companies on the basis of their size, structure, or status. The Corporations Law draws a fundamental distinction between private and public companies. This grouping includes different classes of organisations: the small proprietary company (what used to be called an exempt proprietary company) and the large proprietary company, both created by the *First Corporate Law Simplification Act 1995* (Cth), the public unit trust, and the public corporation. Public companies and the trading of their shares are additionally regulated by, *inter alia*, the Corporations Law, the *Securities Industry Act 1980* (Cth), and the *Australian Securities Commission Act 1989* (Cth), and through their contractual relationship with the Australian Stock Exchange (ASX).[72]

In regulating the fund-raising activities of corporations, the basic prospectus provisions of the Corporations Law have evolved into detailed regulatory regimes covering, *inter alia*, a range of proprietary and equity trusts, debentures, special equity investments (such as employee share plans), and dividend reinvestment schemes. In areas such as these, the Corporations Law is supplemented by regulations, class orders, policy statements, and practice notes.[73]

Likewise, in the area of protection for investors, the Australian regime of continuous disclosure is intended to create a 'disclosure philosophy', eschewing the paternalistic stance of systems in which government bodies judge the merits of an investment proposal (as in some United States state jurisdictions).[74]

Some companies registered under the Corporations Law have special activities that attract additional legislative supervision. For example, banking companies are subject to the *Banking Act 1959* (Cth); life insurance companies are regulated under the *Life Insurance Act 1995* (Cth); companies acting as trustees of superannuation funds can be subject to the *Superannuation Industry (Supervision) Act 1993* (Cth); and public trustee companies are subject to special state legislation.

In addition, companies registered under the Corporations Law but owned or controlled by certain state governments may attract special legislation, such as the *State Owned Corporations Act 1989* (NSW), the *Territory Owned Corporations Act*

---

72 Peta Spender provides an interesting discussion of the legal status of the legislatively endorsed contractual relationship between listed companies and the ASX: P. Spender, 'The Legal Relationship between the Australian Stock Exchange and Listed Companies' (1995) 13 Companies and Securities LJ 240.

73 This is addressed in depth in H. A. J. Ford & R. P. Austin, *Principles of Corporation Law*, 7th edn, Butterworths, Sydney, 1995, chs 10 & 22.

74 See C. G. Goodkind, 'Blue Sky Law: Is There Merit in the Merit Requirement?' [1976] Wisconsin LR 79. One possible justification for the Australian requirement for continuous disclosure may be found in economic theory. According to neo-classical economics, one of the requirements for the efficient operation of the market is 'perfect knowledge'. The laws of supply and demand can only operate effectively in an environment in which information is costless. One way of approximating this in existing imperfect markets is through a continuous disclosure regime, such as that recently implemented in Australia.

1990 (ACT), the *State Owned Enterprises Act 1992* (Vic.), and the *Government Owned Corporations Act 1993* (Qld).[75]

Even if it is accepted that corporate persons should be held socially accountable (just as natural persons are), and that they should acknowledge moral as well as legal constraints upon their conduct, the question of how society can best accomplish these goals remains problematic. This is hardly surprising, given that regulatory regimes aimed at natural persons are not uniformly successful; indeed the recidivism rate suggests that our overall success in this area is limited. It is widely acknowledged that law is, at best, a rough and ready tool for instilling corporate social responsibility. This should not be surprising, given its parallel failure to instil a sense of social responsibility in at least some natural persons. There are several reasons for this. First, law frequently swings into action after the damage has already been done. The overall history of environmental regulation is a compelling illustration. Only after the air is polluted, the waterways degraded, and areas of groundwater contaminated does the political will emerge to regulate the conduct of those responsible. Second, the 'law of unintended consequences' suggests that even proactive regulatory regimes may not always have the consequences that are intended by their proponents. Indeed, they may produce consequences that were not anticipated and that may, in fact, undermine the goals that they were designed to achieve. Further complexities result because law-reform processes normally have substantial input from 'interested parties', and it is hardly surprising that those who are likely to be affected by regulatory changes will be prominent among those participating in the processes.

An alternative suggestion—that corporate structures should be redesigned to explicitly incorporate ethical codes—also has its proponents, although it has been argued that any attempt to embed ethical mandates within corporate decision-making processes will only be achieved at the expense of efficiency and, therefore, profit. The demand for corporate ethical codes and, by extension, for the obligation to foster corporate morality goes much further than simply questions of social responsibility, although these are clearly related. Those who hope that ethical codes will provide the needed stimulus for the development of corporate morality believe that companies should conduct themselves as responsible members of the community, members who try to do what is right irrespective of whether those actions are legally mandated. Ethical codes—codes that specify how the company is to conduct itself towards others—can play an important role in developing this kind of morality, although it is important to understand that the mere presence of a code is no panacea.

If ethical codes form a part of the solution, however, it is not simply the code itself that will provide the answer; it is the extent to which the code can be, and is, successfully embedded in corporate culture and the extent to which it becomes part

---

75 See further S. Bottomley, 'New Legislation for Commonwealth Government Owned Companies—Is It Sufficient?' (1995) 13 CSLJ 331.

of corporate role morality. Many major corporations today have ethicists on the corporate payroll, and ethical codes are the rule rather than the exception. Yet the mere presence of ethicists and of ethical codes has not necessarily enhanced corporate moral agency or altered the behaviour of individual corporate actors. Exxon, for example, had extensive policy documents in respect of the conduct expected of officers and crew on its tankers and a 28-volume disaster-response document dealing with the appropriate response in the event of an oil spill. Both were ignored, and there is no evidence that any form of meaningful monitoring was in place to ensure their enforcement at the time of the *Exxon Valdez* disaster.[76]

Kenneth Arrow discusses the various sorts of mechanisms that may be useful or important in encouraging a climate of social responsibility among corporate actors:

> First, we have legal regulation, as in the case of pollution where laws are passed about the kind of burning that may take place, and about setting maximum standards for emissions. A second category is that of taxes. Economists, with good reason, like to preach taxation as opposed to regulation. The movement to tax polluting emissions is getting underway and there is a fairly widely backed proposal in Congress to tax sulfur dioxide emissions from industrial smokestacks. That is an example of the second kind of institutionalization of social responsibility. The responsibility is made very clear: the violator pays for violations.
>
> A third very old remedy or institution is that of legal liability—the liability of the civil law. One can be sued for damages. Such cases apparently go back to the Middle Ages. Regulation also extends back very far. There was an ordinance in London about the year 1300 prohibiting the burning of coal, because of the smoke nuisance.
>
> The fourth class of institutions is represented by ethical codes. Restraint is achieved not by appealing to each individual's conscience but rather by having some generally understood definition of appropriate behaviour …
>
> [W]hen there is a wide difference in knowledge between the two sides of the market, recognized ethical codes can be … a great contribution to economic efficiency …
>
> A close look reveals that a great deal of economic life depends for its viability on a certain limited degree of ethical commitment. Purely selfish behaviour of individuals is really incompatible with any kind of settled economic life …
>
> Now I've said that ethical codes are desirable. It doesn't follow from that that they will come about … If we seriously expect such codes to develop and to be maintained, we might ask how the agreements develop and, above all, how the codes remain stable. After all, an ethical code, however much it may be in the interest of all, is, as we remarked earlier, not in the interest of any one firm. The code may be of value to the running of the system as a whole, it may be of value to all firms if all firms maintain it, and yet it will be

---

76 Shaw & Barry, pp. 222–4.

to the advantage of any one firm to cheat—in fact the more so, the more other firms are sticking to it.[77]

What is needed, of course, is an ethical code that encourages the development of corporate role moralities that further, rather than undermine, its realisation. In short, an ethical code will successfully alter corporate conduct only if it inhibits the development of corporate role moralities that are prescriptive rather than critical. To the extent that corporate role moralities remain prescriptive—that is, to the extent that they continue to take for granted what classical morality seeks to interrogate (the 'rightness' of the duties prescribed by one's role)—ethical codes will probably remain a dead letter. One of the difficulties with ethical codes is that, unless they encourage critical reflection on practices by agents capable of critical reflection (and we are by no means certain that companies are capable of critical reflection and engagement), they tend to degenerate into lists of rules. When that happens, the outcome is not ethical or moral agency but rule-following (or evasion). Thus, a precondition for the development of an effective code of ethics is the fostering of a critical and reflexive corporate role morality. Such a morality not only evaluates conduct and practices in the context of the corporate role occupied, but also simultaneously evaluates conduct and practices in the context of their effects on the wider environment. The doctor employed by Johns-Manville did not lack an 'ethical code', nor did he lack a 'role morality'.[78] By placing the interests of the firm above the interests of his patients and then rationalising the interests of his patients to accord with those of the firm, he managed to convince himself and others that both corporate interests and his patients' interests would be served by concealing information from the patients about the actual state of their health.

Theories of the corporate body

Running parallel to, and intersecting with, the continuing debate over whether corporations can and should somehow be 'ensouled' is another debate, which is in some ways even more interesting. If the debate about corporate ensoulment is ultimately about how we are to live with the corporations among us and the role of the law in making this possible, this second debate is about which model our legal system should use in order to best describe and proscribe the relationships between the firm's stakeholders. It is a profoundly legal debate and encompasses the fundamental issue of corporate governance. As Stokes notes, 'as an academic discipline [corpo-

---

77   K. J. Arrow, 'Social Responsibility and Economic Efficiency' (1973) 21 *Public Policy*, as reprinted in Shaw & Barry, pp. 239–41. This of course is the classic 'free-rider' problem. If economic transactions are envisaged as a series of 'one-off' transactions, the temptation to 'cheat' is overwhelming. One consequence is repeated re-enactments of what has come to be known as 'the tragedy of the commons'. An interesting feminist approach to the 'free-rider' problem and the 'tragedy of the commons' may be found in C. M. Rose, 'Women and Property: Gaining and Losing Ground' (1992) 78 Virg L Rev 421.

78   See the discussion of the conduct of Johns-Manville on pp. 114–15.

rate law] boasts no long and distinguished pedigree'.[79] Anglo-Australian corporate law (like the company itself) was cobbled together out of ill-assorted (and perhaps ill-fitting) bits and pieces borrowed from agency, from trust, and from partnership law. Through the ingenuity of commercial lawyers and their clients, these elements were engrafted upon the conceptual framework provided by the chartered corporation to create a newfangled commercial entity: the deed-of-settlement company. As Robert Hessen describes the process,

> businessmen and barristers soon devised a second way to acquire corporate features without obtaining a charter from Parliament or the Crown. They did so by combining two common law forms—a partnership and a trust. By designating a few of the potentially numerous partners to be trustees for all the others, with exclusive authority to make contracts with outside parties, they concentrated managerial power in a few hands. Consequently, all other investors could be offered freely transferable partnership interests virtually identical to corporate shares. The success of these unincorporated associations forced Parliament to relent, and in 1844 a permissive enabling act was passed.[80]

Yet while this may have been the practical evolution of the company in British law, the idea of corporate persons or '*persona ficta*', as they were once called, had long since made its way into the common law from the canon law. This conceptual framework was seen as indispensable for the task of dealing with collective entities such as corporations. As William Holdsworth indicates,

> [t]he law knows the natural person. Its rules and its process are fitted to deal with him. They are not fitted to deal with indeterminate groups which exist, and yet show a tendency to crumble when an attempt is made to apply legal rules in detail to themselves and their activities. It is for this reason that the law adopts the device 'of constituting the official character of the holders for the time being of the same office, or the common interest of the persons who for the time being are adventurers in the same undertaking, into an artificial person or ideal subject of legal capacities and duties' ... When once this generalisation had become the accepted theory of the canon law, it was inevitable that it should affect the common law. These personae fictae were with ever increasing frequency litigants in the common law courts; and, when the common lawyers became familiar with them, and with the canonists' theories concerning them, they naturally proceeded to apply these theories to bodies which had nothing to do with the church ... Owing to their manifold activities, the boroughs were the group which, from the point of view of the development of legal doctrine, are the most important. Moreover, they were bodies composed of many members; and, that being so, the body itself stood out with greater distinctness from its individual members.[81]

---

79 Stokes, p. 155.
80 Hessen at 1340.
81 W. S. Holdsworth, *A History of English Law*, as quoted in P. Redmond, *Companies and Securities Law*, 2nd edn, Law Book Company, Sydney, 1992, pp. 26–7.

Because the roots of law's conception of corporate personality are to be found in the ecclesiastical corporation and in the municipal corporation, it is hardly surprising that two concerns have predominated. First, of course, the idea of the corporation as a *persona ficta* engendered a profound and enduring concern with the mechanisms by which that *persona ficta* might express its will, and with how that will might be distinguished from the wills of its controllers and even from those of its members.

Second, concern regarding the mechanisms by which the corporate will might be expressed had formed an intrinsic part of the legal understanding that the corporate person is somehow akin to a body politic. While a good deal of legal lore existed in respect of this understanding, having made its way into the common law from the canon law, it was hardly compatible with the eighteenth- and nineteenth-century desire for a convenient vehicle for commercial enterprise and for harnessing venture capital. As a consequence, the evolving law of the commercial corporation contained schizophrenic elements from the outset. On the one hand, the mechanisms enshrined in the law for internal decision-making were predicated upon an analogy between the corporation and a political entity such as a friendly society or guild. Thus, within the mechanisms for corporate governance, the evolving law enshrined requirements for meetings and for the protection of minority interests. Within Anglo-Australian jurisprudence, the ultimate expression of the company as *persona ficta* may be found in the rule in *Foss v. Harbottle*, also known as the 'proper plaintiff rule', which provides that, where a wrong is done to the company, the company is the proper plaintiff. While scholars such as Robert Hessen make much of the change from 'government chartering of corporations to private contractual creation',[82] the image of the corporation that Hessen suggests has replaced it—that of a nexus of private contracts that is only passively acknowledged by the State—is nonetheless dependent upon the legal fictions that he rejects for many, perhaps most, of its essential attributes.

In the USA, where the contemporary commercial corporation seems to have evolved[83] directly out of the chartered corporation, Andrew Fraser notes that

> the common law doctrines governing the corporation assumed that even the private business corporation should be treated as a body politic, or, in other words, as an association of persons imbued with the civic ethos appropriate to a genuine republican community ...
>
> Once we grasp the political meaning attached to the traditional common law understanding of property it will become apparent that ... the separation of ownership and controls was a necessary step in the growth of the capital market. By factoring out an 'irrelevant' political dimension which had been imported into the investment relationship by the common law, the splitting off of ownership from control made it possible for

---

82 Hessen at 1341.

83 Caution is warranted only because radical libertarian scholars such as Hessen argue that the process by which the modern corporation evolved was, in fact, identical in the USA and England. See Hessen at 1341.

stockholders to relate to the body corporate as simple investors rather than members of what amounted to a political association. The corporate device then came to be valued in terms of its economic utility.[84]

As a consequence, in the USA, the rights ethos underlying republican radicalism united with the commodification of property to strip the corporation of any remaining identity as a body politic. Fraser suggests:

> Once property takes on the form of economic capital—once it is treated by its owner as a mere commodity—it loses its political character and becomes a *social* relation … As each shareholder becomes merely the 'personification' of his individual capital, the notion that every shareholder should have one vote without regard to the size of his capital investment becomes an 'obvious' absurdity. Nor does it make sense any longer to assume that all shareholders must stand in the same relation to the enterprise … The common quality of the world shared by the members of the corporation as a body politic loses its concrete character … The goal of the enterprise becomes profit *per se*, rather than the conduct of a particular form of business activity. That being so, minority shareholders can hardly complain if, for example, a railroad corporation discovers that its surplus capital can be employed more profitably in the purchase of a hotel chain. The doctrine of *ultra vires* loses its meaning and *raison d'etre* once the corporation's only constant aim is to obtain a higher-than-average yield on its capital stock in whatever line of business it chooses to pursue.[85]

If the process in the USA was gradual and marked by both the commodification of the share and the growth of a culture of investors (as opposed to and distinct from members), the process arrived at much the same end in England and, subsequently, Australia, albeit by a very different legal route. When the evolutionary path followed by the United States corporation was closed by the widespread panic over the 'South Sea Bubble', and by the disastrous *Bubble Act 1720*, which followed, English lawyers pursued a very different avenue towards the same fundamental goal: that of providing a vehicle through which investment capital might be harnessed in the service of commercial enterprises. Because corporate charters were not readily available to commercial entities, the deed-of-settlement company was seized upon as a way around the legal difficulties. Armand Dubois notes:

> But for the Crown's illiberality with charters and the reluctance of Parliament to grant private incorporation, incorporated companies might well have become the dominant form of business organisation in 18th century England and the corpus of company law taken a different character. The deed of settlement company, the model of the later registered company, remained in essence a partnership and the principle rules applicable to it were derived from the law of partnership, contract and trusts. With the coming of general incorporation the ancient learning on companies was also assimilated in a complex hybridisation.[86]

84 A. Fraser, 'The Corporation as a Body Politic' (1983) 57 *Telos* 5 at 6–7.

85 Fraser at 31.

86 A. B. Dubois, 'The English Business Company After the Bubble Act 1720–1800', as quoted in Redmond, p. 40.

Models of corporate governance

The British company was cobbled together from ill-assorted borrowings from common law and equity, and given a statutory overlay intended to make it easy to harness this untidy beast into the service of enterprise. Like the United States corporation, it retained the legal paraphernalia of a body politic despite having metamorphosed into something very different. Mary Stokes traces the evolution of British theorising about the 'company' from the early manifestation of the 'fiction/concession' theory. On the 'fiction/concession' theory, Stokes comments:

> This theory treats the company as an artificial entity whose separate legal personality is granted as a privilege by the state. It was a privilege which the state guarded jealously and which was made available to business enterprises whose purposes aimed to benefit the public in general as well as enrich the corporators. Thus many of the early joint-stock enterprises which were granted the privilege of corporate identity were concerned with building and operating canals and railways. What gave legitimacy to these companies was the theory that, as creatures of the state, they were supervised and regulated by the state. In the eighteenth and early nineteenth centuries the theory found its doctrinal expression in the *ultra vires* rule. The *ultra vires* doctrine was used by the courts to keep corporate bodies within the narrowly defined powers granted to them by the statute or charter of incorporation conferring corporate identify upon them. Clearly there is a very strong resemblance between this method of legitimating corporate power and that which still prevails today in respect of administrative bodies. Their powers are granted to them by the state and the courts ensure through the *ultra vires* or jurisdictional principle that they do not act outside their powers. However the fiction/concession theory came under tension once incorporation became freely available on compliance with some simple formalities, for it no longer made sense to treat the incorporation as a special privilege or concession from the state.[87]

In Australia, the enactment of s. 161, granting the corporation all the rights and powers of a natural person, has, of course, taken this particular progression to its logical conclusion. One way of looking at this development is to regard it as belated legislative recognition both of the logic of the modern commercial company and of the consequences of devices such as *Cotman v. Brougham* clauses[88] and *Bell Houses* clauses.[89]

As incorporation gradually became easier, in England (as in the USA), it became increasingly difficult to regard it as a privilege in any coherent sense. In English law,

---

87 Stokes, p. 162.

88 The *Cotman v. Brougham* clause or independent objects clause, as it was also known, was a drafting device intended to ensure that the scope of corporate activity was effectively unlimited. See *Cotsman v. Brougham* [1918] AC 514 at 523.

89 The *Bell Houses* clause simply provided that a company had the power to carry on any business that might conveniently be carried on in connection with, or ancillary to, the business of the company. It originated in *Bell Houses Ltd v. City Wall Properties* [1966] 1 QB 207 and eventually became part of the legislation regulating companies in Australia and the United Kingdom.

given the history of the deed-of-settlement company, it was natural for contractual images to move to the forefront. The evolution of the English company out of the deed-of-settlement company, together with the legacy of the deed form in the memorandum of incorporation and the articles of association, emphasise the 'coming together' of individual property owners as shareholders. Of the contractual theory of corporate nature, Stokes observes:

> The company is a form created by the free agreement amongst the shareholders, much like an extended partnership … This contractual vision of the company focuses on the internal relation of members within the company. It does not say anything explicit about the legitimacy of corporate power in relation to society generally. This is because the more modern justification for corporate power is assumed. That justification is … that the competitive market disciplines the economic power of the company. So the company is regulated both internally and externally by contract …
>
> By adopting a contractual conception of the company the legal model gives as the reason for the vesting of centralized authority to manage the company in the board of directors the contractual agreement of the owners of the company. Thus … the power accorded to corporate managers appears legitimate, being the outcome of ordinary principles of freedom of contract. It reassures us that the hierarchy created within the company does not threaten individual liberty because it is the outcome of a voluntary consensual arrangement … Nevertheless, commentators have argued that the function of … legal rules is to provide a standard set of terms to govern the relationship between the shareholders and the directors, the object being to reduce the transaction costs involved in the parties negotiating a private bargain. In other words these legal rules simply reflect the agreement the parties would have reached if bargaining on these questions had taken place at arm's length.[90]

As Stokes notes, while the law has embraced the contractual model, this model is defective in a number of respects. First, the contractual model makes it difficult, perhaps impossible, to account for one of the central features of company law (and an enduring part of the legacy of the medieval corporation): the idea that the company has an identity distinct from that of its members, and even from that of its members as a general body. Second, as the company has gradually mutated into the multinational corporation, and the member has, for the most part, given way to the investor, the nexus of contracts model of the corporation has become as implausible as the social contract model of the State.

The matter is further complicated by the contractual model's inability to deal with the relationship between the company and other entities because it does not provide any unambiguous conceptual vehicle by which the company may be disaggregated from its shareholders. If the company cannot be disaggregated from its shareholders, the logic of limited liability is undermined. It is also extremely difficult to provide an adequate conceptual foundation for the ability of the company itself

90 Stokes, pp. 162–3.

to enter into a variety of external relationships and to be held accountable for its conduct in those relationships. Thus, albeit inconsistently and incompletely, the contractual model was 'supplemented' by a reworking of Diceyan organicist theory, in which it was posited 'that the company or any group of individuals acting together for a common purpose creates a living organism, or a real person, capable of willing and acting through the people who are its organs just as a natural person wills and acts through their brain, mouth and hands'.[91] Both figure extensively in Anglo-Australian jurisprudence, but neither has provided a mechanism that both legitimates the power actually wielded by modern companies and effectively limits that power, subordinating it to the common good.

---

91 Stokes, p. 163.

THE SEARCH FOR A NEW MODEL: FINDING THE WAY OUT OF, OR FURTHER INTO, THE MIRE?

Introduction

The apparent failure of managerial capitalism to provide an adequate conceptual basis for holding corporations morally accountable has, in recent years, encouraged the development of other ways of theorising corporate accountability. While a number of different models have been suggested, many of them founder upon the proprietary basis of managerial capitalism and its embodiment in contemporary legal regimes.[1] It is worth spending some time on this 'proprietary foundation' and on the reasons why it continues to command support, despite the difficulties that it poses. The first reason is that, within Western legal culture, the link between ownership and control remains theoretically very strong. The legal model of the commercial company is predicated upon a division between ownership and management in which shareholders agree to provide venture capital. It is the obligation of the directors to 'manage' this capital in the 'interests of the company', which in this context are usually identified with those of the 'corporators as a general body'.[2] The interests of the company are at once distinct from those of any individual shareholder (although they are sometimes characterised as those of the hypothetical individual corporator) and from the narrowly commercial interests of the firm.

Attacks upon this model have come from two directions. First, because it is predicated upon a proprietary paradigm, it offers a 'narrow' understanding of the 'interests of the company', effectively limiting the interests that are worthy of recognition to the economic interests of the 'corporators' as a general body. This has led to a tendency to equate the interests of the company with its economic interests, often

---

1   L. Wiseman, 'Shareholder and Company', in S. Fisher (ed.), *The Law of Commercial and Professional Relationships*, FT Law & Tax, Melbourne, 1996, ch. 22, pp. 605, 627.

2   See *Re Smith & Fawcett Ltd* (1942) Ch 304 at 306; *Greenhalgh v. Arderne Cinemas Ltd* [1951] 1 Ch 286 at 291; *AWA Ltd v. Daniels t/a Deloitte Haskins & Sells* (1992) 7 ACSR 759 at 865.

narrowly conceived. Second, where other interests are legally recognised, they have tended to be those based on the financial well-being of the company. Thus the interests of the creditors have been recognised where doubt exists as to corporate solvency.[3] Sometimes (by statute in the United Kingdom and by judicial decision in Canada)[4] the interests of the employees have been brought within the 'interests of the company', but these developments have not yet been replicated in Australia.

The proprietary model underlying corporate law has confined legal developments within narrow and predictable channels. Not surprisingly, these channels have been inhospitable to suggestions that the interests of the company ought to be read, at least in some circumstances, to take the interests of a range of other stakeholders into account. They have also made it difficult to develop a coherent legal framework with the capacity to address two specific forms of corporate misconduct: the tendency of large and economically successful companies to respond to regulation by migrating to more hospitable (that is, less stringently regulated) regulatory climates, and the long-standing difficulty encountered in calling corporate persons to account for torts and crimes.

While these difficulties have, as we saw in the last chapter, vexed the legal community for some time, more recently they have also become the staple fare of literature devoted to business ethics and to the nature of the firm. This chapter will examine some of these recent developments drawing on 'non-legal' sources. We are interested in their capacity to provide an alternative paradigm for legal discourse, one with the capacity to ensure that corporations are held legally and morally accountable for wrongful acts and for conduct that imposes unacceptable detriment upon the wider community. The first of the alternative models we will examine is called 'stakeholder theory'.

Companies and their 'stakeholders'

'Stakeholder theory' is an explicit attempt to broaden the duty base of corporate management to include not only the shareholders as a collective body, but also various other social actors who might be seen, in some sense, as stakeholders in the modern corporation. In a pioneering article, William Evans and R. Edward Freeman[5] argue that the stakeholders in the modern company include consumers, creditors, investors, shareholders and employees. Adopting what they describe as a neo-Kantian approach, one that contrasts dramatically with the largely utilitarian underpinnings of classical economic theory, they argue that

> managers bear a fiduciary relationship to stakeholders. Stakeholders are those groups who have a stake in or claim on the firm. Specifically we include suppliers, customers, employ-

---

3   *Walker v. Wimborne* (1976) 137 CLR 1 at 7.

4   *Companies Act 1985* (UK), s. 309; *Teck Corporation Ltd v. Millar* (1973) 33 DLR (3d) 288 at 314. See also Senate Standing Committee on Legal and Constitutional Affairs, *Report on the Social and Fiduciary Duties and Obligations of Company Directors*, Commonwealth Attorney-General Publication Service, Canberra, 1989.

5   W. M. Evans & R. Edward Freeman, 'A Stakeholder Theory of the Modern Corporation: Kantian Capitalism', in T. L. Beauchamp & N. E. Bowie (eds), *Ethical Theory and Business*, Prentice-Hall, Englewood Cliffs, NJ, 1988, p. 97.

ees, stockholders, and the local community as well as management in its role as agent for these groups. We argue that the legal, economic, political, and moral challenges to the currently received theory of the firm, as a nexus of contracts among the owners of the factors of production and customers, require us to revise this concept along essentially Kantian lines. That is, each of these stakeholder groups has the right not to be treated as a means to some end, and therefore must participate in determining the future direction of the firm in which they have a stake.[6]

Although they acknowledge that their perspective differs greatly not only from the prevailing legal position, but also from many of the central tenets of managerial capitalism, they argue that managerial capitalism has been rendered incoherent and untenable by competing and contradictory legal pressures. While, as we saw in the last chapter, we have a body of judge-made law that has traditionally insisted that the 'interests of the company' are inextricably linked to the economic interests of the shareholders and hence to the pursuit of profit,[7] companies, in Australia as elsewhere, are increasingly constrained by the general law. These constraints operate in a variety of ways. Regulatory regimes aimed at, *inter alia*, consumer protection[8] are making significant inroads upon 'freedom of contract'. Similarly, governments are routinely involved in regulating market conduct, a typical example being provisions aimed at regulating what is broadly termed the 'abuse of market power'.[9]

Evans and Freeman argue that this intervention by the general law is incompatible with the theoretical model provided by managerial capitalism. The internal logic of managerial capitalism suggests that markets can only be self-regulating in an environment in which the firm is solely constrained by market pressures in its dealings with consumers and suppliers. Because the firm is, to an increasing extent, subject to constraints imposed by the general law, the supplier–firm–customer chain essential to this model no longer functions in an unconstrained manner. As a consequence, the operation of supply and demand is disrupted in a way that is incompatible with the operation of Adam Smith's 'invisible hand'. It is, therefore, no longer tenable to argue that market forces are capable of maximising well-being in the way that Adam Smith's thesis demands.

---

6   Evans & Freeman, p. 97. It seems likely that Evans and Freeman were attempting to ally themselves with the various forms of Rawlsian liberalism that, in the decade or so following the publication of *A Theory of Justice*, had a profound influence upon academic legal scholarship.

7   The case law in this area includes *Re Smith & Fawcett Ltd* (1942) Ch 304 at 306; *Greenhalgh v. Arderne Cinemas Ltd* [1951] 1 Ch 286 at 291; *AWA Ltd v. Daniels t/a Deloitte Haskins & Sells* (1992) 7 ACSR 759 at 865. H. A. J. Ford & R. P. Austin, *Principles of Corporations Law*, 7th edn, Butterworths, Sydney, 1995, pp. 259–69 provides an excellent account of the conventional legal position on this vexed area of the law.

8   In Australia, these include part IV of the *Trade Practices Act 1974* (TPA), the Fair Trading Acts in each jurisdiction, and, in some states, additional legislation such as the *Contracts Review Act 1980* (NSW). While these provisions were originally aimed at the protection of consumers, it is clear that in some circumstances their scope is much broader, extending even beyond those who might be characterised, to adopt Paul Finn's pungent phrase, as 'transactionally disadvantaged'.

9   The TPA regulates this aspect of market behaviour in Australia.

Regulation as empowerment: The conventional paradigm inverted

Evans and Freeman put an unusual spin on these commonplace observations. While such observations often provide a natural platform for arguments favouring 'deregulation' so that 'market forces' can once again operate freely, Evans and Freeman suggest that the constraints upon the conduct of market players reflect a deliberate decision by governments to empower wider stakeholders. Collectively, these constraints emphasise that management will no longer be allowed to pursue the interests of shareholders at the expense of customers and suppliers.[10] Because, overall, these changes empower the various groups and individuals who might be seen as having some claim on the firm, they argue that 'the law' is gradually eroding the central premises of managerial capitalism.

Some elements of their argument are persuasive, but we believe that it is essential to understand that, to the extent that their argument holds true, 'the law' is actually sending conflicting messages. In corporate law, the premises of 'managerial capitalism' remain central. With some fairly minimalist exceptions (such as judicial recognition that, in some circumstances, the rights of creditors must be considered in determining the 'interests of the company'[11]), corporate regulators in Australia have steadfastly rejected suggestions that broader interests be recognised, even while the general law struggles to constrain the external activities of corporate persons in pursuit of the public good.[12]

Evans and Freeman argue that the theoretical model of managerial capitalism postulates an economic environment in which the only constraints upon firms are those imposed by market competition, by the operation of the laws of supply and demand. According to the classic market model, the only permissible 'external constraints' are the minimalist liberal prohibitions of force and fraud. The subtext of this argument is that, in an increasingly regulated environment, the forces of supply and demand are no longer free to operate in the way the model requires. Market behaviour is subject to a range of constraints, which distorts the operation of these forces. The increasing prevalence of legal restraints is accompanied by political recognition that the 'invisible hand' of neo-classical economic theory provides an inadequate conceptual model. Externalities, moral hazards, and monopoly power are realities that make this model increasingly untenable. Because it depends upon the existence of a 'perfect market'—and real-world markets do not even begin to approximate perfect markets—the market model is unable to deal with these realities in a consistently meaningful way. Governments,

---

10   Evans & Freeman, p. 99.

11   The traditional position in respect of creditors is that embodied in cases such as *Mills v. Northern Railway of Buenos Aires Co.* (1870) LR 5 Ch App 621 at 628. More recently Australian (and, to some extent, English) courts have held that the interests of creditors, including unsecured creditors, must be considered where insolvency is a real possibility. See, for example, *Walker v. Wimborne* (1976) 137 CLR 1 at 7. Other relevant cases in this area include *Kuwait Asia Bank EC v. National Mutual Life Nominees Ltd* [1990] 3 WLR 297; *Kinsela v. Russell Kinsela Pty Ltd (in liq.)* (1986) 10 ALCR 395. See also Ford & Austin, p. 264.

12   See chapter 5, fn. 49.

therefore, have found it essential to subject corporations, like other market actors, to a range of legal measures intended to foster the public good. This political intervention consciously rejects the allegedly Smithian argument that the operation of unconstrained market competition will achieve the greatest good for the greatest number. According to Evans and Freeman, it also reflects our broader political understandings of the right of each individual 'to be treated, not as a means to some corporate end, but as an end in itself'.[13]

These legal changes create, at the very least, a climate in which it becomes possible, and perhaps even essential, to reconceptualise the 'interests' of the corporation to ensure that its managers incorporate the 'coordination' of stakeholder interests into their understanding of management. Evans and Freeman argue that, if the firm is to 'serve as a vehicle for coordinating stakeholder interests',[14] the following principles must become the 'guiding ideals' of management:

> The corporation should be managed for the benefit of its stakeholders: its customers, suppliers, owners, employees, and local communities. The rights of these groups must be ensured, and, further, the groups must participate, in some sense, in decisions that substantially affect their welfare.
>
> Management bears a fiduciary relationship to stakeholders and to the corporation as an abstract entity. It must act in the interests of the stakeholders as their agent, and it must act in the interests of the corporation to ensure the survival of the firm, safeguarding the long term stakes of each group.[15]

Before we move on to examine the implications of Evans and Freeman's position, a couple of things are worth noting about the operation of these principles. First, as they recognise, there will be times when the interests (and, indeed, the rights) of these groups are in conflict. Their principles offer little in the way of pragmatic guidance as to *how* such conflicts are to be resolved, although they acknowledge that resolution is essential if the firm is to serve as a vehicle for coordinating stakeholder interests. Second, the stakes that are to be coordinated are specifically long-term rather than immediate.[16] The fact that the model is addressing long-term stakes rather than immediate or present interests suggests that there will be times when the stakeholders themselves may be unaware of the precise nature of those interests. People often make complex economic decisions on the basis of their interests as they presently perceive them. We do not have any reason to equate stakeholders' present

---

13 Evans & Freeman, p. 100.

14 A somewhat different spin is put on this idea by A. Wicks, D. Gilbert, & R. E. Freeman in 'A Feminist Reinterpretation of the Stakeholder Concept' (1994) *Business Ethics Quarterly* 475. Compare J. Dobson & J. White, 'Toward the Feminine Firm: An Extension to Thomas White' (1995) 5 *Business Ethics Quarterly* 463 at 473, who argue that the 'feminine firm'—one in which 'virtue ethics theory' is embedded—is economically superior.

15 Evans & Freeman, p. 103.

16 We suspect that the long-term emphasis is essential. For example, a less developed nation might well find it in its 'short-term interests' to permit a facility for processing and disposing of toxic waste products from First World nations. Such a facility would not be in its long-term interests, however.

understanding of their rights and interests with those that, given the benefit of hindsight, could be shown to best protect their stakes in a particular firm.

REVIEW QUESTIONS

1   What are the central tenets of stakeholder theory?
2   Why do the proponents of stakeholder theory argue that it offers a more promising basis for corporate regulation than the traditional proprietary paradigm? What specific interests does it recognise, and how do these interests compete with those recognised by a proprietary analysis?
3   How do the proponents of stakeholder theory 'connect' their arguments to the law? What problems do you think stakeholder theory poses in the context of legal regulation, and how might these be minimised?

Law meets stakeholder theory: A few minor problems

The emphasis on long-term stakes rather than present or immediate interests creates substantial difficulty in translating the 'stakeholder theory of the firm' into a regulatory regime able to ensure that corporate actors (or rather their managers) act as if the corporation is a 'moral agent' that both can and should be held accountable for the consequences of its actions. The traditional recourse of the law in similar circumstances is an 'objective' test or standard, a method of decision-making that is best known in its tort incarnation as the 'reasonable person' test.[17] The use of an objective test would 'suggest' that the relevant 'long-term' stakes are those of the 'reasonable' customer, employee, stockholder, community, and so forth. Similar standards have already made their way into company law, where it becomes necessary to give content to phrases such as 'the interests of the shareholders as a whole'.[18]

Such suggestions are problematical. Often it seems easier to identify 'negative impacts' or invasions of rights than to suggest, even in outline, what long-range stakeholder interests ought to be relevant to particular decisions. A further difficulty—and one that will invite criticism from business organisations and their advocates—is that such criteria lack the clarity and defined edges of 'conventional' economic accounts predicated upon 'wealth-maximisation'. They cannot, as a con-

---

17   The 'reasonable person' test in tort law has been widely criticised. Critics suggest, *inter alia*, that the reasonable person test is insensitive to difference and that it simply provides a framework for individual judges to impose their own views of, in this context, the long-term interests of the reasonable customer. See, for example, D. Donovan & S. M. Wildman, 'Is the Reasonable Man Obsolete? A Critical Perspective on Self-Defence and Provocation' (1981) 14 Loyola of Los Angeles LR 435; C. Forell, 'Reasonable Woman Standard of Care' (1992) 11 UTLR 1; L. M. Finley, 'Breaking Women's Silence in Law: The Dilemma of the Gendered Nature of Legal Reasoning', in D. Kelly Weisberg (ed.), *Feminist Legal Theory: Foundations*, Temple University Press, Philadelphia, 1993, pp. 571–81.

18   The classic example is that used in *Greenhalgh v. Arderne Cinemas Ltd* [1951] 1 Ch 286: the 'individual hypothetical shareholder'. This formulation is very close to a 'reasonable shareholder' test. Unfortunately, as is always the case with such tests, the ambit left for the exercise of 'judicial discretion' is substantial.

sequence, provide adequate guidance for corporate CEOs in terms of practical day-to-day decision-making. The history of corporate law reform in Australia, and in most other jurisdictions, suggests that business organisations and their advocates will both seek and obtain substantial input into any realistic reform process, perhaps the most substantial input. Their first priority has traditionally been a regime that will enable Oliver Wendell Holmes Jr's 'bad man' to determine precisely how close to the wind he can set his sails without running afoul of the regulatory authorities. Certainty of this kind simplifies decision-making and minimises transaction costs. It does not, however, present a particularly useful model for moral accountability.

Disciplinary regimes and their impact

Despite the difficulties noted above, if we examine the various disciplinary regimes that impact upon corporate activities in Australia, it is easy to understand the logic behind the overall thrust of Evans and Freeman's arguments. Leaving aside direct regulation imposed by the *Corporations Law 1990* and its common-law and equitable supplements, at least for the moment, perhaps the most successful (and most revolutionary) of these 'indirect' regulatory regimes is to be found in the *Trade Practices Act 1974* (TPA). In a series of recent cases it has become clear that the 'misleading and deceptive conduct' provisions of the TPA have revolutionised the law of commercial dealings in Australia. While, initially, it was believed that part V of the Act simply expanded the scope of consumer protection in Australia, it has now become clear that its potential ambit is much greater. Commentators have suggested that the TPA and the complementary Fair Trading Acts in each jurisdiction have created a legal climate in which a duty of 'good faith and fair dealing' is on the verge of becoming a part of contract law.[19] In the case of pre-contractual and, even more remarkably, contractual misrepresentations, these statutory provisions have been used to provide redress to third parties, effectively nullifying privity of contract. Evans and Freeman suggest that developments such as these mean that that 'management is not allowed to pursue the interests of stockholders at the expense of customers and suppliers'. While, unlike the USA, Australia has only

---

19 In this context, it is necessary to consider the interaction of innocent misrepresentation, negligent misstatement, and the role of the TPA, ss. 51A, 51AA, 51AB, 52(1), 82, and 87(2), and of the *Fair Trading Act 1989* (Qld), ss. 37, 38(1), 39(1), 99, 100, which mirrors the relevant provisions of the TPA. Equivalent legislation applies in every state and territory in Australia. The relevant legislation is styled the Fair Trading Act in all jurisdictions other than the ACT, where it is styled the *Consumer Affairs and Fair Trading Act 1973*. Its potential impact became clear in *Accounting Systems 2000 (Development) Pty Ltd v. CCH Australia Ltd* (1993) 114 ALR 355. *Accounting Systems* held that the express contractual warranty could amount to a misrepresentation within the terms of the legislation, and that the state legislation could be invoked in the interests of a third party whose interests were harmed by the misrepresentation. We acknowledge that we are making a strong claim. For a more conventional view, see L. Willmott, 'Good Faith in Disclosure', in T. Cockburn & L. Wiseman (eds), *Disclosure Obligations in Business Relationships*, Federation Press, Sydney, 1996.

recently developed strict liability in respect of defective products,[20] here (as in the USA) the legal balance is quietly shifting towards strict liability for representations made in a contractual context. Disciplinary regimes such as these constrain managerial conduct in a number of ways.

The discipline provided by consumer protection legislation and by consumer protection agencies is only one aspect of the limitations that regulatory regimes impose on managerial freedom. Equally significant, but possibly more subtle, are the common-law developments that Paul Finn suggests are increasingly imposing substantive legal constraints upon the 'transactionally advantaged'—that is, those corporate persons whose wealth and power is sufficient to coerce other individuals to act against their own best interests. In Australia, this regime is exemplified by 'the new law of contract'.[21] Even more remarkably, fiduciary concepts are carving out a space for themselves at the heart of commercial arrangements.[22] For Finn, the extraordinary economic and social power wielded by major corporate institutions such as banks is, of itself, sufficient to compel the law to respond. It will do this, Finn argues, by attempting to delimit the scope within which the corporation will be allowed to act.[23]

These legal regimes, variously aimed at consumer protection, environmental protection, and the constraint of the transactionally advantaged, act as checks upon corporate power. In each case, they act upon (law's understanding of) the corporate person from without, seeking to constrain its freedom of action. As disciplinary regimes, rather than 'constitutive regimes', they do not attempt to achieve the same social goal from within by attempting to build the necessary constraints into the internal governance of the corporation. Because they seek to act upon an already imagined ('immortal and invisible') corporate person, rather than to reconceive corporate personality, they endeavour to control an established construct that insistently mocks the bounds of existing constraints. With increasing naturalisation (suggested by the legal developments canvassed in the last chapter), these concerns reinstate the corporate person as an entity beyond the grasp of

---

20 In the USA strict liability developed under the umbrella of tort law. In Australia, it has recently been imposed by statute. See TPA, part IVA.

21 See *Commercial Bank of Australia Ltd v. Amadio* (1983) 151 CLR 447; *West v. AGC (Advances) Ltd* (1986) 5 NSWLR 610; *Walton Stores (Interstate) Ltd v. Maher* (1988) 164 CLR 387 and other similarly expansionary decisions. An extremely useful summary of the developments in this area is provided by J. W. Carter & A. Stewart, 'Commerce and Conscience: The High Court's Developing View of Contract' (1993) 23 WALR 49, which canvasses the relevant case law and provides a useful account of its impact.

22 *Commonwealth Bank of Australia v. Smith* (1992) 102 ALR 453. In acknowledging this, however, we should perhaps give credence to the following dictum: 'But to say that a man is a fiduciary only begins analysis; it gives direction to further inquiry. To whom is he a fiduciary? What obligations does he owe as a fiduciary? In what respects has he failed to discharge these obligations? And what are the consequences of his deviation from duty?' See *SEC v. Chenery Corp.* (1943) 318 US 80 at 85–6 per Frankfurter J.

23 See, for example, P. Finn, 'Contract and the Fiduciary Principle' (1989) 12 UNSWLJ 76; P. Finn, 'Equity and Contract', in Finn (ed.), *Essays on Contract*, Law Book Company, Sydney, 1987, ch. 4. See also S. Fisher, 'General Principles of Obligations', in S. Fisher (ed.), *The Law of Commercial and Professional Relationships*, FT Law & Tax, Melbourne, 1996, ch. 2, pp. 13–48, which provides a useful introduction to some of the principles underlying these developments in the context of the nascent Australian law of obligations.

the (corporations) law—as a nexus of capital[24] that makes full (and possibly disturbing) use of the 'organs' provided by the corporations law, but that cannot be collapsed into those organs.

Leslie Moran reminds us of the artificiality of the corporate person as a juridical subject, which is

> no more than a contrived effect of the lawyer's art or craft. In the artificial person law may be said to simulate legal capacity … Unlike the natural person of the law the artificial person is nothing more than an elaborate disguise, deception, vice, subterfuge as it does not represent any prior person and as such it is neither natural nor real.

Moran goes on to explain that the distinction between the natural and the artificial person of law turns on 'two separate ideas of law':

> [Law as representation] merely makes concrete or visible some prior quality or thing … As such personality in law is the presentation in law of a prior fact or quality of the human subject that is said to be behind or underlying the law … Law as simulation suggests that the phenomenon of law has different characteristics. Here the law is mere image, mere surface, form or appearance … As such it may produce all of those characteristics and qualities attributed to the natural legal subject but there is here no suggestion that this manifestation of capacity is a representation of a prior fact, quality or thing.[25]

The Corporations Law produces an effect, a simulacrum, upon which other regulatory regimes converge. Yet, perhaps because it is precisely that—a simulacrum, a mere effect—the corporation remains able to escape regulation almost at will. A multinational corporation threatened by regulation is able, usually with minimal inconvenience because that contingency was planned for, to migrate from a 'hostile' jurisdiction to one that represents itself as a 'friendly' jurisdiction.[26] Its migration is facilitated because it is a simulacrum and not a person. Unlike would-be human migrants, it does not usually need to seek immigrant status, nor does it confront potential barriers such as race and culture. Rather, particularly in developing countries, its presence will be actively sought. In this context, it is important to recall the passage from Russell Stevenson that was quoted in the last chapter (see pp. 126–7). If, as Stevenson suggests, the corporation cannot be socialised, educated, or shamed,[27]

---

24 Note that the reference is to a 'nexus of capital' rather than to a 'locus of contracts'. The attempt to describe the corporation as a locus of contracts founders upon the inappropriateness of contractual discourse as a descriptor for the relationships between the shareholders and the company. In an economic environment in which the vast majority of traded shares are traded through brokerage firms that hold seats on one of the major stock exchanges, any connection between the individual owner *pro tem* and the company seems fortuitous rather than fundamental to the corporate form.

25 L. J. Moran, 'Corporate Criminal Capacity: Nostalgia for Representation' (1993) 1 *Social & Legal Studies* 171 at 173.

26 Although a more likely response is the mere threat of migration if the 'offensive' elements in the regime are not modified. Should the government yield to political pressure from such corporations, particularly in the case of environmental risks, the resulting cost (such as that of repairing environmental degradation) is often borne by the community at large because the cost has successfully been externalised.

27 R. B. Stevenson Jr, 'Corporations and Social Responsibility: In Search of the Corporate Soul' (1974) 2 *George Washington Law Review* 709 at 713–14.

corporate migration as a response to 'unwanted regulation' should not be surprising, as corporate capacity for loyalty is underdeveloped.

Unlike natural persons, corporations are constitutionally devoid of affect; they lack the ties of blood, culture, and community that make immigration a wrenching experience for most people. To the extent that there is something that it is proper to term 'corporate culture', it is a culture of managerialism, which has become or is in the process of becoming universal. This situation has come about precisely because the corporation is a 'simulacrum'. Natural persons exist within time, space, and culture. They are, by definition, mortal and situated. Corporate persons, at least within the practical and intellectual framework provided by managerial capitalism, exist as 'accumulations of capital', which are presently being put to use in particular ways but which could (in theory at least) be put to other uses without exceptional difficulty should this appear desirable. If economic discourse postulates the 'widget' as the universal product of late capitalism, it is well to remember that the various human and physical 'factors of production' are often treated as equally interchangeable. The role of the manager is to determine the optimal mix of all of the factors of production and to determine the optimal location(s) for the production of particular products.[28]

REVIEW QUESTION

The inability of existing legal regimes to regulate corporate persons effectively is exemplified by the ability of the subsidiaries of multinational corporations to migrate in pursuit of 'agreeable' regulatory regimes. Does stakeholder theory offer a more effective mechanism for holding corporations accountable?

From stakeholder to dual-investor: The community–company interface

From a legal perspective, 'stakeholder' theory poses a number of difficulties. However, despite this, it has successfully made a home for itself in the tool-kit of modern management in the form of the 'stakeholder strategy'.[29] The term 'stakeholder strategy' refers to a public relations campaign by management to convince its stakeholders of their centrality to corporate decision-making. Construction of a 'stakeholder

---

28 W. H. Shaw & V. Barry, provide an account of corporate decision-making in this area in 'Layoffs at Levi', in their *Moral Issues in Business*, 6th edn, Wadsworth Publishing Co., Belmont, Calif, 1995, pp. 231–3.

29 B. Langtry, 'Stakeholders and the Moral Responsibilities of Business' (1994) 4 *Business Ethics Quarterly* 431. Langtry dismisses 'stakeholder' theory as unacceptable on the basis of, *inter alia*, an analogy to the nuclear family and the suggested incoherence of a stakeholder view of the nuclear family. However, this analogy is inappropriate. Legally, there is a fundamental difference between the nuclear family and the corporation. The corporation has been endowed with a form of fictive personality that enables it to function as a legal actor, while the family has social and economic reality. While the family is the target of a variety of regulatory regimes, it lacks legal personality.

strategy' by management is, however, very different both from the normative approach adopted by Evans and Freeman, and from any use that approach might have as a revisionist tool for corporate regulators.

As we saw in the last section, a significant difficulty in moving from the 'normative vision' outlined by Evans and Freeman to its embodiment in a regulatory regime lay in its apparent need for an 'objective' account of the long-term interests of the various stakeholders. A second difficulty—one noted by critics such as Eugene Schlossberger—lies in the dichotomy that 'stakeholder theory' creates between shareholders and stakeholders. To circumvent the unpleasant consequences of this dichotomy and its intimate relationship to (one might even say its dependence upon) the public/private dichotomy, Schlossberger proposes a different model—one that he terms the 'dual-investor model'. According to the dual-investor model, 'there are two types of investors in every business venture: the stockowners (or partners, or sole proprietors), who provide the venture's specific capital, and the society as a whole, which provides ... the "opportunity capital" for the venture. As a result, society is a shareholder in every business venture, though not the same type of shareholder as stockowners'.[30] According to Schlossberger, the singular advantage of dual-investor theory is that it refocuses debate. Instead of postulating a conflict between different sorts of obligations—those owed to the shareholders, who, after all, give to the company, and those owed to stakeholders, who depend upon the company for employment, development, and so forth—dual-investor theory emphasises different sorts of contributions:

> Those who own stock in the corporation provide the specific capital needed for machinery, salaries, buildings, and so forth. But specific capital is not enough to run a modern corporation. No modern business can function without making use of a pre-existing knowledge base, (subsidized) educational system, monetary system, police function, and infrastructure (roads, water mains, sewage systems, etc.). General Motors, Chrysler, and IBM are able to function only by drawing upon the resources society has invested. Let us call this the 'opportunity capital' that society provides. True, these resources may not be invested specifically and exclusively in a particular company, but generations of people have worked very hard to establish the knowledge base and infrastructure upon which any modern corporation draws quite heavily. Indeed, opportunity capital of this kind is as important to a corporation as is the specific capital provided by stockowners or proprietors ... It follows that a corporation has the same kind of fiduciary obligation to society that it does to its stockholders.[31]

Schlossberger goes on to argue that '[b]ecause there are two groups of investors, executives have a dual duty: to make a profit for the shareowners and to give society a return on its opportunity capital. It is this first duty that preserves the "privacy" of private enterprise'.[32]

---

30   E. Schlossberger, 'A New Model of Business: Dual-Investor Theory' (1994) 4 *Business Ethics Quarterly* 459.

31   Schlossberger at 461–2.

32   Schlossberger at 464.

In many ways this provides a much more promising platform for legal analysis than does stakeholder theory. First, by insisting that the obligation to provide society with a return on its opportunity capital is similar to, and as great as, the duty owed to the corporators as a general body, the fiduciary paradigm is extended to society as a whole. This has a number of advantages. For example, we might regard corporate executives as having an obligation, *inter alia*, to manage the affairs of the company in ways that are likely to provide society with a return on its opportunity capital. After all, the law has long understood that corporate executives have an obligation to manage the affairs of the company in ways that seem likely to provide investors with a return on their venture capital. An understanding of this kind mandates a very different approach to 'externalities' and to decisions concerning plant mobility, for example.[33] The various regulatory regimes that impact upon corporate persons can be seen as legal mechanisms to measure the value of the opportunity capital made available to particular companies and to ensure an appropriate return. Rather than an interference with market operation, they can be seen as essential to compel corporate persons to 'internalise' some of the social costs that are often regarded as externalities and discounted in corporate decision-making.

A second, and perhaps more important, long-range consequence is this: dual-investor theory, if tenable, binds the company firmly within the fabric of particular societies. This provides what has, up until now, been lacking: a clear and potentially persuasive meta-theoretical justification for regulatory regimes aimed at curbing the flight or relocation of capital. From a legal perspective, then, dual-investor theory seems to offer avenues by which at least some of the difficulties associated with existing regulatory regimes can be circumvented. If the concept of corporate moral responsibility based upon corporate utilisation of social 'opportunity capital' is accepted, this approach suggests that corporate managers have an obligation to manage the corporation in the joint interests of those who provide its specific venture capital and those who provide its opportunity capital. Some of the consequences of this model are provocative. For example, corporate migration—at least where that migration represents a deliberate decision to evade assuming responsibilities for externalities—may properly be seen not as a rational management decision to minimise costs and maximise profits, but as a breach of fiduciary duty on the part of management. In this way, closing the circle, we return to Moran's image of the corporation as a simulacrum. We have managed, albeit with some difficulty, to devise a model that can incorporate the interests of the wider community within the bounds of corporate interest. In the end, however, this still begs the question. How can we allocate responsibility for corporate conduct within the firm? Still more importantly, how can accountability be built in to corporate decision-making? What avenues are available to ensoul the corporation?

---

33 See fn. 26, above.

REVIEW QUESTIONS

1 How is a stakeholder account different from one that uses the discourse of 'dual-investor' theory?

2 It is interesting to think of the inputs in dual investor theory in the context of how contributions can be 'propertised'. What kinds of inputs are involved in 'opportunity capital'? We are more used to the idea of opportunity costs than to the idea of opportunity capital. How are opportunity costs and opportunity capital related? Is the 'capital' in opportunity capital any less real than that contributed by investors?

3 Can you think of any practical difficulties that might arise in requiring companies to provide society with a reasonable return on its 'opportunity capital'? How might we respond to an argument by corporate managers that the 'fact' of corporate relocation to a Third World country conclusively proves that the 'opportunity capital' provided was unnecessary for corporate purposes?

Ensouling the simulacrum: Agency and morality within the corporate shell

In the last chapter we looked at a number of different conceptions of the nature of the corporation and attempted to tease out some of their implications. We want to return to those models now, reading them against the background of dual-investor theory and in the specific context of whether it is possible to 'ensoul the simulacrum'. Michael Phillips suggests that: 'to be morally responsible for an action, an actor must have performed the action with: (1) a conscious purpose to realize it or its consequences, (2) actual knowledge of its nature or its consequences, or (3) reason to know its nature or consequences'.[34] From a legal perspective, Phillips's model is very useful. His basic test for moral responsibility precisely tracks the parameters of one of the standard tests for legal responsibility: that the act was voluntary and intentional, and that the actor either knew or ought to have known its likely consequences. Yet, if we return to the models that are commonly used to 'describe' the corporation—concession theory, aggregate theory, and real entity theory—none of them is unproblematic in this context.

If, as concession theory suggests, and writers from a variety of perspectives are willing to concede, the corporation is simply an artificial person—a simulacrum created by law—we can no more expect to inculcate even the rudiments of moral responsibility than could Frankenstein. While legal accountability is possible—after all, the law has endowed its fiction with mind and will and organs, thus enabling it to 'act' purposively in the world—these are simply legal fictions. They leave us

---

34 M. J. Phillips, 'Corporate Moral Personhood and Three Conceptions of the Corporation' (1992) 2 *Business Ethics Quarterly* 435 at 437.

where we began, confronting an entity with no body to kick and no soul to damn. Such an entity will be incapable of understanding itself as morally accountable and, more disturbingly, equally incapable of behaving as if it were.[35]

Aggregate theory—like its twentieth-century descendant, 'nexus of contracts' theory—also emphasises that the collectivity is only a convenient mental construct.[36] It is useful as a shorthand description of relationships among discrete individuals but has no real existence:

> [A]ccording to aggregate theory the most important constituents of corporations are human beings … Also, because the collectivities we call corporations seem to have non-human as well as human elements, aggregate theorists sometimes include additional components besides human beings. These include the contracts to form the corporation, other relationships within it, the various intracorporate positions its members fill, and the corporation's internal rules. Such accounts also may incorporate the concession theory by making the corporation's status as a legal fiction one element in the aggregate.
>
> [S]ometimes the component human beings described by aggregate theorists are not flesh-and-blood people, but the utility-maximizing rational actors of economic theory …
>
> The new nexus-of-contracts approach also 'denies the existence of a meaningful corporate entity.' For this reason it—and aggregate theory in general—cannot support the imposition of moral responsibility on corporations. If there is no separate corporate entity, there is nothing to serve as the bearer of distinctively corporate moral obligations. A nonexistent entity cannot act; neither can it form intentions or have knowledge or reason to know anything … According to the aggregate theory, therefore, only individual officers, employees, or other agents can be morally responsible for 'corporate' misdeeds, and that responsibility should be determined under the normal standards applicable to natural persons.[37]

The final contender, 'real entity theory', poses problems of its own, postulating a supra-human entity akin to the *Gessammtperson* or 'group-person', which is described in the following passage from Frederic William Maitland as

> no fiction, no symbol, no piece of the State's machinery, no collective name for individuals, but a living organism and a real person, with body and members and a will of its own. Itself can will, itself can act; it wills and acts by the men who are its organs as a man wills and acts by brain, mouth and hand. It is not a fictitious person: it is a *Gesammtperson*, and its will is a *Gesammtwille*; it is a group-person, and its will is a group-will.[38]

While, on one level, it is easy to see the attraction of a full-blown theory of group-will such as that above, on another level it is frightening.[39] It does, however,

---

35   While the corporation may be obliged to comply with the directives of the regulatory State, regulators simply cannot maintain eternal vigilance. What is required is for corporations to internalise an obligation to obey the law. To date, we have been remarkably unsuccessful in accomplishing this.

36   In this it betrays its conceptual affinities with social contract theory by its insistence that it is the individual that is real rather than the collectivity.

37   Phillips at 439.

38   Frederic William Maitland, as quoted in Phillips at 441.

39   It summons up images of the behaviour of mobs and, perhaps, of Germany under Hitler. The underlying suggestion is of an entity in which the wills of individual human actors are totally submerged in that of the collectivity.

point out exactly what is at stake in the debate over corporate moral personality and goes some way towards delineating the difficulties involved. If the corporation is, as aggregate theory would have it, simply a set of relations among independent individuals, then it has no real existence, no personality of its own. It is a bare creature of law. Unless we can identify one or more individuals who have, as individuals, behaved in a morally (and legally) culpable way, the company cannot be brought to account in any meaningful way. However, if it is—as Maitland (drawing upon Otto Gierke) would have it—a group-person with a group-will, we are confronted by a 'supra-natural' individual of the sort that liberal theorists have been at some pains to avoid.

Even the liberal legal philosopher Ronald Dworkin, who insists that nation states are sufficiently 'real' for their members to be obliged to obey the law, is also at pains to insist that they are not 'real' entities in any meaningful sense and that his view is devoid of 'metaphysical consequences'. Rather, the obligatory nature of laws results from the relationships between citizens, because, says Dworkin, all of its members assume that the rules and the roles within the nation state are equally in the interests of all.[40] He is at some pains to insist that his argument does not entail any kind of 'real entity' metaphysic. Rather, it is a way of coming to terms with, *inter alia*, the idea of obligations of role[41] and, in particular, how obligations of role might be understood in that most unlikely of places, the nation state of late capitalist modernity.

What we want to talk about in this context is whether Dworkin's attempt to give reality to the idea of associative obligations—obligations that people believe they have simply by virtue of belonging to social groups—might help us in understanding the 'reality' of corporate persons, without the disturbing associations that ideas such as a group-mind and group-will conjure up. Dworkin's model explicitly acknowledges limits, something that is advantageous for present purposes. The first of these limits is simple. Using what we like to call his 'Mafia' example, Dworkin insists that 'obligations of role' cease to bind at the point where the group attempts to coerce the individual into violating some basic social norm. The explicit example he gives is where, as a 'condition of membership', a family expects its sons to engage in criminal activities such as murder. Here, the group has forfeited its rights to relational obligations by demanding of its members that they violate some wider social norm. The second, while less dramatic, is also useful. According to Dworkin, where the group no longer extends the benefits of group membership to the individual, any obligations that may have existed lose their force. He also, and interestingly, suggests that, if the conduct embedded in these 'obligations of role' conflicts with

---

40 R. Dworkin, *Law's Empire*, Belknap Press, Cambridge, Mass., 1986. There are a number of difficulties with this model, which have been discussed at length elsewhere. See S. Berns, 'Dworkin's Account of Associative Obligations: New Clothes for an Old Theory?' (1991) 21 WALR 89. Nonetheless, as a model, it may be useful in the corporate context.

41 Obligations of role are also reasonably frightening. Fundamentally, obligations of role are status-based obligations. As such, they pertain not to autonomous and morally independent individuals but to the temporary incumbents of particular social roles: husband and wife, master and servant, ruler and ruled.

other wider social standards, an individual may refuse to comply without denying that the obligations have force. The example he uses is that of a young woman in a patriarchal family who marries without her father's permission. According to Dworkin, while she is entitled to reject her father's demand that he be allowed to select her future husband, she nonetheless owes him an apology and has cause for regret. Dworkin explicitly, therefore, acknowledges that there may be occasions upon which 'obligations of role' may be rejected without forfeiting membership in a social group and without denying their force as obligations.[42]

Against the background of Ronald Dworkin's attempt to provide a sound conceptual basis for the obligations that exist between family members, friends, members of an orchestra, or members of a nation state, it may be useful to return to the image of the colonial jellyfish.[43] Dworkin's model is attractive precisely because it captures some of the complexity of social groups: they 'exist' and act as entities in a very real way, but they are not 'real' in the same way that individual people are real. His account reflects the 'colonial jellyfish' image precisely. In doing so, it offers an account of how corporations can act 'independently' and effectively in ways that are identifiably corporate, and yet are made up of discrete and unique individuals who occupy roles that carry with them substantive obligations. Because of its capacity to capture these complexities, the Dworkinian model clearly delineates the responsibilities of individuals and of the firm. It offers avenues through which accountability can be built in to the system rather than imposed upon it from without.

REVIEW QUESTIONS

1 What aspects of real-entity theory are problematical given our legal and political traditions?
2 How does Dworkin's account of associative obligations differ from the notion of a 'group-mind' or 'group-will' postulated by traditional forms of real-entity theory?

From simulacrum to colonial jellyfish: A Dworkinian model of corporate accountability

Superficially, the model proposed here has a good deal in common with Phillips's attempt to build a real-entity account upon the foundation provided by systems theory. A comparison between the two models should, therefore, prove valuable. Phillips argues that,

---

42 While his choice of example is open to criticism, his model is nonetheless instructive. What it is intended to do is capture some of the complexity of the relationships in which most of us conventionally understand ourselves to have moral obligations. If this model can be applied to corporate entities, it may provide a basis upon which we can hold the corporation accountable where that is appropriate while delineating some of the more problematical aspects of the relationships within the corporation.

43 See chapter 5, fn. 8 (p. 111).

to really characterize a corporation as an aggregate, one has to list and describe all the phenomena it contains. Such an effort would at least have to include the corporation's human personnel, its organizational structure, its decision making processes, the products or services it generates, and the internal and external relations that exist among all of these. Because the internally related parts of this collection would have different qualities outside the collection, we must be careful to describe them as they exist within it. And we also must be careful to exclude from the description all noncorporate actions and mental states—i.e., to describe the human parts as PCAs [persons in their corporate aspects] ...

But what is this 'aggregate' I am depicting? To me, it is more plausibly characterised as a *system* in which all the elements are included and organized. Specifically, a corporation is an assemblage of people and other things unified into a consistent whole by their interrelationship. As pictured above, it *looks* like a system; indeed it resembles a fleshed out organization chart. Also, the two problems that plagued the aggregate theory—the malleability of the corporation's human units and the need to reduce them to PCAs—seem less troublesome if corporations are regarded as systems. If you attribute independent reality to the system as a whole, its elements' variable and fragmented nature is less bothersome than if you must build the system from such elements. Indeed, if the whole is real, one might even expect its elements to appear unstable and incomplete ... [T]his entity has attributes that differ from the sum of its elements' attributes as they existed outside the collectivity. However, it is not clear that this makes the whole either greater than the sum of its parts or morally superior to its parts.[44]

While several aspects of Phillips' system-theory model are interesting (even if we find it difficult to derive any form of moral accountability from an 'organisation chart'[45]), we want to confine our discussion to the idea of PCAs. While Phillips's need for such an idea is clear—particularly since it neatly isolates 'corporate roles' from roles pertaining to other aspects of an individual's life, and thus simplifies analysis enormously—it may also be thought to compartmentalise individual moral accountability sufficiently to compromise it fatally.[46]

---

44 Phillips at 450–1.

45 We do not, of course, deny that an organisation chart can delineate precise lines of authority, but the existence of authority structures (even precise authority structures) does not presuppose moral accountability.

46 This does not, of course, mean that Phillips is wrong. One of the disturbing things about 'organisational behaviour' is the willingness of individuals to act (in pursuit of their corporate goals) in ways that they would, in their private aspects, find appalling and untenable. The conduct of the physician at Johns-Manville discussed in the last chapter (see pp. 114–15) is an excellent case in point. Work by S. Milgram suggests that, when individuals believe that they are acting in ways that are approved by their hierarchical superiors, they are willing to disregard their normal ethical standards and engage in conduct that they would otherwise find repugnant: S. Milgram, *Obedience to Authority: An Experimental View*, Harper & Row, New York, 1974. It is for this reason, among others, that we have some real concerns about the implications of Phillips's system-theory analysis. It may well provide a perceptive, even perspicacious, explanation of some of the difficulties in building 'moral circuitry' into corporate structures; it does not, however, necessarily offer any prospect of overcoming those difficulties. In this context we are also reminded of Alasdair MacIntyre's description of the individual of liberal society: 'The liberal self moves from sphere to sphere compartmentalising its attitudes': A. MacIntyre, *Whose Justice? Which Rationality?* University of Notre Dame Press, Indiana, 1988, p. 345. See also Alasdair MacIntyre, *After Virtue*, University of Notre Dame Press, Indiana, 1981.

Why is the idea of a PCA needed? According to Phillips, while his account identifies the corporation as a 'real' entity, one which differs from the sum of its elements' attributes outside the corporation, this does not necessarily mean that it has either a will or a morality that differs from those of its members. It thus (according to Phillips) becomes important to identify conduct that can be properly attributed to the corporation. A construct such as a PCA helps to compartmentalise the conduct of corporate actors, thus isolating conduct that properly belongs to the corporation from that which is private.[47]

We, however, believe that the notion of a PCA is an unnecessary complication. In most cases, there is little if any difficulty in isolating 'corporate' actions from 'individual' or 'extra-corporate' actions. Where there is 'doubt', it exists either because the liability is 'strict' (that is, without fault)—as is the case where the corporation is held to be vicariously liable for the conduct of an employee—or because there is genuine doubt about whether an individual is acting on his or her own behalf or as a corporate representative.

The idea's superfluousness is particularly clear from a legal perspective. Where it is unclear whether responsibility is individual or corporate, to a lawyer it will always be a question of degree. To resolve the issue it will always be necessary to look at role description, policy, and the context in which action was taken. If we wish, after all the hard work has been done, we can use the idea of a PCA to explain our conclusion that the corporation is liable or not liable as the case may be. If we do that, we are using the idea to explain a conclusion reached by perfectly ordinary forms of legal reasoning. When we ascribe moral responsibility, the process is very similar. While the notion of a PCA may help explain why we made a particular decision, it is not necessary and *does not add anything* to a realistic account of moral responsibility. Where it is unclear whether the corporation is morally (or legally) responsible, that uncertainty arises because it is not clear whether one or several individuals acted as individuals or in their corporate roles. This uncertainty, in turn, may be because they acted 'as individuals' but in response to organisational pressures—to meet particular targets, for example. Once again, the notion of a PCA is of no real assistance when it is most needed.

Dworkin's model, by contrast, is at its most useful in precisely those troubling and uncertain situations in which the lines of accountability are not clear and where, for that reason, we are uncertain whether we are dealing with a deviant individual within the organisational structure or whether the organisational structure is itself deviant and should be held accountable. It suggests that we must begin by identifying the various roles and relationships (Phillips's 'organisation chart' in a more sophisticated guise) that make up our common-sense understanding of what a corporation is and how it works. Here organisation theory can be of assistance—perhaps of greater assistance than the law—in identifying the roles and responsibilities

---

47 In other words, the idea of a PCA reinforces the public/private distinction, ensuring that individual and company remain firmly separated.

within the corporate person and the lines of accountability that they signal. Dworkin suggests that, after we have developed our 'common-sense' understanding of the company and its roles and requirements, a further, critical dimension is needed. It is at this 'second stage' that the greater utility of the Dworkinian model becomes clear. This 'critical dimension' insists that we try to identify an 'ideal type' of corporation using ordinary standards of moral conduct and, in particular, the specific ideal of equality of resources upon which his wider theory is based. When we have identified this 'ideal typical' model, we can use it as a standard against which to measure the roles and relationships within the 'real world' companies with which the law must deal. While the equality that Dworkin's model demands is minimal, it insists that decisions be made in a way that reflects an assumption of the group that the welfare of each of its members is equally important to the welfare of the group as a whole. We believe that this model may have substantial use in today's corporate environment. First, it offers us a way of treating all of those who are a part of the 'corporate jellyfish' as equally important and, in particular, as equally important to the realisation of 'corporate ends'. An application of the Dworkinian model makes it possible to include within the 'corporate jellyfish' not only the various 'corporate organs' as conventionally understood by the law, but also the various 'office holders' within the internal organisational structure of the firm. This kind of account provides theoretical support for tentative legal efforts to suggest that the corporate 'mind and will' may be found at different levels in the corporate hierarchy and in various guises.[48] It also suggests that company employees are among those whose welfare ought to be seen as equally important to the welfare of the group as a whole. This enables us, at both a legal and an organisational level, to build a more complex picture of the interests of the company than is allowed by conventional legal models.

Dworkin's model is useful in another way as well. Because (to the extent it is successful) it neither subordinates the individual to the group, nor deprives the group of identity in order to privilege the interests of individuals, it offers an account in which both the group and the individuals within it can be understood as accountable to wider (similarly constituted) collectivities (and to each other as equal members of those collectivities). It provides the missing foundation for attempts to understand the corporation as a 'citizen'—as a member, in good standing—of wider collectivities, in precisely the same sense that its individual human components are members. This is important. First, it suggests that, to the extent that the community is essential to the company—whether as a market for its products, as a provider of public goods such as power, police, fire services, roads, and education, or as a source of employees (and that it is essential in all of these ways cannot be doubted)—the company itself is obliged to conduct itself as a member in good standing. It must

---

48 See, for example, *Tesco Supermarkets Ltd v. Nattrass* [1972] AC 153; *Canadian Dredge and Dock Co. Ltd v. The Queen* (1985) 19 DLR (4th) 314; *Hamilton v. Whitehead* (1989) 7 ACLC 34. All of these cases, albeit in different ways, emphasise that, in order to locate the 'corporate mind and will' in respect of particular acts and to ascribe responsibility, it is necessary to examine the corporate structure and the ways in which it allocates responsibility.

conduct itself upon the basis that the welfare of other community members and, indeed, of the community as a whole is of equal importance to its own welfare. Second, it reminds us of the complexities of the 'corporate jellyfish', and of the fact that some of the people involved relate to one another both in terms of their corporate roles and in terms of their roles as community members, as citizens, as neighbours, perhaps even as friends.

Most importantly, this line of reasoning provides a model for corporate accountability subtle enough to deal with phenomena such as corporate migration, which have proved intractable in the past. While, clearly, it does not provide a formula by which corporate migration can be prevented,[49] it does suggest why the company's ability to threaten migration when confronted by an unfavourable regulatory regime is so disquieting and so symptomatic of the State's paralysis in an environment increasingly dominated by multinational corporations. Because, traditionally, the company has been legally conceived simply as a *persona ficta* or, as law and economics scholars would have it, as a nexus of contracts, the law has had immense difficulty in coming to terms with the power it wields, and even more difficulty in attempting to constrain the exercise of that power. In legal terms, if the company is understood simply as a *persona ficta*, the law must try to deal with its effects as random occurrences, which have the capacity to destroy the economic basis of communities, perhaps of entire regions. More power is wielded outside the political process than within it in, at least partly because the pressure brought to bear by the company can be, and routinely is, used in ways that circumvent the political process and render it nugatory.

The subtlety of the processes by which corporate persons escape many of the disciplinary regimes to which other citizens are subject is often obscured by the success of those exceptional regimes through which their trading activities are increasingly regulated. Corporate persons are able to use the threat of migration to good effect in, for example, obtaining exemption from pollution control regimes or in encouraging the adoption of 'fast track' approval procedures. It is also clear that taxation and labour relations regimes have a significant bearing upon 'corporate residence'. However, regulation aimed at the goods and services produced by corporate persons, and the methods by which those goods and services are advertised and sold, is proving increasingly successful, although even in this sphere the political will is sometimes lacking.[50] Because the economic power of multinational corporations greatly exceeds that available to any individual, this is hardly surprising.[51]

---

49 Individuals are also free to migrate, and to renounce citizenship.

50 A good example of an area in which the political will has been lacking is the tobacco industry. Despite the enthusiastic use of 'sin taxes', and the gradual elimination of most forms of tobacco advertising, the industry retains sufficient power to deter governments from disallowing tobacco advertising at certain high-profile sporting events, which might well collapse if tobacco sponsorship were to be withdrawn.

51 The United Nations began to take an interest in the activities of multinational corporations more than twenty years ago, endeavouring to develop regulatory regimes to address abuse of market power, to regulate the transfer of technology, and to deal with 'corrupt practices' such as bribery. See L. Robert Primoff, 'International Regulation of Multinational Corporations and Business—The United Nations Takes Aim' (1976) 11 *Journal of International Law and Economics* 287. There is little evidence to date that this has markedly affected corporate conduct.

Corporate illegality: A litmus test for models of corporate accountability

Stephen Yoder suggests that there are three major issues that must be confronted in the process of devising appropriate sanctions for corporate crime. Yoder notes:

> First, there are the inherent moral questions: Is the corporate crime immoral? Should morality make a difference as to whether a criminal law ought to be used as a vehicle for social control? Second, if corporate crime is an appropriate vehicle, the purposes of criminal penalties must be delineated. Are we seeking only deterrence or should we also consider retribution, education and rehabilitation in devising sanctions? Finally, policy makers must make as careful a matching as possible between the purposes identified and the proposals for new and reformed criminal sanctions directed at corporate criminals.[52]

From a policy perspective, an even more important question is whether, in the case of corporate illegality, the imposition of criminal sanctions may not, in the end, be self-defeating, if only because of the difficulties inherent in meeting the appropriate standard of proof. One important distinction between the criminal activity of individuals and that engaged in by corporations is that, in the case of corporations, the impossibility of 'imprisonment' as a sanction may be thought to render the practical distinction between criminal law and civil law minimal in other than symbolic terms. Unsuccessful attempts to prosecute individuals in Australia following the 'profligate' 1980s suggest that, in purely practical terms, the burden of proof will often be beyond the resources of prosecutors, whereas civil penalties might prove effective.

As Yoder acknowledges, 'there is no clear correlation between what is commercially acceptable vs legally acceptable behavior. Activities such as price-fixing and bribery of foreign officials, for example, are well-entrenched in the conventional businessman's "moral code"'.[53] Part of the problem is that the phrase 'corporate crime' is used to cover many different kinds of wrongful conduct, ranging from knowingly marketing a product with a defect that is potentially life threatening[54] to the failure to install or maintain safety equipment on factory premises, or to comply with strict liability provisions in respect of vehicle loadings. Perhaps a more serious problem lies in the reluctance of many individuals, including many judges, to categorise as 'criminal conduct' actions that fall outside current social understandings both of criminality and of the nature of the criminal.[55] If the corporation-as-simulacrum seems insufficiently ensouled for criminal liability, individual corporate agents seem insufficiently 'criminal' (and here the criminal is understood not as a responsible individual but as a social role) to be responsible for the acts with which they might be charged. Corporate liability thus falls between two stools. Commentators such as Lim Wen Ts'ai go further, suggesting that normally it will not be appropriate to impose criminal

---

52   Stephen A. Yoder, 'Comments: Criminal Sanctions for Corporate Illegality' (1978) 69 *Journal of Criminal Law and Criminology* 40 at 41.

53   Yoder at 41.

54   See M. B. Metzger, 'Corporate Criminal Liability for Defective Products: Policies, Problems, and Prospects' (1984) 73(1) Geo LJ 1 at 3.

55   Yoder discusses a number of the reasons why individuals often escape punishment for corporate crime.

liability upon corporations. He suggests that to impose liability routinely upon the corporate body rather than upon the individuals who might appear to be responsible undermines important legal values, such as the principle of individual responsibility, upon which the criminal justice system is based. Ts'ai suggests:

> The large organized corporation is . . . a bureaucracy in the Weberian sense. Weber describes an ideal-type of such an organization as possessing certain typical characteristics: specialization or division of labour; an administration based on files; occupation of offices by individuals, each office having a prescribed sphere of competence; impersonality in decision making; and rules, accompanied by a set of standard operating procedures governing the daily performance of tasks.[56]

In an organisation of this kind, Ts'ai suggests, it is appropriate to deal with individual responsibility in terms of a simple dichotomy: one that contrasts the liability of subordinate officers with that of superior officers. In each case, liability ultimately becomes problematical: in the case of subordinates because, very often, they are not in a position to be free agents (in the moral sense); and in the case of superordinates because they rely upon their subordinates in day-to-day matters, and are involved with goal-setting rather than more mundane activities.

According to Ts'ai, subordinate officers very often act under the constraints imposed by their organisational roles. Because their conduct is often constrained by implicit threats that promotion may be withheld or employment lost if they step outside the confines of their roles, this limits the degree to which they are responsible for conduct that would otherwise be criminal:

> One way in which such a constraint may arise is where a direct order is given to the officer to perform an illegal act. Such an order is often accompanied by an express or implied threat that the officer's promotional prospects or even the officer's job itself could be at stake if he or she disobeys the order. It is well known that 'obeying orders' has seldom been accepted legally as an excuse for committing a crime, but the moral implications of holding a subordinate officer responsible when faced with the above predicament are less clear-cut. Firstly, there is psychological evidence that most people have been so conditioned to obey authority that few can resist its exercise. Secondly, given the fact that most crimes committed on behalf of corporations tend to be of a regulatory nature rather than crimes which are regarded by the community in general as serious moral wrongs—*mala prohibita* as opposed to *mala in se*—it is possible to argue that the act was constructively involuntary.[57]

The kind of person of whom Ts'ai speaks was described by Ganey J in these terms: '[they] were torn between conscience and an approved corporate policy, with the rewarding object of promotion, comfortable security, and large salaries. They were the organization or company man, the conformist who goes along with his

---

56 Lim Wen Ts'ai, 'Corporations and the Devil's Dictionary: The Problem of Individual Responsibility for Corporate Crimes' (1990) Syd LR 311 at 319.

57 Ts'ai at 321.

superiors and finds balm for his conscience in additional comforts and security of his place in the corporate set-up'.[58] The picture becomes bleaker still when Ts'ai considers the liability of superior officers and notes that

> [s]uperior officers . . . tend to delegate matters like designing the mechanisms of task performance to subordinates in order to concentrate on 'strategic' matters such as communications with other firms, corporate policy and goal setting. As such their attention is directed outwards rather than inwards, and their reliance on subordinates to ensure that day to day management is properly conducted is substantial. In cases such as these, it is difficult to find any substantive responsibility on the part of the officers concerned for the commission of the crime, unless it could be said that they *knew of and acquiesced in* the criminal act.[59]

Ts'ai's positivistic model can usefully be contrasted with an expanded version of Dworkin's account of associative obligations. While Dworkin does not attribute any sort of 'supra-individual' personality to collectivities, the collectivity is real nonetheless. The difference lies in his explicit assumption that individuals are not 'consumed' by their obligations of role. Rather, the obligations of role by which they are bound are nullified where these obligations conflict with serious obligations owed as a consequence of membership in a wider collectivity. Where groups themselves are members of wider collectivities,[60] as is the case with corporations, we believe that his account is sufficiently sophisticated to recognise that the collectivity functions as an individual for certain purposes and is itself made up of individuals for other purposes. If this is, in fact, the case, there is no conceptual difficulty in holding the corporation responsible for criminal activity, precisely because its acts are, on one level, individual acts, even while they are, on another, the acts of a collectivity. The question, as always, is whether the act 'belongs', in the relevant sense, to the corporation.[61]

REVIEW QUESTIONS

1   What avenues are available for calling corporate persons to account for criminal or tortious acts?
2   How can a line be drawn between wrongful acts for which the corporation, as such, is responsible and those that are more properly a consequence of individual malfeasance (an individual engaging in what used to be termed 'a frolic of his or her own')?
3   What are some of the factors that make it difficult to 'punish' corporate persons for wrongdoing?

---

58   *New York Times*, 7 February 1961, as quoted by Ts'ai at 322.
59   Ts'ai at 323.
60   We include communities and regions among such collectivities, as well as the more obvious political entities: municipalities, states, and nation states.
61   This need mean no more than whether the purposes involved are corporate purposes or private purposes.

THE LOWERED VEIL:
CORPORATE MORALITY
AND THE COURTS

Introduction

In the last chapter we looked at the conceptual and practical difficulties involved in making the corporation account for wrongdoing. We also explored allied issues, including an emerging ideal of corporate citizenship. The motive for our explorations was the problem of 'corporate individuality'. As you have seen, the law accords the company recognition as a legal person, granting it a personality that is distinct from that of any individual member. In Australia this recognition entitles the corporation to all of the rights and obligations of a natural person,[1] thus ensuring it can carry on its business without let or hindrance. It clears the way for corporate persons to engage in trade and commerce in the same way as natural persons. However, from the perspective of those who deal with corporate citizens, whether as individuals or in some public capacity, dealing with the 'corporate jellyfish'[2] may present unexpected pitfalls. We saw some of these in the last chapter as we began to explore the question of corporate accountability. Because our general laws and institutions have been framed with natural persons in mind, many of them make assumptions and impose requirements that are at odds with the 'nature' of corporate persons. The requirement for a 'mental' element in the criminal law and in certain torts is an obvious example.[3] In the case of corporate wrongdoing, complex issues confront the law as it struggles to allocate responsibility under statutory and common-law rules that were designed with natural persons in mind. These same struggles and issues are intimately bound up with one of the most fundamental doctrines in corporate law. As we begin to explore the 'veil of incorporation' and its impact upon corporate law, we will be particularly concerned with the ways in which this doctrine interacts with the general law.

---

1   In the USA and Canada, despite the absence of a statutory equivalent to s. 161 of the *Corporations Law 1990*, the position is substantively much the same, given that the corporation is entitled to the protection of the Bill of Rights and the Charter of Rights and Freedoms respectively.

2   See fn. 8, p. 111.

When speaking of the legal effects of incorporation and the way in which the corporation must be distinguished both from those who own it and from those who control it, the courts have traditionally relied upon a metaphor: the 'corporate veil'. According to the judges, the endowment of legal personality attendant upon incorporation shrouds the identity and activities of the owners and controllers of the corporation with an impenetrable veil, in this way, perhaps, endowing the fictive corporate body with shape and substance. From the perspective of the legal system more generally, all that is theoretically visible is the 'veiled' body corporate. While the names of shareholders, like the names of directors, are a matter of public record,[4] the law refuses to 'know' them in their corporate aspect, except in exceptional circumstances. So much a part of the contemporary legal scene is this fictive corporate body that we do not always recall that this ghostly presence is of recent origin. According to Paddy Ireland and colleagues,

> [a]n examination of eighteenth and early nineteenth century cases and texts makes it clear that incorporation did *not* at that time entail such a separation. Incorporation did create an entity, the incorporated company, which was legally distinguishable from the people composing it, but there was no suggestion that this entity was 'completely separate' from its members. On the contrary, up to the middle of the nineteenth century incorporated joint stock companies were consistently identified with their component members and were conceptualised not as depersonalised objects but as entities composed of those members merged into one legally distinguishable body.[5]

Only with the House of Lords decision in *Salomon v. Salomon & Co. Ltd* did the corporate body become so 'real' as to obliterate, for most legal purposes, the individuals that animated it. How and why this occurred has become a significant turning point in corporate law. We will return to this history subsequently, both because

---

3   In both criminal law and torts, the law has reacted to this by endeavouring to identify the 'mind and will' of the corporation. It ensouls the simulacrum by attributing to it the mental states of some of its human agents. The classic formulation of this is that of Viscount Haldane in *Lennard's Carrying Co. Ltd v. Asiatic Petroleum Co. Ltd* [1915] AC 705. The *Lennard's* approach has been followed in more recent cases, including *Tesco Supermarkets Ltd v. Natrass* [1972] AC 153; *Universal Telecasters (Qld) Ltd v. Guthrie* (1978) 43 FLR 360; and *Brambles Holdings Ltd v. Carey* (1976) 2 ACLR 176. A rather more subtle approach was adopted in *Re Chisum Services Pty Ltd* (1981) ACLC 292. The court took the view that the search for a 'supermind' within a bank was likely to prove futile. Instead corporate knowledge might be determined from the normal channels of communication within the company. On one level, of course, as Mary Stokes has noted, the search for the corporate soul is simply a manifestation the lingering appeal of the group entity theory of the corporation. On another level, neither we, as individual men and women, nor the law, as our creation, are able to conceive of an entity that acts in a purposive manner and yet is devoid of mind, will, and soul. See M. Stokes, 'Company Law and Legal Theory', in W. Twining (ed.), *Legal Theory and Common Law*, Basil Blackwell, Oxford, 1986, pp. 164–5.

4   While the Corporations Law requires a register of shareholders to be kept, today, given that most shares are traded through brokerage houses, it is not uncommon for shares to be held in 'street names', rather than in the names of the individual investors.

5   P. Ireland, I. Grigg-Spall, & D. Kelly, 'The Conceptual Foundations of Modern Company Law' (1987) *Journal of Law and Society* 149–50, as quoted in R. Tomasic, J. Jackson, & R. Woellner, *Corporation Law: Principles, Policy and Process*, 2nd edn, Butterworths, Sydney, 1992, p. 96.

it is essential to any understanding of the notion of the 'corporate veil' as legal doctrine and because it has shaped corporate law in profound ways.

While most accounts of corporate law begin discussion of the corporate veil with *Salomon's* case, we have chosen to begin with more recent events, both because they highlight the problems that the doctrine poses and because they illustrate the interface of corporate law and general law in a compelling way. The first case we will look at is a small and relatively unimportant aspect of the legal skirmishes presaging the ultimate collapse of Alan Bond's corporate empire. It involved an issue that was seemingly poles apart from corporate politics and corporate veils. The issue before the Australian Broadcasting Tribunal involved an application to renew the broadcasting license for a Brisbane television station, QTQ-9. The licensee, Queensland Television Ltd (QTL), was a subsidiary of Bond Media Ltd. Bond Media Ltd was in turn a subsidiary of Bond Holdings, which was substantially owned by Dallhold Investments Pty Ltd, the Bond family company. Dallhold Investments held together and, through its principal shareholder, Alan Bond, largely controlled the Bond corporate empire. Whatever the practical realities of the Bond empire, at law all of the interlocking companies within it, even Dallhold Investments Pty Ltd, which was 99.9 per cent owned by Bond himself, were independent legal persons, legally separate from each other and from Alan Bond.

In *Alan Bond & Ors v. Australian Broadcasting Tribunal*,[6] the Australian Broadcasting Tribunal revoked QTL's broadcasting license. From a common-sense point of view, its decision remains unremarkable. It concluded upon the facts before it that QTL was, in essence, Alan Bond's puppet, his creature. Because it had formed the view that Alan Bond was not a 'fit and proper person' to hold a broadcasting license, it concluded that QTL, as his puppet, was also not a fit and proper person. As a consequence it was not entitled to hold a broadcasting license. As Roman Tomasic and colleagues tell the story:

> A number of findings led the Tribunal to reach conclusions in this regard. One of these arose out of the fact that Alan Bond had stated to Jana Wendt, on the television program 'A Current Affair', that the then Premier of Queensland had said to him that unless an outstanding defamation claim which the Premier had against the Bond company QTQ-9 in Brisbane, was settled, there might be difficulties in the Bond group of companies continuing to do business in Queensland. Bond therefore agreed to have the matter settled. Subsequently, Mr Aspinall, who was Chief Executive of the Bond Media Division of Bond Holdings and the executive Director of the licensee company, instructed the licensee's solicitors to draw up an agreement whereby an amount of some $400 000 was to be paid to the Premier to settle the defamation claim.
>
> [After hearing this and other similar evidence, t]he tribunal had concluded that:
>   . . . Mr Bond's position within the corporate structure does enable him to initiate and involve himself in management decisions which affect the broadcasting activities within the group . . . Our view is that Mr Bond, through his shareholding, does have

a continuing and substantial interest in the directions and decisions of the various licensee companies. It is also clear that Bond Media occupies an important position in the Bond Group of companies . . .

Mr Bond remains, by virtue of his association with the licensee companies, the only relevant individual in the sense that consideration of his fitness and propriety is relevant to the fitness and propriety of the licensees.[7]

This case puts the dilemma that we confronted in the last chapter in a different perspective. In the last chapter, the question that vexed us was how, or even if, the simulacrum might be 'ensouled'. By eliding the distinction between Alan Bond and the various companies that comprised his corporate pyramid, the Tribunal ensouled it by fiat. To the extent that Alan Bond's corporate empire had a soul, that soul was Alan Bond's. Confronting subsidiaries of the then Bond media empire, the tribunal—not surprisingly, given the distribution of shareholdings, the interlocking directorships, and the comments made in the media by none other than Bond himself—concluded that if Alan Bond himself was not a 'fit and proper person' to hold a television license, then a company that he was in a position to control was, because of that association, not a fit and proper person either. At general law (and, for that matter, as a question of common sense), none of this is surprising.

That Alan Bond's corporate lawyers promptly appealed the decision of the Broadcasting Tribunal is also hardly surprising. After all, QTL, like Bond Media Limited and Bond Holdings, was an independent legal person. While Alan Bond had substantial interests in both (through his family company, Dallhold Investments Pty Ltd) and was a director of Dallhold and the Executive Chairman of Bond Holdings, these were 'ownership' interests. The isolation of ownership and control characteristic of the corporate form meant that whether or not Alan Bond was a fit and proper person to hold a broadcasting license ought to have been legally irrelevant to the fitness of QTL. As a consequence, the Full Federal Court set aside the decision of the Broadcasting Tribunal on appeal, noting that '[t]he Tribunal went astray by equating the fitness and propriety of Mr Bond (or lack of it) with that of the licensees'.

Yet, given what we have learned thus far about corporate persons, it is difficult to understand how a corporate person could ever be a 'fit and proper person'. At the very least, the requirement suggests a capacity to exercise moral judgment, and it seems unlikely that a simulacrum can do this. The underlying paradox is simple. One of the requirements that must be met before a broadcasting license can be granted or renewed is that the licensee must be shown to be a fit and proper person.[8] On the

---

7   Tomasic et al., pp. 104–5 (original emphasis).

8   Requirements of this general character exist in respect of a number of 'statutory privileges'. Admission to the Bar in most jurisdictions requires that the applicant be 'of good fame and character'. Similar requirements exist for those wishing to obtain an abalone license, a liquor license, and so on. All of these requirements first made their way into the law at a time when applicants were, almost universally, 'natural persons'. In the case of 'natural persons' they are reasonably sensible requirements, designed to eliminate potential licensees with criminal records and undesirable connections. Extended to corporate persons, they become profoundly problematic.

facts, the licensee was a corporate person, not a natural person. It is difficult to understand how a corporate person, *as such*, could either qualify as a fit and proper person or fail to do so. Corporations, after all, lack character and have proved impossible to socialise. As noted earlier, '[a]part from its corporators, [the corporation] can have neither thoughts, wishes, or intentions, for it has not mind other than the minds of the corporators'.[9] Yet, in the case of a corporation such as QTL, identifying its mind and will with that of its corporators is of scant assistance. QTL was, after all, a wholly owned subsidiary of Bond Media Limited. If we track its 'personhood' up the pyramid of interlocking companies, disregarding the minority of publicly owned shares along the way, we come at last to Dallhold Investments Pty Ltd and Alan Bond. If we disregard the shadow cast by Bond at every level of the corporate pyramid, all we are likely to find are 'passive investors'. Mary Stokes comments:

> The fact that the shareholders within the large company were increasingly becoming passive investors, irrelevant within the company except for their function in supplying the capital of the company, was entirely consonant with this image of the company. They could be viewed as the organ within the living organism whose task it was to supply the basic necessity of capital without any need to accord them a fuller role within the enterprise.[10]

If it is the directors who must be fit and proper persons, the corporation is endowed with the character of its board. If it is the shareholders who must so qualify, the corporation is endowed with their character. Yet, whichever option we choose, we run the risk of assimilating the corporate body into its various organs. On its own, as 'corporate' person, we have yet to find a way to ensoul the corporation. As such, simply as a corporate person, it can be neither 'fit' nor 'unfit'. Whatever fitness or unfitness it possesses can only arise through 'contamination'.

This last point is important. It encapsulates the paradoxical nature of corporate personality and, indeed, the corporate veil. Wherever the general law requires particular qualifications for engaging in particular activities, and those qualifications demand the capacity to exercise moral judgment, the distinction between the company and its controllers collapses. Irrespective of whether or not the Broadcasting Tribunal had it right, and QTQ-9 was Alan Bond in drag, the Full Federal Court had it wrong, as the High Court was subsequently to acknowledge.[11] The licensees, being corporate persons, could not be 'fit and proper', save by the interposition of some human agency. If the boards of directors of those licensees are to be identified as those whom the law requires to be 'fit and proper persons' for the purposes of licensing arrangements, then surely it would be better that the law mandate an investigation of the individual character of each of the members of each of the boards rather than equate the fitness and propriety of the licensees, as corporate persons, to the degree to which the various boards complied with the statutory and

---

9   *Continental Tyre & Rubber Co. (GB) Ltd v. Daimler Co. Ltd* [1915] 1 KB 893 at 916 per Buckley LJ. By corporators, Lord Justice Buckley clearly meant owners.

10   Stokes, pp. 164–5.

11   See *Australian Broadcasting Tribunal v. Bond* (1990) 94 ALR 11.

common-law requirements of the Corporations Law. The Full Court simply stated that 'the boards of the licensee companies operated in an entirely proper manner and discharged their duties in accordance with the obligations placed upon them by company law'.[12] Yet in the present context to say that the 'boards . . . operated in an entirely proper manner' is to say very little. In the real world of interlocking corporate empires, such as that created by Alan Bond, the directorates of the various corporate entities that make up an empire are likely to be a tightly woven fabric of nominee directors and those who serve on the boards of multiple companies within the group. As was the case with other such groups (Christopher Skase's Qintex, for example), no distinction is made between the interests of companies in the group. And where the linchpin of the conglomerate is the family company of the principal (as was the case with the Bond empire), neither is there a distinction made between the interests of the company and those of its guiding spirit. The realities of such groups are well illustrated by the evidence given in the course of the legal proceedings following the collapse of Christopher Skase's Qintex group. Ms Ferreira, a dealer in the treasury operations department of Schroders Australia, explains:

> In my discussion with either Craig Pratt or Paul Lewis when I confirmed deals undertaken for Qintex, it was not my practice to ask which of the Qintex companies was responsible for the deal. I always treated the client as Qintex and did not differentiate between companies in the group. Paul Lewis and Craig Pratt always talked as being from 'Qintex' without reference to any specific company. To record foreign exchange transactions Schroders needed a client code. I was only aware of one client coding for Qintex which was the coding 'QTLBR1'.[13]

It is worth remembering that during the late 1980s a Bond 'director' giving evidence in a Victorian court explained that he could hardly be expected to recall the details of particular transactions, given that he sat on the boards of numerous companies. Even on the relatively 'sparse' facts presented, we know that a Mr Aspinall, who was Chief Executive of the Bond Media Division of Bond Holdings, was also the Executive Director of the licensee company. There may have been other common directors as well. The common law acknowledges that a nominee director may, at least in some circumstances, look to the benefit of a corporate group as a whole. Pennycuick J noted in the British case *Charterbridge Corp. Ltd v. Lloyd's Bank*:[14]

> As I have already found, the directors of Castleford looked to the benefit of the group as a whole and did not give separate consideration to the benefit of Castleford . . . Each company in the groups is a separate legal entity and the directors of a particular company are not entitled to sacrifice the interest of that company . . . The proper test, in the absence of actual separate consideration, is whether an honest and intelligent man in the

---

12 *Alan Bond & Ors v. Australian Broadcasting Tribunal* (1989) 89 ALR 185.

13 *Qintex Australia Finance Ltd v. Schroders Australia Ltd* (1990) 3 ASCR 267 at 268. It is perhaps worth noting that Qintex, like the various permutations of the Bond empire, was ultimately the emanation of one person: Christopher Skase.

14 [1970] 1 Ch 62.

position of a director of the company concerned, could, in the whole of the existing circumstances, have reasonably believed that the transactions were for the benefit of the company.[15]

Very often, perhaps always, an honest and intelligent person in the position of a director of one company in a corporate group would have difficulty believing anything else. Indeed, a standard this flexible comes close to being no standard at all. Consider the following passage from an empirical study of Australian corporate conduct and of directors' understandings of their roles:

> The triumph of a corporate managerialist ethos over that of legalism was well illustrated by the comment of a Perth based executive director who remarked that:
>
>> We have fifty subsidiaries and I am on forty five. Executive directors on subsidiaries see themselves as part of management and not as an independent Board. We do not think of them as having separate fiduciary duties.
>
> It is clear from this and from other evidence . . . that the group context of corporate life places major strains upon the capacity of directors on subsidiary boards to meet their legal obligations. These strains are evident in the way in which conflicts of interests are dealt with and in the financial transactions between members of the group. The independence of subsidiaries must therefore be seriously questioned. Ultimately, therefore, the capacities of subsidiaries to be good corporate citizens must depend very heavily upon the interrelationships between companies in the group and the sense of responsibility of directors on holding company boards. This leaves little scope for the directors of subsidiary companies to exercise much independent judgment.[16]

Against this background, the insistence of the Full Federal Court that the licensees operated in an entirely proper manner seems disingenuous at best, a narrow and unrealistic legalism at odds with the operating environment of modern corporate empires. This disingenuous quality was undoubtedly acknowledged by the High Court when it held that, irrespective of the fact that the 'boards of the licensee companies operated in an entirely proper manner and discharged their duties in accord with company law', the tribunal was entitled to consider the conduct of Alan Bond, and the fact that he had attempted to mislead the tribunal, in settling the defamation action brought by the then premier of Queensland on exceedingly generous terms. If Alan Bond was not, in the opinion of the tribunal, a fit and proper person for licensing purposes, a company that he had the capacity to influence, perhaps substantially control, was likewise not a fit and proper person.

Yet, as we saw in the last chapter, such is the power of law's understanding of corporate personality that the 'veil of incorporation' retains a stranglehold on contemporary understandings of the corporate individual. The tentative liberalisation in

---

15 [1970] 1 Ch 62 at 74.

16 R. Tomasic & S. Bottomley, *The Fiduciary Duties of Directors in Listed Public Companies: An Empirical Study of Directors' Duties and the Law in Corporate Australia,* Centre for National Corporate Law Research, University of Canberra, Canberra, 1991, p. 10.

the waning days of the Bond empire has not dramatically altered the legal landscape. Indeed, one may properly speculate that it was precisely the impossibility of isolating the individual entities within the 'corporate jellyfish' that has led to the legal refusal to even attempt the task.

Hugh Collins characterises the difficulty that we have been considering as the 'capital boundary problem'. According to Collins,

[f]irms enjoy considerable freedom both in law and in practice to determine the limits of their boundaries. A firm can decide to produce commodities or services within its own organisation or make contracts outside the firm with independent legal entities for the same work to be performed. Furthermore, a firm can operate through numerous corporate entities, corresponding perhaps to different aspects of production, establishing a group of companies managing an economically integrated enterprise. No laws limit this freedom to organise production through external contractual relations with other firms or through subsidiaries.

. . . Although some production processes such as an assembly plant along a conveyor-belt may impel a firm towards vertical integration within a single corporate entity, these constraints do not seem ultimately significant when we recall that in *McDermid v. Nash Dredging & Reclamation Co Ltd* even the crew of a ship could have different employers . . .

One important and general effect of this freedom of capital organisation is that the decision with respect to firm size also has a profound bearing on the potential liabilities of the company as a result of the limitation of legal responsibility to the firm's own actions and omissions. The capital boundary problem which arises consists of this: because the firm determines its own size, it also chooses the limits of its legal responsibilities, which in turn provides an open invitation for the evasion of mandatory legal duties . . .

Perhaps the most significant example of the effects of the limits on legal responsibility in combination with capital's freedom to determine its own size occurs in connection with insolvency of companies. On general principles of legal responsibility, one company cannot be liable for another's debts . . . In the event of the insolvency of one subsidiary company, therefore, the other companies in the group will not in general be liable to creditors, who may go uncompensated as a consequence of the manipulation of capital boundaries. Indeed, a majority shareholder or parent company may provide capital to the subsidiary in the form of secured debt rather than equity, thus achieving priority in English law over unsecured creditors . . .

Here the costs of mismanagement, the risks of undercapitalisation, or liability for hazards such as tort claims by third parties are thrown onto the creditors of the subsidiary firm, rather than being born by the economic organisation which effectively controls the productive operation. Far from being a curious anomaly of English company law, this springs directly from the legal principles of personal and group responsibility, and it illustrates the injustices caused by the capital boundary problem in full swing.[17]

---

17 H. Collins, 'Ascription of Legal Responsibility to Groups in Complex Patterns of Economic Integration' (1990) 53 *Modern Law Review* 731 at 736–8.

Following the corporate collapses of the 1980s, legislative attempts to address at least some consequences of the capital-boundary problem have intensified.[18] In Australia, legislation was enacted in 1992, which provided that a holding company might be liable for the debts of an insolvent subsidiary.[19] Section 588V provides that in circumstances where a subsidiary is either insolvent when it incurs a debt or becomes insolvent as a consequence of incurring that debt, *and* the holding company or one or more of its directors either knew or ought to have known that this would occur, the liquidator of the subsidiary may recover compensation provided that certain conditions are met. The first condition is obvious. The holding company must exercise a degree of control over the affairs of the subsidiary such that it would be reasonable for it to have the relevant knowledge.[20] Second, the statutory provision incorporates what is, in essence, a clean-hands requirement. If the creditor suffering harm or loss was itself aware that insolvency or potential insolvency was present, any compensation paid by the holding company cannot be used to extinguish its debt until all other unsecured debts have been paid in full.[21]

We believe that a similar outcome is also possible through the use of other provisions of the Corporations Law. Personal liability for insolvent trading attaches to a director[22] where the company engages in insolvent trading and the director either knew or ought to have known that this was the case. Because the statutory definition of 'director' in s. 60 explicitly includes a person who habitually acts as a director (a shadow director in other words), it seems likely that, where a holding company directs the actions of a subsidiary, it would run afoul of these provisions and become liable for the debts of the subsidiary. These provisions will be discussed in more detail later.

A little history: Of boots and boot-makers

The concept of legal personality was effectively entrenched in company law by the decision in *Salomon v. Salomon & Co. Ltd*,[23] the facts of which should be familiar to every law student. But there is another story, of course—one rooted in social history. A part of that narrative is recounted below:

---

18 The judiciary also recognise the difficulties involved. A notable example may be found in *Briggs v. James Hardie & Co. Pty Ltd* (1989) 7 ACLC 841. There the plaintiff, who suffered from asbestosis, was compelled to challenge the corporate veil to pursue compensation, the particular subsidiary for which he had worked having gone into liquidation.

19 *Corporate Law Reform Act 1992* (Cth), s. 588V. Legislation having this effect has also been enacted in the United Kingdom.

20 In traditional corporate law terms, the evidence must suggest that it was the 'directing mind and will' of the subsidiary.

21 For a discussion of this provision and its efficacy, see I. Ramsay, 'Holding Company Liability for the Debts of An Insolvent Subsidiary: A Law and Economic Perspective' (1994) 17(2) UNSWLJ 520.

22 See s. 588G–Q of the Corporations Law.

23 [1897] AC 22. See pp. 39–40 for a discussion of the facts of the case.

The hostility to those debenture-holders successfully elbowing out unsecured trade creditors in the boot and shoe industry had already been prominently expressed, notably in the case of the firm of Wolfsky & Co. Ltd, which crashed just before Aron [Salomon]'s firm. The *Shoe and Leather Record* declared that it was,

> . . . another of these discreditable cases in which the Company Acts are availed of to the detriment of the leather trade . . . [where the] company seems to have done a wonderful business in debentures.

Questions respecting a similar case, involving the publishing company, W. Wilfred Head and Marks Ltd, were asked in Parliament around the same time by Reuben Bennett MP, whose Bermondsey firm of S. Barrow & Bros Ltd, leather factors, was, ironically, to rank as one of Aron's company's principal unsecured creditors.

It was no surprise, therefore, when Aron's attempt, early in the legal proceedings, to rank as debenture holder (although subject to Broderip's mortgage) prior to the trade creditors was vigorously criticised. Aron, declared the *Shoe and Leather Record*,

> . . . has been a prominent member of the London shoe trade. He has enjoyed an unblemished reputation for probity, and has been regarded as one of the best men in the Jewish community. It is apparently within his power to preserve that reputation, and we hope he will do so.

By December 1893, the official receiver's report was ready and a meeting of creditors at last held. That meeting was, in the nature of things, a tense and acrimonious affair, with recriminations and accusations flying back and forth . . . Nonetheless, there was a general air of optimism at the meeting that the trade creditors would be paid in full. After all, as the petitioning (i.e. trade) creditors' solicitor pointed out,

> Mr. Salomon was a man of capital when the company was formed some 18 months ago, and doubtless was still a man of capital, seeing that he practically was the company . . .

as well as the major shareholder in a business which all knew to be solvent once Aron's debenture claim was discounted . . .

Commenting on the official receiver's report, a strong editorial in the *Shoe and Leather Record* reiterated much of the incredulity which had characterised its earlier remarks. On Aron's debenture transactions, it commented,

> It is not necessary to impute evil motives to Mr Salomon in regard to this conduct. It is enough to know that the result of these transactions has been to put a considerable sum into the pocket of Mr. Salomon in his personal capacity which properly belongs to the creditors of the same gentleman in his corporate capacity. This is financial juggling with a vengeance.[24]

From this social history we learn that the legitimacy of Aron Salomon's debentures was contested terrain, that the path he ultimately adopted had been taken by others, perhaps numerous others, and that, until Aron Salomon appeared before the House of Lords in *forma pauperis*, its legitimacy was an open question. We also learn

---

24 G. R. Rubin, 'Aron Salomon and his Circle', in J. Adams (ed.), *Essays for Clive Schmitthoff*, Professional Books Ltd, Abingdon, Oxon, 1983, pp. 99, 109–10.

of an era and an industry. Of course, none of this sheds any direct light upon the question of why the House of Lords decided as it did, but it does make it clear that, had not *Salomon* eventually made its way to the House of Lords, another such case would have.

Despite this, the decision was remarkable for several reasons. First, it entrenched in the law the idea that the corporate form was available to sole traders as well as to larger commercial concerns. That aspect of the decision is the more remarkable because the British Parliament had only a short time before rejected the legitimacy of the limited partnership form, suggesting that it did not desire to extend the benefits of limited liability to sole traders and partnerships. Similar arrangements were, as we have seen, already being debated and questioned in Parliament. Second, the particular approach taken to the notion of legal personality enabled individual entrepreneurs to utilise the corporate form for business ventures and to escape financial responsibility for the inevitable failures.

When the case was heard at the Court of Appeal level, Lord Justice Lopes described the company as a 'mere sham' and a mask for a sole trader. By contrast, the House of Lords found that in both fact and law there were seven shareholders, and that, as a consequence, Mr Salomon was entitled both to priority on debentures and to limited liability on debts. Lord Halisbury described the decision of the House of Lords as reflecting the 'will of Parliament'. According to Lord Macnaghten,

> [t]he company had a brief career: it fell upon evil days. Shortly after it was started there seems to have come a period of great depression in the boot and shoe trade. There were strikes of workmen too; and in view of that danger contracts with public bodies, which were the principal source of Mr Salomon's profit, were split up and divided between different firms. The attempts made to push the business on behalf of the new company crammed its warehouses with unsaleable stock. Mr Salomon seems to have done what he could: both he and his wife lent the company money: and then he got his debentures cancelled and reissued to a Mr. Broderip, who advanced him £5000, which he immediately handed over to the company on loan. The temporary relief only hastened ruin. Mr. Broderip's interest was not paid when it became due. He took proceedings at once and got a receiver appointed. Then of course came liquidation and a forced sale of the company's assets. They realised enough to pay Mr Broderip, but not enough to pay the debentures in full; and the unsecured creditors were consequently left out in the cold.[25]

So, we might add, have been their successors. Not only did this decision give full recognition to the concept of independent legal personality, but, far more importantly, it also fostered the development of generations of 'corporate cowboys', entrepreneurs who utilise the corporate form to amass debts in the corporate name and desert failed companies unscathed while pursuing new ventures. Much contemporary reformist legislation—such as the recent provisions in the United Kingdom

---

25 *Salomon v. Salomon & Co. Ltd* [1897] AC 22 at 49–50. It is significant that the alternatives were drawn so starkly. Either the company was a 'mere sham' or it was legitimate.

and Australia, designed to sheet home personal liability where directors allow a company to trade while insolvent—represents a continuing attempt to contain the havoc wreaked by *Salomon* and its numerous progeny. Lawton LJ put the point particularly well in *Rolled Steel Products Ltd v. British Steel Corporation*:[26]

> Stripped of its legal complications, many of which were caused by the way the trial judge dealt with the defendant's applications to amend the pleadings, this case raises issues of fact. When the evidence is looked at in the round, there is revealed an unattractive story of a fairly common kind which shows how some business men manipulate limited liability companies to avoid their financial liabilities and what other business men are driven to do in order to get paid what they are entitled to receive . . . Mr Shenkman had operated behind a screen of small limited liability companies in which he and family interests controlled all the shares. The company which owed Colvilles this huge debt . . . had no assets. Mr Shenkman himself had very few. What assets there were (and they were fairly substantial) were in another company, . . . which had no dealings with Colvilles but into which Mr Shenkman had syphoned by way of a loan about £400,000 of SSS's money which that company should have paid to Colvilles in discharge of its debts. I have much sympathy for BSC. They were being kept out of their money by the legal fiction that RSP was not Mr Shenkman. Unfortunately for them it is a legal fiction which has been recognised by the law for over a hundred years. It is said to have helped the growth of innumerable new businesses. The fact that limited liability has all too often enabled many to enrich themselves at the expense of those who have given credit to the companies they control is the price the business world has to pay for the potentiality for growth and convenience which goes with limited liability.[27]

Through judicial development of the notion of legal personality, two distinct principles ultimately emerged. First, in the classic family company setting, individual entrepreneurs may sell their property to themselves at any price they determine.[28] Second, they may loan to the company the funds needed to pay for the property and treat the transaction as a secured loan, thereby granting themselves priority in a winding-up by virtue of their status as secured creditors.

REVIEW QUESTIONS

1   Read *Salomon v. Salomon* carefully and compare the reasoning in the Court of Appeal with that in the House of Lords. Do you think that it was precedent or policy that impelled the decision in the House of Lords? If the former, try to

---

26   [1985] 3 All ER 52.

27   [1985] 3 All ER 52 at 94–5.

28   The only requirement is that the nature of the transaction and the promoter's interest in it be declared to an 'independent board'. In the absence of an independent board (because in the usual circumstance the promoter is also the principal shareholder and one of the directors), disclosure must be made to the general meeting and the transaction ratified. As was the case in *Salomon*, this is a mere formality in the usual family company.

identify the precedent or precedents used. If the latter, what policy considerations might have been behind this instance of judicial law-making?

2 It may be useful to think about a decision like *Salomon* in terms of the allocation of the social costs of entrepreneurial activity. What do you think might have been the effect of a decision that Aron Salomon was not entitled to recover on his debentures? Is it possible to construct a legal regime that simultaneously encourages entrepreneurial activity and curbs its excesses? How might such a regime be structured?

Now you see it; now you don't: The dance of the corporate veil

In the rest of this chapter, we are going to explore the various legislative and judge-made exceptions to the corporate veil. As we consider the statutory provisions and the case law in this area, it is useful to keep the capital-boundary problem in mind and to consider the various legal developments as attempts to respond to some of its consequences.

Statutory exceptions to the corporate veil

The relevance of the capital-boundary problem to the 'group accounts' provisions of the Corporation Law is clear. These provisions are also the most obvious of the statutory exceptions to the corporate veil. Section 395 of the Corporations Law requires the directors of a holding company to present 'group accounts' at the end of each financial year. These accounts deal with the profit and loss of the group as a whole and the overall state of its affairs, thus enabling a 'true and fair view' of the financial affairs of the holding company. Of course, while s. 395 requires the presentation of 'group accounts', and the information therein is undoubtedly important to financial analysts and others, the financial health of the group as a whole is little comfort to the disappointed creditor of an individual subsidiary.

A number of other provisions in the Corporations Law also have the effect of lifting the corporate veil. These include s. 196 (which removes limited liability where the company carries on business with less than the statutory number of members and has done so for more than 6 months) and s. 219 (which provides that, where a natural person signs a public document or negotiable instrument on behalf of a company, the full name of the company must be included). Section 219(7) provides that, if the company fails to honour the instrument, the person signing is liable. For the most part, these provisions address issues of form rather than substance and are, for that reason, of relatively limited impact.

Taxation law occupies an anomalous position, both statutory and common-law exceptions being relatively commonplace.[29] While the corporate veil may fairly be

---

29 S. Gates, 'Disregarding the Corporate Entity in Favour of Beneficial Ownership and Control' (1983) 12 *Australian Business Law Review* 162 ff discusses the statutory exceptions in the taxation context. At common law as well, the Federal Commissioner of Taxation has traditionally occupied a favourable position. See *Federal Commissioner of Taxation v. Whitford's Beach* (1982) 39 ALR 521.

characterised as 'permeable' when subjected to the gaze of the Federal Commissioner for Taxation, we believe that this has far more to do with the relationship between the Crown and the subject (be that subject a natural person or a corporate person) than with the doctrinal vagaries of corporate law.

Reckless trading: s. 588G–Z

Undoubtedly the most important and far-reaching of the statutory exceptions to the corporate veil are those contained in s. 588G–588Z of the Corporations Law. While s. 588G is parallel to the older s. 592 in a number of its provisions, it is substantially more potent than the earlier provision in that it imposes a statutory duty upon directors to prevent insolvent trading by any company that they manage. This provision is far-reaching in its scope and a departure from tradition in its willingness to impose a positive duty to prevent insolvent trading. A director who fails to comply with this duty may be liable both to a civil penalty and to pay compensation to the company. A creditor who suffers loss as a consequence of a breach of s. 588G may sue the director for the loss suffered. Liability arises where the company has either incurred a debt while insolvent or has been pushed into insolvency by the acquisition of such a debt (where there were reasonable grounds for *suspecting* insolvency) and the company is being wound up. The provision applies only to debts incurred on or after 23 June 1993.

A similar but narrower provision—s. 592—applies where the debt was incurred before 23 June 1993. Provisions such as these are commonly known as reckless- or fraudulent-trading provisions and are aimed at curbing the activities of those who use the corporate form for reckless or unwise business ventures. The present section confers a personal right of action upon both a creditor[30] and a liquidator. In this respect it is broader than its predecessor, which did not provide for recovery by a liquidator.[31]

While these provisions are wide-ranging in their scope, like their predecessor, they place a number of pitfalls in the path of a potential litigant. The most significant of these pitfalls are associated with technicalities in the insolvency rules. The trigger for the operation of the section is whether the errant director or directors failed to ensure that the company did not trade while insolvent, meaning, according to s. 95A, that it did not trade when it was 'unable to pay all its debts, as and when they fall due'. The test is not a balance-sheet test. Rather, it is concerned with liquidity. A company may (at least on paper) have more assets than liabilities, but be unable to pay its debts as and when they fall due. Difficulty arises at least in part because of the necessity to establish that the company was insolvent at the precise point in time when the debt was incurred.[32]

Other issues that may arise in this context involve the director's state of mind. The relevant statutory provision, s. 588G, offers two alternatives. Either the director must have been aware when debt was incurred that reasonable grounds for suspecting

---

30 *Watt & Anor v. 3M Australia Pty Ltd* (1984) 9 ACLR 524.

31 *Ross McConnel Kitchen & Co. Pty Ltd v. Ross & Ors* (1985) 9 ACLR 533.

32 It should be emphasised that this is an extremely formalistic enterprise, which has, in the past, served to prolong litigation and vastly increase the expense involved in determining evidentiary questions.

insolvency existed, or the situation must have been such that a reasonable person in the position of the director would have been aware that reasonable grounds for suspecting insolvency existed. Both those who are actively involved in contravention of the provision and those who are simply 'involved' are caught by the section. According to para. 1229 of the Explanatory Memorandum,

> a court would be expected to look at two separate issues when considering whether the duty had been breached. The first matter would be what circumstances that particular company was in, including the size of the company, the provisions of its articles, the composition of its board and the distribution of work between the board and other officers. The second matter that a court would be expected to look at would be, in the light of the circumstances referred to, what would a reasonable person in the position of director normally be expected to do to ensure that he or she would be aware of any insolvency problem. In particular a court might expect the following:
> * that directors of a large company would ensure that among their number there should be one or more who are talented in the field of corporate financial management;
> * that directors of a large company should read, be able to understand and seek any necessary clarification of the key financial information put before the board, such as a balance sheet and a profit and loss statement;
> * that the board ensure that appropriately skilled people are engaged to carry out the company's accounting functions;
> * that the board would require relevant accounting information to be supplied ahead of regular board meetings at which key financial decisions are to be made, and that, where a significant borrowing is to be undertaken, the management should supply the board with a statement of the company's current financial position as well as the particulars of the way the principle, interest and other charges are to be serviced over the anticipated term of the loan;
> * that the board make arrangements for monitoring the use of any authorisation granted in relation to the use of the company seal, the entering into contracts with financiers or the signing of cheques and bills of exchange; and
> * where the nature of the business may expose the company to a high risk of sudden liquidity restriction, or the company is known by the director to be in a delicate financial position, that extra care and more rigorous safeguards may be adopted.[33]

Taken at face value, the reckless trading provisions represent a significant retreat from the immunity afforded directors by the corporate veil, an immunity bequeathed to us by *Salomon* and remarked upon by Lawton LJ in *Rolled Steel Products v. British Steel*. More significantly still, s. 588V also imposes liability upon holding companies for insolvent trading on the part of subsidiaries. This, we believe, constitutes recognition of the reality of corporate groups.[34] The section provides that a company contravenes s. 588V if:

* the company is a holding company at the time when the subsidiary incurs a debt;

---

33 Explanatory Memorandum to the Corporate Law Reform Bill 1992, para. 1229.

- the subsidiary is insolvent at that time, or the subsidiary becomes insolvent by incurring that debt or by incurring at that time debts including that debt;
- there are reasonable grounds at the time for suspecting that the subsidiary is insolvent or will become insolvent;
- either the holding company or one or more of its directors were aware of these grounds or, having regard to the nature and extent of the corporation's control over the subsidiary's affairs, it is reasonable to expect that a corporation in the holding company's circumstances would have been aware of those grounds or that one or more of the holding company's directors would have been aware of those grounds.[35]

Both in the case of individual directors and in the case of holding companies, the prospect of both civil and criminal liability and joint and several liability for the debt incurred emphasises the magnitude of the retreat in this particular area from the principles expounded in *Salomon*. Kirby P in *Metal Manufacturers Pty Ltd v. Lewis* noted:[36]

> Whether one likes it or not, judges it wise or unwise, sensible or foolish, parliament has provided that in certain circumstances creditors may recover debts from a person who was (relevantly) a director of a company in the circumstances there provided. The obvious purpose of the legislation is not only to provide a means of redress to creditors, lifting the veil of incorporation, where parliament has deemed it appropriate to do so, it is also aimed, by proper concern lest such proceedings subsequently be brought against the directors personally, to instil in them, during times of insolvency or economic difficulty in the corporation, to take particular care in the incurring of debts by the corporation with third parties.[37]

If Parliament has responded to the excesses of the 1980s by devising a set of (financial) circumstances in which the corporate veil ceases to be relevant, those circumstances are limited to circumstances of probable insolvency and, given the restrictive definition of subsidiary in s. 46, have significant limitations. Ian Ramsey has noted:

> This definition has manifest deficiencies. They became obvious during the collapse of the Adelaide Steamship group of companies in 1990–91. Before the collapse, Adelaide Steamship held just under 50 percent of the issued shares of several public companies, including David Jones Ltd. By insisting that these companies were not subsidiaries within

---

34 Having said this, however, we also believe that the provision simply does not go far enough. The classic pyramidal holding company–subsidiary relationship is only one possible structure for a corporate group. To make matters worse, s. 46 of the Corporations Law defines 'subsidiary' in restrictive terms, requiring either the ability to control the composition of the board of the subsidiary or to cast (or control the casting of) more than half of the votes that might be cast in a general meeting of the subsidiary, or the holding of more than half the issued share capital of the subsidiary. Because of this, it is easy enough to avoid the ambit of the provision by electing to adopt a different structure.

35 J. Gooley, *Corporations and Associations Law*, Butterworths, Sydney, 1995, p. 125.

36 (1988) 6 ACLC 725.

37 (1988) 6 ACLC 725 at 727–8.

the meaning of s. 46, the group was able to avoid the obligation to publish consolidated accounts and was also able to report higher levels of apparent profitability than might otherwise have been possible . . .

It is now possible to see why s. 588V presents obvious strategies for evasion. An 'Adsteam' type structure for a group of companies would not be classified as a holding company–subsidiary relationship and therefore would be outside the scope of s. 588V. Another possibility is the establishment of joint ventures to undertake particularly hazardous activities that may result in insolvency . . .

To the extent that restructuring of the way in which business activities are undertaken is a response to s. 588V, we return to Collins' capital boundary problem. As companies are able to determine freely the manner in which they conduct business (that is, whether they conduct business by way of a subsidiary, joint venture or some other means) they can also choose the limits of their legal responsibilities which can lead to evasion of legal rules such as s. 588V.[38]

The regulatory puzzle is further complicated by the fact that the courts have, on the whole, resisted pressure to lift the corporate veil except in compelling circumstances.[39] A further, more serious limitation lies in the fact that liability is restricted to the holding company in circumstances in which the holding company might well be described as the 'directing mind and will' of the corporation. The reality of corporate groups and the complex interrelationships through which their affairs are routinely structured thus continue to escape effective regulation. The continuing failure of the law to address adequately the reality of the 'corporate jellyfish' belies the fact that, as Anthea Nolan notes,

[t]he corporate group rather than its individual constituent entities is now the typical form of business organisation for all but the smallest private enterprises. Despite this, *group responsibility*, the idea that the group should be liable for the obligations of its constituent members, is a concept still virtually unknown to Australian insolvency law. Consequently, where a collection of nominally independent companies are managed as a single enterprise, creditors who happen to deal with the most viable entities in the group may be 'exceptionally astute, or simply unusually fortunate'.[40]

The former chief justice of the Supreme Court of New South Wales, Rogers CJ, has argued both in his judgments[41] and in scholarly writings[42] that current princi-

---

38 I. M. Ramsay, 'Holding Company Liability for the Debts of an Insolvent Subsidiary: A Law and Economics Perspective' (1994) 17 UNSWLJ 520 at 544–5.

39 Surely a part of what is going on here is the almost total lack of either doctrinal or theoretical paradigms for addressing an entity that is simultaneously individual and plural. The legal record in addressing the reality of, *inter alia*, families and pregnant women is not any better. The underlying mind-set is one that insists upon the reality of a stark division between singular and plural, and cannot admit of the possibility that 'entities' exist that are simultaneously singular and plural.

40 A. Nolan, 'The Position of Unsecured Creditors of Corporate Groups: Towards a Group Responsibility Solution which Gives Fairness and Equity a Role' (1993) 11 CSLJ 461 at 464.

41 *Qintex Australian Finance Ltd v. Schroders Australia Ltd* (1990) 3 ACSR 267; *Briggs v. James Hardie & Co. Pty Ltd* (1989) 7 ACLC 841.

42 Justice A. Rogers, 'Comments: Reforming the Law Relating to Limited Liability' (1993) 3(1) AJCL 136.

ples of limited liability, when combined with traditional notions of corporate personality, make a mockery of insolvency law. One can only add that, over time, the efforts of the courts to come to terms with these ideas have done them little credit.

Peek-a-boo, I see you: The corporate veil and the courts

Despite the fact that more than a hundred years have passed since Aron Salomon sold his business to himself, thus passing into legal history, and despite both academic and judicial criticism, the corporate veil has largely remained impenetrable. Generations of judges have contented themselves with criticising its consequences while refusing to do anything that might disturb it.

It is useful to separate out three distinct sets of circumstances in which issues concerning the corporate veil are likely to become critical. The first, and most obvious, set of circumstances is where the underlying issues revolve around corporate structures and corporate finances, particularly when insolvency is looming or when, as with litigation concerning asbestosis, tort claims are pending that may ultimately threaten insolvency.[43] Here, the connection between corporate veil issues and the capital-boundary problem is at its strongest. In these circumstances, the battle over the corporate veil is about whether the efforts of business to erect firewalls to isolate high-risk enterprises or to minimise potential negligence liability will succeed.

The second set of circumstances concerns the potential liability of the corporation, either in crime or in tort, in circumstances where it is necessary to make out a mental element to establish the cause of action.[44] Here, the capital-boundary problem is likely to be of only marginal relevance, if, indeed, it is relevant at all.[45] Problems in this area involve classic issues of corporate governance and corporate accountability. Here the court must look behind the veil if it is to ensoul the simulacrum, and the question becomes this: given that it is necessary for the corporation to have a 'directing mind and will', where is this mind and will to be found?

The third set of circumstances, which may be allied to either the first or the second, involves the conduct of directors and other corporate controllers. Here, typically, a breach of fiduciary duty is alleged. A representative scenario for this third type of circumstance involves the diversion of a corporate opportunity to another corporate person, frequently to another corporate person in which the responsible directors are majority shareholders.[46]

The impact of the 'reckless trading' provisions upon the corporate veil has already been noted. We now turn to the circumstances in which the courts will intervene in the absence of direction from the legislature to lift the corporate veil. While these are conventionally grouped into discrete doctrinal categories—agency,

---

43 Examples include *Qintex Australian Finance Ltd v. Schroders Australia Ltd* (1990) 3 ACSR 267; *Briggs v. James Hardie & Co. Pty Ltd* (1989) 7 ACLC 841; *Rolled Steel Products Ltd v. British Steel Corporation* [1985] 3 All ER 52.

44 See the discussion of corporate criminal liability in C. M. V. Clarkson, 'Kicking Corporate Bodies and Damning Their Souls' (1996) 59 *Modern Law Review* 557.

45 It will, of course, be highly relevant in tort cases where the facts suggest that high-risk activities have been 'quarantined' into an undercapitalised subsidiary, perhaps in one another jurisdiction.

46 A classic example, and one discussed later, is *Wallersteiner v. Moir* [1974] 1 WLR 991.

fraud, group enterprises, trusts, enemy, and taxation (and we will initially follow this tradition for convenience)—we are also interested in whether any clear pattern emerges that triggers the lifting of the corporate veil and whether, as we suspect, there are circumstances in which it is simply not relevant.

The agency gambit: Smith, Stone, & Knight and its progeny

On a number of occasions, British courts have seen fit to lift the corporate veil on agency grounds. In a number of cases this has occurred where failure to lift the veil would substantially disadvantage the corporation.[47] In the best known of these cases—*Smith, Stone, & Knight Ltd v. Birmingham Corporation*[48] and *DHN Food Distributors Ltd v. Tower Hamlets London Borough Council*[49]—the courts were confronted by corporate groups that had organised their business through subsidiaries that were, to all intents and purposes, indistinguishable from departments in a single firm.[50]

In the first of these cases, *Smith, Stone, & Knight Ltd v. Birmingham Corporation*, the company at the centre of the litigation, the Birmingham Waste Co. Ltd, was a wholly owned subsidiary of Smith, Stone, & Knight Ltd. The parent company had followed the commercial practice of setting up a 'distinct' corporate entity for each aspect of its business ventures. While, legally, each of these entities was a separate legal person, they were treated like departments and had, on the evidence, no separate staff, no separate books of account, and no real existence.[51] The Waste Company simply carried out one specific aspect of the holding company's business. When the local authority determined to resume the premises upon which the Waste Company carried out its business, its solicitors seized upon the doctrine of the corporate veil to deny the company compensation (for disturbance of business) to which it would otherwise have been entitled.

How did this curious structure come to exist? According to the facts, the company acquired a partnership business, incorporated it, and continued to run the business as before. The parent company held all but five shares. The remaining five shares were held by the directors of the subsidiary on trust for the company. The parent appointed the directors and took the profits. When the Birmingham Corporation compulsorily acquired the property of the subsidiary, the parent company sought compensation for removal and disturbance of business. Difficulties arose because the parent company owned the property upon which the business of the

---

47 Interestingly, this is the obverse of the capital-boundary problem. In these circumstances, the walls erected between the individual aspects of a single enterprise are being manipulated to disadvantage the corporation. In cases such as these, lifting the corporate veil protects the financial health of the corporate body, rather than serving to undermine the principles of limited liability.

48 [1939] 4 All ER 116.

49 [1976] 1 WLR 852.

50 It is worth emphasising that this is a common pattern of corporate organisation. In such 'corporate groups' the integration of the subsidiary into the parent is virtually total, and the subsidiary has no independent existence.

51 One assumes, however, that sufficient financial records were kept to enable each company to comply with audit and annual accounts requirements.

subsidiary was run, and the site was let at a nominal rental to the subsidiary. As a consequence of this, the Birmingham Corporation could, if it was allowed to use the doctrine as a shield, merely give notice and avoid compensation for disturbance of business. This would enable it to treat the Waste Company as simply a 'tenant at will' and thereby avoid paying compensation to the parent company, the company that, in reality, was carrying on the business. In giving judgment, Atkinson J set out six basic tests for agency in this context:

1   Were the profits the profits of the parent company?
2   Was the management appointed by the parent company?
3   Was the parent the head and brain of the trading venture?[52]
4   Did the parent govern the venture, decide what should be done and what capital embarked?
5   Were the profits made by the skill and direction of the parent?
6   Was the parent in constant and effectual control?

These tests may be summarised in one question: who was really carrying on the business? On the facts of *Smith*, all of these tests were met. As a consequence, the holding company was entitled to compensation for disturbance of business.[53]

The conceptual model upon which the courts relied in *Smith* and in its companion case, *DHN Food Distributors*, has not been adopted by Australian courts, which have generally taken a conservative approach to agency, despite much judicial lamentation about the undesirable consequences of the doctrine.[54] Young J suggested in *Pioneer Concrete Services Ltd v. Yelnah Pty Ltd*[55] that these cases should largely be confined to their own or similar facts and noted that 'merely to read the judgments in the DHN case gives one the impression that it is one of those "too hard" cases in which judges have, for policy reasons, justified the lifting of the corporate veil in that particular case rather than laying down any great new principle'.[56]

It may, however, be precisely because great new principle is possible, if only because of the almost infinite variability of corporate groups and of their structures, and because a profound hostility to any form of collective personality and

---

52   Again we note the prevalence of 'bodily' images: head and brain. We note as well the tendency of the judiciary to lapse into 'familial' rhetoric when discussing the relationship between the holding company and its subsidiary.

53   Two points are worth making in this context. First, although this case is generally cited as an example of a principal–agent relationship between parent and subsidiary, it would be more accurate to describe the subsidiary as a puppet and the parent as the puppeteer. The point of the judgment is that the subsidiary had no independent existence. The reason that the relationship in *Smith, Stone, & Knight* is described as agency is that the rhetoric of puppeteer and puppet is largely reserved for cases such as *Gilford Motor Co. Ltd v. Horne* [1933] Ch 935, where the corporate entity is being manipulated by its controller to enable the controller to escape an obligation to which it would otherwise be subject.

54   The high-water mark of this conservatism is represented by two early High Court cases: *Gorton v. Federal Commissioner of Taxation* (1965) 113 CLR 604; *Ascot Investments Pty Ltd v. Harper* (1981) 55 ALJR 233. It remains to be seen whether a more liberal approach overall is presaged by cases such as *Federal Commissioner of Taxation v. Whitford's Beach Pty Ltd* and *Australian Broadcasting Tribunal v. Bond* (1990) 94 ALR 11.

55   (1987) 5 ACLC 467.

56   (1987) 5 ACLC 467 at 475.

collective responsibility is deeply entrenched in our legal traditions. Damien Considine suggests:

> The expression 'corporate group' is itself an abstraction. It is a concept with definition only when applied. Even then, the generality of the expression is capable of almost infinite application. The usual meaning attributed to 'corporate group' is that of a number of corporations under common ownership and control. How far that meaning takes you depends upon which meaning you choose for 'ownership' or 'control' . . .
>
> The primary reason for the failure of the legal system to understand and effectively regulate corporate groups is the generality inherent in the expression 'corporate group'. It is an abstraction of enormous variety in its expression and application . . .
>
> Distinctions need to be drawn on the basis of, inter alia, the operational structure of each corporation within the group, on the financial relationship between the corporations, the level of dependency in relation to management, the vertical or horizontal position of an individual corporation within the group and the degree of centralisation and autonomy of decision-making. The permutations of group ownership and control are infinite, from 100% subsidiaries to groups where each corporation in the group holds shares in some or all the other corporations in the group, giving the appearance of a corporate group without the classic pyramidal structure . . .
>
> It is not the fact that a corporation owns or controls shares in another corporation or string of corporations which is, in itself, a cause of concern. Rather it is the opportunity for abuse which arises within a corporate group . . . The legal system has not yet recognised an entity larger than a single corporation. The courts have repeatedly stated that the shareholders of one corporation lack locus standi to bring suit against any other corporation.[57]

The ineptitude of the law in dealing with corporate groups is well illustrated by the New South Wales Court of Appeal and High Court decisions in *Hotel Terrigal Pty Ltd v. Latec Investments Ltd*.[58] The judgments at both levels are difficult and ambiguous, and no clear ratio emerges at either level. However, both courts were in agreement that the mortgagee had behaved improperly, both in failing to advertise the auction properly and in taking advantage of the conditions thereby created to arrange for the purchase of the subject property by its subsidiary company.

The facts of *Hotel Terrigal Pty Ltd v. Latec Investments Ltd* are simple and clear enough, if a little distasteful. When the Hotel Terrigal encountered difficulty in maintaining its mortgage repayments on the subject property, the mortgagee exercised its power of sale as, indeed, it was entitled to do. The circumstances surrounding the mortgagee auction were, to say the least, unusual. Little if any advertising had been undertaken, the pre-auction period being curtailed. As a consequence, the auction was almost entirely unattended. As, one presumes, had always been

---

57 D. Considine, 'The Mythology of Corporations and Corporate Groups' (1994) AJCL 215 at 222–3. The jurisprudentially minded will note the echoes of Robert Cover's luminous 'Supreme Court Foreword: Nomos and Narrative' (1983) 97 Harv LR 4. Cover speaks of the courts of the imperial state as 'jurispathic'—law-killing, hacking away at a thousand laws until only the one law of the imperial state remains.

58 [1969] 1 NSWLR 676 (CA); (1965) 113 CLR 265.

intended, the mortgagee then exercised its power by selling the subject property to a wholly owned subsidiary with a board identical to that of the parent company. It goes without saying that there was no 'bargaining at arms length'[59] and that no money ever 'changed hands'.[60] While both the New South Wales Court of Appeal and the High Court had no doubt that the corporate veil should be lifted, the basis for doing so was never entirely clear. Some passages in the judgments of both the Court of Appeal and the High Court suggest that the decision turned upon agency. If this is the case, the argument must be that the parent company acted as the agent of its wholly owned subsidiary in respect of the subsequent purchase, and that this was improper given its role as mortgagee.[61] While some aspects of the judgments apparently turned upon agency, we believe that it is more plausible to suggest that fraud was involved. In essence the mortgagee and the subsidiary sought, by virtue of a degree of legal subterfuge, to acquire a potentially valuable property at the value of the mortgage. The mortgagor thereby lost the opportunity to recoup any of its initial investment, a chance that could only have eventuated in the event of an open and competitive auction.

The ambivalence in the judgments and the lack of a clearly delineated ratio is typical of this area of the law. Despite the compelling nature of the facts, the court was clearly uncomfortable with the idea of tampering with 'corporate individuality' unless it could assimilate the events to some legally familiar doctrine by which the acts of one individual might be thought to have been directed by another individual.[62]

On other occasions, courts have been more reluctant to lift the corporate veil, even where agency arguments might have been thought relevant. One such case was *Harold Holdsworth and Co. (Wakefield) Ltd v. Caddies*.[63] In this case, the appellant had a contract of employment with Harold Holdsworth as its managing director. Because the board was not entirely satisfied with his services, it ordered him to confine his activities to one subsidiary. He subsequently sued for breach of contract. The court rejected the breach of contract argument based upon the corporate veil as being too technical.[64] In effect, the separate legal identities of the individual

---

59 When the traditional contractual metaphor of 'bargaining at arm's length' meets the surreal world of the 'corporate jellyfish', the resultant discontinuities can be hilarious. Similar discontinuities may be found in *Lee v. Lee's Air Farming Ltd* [1961] AC 12 and *Macaura v. Northern Assurance Co. Ltd* [1925] AC 619.

60 All that would have been required was a 'journal transfer'.

61 In these circumstances the identification of agency is puzzling and difficult, particularly since common sense suggests that the problem is that, save for the legal formality of registration, the subsidiary was simply a specific emanation of the parent.

62 Agency ought to be a legally comfortable ground. The common law long ago developed mechanisms to address the sort of 'acting for another' involved in agency arguments, and so, while agency arguments 'lift the veil', they do not dispute the individuality of the corporate entities. They simply insist that one corporate entity acted for another corporate entity or for one of the controllers of a corporate entity.

63 [1957] 1 WLR 352.

64 Why such an argument should be 'too technical' is puzzling. After all, courts encounter no difficulty at all in insisting that the corporate veil should remain firmly in place where shareholders or the liquidator of an insolvent group member have sought to disturb the corporate veil.

companies in the group were simply disregarded, as were the facts that the appellant had been hired to act as managing director of the entire group and that his relegation to one subsidiary constituted a substantial demotion.[65] In *Holdsworth*, as in *Smith, Stone & Knight* (and, as we shall soon see, in *DHN v. London Borough of Tower Hamlets*), the court was remarkably willing to lift the corporate veil where it was in the interests of the corporate group to do so and where it did not tamper with principles of limited liability.

Agency arguments were also invoked in *DHN v. London Borough of Tower Hamlets*. *DHN* was a resumption case, in which the facts were remarkably similar to those in *Smith* some 37 years before. In a sweeping, although not altogether lucid, judgment, Denning LJ treated a group of companies as if it were a partnership and also suggested that the three companies involved were to be treated as one person for the purposes of compensation for disturbance. The case is regarded as authoritative, but exactly what it is authority for is unclear. Some elements in the judgment suggest that agency was the ultimate ground, while other passages suggest that the doctrinal foundation was to be found in a contractual license that, following the (obscure and antiquated) New Zealand decision in *Plimmer v. Wellington*,[66] was irrevocable.

More recently, Australian courts have questioned the rationale behind treating cases such as *DHN* and *Smith, Stone, & Knight* as having precedential value. They have suggested that it is more appropriate to regard them as *sui generis* and to confine them to their own facts. In particular, we should note the comments of Young J in *Pioneer Concrete Services Ltd v. Yelnah Pty Ltd*:[67]

> A very different approach was taken by Rogers AJA, as he then was, in *Briggs v. James Hardie*, a 1989 case. The judgment of Rogers AJA is particularly good and gives an excellent overview of major decisions in this area. It warrants careful examination for this reason, and because of the remarks made by His Honour concerning the dearth of principles governing decision-making in that area.[68]

Lifting the corporate veil: What's a little fraud among friends?

The second major area where judicial lifting of the corporate veil has become commonplace is in cases of fraud or improper conduct. Here, at least where fraud is rel-

---

65 It is important that the court was not prepared to intervene in these circumstances. On one level, it almost seems as if the 'internal management' rule was simply applied to the corporate group, rather than to the individual. At a far deeper level, it is instructive to compare the problem confronting the court in *Holdsworth v. Caddies* with that in *Briggs v. James Hardie*. If one decontextualises them, the issues are identical. In both cases, an attempt was made to manipulate the corporate form to eradicate duties arising in very different contexts: in contract (in the former case) and in tort (in the later case). Why did the court in *Holdsworth v. Caddies* take the view that allowing arguments based upon the corporate veil would be excessively 'technical' where the effect of allowing those arguments would be to allow the managing director to defend his rights against the corporate group? Why was the position apparently different in *Briggs v. James Hardie*? The arguments raised by Hugh Collins in his discussion of the capital boundary problem are significant here. See Collins, at 736–8.

66 (1884) 9 AC 699.

67 (1987) 5 ACLC 467 at 475.

68 See the discussion of this case and the quotation from Rogers AJA on pp. 115–16.

atively clear-cut, the law is uncontentious. The leading authority in the area is *Gilford Motor Co. Ltd v. Horne*.[69] The defendant in the case had been employed by the plaintiff company for 6 years as managing director. His contract of employment contained a non-solicitation clause. The contract was determined consensually after 3 years. The defendant formed a private company to go into direct competition with the plaintiff and proceeded to solicit its clients. The court held that, because the company had been formed to enable him to breach his contract with impunity, its separate personality might safely be disregarded. Injunctions were issued to restrain both the defendant and his company and to enforce the non-solicitation clause. The precise language of the determination was unimportant. On one level, the company could have been described as the 'agent' of the defendant. On another, 'alter ego' seems more appropriate. Either way, it was his creature and, to the extent that it acted at all, it did his bidding.

Wallersteiner v. Moir[70] also dealt with the fraudulent and improper conduct of directors whose actions placed them in breach of their fiduciary duties to the company. Minority shareholders sought redress by means of a derivative action brought for the benefit of the company—an action under an exception to the rule in *Foss v. Harbottle*. The judgment of Lord Denning MR sets out in some detail the consequences of the doctrine of independent legal personality and the difficulties entailed in bringing an action on the company's behalf under one of the exceptions to the rule in *Foss v. Harbottle*.

The West Australian case of *Tate v. Freecorns*[71] is also interesting in this context given that its facts impinge upon the area known as equitable fraud. The facts involved a tort action for personal injury brought against the occupier of a grocery shop. The plaintiff had slipped on a damp area on the floor of the shop, which was inadequately signposted, and fractured her ankle. The occupier was clearly negligent. After the plaintiff contacted her solicitor, substantial correspondence was conducted with the defendant company, which the plaintiff believed, through advertisements and other promotions, to be the occupier of the premises where the accident occurred. While the defendant company denied that it was the occupier, it expressed on several occasions its willingness to negotiate the claim prior to issuance of a writ. When writs were finally issued and the matter came before the court, a claim against any other than the defendant was statute barred because of the effluxion of time.

At trial, evidence was given to establish that the shop was occupied not by the defendant but by a subsidiary of the defendant. The court held that the defendant was estopped by its conduct from denying that it was the occupier. Because it had, through expressing its willingness to negotiate the claim, encouraged the plaintiff to rely upon that willingness to her detriment (the appropriate cause of action having become statute barred), it was required to compensate her. If, however, as this

---

69 [1933] Ch 935.
70 [1974] 1 WLR 991.
71 [1972] WAR 204.

account suggests, the successful cause of action was predicated upon estoppel, the corporate veil becomes almost irrelevant. Estoppel finesses the question of the corporate veil altogether. It does not in any way depend upon the identity of the actual occupier and the relationship of the actual occupier with the defendant.

The court did, however, cite agency as an alternative ground. Here, some of its arguments are interesting and useful in coming to terms with the issues involved in this area. In dealing with the agency arguments, the court made it clear that agency was a question of fact, not law. Whether or not the relationship between the parent company and its subsidiary company was also the relationship of principal and agent fell to be determined according to the evidence led. That relationship, in turn, was largely governed by the formalities of adjectival rather than substantive law. It also means that the search for a principle to guide decision-making is, at least as far as this ground is concerned, a fruitless enterprise. While the status of the true occupier as a wholly owned subsidiary was relevant, it was not decisive. What was required was to examine the conduct of the parties and determine whether, in fact, the holding company acted as the agent of its subsidiary in the matter before the court. The issue was entirely evidentiary. If, ultimately, as *Tate v. Freecorns* insists, agency is simply a factual matter, agency arguments in these circumstances will always be difficult and fraught with ambiguity. We believe that the underlying issue is not truly one of agency, where one entity acts as an agent for one or more others, but the far more difficult and amorphous issue of an ambiguous identity. This problem will not and cannot be resolved unless the courts are willing to accept that, for some purposes at least, putatively separate organisms form part of a unified whole and act as one, and begin to grapple with the consequences of this understanding.

The Australian courts have characteristically displayed a more rigid and inflexible attitude than their counterparts in the United Kingdom and the USA. While a note of realism has crept into at least some judgments in recent cases dealing with the corporate fallout of the 1980s, the prevailing approach does not appear to have become more flexible.[72] Until this occurs, the corporate veil will continue to be lifted in cases of fraud or misleading conduct (as in *Tate v. Freecorns*), but application of the broad agency principles common in other jurisdictions seems unlikely to occur in Australia.

REVIEW QUESTIONS

1   Read *Briggs v. James Hardie* with great care. You might want to think back to the discussion of Johns-Manville's dealings in chapter 5 (see pp. 114–5). Why was the corporate veil an issue? This case exemplifies the degree to which a

---

72   *Pioneer Concrete Services Ltd v. Yelnah Pty Ltd* (1987) 5 ACLC 467 is an apt summary of prevailing judicial sentiment.

doctrine peculiar to company law may have a profound bearing upon litigation in other areas. You might also want to think about the utility of such arrangements from the corporate perspective.

2 Upon what grounds may the corporate veil be lifted by the courts in the United Kingdom? In Australia? In the USA? Do you think that the judge in *Pioneer Concrete* was correct in arguing that *Smith, Stone, & Knight* and similar decisions should be confined to their own facts?

3 Are the courts more willing to lift the corporate veil where doing so will benefit the corporation and where it does not pose any threat to limited liability? Can you think of any reasons why this should play a role in outcomes in this area?

4 Do any clear principles govern judicial decision-making in this area? If questions of agency are purely factual matters and therefore have as much to do with adjectival law as with substantive law, is increasing clarity likely?

5 Is legislative intervention warranted? If so, what issues should be taken into account? What abuses require addressing, and in what ways might it be appropriate to address them?

6 In this area of company law, as in a number of others, the case law is replete with judicial statements decrying the present state of the law and the abuses to which it lends itself. Frequently, judicial comments concerning such abuses are followed by decisions upholding a strict and formalistic approach to the case law, thus ensuring that the abuses noted will, once again, be ratified by the courts. Why is this the case?

Family matters and corporate veils: Money, money, who's got the money?
Incorporation has increasingly become the strategy of choice for wealthy families who wish to arrange their financial affairs so as to enable income-splitting and to minimise the incidence of taxation. This being the case, it is hardly surprising that, from time to time, the Family Court has attempted to lift the corporate veil and to undo the financial arrangements put in place by corporate structures. The following High Court decision—revolving, as it did, around an attempt to ensure that family assets could not be accessed to comply with a judgment of the Family Court—illustrates the difficulties faced by former spouses in attempting to access family assets to which they are entitled by order of the Family Court.

The increasing popularity of the private company as a tax-amelioration device and as a vehicle for the assets and business affairs of affluent families can pose serious problems upon the dissolution of marriage. The potential problems are exacerbated by the structure of the Australian Constitution. Because matters concerning property and property rights are matters that fall within the legislative powers of the several states, while family law falls within a Commonwealth head of power, jurisdictional issues play a substantial role when company meets Family Court. While the Corporations Law has rationalised the area somewhat, at least in terms of enforcement procedures and cross-vesting arrangements, the cross-jurisdictional issues have yet to be fully resolved.

The High Court decision in *Ascot Investments Pty Ltd v. Harper*[73] illustrates the complexities and the potential for abuse in the context of litigation before the Family Court. Upon dissolution of marriage, and following an investigation by the Family Court into the assets of the parties to the marriage, the former husband was ordered to pay a lump sum to the former wife. That sum was to be secured by the transfer of shares in Ascot Investments, the shares being transferred from the former husband to the former wife. The husband refused to comply with the court order and, as a consequence, the Master of the Court executed orders in respect of the transfer. These orders were also ignored.

The history and structure of the company were, to say the least, peculiar. Apparently, the company had been set up for the sole purpose of providing the husband with an 'appropriate' cash flow. The husband had no other assets and no other means of support. The former husband was managing director of the appellant company. There were three other directors, two being adult children of the marriage, and the final director being the husband's former secretary and his lover. The corporate articles gave the board the power to refuse to register a transfer of shares.

At the time that the High Court action commenced, the husband had already served two years in gaol for contempt of court. However, he remained obdurate, and no payment was forthcoming. A majority of the High Court held that the Family Court had erred in ordering registration of the transfer by the company. According to the majority in the High Court, the *Family Law Act 1975* could not apply to third parties (the 'third party' in this case being the corporation) so as to alter their rights.[74] It followed that the Family Court could only deal with the property of the parties to the marriage as it found that property. Where a corporate person was interposed between the property and the parties, the rights and obligations pertaining to the company were fixed by the general law and were a matter for the several states. The legal rights specified in the articles could not be overridden by an order of the Family Court. The High Court also stated that there was no evidence that the company was a sham or a mere alter ego.

In dissent, Murphy J argued that to allow a constitutional power to require transfer of property to be frustrated by the general law was to allow people to immunise themselves against the operation of the federal law. According to Murphy J, there was ample evidence that the husband exercised effective control over the company and that the court would be justified in treating the company as his instrument, particularly since the funds that the husband accessed from the company represented his only assets and his sole means of support. In addressing the particular arrangements in the case, His Honour commented:

> The evidence of his extensive financial dealings with the company justifies the inference that the company is his instrument. It can be inferred (particularly in light of his evasions

---

73 (1981) 55 ALJR 233.

74 See S. Parker, P. Parkinson, & J. Behrens, *Australian Family Law in Context*, Law Book Company, Sydney, 1994, p. 674.

and refusals to answer) that he was channelling from the company to himself through another company known as Parkvale, tens of thousands of dollars which he was spending on racehorses, gambling, travelling and other pursuits. In part of his evidence he referred to a 'pact' with Ascot Investments which:

> 'usually operates along the lines that when I want money I draw it from Ascot Investments. I do not have any other source of income that I can account for, and that is how it is done…'

In addition, there was the affidavit of a Miss Margaret McGregor, who at the time of the hearing was trustee of the shares for the two young children and had been Secretary and a director of the company for many years. The husband's dealings with her also justifies inferences of his control of the company. She was engaged by the husband to assist him in relation to 'his Company'… During that time the arrangements were that she would abide by the husband's directions. Although she was and is trustee of some of the children's shares, under the directions of the husband she breached her duties as trustee by paying into his accounts in the company dividends in respect of the children's shares as 'loans for educational purposes and the like' although there was no accounting to her about what payments were made on behalf of the children. This domination of the company secretary and directory over years and until recently, justifies the inference that the company tolerated the position that her duty was to obey him or obey him as if he were the company, and that he was in control of the company or that it was his alter ego.[75]

REVIEW QUESTIONS

1 What is the doctrine of the 'corporate veil'? To what extent is it appropriate to describe the doctrine as an example of judicial law-making gone mad?

2 Consider reforms that might eliminate the sort of abuses in *Ascot*. Is it appropriate to allow a historic example of judicial law-making to frustrate the clear will of Parliament in an area such as family law?

3 From a purely practical point of view, consider the advice that you might be called upon to provide to clients contemplating establishing a company to run a family business or manage family assets. What potential benefits does the doctrine provide? What potential hazards lurk to trap the unwary?

4 Consider the decision in *Ascot*. If you were called upon to advise a client who sought to establish a similar arrangement for a similar purpose, what ethical considerations, if any, might prove troublesome?

Despite the enactment of cross-vesting provisions in 1987[76] no real legal solution has yet emerged for the problem posed by *Ascot Investments*. The cross-vesting

---

75 (1981) 55 ALJR 233 at 241.

76 *Jurisdiction of Courts (Cross-vesting) Act 1987.*

provisions allow the transfer of proceedings between courts in the various Australian jurisdictions where, for example, the interests of justice so require. While it might be thought that this could alleviate the problems facing a litigant in the position of Ms Harper, the principle set out in *Ascot Investments* recently surfaced in *MJH v. Hannes*,[77] where the New South Wales Court of Appeal made use of it to reject an application to cross-vest a s. 260 Corporations Law dispute to the Family Court. The Court of Appeal deemed it preferable for the s. 260 dispute to be resolved in order that the Family Court should know what property actually belonged to each of the former spouses.[78] The corporate veil, it seems, continues to bewitch the courts, the 'rights' of corporate persons superseding, perhaps obliterating, those of natural persons. The legacy of *Salomon v. Salomon* has proved enduring, in the Family Court as elsewhere.

---

77 (1990) FLC 92–140.
78 The priority given to the determination of property rights is puzzling.

PART 3

THE CORPORATE STATE

8

A SHORT
CONSTITUTIONAL:
THE CORPORATE TEXTS

Introduction: Basic principles of construction

A substantial body of legal scholarship has grown up around the fundamental corporate documents: the memorandum of association and the articles of incorporation. Both the memorandum and articles have parallels in other areas of legal discourse—the memorandum traditionally recording the purposes for which the company was formed[1] (and thus paralleling the statute establishing a city or a university) and the articles setting out the rules by which it is to be governed. However, the rules of construction that have grown up around the corporate texts are subtly different from those used in other areas of the law. Many of these differences reflect the traditional deference of the courts to 'commercial realities' and, in particular, their apparent desire to ensure that their legal interpretation tracks the ordinary understandings of commercial men and women.

Two basic rules of construction apply to the constitutive documents of any company—that is, to the memorandum of association and the articles of incorporation. First, the memorandum is the superior document and prevails over the articles if there is any conflict or inconsistency between them. In many ways it may be described as the company's 'social contract'.[2] Second, while the articles contain the

---

1   The 'purposive' character of the corporate constitution refers back to corporate origins in chartered corporations of the Middle Ages. Corporate charters delineated the purposes for which corporate status was granted, and the *ultra vires* rule ensured that the activities of corporate persons were confined to those specified. For a complete discussion of the docrine and its consequences, see chapter 2, p. 47. See also H. A. J. Ford & R. P. Austin, *Principles of Corporation Law*, 7th edn, Butterworths, Sydney, 1995, ch. 12, pp. 479–501; P. Redmond, *Companies and Securities Law*, Law Book Company, Sydney, 1988, pp. 133–6.

2   A more conventional but less accurate parallel is to a parliamentary Act granting a charter to a university, a hospital, or a city. Such legislation invariably establishes the parameters within which its creature is free to act and delegates certain powers to the new entity, enabling it to enact subordinate legislation, for example. Traditionally, in the corporate context, the memorandum established the objects for which the company was established and the powers that it might exercise. While this is no longer required for the majority of corporate persons, the memorandum continues to be legally foundational and is required to set out the name (and more recently ACN) of the company and its capital structure.

rules by which corporate affairs are to be governed (and thus are akin to legislation), they are to be read as a commercial document, and the words are to be given their ordinary meaning to commercial men and women. The insistence that the articles be read as a commercial document means, in practice, that the courts will avoid a narrow and legalistic reading of individual articles where such a reading conflicts with the expectations that ordinary men and women of commerce are likely to have.

The operation of the first of these rules of construction is illustrated by *Angostura Bitters v. Kerr*.[3] A provision in the memorandum created a reserve fund for the benefit of shareholders. The articles of incorporation also included a provision, art. 119, which set aside a reserve fund for purposes to be determined at the discretion of the board. A reserve fund was duly established. When the board of directors sought to use the fund that it had established for art. 119 purposes, aggrieved shareholders brought action under a provision similar to s. 180 of the *Corporations Law 1990*. Because only one fund had been established, and because the memorandum was the superior document, the Court of Appeal presumed that the fund that had in fact been established had been established in accordance with the provision in the memorandum. On ordinary principles of construction, it followed that a fund that had been established in accordance with the provision in the memorandum was not available for art. 119 purposes.

The operation of the second of these rules of construction is illustrated by *Rayfield v. Hands*.[4] The articles provided that the directors would purchase the shares of members who wished to sell their shareholding. Article 11 was expressed in the following terms: 'members shall inform—directors will purchase'. The normal rules of construction applied to legal documents treat 'shall' as mandatory and 'will' as discretionary. If the provision had been interpreted in accordance with the normal rules of construction, members desiring to sell their shareholding would have been obliged to inform the board of their desire to sell, but the board would have had a discretion as to whether or not to purchase. The court held that the articles were to be read in the ordinary commercial sense rather than as a legal document.[5] It followed that they were to be read so as to validate the intent of the provision. Article 11 was construed so as to give it full effect, and the directors were required to purchase the shares of those members who desired to sell them.

Legally speaking: The nature of the memorandum and articles

As a matter of law, the memorandum and the articles are collectively deemed[6] to have the effect of a contract under seal between the members *inter se* and between

---

3   [1933] AC 550.

4   [1960] Ch 1.

5   Today this kind of interpretation is called a purposive interpretation and has become a commonplace of, *inter alia*, legislative interpretation.

6   Section 180 of the Corporations Law entrenches the common-law understandings in legislation. It is important to recognise that this provision replicates the common law rather than altering it.

the members and the company. The discourse of deeming is very interesting. It represents an open acknowledgment that the 'contract' represented by the memorandum and the articles is a legal fiction, a story the law tells about company structure. Because it is a fiction, a kind of selective disappearing act is possible. Sometimes provisions in the articles (for example, a right to vote in the general meeting) are treated as fully enforceable. At other times, the duties specified by the articles are said to be owed to the company, rather than to the members. When this occurs, the members cannot compel the directors to comply with the provision in question, despite its putative 'contractual force'. As a matter of law, therefore, nexus-of-contracts theory is given some statutory credence, although it may be thought to strain credulity to deem corporate documents a contract between natural persons and the artificial entity created by those documents.

The difficulty here parallels that in some forms of social-contract theory. It is very difficult to explain how an entity that is created by an agreement can be bound by the agreement that created it. The difficulty is a 'foundational' difficulty.[7]

Until 1985, the Australian legislation was awkwardly worded. It maintained the form of an 1844 deed of partnership, and thus disregarded altogether the separate legal personality of the company.[8] The new provision, s. 180, makes it clear that the contract is both between the members *inter se* and between each member and the company. In addition, the Australian provision deems the contract represented by the articles to be between the officers and the company. This addition, a significant substantive reform, may be of substantial significance in the case of a large public company where directors are not necessarily shareholders and where a professionalised managerial elite is in the process of emerging.[9]

A matter of construction: The corporate 'other'

The leading case on the construction of the articles is *Hickman v. Kent or Romney Marsh Sheepbreeders Association*.[10] This early common-law case established the proposition that the articles of association represented a contract between the company and its members. Astbury J asserted that '[a]n outsider to whom rights purport to be given by the Articles in his capacity as such outsider, whether he is or

---

7 This difficulty is characteristic of all forms of social-contract theory other than the Hobbesian. Once one commences to place limitations on the power of the institution created by the social contract, and to insist that those limitations are inherent in the contract itself, one is obliged to explain just how the Frankensteinian monster created by the contract is also controlled by it. The Hobbesian contract provides, of course, a simple alternative. Leviathan was created by contract, but Hobbes does not suggest that it is constrained by that contract.

8 The notion of the separate legal personality of the corporation, as a matter of legal doctrine, is a comparatively recent innovation. Until *Salomon v. Salomon & Co. Ltd* [1897] AC 22, company law, to the extent that there was an independent body of doctrine known as 'company law', was largely recognised for the untidy beast that it was, with doctrines borrowed from agency, from trust, and from contract jostling uneasily for precedence. *Salomon* marked the emergence of company law as a unique and discrete doctrinal entity, one that could and should be theorised about independently.

9 The equivalent provision in the 1961 Australian legislation (*Companies Act 1961*) is s. 62 and that in the comparable English legislation (*Companies Act 1948*) is s. 20. Both are useful for comparison because they highlight the origin of this particular aspect of corporate law in the law of partnership.

10 [1915] 1 Ch 881.

subsequently becomes a member, cannot sue on those Articles treating them as contracts between himself and the company to endorse those rights'. He subsequently emphasised that three principles might be derived from the case law:

> first, that no Article can constitute a contract between the company and a third person; secondly, that no right merely purporting to be given by an Article to a person, whether a member or not, in a capacity other than that of a member, as for instance, as solicitor, promoter, director, can be enforced against the company; and, thirdly, that Articles regulating the rights and obligations of the members generally as such do create rights and obligations between them and the company generally.[11]

In *Hickman v. Kent or Romney Marsh*, one of the provisions in the articles referred any dispute regarding them to arbitration. The English *Arbitration Act 1950*, which was in force at that time, required the written consent of the parties before arbitration. The question before the court was, therefore, whether the relevant article constituted the 'written consent of the parties'. The plaintiffs argued that the article in question amounted to a written agreement to submit to arbitration. This argument was upheld by the court. The case established the following propositions as a part of English common law:

1   Privity of contract applies, and therefore no article may be interpreted as a contract between the company and any third party.

2   The articles do not purport to grant rights to any person, whether a member or not, in any role other than that of member. Other such rights, such as a right to act as company solicitor, are not enforceable against the company. The rights granted by the articles are those of the members generally as members.

3   The articles regulate the rights and obligations both of the members *inter se* and between the members and the company. This last point was further elaborated in *Wood v. Odessa Waterworks Co.*[12] The court held that the company was bound by the articles in the same way and to the same extent as were the members. In *Wood v. Odessa Waterworks*, the board of directors resolved to allow the company to exceed its powers. At the suit of the members, the court granted an injunction to prohibit an act in excess of powers.

Traditionally the courts have given a restrictive interpretation to the s. 180 contract and its precursors,[13] seeking in general to confine the rights granted by the articles to those that can properly be termed proprietary rights. Because the courts have repeatedly held that, for rights to be enforceable, they must be attached to a share as an item of property, it has become important to dissect the rights allegedly granted by the articles to ascertain whether they contain the required proprietary core. A contractual remedy will be denied if it is possible to describe the relevant article as one that sets out the duties owed to the company (for example, by the directors). A

---

11   [1915] 1 Ch D 881 at 897, 900. The operation of privity of contract is interesting in this context.

12   (1889) 42 Ch D 636.

13   It is interesting that the courts have interpreted the s. 180 contract restrictively, given that the tendency in many federations has been for constitutions to be read very widely. The uneasy oscillation between the proprietary paradigm and the political paradigm is, undeniably, a part of the reason for this.

further level of complexity flows from the legal definition of a share as a 'chose in action', a bundle of legal rights and obligations that cannot be reduced to possession and that can only be enforced through legal action. An action under the s. 180 contract sometimes seems akin to a lottery. A plaintiff shareholder can only hope that the particular right that she or he seeks to enforce meets the currently applicable requirements for a proprietary right.

The arbitrary nature of some of the distinctions involved is illustrated by the House of Lords decision in *Prudential Assurance Co. Ltd v. Newman Industries Ltd (No. 2)*,[14] a case that we will examine at some length later. In *Prudential*, the plaintiff sought redress both under an exception to the rule in *Foss v. Harbottle*[15] and under the English equivalent of s. 180. The facts concerned an alleged breach of duty by the directors, which involved a failure on their part to disclose properly certain financial interests to the general meeting. While the articles required the directors to disclose the financial interests in question to the corporators in the general meeting (failure to do so constituting a breach of fiduciary duty on their part), the court held that the disclosure requirement spelt out a duty owed by the directors to the company. Because the duty that had allegedly been breached was owed to the company, and not to the shareholders *qua* shareholders, the company was the 'proper plaintiff' in any legal action seeking to enforce the provision. As a consequence, the individual shareholders were not entitled to avail themselves of s. 20, the English equivalent of s. 180, in order to invalidate the transaction in question. Specifically, the court expressed its vigorous disapproval of an action that sought to use s. 20 (being the English equivalent of s. 180) as a means of evading the operation of the rule in *Foss v. Harbottle*, also known as the 'proper plaintiff' rule.

This approach reflects a fundamental tension in company law generally. Some writers, among them David Wishart,[16] have suggested that the conflict can be resolved only if we abandon the legal fiction that the articles are contractual. Basically, the legal perception that the rights attached to shareholding are proprietary rights is in conflict with the idea of freedom of contract and, indeed, with our understandings of how contract works more generally. Proprietary analysis suggests that the only rights that can emanate from share-ownership are those that somehow track the nature of a share as an item of property. Freedom of contract suggests that the parties to any contract may incorporate any terms they so desire, provided that these do not bring them into conflict with the general law and that, so long as this criterion is met, the content of the provision is irrelevant to its enforcement. It also suggests that the parties involved are fully bound by each and every term. In general, it may be said that the approach of the courts reflects their desire to treat the share as an item of property and to limit the effect of the articles accordingly.

---

14 [1982] Ch 204.

15 See chapter 2, p. 36–7, fn. 46 for an explanation of the rule in *Foss v. Harbottle*. There are exceptions to the operation of this rule, which allow shareholders to bring what is called a derivative action in certain circumstances. The nature and operation of those exceptions will be the subject of the next chapter.

16 D. Wishart, *Company Law in Context*, Oxford University Press, Auckland, 1995. The overall incoherence between the legal regime purporting to regulate the activities of corporate persons and the contractual paradigm is remarkable.

One way of reconciling these apparently competitive paradigms is to acknowledge that it is often appropriate to describe the internal affairs of the company in political terms. According to this approach—one that we find attractive—the corporators are treated as equivalent to citizens, the board of directors as equivalent to an elected government, and the articles as equivalent to the constitution in a constitutional democracy. On this interpretation, it becomes obvious that some provisions specify the rights of individual citizens and others the obligations of elected officials to the State, while still others might be termed procedural or mechanical, expressing appropriate ways of accomplishing desired goals. A political approach emphasises that it is essential to examine the relevant provision and determine its actual function rather than to proceed blindly upon either contractual or proprietary analogues.

While a political analysis most clearly captures the legal complexities of the corporate constitution, the image of the active investor upon which this analysis (and the legal account of corporate governance) is predicated has become dated. Today, an increasing number of large investors, in Australia as elsewhere, are institutional. A substantial majority of non-institutional investors are passive investors, often holding their shares in 'street names' and wholly uninvolved in issues concerning corporate governance. If, in an unoccupied moment, the literature forwarded to them by their brokerage houses attracts their attention, that attention is likely to be limited to completing a proxy form or to indicating a desire to claim a share in the proceeds of a class action suit. The model of shareholders as owners, and specifically as owners within a paradigm of active proprietorship and control, is, today, purely fictive.

Despite this fictive quality, there are real advantages to pursuing a political analysis. A political analysis highlights the tension between a legal model of corporate governance (which mimics many, perhaps most, of the central features of the democratic nation state of late modernity)[17] and a practical reality in which many shareholders are simply passive investors whose shares are held in 'street names' to facilitate easy and rapid transfer.[18] Further complications arise because existing legal regimes are responsible for the regulation of a smorgasbord of different entities. Mostly these regimes are undifferentiated, making the minimal possible distinction between the family company and the multinational. Regulatory targets range from a thinly disguised sole proprietorship at one extreme to the parent company of a modern multinational at the other. It is, *inter alia*, this lack of differentiation in

---

17 It is sometimes thought that tying voting rights to shares rather than to shareholders militates against the coherence of this account. However, the history of property qualifications in both the United Kingdom and Australia reveals that it was not unusual for electors to be entitled to vote in each electorate in which they held property and that votes were essentially attached to landholdings rather than to individuals.

18 Passive investors do not participate in corporate governance, even to the minimal extent suggested by proxy voting. On the other hand, working from within a political paradigm, this may not be unduly bothersome. After all, where voting is not compulsory, as in the USA, voter turnouts are often disappointingly low. Where voting is compulsory, as in Australia, the so-called 'donkey vote' is often a matter of concern. Perhaps passive investors and passive citizens have more in common than one might think.

regulatory regimes that permits the curious hybrid forms that proliferated in Australia in the 1980s. Perhaps the best known of these was Dallhold (Holdings) Pty Ltd, the Bond family company that was the ultimate controller of the pyramid of public and private companies comprising the former Bond corporate empire.

Because of the historicity of law, its bondage to the past, contemporary legal regimes continue to bear the scars of their origins. The Anglo-Australian model is an awkward hybrid of trust, agency, and contract law, cobbled together by business people and barristers to enable English investors and entrepreneurs to compete with those in the USA, where a 'right' to incorporate had become institutionalised. The 'fetishisation' of property, a *leitmotiv* of the common law, took on a new (and potentially disturbing) role as lawyers and judges struggled valiantly to determine the nature and parameters of the 'property' of which the share certificate was the visible symbol. While the law had long been accustomed to dealing with intangibles, traditional legal resources were fragmented by repeated attempts to delineate the proprietary rights acquired through share-ownership.[19] The processes involved are worth looking at, both because of what they tell us about the ways in which the common law understands the property symbolised by the share certificate and because of what they tell us about the liberal understanding of rights as a peculiar form of intangible property.

Voting and property: Voting as property

The most firmly established and unquestioned of the 'proprietary rights' attached to a share is the right to vote. Because the right to vote in meetings of the company has long been recognised by the courts as the fundamental 'proprietary' right pertaining to an individual share, the common law has been extremely reluctant to limit the way in which this right may be exercised. That is, ownership of a share that carries with it a right to vote in general meeting has conventionally entailed an obligation on the part of company to allow individual shareholders to exercise this right in any way they see fit.[20] The seminal[21] decision in *Pender v. Lushington*[22] held that

---

19 The recent High Court decision in *Gambotto v. WCP Ltd* (1995) 16 ACSR 1 suggests that these problems remain with us. See, *inter alia*, M. J. Whincop, 'Gambotto v. WCP Ltd: An Economic Analysis of Alterations to Articles and Expropriation Articles' (1995) 23 ABLR 276.

20 The only exception is where the use made of the vote constitutes a 'fraud on a power'. According to the case law, the doctrine known as a 'fraud on a power' (or 'abuse of voting power') curtails use that may be made of the right to vote where its use is 'a means of securing some personal or particular gain, whether pecuniary or otherwise, which does not fairly arise out of the subjects dealt with by the power and is outside and even inconsistent with the contemplated objects of the power': *Peter's American Delicacy Co. Ltd v. Heath* (1939) 61 CLR 457 at 511 per Dixon J. See also *Crumption v. Morrine Hall Pty Ltd* [1965] NSWR 240, *Clemens v. Clemens Bros Ltd* [1976] 2 All ER 268, *Dutton v. Gorton* (1916) 23 CLR 362. A useful way of understanding the constellation of ideas involved is to use a two-stage approach. In the first stage, the court asks itself whether the decision is such that a reasonable person could, viewing it objectively, believe that it was for the good of the company as a whole. In the second stage, the court asks itself whether the decision was made for that reason or whether there was some other supervening purpose that might render it improper.

21 The use of 'seminal' is deliberate and provocative, not conventional!

22 (1887) 6 Ch D 70.

shareholders may exercise their right to vote in accord with their own self-interest, the motives and purposes behind individual votes being legally irrelevant.[23] The Master of the Rolls, Jessel MR, put the matter thus:

> [I]f these shareholders have a right of property then I think all the arguments which have been addressed to me as to the motives which induced them to exercise it are entirely beside the question … [A] man may be actuated in giving his vote by interests entirely adverse to the interest of the company as a whole. He may think it more for his particular interest that a certain course be taken which may be in the opinion of others adverse to the interests of the company as a whole, but he cannot be restrained from giving his vote in what way he pleases because he is influenced by that motive. There is, if I may say so, no obligation on a shareholder of a company to give his vote merely with a view to what other persons may consider the interests of the company at large. He has a right, if he thinks fit, to give his vote from motives or promptings of what he considers his own individual interest.[24]

While the scope of this understanding of the meaning of ownership has been curtailed somewhat by the equitable principle of abuse of voting power, its lure remains strong. It is, of course, a manifestation of deeply held beliefs about property, about ownership, and about the traditional deference of the common law to proprietary rights and interests. Motive becomes relevant only where the malice of the shareholder collides with the fiduciary obligation binding that same individual as a director (for instance, where a director shareholder is voting as a member of the board of directors). Here, very different rules apply. At this point the conflict between the proprietary right (the exercise of which is unaffected by the malice of the owner) and the equitable fiduciary duty (which binds the director to exercise his vote in the best interests of the company) becomes stark.

Northwest Transportation Co. Ltd v. Beatty[25] illustrates some of the potential complexities and ambiguities that may arise. On the facts, a contract that was both fair and *intra vires* in its terms had been entered by the directors and one of their number as vendor. As is conventional in such circumstances, the vendor-director was required to make full disclosure of his interest to an independent board. Because full and appropriate disclosure had not been made, the company was entitled to avoid the contract if it saw fit. To cure the irregularity and to ensure that the contract was legally enforceable, the board of directors sought ratification of the transaction by the general meeting. The vendor, who was also the majority shareholder, voted in favour of ratification. Despite the apparent impropriety of allowing the vendor to

---

23 It seems likely that courts, in Australia at least, would now be willing to revisit this issue. While the decision in *Pender v. Lushington* resonates awkwardly with the contemporary conscience and with ideas of corporate morality and corporate citizenship, it is entirely consonant with other decisions made during the heyday of legal formalism. Useful comparisons can be made with both *Mogul Steamship Co. Ltd v. McGregor Gow & Co.* (1889) 23 QBD 598 and *Mayor of Bradford v. Pickles* [1895] AC 587 (HL).

24 (1887) 6 Ch D 70 at 75–6.

25 [1938] Ch 708.

vote to expunge his own wrongdoing, the vendor was held to be entitled to exercise his voting right in the general meeting to ratify the contract. While the court acknowledged that he carried a majority of votes in the general meeting, this did not make his vote oppressive, since he was entitled, by definition, to exercise his property rights in any way he saw fit.[26]

Northwest Transportation Co. v. Beatty tacitly established a further principle, which continues to haunt company law: the principle that the court is not to involve itself in the 'internal affairs' of the company, particularly where the affairs under consideration might be thought to involve a matter of commercial judgment. The House of Lords alluded to the possibility of tension between the fiduciary principles governing the conduct of an individual as a director and the total absence of any such principles governing the conduct of the same individual as shareholder. It noted that:

> it would be very undesirable even to appear to relax the rules relating to dealings between trustees and their beneficiaries; on the other hand great confusion would be introduced in to the affairs of joint stock companies if the circumstances of shareholders, voting in that character at general meetings, were to be examined, and their votes practically nullified, if they also stood in some fiduciary relation to the company.[27]

Subsequent courts have interpreted this limitation upon their jurisdiction as having sufficient potency to bar intervention by the courts in any matter that might be thought to require the exercise of commercial or business judgment. Recent cases may have weakened the hard line adopted in this case somewhat, and some members of the judiciary (notably Vinelott J. in the first-instance decision in *Prudential Assurance Co. Ltd v. Newman Industries Ltd*) would be prepared to disallow the votes of an errant director.[28]

Legislative exceptions have also weakened the absolute force of the rule. Section 197 provides that, in class meetings, those voting must consider class interests and not their private interests as individual shareholders. Such a provision becomes extremely important where, for example, a majority of preference shareholders hold both preference and ordinary shares, and the proposal may advantage ordinary shareholders at the expense of preference shareholders. If preference shareholders were to be allowed to vote according to their individual interests as opposed to class interests, a vote in the class meeting might, in fact, defeat the interests of the class as

---

26 The uneasy relationship between 'voting as property' and oppression is worth thinking about. It is also interesting to ponder the question of exactly what would count as 'oppressive' under this definition.

27 *Northwest Transportation v. Beatty* (1887) 12 AC 589 at 600.

28 It is significant that, in recent years, the legislature, the ASC, and the ASX have abrogated the principle in *Northwest Transportation v. Beatty* (1887) 12 AC 589 in a number of ways that operate to exclude the proponents of a shareholder resolution and their associates from voting in certain contexts. The relevant provisions include ss. 623, 243ZF, and 206JA of the Corporations Law. ASC Practice Note 29 is also relevant, as are the following ASX Listing Rules: 3J(3), 3E(a)(a), and 3E(6)(e). While these developments have, to date, largely operated in especially sensitive contexts (such as takeovers, selective buy-back schemes, and reduction of capital), the principle underlying them seems to be gaining in prominence.

such. Put another way, were preference shareholders allowed to pursue their private interests in a class meeting in circumstances where a majority of preference shareholders also held ordinary shares, the interests of those shareholders who did not hold preference shares would never be considered.[29]

The Australian courts have generally been zealous in their preservation of class rights. Surely part of the underlying rationale for this is that, while the 'simple' model of voting as a proprietary right is sometimes *almost* plausible where minority interests are not affected, the potential for 'confusion' or 'commingling' of interests is far greater where structurally different classes of shares are involved. Some of these share classes—for example, cumulative preference shares—are structurally more akin to debt than they are to equity, a fact that goes some way towards explaining why, under most configurations, only ordinary shares are entitled to a vote in general meeting. Unless preference shareholders are required to give priority to the requirements of their class when voting in class meeting, there will be no avenue for the expression of interests that are peculiar to one type of shareholding, and the majority *pro tem* will be able to alter the rights attached to those shares without any impediment.

Further protection for minority interests is statutorily entrenched though sections such as 260 and 460–1, although, as we shall see subsequently, these have been restrictively interpreted. The judiciary has also modified its hard line approach somewhat and allows equitable considerations to supervene in appropriate circumstances.

Clemens v. Clemens Bros [30] is an excellent example of judicial flexibility. The case involved a family company in which the plaintiff held 45 per cent of the issued capital and her aunt held 55 per cent. Each held 100 preference shares. Of 1800 ordinary shares, the plaintiff held 800 and her aunt held 1000. The aunt was one of four directors; the plaintiff was not a director. The directors proposed to increase share capital from £2000 to £3650 by issuing 1650 voting shares. Each of the directors (except for the aunt) were to receive 200 shares, and the balance was to be held by the directors on trust for the employees of the company. Effectively, this move would have reduced the plaintiff's shareholding to 25 per cent of the issued shares. The reduction in her voting power would have entirely destroyed the plaintiff's sole power base within the company: her power to block a special resolution. The case was further complicated by the fact that, for the past 3 years, the directors' emoluments had exceeded the net pre-tax profits, and as a consequence, the plaintiff was persisting with enquiries into company affairs. The court held that the aunt's right to exercise her majority voting power was not unlimited. It could only be exercised subject to equitable constraints:

---

29 Something else is at work here. If class meetings are 'about' anything, they are about granting a voice to particular bundles of rights and interests. It has often been commented that cumulative preference shares, for example, are far more akin to debt than to equity. Where the company is about to embark on a course of action that alters the rights attached to such shares, it is essential that those interests be expressed. If they are not, the ordinary principles of majority rule would deny them expression and would make such shares untenable as an investment proposition.

30 [1976] 2 All ER 268.

But I cannot escape the conclusion that the resolutions have been framed so as to put into the hands of Miss Clemens and her fellow directors complete control of the company and to deprive the plaintiff of her existing rights as a shareholder with more than 25 percent of the votes and greatly reduce her rights under art. 6. They are specifically and carefully designed to ensure not only that the plaintiff can never get control of the company but to deprive her of what has been called her negative control. Whether I say that these proposals are oppressive to the plaintiff or that no one could honestly believe that they are for her benefit matters not. A court of equity will in my judgment regard these considerations as sufficient to prevent the consequences arising from Miss Clemens using her legal right to vote in the way that she has and it would be right for a court of equity to prevent such consequences taking effect.[31]

While this case involved special circumstances, in that it involved a family company and minority rights dominated the reasoning, it does indicate judicial willingness to limit the purposes for which voting rights may be exercised. In essence, the court found that the aunt's primary purpose was to ensure that her niece had no power to block a special resolution. That was not a purpose consistent with the nature of a shareholding. A private vendetta is not a corporate purpose. Using the vote to conduct a personal vendetta could properly be described as a fraud on a power or an abuse of power.

The 'Cheshire cat' contract: Section 180 oddities

The terms of the contract in the articles must always be read subject to the provisions of the legislation, as the legal capacity of the company is always subject to the general law, including the Act. The s. 180 contract has other unique features. These features strengthen arguments that, while it is in some ways akin to a contract, it is not strictly and legally speaking a contract at all. A very useful recent case—which addresses the nature of the articles and canvasses alteration, rectification, class rights, the severability of invalid alterations, and unanimous consent—is *Simon v. HPM Industries*.[32] While only a first-instance decision[33] and not authoritative, it provides both a useful summary of prior case law and a sound discussion of the issues involved, and we shall return to it on several occasions in this chapter.

In general it may be said that rectification is unavailable, even where the terms of the articles fail to accord with the intent of the parties. This was established by *Scott v. Frank F. Scott (London) Ltd*.[34] Thus, in practice, the articles are treated as a contract under seal. There are several reasons for this. First, the articles are a public document. Second, the fact that they are registered with the Australian Securities Commission (ASC) means that the public is entitled both to inspect them and to rely upon their contents. Allowing rectification could potentially prejudice the

---

31 [1976] 2 All ER 268 at 282.

32 (1989) 7 ACLC 772.

33 *Simon* was upheld on appeal in *Herrman v. Simon* (1990) 8 ACLC 1094.

34 [1940] Ch 794.

interests of those who, in the past, relied upon the accuracy of the public record. In *Simon v. HPM Industries,* the court noted on this precise point that:

> The original Articles of association of a company do, in one sense, give effect to private agreements or intentions of the corporators. However, registration of the Articles is required, so that persons dealing with the company can ascertain what are the provisions regulating the affairs of the company. Furthermore, the statutory contract established by the Companies legislation is a contract binding the company, which was not a party to the original agreements or intentions. In those circumstances, it seems that as a matter of principle, a distinction can be drawn between Articles of association and the kinds of documents in relation to which the remedy of rectification is granted ... It might be thought that in a case where there has been a clear mistake, and where it could be shown that there was not risk of any prejudice to third parties who might have relied on the form of the Articles which was registered, the remedy of rectification should be given. However the cases to which I have referred are against this view, and I think I should follow them.[35]

The contract represented by the articles is made on alterable terms. According to s. 176, alteration requires a special resolution and thus a 75 per cent majority vote. The section further provides that a company has at all times the power to alter its articles subject only to the provisions of the legislation. This power may not be excluded, although s. 176, by subsections (2) and (3), provides that this power may be restricted by the memorandum. It reflects the fact that the membership of a company is likely to fluctuate. It is inherently unfair that members should be irrevocably bound by the decisions of former members. As noted earlier, in many ways, the company is like a political organisation, and members ought to remain free to revise the terms of their association whenever they consider it needful.

Predictably in this area of the law there are a number of competing images. We have suggested that lingering associative images are partly why corporate constitutive documents are inherently alterable. These hark back to the legal roots of the modern corporation in the chartered corporation, as exemplified by guilds and boroughs. The image is one of a genuinely consensual association in which decisions are made that ought to reflect the will of those eligible to participate in making them. Another, very different, set of images is relevant as well. In its movement towards modernity, a lasting *leitmotiv* of the common law has been its reluctance to permit the dead hand of the past to constrain present dealings with property. If constitutive documents are set in stone, the understandings and desires of prior generations constrain present dealings, creating additional inefficiencies and impeding dealings with property.

The inherent alterability of the articles is also illustrated by the decision in *Shuttleworth v. Cox Bros & Co. (Maidenhead) Ltd.*[36] The articles provided that the plain-

---

35 (1989) 7 ACLC 772 at 779.
36 [1927] 2 KB 9.

tiff and others were to be 'permanent directors'. The plaintiff was suspected of fiddling the accounts. While six grounds for dismissal had been provided, they did not cover the actions of the plaintiff, and a seventh ground was added by an extraordinary general meeting. The court upheld the plaintiff's dismissal, subject only to the common-law requirement that the alteration be bona fide for the benefit of the company as a whole. Likewise, in *DeVilliers v. Jacobstal Saltworks Ltd*,[37] alteration from time to time was held to be an implied term of the membership contract. On the facts, the plaintiff had been a director for life, and the alteration made him an ordinary director subject to dismissal by a majority vote in general meeting. As H. A. J. Ford & R. P. Austin correctly note:

> The fact that an alteration, complying with the Corporations Law and passed bona fide and not for purposes foreign to the company's operations, affairs and organisation, can disturb existing rights of a member is a sign that articles are not exactly the same as contractual provisions but have some of the characteristics of legislation. They are regulations for the government of a voluntary association of persons. Persons joining subject themselves to the power of a proportion of the total membership to alter in accordance with the constitution, the Corporations Law and the general law the terms of their relationship to each other and each one's relationship to the corporate entity.[38]

Other subtle distinctions play an important role in this area. Where, as is often the case, the articles purport to provide a benefit to a person appointed to serve the company (for example as its solicitor) and the articles are subsequently changed in a way that eliminates the benefit, question may arise as to whether a 'special contract' may have arisen between that person and the company with terms incorporating the relevant provisions in the articles. This can have substantial advantages for the affected individual, since such a contract can only be varied prospectively, while the rights and duties of members and officers can be varied both prospectively and retrospectively.[39] The basis for the distinction is that the articles are simultaneously constitutive and contractual. Because they are constitutive, they are necessarily made on alterable terms. Membership rights and duties are always subject to alteration by the appropriate majority vote. If, on the other hand, non-membership rights and duties become the subject matter of a 'special contract', they can be varied for the future, but not in a way that takes away rights that have previously accrued to that person.

Where the members seek to enforce rights using the s. 180 contract as such, this will only be possible where the rights in question are membership rights—the rights of members as members. The matter was considered at length in the High Court decision in *Heron v. Port Huon Fruitgrowers Assn*.[40] The case dealt with a

---

37 [1959] 3 SALR 873.

38 Ford & Austin, p. 181.

39 See, for example, *Swabey v. Port Darwin Gold Mining Authority* (1889) 1 Meg 385; *New South Wales Medical Defence Union v. Crawford* (1993) 11 ACSR 406.

40 (1922) 30 CLR 315.

farmers' cooperative, its objects being directed towards promoting the sale of the members' fruit. The articles provided that all shareholders, so long as they remained members, must sell their whole crop to the association. If any shareholder failed to do so, that shareholder was required to pay as liquidated damages a specified sum per pound. The articles further provided that shares might only be transferred to bona fide orchardists, and that the association retained the power to refuse to register any transfer. This last provision was deemed void at common law and in restraint of trade.

The High Court considered the nature and meaning of the membership contract at length and concluded that only those articles that were for the regulation of the company could constitute a contract *inter se*. According to the High Court, the provisions that were challenged dealt not with membership and company rights but with a relationship akin to that between an employer and an employee. Because they did not deal with the rights of members *qua* members they did not form part of the s. 180 contract. As Isaacs J put the matter, both concerning the nature of the 'contract' represented by the Articles and whether the provisions in question formed part of that 'contract':

> 'Deemed' indicates a fiction … No doubt such a word used in a contract would be binding on the man who used it, because it is a real contract. But in a document which is not a contract in the same sense, which is only indirectly a contract, and only so by force of other provisions which empower a majority to impose obligations, the case is different. We must then recognize that 'deemed' means to say that although there is no true contract in the ordinary sense, which imports the actual consent of all concerned, this regulation shall, and as so changed from time to time and notwithstanding the absence of consent and even against the will of the minority, be regarded as if they actually consented and so bargained … Having regard to the ambit of the business agency for marketing fruit, it is difficult to see how art. 7, in all its far reaching ramifications, can be said to be confined to a 'regulation for the company'. And it is only such a 'regulation' that can constitute a contract between the company and member as *such*.[41]

Further complications arise in circumstances in which managing directors or directors have separate and independent contracts of service with the company. Such situations were considered in both *Southern Foundries Ltd v. Shirlaw*[42] and *Schindler v. Northern Raincoat Co. Ltd*.[43] In both cases, the articles were altered before the expiry of the separate contracts of service, and the effect of the alteration was to render the plaintiffs ineligible to continue to serve as managing directors. In both, the court was of the view that that, while the companies were free to alter the articles at any time they chose, they were nonetheless liable to pay damages for breach of contract. In effect, although the articles could be altered in a way that

---

41 (1922) 30 CLR 315 at 340–1.

42 [1940] AC 701.

43 [1960] 2 All ER 239.

would place the company in breach of contract, the fact that this had been done could not nullify the legal consequences of breach of contract.[44]

Because s. 180 provides that the statutory contract extends to the officers of the company as well as to members, the position may be very different today from the situation in *Read v. Astoria Garage Pty Ltd*.[45] In that case, no service agreement existed, and the plaintiff's term of office as managing director was terminable without notice. The court held that the plaintiff's occupancy of the post of managing director was not a membership right, nor had it been incorporated in any 'special contract'. As a consequence, the plaintiff was not entitled to compensation for loss of office. While the concrete legal outcome would be different today (because the statutory contract protects officers of the company to the same extent as it does members), the problems and the fine (and the not always persuasive connection between rights that are conferred upon a member or officer as such and other rights) remain with us. The interpretive battle has shifted. The ways in which this distinction functions to render many of the provisions of the articles substantially unenforceable will be addressed later. For the moment it is sufficient to note that members will not be able to enforce any of the provisions contained in corporate articles using s. 180 unless the provision in question can be construed as one that confers rights and obligations upon the members in their role as members.

REVIEW QUESTIONS

1 What basic rules of construction apply to the memorandum and articles?

2 While the articles have been legislatively analogised to a contractual document, judicial interpretation in cases such as *Hickman v. Kent or Romney Marsh Sheepbreeders Association* has been restrictive. In what specific ways have the courts diverged from ordinary contractual principles in interpreting the articles, and what underlying tension does this reflect?

3 Considering the cases that you have read, what sort of rights may be construed as membership rights?

4 In the case of an ordinary contract, what is required if any term is to be altered? What implications does the fact that the articles are inherently alterable have for the analogy to contract?

5 What problem may the inherent alterability of the articles pose for individuals who may have been granted positions or privileges by the articles, and how should such individuals protect themselves?

---

44 This resolution provides a particularly interesting example of the interaction between corporate law and general law. While the constitutive documents of a company can be changed at will, subject only to the relevant majority being attained, this cannot be allowed to prejudice the rights of particular individuals, where those rights are given legally binding expression in the form of an independent contract. As we shall see, the position where no such contract exists is very different.

45 [1952] Ch 637.

Rights and wrongs: What rights are members' rights?

The rights pertaining to a shareholding are, as we have seen, most frequently described as proprietary in nature, yet this term is itself ambiguous. All of us know what property is (at least under our legal system), but very few of us have actually tried to give any systematic account of proprietary rights. It is hardly surprising, then, that some question arises as to those rights that may properly be termed 'proprietary rights'. Likewise, given the paradigm within which corporate law evolved, it is not surprising that the logic underlying the rubric of proprietary rights is hardly transparent. Among the rights that have been identified as proprietary rights are the right to have one's vote counted (*Pender v. Lushington*), the right to a cash dividend (*Wood v. Odessa Waterworks*), and the right to have the prescribed procedure for an election followed (*Papaivanoy v. Greek Orthodox Community*[46]). It is relatively easy to see why the right to a cash dividend (rather than a dividend in the form of, *inter alia*, preference shares) resonates with proprietary overtones. Linking the right to have one's vote counted or to having appropriate electoral procedures followed might seem to draw a much longer bow. On the other hand—and we believe that it is of critical importance in this context—the connection between voting rights and property has an ancient lineage.

Further problems arise from the historicity of the common law. Because these doctrines have evolved at common law, they represent discrete applications, which arose in response to particular factual situations rather than anything with a genuine claim to be a coherent body of declared principle. It seems likely that any contemporary common-law extension of these principles will be ad hoc and inconsistent. Scholars have drawn the distinction between membership rights (which may be enforced under s. 180) and 'outsider rights' (which are unenforceable) in various ways. The classic, sometimes called the narrow, position was that enunciated by Astbury J. in *Hickman v. Kent or Romney Marsh Sheepbreeders Association*:[47]

> An outsider to whom such rights purport to be given by the Articles in his capacity as such outsider, whether he is or subsequently becomes a member, cannot sue on those Articles treating them as contracts between himself and the company to enforce those rights … No right merely purporting to be given to a person, whether a member or not, in a capacity other than that of member, as, for instance solicitor, promoter, or director can be enforced against the company.

Yet, even this restrictive interpretation, as we have seen, did not prevent the terms set forth in the articles being tacitly incorporated into some other contract. Further, even the restrictive approach provides an avenue through which members may restrain some forms of corporate conduct and irregularities.

---

46 [1978] 3 ACLR 801.
47 [1915] 1 Ch 881.

Others, for example Lord Wedderburn,[48] take a much broader view of the s. 180 contract. Writing from a background both as a scholar and as one of England's great commercial judges, he argues in effect that an expansive view of the s. 180 contract is the natural reading. He argues first that, if the rights granted are in fact contractual, then a member should be able to bring a personal action (as opposed to one on behalf of the company under an exception to the rule in *Foss v. Harbottle*) to restrain any breach of the articles whatsoever. After all, it is of the essence of contract that everyone who is a party to a contract ought to be able to enforce it according to all of its terms. For Lord Wedderburn, that is inherent in the nature of contract. It follows that he favours an interpretation in which 'outsider rights' can be indirectly enforced. His interpretation is imbued with classical freedom-of-contract resonances.[49]

Despite the intellectual attraction that Lord Wedderburn's position has exercised and continues to exercise for some scholars, judicial support has been at best scant and inconsistent. Often it is unclear whether judicial reasoning that offers apparent support for the wide view has actually given the conceptual issues any real consideration, or whether judicial language apparently supporting it was wholly driven by pragmatic considerations.[50]

Some apparent judicial support for the 'wide position', as Lord Wedderburn's position is known, may be found in *Quin v. Axtens Ltd & Solomon*.[51] The articles provided that certain transactions could only be embarked upon with the consent of both managing directors. The company purported to enter such a contract, and a member, who was also one of the two managing directors, sought and obtained an injunction restraining the company from embarking upon the transaction in question. In granting the injunction, the court apparently enforced his right as a director.

An alternative interpretation is, however, also available. On this very much narrower and less contentious reading, *Quin v. Axtens Ltd v. Solomon* simply upholds the right of members to have the safeguards for directorial decision-making contained in the articles enforced to the letter. This is a much more moderate approach and one for which there is a degree of judicial support.[52] *Quin v. Axtens Ltd v. Solomon* is a particularly difficult case because of the degree to which the decision turns upon technical procedural details. Because, like many areas of company law, this area is one in which procedural correctness is critical, you will find it helpful to

---

48 K. W. Wedderburn, 'Shareholders' Rights and the Rule in *Foss v. Harbottle*' [1957] CLJ 194; [1958] CLJ 93. We find the wide view compelling.

49 More modern resonances may be found in the notion of the company as a 'nexus of contracts'. The gulf between Lord Wedderburn's classical contractual paradigm and its nexus of contracts sibling is another manifestation of the underlying tensions in corporate law. It is worth thinking about the ideological and conceptual gulf between these two discrete approaches and their very different implications for the legal regime.

50 See, for example, *Kraus v. J. G. Lloyd Pty Ltd* [1965] VR 232, where it was held that a member had the right to have the board of directors of a company properly constituted.

51 [1909] AC 442.

52 Australian support may be found in *Kraus v. J. G. Lloyd Pty Ltd* [1965] VR 232.

read it carefully and to consider whether, given that the director in question was also a member, the action was brought by him as director or as member.

Some additional modern support for the wide view may be found in *Re H. R. Harmer Ltd.*[53] Because the facts of *Re Harmer* involved a small family company, it is difficult to know whether the court simply seized upon the wide view as a useful rationale for its decision, or whether the decision establishes a useful precedent. Generalising from cases involving closely held companies[54] is always perilous. The judiciary is well aware of the difficulties involved in using one statutory and common-law regime to regulate the entitlements in very different entities. Family companies have often been treated as 'quasi-partnerships' because the judiciary is aware that the understandings upon which such companies operate are at variance with the legal regime that purports to govern them. As a consequence, the courts are prepared to consider the actual understandings of the members and the equities between them where this seems appropriate, rather than invariably having recourse to the full rigour of corporate law.

In *Re Harmer*, the board consisted of the father, who was governing director for life, and two sons, each of whom was a director for life. The father was chairman of the board and held a casting vote. He ran the business essentially as he pleased, disregarded the decisions of the board, and considered that he was entitled to do so because he had voting control of the general meeting. While he had originally run the business with skill and zest, and while he was responsible for its success, as he became older his managerial capacities declined. The court took note of the fact that his mental acuity was failing and that his actions tended to be capricious and irrational. The court held that his flagrant disregard for the appropriate procedures and corporate organs amounted to oppression, and that the members were entitled by the articles to have company affairs regulated by the appropriate organ as specified by the articles. Indirectly, therefore, the court was prepared to enforce the English equivalent of the s. 180 contract, although it is significant that it was enforced indirectly rather than directly. It may be that, in some circumstances, an action using the 'oppression remedy'[55] may provide redress where the s. 180 contract will not, although the success of such actions in Australia has varied.[56]

The English section invoked in this case, as with the pre-1984 position in Australia, referred to conduct oppressive to members. In Australia today the legislative bow is drawn much longer, although judicial decision-making has not necessarily taken these ideas on board. Where oppression is argued, it is critical to take note of s. 260(4A), (4B), and (4C), in which the term 'member' is deemed to refer to 'a person who is a member, whether in his capacity as a member or in any other capacity'.

---

53 [1958] 3 All ER 689.

54 Closely held companies include family companies and other private companies in which all of the shares are held by a very restricted number of individuals.

55 Corporations Law, s. 260.

56 A notable failure, and one that signals caution on this front, is the 1984 decision in *Re G. Jeffrey (Men's Store) Pty Ltd* (1984) ACLC 421. (See the discussion of this case in ch. 12 (pp. 320–1).

This provision amounts to statutory acknowledgment of the logic of the wide view and possibly defuses the entire argument where a case for oppression can be made out. In other circumstances, it is likely to be of limited assistance because of the court's traditional reluctance to intervene in commercial decision-making.

A final group of scholars, of whom G. D. Goldberg[57] is probably the best known, have attempted to occupy the middle ground and adopt a moderate position. Goldberg's preferred interpretation is close to the actual language in *Re Harmer*. On this approach, members are entitled to have company affairs conducted by the organ specified in the articles, even if enforcing this right indirectly enforces outsider rights.

An Australian case that tacitly adopted a position close to that advocated by Goldberg is *Kraus v. J. G. Lloyd Pty Ltd*. The facts involved a family feud and two family companies. When one of the two directors died, his widow complained that she was not given the right (granted by the articles) to put the appointment of a replacement to the general meeting. The wife of the other director asserted that she had been validly appointed a life director by her husband, and that this appointment took precedence over the right granted by the articles. The court allowed the widow's action and held that her membership rights were affected. Again, because family relationships and expectations were involved, the potential scope of this precedent is probably limited. As noted earlier, caution must always be exercised in extending precedents developed in the family-company setting to companies that are not closely held.

It is important to understand that both the wide and the moderate views require the action to be brought by a member who alleges that his or her rights as member have been interfered with.[58] Whichever view prevails, therefore, *Eley v. Positive Assurance Co. Ltd*[59] remains authoritative. In *Eley*, a solicitor advanced money to establish a company and was appointed permanent solicitor for life by the articles. At the time of his appointment, he was not a member, although he subsequently became a member. Some time later, the company employed additional solicitors, thus breaching his alleged right to transact all legal business. Eley brought his action as company solicitor, to defend his alleged right to be the sole company solicitor, and the action failed. The court held that the right alleged was not a membership right. Neither, it should be noted, would his position as permanent solicitor come within the general definition of officer so as to enable reliance upon a provision such as the present s. 180. Because Eley had not had the foresight to negotiate a separate service contract with the company, his action failed.

A similar problem arose in *Beatty v. Beatty Ltd*.[60] In *Beatty*, the articles contained an arbitration clause. The plaintiff managing director sought to invoke the arbitration

---

57 G. D. Goldberg, 'Article 80 of Table A of the Companies Act 1948' (1970) 33 MLR 177.

58 The same form is, of course, required where an officer of the company is alleging that her or his rights as an officer have been infringed under the present Australian legislation.

59 (1876) 1 Ex D 88.

60 [1938] Ch 708.

clause when alleging improper remuneration. He failed because the right that he sought to enforce pertained to him as a director, rather than as a member. The common-law position as set out in *Beatty* ought to be compared with the present s. 180, which expressly provides that the s. 180 contract is a contract between the company and each officer. The statutory acknowledgment that the contract runs between the company and each officer in her or his role as officer emphasises that corporate officers are entitled to enforce the provisions of the articles where those provisions explicitly grant them rights in their roles as officers. In this way, s. 180 significantly extends the common law, perhaps in tacit acknowledgment of the fact that many company directors today are not members.

In many of the cases where membership rights were successfully argued, the action took the representative form, being brought on behalf of the member and all other members.[61] The representative form highlights the relationship between the right claimed and membership as such. For this reason, it is probably the key to framing a successful action, and continued use of the representative format is likely to reinforce the modern trend towards a wider understanding of membership rights. As a practical matter, it is essential that any individual who is considering taking up a position with a company should, despite the legislative changes, negotiate a separate service contract. The presence of a provision in the articles that appears to cover the position is never sufficient protection. Because the 'contract' represented by the articles is alterable and protection cannot be successfully entrenched in it, a separate service contract is necessary to ensure the availability of damages if relationships sour and the articles are altered to remove previously entrenched rights.

Rights and obligations: The horizontal relationship between members

The articles govern the relationships of the members *inter se* as well as the relationship between the members and the company. This has been emphasised in numerous decisions. The decision in *Borland's Trustee v. Steel Bros*[62] provides an apt illustration of the way in which this works. The articles provided for the compulsory transfer of a member's shares in certain events (for example, bankruptcy). The articles specified that the member was to be paid a fair price as determined by the articles, and nominated the recipient of the shares. Borland's trustee in bankruptcy sought to evade the operation of the section because he believed that more could be obtained for the shares on the open market. The court held that a share could not be equated to a sum of money. Rather, the share represented the interest of the shareholder in the company, an interest comprising variable rights and liabilities, including in the present circumstances, a duty to transfer the shares in question and to receive a pre-determined sum upon their transfer. Because the trustee in bankruptcy stood in the shoes of the shareholder, he was bound by the rights and obligations that formed part of the property in the shares, exactly as the shareholder had been.

---

61 *Quin v. Axten & Solomon; Pender v. Lushington; Wood v. Odessa Waterworks;* and *Re Harmer Ltd* are useful examples.
62 [1901] 1 Ch 219.

Similarly, in *Rayfield v. Hands*,[63] the duty of the directors to purchase the shares of any member who desired to sell formed an integral part of the package of rights conferred by the shares.

The *inter se* character of the contract was also emphasised in *Peters' American Delicacy Co. Ltd v. Heath*,[64] the leading Australian High Court decision in this area. The facts concerned an alteration of articles and a consequential variation in class rights. In the leading judgment, that of Latham CJ, the High Court emphasised that the articles are a contract between the members concluded on variable terms and, importantly, a contract that recognises the possibility that certain rights may be altered or diminished. It followed that a member as member had no right to complain where such an alteration diminished his or her rights, so long as the action was not oppressive in nature and its bona fides were not in doubt. Both conditions were present on the facts before the High Court. It is important to note, however, that, had the action been oppressive within the language of s. 260 or had the decision not been taken in good faith, the outcome would have been different. Latham CJ set out the relevant principles in full, and this aspect of his judgment is worth reproducing here:

> (1) ... It is not possible, by Articles of association to make an unalterable article ... (2) It follows that the contract between members of the company and between the company and its members which is constituted by the articles must be regarded as containing among its terms a provision that Articles may be altered ... An alteration in a particular case may constitute a breach of contract with a shareholder, but such a breach of contract does not invalidate the resolution to alter the Articles. (3) It follows that where the rights of members of the company depend only upon the Articles it is possible to alter the rights of members or of some only of the members by altering the Articles. The fact that an alteration prejudices or diminishes some of the rights of the shareholders is not in itself a ground for attacking the validity of the alteration ... Any other view would, in effect, make unalterable and permanent any Article of association which conferred rights upon a class of shareholders, or possibly upon any shareholder, if they or he desired that those rights should continue to exist unchanged ... (4) The power to alter the Articles must be exercised bona fide ... (5) It is not for the court to impose upon a company the ideas of the court as to what is for the benefit of the company. It is for the shareholders to determine whether an alteration of the Articles is or is not for the benefit of the company, subject to the proviso that the decision is not such as no reasonable man could have reached ... (6) The benefit of the company as a corporation cannot be adopted as a criterion which is capable of solving all the problems in this branch of the law. An alteration which is made bona fide and for the benefit of the company, if otherwise within power will be good, but it is not the case that it is necessary that shareholders should always have only the benefit of the company in view. In cases where the question which arises is simply a

---

63 [1960] 1 Ch 457.
64 (1939) 61 CLR 457.

question as to the relative rights of different classes of shareholders the problem cannot be solved by regarding merely the benefit of the corporation ... But though a shareholder may vote in his own interests the power of shareholders to alter Articles is limited by the rule that the power must not be exercised fraudulently or for the purpose of oppressing a minority ... (7) When the validity of a resolution of shareholders is challenged, the onus of showing that the power has not been properly exercised is on the party complaining. The court will not presume fraud or oppression or other abuse of power ...

The result of applying these principles is that the special resolution altering the Articles cannot be declared to be invalid merely upon the ground that the original Articles conferred special rights upon the holders of partly paid shares of which the alteration deprived them, or upon the ground that the voting holders of fully paid shares were interested in making the alteration adversely to the holders of partly paid shares. If, however, the resolution was passed fraudulently or oppressively or was so extravagant that no reasonable person could believe it was for the benefit of the company, it should be held to be invalid.[65]

A final decision worth noting in this context is that in *Re Caratti Holding Co. Pty Ltd*,[66] an Australian decision which was subsequently upheld by the Privy Council.[67] The facts involved a partnership that was subsequently incorporated. Caratti had total control and held a life governor's share. Article 32 provided that he had the power to acquire compulsorily the shares of any member. Zampatti had originally been an employee, and later had purchased a 10 per cent partnership share in the business. When the company bought out the original partnership, Zampatti was given 1500 shares at $1500.[68] This was intended to represent, and in fact represented, a 10 per cent share in the company.

At the date of the suit, his interest was worth $400 000, if evaluated upon the basis of the asset backing of the company. Caratti exercised his powers under art. 32, compulsorily acquiring Zampatti's shares at par value. The court held that his conduct was oppressive. According to Burt J, the right of compulsory acquisition was given to Caratti as a member so long as he continued to hold the life governor's share. Both the rights conferred by the s. 180 contract and the rights of pre-emption were rights *inter se*. Thus, upon the construction of the articles, the actions of Caratti were wholly legitimate. This 'contractual legitimacy' did not, however, conclude the matter. Because of the history of the partnership and the relationship between the two men, Caratti's clear attempt to acquire the shares at a gross undervaluation was interpreted by the court as constituting conduct amounting to oppression. The court ordered Caratti to compensate Zampatti for the full asset

---

65 (1939) 61 CLR 457 at 479–82.

66 (1975) 1 ACLR 87.

67 *Re Caratti Holding Co. Pty Ltd* (1978) 23 ALR 655.

68 The par value of these shares was, of course, $1. As is normally the case with shares in closely held companies, particularly closely held companies where the articles vest significant power in the controlling shareholder-director, the shares did not have a market value as such.

value of his holding. The understandings that applied were those subsisting at the date of incorporation, and at that time both men intended that Zampatti should retain his 10 per cent of the business. For Caratti to acquire compulsorily the shares at par value violated this understanding. Like *Harmer*, *Caratti* constituted a clear case of oppression.

A natural justice alternative?

An alternative approach to enforcing membership rights may be through the rules of natural justice.[69] The rules of natural justice have been invoked upon a number of occasions where a member has been expelled by a corporate body and is seeking reinstatement. If it can be established that the act of expulsion constitutes oppression, use of the oppression remedy will probably prove the most cost-effective response. Where the corporate conduct does not amount to oppression, a remedy is less likely to be available. In a number of decisions, articles providing for the expulsion of members have been upheld and the rules of natural justice have been deemed to be inapplicable to incorporated bodies.

Gaiman v. National Association of Mental Health[70] remains the leading decision in this area. In *Gaiman* the court held that all membership rights terminated if a member was requested to resign. An appeal to natural justice failed. It is generally thought that this decision affirms the principle that the rules of natural justice are not available to protect members of corporate persons against deprivation of membership. Of course, if one thinks about the facts of *Gaiman*, the matter might seem rather less clear. The plaintiff was a member of the Church of Scientology. At the time that the case was heard, mainstream mental health professionals routinely denied membership of mental health organisations to scientologists, the basis for the denial being that allowing them membership in orthodox mental health organisations gave unwarranted credence to their beliefs and to their claims for their methodology. Given the facts, there is every reason to regard *Gaiman* as an intensely 'political' decision and to suspect that it may ultimately be confined to its own facts. We do not believe that there is any inherent reason why the rules of natural justice would not be available in an appropriate case.

The court confronted a somewhat similar issue in *Thorborn v. All Nations Club*.[71] Again the plaintiff failed, the rules of natural justice being deemed inapplicable to a social club. Here, the rationale was explicit. Loss of membership did not deprive the plaintiff either of a proprietary right or of her livelihood.[72] Following on from established administrative-law principles, the court was not prepared to extend the protection of natural justice to a plaintiff who did not, in the eyes of the court, have a legally cognisable interest at stake. The entire area is somewhat uncertain. All of the

---

69 For an account of the potential of 'natural justice' as a remedy in this area, see L. Griggs & R. Snell, 'Natural Justice—An Alternative Ground for Intervention and Corporate Decision Making?' (1994) 10 QUTLJ 22–34.

70 [1971] Ch 317.

71 [1975] 1 ACLR 127.

72 This is entirely consistent both with administrative law and with more general common-law principles.

available precedents deal with incorporated associations rather than trading companies. It is difficult to predict the approach of the court if deprivation of membership unequivocally stripped a plaintiff of her or his livelihood or failed to provide compensation for deprivation of proprietary rights.

REVIEW QUESTIONS

1 Consider the various rights that have been held to be proprietary rights in the case law. It is important to read the relevant cases carefully and attempt to understand the judicial reasoning involved. Attempt to formulate a general principle that would serve to provide an overall theory governing the cases you have considered.

2 Consider both the divergent views on the enforceability of the articles and the fact that the successful cases have all been couched in representative form. Why is representative form used, and what does it imply?

3 Can the exercise of powers expressly included in the articles amount to oppression? If so, under what circumstances is it likely to be held that this is the case?

4 What is meant by the term 'natural justice'? You may have to consult a basic administrative law text to find out. Do you think the rules of natural justice ought to apply to at least some of the relationships *inter se*?

5 Reconsider the decision in *Gaiman*. Was this decision predicated upon principled and coherent arguments, or does it ultimately rest upon social policy? Are policy decisions of this kind an appropriate basis for judicial law-making? Is there an alternative?

Alteration of the articles

Section 176 provides for the alteration of articles subject to the provisions of the Corporations Law. Alteration requires a special resolution, although more stringent requirements may be included in the memorandum. Sections 172–3 provide avenues by which the articles may be made virtually unalterable. In addition, certain legal requirements apply: s. 180(3) prohibits any alteration that increases the scope of the liability of members, and where a judgment has been obtained under s. 260, the company has no power to alter the articles in ways which would defeat the judgment of the court.

Special provisions cover class rights.[73] The following constitutes a summary of the major provisions in this area:

1 Where the memorandum and articles do not make any special provisions or declare such rights unalterable, such rights may be altered with the consent of 75 per cent of the members of the affected class.

2 Where class rights are altered or set aside, 10 per cent of the members of the class affected may apply to the court to have the action set aside. Once this step has been taken, the alteration is suspended until, and if, the court confirms it.

---

73 See ss. 197–200.

Consider in this regard the case of *Crumpton v. Morrine Hall Pty Ltd*.[74] The case was concerned with a shareholder in a company who had purchased the shares for the attached rights of tenancy in a home unit. The articles provided that her tenancy could not be determined without the consent in writing of all shareholders. A subsequent alteration to the articles provided as further grounds that the tenancy rights would be terminated if the shareholder sublet the unit. The court held that the articles could not be thus altered without her consent. Given that she had purchased her shares for the attached right of occupancy, the limitation of her right of occupancy significantly curtailed her membership rights, essentially depriving her of the central benefit of membership.

Some further provisions are also relevant in this area. Section 198 provides for alteration where classes are not an issue, and s. 199 deals with class rights in companies without share capital. Section 200 provides that the rights of preference shares in certain respects must be set out in the memorandum or articles. In regard to these provisions, you should also examine the provisions of table A, art. 2–7.

The central legal issue is what constitutes an alteration or variation of shareholder rights. This issue requires judicial determination, and the problems involved in determining whether a particular course of action altered shareholder rights were considered at length in *Greenhalgh v. Arderne Cinemas*.[75] This case was one episode in a lengthy series of legal actions arising out of a bitter faction fight. The litigation continued for over ten years—an expensive pastime, to say the least. The Mallard faction held a bare majority, which was insufficient to alter the articles. As a consequence, an indirect mechanism was adopted to achieve the end sought. By ordinary resolution, 10-shilling shares in the company were split into five 2-shilling shares. Because a majority of 10-shilling shares were held by the Mallard faction, the split gave the Mallard faction the voting power to pass the special resolution sought by it. The court refused to imply any agreement that voting control was beyond interference. It was held that the actual rights attached to the shares were not altered—that is, each share continued to carry the same rights as before, even though the alteration dramatically shifted the balance of power in the general meeting.[76] The result was similar to that in *Peters' American Delicacy Co. v. Heath*, where the fact that the articles were altered so that the distribution of bonus shares depended upon the number of fully paid shares, and not the total number of shares held, was held not to be an alteration such as would prejudice the rights of those shareholders who held partially paid shares. Critically, in both cases, the action was deemed not to constitute a fraud on a minority.

Dixon J outlined the requirements for the application of this latter doctrine in *Peters' American Delicacy Co. v. Heath*. According to His Honour, the purpose of the doctrine is to prevent majority voting power from imposing articles that are

---

74 [1965] NSWLR 240.

75 [1946] 1 All ER 512.

76 While, on initial reading, this decision seems harshly formalistic, it ought to be read against the background litigation. In particular, it should be noted that the plaintiff had achieved the majority he sought to protect by precisely the same mechanism. Read against this history, the decision is, perhaps, unremarkable.

outside those that might reasonably have been contemplated when the company was formed. Examples of improper alterations would include articles supplying major shareholders with goods below cost, those allowing secret profits, and those attempting to pay majority shareholders for their services, thus having the effect of funnelling profits to the majority. Such requirements are in conflict with the concept that shares, and the rights acquired with share-ownership, are proprietary. Attempts to extend the doctrine of fraud on a minority beyond this are fraught with difficulty. Clearly, *Peters'* case limits the scope of voting rights and the purposes for which they may be exercised. Voting rights must be exercised for corporate purposes, and they must be exercised bona fide in the best interests of the company. If a decision is outside what any reasonable person could interpret as being in the interests of the company as a whole, it may be struck down. The rights given may not be exercised capriciously. Dixon J alluded numerous times to the fact that phrases such as 'bona fide for the benefit of the company as a whole' were incapable of precise definition. Likewise, to rely upon phrases such as 'the ordinary principles of justice', 'just and equitable', or 'oppressive' left the whole question to general notions of fairness or the like, which were too vague for judicial guidance.[77] Despite this, he noted:

> If no restraint were laid upon the power of altering Articles of association, it would be possible for a shareholder controlling the necessary voting power so to mould the regulations of a company that its operation would be conducted or its property used so that he would profit either in some other capacity than that of member … or, if as a member, in a special and peculiar way inconsistent with conception of honesty so widely held or professed that departure from them is described, without further analysis, as fraud … The chief reason for denying an unlimited effect to widely expressed powers such as that of altering a company's Articles is the fear or knowledge that an apparently regular exercise of the power may in truth be but a means of securing some personal or particular gain, whether pecuniary or otherwise, which does not fairly arise of the subjects dealt with by the power and is outside and even inconsistent with the contemplated objects of the power … To say that the shareholders forming the majority must consider the advantage of the company as a whole in relation to [changes whose subject matter involves a conflict of interests,] one supposes that in voting each shareholder is to assume an inhuman altruism and consider only the intangible notion of the benefit of the vague abstraction … 'the company as an institution'. An investigation of the thoughts and motives of each shareholder voting with the majority would be an impossible proceeding.[78]

---

77 In more contemporary terms, such terms may operate as screens or masks for the exercise of judicial discretion, allowing a court to draw the line where it believes, rightly or wrongly, that a particular exercise of majority power is wholly unconscionable. An aphorism attributed to the great American judge Oliver Wendell Holmes Jr, suggesting that a law was constitutional unless it made him want to 'puke', bears an astonishing resemblance to the position outlined by Dixon J. Perhaps all we can say is that a majority decision is bona fide unless it (and its consequences) turns the judicial stomach.

78 (1939) 61 CLR 457 at 511–13.

Against this background, the recent High Court decision in *Gambotto v. WCP Ltd* [79] is of substantial interest. The facts involved an alteration to the articles which had the effect of enabling compulsory acquisition of minority shares by a shareholder holding more than 95 per cent of the issued shares. The price was fair, and the court acknowledged that significant taxation and administrative benefits would have accrued to the company were it to become a wholly owned subsidiary of Industrial Equity Ltd. However, the High Court, in a significant extension of prior doctrine, held that it was not sufficient that the alteration be made for a proper purpose. It was also essential that the alteration be fair. According to the majority:

> Fairness in this context has both procedural and substantive elements. The first element, that the process used to expropriate must be fair, requires the majority shareholders to disclose all relevant information leading up to the alteration and it presumably requires the shares to be valued by an independent expert ...
>
> The second element, that the terms of the expropriation itself must be fair, is largely concerned with the price offered for the shares. Thus, an expropriation at less than market value is prima facie unfair, and it would be unusual for a court to be satisfied that a price substantially above market value was not a fair value. That said, it is important to emphasize that a shareholder's interest cannot be valued solely by the current market value of the shares. Whether the price is fair depends on a variety of factors, including assets, market value, dividends, and the nature of the corporation and its likely future.

Significantly, the majority went on to note that 'in the case of expropriation, we consider that the onus lies on those supporting expropriation to show that the power is validly exercised'. [80]

The s. 180 contract is of substantial importance in that it permits members to bring personal actions for wrongs that affect their membership rights. Thus they can circumvent the procedural difficulties involved in the classic minority remedies, such as the exceptions to the rule in *Foss v. Harbottle* and s. 260. Because it has been interpreted narrowly, and because of the courts' reluctance to place a fetter upon commercial decision-making, many 'breaches' of the articles fall outside the scope of the remedy provided.

REVIEW QUESTIONS

1 Study the facts in *Greenhalgh* and *Peters' American Delicacy* carefully. Upon what basis did the court decide in each case that the alteration was not such as to affect membership rights? Do you agree? What does this say about the interpretation given to membership rights?

---

79   (1995) 182 CLR 432.
80   (1994) 182 CLR 432 at 446–7 per Mason CJ and Brennan, Deane, and Dawson JJ.

2 In particular, in *Greenhalgh*, might it have been relevant that the plaintiff had attained his dominant position using precisely the method of which he now complained—that is, an alteration in the share structure?

The articles and the directors

The tenure and status of the directors of public companies is governed by s. 227, irrespective of any provision in the articles. For those private companies that adopt table A, art. 62 has a similar effect. This is often undesirable, particularly in family companies or those formed from a pre-existing partnership—a point to be noted when drafting articles for a proprietary company. Frequently, attempts are made to circumvent these limitations. Perhaps the best known of these circumlocutions is the insertion of a *Bushell v. Faith*[81] clause in the articles. Such a clause provides for the weighting of the votes of the members where an attempt is made to remove certain individuals as directors. In *Bushell v. Faith* the clause was upheld; however, it is unlikely to prevail today in the case of a public company governed by s. 225. It must be noted that *Bushell v. Faith* dealt with a family company, and that the clause provided that, in any attempt to remove a director, that director's shares should carry three votes. There were only three shareholders, each holding 100 shares, making this a classic example of a company that could be destroyed by a personality clash, and one in which the founder might wish to safeguard his position. Whether the founder ought to be allowed to do so is a quite different question, however, and it is one upon which reasonable people may disagree.

Normally, executive and managing directors are protected by service contracts. The effect of these separate service contracts is to entitle those protected to damages in the event of removal from office. Although the director can be removed, the company is liable for breach of contract, it being an implied term of every contract that a parties will not disqualify themselves from performing their contract. The relevant precedents are *Southern Foundries v. Shirlaw* and *Carrier Australasia v. Hunt*.[82] It is crucial to realise that damages for breach of contract are the only remedy that will be available in these circumstances and that, in the absence of a separate contract of service, a director in this position would be entitled to no remedy whatsoever. Even where a separate contract of service exists, specific performance will not be available. The courts will not intervene to enable an individual to maintain his or her position because that would be tantamount to enforcing a personal relationship.

---

81 [1970] 2 WLR 272.
82 (1939) 61 CLR 34.

REVIEW QUESTIONS

1 What special considerations are involved in an alteration of the articles where there are different classes of shares or where the impact appears to affect different members very differently?

2 What is meant by the doctrine of 'fraud on a minority'? Is it possible to formulate a precise definition or a clear statement of the relevant principles in this area? Why do judges in the decided cases regularly allude to the fact that the parameters of the phrase are uncertain? And why do they suggest that even a phrase such as 'bona fide in the best interests of the company' escapes precise explication?

9

A QUESTION OF
GOVERNANCE

Corporate governance is doomed to remain a messy compromise. Decades of modern capitalism have yielded no perfect model; nor will decades more.

The Economist, 30 May 1992.

Introduction

One of the most contentious areas for corporate law in Australia has been that of corporate governance. At the outset we should note that we read 'corporate governance' broadly. Our concern with questions of corporate governance canvasses both the mechanisms by which those responsible for internal governance can be held accountable for their stewardship and the particular issues that arise for corporate governance given the increasing domination of the 'passive investor'.[1] Public attention has focused on this issue for a number of reasons, not least the investigations and prosecutions in the wake of the 'corporate excesses' of the 1980s, which disclosed a number of failures in traditional accountability mechanisms in Australian corporate governance. But this is not to suggest that corporate accountability issues only occurred—or even, perhaps, were only acknowledged—at this time. Rather, the failings of corporate governance have been with us virtually since the inception of the corporate form. Adam Smith summed up the problem nicely. With regard to the investors or 'proprietors' of joint stock companies, he observed that they 'seldom pretend to understand anything of the business of the company; and when the spirit of faction happens not to avail among them, give themselves no trouble about it, but receive contentedly such half yearly or yearly dividend as the directors think proper to make to them'. With regard to the directors, he noted:

> The directors of such companies, however, being the managers of other people's money than of their own, it cannot well be expected, that they should watch over it with the same vigilance with which the partners in a private co-partnery frequently watch over their own ... Negligence and profusion therefore must always prevail more or less, in the management of the affairs of such a company.[2]

---

1 Readers wishing to explore this area in greater depth are encouraged to consult J. E. Parkinson, *Corporate Power and Responsibility: Issues in the Theory of Corporate Law*, Clarendon Press, Oxford, 1993.

2 A. Smith, *Wealth of Nations*, Random House, New York, 1937, p. 699.

These issues—the passivity of shareholders, and the effects of the separation of management and ownership—are continuing themes in corporate-governance debates. The discontent expressed by many people with our current system of governance can, however, be attributed to a variety of factors. 'Each generation', it has been said, 'must conduct the corporate governance debate within the parameters set by the prevailing manifestation of corporatism'.[3] The evolution of the corporate form must, as we suggested in chapter 1, always be kept in mind. But the corporate context also evolves. We have already noted that the corporate excesses of the 1980s and 1990s in Australia were the subject of considerable media attention, which heightened public awareness of the corporate governance debate.[4] It is also tempting to suggest that Australian statutory developments since the late 1970s—such as the *Trade Practices Act 1974* (Cth) (TPA), ss. 52, 51AA, and 51AB—and a corresponding emphasis in the courts on notions of 'unconscionability' raised the institutional awareness of the considerable limitations of traditional corporate accountability mechanisms. Additionally, some commentators identify the rise of finance capitalism[5] and of such institutional investment as superannuation funds (where the individual investor has no choice but to invest) as having a significant impact on the corporate-governance debate. Essentially, the number of individuals who are investing heavily in companies—either indirectly, in the case of institutional investment, or directly—has increased. In particular, consider the recent highly publicised floats of the Commonwealth Bank, GIO Australia, and Woolworths. These encouraged (and were intended to encourage) many people to become investors on the stock exchange and to join the ranks of direct shareholders. This is what Nicholas Renton terms 'the people's capitalism'.[6]

Not all companies, of course, were involved in the corporate excesses of the 1980s. Indeed, the vast majority of Australian companies are family organisations that do not have large public shareholdings. For this reason, some commentators suggest that directors are overregulated. Directors must spend too much time on compliance activities (that is, in meeting the structural and regulatory requirements of the *Corporations Law 1990*) which interferes with the performance activities of the company (that is, the pursuit of profit). Why should a small company, which is essentially an incorporated partnership in which all take part in management, be required to have directors? Company legislation in Australia does not really distinguish between small family businesses and large public corporations. On the other hand, if individuals wish to have the benefits of incorporation, should they not accept the burdens as well?

---

3   M. Lipton, 'Corporate Governance in the Age of Finance Corporatism' (1987) 136 Penn L Rev 1 at 3.

4   N. E. Renton, *Company Directors: Masters or Servants?* Wrightbooks, Melbourne, 1994.

5   That is, the separation of the decision of how to invest from the decision to supply capital for investment. See T. Clark, 'Four Stages of Capitalism: Reflections on Investment Management Treatises' (1981) 94 Harv LR 561.

6   Renton, p. xiii. It is worth noting that, in this respect, Australia is now moving in a direction parallel to that of the USA.

Indeed, much of the criticism of directors and of our current system of regulation sends out somewhat confused signals. On the one hand, there is some criticism of the failure of the current system of directors' duties to deliver satisfactory industrial and economic performance. Others criticise the system for its bias towards short-term economic results, while still others criticise it for failing to provide sufficient control over directors who treat investors, third parties, or shareholders immorally. As we have seen so far, however, it may not be possible to rectify all these criticisms. There is a problem here in having your cake and eating it too. Can we have a system that ensures that directors are accountable, but that also encourages risk-taking and economic expansion? If we demand that directors be accountable, to whom should they be accountable? Who is a stakeholder? If we include creditors and third parties as stakeholders, can a director ever act effectively, or is action paralysed by the number of interests that need to be taken into account?

The objectives of this chapter, then, are first to discuss the division of power between the shareholders and the board, and to consider the implications of that division. Second, we aim to examine the implications of shareholder passivity. Finally, we aim to outline the legal duties of directors and the ways in which those duties are limited by the perceived need to encourage managerial risk-taking and the pursuit of profit. Before we begin, we shall briefly consider the requirements of appointment as a director.

Nice work if you can get it: Requirements of directors

The term 'director' is defined in s. 60 to include a person acting as director, even though he or she may be described by another name, or was not validly appointed or duly authorised to act as a director. This definition also includes a person whose directions or instructions are customarily followed by the directors of a company.[7] P. Lipton and A. Herzberg observe that a director is, by virtue of this definition, not just a person formally appointed to the office. For example, in *Corporate Affairs Commission v. Drysdale*,[8] Drysdale was appointed as a director to fill a casual vacancy on the board. The articles provided that such a director could only hold office until the next annual general meeting. Drysdale would then be allowed to stand for re-election. Drysdale's retirement or re-election was, however, not considered at the general meeting. According to the articles, he was no longer a director of the company. Nevertheless, he continued to participate in the management of the company as if he were a director. The High Court held that, despite the defect in his appointment, he was deemed to be a director and subject to directors' duties.[9]

---

7   Such a person is often referred to as a 'shadow director'. It is worth noting that an entity such as a corporation can be a shadow director within the terms of this section, even though that entity would not be eligible to serve as a director.

8   (1978) 141 CLR 236.

9   P. Lipton & A. Herzberg, *Understanding Company Law*, 5th edn, Law Book Co., Sydney, 1993, p. 298.

Thus, you can see that the Corporations Law is concerned with imposing duties on all those who take part in management of companies. For this reason, many of the duties pertaining to directors' duties are imposed on 'officers'. 'Officer' is defined in s. 9 to include directors, secretaries, executive officers, employees, and managers of insolvent companies, such as receiver managers and liquidators under a voluntary winding-up.

Section 60(2) provides that professional advisers or persons who merely give advice to the directors in the proper performance of their professional functions, or in their business relationship with the directors or the company, are not to be regarded as the 'directors' for the purposes of s. 60(1).

The legislative requirements for eligibility to be appointed as a director are that a person must:

- be a natural person and not a body corporate (s. 221(2))
- be at least 18 years old (s. 228(13))
- not be disqualified from holding office.

The principal grounds for disqualification of individuals for appointment as director are:

- conviction within the previous 5 years on indictment of an offence in connection with the promotion, formation, or management of a body corporate (s. 229(3)(a))
- conviction within the previous 5 years of serious fraud or certain specified offences relating to the management of corporations (s. 229(3)(b)–(d))
- being an insolvent under administration (unless the court grants leave) (s. 229(1))
- disqualification by court order for repeated contraventions of companies and securities industry legislation (s. 230)
- disqualification by court order because of failed companies (s. 599)
- disqualification by the commission after the company is the subject of a liquidator's adverse report (s. 600).

The maximum age limit on directors of public companies (and their subsidiaries) is 72 years. Under s. 228, persons of 72 years of age and over may not be appointed as directors, except by special majority of members at a general meeting. At least 14 days written notice must be given for such a meeting, and the notice must state that the candidate is 72 years old or more and give his or her age.

REVIEW QUESTIONS

1 Do you think that more stringent qualifications should be imposed upon individuals who wish to become company directors? For example, should directors be required to have some minimum standard of business education?

2 Do the age requirements for directors under the Corporations Law contravene anti-discrimination legislation?

What is it that you do? The role of the director

In the introduction, we noted that there have been many criticisms of the regulation of directors since the 1980s, but that these criticisms often tend to be based on conflicting expectations, both of the director's role and of the purposes of regulation. What is it that a director does or, indeed, should do? Is the legitimate role of a company director simply to manage the business? Is the role one of overseeing company policy? Or should the director be an entrepreneurial risk-taker? Your answers to these questions may colour your view of the duties and standards expected of company directors. For instance, on the one hand, it may not be practically possible for a director to be intimately acquainted with the day-to-day operations of a large company, so the imposition of liability for failure in such day-to-day matters may be inappropriate. If the law is too onerous, it may dissuade people from becoming company directors, or it may dissuade existing directors from taking risks. On the other hand, if regulation is insufficient, shareholders, creditors, and other third parties will be (not surprisingly) vocal when faced with directors' dishonesty or incompetence.

To complicate matters further, the diverse nature of companies and the diverse nature of their activities mean that it is difficult to have very clearly defined standards of experience and skill. What we might reasonably expect from the director of a large, public company involved in, say, mining may well be very different from the standards expected of a grocery store owner who is the single director and shareholder in her own company.

The complexity of determining just what it is that directors do, and what standards and duties they should be subject to, was highlighted in the case of *AWA Ltd v. Daniels t/a Deloitte Haskins & Sells*,[10] where Rogers CJ said:

> Foremost amongst [the difficulties that arise in allocating liability to directors, officers, and auditors] is the failure to recognise and admit that many companies today are too big to be supervised and administered by the board of directors except in relation to matters of high policy. The true oversight of the activities of such companies resides with the corporate bureaucracy. Senior management, and in the case of mammoth corporations, even persons lower down the corporate ladder, exercise substantial control of the activities of such corporations involving important decisions and much money. It is something of an anachronism to expect the non executive directors, meeting once a month, to contribute anything much more than decisions on policy, and, in the case of really large corporations, only major policy. This necessarily means, in the execution of

---

10 (1992) 7 ACSR 759; 10 ACLC 933.

policy, senior management is, in the true sense of the word, exercising the powers of decision and of management which in less complex days used to be reserved for the board of directors.[11]

Some commentators have pointed to a gap between the way in which companies actually function and the way in which the law assumes companies to function:

> Because it is inherently undesirable for law and practice to be in a state of visible opposition, the drastic skew between the legal and working models of the board would be of serious concern even if no specific dysfunctional consequences could be perceived. In fact, however, a number of such dysfunctions can be identified. On a relatively particularistic level, many legal rules have been shaped on the premise that the board manages the corporation's business in fact as well as in law. For example, by proceeding from the assumption that officers play a subordinate role to the board, the rules governing the authority of officers frequently embody an unrealistically restrictive view of an officer's power of position. Standards of care, by the same token, often seem to be pitched to the outside director rather than the executive, as if the former were really running the business. In duty of loyalty cases the courts have often given disproportionate weight to the fact that outside directors have approved a transaction in which executives are interested, while the legislatures have sometimes gone so far as to provide that approval by outside directors is sufficient to sterilise an otherwise infected transaction. In a wider context, the skew between belief and reality has led to what might be called the quack-cure problem—the danger that belief in the validity of the received legal model will forestall meaningful regulation by lulling shareholders, legislators, and the public into the illusion (which often seems deliberately conjured up) that a disinterested board is supervising the corporation's affairs.[12]

Why is it that this gap between law and practice has developed? In order to understand this question, it is necessary to consider the way in which directors' duties developed.

A crisis of legitimacy?

In an interesting analysis of the problems associated with the regulation of directors, Mary Stokes argues that these problems are the result of a 'crisis of legitimacy' that arose in respect of companies operating within a liberal democracy. We considered this argument in our earlier discussion of corporate morality. In the context of directors' duties, Stokes's argument is that our system of capitalism assumed that the economic power of the company was regulated, and hence legitimated by a competitive market. But the growth of corporate enterprises meant that this idea of a competitive market was unrealistic. The aggregation of large sums of capital, technological change, and new organisational techniques meant that the firm increased

---

11 (1992) 7 ACSR 759 at 832–3.
12 M. A. Eisenberg, *The Structure of the Corporation*, Little Brown, Boston, 1976.

dramatically in size and the number of firms competing in any particular industry was significantly reduced. Thus, the market structure often ceased to be purely competitive, instead becoming monopolistic or oligopolistic. Furthermore, the company no longer had to accept the market price for its products and could affect that price by varying the output of the products.

Stokes argues that it was the oligopolistic character of product markets that gave those who run the company the discretion to pursue goals other than profit-maximisation. In a perfectly competitive world, it would not be possible for managers to deviate from profit-maximisation norms. The failure of the market, as a result of imperfect competition, to regulate the company as an economic unit is thus inextricably linked with the potentially unrestricted power of corporate managers.

In addition, one of the central features of the market model of legitimisation was the exercise of economic power through exchange transactions in the market. As the company increased in size, however, it became evident that much economic activity was withdrawn from the market sphere and replaced by a hierarchical, bureaucratic elite. The power conferred on business managers by the company was unchecked, and therefore illegitimate within the framework of liberal democracy:

> On a deeper level, the concentration of economic power brought about by the growth in the size of companies, and the oligopolistic nature of product markets undermines some of the traditional justifications for private ownership itself. The concentration of power in the hands of managers of the largest companies could not be seen as the necessary bulwark against the power of the state. Nor could it be argued that private property ensured an efficient allocation of resources, since the market no longer resembled the model of perfect competition.[13]

What, then, was the law's response to this 'crisis of legitimacy'? The first was to intervene in the market in an attempt to ensure that the market resembled (as closely as possible) the paradigm of perfect competition. Thus, the State outlawed monopolistic practices that deviate from that paradigm. Second, company law sought to legitimate the power of corporate managers in two ways. The first method of control arises through the contractual theory of the division of power:

> Although the shareholders no longer exercise the direct control of principles over directors as their agents, the model nevertheless asserts that any danger that the directors might use their considerable discretionary powers to manage the business in their own interests is precluded. It is precluded because the model gives power to the shareholders to appoint and dismiss the directors and the power to supervise them once they are in office. The system of indirect control and accountability is therefore established over the directors as those responsible for the management of the company. This system of indirect control through the internal division of power between the shareholders and the directors is strengthened by providing that the assistance of the courts can be called upon to enforce it.

---

13   M. Stokes, 'Company Law and Legal Theory', in W. Twining (ed.), *Legal Theory and Common Law*, Basil Blackwell, London, 1986, pp. 155, 159.

The second method of control is the application of fiduciary duties to directors. This method

> attempts to balance the desirability of giving to the manager of the company substantial discretionary power so that they have sufficient flexibility to act effectively, whilst at the same time minimising the danger that the existence that such discretion creates, which is that it will be used arbitrarily ... Directors are treated as being in a position analogous to trustees, so powers conferred upon them are given to them in a fiduciary capacity. This means that directors are under a duty to act in the best interests of the shareholders. They cannot place their own interests above those of the shareholders. Fiduciary duties of directors are not merely abstract injunctions to act only in the interests of the shareholders, for they are once again enforceable in the courts.[14]

In the next section we will examine the two mechanisms of control imposed by company law: the division of power between corporate organs, and the imposition of fiduciary duties.

REVIEW QUESTIONS

1   Some commentators argue that the duties of directors should be the subject of private ordering and not State regulation:

> The contractual theory of the corporation states that the corporation is a set of contracts among the participants in the business, including shareholders, managers, creditors, employees and others. The terms of the agency contract include the provisions of state law, which are regarded as a standard form which can be accepted by the parties, or rejected, either by drafting around the provisions or by incorporating, in another state. The corporate contract also specifies the extent to which the parties rely on the competitive pressures from capital, product and managerial labour markets as well as internal incentive structures such as corporate hierarchy, boards of directors, and managerial compensation contracts, to force agents to act in the shareholders' best interests. The policy implication is that private parties to the corporate contract should be free to order their affairs in whatever manner they find appropriate.[15]

Do you agree? What arguments can be made against this point of view? Can you reconcile this view with that of Stokes (above)?

2   The American Law Institute in its Principles of Corporation Governance[16] sets out the functions of the board as follows:

---

14   Stokes, p. 159.

15   H. N. Butler, & L. E. Ribstein, 'Opting out of Fiduciary Duties: A Response to the Anti-contractarians' (1990) 1 Wash LR 17–18.

16   As quoted in L. Griggs, 'The Role of the Board of Directors in Public Corporations' (1994) 11 Aus Bar Rev 214 at 217.

3.01—The management of the business of a publicly held corporation should be conducted by or under the supervision of such principal senior executives as are designated by the board of directors, and by those other officers and employees to whom the management function is delegated by the board or those executives, subject to the functions and powers of the board under 3.02.

3.02(a)—(1) Select, regularly evaluate, fix the compensation of and, where appropriate, replace the principal senior executives.

(2) Oversee the conduct of the corporation's business to evaluate whether the business is being properly managed.

(3) Review and, where appropriate, approve the corporation's financial objectives and major corporate plans and actions.

(4) Review and, where appropriate, approve major changes in, and determinations of other major questions of choice respecting, the appropriate auditing and accounting principles and practices to be used in the preparation of the corporation's financial statements.

(5) Perform such other functions as are prescribed by law, or assigned to the board under a standard of the corporation.

[Section 3.02(b) goes on to provide the board with a number of additional powers, including the power to manage the business of the corporation.]

What role does this model assume that the board of directors plays?

4 Does the use of equity inherently produce an unstable and potentially disloyal shareholder body?

Division of powers

There are, potentially, two governing bodies within the corporation: the directors and the body of shareholders. Often, in small, closely held companies, these bodies will be one and the same. But where this is not the case, who has ultimate control of the company? Under the Corporations Law, certain matters must be decided by the general meeting. For instance, these include:

- altering the memorandum and articles (ss. 172 and 176)
- altering the company's authorised share capital (s. 193(1)(a) and (e))
- consolidating or subdividing the company's shares (s. 193(1)(b) and (d))
- reducing the company's issued share capital (s. 195)
- issuing shares at a discount to nominal value (s. 190)
- altering rights attached to shares (ss. 197–9)
- altering the company's status (pt 2.3, div. 2) or transferring the company's place of incorporation (pt 2.2, div. 4A).

In addition, if a company is listed, Australian Stock Exchange (ASX) listing rules require certain transactions to be sanctioned by the general meeting.[17]

---

17 For instance, where the company's main undertaking is being sold (rule LR 11.1) or where the company is changing its activities (rule LR 11.3).

Outside the statutory and listing rules governing division of power, such division is determined by the memorandum and articles of association, but this division has been problematic.

Servants, masters, or peers?

Although the internal governance of the corporation is recognised as a form of constitutional law, the law's distribution of decision-making power between the board of directors and the shareholders has 'never been well articulated'.[18] In large public companies, of course, the split between ownership and control is most apparent. The tension between the board and shareholders, however, is not confined to the large public company. It is often greatest in small companies where the directors are also shareholders (but not the only shareholders). Here, the opportunity exists for directors to pursue their own interests by exercising their proprietary right to vote for their own benefit, as opposed to corporate ends. In addition, the scope for oppression in such cases is very great. It is essential, because of this potential for directors to pursue their own interests with little (or no) control by shareholders, that directors' duties are clearly formulated and shareholders have effective remedies available to them. This has not, however, tended to be the case. As we shall see, directors' duties are not clearly defined; directors usually control the shareholders' access to corporate information; shareholders must overcome the very practical barrier of costly litigation; and courts have, through the rule in *Foss v. Harbottle* and a restrictive interpretation of the oppression remedy, played a very limited role in the regulation of internal company affairs.[19]

The division of power is mostly commonly defined by table A, art. 66(1), which provides that:

> Subject to the Law and to any other provision of these regulations, the business of the company shall be managed by the directors, wl.o may pay all expenses incurred in promoting and forming the company, and may exercise all such powers of the company as are not, by the Law or by these regulations, required to be exercised by the company in general meeting.

This provision raises two issues. First, in managing the 'business of the company', are directors delegates of the company or coordinate, autonomous bodies to the general meeting? Second, if they are the latter, what functions are included in the term 'business of the company'?

Until the early twentieth century, the law adopted the 'delegation theory' of division of corporate power. Under delegation theory, the general meeting is the fundamental organ of the company and the directors are its delegates or agents. Thus, the

---

18 M. A. Eisenberg, 'The Legal Roles of Shareholder and Management in Modern Corporate Decisionmaking' (1969) 57 Calif LR 1.

19 See chapter 16.

board is subject to the control of the shareholders. A resolution by the general meeting can override the board's decisions. This was the view expressed in *Foss v. Harbottle* by Wigram J:

> The result of these clauses is that the directors are made the governing body, subject to the superior control of the proprietors assembled in general meetings; and, as I understand the Act, the proprietors so assembled have power, due notice being given of the purposes of the meeting, to originate proceedings for any purpose within the scope of the company's powers, as well as to control the directors in any acts which they may have originated. There may possibly be some exceptions to this proposition, but such is the general effect of the provisions of the statute.[20]

Delegation theory originated in the common-law corporations of boroughs and guilds, which could only execute corporate acts at corporate meetings. By the eighteenth century, the deed-of-settlement company operated in such a way that the general meeting was given exclusive consideration of policy or changes of major importance, while the day-to-day conduct of the company's affairs was left to a small group elected by the general meeting and known as 'directors'. Although the precise division of power varied, a common provision was that directors were 'to order, direct, manage and transact all and every of the affairs and things of or belonging to the said company except such matters which ought to be ordered in and done by a General Court of the said Company'. The *Joint Stock Companies Act 1844* (UK) also adopted this form of division of power. The company was required to appoint directors 'for the conduct and superintendence of the affairs of the company' and was enjoined from participating in the management of the company 'otherwise than by means of the directors'.

The operation of this principle is illustrated by *Isle of Wight Railway Co. v. Tahourdin*.[21] In this case, shareholders in the Isle of Wight Railway Company wanted the directors of the company to call a meeting in order to accomplish two aims. The first was to form a committee to enquire into the management of the company, and the second was to remove, if necessary or expedient, any directors and to elect new directors in order to fill the resulting vacancies. Section 90 of the *Companies Clauses Consolidation Act 1845* (UK) (the section considered in *Isle of Wight*) provided for the division of power as follows:

> The directors shall have the management and superintendence of the affairs of the company and they may lawfully exercise all the powers of the company, except as to such matters as are directed by this or the Special Act to be transacted by a general meeting of the company; but all the powers so to be exercised shall be exercised in accordance with and subject to the provisions of this and the Special Act; and the exercise of all such powers shall be subject also to the control and regulation of any general meeting specially convened for the purpose, but not so as to render invalid any act done by the directors prior to any resolution passed by such general meeting.

---

20   (1843) 2 Hare 461 at 492–3.

21   (1884) 25 Ch D 320.

The directors issued a notice of the meeting but did not make any mention of the second issue: that of the election of new officers. The shareholders gave notice to the directors that they would not attend the meeting and proceeded to issue notice of their own meeting. The directors sought both a declaration from the court that the notice convening the shareholders' meeting was invalid and an injunction restraining that meeting. That injunction was granted at first instance, and the shareholders appealed. The directors argued that they had not failed to call the desired meeting and so it was illegal for the shareholders to do so. Where the company had the power to remove the directors, it had to do so at a properly constituted meeting of the company. The shareholders argued that the directors were merely agents of the company and that the shareholders could remove them provided they did so in a lawful manner. The court (Cotton LJ, Lindley LJ, and Fry LJ) upheld the appeal, Cotton LJ stating that:

> It is a very strange thing indeed to prevent shareholders from holding a meeting of the company, when such a meeting is the only way in which they can interfere, if the majority of them think that the course taken by the directors, in a matter which is *intra vires* of the directors, is not for the benefit of the company.[22]

In the court's view, the rule in *Foss v. Harbottle* meant that the court would not interfere on behalf of shareholders unless they had attempted to rectify the problem by calling a general meeting. The board, then, could not prohibit the proposed shareholder meeting.

The contractual theory of the division of power is that the contract of association found in the articles determines the division of power. Thus, if the articles vest power in the directors, and there is no machinery delineated for shareholder control, the general meeting must pass a special resolution to alter the articles before shareholders can interfere. An ordinary resolution of the general meeting cannot overrule a board's decision, nor can it prescribe to the board a particular course of action.

The adoption of this theory is generally traced to the decision in *Automatic Self-Cleansing Filter Syndicate Co. Ltd v. Cunninghame*.[23] The articles of the Automatic Self-Cleansing Filter Syndicate Company gave the board the power to manage the company and specifically to deal with company property subject to such regulations as might be made by extraordinary resolution of the general meeting. The company's memorandum gave, as one of the company's objects, the power to sell its undertaking to another company having similar objects. A shareholder brought a resolution to sell the company property to another company having similar objects, and this was passed at a general meeting by a narrow majority (that majority being composed primarily of the proposing shareholder's votes and those of his friends). At first instance, Warrington J held that the directors were

---

22 (1884) 25 Ch D 320 at 329.
23 [1906] 2 Ch 34.

not bound to put the resolution into effect. On appeal, the company argued that the company was the principal or employer and that the directors were merely agents or servants. The board was therefore bound to obey the general meeting in the absence of oppression or fraud, the company's powers being concurrent with those of the directors. The board argued that, where the articles gave a particular power to the directors, their control was not to be interfered with by the general meeting unless by extraordinary resolution. It would amount to an alteration of the articles to interfere with the exercise of the directors' power by a simple resolution in the general meeting.

The court dismissed the appeal. Collins MR rested his judgment on the bases that to allow the appeal would be unfair to the minority and it would render the article requiring a special resolution to remove the directors otiose. He distinguished the *Isle of Wight* case on the basis that it rested on a different statute. Cozens-Hardy LJ reasoned that there was no right of the court (short of director misconduct) to interfere in the contract of association. In a partnership there would be no right for the court to interfere in similar circumstances. This was not a case, in his view, of a master–servant or principal–agent relationship. Rather, directors were managing partners appointed to fill that post 'by mutual arrangement between [*sic*] all the shareholders: 'You are dealing here, as in the case of a partnership, with parties having individual rights as to which there are mutual stipulations for their common benefit'.[24]

Under the contract theory, then, if the articles give a general power of management to the directors, the general meeting retains only statutory powers and residual powers (that is, the power to act where a board is unwilling or unable to act; the power to ratify the acts of directors and the so-called doctrine of unanimous consent).[25]

The adoption of the contractual view has been problematic for corporate law. As outlined above, the practical effect of the contractual view is that a resolution of the general meeting that takes away the directors' power of management or that interferes with the exercise of that power is inconsistent with table A, art. 66(1). At the least, this view is likely to offend our intuitive ideas of democracy. A board may make significant structural change (such as altering company direction or selling the company undertaking) that is inconsistent with the wishes of the majority. *Cunninghame's* case is an instance of the former problem.[26]

---

24 [1906] 2 Ch 34 at 45.

25 Although delegation theory generally fell out of favour after the decision in the *Auto Self-Cleansing Filter* case, it survived for some years. A year after the decision in the *Auto Self-Cleansing Filter* case, the court adopted the theory in *Marshalls Valve Gear Co. v. Marring Wardle and Co.* [1909] 1 Ch 267 and *Dowse v. Marks* (1913) 13 SR (NSW) 332. See the attempt to reconcile the two theories in *Integrated Medical Technologies Ltd v. Macel Nominees Pty Ltd & Another* (1988) 13 ACLR 110.

26 See also *Wilson v. Miers* (1861) 142 ER 486; *In Re H. H. Vivian and Co. Ltd* [1900] 2 Ch 654.

REVIEW QUESTION

How appropriate is it to use, as Cozens-Hardy LJ did in the *Automatic Self-Cleansing Filter* case, the analogy of partnership in determining intra-company disputes. This analogy is frequently associated with considerations under the 'just and equitable' winding-up clause (see chapter 10). Why, if the company is a separate legal entity, should a partnership analogy be applied at all?

Shareholder control?

But can, and should, shareholders exercise more control over the day-to-day running of the company? In so far as the shareholders' ability to exercise control is concerned, the indiscriminate adoption of art. 66(1) may prevent this. Despite the fact that corporations have freedom to choose their preferred form of organisation, it is often the case that the standard table A, art. 66(1) is adopted for the company. Large public companies and small private, family companies, then, often adopt this division indiscriminately, despite their very different natures and the different expectations of shareholders. It is commonly argued that the shareholders retain ultimate control over the board by their power to alter the articles or to remove the directors, but empirically, this is often not the case. The directors, through proxy voting and their ability to vote in their own self-interest, can often dominate the general meeting. Tom Hadden writes:

> The more usual and accepted conclusion from the available evidence is that shareholders as such have lost all genuine control over the affairs of 'their' companies. The board of directors, or management as a whole, is in a much better position to dominate the affairs of the company both on a day to day basis, as is their duty, and also in general meeting … Management typically controls not only the conduct of meetings but the content of the various resolutions, and in addition is generally in control of the proxy voting system, despite the various attempts both in Britain, and more especially in America, to ensure that the proxy system gives genuine voting power to the mass of shareholders who cannot be expected to attend, nor could be physically accommodated at company meetings.[27]

He concludes that the effect of this is that '[f]or practical purposes the management of any large public company may safely be regarded as a self-perpetuating oligarchy, largely free from effective pressures from their shareholders'.[28] Although writing with regard to the United States situation, Melvin Eisenberg[29] identifies two basic types of private company: one, similar to a partnership, where all shareholders

---

27 T. Hadden, *Company Law and Capitalism*, Weidenfeld & Nicolson, London, 1972, p. 131.

28 Hadden, p. 133.

29 Eisenberg, 'The Legal Roles of Shareholder and Management' at 12.

expect to participate actively in the business and the other where some shareholders do not wish to be active in business. Even in the latter case, he argues, shareholders should have control over 'structural decisions'—that is, 'decisions which, although economic in character, are not made within the general framework or structure of the business as it then exists, but make a substantial change in that structure' (for example, complete liquidation, sale of a substantial proportion of all the assets, or a merger with another business that alters ownership interests and increases, to a significant extent, total size). He further argues that, even in the case of public companies, where many commentators argue that it is impractical to bestow powers of management upon shareholders because it would be unwieldy, shareholders' participation in structural decisions is desirable:

> [A]t the present time one-third of the stock in corporations listed on the New York Stock Exchange is held by highly sophisticated investors with a growing interest in structural changes other than changes in management; ... the proportion of such stock held by such investors will soon reach 40–50 percent; and ... much of the balance of the stock of such corporations seems to be held by wealthy individual shareholders with very substantial shareholdings who may be assumed to be either themselves sophisticated investors or guided by professionals in their investment decisions. Only a small fraction of stock even in publicly held corporations appears to be under the direct ownership of unsophisticated investors with tiny holdings. 'The average shareholder', who holds centre stage in the theories of so many commentators, appears to be only an extra in the real corporate world.[30]

The passive shareholder

Effectively, then, shareholders may have little practical control over directors in the day-to-day running of the company. Their control is indirect, exercised primarily by removing a delinquent director from office. The inability of shareholders to exercise control is one thing. A further question is whether shareholders *would* exercise control if they could. There is considerable evidence that shareholders, at least in public companies, are primarily passive investors, rather than members who have any expectation or desire to participate in the governance of that association.

Some commentators have suggested that the issue of shareholder apathy is no longer relevant because of the holdings of institutional shareholders.[31] The rise in institutional investment means that there is now a body of shareholders in concentrated holdings who have the expertise to control corporate management. Others have drawn different implications from the phenomenon of institutional shareholding. Hadden, for instance, suggests that the issue is made more pressing

---

30 Eisenberg, 'The Legal Roles of Shareholder and Management' at 53.
31 See, further, M. Lipton and Rosenblum, 'A New System of Corporate Governance: The Quinquennial Election of Directors' (1991) 58 Chi L Rev 187; M. L. Rock, 'The Logic and (Uncertain) Significance of Institutional Shareholder Activism' (1991) 79 Geo L Rev 445; P. Black, 'Shareholder Passivity Re-examined' (1990) 79 Geo L Rev 445.

by institutional investment, because shareholders are relegated to the role of 'mere beneficiaries'.

Even where shareholders can participate, it is argued, they do not. But is this an instance of shareholder passivity, or of the effect of barriers to shareholder participation? For instance, Renton notes that, when shareholders are invited to ask questions and comment at the end of the chair's address at an annual general meeting, there is often silence:

> Perhaps the reason for the silence is that many of the people attending such gatherings are very conscious that they are not skilled in company law, in accounting principles, in the economy, in meetings procedure or in public speaking, and also that they really know too little of the company's affairs to want to ask an intelligent question in public. Some shareholders may not even have bothered to read the company's annual report and do not wish to be shown up by raising something which has already been explained in that document.[32]

Of course, management may make conscious efforts to silence shareholders. For instance, in the meeting, management may intimidate or embarrass questioners by drawing attention to the small number of shares they hold or to the short length of time they have been on the register. Alternatively, the chair may insist that all shareholders' questions be asked one after the other, with replies given later as a block, so that the opportunity for appropriate follow-up questions and comments are denied, or meetings may be held at times that are inconvenient, or in locations that are inaccessible.

Even if these barriers to participation are overcome, the normative question remains. *Should* shareholders play a greater role in corporate governance? We have already noted in the introduction to this chapter other commentators' suggestions that it is rational for shareholders to be passive. One only has to consider the costs to shareholders of making themselves informed so as to be able to vote intelligently, the minimal impact of their individual votes, the possibility that other shareholders will 'free ride' on their efforts, and the minimal incremental gain that will flow to them even if they are successful.

In the USA, regulations introduced by the Securities and Exchange Commission require all institutions to play a positive role in corporate governance by exercising their vote instead of remaining silent (or just selling their shares). Anecdotal evidence suggests that this shareholder activism is improving the performance of United States companies.[33]

Such participation may also serve to protect the shareholders themselves from abuse. To some extent, relatively passive shareholders rely on auditors to protect them from loss, both by minimising loss from fraud and by protecting them from investing in an unsound company. But fraud will go on regardless, and although auditors may detect irregularities early, this tends to limit (but not eliminate) the size of the loss.

---

32 Renton, p. 20.
33 Renton, p. 29.

REVIEW QUESTIONS

1 Read the following:

> In the case of a large public company, it would be impossible to vest the management power in shareholders. Indeed, it is difficult to put any form of business decision before shareholders, although occasionally it is necessary to do so because of requirements of the Corporations Law or listing rules. The information necessary for a sound decision is sometimes detailed, complex and confidential. Decisions frequently need to be taken more quickly than is possible if a meeting of shareholders must be convened. The cost of convening a meeting (including preparation, printing, postage, venue and advisers' fees) is very substantial.[34]

Do you agree with this statement? What does it assume about the nature of shareholders? Would it make a difference if the shareholders were primarily institutional investors? Could advances in technology, particularly in the use of the Internet, allow direct decision-making by shareholders? Would this be desirable?

2 Although a number of analysts have traced the problems of accountability to the separation of management and ownership, and to shareholder passivity, as outlined above, some law and economics scholars have drawn different conclusions from the separation thesis. They argue that, rather than being a problem, the separation of the ownership (or risk-bearing) function from the control (or decision-making) function can be seen as a rational response on the part of shareholders. There is no reason why those who supply capital to a corporation should have expertise in (or even a desire to be involved in) managing the company's affairs. In widely held companies, it is cheaper for the shareholders to acquire managers to exercise specialised managerial skills than for the shareholders to become involved themselves. Thus, shareholders are said to be 'rationally ignorant' of management activities, because any active and informed participation would involve large costs and each individual shareholder would have to share the benefits with others who might not contribute to these costs. Not only is it cheaper, but it also makes more sense, because shareholders stand to benefit from the specialised skills of managers.[35] Do you agree?

3 Our system of 'straight voting' (where each member casts one vote per share for a candidate for each vacancy to be filled) enables a bare majority of shares to elect the board. Some states of the USA adopted a system of cumulative voting, in which the number of shares held by a member is multiplied by the number of vacancies; the member can cast all his or her votes for a single candidate or distribute the total among several candidates. This system allows

---

34 H. A. J. Ford & R. P. Austin, *Principles of Corporation Law*, 7th edn, Butterworths, Sydney, 1995, p. 203.

35 M. Jenson & W. Meckling, 'Theory of the Firm: Managerial Behaviour, Agency Costs and Ownership Structure' (1976) 3 J Fin and Ec 305.

for minority representation on the board. It is argued that even the possibility of minority representation encourages directors to pay more attention to the various interests of a corporation. The absence of cumulative voting in Australia can be attributed to the fact that our system of corporate regulation regards the board as a body of supervisory managers who should be united in policy, rather than as representatives of divergent interests. ASX listing rule 3K prevents such a system in a listed company, but cumulative voting could be adopted in the articles of a non-listed company. Do you think that a system of cumulative voting would be advantageous?

Nature of duties

The secret of life is honesty and fair dealing. If you can fake that, you have it made.

Groucho Marx

At the beginning of this chapter, we observed that much of the current round of criticism of the regulation of directors stems from public reaction to the corporate excesses of the 1980s. We also observed that much of this criticism reveals often conflicting expectations of directors. Some have argued against the criticisms levelled at corporate regulation on the basis that only a small proportion of directors behave unethically. This small number attracts a disproportionate amount of media attention. Thus, the criticism of corporate regulation is unwarranted: 'In a general sense this may well be true, but it may also be that a lot of borderline activity has just not come to notice or even that it is being tolerated by shareholders without comment because the companies concerned are doing so well'.[36]

Directors, it can be argued, have ethical obligations to shareholders, employees (current, retrenched, retired, and dependants of deceased employees), lenders, general creditors, suppliers, and customers, and may have implied duties to the community at large (environment and taxation) and to future generations (research and development). But above all, these ethical obligations are ultimately constrained by the profit motive: 'Commercially, it is of little comfort for shareholders of a poorly-performing company to know that their directors, management and auditors are neither negligent nor fraudulent, just not very good at creating and conserving wealth'.[37]

Under the traditional model of corporate governance, the status and concomitant obligations of directors have never been clearly defined. From around 1844, directors were described as 'fiduciaries', but the exact nature and extent of their status as fiduciaries has been unclear. Courts likened directors' status to that of trustees,

---

36 Renton, p. xv.
37 From Independent Working Party into Corporate Governance, *Strictly Boardroom*, Report (F. G. Hilmer, Chair), Business Library, Melbourne, 1993, as quoted in Renton, p. 1. See also N. E. Renton (ed.), *Corporate Practices and Conduct*, Information Australia, Melbourne, 1993.

but directors are not properly trustees because they hold no title to corporate property and different expectations apply to them. Courts likened directors to agents, but directors' powers are wider than those of ordinary agents, and directors are usually free of close supervision by any readily identifiable principal. The search for a suitable analogy went on. Directors were described variously as 'managing partners', 'mandatories', 'fiduciary agents', and 'commercial men managing a trading concern for the benefit of themselves and all others'.

We have already pointed out two factors that are potentially in conflict in relation to the formulation of directors' duties. First, the obligations of directors must be sufficiently general to apply to a very diverse range of corporations. As we observed earlier, the conduct we would expect, for example, from a shopkeeper with a small proprietary, family company would differ considerably from that of the managing director of a large, multinational corporation.

Second, directors are caught in a web of interests created by the company structure. On the one hand, they must manage the corporation for the benefit of their shareholders (and, perhaps, for third parties such as creditors), but on the other, they must take risks and exercise business judgment, and these processes are, in the main, free of assessment by any outside body.

Thus, in order to cater for different sizes and types of corporation and to allow for risk-taking by directors, regulation has been by way of imposing a general minimum standard of conduct: the requirements of due care, skill, and honesty. The standards are intentionally made broad and flexible. The danger is that they become so broad and flexible that they fail to provide effective guidelines for legitimate conduct.

Under the common law and the Corporations Law, directors have the following duties:

- the duty to act honestly and in the best interests of the company (this is often broken down into the subcategories of the duty to avoid a conflict of interest and duty;[38] the duty to avoid competing with the company;[39] the duty to avoid contracts with the company;[40] and the duty not to misuse company opportunities or information[41])
- the duty to act for a proper corporate purpose[42]
- the duty to act with due care and skill.[43]

---

38   *Scottish Co-operative Wholesale Society Ltd v. Meyer* [1959] AC 324; *Re Broadcasting Station 2GB* [1964–5] 2 NSWR 1648

39   *Riteway Express Pty Ltd v. Clayton* (1987) 5 ACLR 1045; *Mordecai v. Mordecai and Others* (1988) 6 ACLC 370.

40   *Baker v. Palm Island Resort Pty Ltd* [1970] Qd R 210; *Hely-Hutchinson v. Brayhead Ltd* [1968] 1 QB 549.

41   *Queensland Mines Ltd v. Hudson* (1978) 52 ALJR 399; *R v. Chew* (1992) 10 ACLC 831; *Grove v. Flavel* (1986) 4 ACLC 654.

42   *Advance Bank of Australia Ltd v. FAI Insurances Australia Ltd* (1987) 5 ACLC 725; *Hannes and Ors v. MJH Pty Ltd and Ors* (1992) 10 ACLC 400; *Bailey v. Mandala Private Hospital Pty Ltd* (1988) ACLC 43; *Whitehouse and Another v. Carlton Hotel Pty Ltd* (1987) 5 ACLC 421; *Darvall v. North Sydney Brick and Tile Co. Ltd and Others (No. 2)* (1989) 7 ACLC 659.

43   *Harlowe's Nominees Pty Ltd v. Woodside (Lakes Entrance) Oil Co. NL* (1968) 121 CLR 483; *AWA Ltd v. Daniels t/a Deloitte Haskins & Sells* (1992) 10 ACLR 933; *(No. 2)* (1992) 10 ACLC 1643.

In addition to the general-law fiduciary duties, and those imposed by the Corporations Law, other legislation—for example, the TPA and the *Income Tax Assessment Act 1936* (Cth)—impose further statutory duties. There is a substantial overlap between fiduciary and statutory duties. Which of the fiduciary or statutory duties should be pleaded depends, among other things, on who is bringing the action (for example, a shareholder, the company itself, or the Australian Securities Commission) and on the remedy sought.

The stakeholders

Before we consider these duties in more detail, we should expand on our observation that it is unclear to whom directors owe their duties. This is a further complicating factor in assessing the effectiveness of accountability mechanisms. At common law, the traditional rule was that these duties were owed only to the company.[44] Lord Greene MR said that directors 'must exercise their discretion bona fide in what they consider—not what the court may consider—to be in the interests of the company, and not for any collateral purpose'.[45] But what is meant by the interests of the company as a whole? Evershed MR put the matter thus: 'the phrase, "the company as a whole" does not (at any rate in such a case as the present) mean the company as a commercial entity distinct from the corporators: it means the corporators as a general body. But can directors exercise their powers for the benefit of the company but to the detriment of the shareholders?'[46]

More recently, it has been suggested that directors' duties may be owed to employees, creditors, related companies, and individual shareholders. The possibility that duties are owed to individual shareholders was canvassed in *Coleman v. Myers*.[47] In this case, shareholders in a family company relied on the directors for advice about a takeover bid by a company owned by one of the directors. It was held that the directors owed a fiduciary duty to the shareholders to disclose any material facts that would affect the shareholders' decision regarding whether to buy or sell.[48] Woodhouse J noted the factors that would give rise to a fiduciary duty to individual shareholders: 'They include, I think, dependence upon information and advice, the existence of a relationship of confidence, the significance of some particular transaction for the parties and, of course, the extent of any positive action taken by or on behalf of the director or directors to promote it'.[49]

An even wider view of directors' duties was expressed by Hodgson J. in *Darvall v. North Sydney Brick and Tile Co. Ltd and Others*:

---

44 *Percival v. Wright* [1902] 2 Ch D 421.

45 *Re Smith & Fawcett Ltd* [1942] 1 All ER 542.

46 *Greenhalgh v. Arderne Cinemas Ltd* [1951] 1 Ch 286.

47 [1977] 2 NZLR 225.

48 See also *Walker v. Wimborne* (1975–76) CLC 40–251; *Hurley and Anor v. BGH Nominees Pty Ltd and Ors (No. 2)* (1984) 2 ACLC 497, where the court held that, in appropriate circumstances, directors of companies that act as trustees owe duties not only to individual shareholders but also to the beneficiaries of the trusts.

49 *Coleman v. Myers* [1977] 2 NZLR 225 at 323.

In my view, it is proper to have regard to the interest of the members of the company, as well as having regard to the interests of the company as a commercial entity. Indeed, it is proper also to have regard to the interests of the creditors of the company. I think it is proper to have regard to the interests of present and future members of the company, on the footing that it would be continued as a going concern.[50]

Hodgson J observed that it was proper to act in the best interests of the company as a commercial entity, even though this may not be in the short-term interests of the shareholders.

In *Walker v. Wimborne*,[51] directors were held liable for misapplication of funds in the course of a breach of duty. Mason J said that 'the directors of a company in discharging their duty to the company must take account of the interest of its shareholders and its creditors. Any failure by the directors to take into account the interests of creditors will have adverse consequences for the company as well as for them'.[52] Consideration of this multiplicity of interests may have one of two effects. Either the interests of the group as a whole may be subverted to the interests of partial groups or action may become impossible as the association becomes atomised by the conflict of interests it creates. James O'Toole, in the context of United States democracy and its implications for corporate management, argues that 'conflict-ridden pluralistic systems regress into stasis; immobilized by the forces of competing factions, they become unable to change in the face of a growing number of intractable problems. On this score, American democracy has recently been criticized as a "trap" in which the self-indulgent pursuit of individual interests precludes any sacrifice for the common good'.[53] On the other hand, if we accept the narrow view—that is, that directors only owe their duties to the company—not only is an individual shareholder often prevented from gaining redress against the wrongdoers under the rule in *Foss v. Harbottle*, but the ability of the community in general to control the immoral or socially irresponsible acts of corporations is also seriously limited.

REVIEW QUESTION

Is the dichotomy between the wide and narrow views of directors' duties analogous to the uncertainty surrounding politician's duties in the nation state? In particular, compare the company/third-party interests dichotomy with difficul-

---

50   (1988) 6 ACLC 154 at 175–6. For another example of the wide view, see *Jeffree v. NCSC* (1989) 15 ACLR 217.

51   (1976) 137 CLR 1.

52   (1976) 137 CLR 1 at 7. See also *Equiticorp Financial Services Ltd v. Equiticorp Financial Services Ltd (NZ) and Ors* (1993) 11 ASCR 642. This wider common-law view is more in accordance with legislative reforms. For instance, in regard to directors and other insiders who deal in securities while in possession of insider information, statutory provisions have replaced the rule in *Percival v. Wright*. In addition, under the Corporations Law, creditors can recover compensation from directors who knowingly allow the company to incur debts that it cannot repay (s. 588G) and where dividends are paid other than out of profits (s. 201).

53   J. O'Toole, *The Executive's Compass*, Oxford University Press, New York, 1993, p. 112.

ties posed for government by the dichotomy of domestic interests and international interests. Consider, too, the way in which politicians owe duties to their parties as well as to their constituents and the nation as a whole—interests that may well be competing.

The duties

Good faith

As fiduciaries, directors must act not only honestly, but also in the best interests of the company. The classic formulation of this duty is to 'act bona fide in what they consider—not what the court may consider—is in the interests of the company'.[54] But this is not merely a subjective duty. Even if a director believes himself to be acting honestly, he may be in breach of duty because he has not properly considered the interests of the company. Under the broad heading of this duty, the director is obliged to:

- act bona fide in the interests of the company
- use powers for their proper purpose
- retain discretionary powers
- avoid actual and potential conflicts of interest and duty.

We shall briefly outline each of these subcategories in turn.

Acting bona fide in the interests of the company

The duty to act bona fide in the interests of the company is a subjective duty—that is, in order to establish a breach of the duty, a complainant must show that the directors did not act in what they honestly believed to be the best interests of the company at the time. This is not necessarily easy to establish, and courts are reluctant to intervene in the commercial decisions of directors. For instance, in *Re Smith & Fawcett Ltd*,[55] Smith and Fawcett formed a company to take over their business. They were the only directors of the company, and the shareholding was divided equally between them. The company's articles provided that the directors had a discretion to refuse to register any transfer of shares. Fawcett died. His executors applied to Smith to be registered as members of the company and to have Fawcett's son (the plaintiff) appointed as director. Smith refused to consent to the registration or the appointment; although he did offer to register 2001 shares and acquire 2000 of these at a price he would fix. The plaintiff rejected this offer. Smith appointed his solicitor as company director. The plaintiff again applied to be registered as a member, but was refused. He then sought to have the company's share register rectified to show that he was the holder of half the company's shares. This application was refused both at first instance and on appeal. Lord Greene MR said:

---

54 *Re Smith & Fawcett Ltd* (1942) Ch 304 at 306 per Lord Greene MR.
55 (1942) Ch 304.

In the present case the principal director has sworn an affidavit which, if accepted, makes it clear that, whether rightly or wrongly, the directors have bona fide considered the interests of the company and come to the conclusion that it would be undesirable to register the transfer of the totality of these shares. Accordingly, on the evidence I am satisfied, as the learned judge was satisfied, that there is no ground shown here for saying that the directors' refusal has been due to anything but a bona fide consideration of the interests of the company as the directors see them. That being so, and that being, on the true construction of the article, the only matter to which the directors have to pay regard, I am of the opinion that the learned judge was right in the conclusion to which he came and that this appeal fails.[56]

Furthermore, determining just what is meant by 'the interests of the company', as we discussed above, is a difficult task. Nevertheless, actions seeking a remedy for failure to act bona fide in the interests of the company have been sustained. Commonly, they occur in small, proprietary companies where directors treat company assets as personal assets or otherwise use company resources for their own benefit.

An instance of this sort of breach can be seen in *Bailey v. Mandala Private Hospital Pty Ltd*,[57] where a director (also the controlling shareholder of the company) arranged for the company to issue shares to his de facto wife so that she would control both the company and the house on his death. A minority shareholder successfully sought a declaration from the court that the share issue was invalid.

In a very different context, this duty can be seen in *ANZ Executors & Trustees Co. Ltd v. Qintex Australia Ltd (recs & mgrs apptd)*.[58] In this case, a parent company covenanted with a financier to obtain guarantees from its wholly owned subsidiaries to support its borrowings. The parent defaulted on its loan repayments, and the financier sought specific performance of the covenant. The subsidiaries, however, were insolvent. Their directors argued that giving the guarantee would be in breach of their fiduciary duty to the subsidiaries' creditors. The court refused to order specific performance on the grounds that the subsidiary's power to guarantee a loan was to be exercised for the benefit of the parent company and not the subsidiary.

REVIEW QUESTION

You may wish to consider the very difficult position of nominee directors. Whose interests should they serve? On the one hand, nominee directors are under a duty to act in the best interests of the company. If they do so to the detriment of their appointer, however, they face the possibility of being

---

56 (1942) Ch 304 at 309.

57 (1987) 12 ACLR 641.

58 [1991] 2 Qd R 360; (1990) 2 ACLR 676; 8 ACLC 980.

removed. Philip Crutchfield[59] suggests that there are three possible approaches to this problem. The first is the strict approach: once appointed, directors must act only in the best interests of the company, in preference to the wishes of appointers.[60] The second approach is to allow a nominee director to have regard to the appointor's interest provided that interest coincides with that of the company.[61] The third approach is to look to the constitutive documents of the company to determine the scope and nature of the fiduciary duty and hence determine the company's 'best interests'. Effectively, in this last scenario, shareholders determine the scope and nature of management obligations.[62] Which of these solutions do you consider to be most appropriate?

Avoiding actual and potential conflicts of interest and duty

The classic formulation of this rule is to be found in *Aberdeen Railway Company v. Blackie Bros* per Lord Cranworth LC:

> A corporate body can only act by agent, and it is, of course, the duty of those agents so to act as best to promote the interests of the corporation whose affairs they are conducting. Such agents have duties to discharge of a fiduciary nature towards their principal. And it is a rule of universal application that no one, having such duties to discharge, shall be allowed to enter into engagements in which he has, or can have, a personal interest conflicting, or which possibly may conflict, with the interests of those whom he is bound to protect. So strictly is this principle adhered to that no question is allowed to be raised as to the fairness or unfairness of a contract so entered into.[63]

This rule encompasses the principles that directors should not contract with the company; that directors should not take bribes or hidden profits; that directors should not misuse corporate funds, corporate opportunities, or corporate information; and that they should not enter into competition with the company. These duties arise under both common law and the Corporations Law.

Thus, the distinction is made between legitimate acts of directors (being those directed to the corporate good), and illegitimate acts (being those directed to the personal good). Corporate regulation, however, as we have observed, was also driven by the desirability of entrepreneurial activity. This distinction between self-interest and the corporate interest, strictly applied, would limit such activity. Lord Herschell stated in *Bray v. Ford* that:

> It is an inflexible rule of a Court of Equity that a person in a fiduciary position ... is not, unless otherwise expressly provided, entitled to make a profit; he is not allowed to put

---

59 P. D. Crutchfield, 'Nominee Directors: The Law and Commercial Reality' (1992) 20 ABLR 109.

60 *Bennetts v. Board of Fire Commissioners of New South Wales* (1967) 87 WN (NSW) 307.

61 See, for instance, *Re Broadcasting Station 2GB Ltd* (1964–65) NSWR 1648 at 1662 per Jacobs J; *Re News Corporation Ltd* (1987) 70 ALR 419 at 436–7 per Bowen LJ.

62 *Levin v. Clark* [1962] NSWR 686; *Berlei Hestia (NZ) Ltd v. Fernyhough* [1980] 2 NZLR 150.

63 (1884) 1 Macq 461 at 471.

himself in a position where his interest and duty conflict. It does not appear to me that this rule is, as has been said, founded on principles of morality. I regard it rather as based on the consideration that, human nature being what it is, there is danger, in such circumstances, of the person holding a fiduciary position being swayed by interest rather than duty, and thus prejudicing those whom he was bound to protect. It has, therefore, been deemed expedient to lay down this positive rule. But I am satisfied that it might be departed from in many cases, without any breach of morality, without any wrong being inflicted and without consciousness of wrongdoing.[64]

The rule against directors acting in their own self-interest is thus not absolute. Taking one area of the duty—that of contracting with the company—as an example, the rule was relaxed in a number of ways: First, directors could contract with the company, provided that the articles allowed them to do so.[65] Second, the rule that directors cannot contract with the company is qualified by the rule that, in order for directors to be in breach of their duty, they must have a 'material interest' in the contract with the company,[66] and this interest must be certain and enforceable, not the mere prospect of deriving a benefit. Third, directors can avoid being in breach of duty if they make full and frank disclosure of their interest in any contract with the company.[67] The original requirement for disclosure was that this disclosure should be made to the general meeting.[68] This, too, has been relaxed in some cases so that disclosure to the board is sufficient.[69]

REVIEW QUESTION

As part of Stage 3 of the Simplification Program, it is proposed that s. 231 be replaced with a requirement that directors of all companies disclose any

---

65 [1896] AC 44 at 51.

65 See, for instance, *Re Automotive & General Industries Ltd* [1975] VR 454, where the relevant articles provided that No contract made by a director with the company and no contract or arrangement entered into by or on behalf of the company, with a company or partnership of or in which any director is a director, member or otherwise is any way interested shall be avoided, nor shall any director so contracting or being so interested be liable to account to the company for any profit realised by any such contract or arrangement by reason only of such director holding his office or of the fiduciary relation thereby established.

The court in this case held that this provision saved contracts made with directors, even though such contract gave rise to a conflict of interests.

66 See Corporations Law, s. 231(2).

67 *Furs Ltd v. Tomkies* (1936) 54 CLR 583; *Regal (Hastings) Ltd v. Gulliver* [1942] 1 All ER 378. In addition, under the Corporations Law, s. 1318(1), officers of a corporation may be relieved from liability if, in any civil proceedings against them for negligence, default, breach of trust, or breach of duty, it appears to the court that they acted honestly and ought fairly to be excused. Where the court grants such relief, the officer may be indemnified under the articles for his or her legal costs in relation to the proceedings under the Corporations Law, s. 241(2).

68 *Furs Ltd v. Tomkies*; *Regal (Hastings) Ltd v. Gulliver*. In addition, a director, although precluded from voting as a director in a resolution to absolve him or herself from a breach of duty, can vote as a shareholder. See *East Pant Du United Lead Mining Co. Ltd v. Merryweather* (1864) 2 H & M 254 at 261; 71 ER 460 at 463, per Sir W. Page Wood VC.

69 *Queensland Mines Ltd v. Hudson* (1978) 52 ALJR 399.

'material personal interests' that they have in the affairs of the company. This is the same requirement as presently exists in s. 232A for directors of public companies. What benefits are likely to flow from this reform?

Duty not to fetter discretions

Directors may, under the corporate constitution, have a variety of discretions. These include the power to engage employees, to buy and sell property, to decide on company borrowings, to issue shares, and so on. In regard to these discretions, directors are under a duty to give adequate consideration when purporting to exercise a particular discretion and are under a duty to retain their discretions. This does not mean, however, that directors cannot appoint agents to act on their behalf, delegate to a managing director, or delegate a matter to a senior management committee, provided that the board gives due consideration to any report the committee might make.[70] At least one commentator has seen this duty as, in essence, otiose:

> The prohibition against fettering a discretion … would have been too onerous a burden on directors if it forbade them from delegating any discretion. But they were not permitted to delegate their discretion in such a way as to exclude their own power to act. This flowed from the nature of their acceptance of power to decide and from the requirement in law that they be responsible. The difficult question was the degree to which the duty restricted directors from making any decision which fettered the company's freedom to act in the future. All decisions are meant to decide for the future and therefore can be seen as fettering the freedom to act. The line between validly deciding and fettering a discretion is arbitrarily drawn, as befits a duty arising from the pragmatic needs of law. Recourse to principle would have revealed that the duty not to fetter discretions was unnecessary from the start: asking whether the purpose of making the decision which purportedly fetters the discretion is proper serves the same function.[71]

The Second Corporate Law Simplification Bill 1995 proposes that directors be allowed to delegate any of their powers to a committee of directors, and that the effect of the committee exercising a power (in accordance with any directions given by the board) is the same as if the board exercised it. This provision will be a 'replaceable rule' so it could be excluded or varied by the company.

Acting for proper purposes

As we have seen, the company's articles confer various powers on directors, such as the power to issue shares, to borrow money, or to hire employees. Directors cannot exercise these powers 'in order to obtain some private advantage or for any purpose foreign to the power'.[72] The approach taken by judges to an allegation of acting for improper purposes is, first, to determine the nature of the power and the purpose

---

70   *AWA Ltd v. Daniels t/a Deloitte Haskins & Sells.*

71   D. Wishart, *Company Law in Context,* Oxford University Press, Auckland, 1994, p. 223.

72   *Mills v. Mills* (1938) 60 CLR 150.

for which it was conferred by reference to the company's articles. Second, the judge will identify the purpose, on the facts, for which the power was exercised and ask what the directors subjectively believed at the time at which they exercised the power. And finally, the judge will seek to determine whether the purpose for which the power was actually exercised was within those permitted.

Difficulties arise where several purposes can be ascribed to a director's actions. In this case, the courts have held that, if the substantial or dominant purpose is improper, the act is invalid.[73] However, in *Whitehouse and Another v. Carlton Hotel Pty Ltd*,[74] the court held that, where there are multiple purposes, the appropriate test is to ask whether the director would not have exercised the power 'but for' that improper purpose.[75] In *Whitehouse*, Carlton Hotel was a family company that was under the control of the father, who was governing director. According to the articles, the governing director had sole power to issue shares. The company capital was divided into three classes of shares: 'A-class' shares held by the father, 'B-class' shares held by the mother, and 'C-class' shares held by the six children. The C-class shares had no voting rights. B-class shares only had voting rights upon the death of the father.

The parents divorced, and the family split, the four daughters siding with their mother, and the two sons with their father. To ensure that the mother and the daughters would not gain control of the company upon his death, the father issued further B-class shares to his sons. The mother had no knowledge of this share allotment, and the issue was not recorded in the company's share register. Some time later, the father and sons had a disagreement. The father purported to annul his allotment of B-class shares. The sons sought rectification of the register. The company argued that the share allotment was invalid on the basis that the governing director had issued the shares for an improper purpose—that is, to ensure that the mother and daughters did not get control of the company after the father's death. The allotment was held invalid, despite the fact that the father may have genuinely believed that the allotment was in the company's interests: 'It is simply no part of the function of the directors as such to favour one shareholder or group of shareholders by exercising a fiduciary power to allot shares for the purpose of diluting the voting power attaching to the issued shares held by some other shareholder or group of shareholders.'[76] Such an allotment is invalid if the wrongful purpose is causative—that is, but for its presence, no allotment would be made.

Allegations of improper purposes most commonly arise in takeover situations (and are covered in chapter 13). They have also arisen in areas such as share issue, as in *Whitehouse*, and directors' refusal to register share transfers.[77]

---

73 *Mills v. Mills.*
74 (1987) 162 CLR 285.
75 This test was applied in *Permanent Building Society (in liq.) v. Wheeler* (1994) 14 ACSR 109.
76 (1987) 162 CLR 285 at 289.
77 See, for instance, *Australian Metropolitan Life Assurance Co. Ltd v. Ure* (1923) 33 CLR 199.

REVIEW QUESTION

Where the directors on a board each act for different purposes, how should the court determine whether a power has been exercised for an improper purpose?[78]

Duty to act honestly

Section 232(2) provides that an officer shall 'act honestly in the exercise of his or her powers and the discharge of the duties of his or her office'. The section corresponds essentially to the fiduciary duty to act bona fide in the best interests of the company as a whole.

In the past judges have been reluctant to find that this section was breached if there was no criminal intent evident on the facts before them.[79] This was because, until 1993, a breach of this section had criminal consequences. Thus, directors were not in breach of s. 232(2) if they believed that they were acting in the company's best interests, even if they were acting for improper purposes.[80] Now, however, criminal consequences only attach where dishonest intent is present.

General law and statutory duties of care

Traditionally, at common law, directors need only exercise that degree of care demanded by their particular level of expertise. For instance, in *Re Brazilian Rubber Estates*, Neville J said:

> One cannot say whether a man has been guilty of negligence, gross or otherwise, unless one can determine what is the extent of the duty which he is alleged to have neglected. A director's duty has been laid down as requiring him to act with such care as is reasonably to be expected from him, having regard to his knowledge and experience. He is, I think, not bound to bring any special qualifications to his office. He may undertake the management of a rubber company in complete ignorance of everything connected with rubber, without incurring responsibility for the mistakes which may result from such ignorance; while if he is acquainted with the rubber business he must give the company the advantage of his knowledge when transacting the company's business. He is not, I think, bound to take any definite part in the conduct of the company's business, but so far as he does undertake it he must use reasonable care in its dispatch.[81]

In the case *of Re City Equitable Fire Insurance Co. Ltd*, Romer J said that a 'director of a life insurance company, for instance, does not guarantee that he has the skill

---

78 See *Harlowe's Nominees Pty Ltd v. Woodside (Lakes Entrance) Oil Co. NL* (1968) 121 CLR 483; *Re Southern Resources Ltd* (1989) 15 ACLR 770.

79 See, for instance, *Marchesi v. Barnes* [1970] VR 434; *Flavel v. Roget* (1990) 8 ACLC 237; *Feil v. Commissioner of Corporate Affairs* (1991) 9 ACLC 811.

80 Note, however, the contrary view expressed in *Australian Growth Resources Corp. Pty Ltd v. van Reesema* (1988) 6 ACLC 529 per King J that s. 232(2) can be breached if directors act for an improper purpose, even if they have acted honestly.

81 [1911] 1 Ch 425 at 437.

of an actuary or of a physician'.[82] At common law, the director was not even required to attend board meetings if this would be inconvenient or onerous. Given the centrality of the corporation to our economic system and the wide-reaching effects that corporate failure can have, we may wish to consider whether this seems reasonable today. Referring to Romer J's example of the director of a life insurance company, Menzies J said (speaking extra-curially):

> [O]f such a director it can properly be demanded that he should have or obtain at least a general understanding of the business of life assurance, that he should know or learn something about the investment of large sums of money in a changing economy, that he should concern himself with important staff problems and that he should bring an informed and independent judgment to bear upon the various matters that come to the board for decision. Any life insurance company appointing a director would expect all of this from him; any person accepting office as director would expect to do as much and, to repeat myself again, what is expected is the best indication of the content of the duty of care that rests upon an office holder.[83]

The standard of care required of company directors has recently been restated by the Corporations Law so as to stress the fact that the test of care and diligence is objective.[84] Section 232(4) provides that an officer of a corporation must exercise the degree of care and diligence that a reasonable person in a like position in a corporation would exercise given the corporation's circumstances. Any assessment of liability will inevitably depend on what we perceive the board's function to be. In *AWA Ltd v. Daniels t/a Deloitte Haskins & Sells*, a company made considerable losses because of the ineffective implementation of the company's foreign-exchange policy. The broad policy on foreign exchange established by the board could not be sufficiently enforced because of lack of internal controls and effective reporting.[85] His Honour held that non-executive directors were entitled to rely on information provided by the company's management and auditors without further inquiry. The Chief Executive, however, who was privy to management information that suggested that internal controls were insufficient, and who failed to investigate the matter further, was in breach of his duty to exercise reasonable care and diligence.[86] Two further decisions—*ASC v. Gallagher*[87] and *Vrisakis v. ASC*[88]—applied the decision

---

82 [1925] Ch 407 at 428.

83 Sir Douglas Menzies, 'Company Directors' (1959) 33 ALJ 156 at 163–4.

84 The section now reads, 'In the exercise of his or her powers and the discharge of his or her duties, an officer of a corporation must exercise the degree of care and diligence that a reasonable person in a like position in a corporation would exercise in the corporation's circumstances'.

85 See quotation from Rogers CJ on pp. 232–3.

86 In *AWA Ltd v. Daniels t/a Deloitte Haskins & Sells (No. 2)*, His Honour refused to relieve this executive from liability on the basis that he made honest errors of judgment: 'honest bungling' was not, in His Honour's view, a sufficient basis for relief.

87 (1993) 11 ACLC 286.

88 (1993) 11 ASCR 162.

in *AWA v. Daniels*. In the former case, Gallagher was a non-executive director of Rothwells. There were a number of problems with Rothwells' loan portfolio, including a very large exposure to related groups and a lack of security for many loans, information of which Gallagher was unaware. Gallagher was charged under the equivalent of s. 232(4) with failing to exercise a reasonable degree of care and diligence by failing to inform himself reasonably about the financial affairs of Rothwells. The magistrate at first instance dismissed the offence. This was upheld on appeal by Pidgeon J, who said that 'the test is basically an objective one in the sense that the question is what an ordinary person, with the knowledge and experience of the defendant, might be expected to have done in the circumstances if he was acting on his own behalf'.[89] In the circumstances, Gallagher was justified in his belief that relevant information would be passed on to him.

In the latter case, Vrisakis was a director appointed as part of the arrangements associated with the rescue package of Rothwells. He was a non-executive director but was an experienced commercial solicitor. He successfully appealed a conviction for breaches of the duty of care and diligence under s. 232(4). It was alleged that Vrisakis had failed to take reasonable steps to ensure that effect was given to the terms of a business plan and management restructure that were contained in the paper prepared by him and adopted by the resolution of the directors of Rothwells at a meeting in 1987.[90] Ipp J said:

> [T]he mere fact that a director participates in conduct that carries with it a foreseeable risk of harm to the interests of the company will not necessarily mean that he has failed to exercise a reasonable degree of care and diligence in the discharge of his duties. The management and direction of companies involve taking decisions and embarking upon actions which may promise much, on the one hand, but which are, at the same time, fraught with risk on the other. That is inherent in the life of industry and commerce; the legislature undoubtedly did not intend by s. 229(2) [now s. 232(4)] to dampen business enterprise and penalise legitimate but unsuccessful entrepreneurial activity. Accordingly, the question whether a director has exercised a reasonable degree of care and diligence can only be answered by balancing the foreseeable risk of harm against the potential benefits that could reasonably have been expected to accrue to the company from the conduct in question.[91]

Does the decision in *AWA v. Daniels* set the standard for directors' duties of care too low? The report of the Royal Commission into the State Bank of South Australia states that:

> The Commissioners' view is that the courts are likely to examine critically any failure by directors to be sufficiently well informed about matters affecting the financial performance and health of their corporations, even if they are non-executive directors ... They

---

89   (1993) 11 ACLC 286 at 298.

90   See K. Whitford, 'The Year that was in Company Law' (1994) 4 AJCL 20; 'Note' (1993) 9 Co Director 6.

91   (1993) 11 ASCR 162 at 212.

assert that it is not enough for directors to pronounce on policy … and emphasise 'the need for directors to be of an inquiring mind'.[92]

These cases show the continued deference of the courts to directors' 'business expertise'. This has been an ongoing tension in our scheme of corporate account-ability. For instance, in the *Harlowe's Nominees* case, the High Court stated that 'Directors in whom are vested the right and duty of deciding where the company's interests lie and how they are to be served may be concerned with a wide range of practical considerations and their judgment if exercised in good faith and not for irrelevant purposes is not open to review by the court'.[93]

This reluctance can, at least in part, be attributed to the public/private dichotomy. The internal workings of companies have traditionally been seen as 'private' matters, so that courts should not intervene in management decisions. This divide is, however, highly questionable in at least two ways. One artificiality in this context is that the so-called 'private' matter of a board's decision can have far-reaching ramifications with regard to a range of third parties, including employees, creditors, and members of the community. Second, this reluctance can be seen to stem from judicial deference to directors' business expertise. This can, in turn, be attributed to the desire to encourage risk-taking, but it is difficult to reconcile this with the notion that directors need not have a particular standard of knowledge or ability.

In addition to the duties that we have discussed so far, the Corporations Law also imposes certain additional statutory duties upon directors, most notably the duty to prevent insolvent trading.

Insolvent trading

As we have seen in the earlier discussion of corporate morality, attaching personal liability for insolvent trading to directors is an attempt to redress the problems caused by *Salomon v. Salomon & Co. Ltd.*[94] While s. 588G is similar to the previous s. 592 in a number of ways, it is considerably more rigorous than the earlier provi-sion in that it imposes a positive duty upon directors to prevent insolvent trading by any company that they manage. Breach of this duty gives rise to a civil penalty and personal liability to pay compensation, and any creditor who suffers loss as a conse-quence of a breach of s. 588G may sue the director for the loss suffered. The aim of this provision is to ensure that directors stop incurring debts and initiate winding-up proceedings if it is reasonably apparent that the company is failing.

In order to incur liability, the following must be shown:

---

92   Royal Commission into the State Bank of South Australia, *First Report* (Hon. S. J. Jacobs, Royal Commissioner), South Australian Government Printer, Adelaide, 1992, p. 43.

93   (1968) 121 CLR 483 at 483.

94   [1897] AC 22.

- An individual was a director at the time that the debt is incurred.
- Either the company is insolvent or the debt will lead the company to become insolvent.
- There are reasonable grounds to suspect that the company was insolvent or would become insolvent at the time that the debt was incurred.
- The director was aware of these grounds (or a reasonable person in a like position in a company in the circumstances of that company would be so aware).
- The director has failed to prevent the company from incurring the debt.

However, the imposition of liability is not absolute. There are a number of potential defences available to a director under s. 588H. These are that:

- the director had reasonable grounds to expect, and did expect, that the company was solvent at the time and would remain solvent even if it incurred the debt
- the director expected that the company was solvent on the basis of information supplied by a subordinate. The director must believe on reasonable grounds that the subordinate was a competent and reliable person who was responsible for providing adequate information about the company's solvency.
- the director, because of illness or some other good reason, did not take part in management at the relevant time
- the director took all reasonable steps to prevent the company from incurring the debt.

REVIEW QUESTIONS

1 Jennifer and Adrian are married and have four children. They are the sole directors and shareholders of Bell Pty Ltd, a company that makes electrical components. Jennifer plays no part in the business at all, being concerned with home duties and the care of children. It appears that Bell has incurred debts while insolvent. Adrian was confident that the company could trade out of its difficulties, but this was not the case. Can Jennifer rely upon the defence of justifiable non-participation in management of the company under s. 588G?

2 In its expectation of solvency, what does s. 588H demand? Must the director have reasonable grounds for making the prediction?[95]

3 Is it fair that s. 588H imposes a blanket defence of reasonable reliance for all companies? Does this allow the directors of small companies to avoid liability in circumstances where one would reasonably expect them to have a more comprehensive knowledge of their companies' finances than would the directors of large companies?

---

95   See *3M Australia Ltd v. Kemish* (1986) 10 ACLR 371; *Commonwealth Bank of Australia v. Friedrich* (1991) 5 ACSR 115.

Civil and criminal consequences of breach of duty

At general law, a breach of the directors' duties most commonly gives rise to damages or compensation, but directors may also, depending on the circumstances, be liable for:

- account of profits
- rescission of a contract where a director has an undisclosed interest in a contract with the company
- declaration of trust and return of property
- claim to an equitable charge over an asset if the company's funds can be traced to that asset.

In addition, directors who are in breach of their duties may find that they are subject to other outcomes, such as termination of their service contracts if the breach amounts to misconduct.

The Corporations Law provides both civil and criminal penalties for breach of directors' duties. The civil penalty provisions apply to breaches of s. 232(2), (4), and (6) (the directors' duties provisions); s. 243ZE(2) and (3) (the related party transactions provisions); s. 318(1) (the accounts provisions); and s. 588G, (the duty to prevent insolvent trading provision). A civil penalty order allows the court to:

- prohibit a person from managing a corporation or impose a fine of up to $200 000
- convict the wrongdoer of a criminal offence, with a maximum penalty of a fine of $200 000 and/or imprisonment for up to 5 years
- make an order that the wrongdoer compensate the corporation.

A criminal penalty can be imposed if there is dishonest intent as described in s. 1317FA.

You may wish to consider how successful these penalties are in deterring wrongful conduct. As we noted earlier, our system of corporate regulation tends to impose provisions upon companies irrespective of their size or nature. A fine of $200 000 may be significant to the director of a small family company, but relatively insignificant to the director of a large public company. And, as we have seen from the Skase saga, many directors of large companies may have the ability to evade prosecution successfully.

In addition, it is possible for directors to be exonerated from liability for at least some breaches of duty. The general meeting has the power to excuse a director's breach of duty by ratifying the director's actions. The general meeting may accept a conflict of interest where full disclosure is made,[96] or they may ratify actions of directors who use their power for improper purposes.[97] They do not, however, have power to ratify where such ratification would constitute a fraud on the minority;[98]

---

96 As in *Regal (Hastings) Ltd v. Gulliver*.
97 As in *Bamford v. Bamford* [1970] Ch 212.
98 *Ngurli Ltd v. McCann* (1953) 90 CLR 425. See also chapter 14.

where the company is near insolvency and ratification would prejudice creditors;[99] where a member's personal right would be infringed;[100] or where the ratification would constitute oppression.

The court also has power to exonerate an allegedly delinquent company director. Under s. 1318, if (in any civil proceedings for 'negligence, default, breach of duty or breach of trust') the defendant can demonstrate that he or she acted honestly and that, having regard to all the circumstances of the case (including those connected with his or her appointment), the defendant ought fairly to be excused for the negligence, default, or breach, the court may relieve the defendant either wholly or in part from his or her liability in such terms as it sees fit.

REVIEW QUESTIONS

1 Are the proceedings under s. 588G (insolvent trading provisions) proceedings for 'negligence, default, breach of duty or breach of trust' as required by s. 1318?[101]

2 Kate is a leading authority on aromatherapy. She was a director of Mother Earth Pty Ltd. While director, she had access to confidential information regarding oil blends as well as a list of clients of Mother Earth. A competitor, Goddess Products, approached Kate and offered her a considerable salary increase, shares in Goddess Products Pty Ltd, and the managing directorship if she would bring her skills, knowledge, and the client list to Goddess Products. Kate did so, resigning from Mother Earth and not disclosing the deal to anyone. Mother Earth suffered significant losses and, having discovered the truth about Kate's resignation, seeks your advice about possible legal actions. What do you advise?

Conclusion

Corporate governance is a messy compromise. It is the site of many tensions. Among these are the tension between risk-taking by directors and protection of shareholders; the tension between corporate regulation and principles of non-intervention; the tension between the company as an ongoing entity and the individuals who comprise it. Directors are, at least in theory, constrained in very specific ways regarding the untoward exercise of their powers: they must act bona fide for the good of the company as a whole; their functions are generally confined to managing 'the business of the company'; and they may be appointed or dismissed by the

---

99   *Kinsela v. Russell Kinsela Pty Ltd (in liq.)* (1986) 4 ACLC 215.

100   *Residues Treatment & Trading Co. Ltd v. Southern Resources Ltd (No. 4)* (1988) 14 ACLR 569.

101   See *Commonwealth Bank of Australia v. Friedrich; Standard Chartered Bank of Australia Ltd v. Antico* (1995) 18 ACSR 1.

shareholders. In reality, however, we have seen that the courts have been unable to explain precisely what 'the interests of the company as a whole' are. We have also seen that 'the business of the company' has never been the subject of rigorous analysis, and that shareholder control is, very often, merely a fiction.

10

FUNERAL RITES:
DISSOLUTION AND DEATH

Introduction

In the last chapter, we discussed the issue of corporate governance. In this chapter we will discuss what could be termed the 'death' of the company. Companies, it is said, have 'perpetual existence'. They maintain the same identity, despite changes to the shareholders. They may exist forever. But this is not to say that the company *will* necessarily exist forever. The corporate entity may be dissolved for a variety of reasons.

The termination of the company form is referred to as 'winding-up' or 'liquidation'. Legally, the term refers to 'a form of external administration under which a liquidator takes control of a company's affairs to discharge its liabilities in preparation for its dissolution'.[1] It commences with a particular act, such as a court order. The company's assets are then liquidated, its creditors paid (to the extent that the assets allow this), and any remaining surplus distributed among its members. The commencement of liquidation does not, of itself, terminate the company. The company is, while being wound up, the same legal person as before. Its control, however, is vested in a liquidator rather than the directors and other officers (who, although a winding-up ends their powers, are still obliged to assist the liquidator). When the process is finalised, the Australian Securities Commission (ASC) strikes the company's name off the register, and the company ceases to exist. The company is now legally 'dead'. Thus, winding-up is a process, rather than an event, and this process may take several months, even years, to complete.

Divorce or euthanasia? Reasons for winding up the company
There are many possible reasons for companies to be wound up. Liquidation is usually undertaken as the result of the insolvency of the company, but this is not always the case. Sometimes it will be a result of the failure to comply with the *Corporations Law 1990* in some significant way.[2] In many cases, the company members will

1   H. A. J. Ford, R. P. Austin, & I. M. Ramsay, *Ford's Principles of Company Law*, 8th edn, Butterworths, Sydney, 1997, p. 1145.
2   In *Re Kurilpa Protestant Hall Pty Ltd* [1946] ST R Qd 170, the court ordered the winding up of a company on the just and equitable ground that the affairs of the company had been conducted since its incorporation in disregard of the *Companies Acts 1931–41* (Qld).

decide to wind up the company based on their mutual recognition that the corporate form has served its purpose, whatever that might be. Alternatively, a winding-up may be requested of the court when the company cannot continue to function because the tensions among the corporators have become so great that unified action is no longer possible. In the first two cases—where the company, as David Wishart puts it, 'ceases to be of social utility'[3]—it is effectively 'euthanased'; in the latter, the more appropriate analogy is that of a divorce:

> [The arrangement between the corporators] was a family arrangement in which their expectation was that they should act in the affairs of the company in a spirit of friendly co-operation for their common benefit and not one in which they contemplated that their rights and relations inter se would be governed by a strict application of the rules of company law. It is not part of my function to attempt to analyse or apportion the reasons for the animosity that has grown up between the parties. The divorce, and the inevitable litigation that has preceded or accompanied it, has in my view, destroyed the relationship of mutual trust and confidence which might otherwise have been expected to subsist between them as members of the same family group. It is no longer possible for them to work together for the common good or to rely, for the protection of their interests and investments in the company, upon the goodwill which they supposed would exist between them. The point has now been reached where such a state of animosity exists between them as precludes all reasonable hope of reconciliation and friendly co-operation in the affairs of the company.[4]

Because of these different reasons for winding up a company, companies may be wound up either voluntarily or compulsorily, by order of the court. Where the members wish to dissolve their business association, they will commonly initiate a members' voluntary liquidation. Where the company makes a formal declaration of solvency, the members are the principal beneficiaries in the distribution of the balance of the company's assets. Thus the State considers it appropriate that members control the liquidation. When the company is insolvent, however, the available assets will be distributed to creditors. In this case, the legislation provides that the creditors should direct the liquidation. It is still possible for the liquidation to be undertaken voluntarily with the consent of the company's members and officers. It is only when the members or officers refuse to wind up their company that an interested party, such as a creditor, need apply to the court for an order for compulsory winding-up.

The objectives of this chapter, then, are to consider the reasons why a company may be wound up and to discuss the ways in which liquidation may occur. We shall begin by outlining the legislative history of winding-up. This history reveals some of the problems posed to various interested parties by a company liquidation. We shall then proceed to discuss the winding-up process, before considering

---

3   D. Wishart, *Company Law in Context*, Oxford University Press, Auckland, 1994, p. 279.
4   *Re Dalkeith Investments Pty Ltd* (1985) 3 ACLC 74 at 79 per McPherson J.

voluntary administration, the role of the liquidator, the effects of liquidation, and finally, dissolution.

Legislative history

In our introduction, we pointed out that winding-up can be a lengthy and complicated process. To a substantial degree, this is the result of the problems caused to creditors by the doctrine of limited liability. Regulation of winding-up seeks to establish a relatively fair and orderly process of realisation and distribution of company assets. But what if there were no doctrine of limited liability? What would happen? In fact, prior to 1844, there was no distinct body of legal principles that could be regarded as the law of company liquidation.[5] All companies, except those that were incorporated by statute or charter, were deed-of-settlement organisations. They were treated for most purposes, including that of winding-up, as large partnerships. This was primarily because there was no widespread use of limited liability.

As you can imagine, this situation was largely unsatisfactory from the members' point of view. They were liable without limit for company debts.[6] Creditors could thus pursue the private assets of any of the members and could continue to do so until any or all of these members were bankrupt. Membership of a joint stock company engaged in trading was sufficient to attract the operation of the bankruptcy laws, which, at this time, were confined to merchants and traders.[7]

But this regulatory situation was not entirely satisfactory from a creditor's viewpoint either. A creditor had little choice but to pursue individual company members, because, to bring proceedings against a company's property, it was necessary to join each and every member of the company as a party. Where there was a large company that had continually changing membership, this was a practical nightmare. A further problem faced by creditors was that, once they brought proceedings against some members, other members (not surprisingly) disposed of their property or left the country in an attempt to avoid liability.

Regulators appreciated these problems, and made some attempt to remedy them. The *Joint Stock Companies Banking Act 1826*[8] was one such attempt. In relation to companies of more than six people carrying on the trade or business of bankers, it enabled the public officers to be sued on behalf of all the members (s. 4). This did not, however, solve the members' problems. Creditors could still proceed against them individually,[9] and members had no way of preventing a future increase in their

---

5   B. H. McPherson, *The Law of Company Liquidation*, 2nd edn, Law Book Company, Sydney, 1980, p. 9.

6   A type of limited liability, coupled with incorporation, was available under the *Chartered Companies Act 1837* (7 Wm IV & 1 Vict, c. 73), but these privileges relied upon the issue of letters patent by the Crown, and the Board of Trade was reluctant to extend these benefits.

7   *Re Hall; ex parte Hall* (1838) 8 LJ Bky 5.

8   7 Geo IV, c. 46.

9   *Re Marston, ex parte Marston* (1839) 9 LJ Bky; *Swift v. Winterbottom* (1873) LR 8 QB 244.

liability once it was certain that the company would fail. At the same time, the necessity of serving and joining all the members frustrated the creditors' attempts to have the company dissolved.[10]

In an attempt to overcome these problems, legislators passed the first major piece of legislation dealing with liquidations: the *Companies' Winding Up Act 1844*.[11] This was '[a]n Act for facilitating the winding up of the affairs of Joint Stock Companies unable to meet their pecuniary engagements'. Its purposes were, first, 'to extend the remedies of creditors against the property of companies; secondly, to facilitate the winding up of companies; and thirdly, to make provision for the discovery of abuses attending the formation and management of companies'.[12]

So that companies could be made bankrupt in a similar manner to individuals, s. 20 provided a process by which a court of bankruptcy could direct the creditors' assignees to apply to Chancery for an order to wind up the company's affairs, and by which it could compel a just contribution from all members towards full payment of the company's debts, liabilities, and the costs of winding-up. In addition, the Act required the court to hold an inquiry into the causes of the company's failure and to provide the Board of Trade with a balance sheet and report detailing the formation and management of the company's affairs (s. 25). On the recommendation of the board, the Crown could then annul the powers and privileges of the company (s. 26), and criminal proceedings could be brought by the attorney-general (s. 27).

You may be able to see from these provisions that the Act was primarily concerned with the rights of creditors. Although the Act did treat the company as a corporate entity in some ways,[13] there was no attempt to introduce limited liability. Thus, although corporate assets constituted the main fund out of which liabilities could be satisfied, any deficit could be made up by recourse to members' individual property.

The *Joint Stock Companies Winding Up Act 1848*[14] allowed members to apply to have a company wound up. It did so by allowing the 'contributories' to present a petition in Chancery for the dissolution and winding-up of a company in any one of a number of events (s. 5). After an order for dissolution and winding-up had been made, the Act provided for the appointment of an official manager (s. 22). The estate and effects of the company vested in this manager (s. 29), who was authorised to bring and defend proceedings in his own name on the company's behalf (s. 50). The Act was amended in 1897[15] to extend its provisions to all partnerships, associations, and companies of seven persons or more, regardless of whether they were incorporated (s. 1). Still, no attempt was made to limit the remedies of creditors against individual members, and many creditors were still disadvantaged. C. A.

---

10   *Van Sandau v. Moore* (1826) 1 Russ 441; *Wheeler v. Van Wait* (1838) 9 Sim 193.

11   7&8 Vict, c. 111.

12   *Re Royal British Bank, ex parte Marcus* (1856) 26 LR Bky 1 at 3 per Turner LJ.

13   For example, under s. 2, the bankruptcy of the company was not to be construed as the bankruptcy of any member of the company in his or her individual capacity.

14   11 & 12 Vict, c. 45.

15   12 & 13 Vict, c. 108.

Cooke notes that the rights of proceeding against individual members only bene-
fited those creditors who could get in first with judgement and execution against an
individual shareholder: 'The mass of small creditors, depositors of funds at the
bank, could only hope for payment of their debts if the process of ascertainment of
the deficiency and call upon the creditors could be carried through'.[16]

The most influential legislative attempt to provide for an orderly and equitable
winding-up came with the *Joint Stock Companies Act 1856*.[17] The Act made two
very important assumptions: that of corporate personality and that of limited liability. Under this legislation, a single system of winding-up could be set in motion by
creditors, contributories, or the company itself (s. 67). There were five prescribed
grounds for winding-up:

1 special resolution passed by the company
2 failure to commence business or a suspension of business for a period of a year
3 reduction in the number of shareholders to fewer than seven
4 inability of the company to pay its debts
5 the loss of three-quarters of the company's capital.

Some changes to this basic scheme of regulation were made by subsequent legislation,[18] but essentially this scheme established the modern form of winding-up as
we know it.[19]

REVIEW QUESTIONS

1 For an instance of the problems caused by inconsistencies between the 1844
   Act and the 1848 Act, see the extraordinary situation that arose in the *Royal
   British Bank* case. Here competition arose between an official manager (representing the members), who applied to the Court of Chancery for a winding-
   up, and the assignee (representing the creditors), who took steps to declare
   the company bankrupt. The resulting litigation can be found in *Aitcherson v.
   Lee;*[20] *Re Royal British Bank, ex parte Marcus;*[21] and *Re Royal British Bank,
   ex parte Shore.*[22] How was the inconsistency finally resolved?
2 Compare the grounds for winding-up that are specified in the Joint Stock
   Companies Act 1856 (above) with the grounds for winding up in the Corporations Law. What similarities are there? What significant changes have
   been made? What do these changes suggest about society's attitudes to the
   conduct of companies?

---

16 C. A. Cooke, *Corporation, Trust and Company*, Manchester University Press, Manchester, 1950, p. 150.
17 19 & 20 Vict, c. 47.
18 For example, the *Companies (Winding Up) Act 1890* (53 & 54 Vict, c. 63); *Companies Act 1929* (19 & 20 Geo V,
    c. 23).
19 McPherson, pp. 9–17.
20 (1856) 28 LJ (OS) 115.
21 (1856) 26 LJ Bky 1.
22 (1857) 26 LJ Bky 17; 28 LJ (OS) 224.

The end is near: the processes of winding-up

We have seen that our current regulatory scheme of winding-up is based upon mid-nineteenth century legislation. It falls now to consider the main features of this process. A winding-up proceeds, essentially, as follows. First, the act initiating the process takes place—that is, either the company passes a resolution or the court makes an order for the company to be wound up. A liquidator is then appointed, and control of the company passes to him or her. The liquidator converts all the company's assets into cash, obtains sufficient uncalled capital as is necessary to pay debts, and pays out all creditors. If the assets and uncalled capital are insufficient, the liquidator pays the creditors in order of priorities set out in the Corporations Law. If (after payment of winding-up expenses and payment out of all creditors) any surplus remains, this is then distributed to the shareholders in accordance with the memorandum and articles.[23] Only after all this has occurred is the company dissolved. Most commonly, a company will be wound up on that most serious of company wrongdoings: insolvency.

Insolvency

If the commercial company's *raison d'être* is profit-making, then its existence can no longer be justified if it becomes insolvent. This is recognised by the Corporations Law, which provides that a court may wind up an insolvent company under s. 495A. A number of parties may apply to the court for a winding-up order, including the company itself, a creditor (secured, prospective, or contingent), a contributory, a director, a liquidator or provisional liquidator, the ASC, and certain prescribed agencies (for instance, the insurance and superannuation commissioner has been prescribed).

The aim of the winding-up in insolvency is to provide a procedure that ensures an orderly distribution of property among the creditors. It is, essentially, a remedy of last resort. The liquidation of a company on the grounds of insolvency is undertaken in cases where there is no real prospect of the company trading out of its difficulties. If there is any prospect that the difficulties may be overcome, alternative remedies (such as the appointment of a receiver, or voluntary administration) may be attempted. From a creditor's viewpoint, liquidation is usually a compromise. The creditor accepts that she or he will probably not recover the full amount of the debt, but at least liquidation provides an orderly process of realising and distributing the company's assets.

In insolvency situations, the process of liquidation closely resembles the administration of a bankrupt person's estate under the *Bankruptcy Act 1966* (Cth), although this Act is confined to insolvency on the part of natural persons.[24] The major differences between bankruptcy and company liquidation are the result of attempts to prevent the unscrupulous from exploiting limited liability. Those who control a

---

23 P. Latimer, *Australian Business Law*, 16th edn, CCH, Sydney, 1997, p. 646.

24 P. Gillies, *The New Corporations Law*, 2nd edn, Federation Press, Sydney, 1992, p. 431

company may, for instance, create a fixed or floating charge in their own favour so that assets remain in their personal possession. They may make inflated payments to themselves in their capacities as directors or managers, or they might repay loans or deposits made by them to the company in preference to (and thus to the prejudice of) ordinary creditors.

REVIEW QUESTIONS

1 One important difference between the procedures relating to personal bank-ruptcy, on the one hand, and winding-up on the grounds of insolvency, on the other, is that the objective of the bankruptcy administration is to discharge individuals from their debts and to allow them a 'new start' in commercial life. The outcome for the company is quite different. The company ceases to exist at all. Why are these outcomes so divergent?

2 What does it mean when it is said that insolvency is an 'inability to pay debts as and when they fall due'?[25] How does one distinguish between 'a tem-porary lack of liquidity' and insolvency? See *Re Timbatec Pty Ltd*.[26]

3 Should creditors be protected under the Corporations Law? Why are normal contractual principles considered to be insufficient to protect creditors? When will the interests of shareholders and the interests of creditors conflict?[27] Does the separation of ownership and control that occurs within many companies serve to protect creditors?

4 Why are the courts reluctant to allow creditors to interfere with the administra-tion of solvent companies? What is the alternative to such interference?[28]

5 What changes to the standing of unsecured creditors will the Second Cor-porate Law Simplification Bill 1995 bring about? See, in particular, the pro-posed s. 1324(1A) and (1B).

Proof of insolvency

The definitions of 'solvency' and 'insolvency' are to be found in s. 95A.[29] Accord-ing to these definitions, a company is solvent only if it is able to pay all its debts as and when they become due and payable. A company that is not solvent is deemed insolvent. The term 'own money' includes funds to which the company has access within a reasonable period through borrowing, or through mortgaging or selling

---

25 See *Sandell v. Porter* (1966) 115 CLR 666.

26 (1974) 4 ALR 12.

27 See C. W. Smith & J. B. Warner, 'On Financial Contracting: An Analysis of Bond Covenants' (1979) 7 *Journal of Financial Economics* 7.

28 See *National Australia Bank Ltd v. Bond Brewing Holdings Ltd* (1990) 1 ACSR 405; [1991] 1 VR 386.

29 The definition is similar to that of 'personal bankruptcy'. See *Sandell v. Porter*.

assets. The test in 95A is that of 'commercial' as opposed to 'balance-sheet' solvency. For the purposes of 'commercial' insolvency, an applicant does not need to show that liabilities exceed assets (that is, 'financial' or 'balance-sheet' insolvency).[30] Instead, the applicant may prove insolvency by a failure to honour bills of exchange, for example, or by showing a large number of outstanding debts and unsatisfied judgments.[31]

Applicants for a winding-up order on the grounds of insolvency can prove their case by any admissible evidence, but there are certain situations where the courts will presume insolvency. Under 459C(2), there is a rebuttable presumption of insolvency where the company fails to comply with a statutory demand, where execution is returned unsatisfied, or where an action is brought to enforce a floating charge by appointment of a receiver (by the chargee or a court) or by the chargee going into possession. The application must be brought within three months of the event that gives rise to the reason.

Statutory demand

Under the procedure of statutory demand, a creditor who is owed at least $2000 (where that amount is due and payable) serves a notice on the company requiring payment of the sum due within 21 days. If the company fails to pay the sum to the reasonable satisfaction of the creditor, it is deemed to be unable to pay its debts. The requirements of a demand notice are set out in s. 459E. The creditor's claim must be a debt.[32] If any dispute arises and a company wishes to challenge a notice of demand, s. 459G provides that it must apply to the court.

In the past, there has been some divergence on the required level of compliance with the requirements of that section. In some cases, courts have held that, because of the serious consequences involved, strict compliance with the legislation is necessary.[33] Other courts have taken a more purposive approach and have been prepared to forgive minor procedural errors in the demand. Section 459J now gives legislative recognition to the purposive approach.

Unsatisfied judgment

Under the procedure relating to unsatisfied judgments (s. 459C(2)(b)), a company is deemed unable to pay its debts if execution, another form of issued process, or a decree or order of any court in favour of a creditor is returned unsatisfied (either in whole or in part). This is a less popular means of proving insolvency because the creditor will first experience the delay and expense of getting a judgment and then of seeking its execution. Under s. 459D(2), an applicant can prove insolvency by other means.[34]

---

30 *Re Tweeds Garages Ltd* [1962] Ch 406.
31 *Re Federal Land Company* (1889) 15 VLR 145.
32 For instance, it cannot be an amount due as damages: *Murdoch Constructions Pty Ltd v. Learnton Nominees Pty Ltd* (1983) 7 ACLR 422.
33 *Re Willes Trading Pty Ltd* (1978) 3 ACLR 582.
34 *Re Turf Enterprises* [1975] Qd R 266.

According to the wording of s. 459A and B, the courts retain a discretion to refuse an insolvency order. Orders have been refused in the exercise of the court's discretion in a number of circumstances. First, orders are refused where the debt owed is less than the statutory minimum for the statutory demand procedure. The Corporations Law does not stipulate a minimum amount of debt unless the statutory demand procedure is used, but the courts have decided that, in some cases, small debts should not be the basis of claims.[35] Second, if there is a bona fide dispute regarding the existence of the debt, which is made on substantial grounds, the court will exercise its discretion to refuse to issue an insolvency order.[36] This can only take place if the company is not otherwise insolvent and the dispute is about the existence (rather than the amount) of the debt.[37]

Other grounds for winding-up

Although common, insolvency is not the only ground for a winding-up. The court may also wind up the company on other grounds specified in s. 461. These are that:

- the company has resolved by special resolution to be wound up by the court
- default has been made in lodging the statutory report or in holding the statutory meeting
- the company has not commenced business for a year after incorporation or has suspended its business for a year
- the number of members has fallen below the statutory minimum
- directors have acted in the affairs of the company or affairs of the company have been conducted in a manner that is oppressive
- the court is of the opinion that it is just and equitable that the company be wound up.

The 'just and equitable' ground for winding up a company has proved to be a contentious area of the law. We turn now to consider the issues relating to this aspect of winding-up.

REVIEW QUESTION

A company may be wound up if it acts oppressively or unfairly in dealing with its members, but it is interesting to note that the failure of a company to treat outsiders morally or ethically is, in general, not a ground for winding-up. Should it be? In what circumstances?

---

35 It is not clear whether the value of debts should be less than the minimum required under the statutory demand procedure. See *FAI Insurances Ltd v. Goldleaf Interior Decorator Pty Ltd* (1988) 14 ACLR 285.

36 *Re KL Tractors Ltd* [1954] VLR 505.

37 *National Mutual Life Association of Australasia Ltd v. Oasis Developments Pty Ltd* (1983) 7 ACLR 758; *Re Tweeds Garages Ltd.*

The vexed problems of s. 461

Under s. 491, a company can resolve by special resolution to have itself voluntarily wound up. But, as a special majority is required to pass the necessary resolution, a minority shareholder without the required support cannot rely on this mechanism. Such a minority member may, however, seek to rely on the basis of oppression (discussed in chapter 14) or on the basis of s. 461, the just and equitable winding-up.

Cases decided under s. 461 tend to be contentious. There are two main reasons for this. The first reason is that the company is often a viable (and sometimes highly profitable) commercial entity when a minority shareholder seeks to wind it up. There are thus inherent policy tensions between the desirability of encouraging the ongoing existence of a moneymaking entity and the objective of ensuring that individuals are treated fairly. The second reason is that judges have tended to look behind the corporate identity to the individuals who operate within the corporate structure. Because of this, considerations that seem more appropriate to a partnership setting are often alluded to, and these do not sit easily within the corporate structure.

When is a partnership not a partnership? When it's a company!

Section 461(k) is derived from s. 5(8) of the *Joint Stock Companies Winding Up Act 1848* (UK). The section, in turn, has its origins in partnership law, and judges have tended to apply quasi-partnership principles in this area, despite the well-accepted rule of separate legal identity. This section confers power on the courts to do what is just and equitable. It does not, however, stipulate the criteria for either justice or equity.[38] Many cases have been decided on the basis of the elusive idea of 'commercial morality':

> One could imagine a case in which a board of directors quite properly decided that no dividend should be declared; that might force an elderly indigent shareholder on to the old age pension and so be unfair to him, but we would think that few people would regard it as a ground for winding up the company. On the other hand, most people might think otherwise about a board of directors which used its voting power (in a case in which it could do so) consistently to refuse to pay dividends and at the same time to authorise the payment to itself of extravagant sums by way of directors' remuneration. That would be a breach of commercial morality, and perhaps that is what the subsection is directed against.[39]

The classic case of the application of the just and equitable principle is often considered to be *Ebrahimi v. Westbourne Galleries Ltd.*[40] In this case, E and N were originally partners in a business, and then converted their partnership to a company.

---

38 See Burt J in *Millheim v. Barewa Oil and Mining NL* [1971] WAR 65 at 67.

39 *Re Weedman's Ltd* [1974] Qd R 377 at 398 per Lucas J.

40 [1973] AC 360 at 379. For recent examples of the application of the 'just and equitable' winding-up clause, see *Kikotovich Constructions Pty Ltd v. Wallington* (1995) 17 ACSR 478; 13 ACLC 1113; *McMillan v. Toledo Enterprises International Pty Ltd* (1995) 18 ACSR 603.

E and N were the first directors of this company. Under the company constitution, the members in general meeting had the express power to remove a director by ordinary resolution. N's son, G, was made a director. N and G had the majority of votes at the general meeting. The company was successful, and profits were distributed as directors' remuneration, but dividends were never paid. E and N had a disagreement, and the members in general meeting passed a resolution to remove E as director. E brought an action alleging oppression, petitioning for an order to have N and G either purchase his shares or sell their shares to him. Alternatively, he petitioned for a just and equitable winding-up. The House of Lords upheld the first-instance decision of Plowman J that the company be wound up. Their Lordships found that small, closely held companies were analogous to partnerships, and that people do not enter partnerships without a degree of trust and confidence in each other. When that trust and confidence is gone, it may be appropriate to wind up the company. Lord Wilberforce said that 'there is room in company law for recognition of the fact that behind [the company] or amongst it, there are individuals, with rights, expectations and obligations *inter se* which are not necessarily submerged in the company structure'.

But is this appropriate? The idea of applying partnership principles seems inconsistent with the separate entity doctrine established in *Salomon v. Salomon*. Wishart argues:

It seems odd that company law accepts the similarity at this point while denying it at all others. Furthermore, since rights are in this context either agreed or conferred by law, justice and fairness should have the agreement and the law as their standards. The agreement is to be a company and to have company law applied. A choice not to be subject to partnership law has been made. The application of partnership law should have a rationale other than mere factual similarity.[41]

Indeed, this was even acknowledged in *Ebrahami*:

To refer, as so many of the cases do, to 'quasi partnerships' or 'in substance partnerships' may be convenient but may also be confusing. It may be convenient because it is the law of partnership which has developed the conceptions of probity, good faith and mutual confidence, and the remedies where these are absent, which become relevant once such factors as We have mentioned are found to exist: the words 'just and equitable' sum these up in the law of partnership itself. And in many, but not necessarily all, cases there has been a pre-existing partnership the obligations of which it is reasonable to suppose continue to underlie the new company structure. But the expressions may be confusing if they obscure, or deny, the fact that the parties (possibly former partners) are now co-members in a company, who have accepted, in law, new obligations. A company, however small, however domestic, is a company, not a partnership or even a quasi-partnership and it is through the just and equitable clause that obligations, common to partnership relations, may come in.[42]

---

41 Wishart, p. 280.
42 [1973] AC 360 at 379–80 per Lord Wilberforce.

Fairness v. profit

These cases, as we pointed out earlier, are further complicated by the court's extreme reluctance to wind up a profitable company. In *Re Dalkeith Investments Pty Ltd*,[43] a divorce between two major shareholders resulted in a breakdown in the mutual trust and confidence among members. As this was irreconcilable, the applicant shareholder was entitled to have the company wound up under what is now s. 461(k). However, McPherson J said (at 79) that 'the effect of s. 367(3) [now s. 467(4)] of the Act is, as we see it, that winding-up is to be regarded as a remedy of last resort and one which ought not to be granted if some other less drastic form of relief is available and appropriate'. On this basis, a remedy under s. 260 was granted for the purchase of the minority member's shares by the majority. A winding-up would have been prejudicial to the shareholders other than the applicant. The company was profitable and held considerable net assets and should not unnecessarily be brought to an end. The Privy Council stated the principle very succinctly: 'to wind up a successful and prosperous company and one which is properly managed must clearly be an extreme step and must require a strong case to be made'.[44]

In some cases, the fact that the company is solvent has not deterred the court from making a winding-up order. For instance, in *Bernhardt v. Beau Rivage Pty Ltd*,[45] a solvent company was ordered to be wound up. Because the company's substratum had disappeared, a minority shareholder sought to wind up the company on the 'just and equitable' ground. A majority's offer to purchase his shares was refused. The court found that the minority shareholder was not acting unreasonably because he could have obtained a greater return more promptly if his winding-up application had been granted.

Despite instances such as this, in which the court has seen fit to wind up the company, the judicial reluctance to wind up a solvent company means that a just and equitable winding-up may not be an effective remedy for the minority shareholder. Certainly, the order enables a shareholder to have a liquidator recover company property and distribute the surplus (if any) among members. But in practice, the court, before making an order under the 'just and equitable' clause, will ordinarily adjourn or suspend its order in the hope that the parties will come to some compromise before the formal order is made. In fact, where a shareholder applies for a winding-up order on the 'just and equitable' ground but is entitled to relief by some other means, that shareholder may lose her or his entitlement to a winding-up under s. 461(k) if the court considers that it is unreasonable not to pursue that alternative remedy.[46]

---

43 (1985) 3 ACLC 74.

44 *Cumberland Holdings Ltd v. Washington Soul Pattinson & Co. Ltd* (1977) 13 ALR 561 at 566–7 (Privy Council) per Lord Wilberforce.

45 (1989) 7 ACLC 639.

46 See *Re a Company Pty Ltd* [1983] 1 WLR 927.

The appropriateness and effectiveness of the remedy for a minority shareholder was considered in *Alessi v. The Original Art Co. Pty Ltd.*[47] In this case, Young J thought it proper to appoint a liquidator in a situation where a shareholder and director of a company that operated as a 'quasi-partnership' sought to have the company wound up on the 'just and equitable' ground. His Honour held that it would normally be unreasonable to wind up a company in circumstances where it is clearly solvent or where the shareholders could sell their shares on the stock exchange for a fair value.

In considering whether to order the company to be wound up, however, Young J said that it was appropriate to bear in mind the capacity of shareholders to buy others out. At the same time, it was important that any alternative remedy should effectively give relief. Thus the amount of money available to the plaintiff if an order for compulsory purchase is made should be considered by the court to be adequate in the circumstances.

Cases decided under the 'just and equitable' winding-up clause have been categorised into four groups:

1 failure of the substratum
2 deadlock in the operation or management of the company
3 fraud in formation
4 misconduct by directors.

Failure of the substratum

The expression 'failure of the substratum' is attributed to Lord Cairns LJ in *Re Suburban Hotel Co.*,[48] but perhaps the best known Australian case of this type is *Re Tivoli Freeholds Ltd.*[49] Here an action for failure of the substratum was brought when a company that was formed to run a theatre had become involved, essentially, in corporate raiding.

A minority shareholder—who, with supporters, controlled 42 per cent of the company's shares—petitioned the court for the company to be wound up. This action was based on both the ground of oppression and the 'just and equitable' ground. The court did not find oppression, but it did find that it was just and equitable for the company to be wound up on the basis that the company was acting outside what could fairly be regarded as having been within the general intention and common understanding of the members when they became members.

Menhennitt J said (at 468–9) that the concept of a failure of substratum was subsumed within a broader principle:

> It has been recognised that it may be just and equitable to wind a company up if the company engages in acts which are entirely outside what can fairly be regarded as having been

---

47 (1989) 7 ACLC 595.
48 (1867) 2 Ch P 73.
49 [1972] VR 445.

within the general intention and common understanding of the members when they became members ... The cases on loss or failures of substratum are an illustration of this small basic concept, for example, *Re Wondoflex Textiles Pty Ltd.* This more basic concept is not, it seems to me, confined to cases of 'partnership' companies or 'main object' companies. Whilst it may be easier to find the general intention and common understanding in those cases, We can see no reason in principle why it should be confined to such cases and We are not aware of any decision that it is so confined.

Essentially, then, this ground refers to situations where the purpose for incorporation is being so ignored that the company should be wound up.

REVIEW QUESTIONS

1 Davos Pty Ltd is a company that produces environmentally friendly cleaning products. Its directors are Sally, Neil, and Paul, and its shareholders are Sally, Neil, Paul, and Lorraine. Sally and Neil, who together hold 58 per cent of the shares in Davos, sell their shareholdings to Graeme. Graeme wants to change the direction of the company so that it produces cheaper, but decidedly environmentally unfriendly, cleaning products. Lorraine has considerable ethical difficulty with this new direction and comes to you for advice. What do you advise?

2 What is the difference between the doctrine of failure of the substratum and that of *ultra vires*?

Deadlock

Deadlock in the operation of management—that is, where a company cannot serve its purpose because of a disagreement—may result in a just and equitable winding-up.[50] Although determining what amounts to a deadlock is a question of fact, a dispute must go beyond what may be termed a 'domestic quarrel'.[51] For instance, in *Re Yenidje Tobacco Co. Ltd*,[52] R and W were tobacconists who formed a private company. They were the sole shareholders and directors. The articles provided for equal voting powers, that one director was sufficient to form a quorum, and that the issue was to be put to arbitration if a deadlock arose. When differences arose and the matter went to arbitration (at considerable cost), R refused to abide by the arbitrator's decision. Relationships became hostile, and the parties communicated only through an intermediary. W brought an action alleging failure of substratum and seeking a winding-up, despite the company's prosperity. Cosens-Hardy MR held that it was

---

50 See *Re Macman Pty Ltd* (1992) 10 ACLC 287; *Wagner v. International Health Promotions Pty Ltd* (1994) 14 ACSR 466.

51 *Symington v. Symington's Quarries Ltd* (1906) 8 F 121 at 129 per Lord Dunedin. See also *Morgan v. 45 Flers Avenue Pty Ltd* (1986) 10 ACLR 692.

52 [1916] 2 Ch 426.

necessary to consider the precise position of such a company and the degree to which it was proper to call it a partnership in the guise of a private company. As under partnership law the factual situation amounted to grounds for dissolving the partnership, he was prepared to consider the applicability of such principles to the company structure. Under partnership law, all that is required for a dissolution is that the partners be unable to place that degree of confidence in one another that each has a right to expect. The breakdown in mutual confidence must not be caused by the party seeking to take advantage of it. His Honour stated that 'in a case like this we are bound to say that circumstances which would justify the winding-up of a partnership between these two by legal action are circumstances which should induce the court to exercise its jurisdiction and order the company wound up'.[53]

At the basis of the judicial interpretation of the 'just and equitable' winding-up clause is this idea of a fundamental breakdown in confidence within the company, analogous to the breakdown of trust and confidence between partners. This idea was examined in *Carpenter v. Carpenter Grazing Co. Pty Ltd.*[54] In this case, the court declared a share allotment invalid because it was not in the interests of the company as a whole, but it refused to wind up the company. Although the company was a small, family company, it was not a quasi-partnership as in *Ebrahimi*. The company was set up by a father in such a way that he had control of management but his children only had an equity interest. This meant that the company was not analogous to a partnership, as a partnership presumes that all partners have a right to participate in management. The fact that there had been a dispute over respective shareholdings did not of itself show an irretrievable breakdown of confidence, nor did it represent a deadlock between family members.[55]

Lack of probity, or impropriety leading to a loss of confidence in company management

Investment is discouraged if management cannot be trusted with members' assets (and particularly in cases where it is difficult to remove a delinquent director). Thus, a company will be wound up where there is a lack of probity or impropriety on the part of management. For instance, where a company has been incorporated to carry out a fraud, it is a ground for a just and equitable winding-up.[56] Similarly, misconduct by the directors may justify a winding-up, but the minority shareholder must establish that the lack of confidence goes beyond mere disagreement with management decisions. For instance, in *Loch v. John Blackwood Ltd,*[57] the Privy Council upheld an order for the winding-up of a company on the 'just and equitable' ground because the managing director had conducted the company's business as if it were

---

53 [1916] 2 Ch 426 at 432.

54 (1986) 4 ACLC 18.

55 P. Lipton & A. Herzberg, *Understanding Company Law*, 5th edn, Law Book Co., Sydney, 1993, p. 530.

56 *Re Thomas Edward Brinsmead & Sons* [1897] 1 Ch 45; *Re London & County Coal Co.* (1886) 3 LR Eq 355; *In the Matter of the Neath Harbour Smelting & Rolling Works Ltd* (1886) 2 TLR 336.

57 [1924] AC 783.

his own. His lack of probity justified the minority shareholders' lack of confidence in his management:

> It is undoubtedly true that at the foundation of applications for winding up on the 'just and equitable' rule, there must lie a justifiable lack of confidence in the conduct and management of the company's affairs. But this lack of confidence must be grounded on conduct of directors, not in regard to the private life or affairs, but in regard to the company's business. Furthermore, the lack of confidence must spring not from dissatisfaction at being outvoted on the business affairs or on what is called the domestic policy of the company. On the other hand, whenever the lack of confidence is rested on a lack of probity in the conduct of the company's affairs, then the former is justified by the latter and it is, under the statute, just and equitable that the company be wound up.[58]

REVIEW QUESTIONS

1 The Bread Factory Bakery Pty Ltd is, at present, a solvent company. Its principal shareholders are members of the Ellis family. However, it borrowed heavily to buy and install new dough-breaking machinery 3 months ago. It must repay the loan it took out to purchase the machinery within 12 months, but at this point it does not have the necessary capital to do so. The company wishes to wind up, as a result of the ill health of one of its directors and shareholders, Rene Ellis. How would you advise the directors?

2 Many of the successful cases under s. 461 have involved quasi-partnership considerations, despite judicial efforts to suggest that these are something else. Should these play a role in judicial decision-making in this area? Justify your answer.

3 Jane and Richard converted their partnership to a company to run their clothing wholesale business. Although there is nothing in the company constitution about the division of responsibility between them, Jane takes responsibility for ordering and accounts, while Richard takes care of sales and staff management. The business is extremely successful, and Jane and Richard decide to float their company on the stock exchange. The company continues to be extremely successful, but Richard is now very unhappy because Jane has assumed control of staffing, in contravention of their original understanding. Can Richard bring an action for a just and equitable winding-up?

4 Does a plaintiff in a 'just and equitable' winding-up action have to come to the court with 'clean hands'?[59]

---

58 [1924] AC 783 at 788 per Lord Shaw.
59 See *Ruut v. Head* (1996) 20 ACSR 160.

A voluntary winding-up

Not all windings-up are as acrimonious as some of the ones discussed in the cases above. In some cases, members will wish to wind up the company where, for instance, the company purpose has been served and the association is no longer needed. A members' voluntary winding-up is governed by s. 494 of the Corporations Law. Importantly, the procedure is only available if a company is solvent, and to this end, the members must make a declaration of the company's solvency.[60] The purpose of this declaration is to prevent abuse of the voluntary winding-up procedure where a company is actually insolvent. Because there is less supervision by the courts (and less protection for creditors) in a voluntary winding-up procedure, it is appropriate that members be required to provide assurances of solvency.

In order to institute a members' voluntary winding-up, the conditions in s. 494(3) must be complied with. If they are not, the provisions of a creditors' voluntary winding-up apply.[61] A statement of affairs must be attached to the declaration of solvency. This should show the property of the company, the total amount expected to be realised from it, and the liabilities and estimated expenses of winding-up. This statement must comply with s. 494(2), and a director who makes such a declaration must have reasonable grounds for forming the declared opinion.[62]

Section 513B(e) provides that the winding-up generally starts on the day that the members pass the special resolution to wind up the company. The commencement date for a winding-up is important, because from that point, the operations of the company are concerned only with the liquidation process, and the law imposes special restrictions on the company and its officers.[63] With regard to the conduct and the calling of a meeting to pass a special resolution, the usual rules regarding meetings apply.[64] A resolution is irrevocable once it is properly passed.[65]

Voluntary winding-up: A creditors' voluntary winding-up

A creditors' voluntary winding-up occurs where a company is insolvent. In this case, the creditors' interests are at stake. The creditors appoint the liquidator (ss. 496(5) and 499(1)), fix his or her remuneration (s. 499(3)), and supervise the liquidator's conduct of the liquidation (s. 506(1)(a)). It is important to realise that, despite its name, a creditors' voluntary winding-up is not initiated by the creditors. Rather, a members' voluntary winding-up is converted to a creditors' voluntary winding-up if the company is insolvent. This process can occur in one of two ways. First, it can occur where there is no declaration of solvency—that is, the members have started

---

60 Corporations Law, s. 494(1). See *Re Kyra Nominees Pty Ltd* (1980) 5 ACLR 60.

61 *Re Kyra Nominees Pty Ltd.*

62 Corporations Law, s. 494(4).

63 Section 513B provides for other dates to be deemed the commencement date if other external administrations have begun before this.

64 Corporations Law, s. 253(1).

65 *Ross v. P. J. Harringa* [1970] NZLR 170.

to voluntarily wind up the company, but the directors do not make and lodge their declaration of solvency under s. 494. Second, it can occur where members have appointed a liquidator and that liquidator is of the opinion that the company cannot pay its debts in full within the period stated in the declaration of solvency. In this case, the liquidator convenes a meeting of creditors according to s. 496(1) and puts before that creditors' meeting a statement of the company's assets and liabilities. Where this procedure is followed, the liquidator must also advise the creditors of their right to appoint a new liquidator under s. 496(5). From the date of this meeting, the liquidation then proceeds as a creditors' voluntary winding-up.[66]

Voluntary administration

Not all companies in financial difficulties are wound up. Other options are available. These include receivership,[67] creditors' schemes of arrangements,[68] and voluntary administration. Voluntary administration allows the directors to appoint an administrator to help a struggling company to trade out of its financial difficulties.[69] The object of a period of voluntary administration is to give a failing company a chance of survival or, if this is not possible, to maximise the return to the company creditors.[70] During the period of administration, s. 440A–G protects the company from actions by creditors: 'Until the introduction of voluntary administration in June 1991, the only equivalent procedure available to a company and its creditors was a creditors' scheme of arrangement.[71] Voluntary administration now offers a far quicker and cheaper alternative'.[72]

There are a number of potential outcomes of voluntary administration. Because of an improvement in the company's operations, there may be a higher return to creditors than as a result of a liquidation. Alternatively, the company may be sold as a going concern.[73] The scheme also offers certain other advantages—for instance, directors have an incentive to assist the liquidator. The scheme also overcomes a practice that was widespread, whereby directors of a

---

66 Corporations Law, s. 496(6) and (8).

67 Receivership is usually set up by a secured creditor who appoints an insolvency practitioner as receiver to enforce the security. The receiver acts primarily for that creditor's benefit. A receivership may be general (for example, where the property forming the security is the company's business and the whole, or most, of its property) or particular (for example, where the receiver is appointed to take control of specific property and there is no reason for the directors to renounce control).

68 'Creditors' schemes of arrangement are relatively uncommon, in contrast with schemes of arrangement with members, which have been influential in effecting solvent company reorganisations. Official management was a form of external administration of companies that was not used very often. The scheme was repealed in June 1993': L. Griffiths & S. Woodward, *Corporations Law Workbook*, 3rd edn, Law Book Co., Sydney, 1996, p. 404.

69 Voluntary administration is covered by part 5.3A of the Corporations Law.

70 Corporations Law, s. 435A. On voluntary administration generally, see C. Anderson & D. Morrison, 'Voluntary Administrations and their Effect on the Use of Schemes of Arrangement' (1994) 2 Insol LJ 195; K. Lightman, 'Voluntary Administration: The New Wave or the New Waif in Insolvency Law' (1994) 2 Insol LJ 59.

71 Under this scheme, directors gave up direction to an insolvency practitioner appointed to administer the company in accordance with a scheme agreed to by the creditors. Establishment of such a scheme was subject to considerable delay, as not only did the creditors have to meet, but the scheme also had to be court-approved.

72 Griffiths & Woodward, p. 405.

73 See *Brash Holdings Ltd v. Shafir* (1994) 14 ACSR 192; 12 ACLC 619

company facing financial difficulties would simply transfer the company assets to a new company and carry on business much as before, thus effectively frustrating the claims of creditors.[74]

Lorraine Griffiths and Susan Woodward provide a succint summary of the law relating to voluntary administration.[75] The company may appoint an administrator when the directors resolve that the company is insolvent (or likely to become so) and it is appropriate to appoint an administrator.[76] There is a strong incentive for directors to appoint an administrator if the company's solvency is in doubt. This incentive is provided by both the insolvent trading provision and similar provisions found in the *Income Tax Assessment Act 1936* (Cth),[77] which impose personal liability on directors for insolvent trading.

Others parties may also appoint an administrator. These include a liquidator or provisional liquidator (per s. 436B) and a chargee, who is entitled to enforce a charge over the whole, or substantially the whole, of the company's property (per s. 436C). In the latter case, the chargee is usually a bank or other financial institution that has a security or mortgage over company assets:

> In terms of qualifications, an administrator must be a registered liquidator who is independent of the company (see s. 448A–D). His or her job is to investigate the financial position of the company and to decide on a course of action that is in the best interests of the creditors.[78] In order to carry out the investigation, the administrator effectively displaces the directors, whose powers are suspended (s. 437C), and is given wide powers to take control of the company's business (see ss. 437A and 442A). Administrators are liable under the Corporations Law as officers of the company.[79]

Administrators are also personally liable for certain categories of debts incurred during the administration period, but s. 443D provides right of indemnity out of the assets of the company for all debts for which they are liable. Sections 443E and 443D provide that this right of indemnity takes priority over all other debts of the company (with certain exceptions relating to secured creditors) and that it is secured by a lien over the company's property.

Within 5 business days of appointment, s. 436E provides that the administrator must convene a meeting of the creditors to determine whether to replace the administrator or to form a consultative committee of creditors:

> Within 21 days of appointment, s. 439A requires the administrator to convene a second meeting of creditors to decide on the company's future.[80] The administrator must submit a detailed report to creditors for the purposes of the second meeting, including a statement

---

74   Such directors breach their fiduciary duties, but any redress would require costly and often lengthy litigation.

75   Griffiths & Woodward, pp. 406–7.

76   Corporations Law, s. 436A(1).

77   See s. 222AFA–ARA.

78   Corporations Law, s. 438A.

79   Griffiths & Woodward, p. 406.

80   The time limits imposed for the steps in the voluntary administration are strict. Some of the time limits can be extended by application to the court. See *Mann v. Abruzzi Sports Club* (1994) 12 ACLC 137.

of the administrator's opinion about each of the options. The administrator must give his or her opinion on:

- whether to enter into a deed of arrangement
- whether the administration should end and the company revert to the control of its directors, or
- whether the company should be wound up.[81]

The company may resolve to wind up at various stages of the administration (for example, at the second creditors' meeting or at a meeting terminating the deed of arrangement). Transition to winding-up can also occur under s. 446A when certain deadlines are not met.

REVIEW QUESTION

The Australian Law Reform Commission (ALRC) published the *Report on General Insolvency Inquiry*, in which it stated that the aim of the voluntary administration proposal would be

> to provide for a period of containment to enable the property and the business of the company to be investigated and assessed to determine the most appropriate form of administration. The meeting of creditors may resolve that the company make a deed of company arrangement. Alternatively, if the creditors resolve that the company should be wound up in insolvency that is implemented without further delay or unnecessary cost. This offers an integrated process which is not available under existing companies legislation. It is a more accessible form of procedure and may encourage financially troubled companies to seek an early administration.[82]

Does the scheme of voluntary administration effectively achieve these aims? Look at the previously available options. What were their shortcomings?

The liquidator

Where, however, a liquidation must take place, a liquidator will be appointed. It is the liquidator's job to carry out the winding-up process that leads to the eventual dissolution of the company. Unlike a voluntary administration, in a liquidation, the liquidator cannot help the company to trade out of its difficulties.

The liquidator is appointed by the court (in the case of a court or compulsory liquidation), nominated by the creditors or members (in a creditors' voluntary winding-up), or appointed by the members (in a members' voluntary winding-up). Liquidators must possess appropriate experience, capacity, and qualifications, and they must be registered with the Australian Securities Commission (ASC).[83] Their

---

81 Griffiths & Woodward, p. 407.

82 Australian Law Reform Commission, *Report on General Insolvency Inquiry*, Report no. 45, vol. 1, ALRC, Sydney, para. 22.

83 Corporations Law, ss. 532, 1278, 1279, 1282 deal with the qualifications of liquidators and the registration requirement.

principal duties were outlined in *Re Partridge; ex parte McDonald*: 'to take possession of and protect the assets, to make lists of contributories and creditors, to have disputed cases adjudicated upon, to realise the assets and to apply the proceeds in due course of administration amongst the creditors and contributories'.[84]

The liquidator is an agent of the company[85] and thus owes a fiduciary duty to the company. The nature of this duty can be seen in the comprehensive statement of the role and duties of the liquidator that was given by Marks J in *Commissioner for Corporate Affairs v. Harvey*:

> The duties of the liquidator need to be clearly understood. Fundamentally he must administer the estate strictly in accordance with the duties and obligations specifically imposed on him by the *Companies Act* and its Rules. It is obvious that everything to be done in a competent administration is not and cannot be specifically prescribed. Preserving the assets, giving proper attention to the administration, acting with due dispatch and ensuring adequate knowledge and understanding of the affairs of the companies are matters of common sense. If there is a difficulty at any stage of the administration then it is the clear duty of the liquidator to inform the court and take directions.[86]

In *Re Allebart Pty Ltd*, Street J elaborated more fully on the way in which the liquidator's duty to investigate the affairs of the company interacted with the requirement that strict impartiality be maintained:

> A court winding-up involves more than a mere realisation of the assets and distribution of proceeds. The official liquidator is an officer of the court, and as such he has public responsibilities to investigate past activities connected with the company, and, in appropriate cases, to initiate such further proceedings, civil or criminal, connected therewith as the circumstances may dictate ...
>
> I have already stated my view that in no degree or in no respect is the conduct of the petitioner in the present windings up open to legitimate criticism. It has, quite justifiably, urged on the official liquidator and made funds available to him ... A liquidator is bound to be on guard lest he compromise his position of independence and impartiality in all respects in the discharge of his functions as an officer of the court administering the winding up of a company. Not only is it his prerogative to decide what steps should be taken, but it is his duty to exercise himself, according to the dictates of his own opinions, what should and what should not be done in the course of any given winding up ... Where he draws upon financial assistance from a creditor, it is incumbent upon him to ensure that he does not place in jeopardy his independence in the discharge of his duties. It is indispensable that in point of substance the liquidator's independence should be preserved; and it is undesirable that a liquidator should permit a situation to develop in which it might appear that he has yielded up in any degree whatever his exclusive independent control in the decision-making processes and administration of winding up.[87]

---

84   (1961) 61 SR (NSW) 622 at 622, as cited in Latimer, p. 648.

85   *CCA(Vic) v. Harvey* [1980] VR 669 at 695; (1979) 4 ACLR 259; CLC 40–564.

86   [1980] VR 669 at 691 per Marks J.

87   [1971] 1 NSWLR 24 at 26–8 per Street J.

The nature of the liquidator's role and the fact that the actual winding-up is carried out by the court impose further obligations:

> An official liquidator is an officer of the court (Supreme Court (Companies) Act Rules, r. 74(1)).
>
> In a compulsory winding up his office stems from appointment by the court. He is clearly not an employee of the court but the nature of the appointment makes him a representative of it. As Street J said in *Duffy v. Super Centre Development Corp Ltd* [1967] 1 NSWR 382 at 383, the decisions the liquidator makes from time to time are in effect made under the authority of the court itself. The winding up is by the court which for the purposes the liquidator is its representative. As such he is entrusted with the reputation of the court for impartial and proper dispatch of duties. No lesser standard in that regard is to be expected of the liquidator than of a court or a judge.
>
> When a winding up occurs, the financial outcome for creditors and contributories is dependent, amongst other things, on honest administration. It is the trust which those persons are obliged to place in the liquidator to preserve the assets and act faithfully and fairly that defines the weight of the duties owed and the strictness with which his conduct must be considered by the court.
>
> The law in the circumstances regards such duties as fiduciary although clearly it will not interfere with bona fide exercise of discretions which are not beyond the acts or omissions of a reasonable man.[88]

As you can see from this statement, it is most important that a liquidator is impartial. A liquidator that is seen to have an interest in the company, or has a previous association with someone interested in the winding-up, is liable to be removed by the court and a new liquidator appointed.[89]

Section 477(1) provides that a liquidator may:
- carry on the business of the company so far as it is necessary for the beneficial disposal or winding-up of that business
- pay any class of creditors in full (subject to the priority provisions contained in s. 538)
- make any compromise or arrangement with creditors or with persons claiming to be creditors
- compromise any calls and liabilities to call, any debts and liabilities capable of resulting in debts, and any claims (present or future, certain or contingent, ascertained or sounding only in damages) subsisting or supposed to subsist between the company and a contributory or debtor or person apprehending liability to the company.

Under s. 477(2), the liquidator also has the power to bring or defend legal proceedings, or to appoint a solicitor. The liquidator is also empowered by the Cor-

---

88 *Commissioner for Corporate Affairs v. Harvey* [1980] VR 669 at 695–6 per Marks J.
89 Corporations Law, s. 503. See further *Commonwealth v. O'Reilly* [1984] VR 931; (1984) 52 ALR 631; 8 ACLR 804; 2 ACLC 190; *Re Biposo Pty Ltd; Condon v. Rogers* (1995) 17 ACSR 730; 13 ACLC 1271.

porations Law and Rules of Court to examine the activities of former directors, make calls on shares, or reject proofs of debt.

REVIEW QUESTIONS

1 Susan is a creditor of Glodry Pty Ltd, a company that manufactured a quick-drying synthetic fabric. Unfortunately, the company was wound up for insolvency. Carl was appointed official liquidator of Glodry. Susan received 40 cents in the dollar for the money owing to her. However, Susan has just discovered that Carl dishonestly used funds from Glodry to make unauthorised payments to Merrywether Pty Ltd, his own company. He also used funds from Glodry to pay for his personal expenses during the liquidation. Susan now comes to you for advice. What remedies, if any, does she have against Carl?

2 Can a liquidator delegate the liquidation to someone else?[90]

3 Jack and Max are unsecured creditors of Kasper Pty Ltd, which is in liquidation. They assisted the liquidator by contributing money to a 'fighting fund' to pursue the directors of Kasper (Jessica and Alison) for breach of their duty of honesty under s. 232. Are Jack and Max entitled to a larger dividend than unsecured creditors who refused to contribute to the fund?[91]

Payment of debts on liquidation

The distribution of company assets can commence after the assets have been collected and the time fixed for proving of claims has passed. The fund from which liabilities are to be paid consists of assets that are beneficially owned by the company when the winding-up order is made, subject to the rights of secured creditors, and assets that come into the company's beneficial ownership after the winding-up order. The liquidator can enlarge this fund by taking legal proceedings to recover property or money that the company disposed of before liquidation, or compensation to which it is entitled for some wrong done to it. Specifically, the company's fund can be enlarged in the following ways:

* *voidable transactions* (Transactions that are voidable within the meaning of pt 5.7B include uncommercial transactions where the company is insolvent[92] and unfair preferences that are made to some creditors when the company is insolvent.[93])

---

90 See *Re Ah Toy* (1986) 4 ACLC 480.

91 See *Re Kyra Nominees Pty Ltd* (1987) 5 ACLC 811.

92 Under s. 588FB, an uncommercial transaction is one that the hypothetical reasonable person in the company's circumstances would not have entered into. See *Walker v. Nicolay* (1991) 4 ACSR 309; *Re Action Waste Collections Pty Ltd (in liq.)* [1981] VR 691; (1981) 38 ALR 199; 5 ACLR 673. For a general discussion of this area, see A. Keay, 'Liquidators' Avoidance of Uncommercial Transactions' (1996) 70 ALJ 390.

93 An unfair preference is a transaction between the company and a creditor whereby the creditor receives more for an unsecured debt than would have been received if the creditor had had to prove for it in the winding-up. See *Airservices Australia v. Ferrier* (1996) 137 ALR 609; 21 ACSR 1; *Richardson v. Commercial Banking Co. of Sydney Ltd* (1952) 85 CLR 110 at 133.

- *compensation from directors or other company officers for breach of duty* (Under s. 598, the company may receive compensation from directors or officers who breach their duties under s. 232. Under s. 588G, directors may be liable to compensate the company where they fail in their duty to prevent insolvent trading.)
- *recovery or property or compensation from persons liable as constructive trustees* (This covers situations where third parties receive company property from directors knowing of their breach of fiduciary duty, or where third parties knowingly assist the directors to commit a dishonest breach of their fiduciary duty.)
- *invalid charges* (In some cases, the company will be wound up free of certain charges. These include specific floating charges under s. 588FJ, charges on the company's property that were required to be registered but notice of which was not lodged within the prescribed time under s. 266, and charges given to company officers or their associates and enforced within 6 months of creation without the court's leave under s. 267.)
- *calls on contributories* (As we saw in chapter 3, in some cases of limited-liability companies with share capital, or in cases of companies that are unlimited or limited by guarantee, calls can be made on contributories.)
- *recovery from execution creditors* (Section 569 provides that, in some instances, amounts can be recovered from creditors who enforced a judgment against the company in the 6 months prior to the winding-up.)

Section 555 provides that debts are to be ranked equally, but if the property of the company is insufficient to meet these in full, they should be paid rateably. In s. 556, however, there is a statutory order of payment for unsecured creditors. Under this section, first priority is given to the costs incurred in the winding-up process.[94] The claims of employees incurred before the beginning of winding-up are next in the order of priority and must be paid before claims of other unsecured creditors.

REVIEW QUESTIONS

1 In 1988, the ALRC recommended that an Insolvent (Assetless) Companies Fund be established.[95] This fund would be financed by a levy on all companies at the time of filing their annual return. The fund would be administered by the ASC and would provide funds for the costs of winding-up and any investigation that may be required in respect of companies with assets below a prescribed level. This scheme has not been implemented. Should it be? What advantages and disadvantages can you see in such a scheme?

2 Do you agree that employees' claims should be given priority over other unsecured creditors, such as independent contractors or small business operators? Would it be appropriate to require employers to contribute to a wage-earner

---

94 *Re Universal Distributing Co. Ltd (in liq.)* (1933) 48 CLR 171.
95 See ALRC, paras 349ff.

protection fund, from which employees of an insolvent employer could claim moneys owing to them? What disadvantages could you see in such a scheme?[96]

3 What is a 'relation back day'?

4 Evolve Pty Ltd was insolvent. It owned, *inter alia*, a warehouse in suburban Melbourne. Evolve defaulted in its payments under the mortgage on the warehouse. In order to avoid a mortgagee's sale, Evolve borrowed $50 000 from Tyree Pty Ltd, a company owned by one of Evolve's directors, Gary Rogers. The threatened mortgagee's sale was averted. Six months later, the warehouse was sold. The proceeds were used to repay Tyree, and the balance was used to discharge the mortgage. Evolve has gone into liquidation, and the liquidator comes to you for advice. She wishes to know if she can recover the $50 000 from Tyree as being a voidable preference. What do you advise her?[97]

Effects of winding-up

We have seen that companies may be wound up for different reasons, and, accordingly, different methods of winding-up are provided for by the common law. But, as we pointed out earlier, a company does not automatically cease to exist on the institution of winding-up. After liquidation commences, the company still exists as a separate legal entity. In a voluntary winding-up, under s. 493, the company ceases business except as is necessary for winding-up. There is no corresponding provision for compulsory winding-up, but it is assumed that it does not affect the corporate status of the company.[98] According to s. 474(1), the company does not have the beneficial ownership of property. In a compulsory winding-up, any disposition of property[99] (other than that which is exempt) made after the commencement of winding-up is void, unless the court orders otherwise.[100] We have seen that, in a voluntary winding-up, the powers of the directors ordinarily cease on the appointment of a liquidator.[101] In a compulsory liquidation, the powers of officers[102] of the company also cease on the appointment of the liquidator.[103]

Ordinarily, winding-up does not terminate any contracts that a company might be involved in, although this may depend upon the nature and terms of the contract

96   See ALRC, paras 721–7.

97   See *Re Hamilton View Pty Ltd* [1979] ACLC 32 036.

98   *Reigate v. Union Manufacturing Co.* [1918] 1 KB 592.

99   The words 'disposition of property' are given a wide meaning: *Re Margart Pty Ltd (in liq.)* (1984) 9 ACLR 269.

100 The exercise of the court's discretion to validate a disposition is discussed in *Tellsa Furniture Pty Ltd v. Glendave Nominees Pty Ltd* (1987) 9 NSWLR 254 at 260 per Priestly J. See also Corporations Law, s. 468(2) and (3).

101 Corporations Law, ss. 495(2) and 499(4).

102 'Officer' is defined in Corporations Law, s. 82A.

103 Corporations Law, s. 471A(1).

in question.[104] The exception to this rule is that a compulsory winding-up order constitutes a notice of dismissal for employees.[105] In a compulsory winding-up, share transfers made after winding-up commences are void unless otherwise ordered by the court under s. 468(1) or by the liquidator in a voluntary winding-up.[106]

Winding-up may have an effect on proceedings against the company. Section 471B provides that, where a winding-up order is made by the court or a provisional liquidator is appointed, a plaintiff cannot begin or continue with a civil procedure in a court against the company.[107] Courts, however, have granted exceptions to this rule where, for instance, a plaintiff is claiming his or her own property[108] or where the balance of convenience favours the action continuing.[109] A similar provision[110] can be found in relation to a voluntary winding-up.

Dissolution

Dissolution following compulsory winding-up

Actual dissolution in this case may occur in one of two ways. First, the liquidator applies to the court to be released and to have the company dissolved according to s. 480. Second, liquidation may occur under the terms of s. 572 where the ASC has reasonable cause to believe the following: that no liquidator is acting; that the affairs of the company are fully wound up and the liquidator has been in default for 6 months in lodging any required return; that the affairs of the company are fully wound up and there are no assets; or that there are insufficient assets available to pay the costs of getting a court order for dissolution under s. 480.

The liquidator will apply to the court when she or he has, as far as is practicable, realised all the company's property, distributed a final dividend (if any) to the creditors, adjusted the rights of the contributories among themselves, and made a final return (again, if any) to the contributories. If the liquidator does not apply for an order that the company be dissolved, the company may later be dissolved under ss. 572 and 574.

Dissolution following voluntary winding-up

In this case, the liquidator makes an account showing how the company's property has been disposed of and the winding-up conducted. She or he then calls a

---

104 *Re Tru Grain Co.* [1921] VLR 653. The liquidator may, however, be able to disclaim a contract that is onerous for the company if the court gives leave to do so: Corporations Law, s. 568(1B).

105 *Re Standard Salt and Alkali Ltd* [1934] SASR 168. However, this is not necessarily the case in a voluntary winding-up: *Midland Counties Bank v. Attwood* [1905] 1 Ch 357.

106 Corporations Law, s. 493(2).

107 *R. A. Ringwood Pty Ltd v. Lower* [1968] SASR 454. This can, of course, have significant consequences in circumstances such as those surrounding the 'asbestosis' cases (see pp. 114–15). There are substantial incentives for subsidiary companies involved in hazardous activities to be 'under-capitalised'. This minimises the depletion of group resources through settling claims or paying out awards of damages.

108 *Re David Lloyd & Co.* [1877] 6 Ch D 339.

109 *Re Gordon Grant and Grant Pty Ltd (in liq.)* (1982) 6 ACLR 727.

110 Corporations Law, s. 500(2).

meeting of the company or, in a creditors' voluntary winding-up, a meeting of the members and the creditors, and lays the account before the meeting.[111] Within 7 days of this meeting, the liquidator lodges a return of the holding of the meeting and a copy of the account with the ASC. After 3 months have elapsed, the company is dissolved automatically.

Under ss. 572 and 574, a company that has undergone a voluntary winding-up may also be dissolved where the ASC has reasonable cause to believe that no liquidator is acting, or that the company's affairs are fully wound up and the liquidator has been in default for 6 months in lodging any return required.

Consequences of dissolution

Upon dissolution, the company ceases to be a legal person and is treated as dissolved by the courts, both within and outside the place of incorporation.[112] The debts and other obligations of the company are extinguished. The liquidator's power in relation to the company ceases, as does the liquidator's statutory duty to the creditors and the contributories.

Any outstanding property of a dissolved company vests in the ASC under ss. 576 and 1336.[113] The ASC has power to sell the property and apply the proceeds to the costs of sale. The surplus is to be dealt with under pt 9.7 of the Corporations Law and paid into an unclaimed money account per s. 577. Ordinarily, liquidators must retain the company's books and the papers relevant to the liquidation for 5 years from the date of dissolution. However, in a compulsory winding-up, these may be destroyed within that time with the approval of the court. Section 542 covers voluntary liquidations. The books may be destroyed by direction of the company in general meeting (with the ASC's consent) in a members' voluntary winding-up, and by direction of the committee of inspection or the creditors (with the consent in each case of the ASC) in a creditors' voluntary winding-up. Section 262A of the Income Tax Assessment Act requires business records to be retained for 7 years, but does not require the preservation of records of a company that has gone into liquidation and been finally dissolved. Books of the company, other than those that the liquidator must retain, are retained by the last directors for 3 years after the date of dissolution.[114]

REVIEW QUESTIONS

1   The Second Corporate Law Simplification Bill changes the terminology in this area from 'dissolution' to 'deregistration'. Under the proposed s. 601AD, the company will cease to exist on deregistration, which will be voluntary, ASC-initiated, or ordered by the Federal or Supreme Court. Which term do you consider to be more appropriate? Why?

---

111 Corporations Law, s. 509.

112 *United Service Insurance Co. Ltd v. Lang* (1935) 35 SR (NSW) 487.

113 *Vitamins Australia Ltd v. Beta-Carotene Industries Pty Ltd* (1987) 5 ACLC 802 at 808.

114 Ford et al., p. 1196.

2 Under the Second Corporate Law Simplification Bill, s. 601AD, in what circumstances will the ASC be able to 'deregister' a company?

Conclusion

Thus, we have seen that, although companies are argued to have 'perpetual existence', they may be brought to an end under a variety of circumstances. In some situations, particularly where the company is wound up on the grounds of oppression
or on the 'just and equitable' ground, the winding-up of the company is analogous
to a divorce. In other circumstances, particularly where the company ceases to be of
'social utility', the company's demise is more analogous to euthanasia, particularly
where the company is guilty of the ultimate corporate wrong: insolvency. Regulation in this area is primarily concerned with an orderly and equitable gathering and
distribution of company property. This is necessary primarily because of the abuses
that can arise because of the doctrine of limited liability. To ensure that all parties are
treated fairly, within the constraints of limited liability and corporate personality,
the process of winding-up can take considerable time and effort.

PART 4

THE CORPORATE (T)RADER

11

MONEY MATTERS:
THE STRUCTURE OF
DEBT CAPITAL

Corporate empires: Corporate debts

While it is conventional to begin the examination of corporate finance with an exploration of the workings of share capital and the various forms it may take, as a generalisation it is safe to say that debt finance is, for a majority of companies, vastly more significant as a source of operating funds than is equity finance.[1] In the case of many proprietary companies, this should be obvious.[2] The law allows incorporation with an absolute minimum of equity capital, hence the expression 'two-dollar company'. In such circumstances, the business of the company is necessarily conducted with borrowed funds.

The same is equally true, but vastly less obvious, in the case of many public companies. Many of the corporate empires of the 1980s[3] were largely constructed upon the basis of debt finance rather than equity finance. The ready availability of loan finance, and the ease with which further loans could be accessed, made debt finance substantially more attractive for corporate expansion than were attempts to raise further capital through equity. Reliance upon debt rather than equity as a source of finance had a further attraction in the context of the entrepreneurship that flourished at this time. Whereas reliance upon equity finance tends to dilute control and thus to reduce the power of the individual entrepreneur, debt finance avoids this, although substantial creditors sometimes insist upon representation upon corporate boards through the medium of nominee directorships. Maintaining control is seen as important where the entrepreneur desires to maximise freedom of action and the ability to respond to changing market conditions.

In this chapter we propose to focus upon the various avenues through which the company is able to access debt capital and to examine some of the associated policy

---

1   It is important not to overemphasise the distinction between debt capital and equity capital. On one level, the distinction is largely a matter of accounting practice.

2   Indeed, the reasons for this were spelt out in the passage from Gilbert and Sullivan quoted on p. 11.

3   See chapter 7.

issues. Broadly, there are two major forms of debt financing available to companies: the charge[4] and the unsecured debenture.[5] Note that companies are able to access all of the forms of credit available to the ordinary consumer. When a company secures goods or services from natural or corporate persons, it may well secure these upon some form of extended terms exactly as do natural persons. Similarly, corporate persons frequently utilise facilities such as credit cards in many of the same ways and for the same purposes as do natural persons. Other forms of debt finance are also unremarkable. For example, overdrafts are used by corporate persons in the same way as they are used by sole traders or partnerships. These credit relationships are governed by the laws concerning contract (and property, where security is required) in exactly the same ways as are credit relationships involving natural persons or partnerships.

The familiarity of many of these conventional ways of accessing debt finance obscures many of the features of corporate finance that are not only unique to corporate persons but also paradoxical. In the initial paragraphs of this chapter we drew a distinction between equity capital and debt capital. Many people believe that this is an obvious distinction. After all, we all know the difference between the money that we ourselves have amassed (whether it be money in a savings or checking account or our 'part ownership' of a motor vehicle or a house) and that which we owe, whether by way of mortgage, hire purchase, or credit card debt. In the world of corporate finance, the distinction is much less obvious, and in some cases, the line between equity finance and debt finance is hopelessly blurred. Convertible financial instruments[6] are commonplace in modern financial markets. Thus, instruments that begin their lives as 'debt' may subsequently become 'equity'. Similarly, some instruments that are technically equity are almost indistinguishable from debt. In the next chapter, when we begin to examine the different classes of shares that are traded on financial markets, we will look at 'preference shares' and at their role in corporate finance. Preference shares are a curious hybrid. While—being shares in the company—they are a form of equity finance, they function in ways that make them almost indistinguishable from debt finance.

The blurring of the boundaries between equity and debt becomes even more apparent when we look at one of the classic mechanisms used to interrogate the financial well-being of the company: its 'gearing'. Gearing is expressed in terms of a ratio that compares the company's reliance upon debt finance with its reliance upon

---

4   'Charge' is being used very broadly in this discussion and includes a legal mortgage. For an overview of different types of charges and the rules that govern them, see J. H. Farrar & L. G. S. Trotman, 'Charges', in *Australian Corporation Law*, Butterworths, Sydney, chapter 3.5, p. 35 011.

5   A debenture is simply an acknowledgment of debt. Section 9 of the *Corporations Law 1990* defines a debenture as a document acknowledging a debt. Because of the breadth of this definition, s. 1045 requires a specific statement, which indicates whether it provides evidence of an unsecured note, mortgage debenture (where there is a statement that the loan is secured by a registered or registrable first mortgage over land, up to a specified value), or debenture. It should be noted that United States discourse uses the term 'bond' rather than debenture, hence the familiar 1980s expression 'junk bonds'.

6   Convertible debentures are specifically provided for by the Corporations Law, s. 9. These entitle the debenture holder to convert the debenture into shares.

equity finance. Put in those terms, it might appear that, to determine the 'gearing' of a company, all that is required is a simple comparison between the level of equity finance (that is, issued shares) and debt finance. The position is not that straightforward, however. When calculating the gearing ratio of a company, preference shares are properly treated as debt finance rather than as equity finance. Thus the issued capital of many companies is divided between equity finance (ordinary shares) and debt finance (preference shares).[7] If a company relies heavily on debt finance rather than on equity finance, it is said to be 'highly geared', or 'highly leveraged'. Many companies pursuing speculative investment strategies or entrepreneurial ventures favour relatively high gearing levels. When a company is highly geared, it is able to develop very rapidly by accessing funds that vastly exceed the equity capital available to it and by reaping the rewards of the extra leverage that this form of finance makes available. This strategy enables it to maximise the potential return to its investors, although it also maximises the risks.[8]

Corporate finance has also developed its own vocabulary and its own unique forms of debt finance. We will be looking at these vehicles in more detail later in this chapter. Here we want simply to mention them as part of our overall introduction to debt finance. Some elements of this vocabulary have made their way into the popular press—'junk bonds',[9] for example. Others remain obscure and 'lawyerly', such as debentures and 'floating charges'. All of these forms of debt capital make a significant contribution to the life-blood of companies, both large and small.

We will begin by taking a 'bird's eye' view of the role of credit in the modern company and will try to familiarise ourselves with the language of credit and with some of the issues that may arise. This will involve a review of some basic ideas that are usually canvassed in contract and in property law. Second, we will look at some forms of credit that are unique to corporations, and at the issues that arise when

---

7   For a full discussion of the nature of preference shares and the ways in which they are more akin to debt finance than to equity finance, see chapter 12.

8   These risks are particularly high where the company pursues highly speculative and/or volatile investments with borrowed funds. The gearing practices that prevailed during the 1980s were a substantial factor in the corporate failures sparked by the collapse of the share market on 'Black Monday' in 1987. Companies whose asset base was heavily dependent upon the vagaries of the share market (particularly where the shares had been purchased on margin) were exceptionally vulnerable.

9   While the official Australian term for 'junk bonds' is the rather pedantic 'deferred unsecured notes', the term 'junk bonds' rapidly made its way into both the popular and the financial press. Junk bonds are a form of deferred or subordinated debt, sometimes referred to as 'mezzanine finance'. Subordinated debt arrangements enable the corporation to create hierarchies of creditors. Where this is done, close associates of the borrowing company defer their entitlements to repayment to encourage outsiders to provide finance. Ultimately, these contractual arrangements enable unsecured creditors to arrange for a priority of entitlement to repayment among themselves. Just as preference shares became almost indistinguishable from many forms of loan finance—a fact recognised by their placement on the debit ledger in calculating the gearing ratio of the company—'junk bonds' (being the most junior of junior debt) become almost indistinguishable from equity finance. In the Australian market they have been treated as substantially interchangeable with shares in some circumstances, particularly where this facilitates evading the provisions of other regulatory regimes. On the use of subordinated debt and the interpretation of subordination provisions, see *United States Trust Co. of New York and Ors v. Australia & New Zealand Banking Group Ltd* (1993) 11 ACSR 7.

these creative forms of financing come before the courts. Finally, we will explore the interface between the use of various forms of credit and the market price of different classes of shares, and we will look at a number of policy issues that arise in this context. This chapter is not intended to make its readers experts in the area of debt finance. It is intended to provide a broadly based introduction to the forms of debt finance available to corporate actors and an understanding of the policy framework within which concerns have been raised about the legitimacy and appropriateness of these forms of finance.

REVIEW QUESTIONS

1 List all of the different forms of credit with which you are familiar. How many of them seem well adapted for business use?
2 Do you think that the ability, through limited liability, to minimise personal financial exposure (in the case of a small proprietary company) encourages a more risk-taking approach to management than would be the case if a sole trader or partnership were involved?
3 Consider a group of interlocking companies in which some of the individual elements pursue a strategy (perhaps as a matter of group policy) of being highly geared, while other elements pursue more conventional (and therefore less potentially profitable and less risky) strategies. Do you think that the *Corporations Law 1990* ought to allow creditors of the highly geared elements to recover from other companies in the group if an insolvent liquidation occurs? What policy judgments might encourage you to answer this question in the affirmative? What countervailing policy judgments might encourage a negative response?

The machinery of 'credit'

Today it is no more possible for a business to operate without reliance upon credit than it is for an individual to do so. One of the most significant strategic decisions made by any manager concerns the extent to which the business will depend upon its own resources for its day-to-day operations and the extent to which it may find it preferable (or even essential) to rely upon various forms of credit.[10] Even where a company is not highly geared, it will often be advisable for it to rely upon credit finance, *inter alia*, to smooth out uneven patches in its cash flow and to enable it to function effectively in the market. The judicious use of debt capital may also permit the company to expand much more rapidly than would otherwise be the case.

---

10 Obviously, matters become even more complex where the company is part of a group of companies that moves its resources from entity to entity as required. We looked at some examples when we considered the 'corporate veil' and the circumstances in which the courts will disregard it in chapter 7.

Corporations are able to access a bewildering array of debt finance. Obvious, and simple, forms of finance include revolving credit arrangements such as overdrafts or deferred payment arrangements with suppliers. These enable the company to meet its ongoing obligations, such as the payment of its employees and suppliers, while itself awaiting payment for services rendered. Other obvious forms are the credit cards that many companies issue to their executive officers, and various other forms of unsecured borrowing.

While such arrangements have obvious advantages from the perspective of a company seeking finance, they have obvious disadvantages from the point of view of prospective creditors. First, the debts involved are typically unsecured. The contractual arrangements creating the debt will almost invariably specify the manner and the date upon which repayment is due, but because no security is held, repayment may be difficult to procure if the company faces uncertain financial times.[11] The ordinary legal mechanisms[12] for enforcing payment by a defaulting debtor are relatively costly and, unless implemented in a proactive manner, likely to leave the unsecured creditor ranked *pari passu* in an insolvent liquidation.[13]

From the perspective of the creditor, therefore, it is desirable for the debt to be secured rather than unsecured. One standard definition of 'security' is that provided by E. I. Sykes:

> For the practical purposes of the ordinary security given to secure the repayment of money lent or the payment of money owed, it is probable that a security can be defined as an interest vested in a person called 'the creditor' in certain property owned by another called 'the debtor', whereby certain rights are made available to the creditor over such property in order to satisfy an obligation personally owed or recognised as being owed to the creditor by the debtor or some other person. This is wide enough to comprehend the case of a security by a guarantor.[14]

---

11 So far as the various unsecured forms of finance available to corporate persons are concerned, no meaningful distinction can be made between companies and sole traders or partnerships. Liquidation (in the case of insolvent companies) and bankruptcy (in the case of insolvent individuals) are, in Australia, distinct legal regimes, but in terms of their impact upon unsecured creditors, the position is identical. To the extent that a distinction is possible, it is simply that corporations frequently have a far wider range of creditors than do individuals. This is, in part, a consequence of the protection afforded by limited liability and its potential to encourage a predisposition towards risk-positive behaviour.

12 Judgment may be sought in the court, and when judgment is given, recourse to execution proceedings against the property of the company, or to garnishee proceedings against money or property owed to the company, must be had. If such proceedings are pushed by a number of unsecured creditors simultaneously, the company may be forced into insolvent liquidation. When this happens, creditors are unlikely to recover fully; indeed, if the company is truly over extended, unsecured creditors may recover less than 25 cents in the dollar.

13 It should be noted that banks and other large institutions are somewhat less likely to wind up in this position than are trade creditors and the like. As we shall see later, institutional creditors often attempt to protect their interests through mechanisms that assimilate unsecured debt to secured debt. It is also worth noting that it is probably somewhat more common for unsecured creditors to play the liquidation card than it is for them to pursue bankruptcy proceedings against an individual.

14 E. I. Sykes & S. Walker (eds), *The Law of Securities: An Account of the Law Pertaining to Securities over Real and Personal Property under the Laws of the Australian Jurisdictions*, 5th edn, Law Book Company, Sydney, 1993, p. 12. For further attempts at definition, see S. Fisher, *Commercial and Personal Property Law*, Butterworths, Sydney, 1997, para. 8.2.

Undeniably, the discourse of 'security' has its ambiguities, the term security being used (more or less interchangeably) to describe the bundle of rights created by way of debenture or mortgage, the property over which the rights are created, and even, upon occasion, the instrument creating the interest. These slippages in language are a consequence of our cultural understandings of property and, in particular, of the distinctions such as those between rights *in personam* and rights *in rem*, and those between choses in possession and choses in action. Our culture and our legal traditions distinguish sharply between 'obligations' and 'property'. For instance, a distinction is be drawn between, on the one hand, the obligations created by documents purporting to create rights in the creditor over either real or personal property of the debtor and, on the other hand, the property that is the subject of those rights. This is exemplified by the fact that, under the Corporations Law, charges over both real and personal property must be 'registered'[15] if they are to have the desired effect of converting an unsecured debt into a secured debt.[16] If the charges are not registered, the words of the document will not be sufficient to entitle the creditor to take its place among the secured creditors in an insolvent liquidation, and thus it is unlikely to recover the full amount owed.[17]

REVIEW QUESTIONS

1   What is the distinction between rights *in personam* and rights *in rem*? (If you are uncertain about this distinction, it may help to consult a standard property text.) Why might this distinction be critical in the context of a discussion of the uses (and abuses) of debt capital?

---

15   See pt 3.5 of the Corporations Law. Registration 'perfects' a security interest—that is, renders it binding upon persons other than those who are immediately a party to it. Such requirements became a part of corporations law at the turn of the century, the intention being that registration of a charge would give notice to those consulting the register of the existence and nature of the security interests contained therein. The present legislative provisions rank the securities, and careful attention to the detail of the provisions, especially s. 262(1), is essential. Not surprisingly, there has been substantial litigation in this area. By way of illustration of the issues that may arise, see *Australian Central Credit Union v. Commonwealth Bank of Australia* (1991) 9 ACLC 396; *Bailey v. Manos Breeder Farms Pty Ltd* (1990) 8 ACLC 1116; *Equus Financial Services Ltd v. Boambee Bay Resort Pty Ltd (in liq.)* (1991) 9 ACLC 779.

16   While, as we shall see shortly, the forms of security utilised in corporate transactions are much more varied than those available to individuals and to non-corporate enterprises, a properly registered security generally functions in much the same way as familiar securities, such as a home loan or mortgage. The documentation specifies that the lender has a particular limited interest in property, the title to which is held by the borrower. Should the borrower default in its obligations under the security, the lender is typically entitled to take possession of the security provided and to sell it to recover the funds advanced by way of loan. It goes without saying that, if the property realises more than the amount of the security and any outstanding interest, the balance must be returned to the borrower (if it is solvent) or to the liquidator (if the borrower is insolvent). In an insolvent liquidation, any such surplus will be available either to any secondary secured creditors over the same subject matter or to the unsecured creditors *pari passu*.

17   An unregistered charge is simply a contract. As such, it is unable to bind third parties.

2 Think about your present legal rights to goods and services. Try to classify those rights into choses in action and choses in possession. Into which category would you place your right to 'quiet possession' of the flat or house in which you live, your right to your car, your rights under a contract entitling you to security services for your home or office?

3 Is the entitlement of a creditor to repayment of an unsecured debt a chose in action or a chose in possession?

Giving security: Mortgages and charges

Because this area of the law is complex and technical, we want to begin our consideration of it by looking at a form of security that should be familiar: a mortgage over real property.[18] Most people rely upon mortgages to enable them to purchase their homes. Corporate persons rely upon registered mortgages for much the same purpose: to enable them to purchase property upon which to carry on their business activities.

In its classical general law form, the mortgage deed transferred all of the legal rights of the debtor (mortgagor) in the mortgaged property to the creditor (mortgagee) subject to a contractual condition that the subject property be retransferred to the debtor when the debt was completely repaid. Under Torrens title (which has largely superseded general law title in all Australian jurisdictions[19]), while the term 'mortgage' continues to be used, what is actually created under the legislation is a *charge*, under the terms of which the creditor acquires a bundle of specified rights against the subject property which can be exercised under specified conditions.

While the distinction between a mortgage and a charge is highly technical, it is useful to bear it in mind when examining corporate finance. In a mortgage (which can, in principle, be held over any property, whether real or personal), the mortgagor transfers all of his or her legal and equitable rights in the subject property to the mortgagee. At common law, all that the mortgagor retained was a contractual right to have the property transferred back when the debt was repaid in full. This left the mortgagor in a vulnerable position and led to intervention by the courts of equity. As a consequence of equity's intervention, this contractual right vested in the mortgagor by the deed of mortgage became known as the mortgagor's 'equity of redemption'. The equity of redemption was itself deemed by the courts of equity to be a species of proprietary right.

The position with respect to a charge is very different. Where a charge is issued, the individual or institution holding the charge gains rights against the property that is subject to the charge, rather than an actual interest in the subject property.

---

18 Technically, of course, under the Torrens system of registration, a legal mortgage is a charge rather than an actual mortgage, as was the case at common law; however, this technicality is widely ignored in both ordinary and legal discourse.

19 While real property held under the general law (and not registered under the Torrens system) continues to exist in some Australian jurisdictions, all Australian real property is gradually being brought under the Torrens system as it is transferred upon sale or upon the death of the owner.

Charges gain their force against third parties by virtue of the act of registration, not by the execution of the documents creating them.[20] A charge that is not registered, therefore, will not bind those who are not parties to it. Unlike mortgages, charges are creatures of equity. As a consequence, there is no such thing as a 'legal charge', although statutory regimes may make provision for registering charges and specify the consequences of registration (and of the failure to do so).

Mortgages can be either legal or equitable. Over the centuries, the common law had developed quite precise rules about the nature of interests that could be characterised as 'proprietary',[21] and about the documentary evidence that was required to effect a legal mortgage and the terms that were appropriate. Future property could not be mortgaged. The rigidity of the common law in this area led, as was the case in other areas of the law, to the intervention of the courts of equity. As they did not regard themselves as constrained by the niceties of form, they were prepared to enforce dispositions of property that failed to meet the common-law requirements. The courts of equity also developed alternative conventions concerning the actions that were sufficient to give rise to an equitable mortgage. Equity's jurisdiction, unlike that of the common law, extended to future property, thus covering a situation such as that arising in *Holroyd v. Marshall*.[22] According to the Lord Chancellor,

> if a vendor or mortgagor agrees to sell or mortgage property, real or personal, of which he is not possessed at the time, and he receives the consideration for the contract, and afterwards becomes possessed of property answering the description in the contract, there is no doubt that a court of equity would compel him to perform the contract, and that the contract would, in equity, transfer the beneficial interest to the mortgagee or purchaser immediately on the property being acquired. This, of course, assumes that the supposed contract is one of that class of which a court of equity should decree the specific performance. If it be so, then immediately on the acquisition of the property described the vendor or mortgagor would hold it in trust for the purchaser or mortgagee, according to the terms of the contract. For if a contract be in other respects good and fit to be performed, and the consideration has been received, incapacity to perform it at the time of its execution will be no answer when the means of doing so are afterwards obtained.[23]

---

20 Division 2 of the Corporations Law deals with the registration of charges. See ss. 262–82. Section 9 contains a definition of the term 'floating charge', and further particulars in respect of this category of charge may be found in ss. 556, 561, 588FJ. On charges generally, see L. Taylor, 'What a Company Charge Does not Reveal—The Financier's Perspective' (1992) CSLJ 396 and I. Cameron, 'Company Charges and the Australian Law Reform Commission: Scrutinising "The Department of Utter Confusion"' (1994) 12 CSLJ 357.

21 The discussion in *Mabo and Ors v. Queensland (No. 2)* (1991–92) 175 CLR 1 epitomises the technical and limited nature of the sorts of interests that the common law recognised as rights of property. These technical rules meant that many interests that we think of as proprietary interests were excluded. Such interests could not become subject to a legal mortgage, although they could be charged in various other ways.

22 (1862) 10 HLC 191; 11 ER 999.

23 (1862) 10 HLC 191 at 211. The recognition of the capacity to mortgage future property paved the way for recognition of floating charges. However, the capacity to mortgage future property by way of fixed charge remains. It is a matter of interpretation whether a given document creates a fixed or a floating charge. See *Re New Bullas Trading Ltd* (1994) 12 ACLC 3203; BCC 36.

Charges, on the other hand, are not creatures of the common law but of the courts of equity, although statutory charges exist pursuant to legislation. As noted earlier, where a charge has been created, its holder does not gain any right in the property that is subject to the charge, although its holder does gain rights 'against' that property. As we enter the realm of charges, we meet one of the forms of finance that is generally considered to be unique to corporate persons:[24] the floating charge. Floating charges will be looked at in some detail in the next section. They have a number of unique features, and they are, and have been, the subject of substantial controversy in the courts.

REVIEW QUESTIONS

1 Explain the difference between a mortgage and a charge in your own words. Those of you who have already studied the real property law will be familiar with the terminology associated with general law mortgages.
2 Do you think that it makes any difference whether a creditor has a right in specified property or a right to institute proceedings against specified property? If so, what difference might it make?
3 Think about the distinction between rights *in personam* and rights *in rem*. Is a registered charge a chose in action or a chose in possession? How do you know?
4 What happens if the person or institution holding a charge fails to register it? Why does the law allow so much to turn on the act of registration?

Equity triumphs: The invention of the floating charge
If charges as a general category are creatures of equity, the floating charge epitomises the creativity of equity's practitioners. It is, perhaps, the ultimate commercial financial vehicle. As it initially developed in the courts of equity,[25] the floating charge enabled a business to offer its entire 'undertaking' as security for a loan. This development was very important for a number of reasons. First, in the case of many businesses, including small and medium sized commercial ventures, much of the capital

---

24 While it is generally thought that only corporate persons can create floating charges, it is difficult to ascertain the foundation for this belief. Certainly there does not appear to be any characteristic or quality unique to corporate personality that would enable the company to exercise capacities that natural persons are unable to exercise.

25 The first known judicial recognition by Chancery occurred in *Re Panama, New Zealand and Australian Royal Mail Co.* (1870) Ch App 318, although the juridical nature of the new device remained in substantial doubt until the early twentieth century. The critical cases in this development are *Re Yorkshire Woolcombers Assoc. Ltd* [1903] 2 Ch 284; *Illingworth v. Houldsworth* [1904] AC 355; *Evans v. Rival Granite Quarries Ltd* [1910] 2 KB 979. For a general (albeit traditional and conservative) discussion of the floating charge, see W. J. Gough, 'The Floating Charge: Traditional Themes and New Directions', in P. D. Finn (ed.), *Equity and Commercial Relationships*, Law Book Company, Sydney, 1987, p. 239. See also J. Ricketts, 'Automatic Refloatation of a Crystallised Floating Charge' (1992) 22 WALR 430; J. O'Donovan, 'Re New Bullas Trading Ltd—The Evolving Floating Charge' (1995) 13 CSLJ 203. A series of brief notes on corporate insolvency by S. Cameron & M. Betjeman in (1995) 13 CSLJ 393–6 is also useful.

of the business is tied up in its stock in trade. Because the stock in trade of a business is continually changing—as merchandise is sold and replaced by newly acquired (or manufactured) goods—it might appear that it would be extremely difficult to utilise it as security in securing further debt capital. Similarly, in the ordinary course of its trade, a business is likely to amass a number of debts—that is, money owed to the company for goods and services provided by it. Both the stock in trade of a company and its debts may be worth substantial amounts of money. However, these assets are continually changing in the normal course of the company's business.

Equity practitioners sought to provide financial vehicles that could fill this gap. They sought to develop security instruments that were sufficiently flexible to permit the enterprise to carry out its trade unimpeded so long as its commitments under the instrument were met on a regular basis. But at the same time, these interests had to be capable of allowing the holder of the charge to realise the value of the stock in trade or of the money owed to the company should the company default under the terms of the charge. Over time the interaction between equity practitioners and the courts created the instrument that we today know as the 'floating charge'.[26] According to Hoffman J,

> [t]he floating charge was invented by Victorian lawyers to enable manufacturing and trading companies to raise loan capital on debentures. It could offer the security of a charge over the whole of the company's undertaking without inhibiting its ability to trade. But the mirror image of these advantages was the potential prejudice to the general body of creditors, who might know nothing of the floating charge but find that all the company's assets, including the very goods which they had just delivered on credit, had been swept up by the debenture holder. The public interest requires a balancing of the advantages to the economy of facilitating the borrowing of money against the possibility injustice to unsecured creditors.[27]

In this section we will explore the development of the floating charge and the terms of art that are associated with its operation. We will also explore some of the mechanisms that have been developed to enhance the efficacy of floating charges from the perspective of the charge-holder.

From the perspective of a company attempting to secure additional working capital, and with a substantial proportion of its existing capital tied up in its stock in trade, it is easy to see the attraction of an instrument such as a floating charge. But one might think that such a vehicle would be comparatively unattractive to those providing finance, given that, to serve its purpose, it must allow the company's normal business operations to proceed undisturbed. Most ordinary people would, we

---

26 The case law concerning floating charges is abundant, and growing rapidly. Much of the litigation centres on determining the priorities among floating charges and other forms of debt. For a representative sample of the kinds of issues that may arise, see *Crawford v. Australia & New Zealand Banking Group Ltd & Ors* (1994) 12 ACLC 957; *McIntosh v. Turner Corporation Ltd (in liq.)* (1995) 13 ACLC 1314; *Australian Central Credit Union v. Commonwealth Bank of Australia* (1991) 9 ACLC 396.

27 *Re Brightlife Ltd* [1987] 1 Ch 200 at 214.

suspect, find the idea of using property that one intends to sell as security for a loan puzzling, even faintly dishonest.

The courts speak of floating charges as 'hovering' or 'floating'[28] over the assets of the company until some event (either specified in the instrument creating the charge or undertaken by the charge-holder) causes it to 'crystallise' or fix upon the particular assets held at a particular point in time.[29] The following description by Buckley LJ expresses its character well:

> A floating security is not a future security; it is a present security, which presently affects all the assets of the company expressed to be included in it. On the other hand, it is not specific security; the holder cannot affirm that the assets are specifically mortgaged to him. The assets are mortgaged in such a way that the mortgagor can deal with them without the concurrence of the mortgagee. A floating security is not a specific mortgage of the assets, plus a licence to the mortgagor to dispose of them in the course of his business, but is a floating mortgage applying to every item comprised in the security but not specifically affecting any item until some event occurs or some act on the part of the mortgagee is done which causes it to crystallise into a fixed security. Mr Shearman argued that it was competent to the mortgagee to intervene at any moment and to say that he withdrew the licence as regards any particular item. That is not in my opinion the nature of the security; it is a mortgage presently affecting all the items expressed to be included in it, but not specifically affecting any item till the happening of the event which causes the security to crystallise as regards all the items. This crystallisation may be brought about in various ways. A receiver may be appointed, or the company may go into liquidation and a liquidator be appointed, or any event may happen which is defined as bringing to an end the licence to the company to carry on business. There is no case in which it has been affirmed that a mortgagee of this description may at any moment forbid the company to sell a particular piece of property or may take it himself and keep it, and leave the licensee to carry on the business subsisting as regards everything else. This would be inconsistent with the real bargain between the parties, which is that the mortgagee gives authority to the company to use all its property until the licence to carry on business comes to an end.[30]

Because of this 'hovering' quality, and because such an instrument characteristically covers many discrete items of property, it is common for the document creating the charge to endeavour to restrict the power of the grantor to create further securities in competition to it. The restrictive clauses used for this purpose are

---

28 An early characterisation is that of Lord Macnaghten in *Illingworth v. Houldsworth* at 358: 'a floating charge … is ambulatory and shifting in its nature, hovering over and so to speak floating with the property which it is intended to affect until some event occurs or some act is done which causes it to settle and fasten on the subject of the charge within its reach and grasp'.

29 Not surprisingly, litigation concerning crystallisation abounds. See *National Australia Bank Ltd & Anor v. Composite Buyers Ltd & Ors* (1991) 6 ACSR 94; *Re Obie Pty Ltd (No. 2)* (1984) ACLC 67; *Fire Nymph Products Ltd v. The Heating Centre Pty Ltd (in liq.) & Ors* (1992) 10 ACLC 629 (discussed at length later in this chapter).

30 *Re Evans v. Rival Granite Quarries Ltd* at 999–1000.

covenants not to do particular acts.[31] Such covenants are believed to be an essential element in an effective floating charge because otherwise there would be no limitation upon the right of the company to create specific mortgages and/or charges over the goods subject to the floating charge. While early case law regarding floating charges[32] did not specifically acknowledge this capacity, it was recognised well before the turn of the century.[33] To complicate matters further, while it has been thought, since *Re Benjamin Cope & Sons Ltd*,[34] that a company could not create a floating charge ranking prior to or *pari passu* with an existing floating charge, later case law confused the issue somewhat and suggested that a subsequent floating charge over only part of the assets could be so ranked. John Farrar and Lindsay Trotman suggest:

> Because of the latitude shown by the courts to companies who have created floating charges, it has become the general practice to insert a clause forbidding the creation of any mortgage or charge ranking in priority to or *pari passu* with the floating charge … Such a clause is on its face a restriction on dealing in the course of business. The courts nevertheless proceed on the assumption that it is valid although they recognise that it must be strictly construed. In no case does the validity of such a clause appear to have been challenged …
>
> Conversely, a point which would still seem tenable is that the subsequent mortgage must be granted by the company in good faith and in the ordinary course of business. It is strongly arguable that the subsequent mortgage, being granted in breach of the restrictive clause, can be neither. In other words, it is arguable that it is evidence of equitable fraud by the company.
>
> Where a restrictive clause is used outside a debenture and as a substitute for secured indebtedness it is commonly called a negative pledge …
>
> It is now clearly established that knowledge of the existence of such a clause in a debenture operates in equity to prevent a subsequent mortgagee obtaining priority. This seems to be consistent with the equitable fraud argument. The onus appears to be on the subsequent chargee to prove that he is a bona fide chargee for value without notice, not on the first chargee to prove that he has knowledge or notice.[35]

---

31 For a discussion of such covenants in the Scottish context, see *AIB Finance Ltd v. Bank of Scotland* [1995] BCLC 185. In England see *Griffiths v. Yorkshire Bank plc* [1994] 1 WLR 1427. More generally, see R. Grantham, 'Priorities and Floating Charges' (1996) NZLJ 126. The debate in England and Scotland would presently appear to centre on the nature of the chargee's interest. See *Bond Brewing Holdings v. National Australia Bank* [1990] ACLC 330. See also J. Stone, 'Negative Pledges and the Tort of Interference with Contractual Relations' (1991) NZLR 411. Stone suggests that a subsequent secured lender (with knowledge of the pledge) may become liable in the tort of interference with contractual relations, but acknowledges that this remedy is likely to be of minimal value since its only likely effect, where the borrower is insolvent, is to defeat the security of the subsequent lender and increase the asset pool (if any) available to unsecured creditors.

32 *Re Panama, New Zealand and Australian Royal Mail Co.* is typical in this regard.

33 *Re Florence Land Co.: Ex parte Moor* (1878) 10 Ch D 530.

34 [1914] 1 Ch 800 at 806. See also *Smith v. English and Scottish Mercantile Investment Trust* [1896] WN 86; (1896) 40 SJ 717.

35 Farrar & Trotman, 35 110. For the statutory position, see Corporations Law, s. 279(3), which provides for registration of the details of the prohibition on the creation of subsequent fixed charges. The prohibition must be registered before it can have effect.

More complex financial arrangements may involve the issue of a series of debentures or debenture stock to many different individuals. In order to avoid the patent inconvenience of a plurality of creditors, a trustee[36] will be appointed to act on behalf of the lenders by the debenture trust deed. Such a deed is essential where the company wishes to solicit subscriptions for debentures. Clifford Smith and Jerold Warner describe the ways in which, in the USA, bond covenants can be used to minimise the risk that companies would act so as to advantage shareholders at the expense of bondholders:

> We selected a random sample of eighty-seven public issues of debt which were registered with the Securities and Exchange Commission between January 1974 and December 1975 ... Standardized provisions ... are used frequently: 90.8 percent of the bonds contain restrictions on the issuance of additional debt, 23.0 percent have restrictions on dividend payments, 39.1 percent restrict merger activities, and 35.6 percent constrain the firm's disposition of assets.[37]

Such covenants are, of course, equally useful in Australia.

During the period when the courts of equity were developing the doctrines that governed priorities in relation to floating charges, these charges were commonly granted over the whole of the enterprise. This formulation compelled the courts to elucidate the relationship between floating charges and other forms of security. Clearly, floating charges could not take priority either over fixed charges that were earlier in time or over prior legal mortgages. The priorities with regard to floating charges and other forms of debt were not, at the outset, entirely settled. It became clear fairly early that floating charges were a form of secured debt and that their holders therefore took priority over all species of unsecured creditor.[38] The exact operation of these instruments, and the mechanisms by which they crystallised, evolved gradually through judicial decisions, although a number of areas of ambiguity remain.

By 1903 many of the initial ambiguities were coming sharply into focus. In *Re Yorkshire Woolcombers Assoc. Ltd*,[39] the association had created a floating charge over its entire undertaking. This charge did not incorporate a negative pledge—that is, a clause that specified that the association was not to create any charge in priority to itself. Needing further finance, the association purported to create a charge over 'all and singular the book and other debts now owing to the association, and also all and singular the book and other debts which may at any time during the continuance of

---

36 Corporation Law, s. 1052 specifies who shall be eligible to serve as a trustee for such a debenture deed.

37 C. W. Smith Jr & J. B. Warner, 'On Financial Contracting: An Analysis of Bond Covenants', in R. Romano, *Foundations of Corporate Law*, Oxford University Press, New York, 1993, pp. 127, 128.

38 *Re Panama, New Zealand and Australian Royal Mail Co.*; *English and Scottish Mercantile Investment Company* [1892] 2 QB 1. In the latter case, the debenture instrument contained the following clause: 'This debenture is one of a series of 200 debentures ... all to rank pari passu as a first charge on the property hereby charged, without any preference or priority one over another; and the charge hereby created is to be a floating security, but so that the Corporation is not to be at liberty to create any mortgage or charge in priority to the said debentures'.

39 [1903] 2 Ch 284.

this security become owing to the association'.[40] When the matter came before the English Court of Appeal, Romer LJ was required to determine whether the charge created thereby was floating or fixed. According to the Lord Justice:

> Under s. 14 of the *Companies Act* of 1900, for a charge to be a 'floating charge on the undertaking or property of the company' within the meaning of the words used in that section, it cannot, I think, be properly contended that it is essential that the charge must be on the whole undertaking, or on the whole property, of the company ... [W]hen the courts have to consider whether the charge is a floating one ... one must, I think, deal with the question of substance to be answered according to the circumstances of each particular case. I certainly do not intend to attempt to give an exact definition of the term 'floating charge,' ... but I certainly think that if a charge has the three characteristics that I am about to mention it is a floating charge. (1) If it is a charge on a class of assets of a company present and future; (2) if that class is one which in the ordinary course of the business of the company, would be changing from time to time; and (3) if you find that by the charge it is contemplated that, until some further step is taken by or on behalf of those interested in the charge, the company may carry on its business in the ordinary way as far as concerns the particular class of assets I am dealing with.
>
> In the present case those three characteristics do in my opinion distinguish the charge we have to consider. In the first place, the charge is one upon all the debts of the company present and future, not even limiting them (though I do not think it makes any difference) to the trade debts. In the second place, it obviously contemplates a class of asset which, in the ordinary course of the life of the company, must continually, and of necessity, change; and thirdly, in the present case, if I look at the deed which created the charge here, to my mind it clearly contemplated that until some step is taken by or on behalf of those who are to have the benefit of the charge, the company would be able to receive the debts due the company in its ordinary course of business, and to deal with them for the ordinary purposes of the business.[41]

In the early cases, floating charges were thought to require both a specific and identifiable event, and the intervention of the chargee in order for crystallisation to occur. Gradually it was recognised that crystallisation was 'automatically' brought about by events such as the appointment of a receiver under a prior fixed charge, the appointment of a liquidator, or any other event that brought the business of the company to a halt. Once it was recognised that crystallisation could occur without the intervention of the chargee, draftspersons sought to specify in the charges themselves events that would bring about crystallisation, thus enhancing the value of the security to the chargee.

---

40   [1903] 2 Ch 284 at 294–5.

41   [1903] 2 Ch 284 at 294–5. It is worth considering whether the association actually intended to create a second floating charge or whether, in fact, it intended to create a fixed charge over a particular class of property (book debts, present and future). Some commentators have expressed concern that this decision effectively eliminated the utility of fixed charges over future property. This does not seem to be the case. See *Re New Bullas Trading Ltd.*

Conceptual questions and practical realities

The law has, since equity first recognised the floating charge, accepted that, after crystallisation, the chargee is entitled to rank as a secured creditor, but the nature of the charge-holder's 'pre-crystallisation' interest in the property charged is far from clear. Some recognised authorities[42] suggest that, until crystallisation occurs, a floating charge is incapable of creating any equitable interest except for, perhaps, a 'mere equity' arising out of the contract. On the other hand, in *Landall Holdings Ltd v. Caratti*,[43] the Supreme Court in Western Australia held that, where such a charge extends to real property, it creates an interest in land for the purposes of the Statute of Frauds, irrespective of whether crystallisation has occurred. It seems to us difficult to dispute that some form of 'security interest' is inherent in the charge itself,[44] irrespective of whether crystallisation has occurred. Should the company engage in a transaction that is outside of the ordinary course of its business, that transaction becomes subject to the charge. In such circumstances, the question of whether or not the charge has crystallised is immaterial.

Further troubling questions concern the conceptual basis of the company's entitlement to carry on business and to deal with the subject matter of the charge. Historically, two theories were used to account for this: the 'licence' theory[45] and the 'mortgage of future assets' theory. The first, and older, theory accounted for the company's power to enter a deal with the charged property by means of an implied licence.[46] The second theory accounts for the existence of power by pointing to the fact that the charge cannot attach or fix to any particular assets until crystallisation has occurred. It is argued that the charge cannot, therefore, provide any impediment to dealing, since it does not touch upon any particular asset. In the next section, we will begin to examine how floating charges operate in practice and the way in which they interact with other forms of corporate finance through an examination of *Fire Nymph Products Ltd v. The Heating Centre Pty Ltd*.[47]

The Fire Nymph saga: A little dodgy dealing among friends

The *Fire Nymph* saga[48] illustrates both the complexity of such arrangements and the way in which floating charges and *Romalpa* clauses interact. Fire Nymph had been

---

42 Gough, p. 250. See also *Tricontinental Corp. Ltd v. Federal Commissioner of Taxation* (1987) ACLR 421. Gough is a particularly ardent opponent of the implied licence theory.

43 [1979] WAR 97.

44 In this context we presume registration. We leave open the question of whether this amounts to any more than the sort of defeasible interest discussed in n. 31 of this chapter. For an interesting addition to the debate, see S. Worthington, 'Floating Charges—An Alternative Theory' (1994) 53 Cambridge LJ 81. She argues that a floating charge ought to be seen as a fixed charge, which is defeasible when the charger deals with the assets in ways that are consistent with the licence granted by the charge.

45 For a recent discussion of the licence theory, see J. C. Nkala, 'Some Aspects of the Jurisprudence of the Floating Charge' (1993) 11 CSLJ 301.

46 While this thesis appealed to some academics, it found little favour among judges. Some support may be found in *Reynolds Bros (Motors) Pty Ltd v. Esanda Ltd* (1984) 8 ACLR 422; 1 ACLC 1333.

47 (1988) 14 ACLR 274 (first instance); *Fire Nymph Products Ltd v. The Heating Centre Pty Ltd (in liq.) and Ors*, unreported, 1989, no. CA 40598,1992 NSW Lexis 7510; BC9203017 (Full Court NSW Supreme Court).

48 *Fire Nymph* is discussed in M. Sneddon, 'Automatic Crystallisation of Floating Charges—Catching a Disposition which Triggers the Crystallisation' (1993) 21 ABLR 152.

in the business of manufacturing heating appliances, and The Heating Centre acted as a retail and wholesale supplier of such appliances. After both companies fell on hard times in 1986, they entered into a transaction under the following terms:

1   Fire Nymph Products Limited (In Receivership)(FN) will take back from The Heating Centre Pty Limited (HC) all units supplied to date by FN to HC.

2   It is acknowledged that FN has full title to the product. Possession of the product, however, shall remain with HC as bailee for FN. The product is to be separately stored and HC will maintain it in the form in which it was despatched by FN. Risk in the product will remain with HC until payment by HC in accordance with this agreement.

3   HC is authorised to sell the product and will use its best endeavours to sell it as soon as possible. HC will put into an account specified by FN or its receivers a sum equivalent to the proceeds of the sale of any product sold (after deduction of sales tax) on the day following the date of sale of such product (whether or not HC has, at that point, received payment from the purchaser). Any such proceeds of sale held by HC for any reason are held by them as trustee for FN until payment into that account.[49]

The question before the court was whether this remarkable transaction fell within the natural meaning of the phrase 'ordinary course of its ordinary business'. Not surprisingly, the trial judge held that this transaction could not be characterised as falling within the ordinary business of the company. According to the trial judge, the transaction was a sham. The Heating Centre was insolvent. The transaction was intended to enable Fire Nymph to recover its funds from an insolvent debtor and still make use of the sale facilities of the debtor to maximise the return it hoped to receive. There was nothing ordinary about the transaction at all, given the surrounding circumstances. As is clear from the terms of the transaction as quoted above, the facts in *Fire Nymph Products Ltd* involved not only a mortgage deed by way of floating charge containing an automatic crystallisation clause, but also a clause clearly intended to have the (retrospective) effect of a *Romalpa* (retention of title) clause[50] in the transaction that was alleged to bring about crystallisation.

Understandably, given the complexity of some of the legal issues, the case was appealed. To understand the basis for the appeal, it is necessary to examine the terms of the mortgage deed closely. The clause reproduced below formed part of the mortgage deed between The Heating Centre Pty Ltd, as mortgagor, and AGC (Advances) Ltd:

IT IS HEREBY DECLARED that the charge hereby created shall operate as a first fixed charge as regards all real and leasehold property ... and shall operate as a floating secu-

---

49   Unreported, 1989, no. CA 40598, 1992 NSW Lexis 7510; BC9203017 (Full Court NSW Supreme Court) at 6.

50   As Rogers CJ noted, 'It may well be that part of the result sought to be achieved by the September transaction was to put FN in the position in which it would have been had there been a Romalpa provision in the contract under which supplies had been obtained in 1986': unreported, 1989, no. CA 40598, 1992 NSW Lexis 7510; BC9203017 (Full Court NSW Supreme Court) at 6.

rity only as regards all other assets hereby charged BUT SO THAT the Mortgagor is not to be at liberty to create any mortgage or charge in priority to or pari passu with the Charge created by this Deed except with the consent in writing of the Mortgagee AND THAT if the Mortgagor shall deal with any or all of the Mortgaged Property other than in the ordinary course of its ordinary business then the floating charge hereby created shall ipso facto become fixed to all of the Mortgaged Property at the moment immediately prior to such dealing and at that point of time the Mortgagee shall be deemed to have intervened and to have exercised all or any of its rights of intervention in respect of all the Mortgaged Property.[51]

Gleeson CJ had this to say about the terms in which this clause was framed and, in particular, about its attempt to ensure that the event that triggered crystallisation was itself caught by that crystallisation:

> The practical result sought to be achieved by the clause is obvious enough. The drafting is intended to produce the consequence that the extraordinary dealing that results in crystallisation will not itself escape the consequences of such crystallisation. The language used to give effect to that intention has about it some infelicities. To say that the charge 'shall ipso facto become fixed … at the moment immediately prior to such dealing' involves an element of temporal incongruity. Using belt as well as braces, the clause then goes on to say that 'at that point in time the mortgagee shall be deemed to have intervened'. The repeated references in CL3.1 to the charge fixing, or intervention being deemed to have occurred, 'immediately prior' or 'at the moment immediately prior' to the relevant dealing suggests a concern with the issue of priorities.

His Honour continued:

> I cannot accept that there is a conceptual impossibility involved in making a charge become fixed, and attached to specific property, contemporaneously with the event that brings that about. I do not accept that it is in the nature of crystallisation of a charge that it can only occur after the happening of the event which, by contract, produces crystallisation. To put the same proposition in another way, I do not accept that, in the contemplation of law, the two things must occur in sequence or that the law necessarily perceives a relevant interval of time between the two … The essence of crystallisation is that a charge fixes upon certain specific property, and that the mortgagor company's contractual right as against the chargee to dispose of the property comes to an end. Where that right, whether flowing from the practical consequences of a negative stipulation, or what is sometimes referred to as an implied licence, is a right to deal with the subject property in the ordinary course of business, and the charge provides that a dealing other than in the ordinary course of business crystallises the charge, then it must be possible for the parties to agree that if the company engages in an impermissible dealing of a kind that crystallises the charge, the charge will attach to the property the subject of the impermissible dealing. It is not a sufficient objection to this to say

---

51   Unreported, 1989, no. CA 40598, 1992 NSW Lexis 7510; BC9203017 (Full Court NSW Supreme Court) at 10.

that such a result could possibly be unfair to third parties. We are dealing with the operation of a contract, and there is nothing in legal theory that prevents parties from making a contract that might produce results adverse to third parties.[52]

Among the stock in trade that was the subject matter of the charge were a number of heating units manufactured by Fire Nymph Products Ltd. The issue before the court was whether these heating units were caught by the crystallisation of the charge or whether they escaped its net. Whereas Gleeson CJ held that it was open for the parties to specify that a dealing that triggered crystallisation could also be caught by crystallisation, Sheller and Handley JJA resolved the matter a different way. According to Their Honours,

> this argument fails not because of the attempt in CL3 to backdate crystallisation but because it is of the essence of a floating charge that the chargor enjoys the advantage of being able to trade and dispose of assets in the course of trade only so long as it is done in the ordinary course of business … In my opinion a dealing with assets then subject to a floating charge otherwise than with a view to carrying on the chargor's business is a crystallising event. The effect of such a dealing is that the assets pass to the disponee subject to a fixed charge.[53]

REVIEW QUESTIONS

1 What are the terms of the 'negative pledge' incorporated in this floating charge? Why are these terms necessary?

2 What event was specified to cause crystallisation? Can you think of any reasons why this might be problematical? Do you think that the courts should uphold an 'automatic crystallisation' clause written in these terms? What sorts of reasons for and against can you give?

3 Consider the circumstance where such a clause is in place and those with whom the company trades have provided goods on credit. If the goods are among those covered by the floating charge, as is usually the case, what, if any, redress does the unsatisfied trade creditor have if the goods are among those seized by the holder of the charge?[54]

4 In practical terms, is there any difference between the approach of Gleeson CJ and that of Sheller and Handley JJA?

---

52 Unreported, 1989, no. CA 40598, 1992 NSW Lexis 7510; BC9203017 (Full Court NSW Supreme Court) at 9. As His Honour notes, there is nothing in legal theory that prevents parties from making a contract that produces results adverse to third parties. It might be thought, however, that such a contract could be deemed *contra bones mores*, at least where the adverse effect is consciously sought.

53 Unreported Judgment of the New South Wales Supreme Court, no. CA 40598 of 1989, 1992 NSW Lexis 7510; BC9203017 (Full Court Supreme Court) at 14–15.

54 Some of you may recall learning about *Romalpa* clauses when you studied the law of contract. If the goods in question were, or purported to be, covered by a *Romalpa* clause, how might this affect the situation? The interaction between *Romalpa* clauses and floating charges is, in fact, both interesting and complex, and a substantial body of literature exists with respect to this interaction. See, for example, Taylor at 396; B. Collier, 'Romalpa Clauses: A Question of Title' (1989) 60 (2) Chartered Accountant 42; P. Rozenburg, 'Retention of Title Clauses, Company Charges, and Security Interests' (1989) 7 (3) CSLJ 409.

Financial (mis)deeds: Off-balance sheet accounting

During the 1980s, the financial press routinely alluded to the prevalence of practices that were collectively termed 'off-balance sheet accounting'. Because many of these practices remain current, and because cases dealing with some of them are still before the courts, we want to take some time to examine them. In the simplest possible terms, the term 'off-balance sheet accounting' refers to a group of accounting practices with both the intent and the effect of understating the liabilities of a firm in its published accounts. The practice of off-balance sheet accounting was a response on the part of corporate managers to the routine presence of provisions in either its constitutive documents or in loan documents that

> require it to maintain a certain level of liquidity, or to work within specified debt–equity ratios, or to limit external borrowings. Off-balance sheet financing reflects managers' wish to get around these 'covenants'. During the 1980s many Australian corporations raised funds through borrowings, and accordingly would have been subject to restrictions required by lenders in terms of 'negative pledge' or other borrowing arrangements.[55]

Necessity being, as always, the mother of invention, corporate accountants and managers devised a number of mechanisms to provide 'cosmetic enhancement' for corporate accounts. Some of these devices are extraordinarily simple. A straightforward practice such as clearing current liabilities shortly before the balance date can effect a remarkable transformation in the current ratio (the ratio of current assets to current liabilities), while having no impact whatsoever upon the underlying solvency and/or liquidity of the company.

Other practices are more complex and controversial. The debates over the appropriateness of the classification of convertible debentures or notes fall into this category. Convertible debentures and notes offer redemption through share-issue as an alternative to repayment of the amount outstanding. Several different forms are possible. Where they are issued as mandatory convertible securities, the company is entitled to convert the securities to shares when the specified date or event occurs, irrespective of the debenture holder giving consent. Where they are convertible at the option of the holder, the process is not automatic, and the process must be initiated by the company.[56] In the present context, the practice of a number of entrepreneurial companies in treating convertible notes as equity provides a further illustration of the 'fuzziness' of the distinction between debt finance and equity finance.[57]

A company that was keen to enhance its apparent debt–equity ratio (its gearing) was thus given a number of options. According to R. G. Walker, '[m]any leading

---

55 R. G. Walker, 'Off-Balance Sheet Financing' (1991) 15 *UNSWLJ* 196 at 197. The references cited therein provide an overview of the recent literature on this topic.

56 *Precision Data Holdings Ltd v. Titan Hills Australia Ltd* (1990) 2 ACSR 707 at 723.

57 Not surprisingly, this very 'fuzziness' has encouraged some companies to attempt to evade standard legal prohibitions, such as the prohibition on issuing shares at a discount. See discussion of *Mosley v. Koffyfontein Mines Ltd* [1904] 2 Ch 108 in H. A. J. Ford & R. P. Austin, *Principles of Corporation Law*, 7th edn, Butterworths, Sydney, 1995, p. 682.

Australian 'entrepreneurial' corporations chose to report convertible notes as share-holders' equity, thus enhancing reported debt–equity ratios'.[58] Walker discusses some of the reasons for these practices:

It seems likely that one of these is simply that directors and company officers may sometimes desire to convey an illusion of financial prudence and managerial success. Rapidly increasing levels of debt relative to aggregate shareholders' funds may convey the impression that managers are adopting risky financial strategies. Even though some of the transactions used to keep debt off balance sheet may be described in the accounts in a form that it is interpretable by skilled analysis, managers may still act on the assumption that lenders or investors may not fully comprehend the significance of those disclosures. Managers may believe that many readers of financial statements may be fixated with reported income, or with the key financial indicators reported in annual reports or in the print media.

This alternative interpretation is not looked on with favour by those who invoke references to the supposed 'efficiency' of the securities markets. Some commentators suggest that managers who undertake these activities are wasting their time—since the market can see through their choice of accounting policies.

However, whatever inferences are drawn from the findings of empirical research studies into reactions to accounting disclosures, it is inescapable that those studies are concerned with aggregate market behaviour, and not with the way in which individuals make judgments on the basis of published financial reports.

It is difficult to describe the main techniques used in off-balance sheet financing with any confidence: after all, the aim is to conceal debt, and parties engaged in such practices are hardly likely to flaunt their success in the art of concealment. Consequently, empirical evidence of successful off-balance sheet financing is, by definition, unavailable. However one can speculate: and in this spirit it is suggested that the main techniques recently used in Australia in the cause of off-balance sheet financing were the following:

(i)   Leasing
(ii) Non-consolidation of finance subsidiaries
(iii) Non-consolidation of 'subsidiaries' through the use of trusts as part of a group structure, shares with differential voting rights, or other devices
(iv) Asset and liability 'set-offs'
(v)   Complex transactions.[59]

Each of these approaches provides a mechanism for the selective provision of information and thus can be used to assist the manager who wishes to present information in ways that may enhance the image of the company with, for example, the investment community. Some of the approaches are straightforward; others are complex and subtle.

Standard accounting practice has long accepted a distinction between 'operating leases' and 'finance leases'. Operating leases are off balance sheet, with lease pay-

---

58   Walker at 197.
59   Walker at 198–9.

ments merely appearing as current period expenses. Finance leases are very different, the transaction typically being seen as the acquisition of an asset on credit terms and that situation being reflected upon the face of the balance sheet. A manager who was concerned with the 'image' conveyed by the balance sheet would, obviously, be eager to structure lease arrangements in a way that ensured that corporate accounts would treat a majority of outstanding leases as 'operating leases'.[60]

Not surprisingly, corporate structure also provides a fertile field for further exercises in creative accounting. As you are aware, where companies adopt complex and interlocking structures involving numerous subsidiaries, they are required by the Corporations Law[61] to lodge group accounts with the Australian Securities Commission (ASC). Until the issue of Australian Accounting Standards (AAS) 24 and Australian Accounting Standards Board (AASB) 1024 in 1990, there were no specific guidelines for financial accountants in this area. Managers developed a convention among themselves that consolidated statements were not required to include the financial details of any subsidiary whose activities were 'inconsistent' with those of other members of the group. Because, initially, there were no applicable accounting standards, many companies excluded their 'financial subsidiaries' from their consolidated accounts. Since these finance companies were often highly leveraged, this had a substantial effect on the apparent debt–equity ratio of the group. During the 1980s, mechanisms such as these were commonly used to great advantage. In the rash of regulation that followed the corporate collapses of the 1980s, this practice was outlawed by AASB 1024, however, arguments continued for some time about the need to include another group of subsidiaries: those whose primary business involved the provision of life insurance.[62]

REVIEW QUESTIONS

1 Practices such as those sketched above are largely regulated (and outlawed) through professional associations, rather than legally. Do you think that self-regulation (on the part of accounting professionals) in this area is appropriate? What are the advantages and disadvantages?

2 If, as seems likely, the various forms of off-balance sheet financing described above are partly motivated by the limitations on borrowing set down in the constitutive documents of most companies, one of the central issues is the degree to which it is desirable to compel management to be accountable to the shareholders. To what extent do you believe that corporate management ought to be accountable to the shareholders for its choices in respect of the most appropriate structure (including financial structure) for the enterprise? Why?

---

60 It is hardly surprising that lessors and lessees have very different perspectives, with lessees tending to regard a majority of leases as operating leases, while lessors take a somewhat different view.

61 Section 266(1) sets out the requirements for group accounts.

62 See Walker at 205. According to Walker, this argument is based on the idea that it would be misleading to treat resources held for the beneficiaries of life-insurance policies as assets in the consolidated accounts.

Hybrid schemes: Investment without participation

Dual-class ordinary shares

During the last two decades, a variety of new commercial vehicles have developed as mechanisms for investment and market exploration. Some of these represent reworkings of conventional, even traditional, corporate structures, such as the issue of dual-class ordinary shares.[63] On the face of it, there is nothing unusual in the issue of dual-class ordinary shares, which is one avenue that the founder or founders of a proprietary company may utilise to maintain control while allowing for wider membership—that is, membership outside the immediate family group. Likewise, when companies that began their lives as closely held proprietary companies 'went public', it was not uncommon for this structure to be retained, particularly where the company continued to be closely associated with the name and fortunes of its founding genius.

Far more interesting is the trend that has recently developed in the USA, in which public companies alter an existing capital structure to provide for two classes of ordinary shares. The attractions of such a device, for management at least, are worth exploring. Where one class has substantially enhanced voting rights and the other class limited voting rights, the first and obvious effect of this development is to effectively separate economic participation from corporate governance. A second effect is more subtle, but clearly indicates one of the reasons for the popularity of dual-class structures. As Gordon notes, '[i]f management and its allies hold the voting stock necessary to elect directors, a hostile [takeover] bid becomes practically impossible'.[64]

Other enterprises break new ground while reworking half-forgotten forms to achieve new commercial ends. For example, the joint stock company can be seen as the precursor of the contemporary trading trust. Similarly, contemporary conglomerates can minimise their reliance upon corporate entities by conducting some or all of their business activities through alternative forms. Among the devices that can be used are trading trusts, joint ventures, and partnership arrangements, whether general or limited. Through commercial forms such as these, the limitations upon borrowing that are conventionally entrenched in corporate documents can be simply evaded. These forms may also substantially enhance management discretion in other areas by ensuring that control remains confined within the 'management group'.

Leveraged buyout organisations

A classic example of this kind of creativity may be found in one of the more sophisticated of the 'new' organisational forms fostered in the boom days of the 1980s: the leveraged buyout (LBO) organisation. An LBO organisation is, in the simplest pos-

---

63 The United States term for this is 'dual-class common stock'.

64 J. N. Gordon, 'Dual Class Common Stock and the Problem of Shareholder Choice', in Romano, p. 200.

sible terms, a commercial entity, the activities of which are almost exclusively financed by debt capital rather than equity capital. Typically, in an LBO organisation, the debt–value ratio will average close to 90 per cent. As their name suggests, LBO organisations were frequently used as takeover vehicles. Their debt–equity ratio made them ideal as corporate raiders, since management funds could be used in a highly strategic manner and the leverage gained by the extensive use of debt finance served as a multiplier factor. It is hardly surprising that bond-holders in likely takeover targets frequently sought to protect their interests by mitigating the risks associated with leveraged buyouts through the use of protective covenants.[65] It has been suggested that

> many large industrial companies have issued debt during [the late 1980s] that contains either 'poison put' provisions (that is provisions that give bondholders a right to sell their bonds back to the issuer at par if a change of control occurs) or provisions that require issuers to increase the coupon payments on their bonds (in order to maintain the pre-takeover value of the bonds) if there is a change in control.
>
> In addition to contracting for explicit protection against the risk of leveraged buyouts, bondholders can mitigate this risk in at least two other ways. First, convertible bonds provide bondholders with the opportunity to participate in the gains associated with leveraged buyouts (if, of course, the conversion price is less than the price offered in the buyout). Bondholders also can hedge the risks associated with leveraged buyouts by simultaneously owning both the bonds and stocks of the same issuers.[66]

A new commercial 'creature', the LBO association (combining an LBO organisation with other entities), gradually developed as a consequence of the success of some of these LBO organisations. The LBO association combines partnership, limited partnership, and corporate forms in one entity. The management adopts the form of a general partnership and typically has large equity input. The numbers of partners will characteristically be limited, usually to about ten. The individual 'buyout funds' are structured as limited partnerships.[67] Simon Fisher describes limited partnerships in these terms:

> Limited partnerships do not follow the scheme of general law partnerships. With the consent of the general partners, a limited partner may assign the limited partner's share in the

---

65 Among the most significant of these risks was the fact that the new management had little, if any, incentive to manage the target company in a way that was favourable to the bondholders.

66 K. Lehn & A. Poulson, 'Contractual Resolution of Bondholder-Stockholder Conflicts in Leveraged Buyouts', in Romano, pp. 133, 134.

67 Limited partnerships exist in many, but not all, common-law jurisdictions. They are available, albeit with some restrictions, in Queensland, New South Wales, Tasmania, Victoria, and Western Australia. See *Partnerships (Limited Liability) Act 1988* (Qld); *Partnerships (Limited Liability) Act 1988* (NSW); *Limited Partnerships Act 1908* (Tas.); *Partnership Act 1958* (Vic.), pt 3; *Limited Partnerships Act 1909* (WA). Such legislation is not currently available in other Australian jurisdictions. Legislation providing for limited partnerships is also in force in New Zealand and the United Kingdom. Until the new corporate forms of the 1980s, their popularity had been waning in most jurisdictions. They are akin to the continental *société en commandite*.

partnership to an assignee, who is taken to be a limited partner in substitution for the rights and obligations of the assignor … The corollary of assignment of an interest in a limited partnership is the admission of new partners. The legislation provides that subject to the terms of any agreement between the partners in the limited partnership, a person may be admitted as a partner in the partnership without the consent of any limited partner. This feature seems to deny to limited partnerships the significance of the relationship of personal confidence which is a hallmark of the general law partnership, at least when it comes to the admission of new partners. This reflects once more, it is suggested, the nature of the limited partnership as an investment vehicle.[68]

It is easy to see the utility of a senior management structured as a partnership with the non-debt venture capital provided, in the first instance, by the general partners and, in the second instance, by the limited partners, who function as passive investors. While the limited partners are unable to exercise any direct control, because the general partners stand in a fiduciary relationship to them, the general partners are bound to act so as to further the interests of the limited partners taken as a group. Jensen describes LBO associations as

> a new model of general management. These organizations are similar in many respects to diversified conglomerates or to the Japanese groups of firms known as 'keiretsu' …
>
> LBO associations … are run by partnerships instead of the headquarters office in the typical large, multibusiness diversified corporation. These partnerships perform the monitoring and peak coordination function with a staff numbering in the tens of people, and replace the typical corporate headquarters staff of thousands. The leaders of these partnerships have large equity ownership in the outcomes and direct fiduciary relations as general partners to the limited partner investors in their buyout funds …
>
> In addition, the contractual relation between the partnership headquarters and the suppliers of capital to the buyout funds is very different from that between the corporate headquarters and stockholders in the diversified firm. The buyout funds are organized as limited partnerships, in which the managers of the partnership headquarters are the general partners. Unlike the diversified firm, the contract with the limited partners denies partnership headquarters the right to transfer cash or other resources from one LBO business unit to another. Generally all cash payouts from each LBO business unit must be paid out directly to the limited partners of the buyout funds. This reduces the waste of free cash flow that is so prevalent in diversified corporations.[69]

The 'buyout funds', typically making extensive use of debt finance, are highly effective and efficient as corporate raiders, amassing control of one or more targets, which provide the funds for further activity and for returns to the limited partners as well as the general partners. It is worth noting, if only in passing, that

---

68   S. Fisher, 'Partnership', in S. Fisher (ed.), *The Law of Commercial and Professional Relationships*, FT Law & Tax, Melbourne, 1996, ch. 19, pp. 493, 503.

69   M. C. Jensen, 'Active Investors, LBOs, and the Privatization of Bankruptcy', in Romano, pp. 220–1.

the LBOs raise very different governance issues from those we looked at earlier.[70] Because they are organised on the basis of partnership, rather than as corporate entities, the relationships within them are governed by fiduciary principles to a much greater extent than is the case with corporate persons. As a consequence, the duty that theorists such as Milton Friedman[71] suggest is owed to shareholders as a consequence of the corporation–shareholder relationship (but that has little, if any, legal foundation) is transformed into a classical fiduciary relationship. Because the managing partners in a leveraged buyout association stand in a fiduciary relationship to the limited partners in each individual LBO business unit, there is a substantial incentive for them to maintain strict financial separation between the individual LBO business units. The particular dynamics of the relationship and the fact that the managing partners typically are heavily committed to the entities that they are managing encourages a more hands-on style of management. In the present context they provide a useful and interesting example of a commercial form that originally evolved to escape the limitations on borrowing that was characteristic of limited liability companies. Needless to say, they also enable management to maintain tight hands-on control and to limit its own exposure to the possibility of takeover and thus to a change of management.

REVIEW QUESTIONS

1 Compare the structure of the LBO association to the corporate conglomerates that flourished in Australia during the 1980s. Which structure affords the greatest flexibility and most successfully maximises the ability of the individual entrepreneur to respond to market opportunities and changes? What are the advantages and disadvantages of each?[72]

2 In chapter 5 we looked briefly at the structure of Alan Bond's corporate empire. We also looked at some of the issues surrounding Christopher Skase's empire. Do you think an LBO association might have provided a more appropriate structure for corporate empires such as those developed by Bond and Skase? Why or why not?

---

70 See, generally, the discussion in chs 4–7. In Australia the rights and responsibilities of both general partners and limited partners are governed by legislation in the various states. At present, the utility of devices such as LBO associations is limited in Australia, both because not all jurisdictions make the limited partnership form available to investors and because of the restrictions upon its use, even in those jurisdictions where it is technically available.

71 See ch 5, fn. 52 (p. 128).

72 It may help for you to read P. Redmond, *Companies and Securities Law*, Law Book Company, Sydney, 1988, pp. 3–24.

12

A Matter of Money: Equity Capital

Looking at share ownership: What interest does a share represent?

When we considered the 'corporate constitution' and the readings that courts in the United Kingdom and in Australia have given to the documents of which it is comprised, we looked at the way in which judicial readings of these texts tracked the idea of property. We saw how the legal enforceability of provisions of the articles, for example, turned upon whether the particular provision had the requisite 'proprietary character'. In this chapter we will be looking much more closely at the way in which the law regulates the financial affairs of the company, and at the nature of shares and of share capital.

We will begin our exploration of the nature of share capital by looking at the statutory definition provided by the *Corporations Law 1990*. Section 9 defines 'share' as a share in the share capital—the interest of a shareholder in the company as measured by a sum of money. Two things are immediately apparent. The first is that readers who did not understand what a share was before they consulted the definition section would be none the wiser after doing so. The second point—made indirectly rather than directly—is that, whatever a share is, it is not simply a sum of money. Rather, the 'price' of the share is one 'measure' of a shareholder's interest in the company (and its fortunes).[1] The statutory definition is substantially drawn from that provided by the court in *Borland's Trustee v. Steel Bros & Co. Ltd*[2] and effectively replicates the approach of the common law.

Part 7.13 of the Corporations Law offers somewhat more detail, with s. 1085 identifying shares as personalty and specifying that the *lex situs*, or location, of the shares is the place where the register or branch register is kept. This information becomes critical in a conflict of laws situation. Legally, a share is a chose in action. Share ownership gives no right to any specific share in the assets of the company; indeed, even where one shareholder owns all of the outstanding shares, he or she is

---

1   A share is not a thing (chose in possession), but rather a set of rights, obligations, and possibilities (chose in action). As such, it cannot be reduced to physical possession, although the 'sign' of ownership, the share certificate, can be.

2   [1901] 1 Ch 279.

not thereby entitled to regard the assets of the company as his or her own. This proposition is clearly illustrated by *Macaura v. Northern Assurance Co. Ltd.*[3] The plaintiff, Macaura, owned a timber estate, which he subsequently sold to his private company in exchange for fully paid shares. Through an oversight, the insurance policy on the timber remained in his own name. When he attempted to claim on the insurance, all of the timber having been destroyed in a fire, his claim was rejected by the insurer. According to Lord Buckmaster,

> [t]he appellant could only insure either as a creditor or as a shareholder in the company … As a creditor his position appears to me quite incapable of supporting the claim … Turning now to his position as shareholder, this must be independent of the extent of his share interest. If he were entitled to insure holding all the shares in the company, each shareholder would be equally entitled, if the shares were all in separate hands. Now, no shareholder has any right to any item of property owned by the company for he has no legal or equitable interest therein.[4]

Subsequently, Lord Buckmaster elaborated further on this theme and noted:

> The debt was not exposed to fire nor were the shares, and the fact that he was virtually the company's only creditor, while the timber was its only asset, seems to me to make no difference. He stood in no 'legal or equitable relation to' the timber at all. He had no 'concern in' the subject insured. His relation was to the company, not to its goods, and after the fire he was directly prejudiced by the paucity of the company's assets, not by the fire.[5]

The 'inequity' one perceives in *Macaura v. Northern Assurance Co. Ltd*[6] is the inverse of that in *Salomon v. Salomon & Co. Ltd.*[7] If, in *Salomon*, the separate legal personality of the company enabled Aron Salomon to recover upon the debentures that he held at the expense of the company's unsecured creditors, in *Macaura* the defendant insurance company was able to avoid Macaura's claim under the contract of insurance, as Macaura lacked any insurable interest in the subject property. In both, the corporate veil concealed the relationship between entrepreneur and company, and what had been created as a commercial vehicle achieved a life of its own and an independent identity.

Today, the distinction between share-ownership and a share in the assets of the company often becomes a critical point of contention in litigation concerning family companies, whether under the oppression remedy (Corporations Law, s. 260) or

---

3   [1925] AC 619.

4   [1925] AC 619 at 625–8.

5   [1925] AC 619 at 630. Despite the logic of the reasoning, we should not lose sight of the fact that Mr Macaura was, for all intents and purposes, both the only shareholder and the sole creditor of the company. His failure to reinsure in the name of the company, thus protecting its goods against loss, meant that he had paid for insurance on goods that he did not own, and the company was unable to claim when the goods were destroyed since it had not insured them. The only winner would appear to have been the insurance company, which was able, through a legal technicality, to avoid meeting the commitments it had undertaken when it provided the insurance.

6   In this context it is worth noting that the 'inequity' in question has been statutorily eliminated in Australia by virtue of the *Insurance Contracts Act 1984*, ss. 16–17.

7   [1897] AC 22.

in an action for a just and equitable winding-up under s. 460. *Re G. Jeffrey (Men's Store) Pty Ltd*[8] illustrates the potential pitfalls. The company had been established by the father of the two protagonists. It controlled a substantial proportion of the family assets and thus a substantial proportion of the wealth inherited by the two principal protagonists. The father had been the majority shareholder and governing director of the company. Upon his death, each of his two sons received 30 per cent of the shares, while his widow received 20 per cent and each daughter 10 per cent. Richard became the managing director of the women's wear division, and Anthony became the managing director of the men's wear division. Subsequently, Anthony resigned as managing director of the men's wear division, and Richard took over. Anthony was no longer employed by the company, although he retained his shares. Richard subsequently obtained the shareholding of one of his sisters, a move that gave him effective control, since their mother invariably voted with Richard or gave him her proxy. Anthony complained of Richard's authoritarian attitude, of his own inability as a director to secure profitable investment of surplus funds, and of the dividend structure. He continually pressed his brother to purchase his shares, but the offer received was unrealistic in light of the asset backing of the company. The articles empowered the managing director to exercise all the powers of the board, and Richard did so without hesitation.[9] According to Crockett J:

> In his evidence Richard candidly admitted that he considered himself to be sole arbiter of policy as well as of management decisions and that he proceeded as he thought proper simply because he knew he could not be prevented from doing so. It is plain he believes his brother's directorships to be an incubus upon both companies' operations and that in the case of each company the board is an ineffectual mechanism so that it should be, and in fact is, disregarded except for the performance of the very minimum of necessary formal functions. In other words, he treats the businesses as though they were his own, imposing an autocratic control over them and ignoring as far as possible the corporate structure in which each is housed.[10]

Despite this evidence, which was not significantly contradicted, Crockett J considered that Anthony's only significant complaint was concerning the dividend structure, and this was, according to His Honour, based upon proper commercial considerations. While, admittedly, the plaintiff was 'locked in', no member of the family was prepared to buy him out at a price that reflected the value of his inheritance. This followed from the structure of the company and not from the conduct of his brother. The critical point here is that, when the plaintiff inherited shares in the company that his father had established, what he inherited was a bundle of rights and obligations, not an interest in the property held by the

---

8　(1984) 2 ACLC 421.

9　This was a common practice in family companies that were effectively 'one person' companies but that were required by the previous legislation to have a minimum of two directors in order to comply with the legislation. It enabled the founding shareholder to control the company 'as if' it were a sole proprietorship.

10　(1984) 2 ACLC 421 at 423. A similar line of reasoning was pursued by Lord Grantchester in *Re a Company Pty Ltd* [1983] Ch 178.

company. He had, in other words, a 'share' in the company's fortunes. Because he simply inherited a bundle of rights and obligations, their nature was that set out in the constitutive documents of the company. The court would not intervene in order to compel other family members to purchase his shares at the proportion of the asset value of the company that they represented because, *inter alia*, such a ruling had the potential to destroy the company. His inheritance, therefore, was neither more nor less than the bundle of rights and obligations set out in the relevant corporate documents.

REVIEW QUESTIONS

1 Family feuds—whether arising as a consequence of a falling out between siblings who have inherited shares and directorships in a family company, or as a consequence of a marital breakdown—are endemic in this area of company law. How should the law handle situations such as that in *Jeffrey* and in its English counterpart, *Re a Company*?

2 The common law has gradually sought to eliminate fetters upon the alienation of property, the ostensible reason being its reluctance to have the present generation constrained by the 'dead hand' of the past. Is it appropriate for a testator to be able to achieve through the medium of a family company what could not be achieved through other mechanisms?

Learning the language of equity capital

Those who listen to the financial reports on television or read the financial pages of the newspapers will be aware that the share-market—or stockmarket, as it is also called—has developed a language of its own. The purpose of this section is to introduce you to some of the more important elements of this language from a legal point of view.

In the commercial companies with which this book is largely concerned, the ability to raise capital is fundamental to corporate activities. The word 'capital' itself has a variable meaning. In common parlance, 'capital' refers either to the value of the outstanding securities or to the net assets of the company.[11] The memorandum of association of every company is presently[12] required by the Corporations Law, s. 117 to specify the amount of share capital available to the company at the time of registration. This amount is known as the 'registered capital', and it simply indicates the capital that is theoretically available to the company at its 'birth'. For example, the memorandum of a company might specify that its registered capital is $100 000. The memorandum might specify further that this registered capital is made up of 100 000 shares with a par value of $1. Each new

---

11 These two are, it should be noted, totally different.

12 These requirements will change for newly registered companies with the enactment of the Second Corporate Law Simplification Bill.

company is required by s. 117(1)(b) to disclose its registered capital, but under the current legal regime, a company can lawfully be registered with an 'issued capital' of only $2 in the form of two $1 shares. There is no necessary equivalence between the registered capital and the issued capital; indeed they are usually very different.

The memorandum may also specify the authorised capital of the company. The authorised capital is the dollar limit up to which the company may issue shares in order to raise money for its operations. The authorised capital is meaningless in financial terms. It is not uncommon for a company to have authorised capital of $10 000 000 and issued capital of only $2. While the authorised capital as specified in the memorandum is supposed to establish an upper limit, beyond which the company may not issue shares, this is easily overridden. In practice, a company can increase its authorised capital by resolution in general meeting,[13] provided that the articles so permit. Finally, another term that may be used in the memorandum is 'nominal capital'. As the meaning of the word 'nominal' suggests, this term acknowledges what is, in fact, the case: that the figure specified is unlikely to be of any assistance in determining the financial stability or well-being of the company.

The memorandum also specifies the nominal or par value of the shares. Under normal circumstances, neither the authorised capital nor the par value of the shares has any real significance. As should be clear from the paragraphs above, none of these figures actually tell us very much if we want to find out about the financial well-being of the company. The only figure that provides any information at all about the financial position of the company is its 'issued capital'. The term 'issued capital', as we saw above, refers to the value of the shares that have actually been issued by the company. Yet even here, the bare statement that a company has $200 000 of issued capital in the form of shares of $1 par value does not indicate that the company has actually received $200 000 of equity capital. In large public companies, shares are issued to raise funds for the company. At the time when they are issued, shares may be either 'called' (paid-up) or 'uncalled' (partially unpaid).[14] Thus, a company may have issued 200 000 shares with only 40 cents in the dollar paid up on each share. This means that 60 cents per share remains to be paid up. The figures that are of interest to creditors and to others with an interest in establishing the financial well-being of the company are the paid-up capital and the unpaid or uncalled capital.[15] In the case of the example above, the paid-up capital of

---

13 Corporations Law, s. 193(1)(a).

14 While this is unusual today, it remains possible, although the Second Corporate Law Simplification Bill recommends the abolition of the concept of par value. Once this occurs, questions of par value and the distinction between called and uncalled capital will be eliminated for newly formed companies, although they will remain relevant to companies formed before the abolition of par value.

15 These terms differ slightly in meaning, although they convey similar information. Unpaid capital simply refers to the amount as yet outstanding on the shares. It is used where the company has made a 'call' on its shares. A call is a demand that a certain proportion of the unpaid amount owing on each share be paid. Thus, where shares were issued partly paid at, say, 40 cents in the dollar, the company may at some point make a further 'call', or 'demand for money', in the amount of 20 cents in the dollar. The company would do this where it desired to raise funds for further projects. The 'unpaid' capital in such a case would be 40 cents in the dollar. Uncalled capital is used where the company has made no call beyond the original payment of 40 cents in the dollar.

the company is $80 000, while its uncalled capital is $120 000. Uncalled capital represents a reserve for creditors and may be charged to raise loan funds.[16] All uncalled funds must be called in at liquidation so that company debts can be settled and capital returned to the shareholders (in a solvent liquidation). Today, it has become relatively uncommon for shares to be partly paid unless the company is a no liability[17] company, but there is no legal bar and a company may, if it wishes, issue its shares partly paid.

In ordinary discourse, 'shares' and 'stock' are roughly equivalent terms, and we will generally use them interchangeably. There is a technical difference, in that stock is divisible while shares are not, but this difference is of minimal significance in this context. The Corporations Law, s. 197(1) provides for the issue of different classes of shares, should the directors so desire and the articles so permit. Different classes of shares represent different bundles of rights and entitlements. For example, while ordinary shares usually carry one vote each in the general meeting, in some small companies there may be different classes of ordinary shares with different voting rights. Sometimes the articles will provide that, in certain matters, some shares carry five votes, for example, rather than the usual one. Other classes of shares typically do not carry any voting rights. Another important distinction between different classes of shares is likely to be in terms of dividend entitlements. In some companies, different classes may also differ in the priority that they receive in respect of return of capital upon winding-up or in respect of their entitlement to share in any surplus in a solvent liquidation. We will look at those differences in a little more detail later.

The most usual classes of shares are ordinary shares and preference shares. Most of the shares traded on stock exchanges are ordinary shares, although preference shares are also traded both on the various exchanges and over the counter. Ordinary shares typically carry one vote per share in general meeting. When most of us think of share-ownership, we think of ordinary shares. In general, for an ordinary share to attract a dividend, the company must show a profit in its annual accounts *and* the board of directors must have declared a dividend of a specified amount.

Preference shares are very different. While today, preference shares are often replaced by debentures, they retain some importance in proprietary companies and have been used in corporate empires where the principal shareholders desire to raise equity capital without compromising their control of the company in general meeting. Preference shares typically do not carry any voting rights in the general meeting, although preference shareholders will be entitled to vote when special class meetings are called. Although they typically lack voting rights, preference shares usually carry rights to dividend payments that take precedence over those of ordinary shareholders, giving them their name. By convention, they provide for dividends at a

---

16 Charged means 'mortgaged' or offered as security for a loan.

17 Under the Second Corporate Law Simplification Bill, no liability companies will cease to exist since, with the abolition of par value and the notion of uncalled capital, there will be no such thing as a 'no liability' company, all companies being in effect 'no liability' companies.

fixed rate expressed as a percentage, which is sometimes called the 'coupon rate'. This sets them apart markedly from ordinary shares, where should there be a profit, the board of directors determines the appropriate level of dividend and may decide that a dividend is not appropriate, despite the existence of a profit.

Preference shares may be either cumulative or non-cumulative. If cumulative preference shares have been issued, the right to a dividend at the specified rate accumulates during any period when the company is unable to pay any dividend because of its failure to make a profit. Thus, even if a company were unable to pay any dividend for a period of years, the dividend entitlements of cumulative preference shareholders would continue to accumulate.[18] If the company again became profitable, the preference shareholders would be entitled to be paid the entire accumulated amount of dividend owing before the ordinary shareholders would receive any return on their investment.

Some preference shares are 'redeemable'. This means that they have a fixed date of maturity. For example, a company may issue redeemable cumulative preference shares with a 7.5 per cent coupon rate and a term of 7 years. This means that the company must redeem (buy out) these shares no later than 7 years after the date of issue. Because of these peculiarities, and because of the interpretative practices of the courts, cumulative preference shares are often described as being closer to debt capital than they are to equity capital. The fixed rate of dividend expressed as a percentage and the provision for unpaid dividends to accumulate seem much more like entitlements under a debenture agreement, for example, than a form of equity. The same is true of features such as a fixed date of maturity. Redeemable cumulative preference shares, in particular, differ from debenture agreements only in that they are entitled to participate in class meetings and in that, should the company be liquidated, their holders would not have their capital returned until all creditors (including debenture-holders, who normally rank as secured creditors) have been satisfied in full.[19]

Sometimes deferred shares, also called founder's shares or management shares, may also be issued. Where these are issued, any entitlement to dividend payments is deferred until dividends have been paid to ordinary shareholders. Such shares were formerly issued where there was a desire to increase confidence in the soundness of the company and its management. They are relatively uncommon today, perhaps because the 'personal' style of management characteristic of early corporate capitalism has largely given way to a more professional and less personal style.

---

18 This differentiates preference shares sharply from ordinary shares, where there is no dividend 'entitlement' as such, although the directors may, in years when the accounts disclose a profit, declare an appropriate dividend.

19 It is, however, important to bear in mind that today it is hardly unusual for a nominee director to represent the interests of a substantial debenture-holder on the board of directors and that Australian courts have acknowledged that, particularly where a company is in financial difficulty, the interests of the company may include the interests of its creditors. See *Walker v. Wimborne* (1976) 137 CLR 1; *Kinsela v. Russell Kinsela Pty Ltd (in liq.)* (1986) 10 ACLR 395; *Grove v. Flavel* (1986) 4 ACLC 654.

REVIEW QUESTIONS

1 What is a share?
2 What is the legal distinction between personalty and realty? How are shares classified?
3 Be sure that you understand the meaning of the following terms and know why they are important:
   • *lex situ*
   • chose in action
   • ordinary share
   • cumulative preference share
   • non-cumulative preference share
   • deferred, founder's, or management share
   • debenture
   • capital
   • authorised capital
   • issued capital
   • par value

Legal requirements: Corporate financial structure

Section 209 of the Corporations Law requires every company to maintain a register of its members. It also specifies the particulars that must be included in the register. The register must contain the names and addresses of all of the members, the number of shares held by each member together with their identifying numbers, the numbers of the relevant share certificates, and the amount that has been paid or has been agreed to be paid as consideration. Also required, and often of critical importance, is the date that the shareholder was entered in the register as a member and the date of cessation of membership for all who have ceased to be members within the past 7 years. The law requires the company to keep the register at either the registered office or the principal place of business of the company. Because the register must be available during ordinary business hours, it has become common for a solicitor's or accountant's premises to be named as the registered office of the company.[20]

The company secretary is responsible for ensuring that the register is kept up to date and accurate. Section 210 provides that members may inspect the register free of charge at any time, while non-members may inspect the register upon payment of the stipulated charge. The register may be closed for a period of not more than 30 days in each financial year (s. 210(1)). This enables the register to be checked and allows the company secretary to update the register to accurately reflect current membership. While the register is closed, no changes in membership may occur.

---

20 The registered office of a company is of substantial legal importance. For example, legal documents (such as writs and summons) delivered to the registered office will be deemed to have been served upon the company.

This is ordinarily done at the close of the financial year and provides an opportunity for the company to update its records.

Legally, the register is an extremely important document. Section 209(4) of the Corporations Law provides that the register is prima facie evidence of the matters entered therein, although this presumption of fact may be unseated by evidence of either a fraudulent or an innocent misrepresentation. Where there has been a misrepresentation, s. 212 provides for rectification. The operation of this rule is illustrated by *Re Clifton Springs Hotel Ltd.*[21] The plaintiff applied for shares in the company, and paid his application and allotment money. His name was entered in the register. He was given no notice of his acceptance as a member, although he did receive notice of an extraordinary general meeting. When the company entered liquidation, the plaintiff's name was entered in the settled list of contributories. He was, therefore, liable to pay the amount uncalled on his shares. Although the minute book did not contain any record of the minute of allotment, the liquidator relied upon the evidence provided by the register, and the court accepted this evidence.

The allotment of share certificates is provided for by the Corporations Law, ss. 1086–9 and 1096.[22] The law provides that when a company issues new shares the shares must be available for delivery within 2 months of being allotted. In issuing the certificate, the company asserts that the person named thereon is entitled to the certificate[23] and that the amount certified as having been paid has, in fact, been paid. This principle becomes fundamental where a third party has acted on the strength of the certificate in advancing money by way of loan or in agreeing to purchase the shares. Where the company, without negligence or fraud, has erroneously asserted that a particular individual is the owner, a third party who has relied upon the certificate and who has been prejudiced thereby will be awarded damages for any harm or loss sustained as a consequence of the representation. The company is estopped from denying the representations constituted by the face of the certificate. The third party is, therefore, entitled to demand that the company retain or enter that individual's name on the register. If the shares have subsequently been issued to a fourth party, the company must pay as liquidated damages the value of the shares at the time that the third party became entitled to them plus interest on that sum. These principles are not unseated merely because of fraud on the part of the third party.[24]

A remedy will, obviously, also be available where the person to whom the certificate was initially issued has been the victim, rather than the perpetrator, of a fraud. In *Balkis Consolidated Ltd v. Tomkinson*,[25] Tomkinson had been deceived by both the transferor and the servants of the company. When a third party purchasing from him was unable to secure registration, Tomkinson was forced to purchase shares on

---

21   [1939] VLR 27.

22   We are speaking here of the issue of new shares by the company, not of the transfer by sale of existing shares.

23   *Re Bahia & San Franciscan Rail Co.* (1868) LR 3 QB 584.

24   *Re Bahia & San Franciscan Rail Co.*

25   [1893] AC 396.

the market to satisfy his contract. He was held to be entitled to damages for the harm incurred thereby. A remedy will also be available where reliance upon the certificate has disentitled an innocent shareholder to a remedy that would have been available but that had been lost through effluxion of time.[26]

Despite the centrality of the register and its probative value, the information contained in it has one extremely important limitation. While the register is the authoritative record of share ownership, it records only legal ownership. It is completely silent about beneficial ownership. This emphasises that the register's principle function is to establish the identities of those who are apparently entitled to deal with the shares described in it, rather than those on whose behalf they are held. While shares may be held on trust,[27] the Corporations Law provides by s. 213(8) that, subject to a limited range of exceptions, notice of trust need not be entered on the register. The register is completely silent both regarding whether or not particular shares or parcels of shares are held on trust and regarding the identity of the beneficial owner or owners. The statutory exceptions apply to personal representatives, trustees supervising the affairs of legal incompetents, and the official trustee in bankruptcy. The policy objectives behind these exceptions are obvious.

This 'gap' in the public record has, over the years, amply fulfilled its potential for mischief. Where establishing that the wrongdoers are able to control the company is critical to a successful cause of action (as in an action under one of the exceptions to the rule in *Foss v. Harbottle*[28]), courts are normally reluctant to go behind the face of the register and recognise actual control as opposed to apparent control. The failure of the register to disclose beneficial ownership also has the potential to conceal a conflict of interest where question arises about whether directors have breached their fiduciary duties in particular transactions. Indeed, given the complexity of modern corporate structures, and the webs of interlocking shareholdings binding those structures together, those actually holding the beneficial interest in shares and, not infrequently, controlling the votes of those shares through a contractual arrangement with the legal owner, may not be known either to other corporators or to corporate management.

REVIEW QUESTIONS

1 What is the register, and what information is it required to contain?
2 What is the legal importance of the register?
3 Which corporate officer is responsible for maintaining the register?
4 Should the law be changed to ensure that the ownership of both the legal and the beneficial interest is recorded in the register? What arguments might be made in

---

26 *Dixon v. Kennaway & Co.* [1901] 1 Ch 833.

27 As you may recall, where property is held by one person on trust for one or more others, legal and beneficial ownership are separated.

28 (1843) 2 Hare 461.

favour of requiring both legal and beneficial ownership to be notified on the face of the register? What are the arguments against such a development?

5 Might this be an area where one rule might be appropriate for a publicly listed company and another for a proprietary company? Can you think of any reasons why this might be the case?

6 If, as a matter of policy, different rules are appropriate for public companies and for private companies, how should the law deal with corporate groups in which some companies are publicly held while others are closely held private companies?

The allotment of shares

We can learn a great deal about the law's understanding of the nature of the 'share as property' by examining the way in which an allotment of shares has been characterised in, for example, taxation law. The leading Australian case on this issue is the High Court decision in *Federal Commissioner of Taxation v. St Helen's Farm*.[29] The High Court held that the allotment of shares does not constitute a disposition of property. Neither does the consideration passing from the allottee to the company constitute a price. According to Barwick CJ, for the majority:

> I am quite satisfied that … the Assessment Act does not make the allotment and issue of a share in the capital of an incorporated company a disposition by that company of property to the allottee and, further, that the allotment money paid or payable by the allottee in respect of the allotment and issue of the share does not constitute a consideration passing from the allottee to the company for the disposition of property by the company to the allottee; in other words, does not constitute a price … Until allotment and issue, which includes the entry of the allottee's name on the share register in respect of the allotted share or shares, there is no property in the unissued shares; and, in particular, there is not then, or for that matter at any other time, any property or proprietorial right in or of the company in the unissued shares in its capital. The company has the capacity to allot and issue shares in the capital up to the amount of that capital, its nominal capital. But that capital is not the property of the company. Indeed, when allotted and issued, the nominal amount of the issued share or shares constitutes in accounting terms a liability of the company. But it is not property which comes to the allottee from, or by transfer from, the company. It is property which comes into existence by the allotment and issue or, more precisely, which is the consequences of such allotment and issue. The property consists of rights which may thereafter be exercised by virtue of the membership of the company thus gained and in accordance with its Memorandum and Articles of Association.[30]

The reasoning proceeds upon the basis that, until allotment, there is no property in unissued shares, nor does the company have any proprietary right in shares

---

29 (1981) 81 ATC 4040.
30 81 ATC 4040 at 4042.

of its own capital. Instead, the company has a 'bare capacity' to issue shares up to the amount of the nominal capital. The property comes into being through being issued—the property consisting of exercisable rights. This emphasises both the incorporeal nature of the property in shares and the fact that shares are choses in action. The register, and indeed the share certificate itself, does no more than signify that the person named therein is legally entitled to exercise the rights associated with share-ownership and can be legally compelled to fulfil the obligations of share-ownership.[31]

Share transfer, by contrast, deals with property that has already come into existence. The property in shares can be transferred in a number of different ways. It is important to distinguish a transfer of shares, which constitutes an attempt to make a sale and hence a transfer of ownership rights from the transmission of shares by operation of law, as occurs upon death or bankruptcy. In this context it is important to think very carefully about the nature of the property represented by a share certificate. If you are clear about the fact that the property in question consists of legal rights and obligations rather than anything more tangible, these legal peculiarities will begin to make some sense.

Restrictions on the alienation of shares, such as those contained in table A, articles 19–25 and in the Corporations Law,[32] form an intrinsic part of the property represented by the share. As a consequence, such restrictions do not constitute fetters on the alienation of a pre-existing property right but are one aspect of the right itself. This point is important in light of the common law's lengthy struggle to eliminate, so far as is possible, fetters on the alienation of property and the legal association of alienability with our ideas of property.[33] Otherwise, the provision that the legislation makes for the imposition of restrictions upon the alienation of shares may seem curious (or even arcane). Once it is understood that the restrictions upon the alienation of shares are a part of the property in the share, the potential for conflict disappears. Shares are simply a bundle of rights and correlative obligations. There is no 'property' external to these rights and obligations that could possibly be fettered by the incorporation of restrictions upon alienation among those rights and obligations.[34]

---

31 On share-issue, see Corporations Law, ss. 124, 184, 187, 194, 223. See also table A, articles 2 & 38.

32 ss. 213, 1085, 1089–93, 1100–4.

33 One might want to contrast the law's recalcitrant and tardy progress towards recognising common-law native title with its easy acceptance of the sort of property represented by the share certificate. Clearly, the real stumbling block was not the fetters on alienation inherent in indigenous conceptions of property, but the absence of individual control and the right to exclude others from enjoyment of that property. Indirectly, another very different point is made. Property is not a natural entity, a given, but a legal and political construct. Property is what the law has made it. Compare R. Dworkin, *Law's Empire*, Belknap Press, Cambridge, 1986, pp. 276–312 with R. Nozick, *Anarchy, State and Utopia*, Basil Blackwell, Oxford, 1974, pp. 153–82.

34 This does not, however, answer the question asked earlier. Where the laws of inheritance are used effectively to produce 'inalienable' property (which enables one sibling to compel another sibling to accede in decisions), there are a number of unresolved policy questions. Given the prevalence of litigation on such issues, and its costs, and given the deleterious effect the corporate setting can have on ordinary human relationships, it may be desirable for an alternative regime to be devised for family companies.

Borland's Trustee v. Steel Bros & Co. Ltd provides an excellent example of the way this principle operates in practice. The articles contained a provision that the board might compulsorily acquire shares at a specified consideration, the operation of the provision being triggered by certain specified events. One such triggering event was the bankruptcy of the registered owner. After Borland became bankrupt, his trustee in bankruptcy sought to challenge the provision and have himself registered as owner, believing that the shares could be sold for a better price on the open market. The court upheld the provision, and the shares were acquired by the board. Similar provisions were upheld in *Lyle & Scott Ltd v. Scott's Trustee*[35] and in *Scott's Trustees v. British Investment Trust Ltd*.[36] Because the articles made provision for the event that in fact occurred, and because the trustee in bankruptcy stood in the place of Borland and therefore was bound by the provision in the articles exactly as Borland had been, the provision was given full effect.

In *Re Swaledale Cleaners*,[37] the articles gave the directors absolute and uncontrolled discretion to refuse to register any transfer of shares. The articles provided further that notice of refusal was to be sent to the transferee within 2 months of lodgment. Both H, who held 5000 shares and A, who held 500 shares, were deceased. Their executors sought to transfer the shares to the applicant, who also held 500 shares. The applicant and Major Swaledale, who held 4000 shares, were the sole directors, although the applicant had not been re-elected at the annual general meeting, leaving the board without a quorum. The sole director was empowered by the articles to appoint a second director and to call a general meeting. At the meeting at which the applicant lost his seat, he formally requested registration of the transfer, and this was refused in a minute by Major Swaledale, although no resolution was passed to that effect. When the applicant subsequently applied for rectification of the register, Major Swaledale appointed another director and the board formally refused the request. Four months elapsed before the formal refusal. A delay of this magnitude was held to be unacceptable. The court held that the shareholder had a prima facie right to a transfer. Although the articles allowed the directors to refuse to register a transfer, it was essential that the power be exercised within a reasonable time. Here 4 months had passed between the formal request for registration of the transfer and the formal refusal. The right to transfer had been lost through excessive delay.[38]

REVIEW QUESTIONS

1 Distinguish carefully between an allotment of shares, a transfer of shares, and transmission of shares by operation of law. What legal incidents attend each transaction, and why are these distinctions important?

---

35 [1959] 2 All ER 661.

36 [1959] AC 763.

37 [1968] 1 WLR 1710.

38 This is an example of the equitable principle of laches, acquiescence, and delay.

2 How does the law conceptualise the 'property' in a share? At what point does this property arise, and what are its characteristics?

Classes of shares

As noted earlier, a company may issue shares that belong to several different classes. The rights that attach to share-ownership will vary according to class and should be defined by the memorandum.[39] Because it is common for corporate documents to be sloppily drafted,[40] the courts developed a number of presumptions to assist them in fleshing out the entitlements of different classes where, for example, a solvent liquidation has occurred and it is necessary to return capital to the shareholders. In general, upon return of share capital in a liquidation, there is a basic presumption of equality. This presumption applies irrespective of the amounts paid up on the shares because each share carries equal rights and liabilities. The *locus classicus* in this area is the 1899 House of Lords decision in *Birch v. Cropper*.[41] A company had share capital consisting of partly paid ordinary shares and fully paid preference shares. In liquidation the assets were more than sufficient to repay to both classes the amount paid up on their shares. Preference shareholders sought an order that the surplus be distributed in proportion to the amount paid up on the shares, a distribution that would favour their interests, all preference shares being fully paid. Ordinary shareholders, for their part, sought to deny preference shareholders the right to participate in the surplus. The court held that the surplus should be divided in proportion to the number of shares held. Each share represented the same fraction of ownership in the company irrespective of whether or not the shares were paid up. According to Lord Macnaghten:

> The ordinary shareholders say that the preference shareholders are entitled to a return of their capital, with 5 per cent interest up to the day of payment, and to nothing more. That is treating them as if they were debentureholders, liable to be paid off at a moment's notice. Then they say that at the utmost the preference shareholders are only entitled to the capital value of a perpetual annuity of 5 per cent upon the amounts paid up by them. That is treating them as if they were holders of irredeemable debentures. But they are not debentureholders at all. For some reason or other the company invited them to come in as shareholders, and they must be treated as having all the rights of shareholders, except so far as they renounced those rights on their admission to the company. There was an express bargain made as to their rights in respect of the profits arising from the business of

---

39 See Corporations Law, ss. 196, 200 & 256(1)(c).

40 In the past, corporate documents were frequently drafted without the benefit of legal advice. Such amateur drafting frequently led to litigation. Even where legal advice has been sought, a number of traps remain. Because many solicitors simply adapt the corporate documents supplied with a 'shelf company' to a client's purposes, it is often necessary to modify standard-form articles. Where this is done, inconsistencies often arise and cause substantial difficulties in the event of conflict.

41 (1897) 14 AC 525.

the company. But there was no bargain—no provision of any sort—affecting their rights as shareholders in the capital of the company.[42]

With any shareholding there is a basic presumption of equality regarding income, dividends, net capital, meetings, voting rights, and liability. This presumption is rebuttable where a company has issued different classes of shares. The decision to issue shares carrying different entitlements is internal and has nothing to do with stock-exchange regulations. A class structure may be adopted for a number of different reasons: to confine control, to assist in raising capital (as, for example, with preference shares), or to instil confidence (as with founder's shares). Where different classes are issued, the rights regarding repayment of capital, dividends, voting rights, and priority in liquidation may also be varied.[43] The specifications in the articles may not be complete, particularly where the articles are 'home-drafted', and so over the years the courts have developed complex judicial presumptions to deal with those cases where specific incidents are not set out in the articles as fully as is appropriate. Among these presumptions are:

1   a presumption that preference shares are cumulative as to dividend[44]
2   a presumption that, where there is a right to priority as to dividend, there is no right to surplus property in liquidation[45]
3   a presumption that, where there is a preference as to the repayment of capital, there is no right to share in a surplus on winding-up.[46]

Redeemable preference shares

Redeemable preference shares require special consideration for a number of reasons. Because of their unusual features, the Corporations Law makes specific

---

42   (1897) 14 AC 525 at 546. The language of the judgment is worth careful attention. Phrases such as 'come in as shareholders' clearly hold up an image of the company as a 'company of merchant adventurers', perhaps drawing upon earlier incarnations, including chartered corporations such as the Hudson Bay Company, the East India Company, and their descendant, the joint stock company. While the joint stock company had been replaced, by the time *Birch v. Cropper* was heard, by an entity indistinguishable from the modern corporation, presumptions that originated in the guilds of the Middle Ages continued to dominate judicial rhetoric. We do not think a judge today would speak of 'inviting'.

43   See Corporations Law, s. 200. The law provides that the rights attached to each class of shares must be specified in the memorandum or articles. However, just what the consequences of a failure in this regard are intended to be is not specified clearly. Human nature being what it is, occasions are likely to arise in which the rights are incompletely specified—that is, the rights may not address all possible axes along which variation can occur. When this occurs, we believe that the common-law presumptions developed by the courts will provide a fall-back position.

44   *Webb v. Earle* (1875) LR 20 Eq 556. This presumption may, of course, be rebutted by terms that indicate that preference shareholders may only look to profits for the current year for their dividend entitlement. See *Staples v. Eastman Photographic Materials Co.* [1896] 2 Ch 303.

45   See, for example, *Will v. United Lankat Plantations Co. Ltd* [1914] AC 11. This effectively treats preference shares as though they were equivalent to debentures—as an investment for fixed return, rather than one more intimately tied to the fortunes of the company.

46   See *Scottish Insurance Corp. Ltd v. Wilsons and Clyde Coal Co. Ltd* [1949] AC 462; *Re Isle of Thanet Electricity Supply Co. Ltd* [1950] Ch 161. Generally on this area, see *Dimbula Valley (Ceylon) Tea Co. Ltd v. Laurie* [1961] Ch 353. The judgment of Buckley J provides an excellent summary of the case law and a clear exposition of the principles that the courts use in interpreting the memorandum and articles in such circumstances.

provision regarding redeemable preference shares.[47] Many companies find the issue of redeemable preference shares an attractive proposition. Because they offer a seemingly more secure return, it is thought that they may attract investors where market conditions make the ordinary shares of the company relatively unattractive. They are preferable to debentures as a means of securing new funds, as dividends are not payable where the company is operating at a loss, although, of course the unpaid dividends will continue to accumulate where cumulative preference shares have been issued.

From a corporate perspective, redeemable preference shares are attractive because they are substitutable for debentures. Because they are similar to debentures in many respects, particularly in that they are redeemable after a term of years and pay a fixed rate of interest, they may also be used to enable companies to evade limits on borrowing contained in the memorandum and articles. If a company desires additional capital above and beyond that which may legitimately be borrowed, it may well be simpler and more effective for the company to issue redeemable preference shares than it is for it to secure the necessary special majority to alter the memorandum or articles. The value of redeemable preference shares to investors is, however, limited by the fixed rate of dividend and the fact that the preference granted is only over ordinary shares, and not over charges and debentures. A further disadvantage is that excessive use of redeemable preference shares leads to capital being excessively highly geared,[48] and this can potentially put the company a difficult financial position during uncertain financial times. During the 1980s entrepreneurs made a number of attempts to explore the use of preference shares as an alternative form of financing.[49]

The mechanics of share issue

Shares may be issued in several different ways. In a public issue (available only to a limited company), the offer is made to the public through a prospectus. Prospectuses today are strictly controlled with regard to their contents and the information

---

47 Corporations Law, s. 192(5) provides that, where redeemable preference shares are redeemed, an amount equivalent to their nominal value shall be transferred out of the profits that are otherwise available for dividends to a capital redemption reserve.

48 This feature provides further evidence of their kinship to debt finance. The use of redeemable preference shares leads to the company being highly geared because, like other forms of debt finance, they have a fixed redemption date. Where a company is unable to redeem its redeemable preferences shares when the redemption arrives (and is unable to persuade its redeemable preference shareholders to convert their shares to another form of finance), it would appear that their only recourse is to have the company wound up, a step that would bring their interests into direct conflict with those of the creditors. In such circumstances, given that the Corporations Law is silent, the courts would be forced to decide upon policy grounds, such as the protection of creditors' interests.

49 P. Redmond, *Companies and Securities Law*, Law Book Company, Sydney, 1988, pp. 616–17 provides case studies on the use that BHP and Fairfax made of preference shares. The Fairfax proposal, while never finalised, was particularly interesting because it involved an attempt to raise capital by issuing preference shares in order to avoid diluting the control of the Fairfax family.

presented in them.[50] In a public issue, the company offers new shares to the public in order to raise money. Such shares may be offered either at par value,[51] or, more commonly, at a 'premium'—a specified sum above par value, which is related to the existing market price at which shares in the company are currently traded on the stock exchange. As we have seen on a number of occasions in recent years, high-profile companies that have been newly floated on the share-market may also command a significant premium. Recent examples include former government entities, such as the newly privatised Commonwealth Bank and Qantas.[52]

Rights and bonus issues are very different from a public issue. No prospectus is required. Unlike a public issue, both rights issues and bonus issues are made to existing shareholders and debenture holders on terms that are favourable to members. A rights issue raises new capital for the company. In a rights issue, which occurs where the company shares have a market price above par value, the shares are offered to members at a discount against market price. Thus, for example, if the market price were $4.25, the rights issue might set a price of $2.85 per share. A rights issue may either be renounceable or non-renounceable. A non-renounceable rights issue may only be subscribed to by the specific members to whom the offer is made. Where the offer is renounceable, however, those receiving the offer may, if they desire, 'renounce' their rights in favour of nominees. Where a renounceable rights offer is made, rights can be traded. In some cases, rights have been openly traded upon stock exchanges. In the context of the Corporations Law, this raises a number of difficult questions. One such question is whether an issue of renounceable rights constitutes an offer to the public. Section 1017A provides that a prospectus is exempt from registration where the shares are issued to existing members of the corporation. While a renounceable rights issue is offered to existing members, the capacity of those members to transfer their entitlement to nominees suggests that such an issue may go beyond the parameters of what is allowed. In such circumstances, it seems to be essential to ensure that the prospectus for the issue was registered—a formality that might reduce the attractiveness of a rights offer as a mechanism.

While a bonus issue is also an issue to existing members, it does not raise new capital. In a bonus issue, funds from the capital redemption reserve or the share premium account are converted into shares, and the shares are issued at no cost to members, often in lieu of a dividend payment in cash. It is clear that a bonus

---

50 Corporations Law, s. 1021. See also ss. 1025–32, 1020AI, 96, 1005–12, 996. This area of the law is highly technical and tightly regulated. It should be noted that, historically, regulation of the contents of the prospectus was somewhat lax. See, for example, *Derry v. Peek* (1889) 14 AC 337 at 376. After a series of cases involving fraud and misrepresentation, Parliament imposed reasonably stringent standards.

51 Under the Second Corporate Law Simplification Bill, the concept of par value will be abolished for new companies, although this will not affect the position with respect to existing companies. This in turn will, as you saw in chapter 3, render both the prohibition on discounting and the notion of issuing at a premium redundant.

52 If the reforms recommended in the Second Corporate Law Simplification Bill become law, new issues of shares will be floated at a price that estimates the price that they will command when traded. While the distinction between issue at par value and issue at a premium will disappear, it is likely that the process by which an 'offer price' is fixed will not alter significantly.

issue does not constitute an offer to the public such as to be caught by the prospectus requirements.

In principle, shares are fully transferable. Their transferability may be restricted by the articles, as was the case in *Borland's Trustee v. Steel Bros*. Restrictions of this kind, which are usual in private companies, are invariably caught by the *contra proferentum* rule. Where the directors exercise their discretion and refuse to register a transfer of shares, ss. 1090–4 of the Corporations Law may be invoked. These sections provide that either the transferee or the transmittee may apply to the court for relief, and that the court has discretion to make such an order as it deems fit, including an order that the company purchase its own shares. Where the articles grant a power of refusal to the directors, s. 461 may be invoked in a demand for a just and equitable winding-up.[53]

Shares may, of course, also be transmitted by the operation of law. Where a false or misleading statement is made regarding transfer, or where a mistake is present, the normal rules of contract law apply, and an action in negligent misstatement may be available in appropriate circumstances. Both the Commonwealth *Trade Practices Act 1974* (TPA), s. 52, and s. 999 of the Corporations Law may be available.

REVIEW QUESTIONS

1 What basic legal presumption governs shareholdings?
2 Why might a company disturb this presumption by issuing different classes of shares?
3 If corporate management fails to specify the specific incidents attached to each class of shares fully, what judicial presumptions operate?
4 What is a public issue? How may such an issue be made?
5 What is a rights issue? What is the difference between a renounceable rights issue and a non-renounceable rights issue, and what potential regulatory problem does this pose?
6 What is a bonus issue, and how does it differ from a rights issue?
7 What are some of the ways in which shares can be transmitted by operation of law?

Allotment

The prospectus

Chapter 7 of the Corporations Law governs prospectuses, securities, and charges. Sections 1017–32, 9, 65, 1020A, 96, 1005–12, and 1035–43 are particularly relevant to prospectuses. Note should be taken of s. 1031, which covers allotments for

---

53 See *Ibrahimi v. Westbourne Galleries Ltd* [1973] AC 360 and other cases on s. 461 and overseas equivalents.

which the prospectus indicates that an application has been made for quotation on the stockmarket. Section 996 prohibits an allotment unless a minimum subscription has been received. It is usual for a new issue to be underwritten by a brokerage firm, and where this is the case, the brokerage house will handle the necessary formalities and will take up any shortfall from the minimum subscription level. All subscription money received in respect of a new issue must be kept in a trust account until the minimum subscription level is reached. If this level is not reached, the company must repay applicants according to the terms of s. 1036. This section provides that, where repayment has been made within 7 days, no interest is required. If repayment is not effected within 7 days, the directors are jointly and severally liable to repay with interest at 8 per cent. Section 1036 is a penal provision. Section 187 requires the company to lodge a return of allotment with the Australian Securities Commission (ASC) and provides that the court may validate improperly issued shares under specified circumstances.

A share-allotment may be acquired by subscription to the memorandum, by application, or by transfer. Where the allotment is acquired by subscription, the process is self-contained, and the date of membership is the date of the company's legal 'birth'. In the case of both application and transfer, the date of membership is the date of entry in the share register. The rules governing allotment are contractual, and the actual share appropriation must be made by a resolution by the board of directors of the company. The prospectus constitutes an invitation to treat, the actual application for shares being the offer. To apply for shares, the prospective shareholder must complete the application form accompanying the prospectus and submit this form together with 5 per cent of the purchase price of the shares. The application must be made within a reasonable time or the prospectus will lapse. The application form is a standard form contract that invariably includes a clause whereby the applicant agrees to take a stated number of shares or such lesser number of shares as the company sees fit. Such a clause is essential to cover the case where, as a result of substantial demand, the allotment is oversubscribed. If an allotment is oversubscribed, the shares actually allotted to each applicant are proportional to those stated on the application in the prospectus as applied for. The contract is complete when the acceptance letter is posted (the postal acceptance rule applying).[54]

While the contract is complete upon acceptance and the new allottee is, therefore, liable to pay calls,[55] the allottee does not become a member of the company until her or his name has been entered on the register. During the period between acceptance and the minute of allotment entering the shareholders name on the register, the allottee has liabilities under the contract but does not enjoy membership rights. While it seems somewhat unfair that allottees can become subject to the obligations of membership at a time when they are not entitled to the rights conferred, in practice this is likely to be of minimal importance—a development

---

54 See *Household Fire & Carriage Accident Insurance Co. v. Grant* (1879) 4 Ex D 216.

55 *Household Fire & Carriage Accident Insurance Co. v. Grant.*

highlighting the ascendancy of contract over association. With the replacement of the 'merchant adventurer' of the British East India Company by the passive investor of the modern multinational, it appears that contract's ascendancy over association has finally been completed.

Issue at a premium

In the case of an established company, it is normal for shares to be issued at a premium—that is, a price that is above the par value of the shares.[56] Very often the premium will reflect the price at which existing shares are traded. At common law, the premium (or proportion of the purchase price above par value) was not treated as a part of the capital, and such premiums could be paid as dividends. Section 191 of the Corporations Law requires the premium to be transferred to a special account to be known as the 'share premium account'. Apart from the exceptions in s. 195(6), all provisions concerning the reduction of capital apply. The share premium account may be used to pay up unissued shares to issue to members as bonus shares, to pay up the unpaid balance on members' shares, and for dividends paid in the form of shares.

This area is not without its ambiguities. For example, in *Re Driffield Gas Line Company*,[57] a company entered liquidation. After all creditors were paid, sufficient funds remained to return all paid-up capital to shareholders. This distribution was made according to the nominal cost (or par value) of the shares, and the premiums paid were disregarded. A court deemed this form of distribution to be fair and proper, despite the apparent inequities.[58] Similarly in *Niemann v. Smedley*[59] it was held that, where shares were issued at a premium and the assets in liquidation proved insufficient to meet the liabilities, shareholders were not liable for calls on the unpaid premiums. Given that, with the exception of closely held private companies, it is uncommon for shares to trade at their par value, this approach seems unrealistic, although it illustrates the degree to which the law is wedded to formal equality.

---

56 For new companies, this concept will be meaningless when and if the Second Corporate Law Simplification Bill becomes law. It will, of course, continue to be relevant in the case of companies incorporated before enactment.

57 [1898] 1 Ch 451.

58 There is an interesting disjuncture here between par value and market value. Par value has had a kind of reality for the law, which market value does not. Par value is 'legal value', 'official', settled, and authoritatively determined. Market value is unstable, chimerical, subject to variation without legally cognisable cause. In such circumstances, depending upon the funds available, what *Re Driffield Gas Line Company* suggests is that par value ought to be returned to all shareholders, thus maintaining the fiction of equality despite the clear evidence (in terms of a premium paid) of inequality. If, after return of capital, a surplus still exists, that surplus will fall to be distributed in accordance with the priorities set out in the memorandum or articles. In market terms, there will be a clear inequality of return; in legal terms, formal equality is maintained. In this context as in others, formal equality (the equality of law) defeats substantive equality (the equality of the market). Although this is a familiar phenomenon, its effect in this context is remarkable. We are all familiar with the more usual case in which lack of resources limits access to formally equal rights. Here, formal equality has traditionally denied recovery of resources actually committed.

59 [1973] VR 769.

The prohibition on discounting [60]

Sections 190[61] and 203–4 of the Corporations Law deal with the prohibition, except in the circumstances specified, on issuing shares at a discount—that is, below par value. The legal prohibition has its origin in the requirement that capital be maintained to provide a reserve for creditors. Allowing discounting would dilute the capital structure of the company, allowing the 'real time' value of its issued capital to fall below the 'legal' value inscribed on the face of its corporate documents. Section 204 provides for the payment of brokerage fees out of share capital, subject to certain limits and controls, while s. 190(1) deals with discounting by no liability companies.[62]

There are a number of different conceptual strands to this issue. One, at least in theory, lies in the desirability of ensuring that the public documents of the company accurately represent the capital actually ventured upon corporate business. Another very different strand has to do with the relationship among the company's shareholders themselves and the need to maintain equality in this relationship. This latter conceptual strand came before the English courts in *Welton v. Saffrey*.[63] The facts of the case concerned the winding-up of a solvent company in which some of the shares had been issued at a discount. Those shareholders who had obtained shares at a discount were obligated to pay calls on the shares before the rights among themselves were adjusted. The aim was to secure fairness as between the shareholders. Although the practice is statutorily prohibited today, a number of mechanisms have developed by which it can be evaded,[64] as we shall see later.

Ooregum Gold Mining Co. of India Ltd v. Roper[65] provides the classic statement of the rationale behind the prohibition on discounting and was a watershed in the development of the modern law. A company in a generally depressed market was seeking finance through preference shares, its ordinary shares having proved unattractive. The shares had a nominal value of £1 and were issued with 15 shillings credited as paid. Effectively the shares were issued for 5 shillings. Lord Watson emphasised that

---

60 When the idea of 'par value' is eliminated, the notion of 'discounting' will disappear. See the Second Corporate Law Simplification Bill.

61 In *Re Esmeralda Exploration Ltd* (1991) 105 ALR 239; 33 FCR 192 the court enumerated some of the factors that were relevant to confirming a resolution to issue shares at a discount. Conditions may also be imposed, as in *Re Air North West Pty Ltd* (1988) 6 ACLC 1143.

62 In this context it should be noted that the prohibition on discounting has been held to be irrelevant to no liability companies. See *New Good Hope Consolidated Gold Mines NL v. Stutterd* [1916] VLR 580.

63 [1897] AC 229.

64 It is useful and interesting to compare the putative concern with equality among members themselves evidenced by *Welton v. Saffrey* with the apparent lack of concern in *Re Driffield*. In the former case, what the court described as concern for equality among members themselves may be read as concern with the integrity and accuracy of the constitutive documents of the company. In the later, the apparent lack of concern masked the courts unease at claims lacking formal verifiability—lacking the evidence provided by the constitutive documents of the company. Both equality and inequality can only be read through the foundational texts of the company. Once the texts are abandoned for the vagaries of the market, equality is irrelevant, and the courts will not probe behind the documents in search of 'business realities'.

65 [1892] AC 125.

these enactments read together indicate the intention of the Legislature that every member who takes shares from the company in return for cash shall either pay or become liable to contribute their full nominal value ... Consequently, if shares are issued against money, it appears to me that any payment to the company less than the nominal amount of the share must, by force of the statute, and notwithstanding any agreement to the contrary, be treated as a payment to account, the member remaining liable to contribute the balance, when duly called for [Where the shares are issued against other goods or services, His Lordship observed that] the Court would doubtless refuse effect to a colourable transaction, entered into for the purpose or with the obvious result of enabling the company to issue its shares at a discount; but it has been ruled that, so long as the company honestly regards the consideration given as fairly representing the nominal value of the shares in cash, its estimate ought not to be critically examined. That state of the law is certainly calculated to induce companies who are in want of money, and whose shares are unsaleable except at a discount, to pay extravagant prices for goods or work to persons who are willing to take payment in shares.[66]

Lord Watson's judgment purported to reflect the parliamentary intent that every person taking shares should be liable up to the full nominal value of the shares. Where the shares were offered at a discount, the liability remained, and calls could be made in liquidation. Again the emphasis is upon the public documents, the sanctity of the foundational texts. Where the texts are undermined—where they become no more certain than the vagaries of the market (as would surely be the case if discounting were openly allowed)—the court would lack a certain foundation from which to commence its deliberations. While the courts emphasise the importance of the memorandum and articles as a public record, we believe that they are of far greater importance as evidentiary texts—as 'best evidence'. Through reliance upon these foundational texts, the courts are able to avoid sitting in judgment upon decisions made for 'commercial' reasons.

Despite the apparent strictness of the rule, where the full cash value is paid, a portion thereof may be returned for repayment of indebtedness for goods and services. Here the disjuncture between the texts and the need to preserve their integrity and authority, on one hand, and the 'real world' of markets and commercial transactions, on the other, is highlighted. If the court will insist (and almost invariably it does) that the value upon the face of the constitutive documents of the company is the only value it will recognise as meaningful, it will also (paradoxically) refuse to question the 'legitimacy' of commercial dealings, even where those dealings effectively undermine the rule that it insists it is upholding. While the court will frequently acknowledge, as did Lord Watson, the potential for abuse afforded by payment in kind rather than in cash, it will not intervene.

The potential for abuse of this kind was realised in *Re Wragg Ltd*,[67] a classic 'Salomon' scenario in which a partnership sold its business to the company at a gross overvaluation. When the company became insolvent and entered liquidation, the

---

66 [1892] AC 125 at 136–7.

67 [1897] 1 Ch 796.

liquidator sought to establish that the shares were not fully paid. *Ooregum* was cited, but to no avail. The court held that there was no law that overrode the capacity of a company to pay any price it saw fit for a business, despite the fact that the overvalue amounted to £11 000, which was known by both the vendors and the purchasers. The court held that the onus was on the person alleging the transaction to be colourable—in this case the liquidator—to establish fraud. The artificiality of describing the situation where a partnership sells its business (including in the purchase price a quantum reflecting the good will of the business) to a company controlled by the former partners as one where the company 'paid and was entitled to pay a price it deemed appropriate for the business' is nothing short of remarkable. It is, however, in keeping with the traditional approach of the courts to matters of this kind and, in particular, in keeping with the settled judicial doctrine that the court will not examine the business of the company where to do so would involve it in matters of 'commercial judgment'.[68]

Section 187 of the Corporations Law attempts to impose some controls on transactions of this sort. It requires that a copy of any contract for non-cash consideration must be lodged with the ASC. Where the contract is not reduced to writing, a statement of particulars must be lodged. While these requirements ensure that such transactions become part of the public record, and thus available to those who choose to deal with the company (a reform that may help to curb the most flagrant abuses), such provisions do nothing to resolve the underlying problems. Those underlying problems have three sources. First, they reflect the ways in which the courts have constructed the idea of separate legal personality and the nature of the barrier that the corporate veil imposes between the knowledge of the corporators as individuals and the company's knowledge.[69] Second, they reflect the time-honoured refusal of the courts to question the directors' conduct of the business of the company, such conduct being a matter of business judgment. Finally, and most significantly in the case of the closely held corporation, they reflect the unreality of a knowledge system that suggests that the directors of a company can, as directors, disregard their own interests as individuals. It is this unreality that enables the courts to complacently hold that 'so long as the company honestly regards the consideration given as fairly representing the nominal value of the shares in cash, its estimate ought not to be critically examined'.[70]

In English law, the emphasis is upon the intent, and the provisions are given a purposive reading. Both *Ooregum* and *Welton v. Saffrey* contained strong dissenting judgments, which suggested that the company ought to be allowed to

---

68 The 'business judgment rule', as this general principle is called in the USA, states that, where the probity or otherwise of a transaction or a series of transactions can plausibly be seen as matters of 'commercial judgment', the courts will not intervene, nor will they go behind the surface of the transaction and endeavour to establish its colourability.

69 As Alasdair MacIntyre noted in a rather different context, '[t]he liberal self moves from sphere to sphere compartmentalising its attitudes': A. MacIntyre, *Whose Justice? Which Rationality?*, University of Notre Dame Press, Notre Dame, 1988, pp. 346–7.

70 *Ooregum Gold Mining Co. of India Ltd v. Roper* at 137.

discount where this was permitted by the articles and if the balance was liable to be made up in an insolvent liquidation. A clear distinction was made between the obligation of the company to third parties and the rights of the members among themselves. Had this perspective been adopted by the court as a whole, it would have been possible for shares to be issued at a discount provided that calls were paid in the event of an insolvent liquidation. In a solvent liquidation, discounted shares would be entitled to participate on an equal footing. This position is fundamentally logical. Where shares are traded on the market, no distinction is made between a purchaser at par value and one who purchases at a premium. No reason exists, therefore, for distinguishing between a purchaser at a discount and one at par value. If the rationale behind the prohibition is simply to protect the interests of creditors in an insolvent liquidation, a blanket prohibition would seem unnecessary, perhaps even counter-productive.

Some Australian support for this overall line of reasoning may be found in the judgment of Dixon J (as he then was) in *King v. Tait*.[71] The facts concerned a company in liquidation. The articles provided that the assets exclusive of uncalled capital should be distributed in proportion to the shares held, irrespective of whether those shares were fully or partly paid. The relevant article was deemed valid, and the distribution was made in accord with the shares held. Those who had paid advances upon calls were not entitled to recoup their advances. This interpretative approach suggests that the prohibition upon discounting exists solely to protect creditors and outsiders. The central issue is one of commercial morality.

Relationships among the members themselves, on the other hand, are purely contractual. Within the paradigm of equal contracting parties dealing with one another at arm's length, the price paid for the shares is immaterial. The only material facts regarding their relationships concern the rights and obligations incorporated in the memorandum and articles. Dixon J began by summarising the liquidation agreement confirmed by the court. He then went on to discuss the general law approach, and finally he referred to the article ultimately validated by the court and described its effect:

> [The liquidation agreement] provided that [the assets] should be allotted by the purchasing company to the shareholders of the liquidating company in proportion to the amount paid by them in the capital of the latter. It went on to provide that the allotment should be on the basis of the amount actually paid up as capital, whether in respect of fully paid or partly paid up shares. Now such a method of distributing assets in excess of those applied in the discharge of debts and costs of winding up is not in accord with the general law, which, in the absence of specific provision requires that the capital shall be equalized as a first step and then the fund shall be distributed according to the number of shares. The plan, therefore, needed the authority of some regulation of the company ... In point of fact an article existed which prescribed a mode of distribution completely inconsistent with that provided by the agreement. [The article in question provided for distribution in

---

71 (1936) 57 CLR 715.

proportion to shares held, whether partly paid or fully paid and provided that all shares were to rank equally, with no calls to be made.] Do the Acts contain anything which invalidates such an attempt to give the shareholders an interest in the net assets according to the number of their shares without taking into account the discrepancy between the amount subscribed and the amount paid-up? In my opinion they do not.[72]

Section 190(2) provides complex mechanisms for discounting, and covers the rate, the time limit, and a requirement that discounted shares be offered to existing members in proportion to holdings in preference to outsiders. But the provisions are rarely used. Because the statutory procedures are complex and cumbersome, it is much simpler to create a new class of shares with special privileges and to offer them at par value. This whole area is extremely formalistic. Reform proposals are regularly mooted. For example, the Gedge Committee suggested the abolition of the concept of par value, and its abolition is one of the recommendations of the Second Corporate Law Simplification Bill 1995. The entire concept of par value has no basis in reality and bears no relationship to the asset backing of the company. In some jurisdictions—for example, the USA—no equivalent to par value exists, and pricing is entirely market-driven.

REVIEW QUESTIONS

1 What is the rationale behind the prohibition on discounting? Should this prohibition be retained in light of the fact that companies may now purchase their own shares under appropriate circumstances?
2 What value, if any, does the concept of par value have in the modern commercial world? Would the abandonment of this concept be in any sense problematical or cause commercial inconvenience? Put another way, should companies be required to maintain certain levels of financial backing to be allowed to trade?
3 If par value is abolished, what effect is this likely to have upon the reasoning of the courts in matters such as those we have been considering?
4 What policy issues in this area are likely to be relevant when the Second Corporate Law Simplification Bill becomes law?

Alteration of share capital

The basic rule is that share capital must be maintained. This rule is subject to a number of exceptions and qualifications. An increase in authorised capital is always possible. The power to increase the authorised capital is vested in the board.[73] In

---

72 (1936) 57 CLR 715 at 739–44.

73 *Hogg v. Cramphorn* [1967] Ch 254; *Mills v. Mills* (1938) 60 CLR 150; *Harlowe's Nominees Pty Ltd v. Woodside (Lakes Entrance) Oil Co. NL* (1968) 121 CLR 483.

Harlowe's Nominees Pty Ltd v. Woodside (Lakes Entrance) Oil Co. NL, the leading judgment put the relevant considerations particularly clearly:

> The principle is that although primarily the power is given to enable capital to be raised when required for the purposes of the company, there may be occasions when the directors may fairly and properly issue shares for other reasons, so long as those reasons relate to a purpose of benefiting the company as a whole, as distinguished from a purpose, for example, of maintaining control of the company in the hands of the directors themselves or their friends ... *Directors in whom are vested the right and the duty of deciding where the company's interests lie and how they are to be served may be concerned with a wide range of practical considerations and their judgment, if exercised in good faith and not for irrelevant purposes, is not open to review in the courts.*[74]

The fundamental fiduciary requirement is that the increase must be in the best interests of the company as a whole. Thus it would be improper for the directors to endeavour to increase authorised capital to enable them to allot shares to a 'white knight' in order to avert a takeover bid and thereby maintain their own position. On the other hand, as on the facts in *Harlowe's Nominees*, it is entirely proper for directors to issue shares to strengthen a relationship with another company with which it has been involved in a joint venture, even if this has the 'incidental' effect of averting a takeover bid. Section 193 provides that authorised capital may be increased by an ordinary resolution, and that notice of any such increase must be lodged with the ASC.

Reduction of authorised capital is a much more complicated issue. Certain basic mechanisms intended to facilitate this have been incorporated in the Corporations Law and in the articles. Section 193(e) provides that the cancellation of unissued shares does not constitute a reduction of capital. The cancellation of shares that are forfeited where a shareholder fails to pay calls[75] is likewise not deemed a reduction of capital. Apart from these special cases, all reductions of capital require the approval of the court.[76] The court will, subject to equitable considerations, allow a reduction of capital in three general sets of circumstances: where the company has experienced significant losses, where it has capital in excess of requirements, or where it is reorganising its capital structure.

Loss reduction

Where the company has experienced losses to the extent that its net assets fall below the value of issued share capital, a loss reduction may be appropriate. In such a case,

---

74 (1968) 121 CLR 483 at 493 (emphasis added). This is, of course, one iteration of the 'business judgment rule' discussed earlier in this chapter. The judgment as a whole is a classic illustration of the reluctance of the courts to become involved in the 'private' judgments of corporate managers. The emphasis upon the bona fides of the directors highlights the problematical nature of any challenge. For a successful challenge to be made to such an issue, it would be necessary for the plaintiffs to argue that the issue was not made in good faith, effectively impugning the integrity of the board. In general, litigation involving allegations of a breach of directors' duties avoids the question of bona fides wherever possible because of the probative difficulties.

75 See arts 26–33, table A.

76 This will no longer be the case if the Second Corporate Law Simplification Law is enacted.

the issued share capital may be reduced to the extent that share capital outstanding reflects the true asset backing of the company. Where this occurs, nominal value and asset value will be equivalent.

Capital in excess of requirements

Sometimes where a company is overcapitalised, possibly because of internal reorganisation or restructuring, it may be appropriate to return capital to shareholders. In *Re Fowlers Vacola Manufacturing Co. Ltd*,[77] the company had been running a fruit-canning business as an adjunct to its primary business. For a number of years, this division had incurred substantial losses, and as a consequence, the company determined to abandon it. Following the abandonment of the canning division, the company was left with capital of some £303 750 in excess of its needs and desired to return this capital to its shareholders. The company sought to accomplish this by returning 7 shillings 6 pence per ordinary 10 shilling share and reducing the nominal value of ordinary shares from 10 shillings to 2 shillings, 6 pence. The court held that a reduction of this type was prima facie unfair unless the restructuring was done in accordance with priorities upon winding-up. According to Little J,

> [i]t does not mean, of course that a reduction involving a return of capital other than in accordance with priorities on winding up, must, or should in all circumstances be regarded as unfair or inequitable. But the practice … based as it is on the analogy of priorities in a winding up, is at least a guide to what may be regarded as prima facie fair and equitable in cases of payment off of surplus capital, as well as in cases of loss reduction …
>
> In the present case, the preference shareholders are not to participate even on an equal basis with the ordinary shareholders in the return of capital. They do not participate at all. They have not had the opportunity to express their views, let alone have they given their assent, at a separate meeting of the class … I can see nothing in the circumstances which in the interests of the company or in the interests of fairness as between classes requires or warrants the exclusion of the preference shareholders from participation in the contemplated return of capital. Bearing in mind the priority given on winding up I should have thought that in the circumstances of this case fairness called for at least equality in treatment of the classes.[78]

Reorganisation of capital structure

A company may seek to reorganise its capital structure for many different reasons. In times of low interest rates, a prosperous company may prefer to borrow on the market rather than rely on shareholders' funds. If commercial loans are available at 9–10 per cent and the interest rate on redeemable preference shares stands at 14–15 per cent, it may be more appropriate to redeem the shares and seek to borrow at a favourable rate. While this can be a dangerous practice, leaving the company excessively vulnerable to market and interest movements, some companies may find it a useful strategy.

---

77   [1966] VR 97.
78   [1966] VR 97 at 105–6.

Re Holder's Investment Trusts[79] provides a good example of the way in which these matters may come before the courts. The company could not afford to redeem its preference shares as the date for redemption approached. Seeking to postpone the day of reckoning, it proposed a restructuring scheme, which involved cancelling the preference shares and substituting unsecured stock. It sought to make this proposition attractive to its preference shareholders by offering an additional 1 per cent interest on unsecured stock. The proponents of the scheme held both redeemable preference shares and unsecured stock. The proposal offered substantial advantages to those who held both preference shares and stock. The proponents had not, however, considered the interests of investors who only held preference shares. When the company sought the approval of the court for the restructuring, as it was required by law to do, Megarry J emphasised that approval was discretionary and that the court would only approve a restructuring of capital where it had assured itself that the plan was fair as it operates between the classes themselves. Since the proponent of the restructuring was the company, it followed, according to Megarry J, that the onus was on the company to satisfy the court that this was the case.[80]

Section 195 allows for any type of reduction provided that the articles authorise the method chosen, a special resolution has been passed, and the plan is confirmed by the court. Three forms of reduction are suggested by the legislation:

1 The company may extinguish or reduce the liability on partly paid shares by reducing their nominal value.
2 In a loss reduction, the company may cancel that proportion of paid-up shares that are not represented by available assets.
3 The company may pay off capital in excess of current needs.

The appropriate procedures must be adhered to stringently. Application is to be made to the court by summons as provided in the Rules of the Supreme Court. Section 195(3) provides that the creditors may object, and s. 195(10) provides that, if any creditors are unaware of the reduction, members must contribute as if the reduction was not made. A *discretion* is vested in the court, and the requirements of s. 195 must be complied with.[81] Approval by the court of any proposed reduction in capital is wholly discretionary, and the court will evaluate each proposed reduction on its merits, an overriding concern being whether or not the proposed reduction is fair as it operates between members themselves.

Class rights

The Australian courts have generally taken an extremely proactive stance towards the protection of class rights, and class rights must always be considered if an alteration of share capital is proposed. As we saw above, the proposed restructuring was

---

79 [1971] 1 WLR 584.

80 This is, of course, simply an application of the ordinary rule that the onus of proof lies upon the proponent of the proposition before the court.

81 For a discussion of the parameters of that discretion, see *Nicron Resources Ltd* (1992) 8 ACSR 219; *Ex parte Westburn Sugar Refineries Ltd* [1951] AC 625.

disallowed in *Re Holder's Investment Trust* because the proponents of the plan had failed to consider the interests of those who held only preference shares, and had not afforded them an opportunity to consider the proposed restructuring and to vote on it independently.

A similar approach was taken by the Australian High Court in *Re Fowler's Vacuola*. Because the company wished to close down its canning division, it had capital in excess of its requirements, although it had made an operating loss for the past 2 years. When it sought to exclude preference shareholders from a proposed return of capital, the court disallowed its proposal. The proposal put forward by the company did not accord with the priorities on winding-up, which gave preference in return of capital to preference shareholders. No class meetings had been held because formal class rights were not altered by the proposal. Given the interpretative paradigms adopted by the Australian courts, it will never suffice simply to rest on an assertion that class rights have not been altered. Rather, the company has an obligation to consider whether the proposal impacts equally upon all classes of shares, and if it does not, it is essential that the disadvantaged shareholders be afforded an opportunity to consider the proposal independently.

Although Australian courts have generally been assiduous in protecting class rights, some elements of their reasoning, in fact, provide less than wholly satisfactory protection. While *Re Fowler's Vacuola* typifies the Australian approach to class rights, procedurally it offers less satisfactory protection for minority interests than does the approach adopted by the House of Lords in *Re Holder's Investment Trust*. The critical difference involves the location of the onus of proof. In *Holder's*, the House of Lords approached the matter on the basis that the onus of proof lay upon the company to establish that its proposal was fair as it operated among the classes themselves. In *Fowler's Vacuola*, the High Court proceeded upon the basis that the onus lay upon the complaining shareholders to establish unfairness.

In practical terms, this question is extremely important. Where the facts are evenly balanced, the party who has the onus of proof is likely to be at a disadvantage. It is much more difficult to put forward a convincing argument on issues such as the fairness or otherwise of a proposed scheme than it is to rebut an argument put by opposing counsel. Because the legislation requires the company to apply to the court for confirmation of the scheme (Corporations Law, s. 195), the onus appears to lie upon the company to establish the fairness of any proposal for reduction of capital as it operates among the members themselves. The normal rule is that, to make its case, the party approaching the court must establish the facts upon which that party relies. It is also important to note that the burden of proof shifts constantly during the trial as evidence is led and the necessity arises to rebut it. A company might, for example, cite the approval of a class meeting as prima facie evidence that a proposed reduction was fair as it operates among the members themselves. It has, thereby, discharged its initial onus; however, this evidence might itself be rebutted by further evidence that a particular group of preference shareholders was prejudiced by the proposed scheme, even while the class as a whole accepted it. At this point, it would be necessary for the company to produce further evidence to convince the court of the fairness of the proposed reduction. We believe that *Holder's* was correct on this point and ought to be followed, while the approach adopted in *Re Fowlers Vacuola* seems profoundly at variance with the overall goal of protecting class rights.

The concept of fairness between classes is heavily influenced by the articles. *Scottish Insurance Corp. Ltd v. Wilsons and Clyde Coal Co. Ltd* [82] analysed the issues involved in fairness among the classes in substantial detail. The facts of the case involved a company that was due to be nationalised and that sought to reduce itself to a bare legal shell before the receipt of compensation. To accomplish this end, the company sought to pay out preference shareholders. The preference shareholders objected, as they hoped for a higher return from the compensation payments. The compensation payment in respect of nationalisation was likely to be substantial, and it was apparent that, even after all creditors were satisfied and the capital returned to all members, surplus funds would remain. The preference shareholders sought to postpone the return of capital in order to participate in the surplus to be distributed after creditors were satisfied and capital returned. The court held that, because the articles gave the preference shareholders no right to share in any surplus on liquidation, such a right did not exist. In light of that analysis, the proposed reduction was deemed fair as it operated among the classes themselves. As Lord Simonds put the matter,

> [t]he company has at a stroke been deprived of the enterprise and undertaking which it has built up over many years: it is irrelevant for this purpose that the stroke is delivered by an Act of Parliament which at the same time provides some compensation. Nor can it affect the rights of the parties that the only reason why there is money available for repayment of capital is that the company has no longer an undertaking to carry on. Year by year the 7 per cent preference dividend has been paid; of the balance of the profits some part has been distributed to the ordinary stockholders, the rest has been conserved in the business. If I ask whether year by year the directors were content to recommend, the company in general meeting to vote, a dividend which has left a margin of resources, in order that the preference stockholders might in addition to repayment of their capital share also in surplus assets, I think that directors and company alike would give an emphatic negative. And they would, I think, add that they have always had it in their power, and have it still … to see that what they had saved for themselves they do not share with others … Reading these articles as a whole with such familiarity with the topic as the years have brought, I would not hesitate to say, first, that the last thing a preference stockholder would expect to get … would be a share of surplus assets, and that such a share would be a windfall beyond his reasonable expectations and, second, that he had at all times the knowledge by reference in art. 139 to the payment off of the preference capital, that at least he ran the risk, if the company's circumstances admitted, of such a reduction as is now proposed being submitted for confirmation by the court. Whether a man lends

---

82   [1949] AC 462.

money to a company at 7 per cent or subscribes for its shares carrying a cumulative preferential dividend at that rate, I do not think that he can complain of unfairness if the company, being in a position lawfully to do so, proposes to pay him off.[83]

The considerations influencing the court's discretion were set out by Lord Reid in *Ex parte Westburn Sugar Refineries Ltd.*[84] According to Lord Reid, the court was to consider the interests of creditors, the equities among members themselves, and the public interest, as well as the interests of those who might form a connection with the company in the future. On the facts before him, Lord Reid was satisfied that the scheme was proper, despite the presence of a collateral purpose to avoid a threatened nationalisation. It was permissible to seek to avoid a prospect that would be deleterious to the company, including the prospect of substantial amounts of taxation. The court further held that the repayments could be made in the form of assets other than cash. It was considered to be irrelevant that the assets exceeded the nominal amount of the reduction. The assets need not be valued. According to Lord Radcliffe, the public interest only required that the liquidity position of the company be strong. Other allowable reductions may include compromising a bona fide claim—that is, choosing not to pursue a legal remedy, through litigation or otherwise, that is available to the company and would be financially advantageous to it.[85]

REVIEW QUESTIONS

1 Why might a company find it necessary or desirable to reduce its issued capital?
2 In what ways may such a reduction be accomplished, and what legal proceedings are involved?
3 What matters are relevant to the exercise of the court's discretion where a reduction is sought?
4 Why is the location of the onus of proof important in this area?

Financial assistance in the purchase of the shares of the company

This area is highly contentious and routinely politicised. The approach taken to this area is very much a function of the overall political theory held by the government of the day. The law in this area was substantially reformed in both 1980 and 1981. It should be noted that the prohibition on giving financial assistance does not exist in the USA, despite the fact that the law in most United States jurisdictions is stricter overall and such restrictions are frequently attacked as inefficient and unnecessarily restrictive. It is, however, significant to note that, while the current Australian law allows a company to purchase its own shares subject to meeting the

---

83 [1949] AC 462 at 486–7.
84 [1951] AC 625.
85 For a further judicial analysis of this area, see *Re Elders IXL Ltd* (1985) 9 ACLR 280.

requirements of s. 206AAA and the following subsections, the ban on giving financial assistance in the purchase of the shares of the company has not been abolished.

The statutory rules are derived from the common law and first surfaced in *Trevor v. Whitworth*.[86] The company was a manufacturing company. Provisions in the company's articles allowed it to purchase its own shares. A shareholder applied to the liquidator for the balance owed to him by the company on such a purchase. The House of Lords held that it was illegal for a company to purchase its own shares on the ground that it was essential to protect the funds upon which creditors relied. This view prevailed. Remarkably, the rationale in *Trevor v. Whitworth* remains the basis for the legislative provisions, despite the fact that it is now lawful for a company to purchase its own shares provided that it complies with the relevant provisions. In spite of the legislative changes, the bar on giving financial assistance remains firmly in place. The provision was first enacted in the *United Companies Act 1961* (UK), s. 67. The current provisions are ss. 129–30. The Green Committee (in the United Kingdom) described the practice it sought to curb in the following terms:

1   A syndicate agrees to purchase sufficient shares to gain control from existing shareholders.
2   Bridging finance is required to complete the purchase.
3   The new controllers appoint their own board.
4   The syndicate nominees on the board loan the syndicate sufficient funds to cover the bridging finance.[87]

In the view of the committee, such practices offended against the spirit of *Trevor v. Whitworth*. While this is the 'received wisdom' in this area, we need to ask whether the restrictions are necessary and whether they can be justified. Where a company purchases its own shares (as is now allowed), such shares have no value in liquidation. Giving financial assistance only reduces the available assets if the transaction disadvantages the company—that is, if the transaction is not one that would have been entered by independent parties dealing at arm's length. Whether or not the available assets are reduced is a question of fact. Relevant considerations undoubtedly include the interest rate on the loan, the security offered, and the documentation. There is no apparent disadvantage if the loan is fully secured and given at proper commercial rates. Where, on the other hand, there is no security, or the security that is offered is overvalued or insufficient and the rate is significantly less than would apply in a commercial transaction, the position is very different. It follows that disadvantage arises if, and only if, the loan in question is made without appropriate security, is made at below market rates of interest, or is undocumented.

The leading Australian case on the requirement that capital be maintained is *ANZ Executors & Trustee Co. Ltd v. Qintex Australia Ltd*.[88] This case was part of

---

86   (1887) 12 AC 409 (CA).
87   Company Law Amendment Committee (the 'Green Committee'), *Report 1925–26*, Cmd 2657, HMSO, London, 1926, para. 25.
88   (1990) 2 ACSR 676.

the litigation resulting from the collapse of the Qintex group. Qintex had borrowed more than $185 million on the strength of three unsecured notes. The trust deeds under which the notes were issued contained a clause under which Qintex agreed to procure any of its ninety-five subsidiaries to become guarantors in respect of the debts under the deeds. After the collapse of the parent company, the ANZ sought to enforce the covenants. The subsidiaries were also insolvent, but in the case of some of the subsidiaries, the available assets may have exceeded the liabilities. When the ANZ argued that Qintex could compel the subsidiaries (which were not wholly owned) to execute the guarantees, the Supreme Court of Queensland responded in this way:

> But a shareholder's freedom to exercise his vote as he pleases does not mean that in law he can accomplish everything that takes his fancy. The right to vote is, it is true, a species of property that can be exercised at will, and it may confer control over the affairs and property of the company; but it does not follow that the holder may always do whatever he likes with the corporate assets …
>
> For this reason there are some things that shareholders cannot do. Quite apart from specific statutory prohibition, they cannot authorise dividends to be paid out of capital; or the company to purchase its own shares; or the unrestricted return of capital to shareholders …
>
> If an insolvent company may not properly give assets to its members, it is difficult to see why it should be able to give them to anyone else.[89]

The current provisions provide for a consent procedure to soften the strictures somewhat (Corporations Law, s. 205(10)). The prohibition on the provision of financial assistance in the purchase of shares contains three basic elements:

1 'directly or indirectly giving assistance for the purpose of, or in connection with', the acquisition of shares or units of shares, whether proposed or actual
2 giving direct or indirect assistance in connection with the acquisition of shares or units of shares, whether proposed or actual
3 lending money directly or indirectly on the security of shares in the company.

Within the terms of the section, acquisition is wider than purchase (s. 205(16)). This represents an extension of the previous legislation. The legislation incorporates shares and units of shares, options, and all rights, whether of a legal or an equitable nature. The provisions of s. 205(2) apply whether what is involved is the making of a loan, the giving of a guarantee, the provision of security, or the release of an obligation (s. 205(2)). The existence of a subsidiary–holding company relationship must be determined on the date that assistance is given (s. 205(1)(c)(ii)).[90]

Courts have adopted two different interpretive paradigms when addressing provisions such as s. 205(1)(c)(ii). The classic approach—adopted in the United Kingdom in *Belmont Finance Corp. Ltd v. Williams Furniture Ltd (No. 2)*[91]—seeks to

---

89   (1990) 2 ACSR 676 at 682–4.

90   See also *Bond Corp. Holdings Ltd v. White Industries Ltd* [1980] 2 NSWLR 351.

91   [1980] 1 All ER 393.

determine whether or not the provision of assistance 'enabled' the transaction to be moved forward. This approach is often referred to in the literature as the 'wide' approach. If the 'assistance', however provided, enabled the transaction, whether in whole or in part, then the transaction falls within the provision. The second interpretative paradigm examines whether or not the giving of assistance has 'impoverished' the company. The impoverishment approach is much narrower.

The classic example of the impoverishment approach is the New Zealand case *Re Wellington Publishing Company Ltd.*[92] Following a successful takeover, the new board of directors authorised the payment of a dividend to shareholders. The dividend was properly paid, the company enjoying a significant profit. The dividends received by the new directors were then used to pay for the shares that they had purchased. The legislation in New Zealand, as in Australia (Corporations Law, s. 205(8)), makes an exception for assistance given in the form of a dividend, and this manoeuvre was, therefore, entirely legal. In this context, it is important to distinguish between the legality and the fiscal propriety of the dividend. The law, it should be remembered, allows some dividends that no accountant would consider proper. For example, the law permits the payment of dividends out of current revenue profits without making good prior revenue losses. The law also tolerates the failure to make provision for the loss or depreciation of fixed assets, allowing a dividend to be paid upon the basis of profits derived from the revaluation of those assets. The dividends in *Re Wellington* were, however, 'normal'—that is, they arose out of profits in the ordinary way. It was held that the transaction involved did not constitute providing financial assistance in the purchase of shares in the company. It is important to be aware that this decision is extremely easy to distinguish in the following respects:

1   The company was clearly solvent after payment of the dividend.
2   There were no minority shareholders involved.
3   The finding by the judge that the payment of a dividend did not ordinarily constitute assistance constituted a substantial concession.
4   The dividend was declared out of a revenue reserve.

The new section was considered in *Re Myer Retail Investments Ltd.*[93] The decision broke little new ground, the court simply accepting the view of McGurney J in *E. H. Dey Pty Ltd v. Dey*[94] that the word 'otherwise' was to be given its natural meaning: 'in any other way'. It follows that 'otherwise' was not to be read *ejusdem generis* to loans, guarantees, and so on. The prohibition on the giving of assistance is, therefore, extremely broad, the legislation being intended to capture all possible avenues through which assistance may be given.

Section 205(3)–(4) emphasises that a substantial purpose is all that is needed. Thus it covers the situation where A Ltd enters a transaction with B Ltd and part of the purpose is to put A in funds to acquire shares. Subsection (4) requires the

---

92   [1973] 1 NZLR 133.
93   (1983) 1 ACLC 990 at 995ff.
94   [1966] VR 464.

company to be aware of the transaction—that is, the appropriate corporate organ must have actual knowledge of the transaction. Constructive knowledge is not sufficient. These provisions are difficult to reconcile with s. 185(1), which provides that no company may be a member of its own holding company. The structure of s. 185(1) would appear to make an acquisition of this nature void, while breaches of s. 205 appear to be voidable rather than void.[95] The conflict was discussed in *Bond Corp. Pty Ltd v. White Industries Ltd.*

The exception in s. 205(8) is new. It covers those companies whose ordinary business concerns the lending of money and situations where the loan is made to facilitate the acquisition of shares by employees. Section 205(10)–(14) provides a consent procedure. While the procedure appears useful (if expensive), it is not frequently used.

Where s. 205 is breached, corporate officers involved in the breach are guilty of an offence carrying a penalty of $10 000 or 2 years' imprisonment. The current provision differs from its precursors in the Uniform Companies Acts[96] because the present provision explicitly exempts the company (as distinct from its officers) from criminal liability.[97] The penalty is $10 000 or 2 years in prison. The officers involved in the contravention are also required to compensate those who suffer loss as a consequence of the contravention. It is important to be aware that this includes compensation to the company where it suffers harm or loss as a consequence of breach. Relief under s. 1318 may be available if the officers involved in a contravention can establish that they acted honestly and reasonably, and ought fairly to be excused.

The civil consequences of a breach are identified by s. 206. This section substantially reforms the previous legislation. The former legislation often operated to the disadvantage of the company because it was silent on the contractual consequences of the provision. The practical consequence of this, as shown by *Dressy Frocks v. Bosch*,[98] was that all such contracts were void for illegality. As a consequence, the company could not sue to recover the moneys loaned under such contracts. The current legislation makes the loans voidable at the option of the company, save where it is necessary to avoid them to protect innocent third parties. From a practical perspective, it is important to note that the rights and liabilities provided for by the section are expressly stated to be in addition to, and not in derogation from, any

---

95 On this point, and the potential conflict, see *Bond Corp. Pty Ltd v. White Industries Ltd.* On the interpretation of s. 185 and its precursors, see *Dressy Frocks Pty Ltd v. Bosch* (1951) 51 SR (NSW) 390; *Shearer Transport Co. Pty Ltd v. McGrath* [1956] VLR 316; *E. H. Dey Pty Ltd v. Dey.*

96 See various Uniform Companies Acts listed in the Table of Statutes under each Australian state or territory.

97 Section 205(5) provides that the company does not incur criminal liability by virtue of a breach of the provision. Under the former provision—Uniform Companies Act, s. 67—both the company and its responsible officers incurred criminal penalties. Section 205(5) provides that every officer who aids, abets, or induces the contravention, who is in any way knowingly concerned with it, or who is a party to it is liable. See *Mudge v. Wolstenholme* [1965] VR 707, in which O'Brien J noted that knowing contravention simply requires that the officers be aware of the facts upon which the contravention depends. The officers need not be aware that those facts constitute a breach of the provision.

98 (1951) 51 SR (NSW) 390.

other rights and liabilities that may be available under the common law
(s. 206(15)). As was made clear by *Belmont v. Williams*, among the remedies available may be those afforded by the tort of conspiracy. A constructive trust may also
arise in appropriate circumstances.[99]

REVIEW QUESTIONS

1 What is the legal basis for the prohibition against giving financial assistance
   in the purchase of the shares of the company?
2 What sorts of transaction does the statutory prohibition encompass?
3 Read the relevant case law and consider whether such practices ought to be
   allowed. Do you think that the present provisions represent the most effective
   and efficient way of dealing with the problem?
4 What is the distinction between a void transaction and one that is merely
   voidable?

Dividends

In company law, dividends are defined as payments made out of profits. While
the law specifies that dividends may only be paid out of profits, no legal controls
exist—apart, perhaps, from s. 260(1)(a)(ii) or the doctrine of 'fraud on a minority'. In *Re Weedman's Ltd*,[100] Lucas J observed that, where the question of the propriety of a failure to declare dividends comes before the courts, the real issue is
whether the failure can be characterised as a breach of commercial morality. Thus,
even where profits are available, the mere failure to declare a dividend will not be
sufficient to establish that such failure was in any way improper. Something more
is needed—for example, a failure to pay a dividend coupled with extravagant
director's remuneration or the payment of large bonuses to favoured employees.
The question is only likely to arise in closely held companies where individuals are
unable to readily extricate their investments from the corporate structure. In a
public company, persistent failure to declare dividends is likely to have an adverse
effect upon share prices. Because of market pressures, it is far more common for
public companies to pay dividends in questionable circumstances than it is for a
dividend to be improperly withheld.[101]

The former taxation law encouraged the proprietors of private companies
to eschew payment of dividends, despite the availability of profits. There were substantial taxation advantages to be had in allowing profits to accumulate and then

---

99   See *Consul Development Pty Ltd v. DPC Estates Ltd* (1975) 132 CLR 373 for discussion of the requirements of a
     constructive trust in Australian law. A constructive trust was also available in *Belmont v. Williams*.
100 [1974] Qd R 377.
101 The law does, however, require that the financial statements of the company accord with the appropriate
     accounting standards. See s. 298(1) and the AASB standards.

winding up the company and distributing the surplus among shareholders.[102] The present taxation legislation imposes specific requirements upon private companies regarding dividend payments. These requirements are designed to limit the usefulness of these companies as tax shelters and to curb the practice of salting away the profits and distributing them when the company is liquidated. Once we move beyond measures implemented to limit the success of tax-avoidance schemes, dividend policy is an internal matter and one requiring the exercise of commercial judgment. In normal circumstances, the court will not intervene.[103] The articles typically make provision for the allocation of dividends. The sample articles provided by table A empower the general meeting to declare dividends and determine the appropriate level.[104] The form adopted in table A has proved unpopular with most companies, and it is more usual for the power to be vested in the board of directors.

Dividends may only be paid out of profits. However, the term 'profits' is notoriously flexible in corporate practice. In *Australasian Oil Exploration Ltd v. Lachberg*,[105] a company in serious financial difficulty agreed to sell its most valuable asset—its whole shareholding in a second company—to a third company formed to acquire the shareholding. The terms provided that the shares were to be acquired for their cash value, which was less than their asset value. The price was met through the issue of shares by the purchaser to the vendor upon certain conditions. The agreement was held void in that it constituted an unauthorised distribution of the capital of the vendor among the shareholders and was, therefore, *ultra vires*. The High Court held that a company has no capital profits available to pay a dividend unless there has been an accretion to paid-up capital. Counsel argued that,

> if a company engages in a transaction whereby it disposes, otherwise than in the course of its trading or business activities, of a single capital asset for a price in excess of the value at which that asset stands in its books, it may lawfully distribute the casual profit so made among its shareholders whatever the capital position of the company might otherwise be. [Dixon CJ, and McTiernan & Taylor JJ rejected this argument, stating that it] is enough on this point to say that a company has no capital profits available for dividend purposes unless upon a balance of account it appears that there has been an accretion to the paid up capital.[106]

---

102   Here, of course, we are referring to the 'bottom of the harbour' schemes of the early 1980s. Before the introduction of the current capital gains tax regime, it was more tax effective for high-income earners to allow profits to accumulate rather than to distribute them in the form of a dividend. When a substantial fund had accumulated, the company was liquidated and the profit remaining after all accounts were settled would simply be distributed as 'surplus', thus escaping the taxation net. A new company could then be established and the process repeated.

103   See, for example, *Re G. Jeffrey (Men's Store) Pty Ltd*. While the court agreed that the plaintiff shareholder was locked in, it considered that his only real complaint was based upon dividend policy and that dividend policy was predicated upon proper commercial considerations. It followed that he could not recover. A similar approach was taken in *Re a Company Pty Ltd; Thomas v. H. W. Thomas Ltd* (1984) 2 ACLC 610.

104   Table A, art. 86(1)–(2).

105   (1958) 101 CLR 119.

106   (1958) 101 CLR 119 at 133. See also Corporations Law, ss. 191, 201. Dividends are only to be paid out of profits or pursuant to s. 191 in the form of bonus shares. Section 202 is also relevant here, but only applies where construction must be completed before the commencement of profit-making activity. If dividends are paid that exceed allowable profits, s. 201(2) provides that the officers responsible are guilty of a breach and are liable to the creditors of the company up to the amount that the dividends exceed available profits.

The real difficulty arises from the amplitude given to the term 'profits'. In *Blackburn v. Industrial Equity Ltd*,[107] a company declared dividends, including a special distribution that involved a cash payment to the parent company and a share issue to other shareholders. This was invalidated on the basis that the payment represented a dividend for the year ending 30 June 1975 and the company lacked sufficient operating profit for the relevant year. It was immaterial that ample funds would have been available had the company revalued its assets. In addition, the court deemed it improper that the company distinguished among its shareholders.

A similar situation arose in *Marra Developments Ltd v. Rofe*.[108] A dividend was declared and fell due on 16 December 1974. After declaration of the dividend, but before payment, the company revalued its pastoral properties downward. The value of the shares was written down by £21 220 117. As a consequence of the revaluation, the accounts showed accumulated losses. The court held that, at the time the dividend was declared, the accounts revealed that sufficient funds were available. The dividend was properly declared out of profits. There was no obligation on the company to have regard to the next accounting period. The directors might have sought a declaration from the court that the dividend declaration was void, but they could not elect the dividend as a debt that the company need not pay. Two principles emerged from this decision:

1 It is not necessary that profits be available at the date when a dividend falls due to be paid. Unavailability of profits at this date will not convert a validly declared dividend into a payment out of capital.

2 Despite the fact that the payment of a dividend is postponed to the interests of creditors during liquidation, this does not affect the position while the company is still carrying on business. A dividend that has been validly declared but not paid represents a debt owed to the shareholders.

It is important to understand that the term 'profits' is only meaningful in the context of the accounts of the company. Corporations Law, ss. 316 and 326 cover the responsibility of the company to present annual accounts; however, the legislation does not impose accounting methods. Most companies, although by no means all, value their fixed assets by the historic cost method—that is, by their cost price. Other assets, such as stock in trade, require different modes of valuation, and the choice of method may determine whether the accounts of the company show a profit or a loss for the year in question.

The legal nature of the term 'profits' came before the courts in *Re Spanish Prospecting Company Ltd*.[109] Here P and V were servants of the company. They were entitled to a fixed sum, which might only be drawn out of profits. In liquidation, P and V sought payment in full out of the surplus available for distribution. According to Fletcher-Moulton LJ, 'profit' implies a comparison between the state of the business at two dates. It represents the amount of gain in a year. Thus it involves a

---

107   (1980) CLC 40-064.
108   [1977] 2 NSWLR 616.
109   [1911] 1 Ch 92.

comparison of assets, and this means that the assets must be valued and not merely enumerated. As His Lordship stated,

> Even if the assets were identical at the two periods it would by no means follow that there had been neither gain nor loss … A stock of fashionable goods is worth much more than the same stock when the fashion has changed. And to a lesser degree but no less certainly the same considerations must apply to buildings, plant and other fixed assets used in the business …
>
> To follow out the strict consequences of the legal conception in making out the accounts of the year would often be very difficult in practice … Hence certain assumptions have become so customary in drawing up balance-sheets and profit and loss accounts that it may almost be said to require special circumstances to induce parties to depart from them. For instance, it is usual to exclude gains and losses arising from causes not directly connected with the business of the company, such, for instance, as a rise in the market value of land occupied by the company. The value assigned to trade buildings and plant is usually fixed according to an arbitrary rule by which they are originally taken at their actual cost and are assumed to have depreciated by a certain percentage each year … These, however, are merely variations of practice by individuals. They rest on no settled principle.[110]

The strict meaning given here is, as His Lordship acknowledged, rare in actual accounts inasmuch as it incorporates gains and losses not directly concerned with the business of the company—for example, an increase in the value of the real property of the company, or a diminution in the value of its stock in trade because the merchandise has become outdated. There are many practical problems. The valuation of stock in trade and the appreciation and depreciation of fixed assets pose vexed questions, and there is no general agreement about the 'proper' or even the most 'appropriate' approach to valuation. There is no standard method. In general, if total assets are compared, any increase can be regarded as a profit.

There is no legal requirement to make up for lost fixed assets or for losses of a prior accounting period before a profit is declared. Even some commercial people regard this standard as excessively permissive. The early legal doctrine suggested that the ruling principle was maintenance of capital and that a dividend could not be paid if its effect was to reduce the assets below the level of liabilities. This came to be known as the rule in *Flitcroft's* case. Today this attitude—which was basically protective of the interests of creditors—has been replaced by one reflective of *laissez faire* philosophy.

The modern approach emerged in *Lee v. Neuchatel Asphalte Co. Ltd.*[111] A company had been formed to work wasting assets[112]—specifically, asphalt mines. The

---

110   [1911] 1 Ch 92 at 98–101.

111   (1899) 41 Ch D 1.

112   As should be clear from the context, a wasting asset is one that is liable to be exhausted by the company's business activities. Extractive industries characteristically involve wasting assets, in that the company's core enterprise diminishes in value each year as the reserves are exhausted. Eventually all that remains is the obligation (today often imposed by government) to restore the site upon which the activity occurred.

plaintiff argued that a reserve fund established by the articles should be used to replace wasting assets, although the articles did not so specify. The argument failed. Lord Justice Lindley held that to insist on such a rule would 'paralyze the trade of the country'. The law did not specify how profits were to be calculated, and there was no requirement to make up lost capital. The proper course fell for determination by commercial people, a classic example of judicial deference to commercial decision-making. His Lordship continued:

> As I pointed out in the course of the argument, and I repeat now, suppose a company is formed to start a daily newspaper; supposing it sinks £250 000 before the receipts from sales and advertisements equal the current expenses, and supposing it then goes on, is it to be said that the company must come to a stop, or that it cannot divide profits until it has replaced its £250 000, which has been sunk in building up a property which if put up for sale would perhaps not yield £10 000? That is a business matter left to business men. If they think their prospects of success are considerable, so long as they pay their creditors, there is no reason why they should not go on and divide profits, so far as I can see, although every shilling of the capital may be lost. What it means is simply this: that if you want to find out how you stand, whether you have lost your money or not, you must bring your capital into account somehow or other. But supposing at the winding up of the concern the capital is all gone, and the creditors are paid, and there is nothing to divide, who is the debtor? No one is debtor to any one. If there is any surplus to divide, then, and not before is the company debtor to the shareholders for their aliquot portions of that surplus.[113]

With respect to the proper approach to wasting assets, Lindley LJ commented:

> If a company is formed to acquire and work a property of a wasting nature, for example, a mine, a quarry, or a patent, the capital expended in acquiring the property may be regarded as sunk and gone and if the company retains assets sufficient to pay its debts, it appears to me that there is nothing whatever in the Act to prevent any excess of money obtained by working the property over the cost of working it, from being divided amongst the shareholders, and this in my opinion is true, although some portion of the property itself is sold, and in some sense the capital is thereby diminished.[114]

The effect of the *laissez faire* approach was to undermine the doctrine of maintenance of capital. It should be noted that the approach taken in this case has never been popular with accountants and falls well below generally accepted standards of accounting practice.

A subsequent decision, that in *Bond v. Barrow Haematite Steel Co.*,[115] did little to clarify matters or produce a more sensible approach. In that case, which again involved mining interests, the court relied upon a distinction between fixed capital and circulating capital.[116] The court held—defying both logic and common

---

113   (1889) 41 Ch D 1 at 22–3.
114   (1889) 41 Ch D 1 at 24.
115   [1902] 1 Ch 353.
116   Fixed assets are those that are intended as a permanent or nearly permanent part of the company's infrastructure. Circulating assets are those that are intended to be sold or lent out and replaced with others.

sense, it would seem—that mine leases represented circulating capital, whereas owned mines represented fixed capital. No general principles could be established, and each case must be determined on the basis of expert evidence. According to Farrell LJ, while fixed capital might be sunk and lost, circulating capital must be maintained. No distinction was to be made between realised and estimated loss. The court emphasised that the proposition that dividends must not be paid out of capital, and the proposition that dividends may only be paid out of profits are wholly distinct. A company with a balance to the credit side of its profit–loss account is not bound to apply such balance to an established deficiency in capital assets. No hard and fast rule was possible.

In *Amonia Soda Co. v. Chamberlain*,[117] Swinfen-Eady LJ elaborated upon the distinction between fixed and circulating capital. According to His Lordship, the distinction depended upon the particular nature of the business involved. For example, in a trustee company, the investment fund represented fixed capital. In a manufacturing company, the plant and machinery represented fixed capital. These items were intended to form a permanent part of the company structure. Those assets that were intended to be sold, lent out, and replaced with others were circulating capital. The question of wasting assets, such as mines, was not addressed. According to the Lord Justice, the argument put by the plaintiff—that, although the dividend was paid out of net profits for the accounting period, prior losses had not been made up—was unsound. It could not be said that there were no profits until prior losses had been made up. The directors had no obligation to recoup fixed capital. If there were losses prior to any profits, these were necessarily losses of fixed capital.

A number of the problems involved follow from the fact that the revenue accounts are not understood as continuous, but rather as applying to discrete 1-year periods. The balance sheet is a historic document. While some authority exists that depreciation should be allowed for, the overall picture is far from clear. Further problems accompany any revaluation. For example, it may be questioned whether a company with extensive land holdings should be allowed to revalue its capital assets and, on the basis of that revaluation, declare a dividend. However, where a fixed asset is sold and the profit realised, the profit is available for distribution as dividends, and some argue upon this basis that the same ought to apply upon revaluation, at least where certain controls upon revaluation exist.

Where an asset is sold, different modes of valuation can be used to bring the profit to account. Consider the distinction between historic cost and book valuation. Where real property has been valued by the historic cost method and has been owned by the company for a number of years, the 'profit' realised upon sale is likely to be substantial. Where, on the other hand, book valuation is used and the real property has been revalued regularly (let us say every 5 years), the 'profit' realised upon sale is likely to be much less. Even if two different companies bought land at the same price and realised their investment at the same time and

---

117   [1918] 1 Ch 266.

for the same price, these two modes of valuation would produce dramatically different profit statements.

The argument has been put that, since profit upon sale generates funds available for dividend payment, paper profits from revaluation should do the same. On this point, English and Scottish law diverge. Such dividends are barred by Scottish law, and this approach was favoured by the Jenkins Committee. The English position, and that generally followed in Australia, is typified by *Dimbula Valley (Ceylon) Tea Co. Ltd v. Laurie.*[118] Buckley LJ held that such dividends were permissible, subject to certain controls. The revaluation must be bona fide, the assets in question must not be subject to short-term fluctuations, and the payment must be permitted by the articles. In Australia, *Industrial Equity v. Blackburn*[119] added a further control. The revaluation must be a general revaluation, not one of isolated assets. Further, in revaluation, any decline must be set off against the appreciation realised. While these controls are useful, they do not resolve the underlying conflicts. In particular, given the distinction between fixed and circulating capital, they do little to standardise accounting methods and the inevitable legal ramifications.

REVIEW QUESTIONS

1 What is meant in company law by the term 'profits'?
2 Does this meaning lead to sound judicial reasoning, or is it fundamentally flawed?[120]
3 Consider the distinction between fixed capital and circulating capital upon which much of the early case law was based? Is this distinction logical? Is it possible to make a sensible distinction between fixed capital and circulating capital?
4 How might this area of the law be reformed statutorily? What factors must be considered if any such reform is to be workable?

---

118   [1961] 1 Ch 353.
119   (1977) 137 CLR 567.
120   In this context, it might be helpful to read L. C. B. Gower, *Principles of Modern Company Law*, 4th edn, Stevens & Sons, London, 1979, p. 513.

13

ENTER THE MAZE:
TAKEOVER REGULATION

In law, 'takeover' refers to a change in the control of a company. A takeover may or may not be a consensual transaction. It is not always a 'marriage'. Rather, the threat of a change in control frequently attracts resistance from the directors of the 'target' company. After all, customarily, they stand to lose their positions. The popular language of takeovers—for instance, as used in the media—is the language of combat. We speak of the 'takeover battle', the 'hostile bid', 'knights', 'raiders', 'targets', and 'defensive strategies'. These are images of violence. This is a discourse that reflects a Hobbesian conception of a competitive and hostile environment. It is also an extraordinarily colourful language, perhaps the most colourful in all of commercial law:

> The ABC Company issues 'golden parachutes' to its executives and pursues a 'scorched earth' policy by selling its 'crown jewels' and issuing a 'poison pill' to its shareholders, all in an attempt to foil a takeover bid by Mr Z, a well-known 'shark' and 'greenmailer' who floats junk bonds with abandon. When Mr Z persists, a white knight, otherwise known as Company X, arrives to fend off the hostile attack.[1]

While the controllers of each company are the primary protagonists, there are often other active players in this battle. Ordinarily, the battle for control is determined by the transfer of shares. As Adolf Berle and Gardiner Means[2] point out, a common characteristic of companies is the separation of ownership and control. In the takeover situation, there is, therefore, often a conflict of interests between the

---

1   J. C. Coffee Jr, L. Lowenstein, & S. Rose-Ackerman, *Knights, Raiders and Targets: The Impact of the Hostile Takeover*, Oxford University Press, New York, 1988, p. 3. Coffee et al. provide a helpful translation of that passage:

> The ABC Company seeks to fend off a hostile takeover by giving its executives generous severance agreements, selling highly profitable divisions, and issuing a security that will permit shareholders other than Mr Z to exchange their shares for a package of securities at a very favorable exchange ratio that may deter a takeover bid. The aggressive Mr Z finances his bid by issuing high-risk debt backed by the assets of the firm he is trying to acquire. He is known as a person who sometimes buys a substantial part of a company and then lets himself be bought out at a higher price by a friendly bidder, such as Company X.

2   A. A. Berle & G. C. Means, *The Modern Corporation and Private Property*, revised edn, Harcourt, Brace and World, New York, 1968.

owners of the company and the company management. The steps that management take to resist the takeover may not ensure the best financial outcome for the shareholders.

Shares are property, and hence wealth. Because property is such a fundamental concern of liberal democracies, the takeover attracts a high degree of government intervention. The State seeks to protect that private right of property, to ensure that shareholders (the property owners) are protected, *inter alia*, from unequal treatment, from inadequate information, and from such wealth-depleting activities as asset-stripping. Regulators, then, seek to control the battlefield on which the takeover war takes place and to determine the legitimacy or otherwise of the tactics:

> There is, as it seems to me, no doubt that a predominant theme of the Code is to ensure that all shareholders in a target company are treated fairly; that all have an opportunity to dispose of their shares to the offeror, whether or not the offer has been directed to them, and if so directed whether or not it has been accepted; and that minority or non-accepting shareholders are no longer faced with the choice of either being 'locked in' to a company under new control, or throwing themselves upon the mercy of the market place to dispose of their shares. So much appears from the provisions of ss. 42 and 43 [equivalent to ss. 701 and 703 of the *Corporations Law 1990*] as they relate to non accepting offerees … [T]hey are given the right to require acquisition of their shares, after the offer has closed, on terms of the takeover offer, if the offeror has not achieved the right of compulsory acquisition on those same terms, and there are elaborate statutory provisions designed to establish the fairness of the offer. The value of the Code to these minority of non-assenting shareholders is that, without this statutory protection, the market might well discount the value of their minority shareholding.[3]

The discourse imagines a vulnerable minority shareholder, but in very many takeovers, that shareholder is an institutional investor or another corporation, which is hardly a powerless entity. In what ways, we might ask, are different groups of minority shareholders vulnerable? To what extent may institutional minority shareholders be active participants in the takeover battle—protagonists whose interests may accord with those of the raider or with those of the target, depending upon the particular circumstances of the case?[4]

But there are other considerations involved in takeovers, apart from the protection of individual (including corporate individual) property rights. Some of these considerations involve Australia's competitiveness and its economic efficiency. If it is, in fact, the case that takeover activity, as a general rule, reduces the number of players in the market, then regulatory regimes may be designed to minimise

---

3   *Mercantile Mutual Life Insurance Co. Ltd v. Actraint No. 85 Pty Ltd (No. 2)* (1990) 8 ACLC 138 at 145 per Jacobs J, considering the policy of the predecessor of Corporations Law, s. 703.

4   As is often the case with regulatory regimes designed to protect 'consumers' (in this case consumers of particular types of investment products), a regulatory regime predicated upon the needs of a hypothetical 'individual shareholder' is likely to provide an unnecessary level of protection where more sophisticated institutional and corporate shareholders are concerned.

takeover activity for reasons other than the protection of minority shareholders. For instance, fewer companies in the market-place may mean less economic competition and increased levels of industrial concentration, which are undesirable for other reasons. Takeovers may also increase managerial efficiency or effect economies of scale.[5] Where the takeover target is poorly managed and/or uncompetitive, takeover activity may enhance productivity overall by eliminating inefficient players from the market. These considerations relate to the various facets of the liberal conception of a free and competitive market.

Other considerations relate to the national economic interest. One such consideration involves the extent to which foreign interests should be permitted to own and or control corporations. As, increasingly, we move into the era of the 'global market', international players may wish to gain a foothold in Australian industry through takeover activity. Depending upon the particular industry involved, this may occasion high levels of concern, as is the case with media-ownership. Where this is the case, other regulatory regimes interact with the regulation of takeover activity. Sometimes, popular concern regarding 'foreign ownership' and control arises because the target company is an 'Australian icon', as was the case with Arnott's Biscuits. Where this is the case, popular sentiment will often play a significant, although rarely determinative, role.

There are many tensions here. Not least is the paradox in which business interests demand a 'free and competitive' market (that is, a market free of government intervention), on the one hand, and, on the other, government intervention to protect those same interests from, for example, foreign takeovers.[6] In seeking to accommodate these various tensions, takeovers regulation becomes complex and difficult.[7]

If takeovers are battles, the regulatory scheme has created a strange battlefield. The regulation of takeovers, it has been said, is a statutory maze, and this is true in at least two senses: First, there are a great number of statutory provisions and general law rules that impact upon takeovers. Second, much of the legislative regulation, particularly Corporations Law, ch. 6, is couched in highly prescriptive and complex legal language. Strangely, despite the fact that the everyday language of takeovers is

---

5   What controls are warranted, and how are they best defined and enforced? Various attempts have been made to analyse the effects of takeovers. However, the outcomes tend to vary with the methodology used. Possible approaches include accounting (post-takeover profitability), economic (enterprise efficiency), financial (share-price changes), and managerial (relatedness and diversification studies) approaches. Look, for instance, at the different outcomes in F. McDougall & D. Round, *The Effects of Mergers and Takeovers in Australia*, Information Australia, Melbourne, 1986 (accounting approach), and S. Bishop, P. Dodd, & R. Office, *Australian Takeovers: The Evidence 1972–1985*, Centre for Independent Studies, Sydney, 1987 (financial).

6   It is worth noting that business demands for deregulation are frequently muted in this context, at least on the part of local players. Overseas interests may well complain loudly about an uneven playing field.

7   Takeovers may have social costs as well. Certainly it has been suggested that they are capable of paralysing industry and that this has enormous flow-on costs. Arguments in favour of minimum regulation suggest that takeovers are very useful in culling 'weak' and inefficient management and replacing it with strong, entrepreneurial management. This has not always proved to be the case in Australia, where takeover targets have been targeted because they provide a ready source of liquid funds that can be used to finance further takeover bids. Where the target company is seen simply as a source of cash, it represents an industry that is lost to the market-place.

the language of battle, this is not the language used in the statutes or cases. Rather, the inherently adversarial nature of the takeover is masked by a wealth of passive and abstract legalisms: 'relevant interest', 'associate', 'entitlement', 'substantial interest', 'acquisition of shares'.

The metaphor of the maze, then, is apt. But there are many types of maze. What maze image best describes the takeover battlefield created by regulators? Is it a maze of mirrors, such as you might find in an old fun park, at once both gaudy and sinister? As individual combatants step into the maze, they are confronted by endless reflections reaching back infinitely. Some of the mirrors distort their image, now making them smaller, now taller, as they make their way through. Or is the maze that of the laboratory, a tiny city of white walls filled with rats? Scientists make the maze ever more complicated. Yet, each time they do, the combatants, now laboratory rats, learn, grow smarter, and find their way out. Or is the regulation of takeovers best likened to a garden maze of yew hedges, redolent of Victorian decadence? The combatants enter its neat, precise clipped hedges, which are at once indicative of obsessive regulation and of concealment—hiding the dark and the bizarre.

Recently, proposals have been put forward to simplify the takeovers provisions. The objects of these proposals are to develop takeover provisions that are easier to understand and apply, to reduce compliance costs, to improve information about takeovers, and to ensure that compulsory acquisitions are easier. Will these proposals be effective in reducing the current state of complexity? Choose your maze, and begin to map your way out. The centre of the maze is ch. 6 of the Corporations Law. Branching out from the centre are the other provisions of the Corporations Law, the general-law duties of directors, the *Foreign Acquisitions and Takeovers Act 1995* (Cth), the *Trade Practices Act 1974* (Cth) (TPA), the Australian Securities Commission (ASC) Listing Rules, and various other legislative provisions. Begin!

REVIEW QUESTION

In what ways could one achieve control of a company without a takeover? In what situations may a takeover be effected without a transfer of shares?

The centre of the maze: Corporations Law, ch. 6

At the centre of the maze are the complex provisions of the Corporations Law, ch. 6, the primary objective of which is to regulate the process of change in control by transfer of shares in such a way as to protect the non-controlling shareholders of target companies. Often, those who seek a controlling interest in a company will pay a premium for that control. Berle argues that the value of the control function of a corporation should be treated as 'belonging' to the corporation—that is, in his view, 'control is an asset'.[8] If we accept Berle's premise, it becomes possible to argue that a controlling shareholder occupies a fiduciary position and should not, because of that position, be able to obtain a control premium for her or his own use. Alternatively, it could also be argued that a controlling shareholder has a duty to the other shareholders to provide them with an *equal opportunity* to sell before the controlling shareholder sells her or his shares. The latter argument was originally one of the primary rationales for the regulatory scheme imposed by ch. 6:

16   We agree with the general principle that if a natural person or corporation wishes to acquire control of a company by making a general offer to acquire all the shares, or a proportion sufficient to enable him to exercise voting control, limitations should be placed on his freedom of action so far as is necessary to ensure:

(i)   that his identity is known to the shareholders and directors;

(ii) that the shareholders and directors have a reasonable time in which to consider the proposal;

(iii) that the offeror is required to give such information as is necessary to enable the shareholders to form a judgment on the merits of the proposal and in particular, where the offeror offers shares or interests in a corporation, that the kind of information which would ordinarily be provided in a prospectus is furnished to the offeree shareholders;

(iv) that so far as is practicable, each shareholder should have an equal opportunity to participate in the benefits offered.[9]

A number of justifications can be given for this policy. First, it can be argued that small shareholders are particularly at risk of being excluded from participation in the control premium, because control of the target may be transferred when the bidder purchases the holdings of a small number of large shareholders at premium prices, and small shareholders may have no opportunity to sell. Second, after control in shares is transferred, corporate business may be conducted in a way that is disadvantageous to minority shareholder interests. Third, if the bidder does not acquire all the shares, the business is worth more than the bidder has paid and therefore the acquisition is partially financed by those shareholders from whom the bidder does not buy. Finally, it may be argued that the sale of shares allows the investor to realise a profit on the investment, and every shareholder should share proportionately in that profit.

---

8   Berle & Means, p. 216. For discussions of the issue of the 'control premium', see *Perlman v. Feldman* (1955) 219F 2d 173; 349 US 952; *James v. Ahmanson & Co.* (1969) 460 P 2d 464 (Cal Sup Ct). See also W. D. Andrews, 'The Stockholder's Right to Equal Opportunity in the Sale of Shares' (1965) 78 Harv LR 505. On the subject of partial offers, see J. C. Coffee 'Partial Justice: Balancing Fairness and Efficiency in the Conduct of Partial Takeover Offers' (1985) 3 CSLJ 216; and Companies and Securities Law Review Committee (CSLRC), *Report to the Ministerial Council on Partial Takeover Bids*, CSLRC, Sydney, 1985. The sense of this premise is impossible to deny. Within the corporate setting, control is often the ultimate prize. In takeover battles, the controlling shareholders will be courted. If they hold out, they may be able to demand a substantial premium for their shares.

9   Company Law Advisory Committee to the Standing Committee of Attorneys-General (Eggleston Committee), *Second Interim Report*, Commonwealth Government Printer, 1969, p. 26.

Despite the fact that equality of opportunity theory is enshrined in the legislation (see, for instance, Corporations Law, ss. 703, 731, and 733(d)), there has been a gradual shift in the overall legislative approach from equality of opportunity to formal equality since the adoption of the recommendations of the Eggleston Committee in the *Companies (Acquisitions of Shares) Code*. In general terms, the primary emphasis of the legislation is still to protect shareholders in a takeover target from unfair treatment. This is done by ensuring that shareholders are given information enabling them to make an informed decision on whether to accept the offer, and by ensuring that they are given an equal opportunity to accept the offer, having been given sufficient time to think about it. Provisions directed towards these ends attempt to map equality of opportunity onto the battlefield. More recently, provisions have been enacted with a very different goal in mind: that of ensuring that shareholders actually receive formally *equal* treatment. Thus procedures have been developed to prevent more powerful shareholders (often directors and controllers, along with institutional or more substantial investors) from obtaining higher prices than other shareholders. Provisions have been enacted that require that a higher price be extended to all those accepting under a formal takeover offer. The legislative framework regulating the conduct of takeovers ultimately requires that no person should gain a controlling interest without offering to acquire the remaining shares.[10]

REVIEW QUESTIONS

1 Do you agree with the equality of opportunity argument? If there is a tendency for a controller to treat minority shareholders unfairly, is it best to prevent the acquisition from occurring, or would it be preferable to strengthen the minority's remedies for oppression?

2 Is it fair to impose restrictions on the proprietary rights of controlling shareholders? If a controlling shareholder has secured control by means of entrepreneurial talent and expense, should the legislation prevent that individual (or entity) from selling control at a premium, given that it was possible for all other shareholders to exercise the same degree of initiative? Does it make a difference to your answer that many minority shareholders are, in fact, often powerful corporations or institutional investors? Why or why not?

Since the late 1960s,[11] a hybrid method has been used in attempts to ensure equality of opportunity in the Australian context. This method is at once a mixture of equity and public law elements, a blend of the United States and British

---

10 For a discussion of the movement from equality of opportunity to formal equality, see L. A. Bebchuk, 'Towards Undistorted Choice and Equal Treatment in Corporate Takeovers' (1985) 98 Harv LR 1693.

11 The first serious attempt at the regulation of takeovers followed the Eggleston Committee's *Second Interim Report* in 1969.

approaches. Before enactment of the uniform companies legislation in 1961–62, the early Australian laws on takeovers were based on 'pause and publicity', and were largely ineffective. The Uniform Companies Acts themselves had only two sections dealing directly with takeovers: ss. 184 and 185. The legislation required a bidder to give the target company prescribed information about the proposed offers, so that the target company could inform its shareholders about the board's response. This legislation regulated 'offers' or 'invitations' outside the ordinary course of stock-exchange trading. Technical interpretations of 'offer' and 'invitation' allowed bidders to make unregulated announcements, and shareholders were stampeded into rushed sales. There was concern about, *inter alia*, avoidance of these sections.

Following the Eggleston Committee's *Second Interim Report* in 1969, s. 184 was repealed and twenty-five new sub-sections (s. 180 A–Y) were inserted into the Uniform Companies Act. The new statutory takeover procedure, however, did not apply to purchases made in the ordinary course of trading on a stock exchange. Thus, the legislation inadvertently encouraged 'dawn raids'. In a 'dawn raid', the takeover offeror persuaded key institutional and other large shareholders to sell on-market. This enabled the offeror to accumulate a very large parcel of shares in a short time. Small shareholders did not know what was happening and had no opportunity to tender their shares. Because they occupied a minority position in the company, control had passed at a premium in which they had no chance to participate. This undermined the equality of opportunity that the Act had tried to put into place.

In an attempt to remedy this and other perceived defects of the Uniform Companies Act, the Companies (Acquisition of Shares) Code came into effect on 1 July 1981.[12] But the Companies (Acquisitions of Shares) Code was itself amended even before it came into operation. In a harbinger of what was to come, the drafted legal rules had become so complex that they had to be tempered by vesting a series of discretions in the National Companies and Securities Commission (NCSC). The legislation was further amended on no less than eight occasions between 1981 and 1987.

The corporate regulators attempted, in the Companies (Acquisitions of Shares) Code, to blend the prescriptive United States scheme with the self-regulatory approach taken in the United Kingdom. There were, however, a number of criticisms of the Companies (Acquisitions of Shares) Code. It made takeovers too difficult and allowed too many opportunities for defensive tactics. Thus, it was argued, inefficient management might be protected from competition, and the detention of valuable resources in inefficient industries could be sustained. Furthermore, the Code sought to regulate primarily through extravagantly detailed provisions (that is, through an extremely formalistic black-letter law approach). Such an approach is doomed to failure because it inevitably encourages the development of ingenious

---

12 Despite its title, it was not a Code in the true sense. While vastly more complex than its predecessor, it did not represent a radical rethink of the nature of the problem and the possible solutions, but an attempt to blend two very different types of regulatory regime.

devices, which can be and often are successfully used to evade the provisions. The tendency to invite avoidance is exacerbated in that the complexity and detail of the scheme discourages judicial creativity, as does the absence of any apparent space for the exercise of discretion by the courts. Inevitably, it is argued, such a scheme encourages narrow judicial interpretation. As a consequence, any response to changing conditions can only come by way of legislative action. This encourages a legislative cycle in which each new flurry of amendment offers little more than a belated attempt to eliminate the 'loopholes' discovered by those seeking to evade regulation. This may be contrasted with jurisdictions where the primary elements are discretionary (for example, the United Kingdom).

Despite these criticisms, the basic structure of the Companies (Acquisitions of Shares) Code has been preserved in the Corporations Law, ch. 6. The Corporations Law modified the Code principally by establishing the Corporations and Securities Panel, which may, on the application of the ASC, declare an acquisition or conduct to be unacceptable. This power had earlier resided in the ASC.[13] Establishment of the Corporations and Securities Panel was necessitated by ongoing criticism of the fact that the previous regulator was empowered to declare certain acquisitions and conduct unacceptable as well as to investigate and to prosecute corporate misconduct. This blurring of prosecutorial and judicial functions was believed by many to be incompatible with the adversarial context in which Australian corporate regulation operates and at variance with established common-law principles.

Regulators have attempted to confer explicit and highly specific legal rights on the parties involved in a takeover, rather than to rely on the uncertain application of the self-regulatory principles of a Code. Discretion to waive or modify the takeover rules (and to declare 'unacceptable' certain kinds of acquisition and conduct that may not literally transgress the letter of the law) was vested in the ASC and the Corporations and Securities Panel in order to meet the need for regulatory flexibility. The principal discretions are contained in ss. 728, 730,[14] and 732 (see also ss. 644(3) and (4)).[15] The ASC may also intervene in any proceedings relating to any matter arising under the Corporations Law (s. 1330).

In a recent proposal, the Attorney-General has suggested changes to the current regime.[16] Under the present regime, one weapon against a hostile takeover that a target company or rival bidder has is to seek a merits review by the Administrative

---

13 Under s. 733, the ASC may apply to the Corporations and Securities Panel within 90 days for a declaration where it appears that unacceptable circumstances have or may have occurred in relation to the acquisition of shares or as a result of conduct engaged in by a person in relation to shares. The circumstances in which the acquisition or conduct may be declared unacceptable are set out in s. 732. The Panel may make interim orders (ss. 733A and 733B) as well as other orders to protect the rights or interest of persons (s. 734(2)). See *Elders IXL Ltd v. NCSC* (1986) 4 ACLR 465; *Re Titan Hills Australia Ltd* (1992) 10 ACLR 131.

14 The operation of a statutory predecessor of these sections is illustrated by *TNT v. NCSC* (1986) 4 ACLR 624.

15 Like the Securities and Exchange Commission in the USA, the ASC produces policy statements, practice notes, and other material, which indicate how the discretions will be exercised.

16 Corporations Law Simplification Task Force, 'Takeovers—Proposals for Simplification', reproduced in full in (1990) 3 *Australian Corporations and Securities Law Reporter* 803 588.

Appeals Tribunal (AAT) in respect of a decision by the ASC to approve a modification of ch. 6. The Task Force argues that it is undesirable to allow a merits review by the AAT to be used to frustrate hostile takeovers. Thus, the task force suggests that the AAT should be stripped of its jurisdiction to review decisions of the ASC under ss. 728 and 730 where these decisions are made in relation to takeover bids and decisions made under ss. 644 and 733.[17] In addition, the Task Force intends to amend s. 732 to give the Corporations and Securities Panel jurisdiction in cases where relatively small parcels of shares are used to influence the outcome of a battle for corporate control or where a person's exercise of corporate control does not coincide with specific acquisitions of shares:

> Indeed, it is difficult to see why this aspect of the provision has survived this long. Essentially it is a restatement of principles formulated by the Eggleston Committee, which at the time did not envisage that the legislation that was to follow would regulate not only takeovers, but acquisitions of voting shares in general. That being the case, the drafters of the Companies (Acquisition of Shares) Code had either overlooked the fact, or had intended that unacceptable circumstances be limited to situations where large parcels of shares are acquired with a view to gaining control of a company. Whatever the case, there seems to be no reason why the anti-avoidance role of the Panel should not extend to any conduct contrary to the policy objectives of Ch 6.[18]

REVIEW QUESTIONS

1   In *Elders IXL Ltd v. NCSC*,[19] the NCSC argued that the purchase by Hawkins's company of 4.4 per cent in BHP at a time when it was thought that Elders was interested in acquiring a controlling interest in BHP indicated that Hawkins intended to assist Elders against BHP. Thus, it appeared that Elders might in turn assist him in relation to his interest in a company in which they both held shares. The NCSC argued that there had been an unacceptable acquisition and alleged that Hawkins was associated with Elders in connection with the acquisition of BHP shares by Hawkins. This argument was based on the idea that an association may be a proposal in the mind of one person that has not yet been (and may never be) communicated to another. In relation to this argument, Marks J said:

> The purpose of the [Takeovers] Code is to regulate takeover activity. The purpose of [s. 12] is to identify the size of a relevant shareholding for the purposes of the restriction imposed by [s. 615]. Necessarily [s. 12] is concerned with real combinations and real aggregations which, one way or another, truly exist. It is not con-

---

17   This would not, however, affect judicial review under the *Administrative Decisions (Judicial Review) Act 1977*. What it would do is eliminate one defensive tactic and, it may be argued, prevent the manipulation of the merits review process in a manner that is inconsistent with the aims of the merit review process.

18   M. Kollar, 'Takeover Rules to be Made Simpler' (1996) 3 ACN 33.

19   (1986) 10 ACLR 719.

cerned to fantasise combinations by adding to a holding that of another person, who has no real connection, potential or otherwise with the first.

Do you agree? What, if any, dangers do you see in such 'fantasising' by corporate regulators?

2 The Task Force suggests that,

[a]t present, only the ASC can refer a matter to the Panel. This restriction is inherent in the purpose for which it was created. It has the advantage of preventing a party from using a reference to the Panel as a defensive or spoiling strategy. However, it has been suggested that interested parties should have a direct right of access to the Panel. This would lead to the Panel assuming a general role in reviewing conduct in relation to takeovers.

Should an interested person be able to refer a matter directly to the Panel?

A brief tour of the centre of the maze

Chapter 6 of the Corporations Law does not set out any general statement of its objectives. The principal reason for this is that controversy continues to surround the principle of equality of shareholder opportunity. In general, however, the objects of the regulatory regime can be found in s. 731. The takeover provisions should be interpreted in light of these objects.[20]

The key provision in ch. 6 is s. 615.[21] This provides that an acquisition that allows the bidder to control more than 20 per cent of the voting shares in the target should be regulated. Once the bidder reaches the 20 per cent threshold, further acquisitions are supervised until 90 per cent of the target is acquired. There is nothing 'magical' about the 20 per cent figure. This threshold has been controversial, and other figures have been mooted over the years. At the time of the publication of the Eggleston Committee's *Second Interim Report* in 1969, the proportion specified in the Uniform Companies Act, s. 184, was one-third. The Committee itself recommended a figure of 15 per cent. That figure was introduced in 1971 and remained until 1981. In recent years in the USA, an acquisition of 5 per cent may be regarded as a significant step towards control.

In essence, under ch. 6, an offeror cannot acquire more than 20 per cent of voting shares in a target unless on of the following events takes place:
- A formal takeover bid (scheme) is made.
- A formal takeover announcement is made.
- Acquisitions are made by way of a so-called 'creeping takeover'.
- The approval of the target's shareholders is obtained at a meeting at which the offeror and its associates do not vote.[22]

---

20 *Niord Pty Ltd v. Adelaide Petroleum NL* (1990) 2 ACSR 347 at 357.

21 On the general purpose of the predecessor of s. 615, see *Afro-West Mining Ltd v. Australian Mining Investments Ltd* (1988) 14 ACLR 709.

22 Note also the exceptions in Corporations Law, ss. 619, 622, 629, and 633(c).

A 'takeover scheme' is a procedure whereby a formal, written 'Part A offer' is made to members of a target company (either all the members or all the members of a particular class of shares) and a written 'Part B statement' is made by the latter in reply.[23] In summary, the procedure is as follows:

- The bidder prepares a Part A statement that complies with Corporations Law, s. 750. The statement must disclose all information that is known to the bidder and that is material to the target company shareholder's decision whether or not to accept the offer.[24]
- This statement and a copy of the proposed offer must be registered with the ASC 21 days after both documents are served on the target company (s. 644(1)).
- The ASC must be notified of this service (s. 637(2)) on the day that the Part A statement is served on the target company.
- If the company is listed on a stock exchange, a copy of the statement must also be served on the company's home exchange (s. 637(2)).
- Once these formalities are complied with, written offers, accompanied by the Part A statement, are sent to the shareholders of the target company (s. 638(2)).
- The target company prepares a Part B statement in reply (s. 647). This sets out reasons to accept or reject the offer and any information material to the shareholder's decision in compliance with Part B of s. 750.
- The Part B statement is lodged with the ASC and, where the company is a listed public company, the stock exchange on the same day that it is given to the offeror (s. 647(4)). Experts' reports may accompany a Part B statement (s. 647(3)). In some circumstances, for example where the bidder is a director of the target company, the Part B statement must be accompanied by an independent expert's report that states, *inter alia*, whether, in the expert's opinion, the takeover offer is fair and reasonable (s. 648).[25]

REVIEW QUESTIONS

1 In making the Part B statement, directors of a target company must disclose information that is material to a target shareholder's decision and must not include material that is deceptive or misleading. In *Unity APA Ltd v. Humes Ltd*,[26] a target company delivered a Part B statement based on unaudited figures. Two items of extraordinary loss totalling $13 million had not been shown. The court held that the information was not material to the decision by a shareholder regarding whether or not to accept the takeover offer. The losses in question did not relate to the operating profit of the company. Beach J said at 637:

---

23 See *Clements Marshall Consolidated Ltd v. ENT Ltd* (1988) 6 ACLR 389.

24 The court can amend the statement where it contains errors (see *Elkington v. Vockbay Pty Ltd* (1993) 11 ACLR 591) or order that additional information be forwarded so as to clarify it (*Target Petroleum NL v. Petroz NL* (1987) 5 ACLR 687).

25 Special provisions exist for variations of the takeover offer: ss. 654–61; see also 'Variation of Takeover Offers' (ASC practice note 4) (1991) 1 *Australian Securities Commission Releases* 28 at 141.

26 (1986) 4 ACLR 635.

One might ask what information is material to a shareholder in arriving at such a decision. I would have thought the first thing a shareholder is concerned to ascertain is the present value of his shares. If the shares are listed on a stock exchange he will have little difficulty in ascertaining their present market value. But their present market value is not the only fact he will have regard to. He will also want to know what the asset backing of the shares is, what the profitability of the company has been and is likely to be in the future, and what financial benefits he is likely to receive in the way of dividends, bonus issues and the like if the takeover succeeds on the one hand, or fails on the other. Equipped with that information, he will be able to evaluate the offer made.

Do you agree with this decision? Is this information sufficient? If you were a shareholder making such a decision, would you consider a loss of $13 million material?

2   What is a 'Part B statement'? What purpose do Part A and Part B statements serve? For whose benefit was the statutory process of regulation devised?

In a takeover announcement, a person (either legal or natural) instructs an 'appropriate dealer' at a 'relevant official meeting' of the stock exchange to make an on-market bid pursuant to a takeover announcement.[27] The procedure is only available where the target company is a listed public company and certain criteria relating to shareholding are satisfied by the bidder (s. 674). The announcement is an offer to buy all shares (or, alternatively, all shares of a specified class) in a target company. The offer must remain open or live for a minimum period of 1 month (or up to 6 months with the ASC's consent) at or above a specified minimum price, which is set at the highest cash price the bidder has agreed to pay or has paid in the last 4 months (s. 676(1)).[28] The procedure once the announcement is made may be summarised as follows:

• The offeror serves a Part C statement on the target company on the day that the announcement is made.[29]
• At the same time, a copy is also served on the company's home stock exchange.
• Within 14 days of the announcement, the bidder must send a copy to the target company's shareholders (s. 679(1)).
• Within 14 days of receipt of the Part C statement, the target company must prepare and serve a Part D statement in reply on its home stock exchange. The Part D statement provides reasons why the directors of the target company have decided to accept or reject the offeror's offer.[30]

---

27   Corporations Law, s. 603. Note the contrived and technical discourse. Careful attention must be paid to the meanings of specific terms and to their interpretation in the case law.

28   Section 677 allows the bidder to increase her or his price in some circumstances: see *ICAL Ltd v. McCaughan Dyson & Co. Ltd (No. 2)* (1987) 5 ACLR 969.

29   The Part C statement must comply with s. 750, as must the Part D statement, which will be prepared by the target company in reply.

30   The Part D statement must conform with the Corporations Law, s. 750. Section 683 details the process for serving the Part D statement.

- On the day that the Part D statement is served on the target company's home stock exchange, a copy of the statement must be lodged with the ASC and provided to the bidder.

REVIEW QUESTIONS

1 Robert Baxt[31] notes that the on-market procedure was very popular when it was first introduced, but a number of brokers devised a system (the 'one cent punt') whereby they could gamble on a rising price by purchasing shares at a price slightly above the offer price, the offer price providing them with a convenient market floor, which made purchases almost riskless. The effect was to make it commercially necessary for the offeror to increase the price. Do you think that the exploitation of loopholes is an inherent disadvantage of an intricately drafted regulatory scheme such as the Corporations Law, ch. 6? Do such schemes adequately protect potentially vulnerable shareholders? (In considering this question, you may wish to reconsider the image of the laboratory rats given at the beginning of the chapter.)

2 What are the differences between a 'takeover bid', a 'takeover offer', a 'takeover scheme', and a 'takeover announcement'?

3 What are the risks inherent in making a takeover bid that has only a marginal chance of success?

One final form of takeover activity deserves special mention, not least because it represents an isolated exception to the regulatory 'overkill' that characterises 'the maze'. A 'creeping takeover' is governed (if that term is apposite) by Corporations Law, s. 618. Under this provision, a bidder can acquire not more than 3 per cent of the voting shares in a target company every 6 months. The bidder must have been entitled to more than 19 per cent of the shares for a continuous period of at least 6 months before the commencement of the 'creeping takeover'. Unlike the procedures to be followed in making a takeover bid or announcement, the bidder does not have to disclose any information to the shareholders of the target company, and the target company does not have to respond. This relative lack of regulation is believed to be consistent with the objectives of the takeovers legislation because the shareholders have ample time to decide whether to sell their shares.[32]

Often a bidder does not acquire all the shares of a target company. Division 6 of part 6.5, s. 703 upholds the theory of equality of opportunity and deals with this situation in two ways. It provides that remaining shareholders may require the bid-

---

31   Quoted in J. Farrar, 'Fuzzy Law: The Modernization of Corporate Laws and the Privatisation of Takeover Regulation' in J. Farrar (ed.), *Takeovers: Institutional Investors and the Modernization of Corporate Laws*, Oxford University Press, Auckland, 1993, p. 157.

32   But is this necessarily the case where small investors are concerned? What kinds of knowledge and attention to detail are assumed by the regulatory 'vacuum' surrounding the creeping takeover?

der to buy them out, and it enables a successful bidder to compulsorily acquire any outstanding shares. When a bidder becomes entitled to 90 per cent or more of the target, it must give the remaining shareholders an opportunity to sell out at the takeover price. The bidder is required to notify these shareholders that it has attained 90 per cent of the target within 1 month after the offers close. These shareholders have 3 months to require the bidder to buy their shares. The notice must be accompanied by the report of an independent expert.[33] Under s. 701, a bidder who attains 90 per cent of the target company can acquire all the shares included in the class of shares for which offers were made, subject to the satisfaction of certain criteria (unless the bidder held 10 per cent or more of the class of shares sought before she or he made the bid).

Recently, a dissenting shareholder challenged the constitutional validity of the Corporations Law, s. 701. Mr Gambotto was a shareholder in Resolute Resources Ltd (Resolute). Resolute Samantha Ltd (Samantha) launched a takeover scheme to acquire all the shares in Resolute. Gambotto declined Samantha's offer to acquire his shares, but Samantha's offers were accepted by enough shareholders to make Gambotto a dissenting offeree for the purposes of the compulsory acquisition provisions. So as to invoke these provisions, Samantha gave Gambotto notice that it desired to acquire the outstanding shares that he held. Gambotto applied to the High Court for a declaration that the compulsory acquisition provisions in the Corporations Law were invalid, arguing that there was an implied principle in the Constitution that state and Commonwealth parliaments could not pass laws for the compulsory acquisition of property. He argued that this could be implied from s. 51(xxxi) of the Constitution (the provision governing the Commonwealth's ability to make laws for the acquisition of property on just terms) and from s. 92 (guarantee of free trade, commerce, and intercourse among the states).

Gummow J held that s. 701 was valid. His Honour said that no general principle could be extracted from the Constitution that imposed a restraint upon the legislative power to enact a law for the compulsory acquisition of property. The principle argued for by Gambotto was far broader than any expressly imposed upon the Commonwealth by s. 51(xxxi). It was not conceivable that the Constitution imposed a restraint upon state legislation that was greater than that imposed upon the Commonwealth in that respect.[34]

Chapter 6 of the Corporations Law is an intricate web of legal terms that have been carefully defined in the legislation and that are mutually interdependent. These terms have been interpreted literally by the courts:

---

33 *Kingston v. Keprose Pty Ltd (No. 2)* (1988) 6 ACLR 111.

34 *Gambotto v. Resolute Samantha Ltd; Gambotto & Ors v. Beach Petroleum NL* (1995) 13 ACLR 342. One way of resisting a compulsory acquisition was by means of 'share-splitting'. Although these schemes are not considered 'illegal', the ASC can effectively negate such schemes, based on the Eggleston Committee's principles. See *Peninsula Gold Pty Ltd v. Australian Securities Commission* (1996) 19 ACSR 703. For an interesting discussion of some of the issues involved, see M. J. Whincop, 'Gambotto v. WCP Ltd: An Economic Analysis of Alterations to Articles and Expropriation Articles' (1995) 23 ABLR 276. See also I. Ramsay (ed.), *Gambotto v. WCP Ltd*, Centre for Corporate Law and Securities Regulation, University of Melbourne, Melbourne, 1996.

Australian courts have traditionally adopted a literal approach to the interpretation of statutes, especially where criminal sanctions are created or valuable property rights are involved. Our legal history has shown that devices for the avoidance of statutory prohibitions, which might be struck down in other countries as contrary to the spirit of the legislation although literally permitted, have sometimes succeeded. Consequently, the drafters of legislation have been challenged to define prohibitions in such precise language that avoidance devices are negatived. The result of this drafting approach, dramatically illustrated in Ch 6, is lengthy and complex legislation. On the one hand, the drafting approach challenges legislators to identify and state the exact scope of prohibitions and to anticipate attempts at avoidance, and consequently the Australian drafting can provide some salutary lessons for others.[35]

Consider the 'core' of ch. 6: the central prohibitions in s. 615. These revolve around 'control' (*de jure* or de facto) and hinge on the 'acquisition of shares', which is defined in Corporations Law, s. 51.[36] The definition has two limbs. First, a person acquires shares in a body corporate only if the person acquires *a relevant interest* in those shares as a result of a transaction entered into by or on behalf of the person in relation to those shares, to any other securities of that body corporate, or to securities of any other body corporate. Under the second limb, a person acquires shares in a body corporate if the person acquires any legal or equitable interest in securities of that body corporate or any other corporation and, as a result of the acquisition, another person acquires a relevant interest in those shares.

Under the Corporations Law, s. 31, a relevant interest exists where a person has either power to vote in respect of a voting share or power to dispose of a share. In turn, the power to vote in respect of a share means power to exercise, or control the exercise of, the right to vote attached to the share (s. 30(2)). Power to dispose of a share includes reference to the power to exercise control over the disposal of a share (s. 30(3)). 'Power or control' is widely defined, as is 'relevant agreement' (ss. 30(4) and 9). The extent or nature of power over voting or disposal is immaterial.[37]

The problems of a regulatory scheme that relies heavily on such 'black-letter' provisions, and the problems that can be caused by a literal interpretation of those provisions, are well illustrated by *North Sydney Brick and Tile Co. Ltd v. Darvall*.[38] Darvall and others sought to acquire all the shares in North Sydney Brick and Tile Co. Darvall prepared a Part A statement, which was defective in certain respects. Darvall argued that, because the articles of the company conferred a pre-emptive right upon each member, a Part A statement was not necessary. It followed that, if

---

35 On the issue of interpretation, see *OPSM Industries Ltd v. NCSC* (1982) 1 ACLR 479, which held that the Companies (Acquisitions of Shares) Code, s. 58 (now Corporations Law, s. 730) is to be read 'broadly and literally'.

36 The breadth of s. 51 is illustrated by *NCSC v. Brierley Investments Ltd* (1988) 14 ACLR 177. In this case, company B purchased 30 per cent of company R's shares. This was held to constitute an unlawful acquisition of shares in company W. Sections 32 and 33 deemed R to have control of a chain of companies, the last of which owned a parcel of shares in W. When B purchased the shares in R, it was, therefore, indirectly acquiring a relevant interest in W.

37 *Re Kornblums Furnishings Ltd* (1981) 6 ACLR 25.

38 (1986) 5 NSWLR 681.

the Part A statement did not comply with the legislation, its failure to do so did not have legal implications. More specifically, the argument was that Darvall already held more than the 20 per cent of the issued shares in the company and, as a consequence, s. 11 of the Companies (Acquisitions of Shares) Code was not contravened. Fleshed out, the argument put by Darvall took the following form. Darvall held shares in the company. Because the company articles restricted the manner in which shareholders could dispose of the shares, Darvall held a 'relevant interest' in all the shares of the company. It followed that Darvall was already entitled to more than the prescribed percentage of shares.

In response to this argument, Mahoney JA said:

> The company's submission is that the right which these articles give Mr Darvall constitute the '*power ... to exercise control over the disposal of*' any share in the company other than his own, within s. 9(1)(b).
>
> Whether the articles have this operation depends in the first instance, upon the meaning to be given to 'control' in s. 9(1)(b). 'Control' is a word which has a number of possible meanings. It has been described as a word of wide and ambiguous import: *Bank of NSW v. Cth* (1948) 76 CLR 1 at 385 per Dixon J. However, in many contexts, it is difficult to find a convenient substitute for it. In its essential meaning in this context, it looks to the doing of something, viz., the disposition of a share; and to the power which another person has to restrict or prevent the doing of it in some or all of those ways or circumstances. In this sense it looks to two things: the things that may be done by way of restriction or prevention; and the part which the person in question plays in the doing of them.[39]

It was held that s. 11(1) did not apply and that therefore Darvall did not need to follow the procedure of preparing a Part A statement.

Glass JA noted that it was argued that some restriction should be placed on the meaning of 'control' to avoid absurd consequences. Such consequences included:

- each shareholder would be entitled to 100 per cent of the voting shares in the company within the meaning of s. 11(1) and each shareholder would be simultaneously entitled to the same percentage;
- no person could acquire a single share in the company except by following the statutory takeover procedure.

But he continued:

> But upon reflection I am satisfied that it would be wrong to impute to the legislature an intention to avoid these consequences on the assumption that the impact of the Code in all its ramifications had been fully appreciated. To exclude them in the process of construction by imputing to the legislature foresight of such consequences and an intention to avoid them would not in my opinion be warranted.[40]

---

39 (1986) 5 NSWLR 681 at 689 (emphasis added).
40 (1986) 5 NSWLR 681 at 685.

REVIEW QUESTIONS

1 Mort is a shareholder in Barkers Parkers Pty Ltd, which owns 9 per cent of the shares in a number of listed companies, including Australian Parking Stations Ltd. Mort has also bought shares in Australian Parking Stations and now owns some 18 per cent of the issued shares in that company. Advise Mort of the consequences of his acquisition.

2 Compare the decisions in *North Sydney Brick & Tile Co. Ltd v. Darvall* and *Foodland Associated Ltd v. Garina Pty Ltd*.[41] How can these cases be reconciled? Do you agree with Wallace J's finding in *Garina* that the articles were not pre-emptive? Is this a valid point of distinction between the cases?

3 If the concept of a relevant interest is related to power, rather than ownership, could more than one person have a relevant interest in a share? If so, in what circumstances?[42]

4 In what circumstances may a relevant interest be disregarded? (See Corporations Law, ss. 38–43.)

In some circumstances, a relevant interest will be deemed to arise. For instance, s. 34 provides that where—on performance of the relevant agreement, enforcement of the right, or exercise of the option—a person would have a relevant interest in the share, then the person will be deemed to have the relevant interest at the time that the agreement was entered into or the right or option granted. In *Re Adelaide Holdings Ltd*,[43] Pan D'Or Mining NL brought proceedings to wind up Adelaide Holdings Ltd. Pan D'Or owned a number of shares in Archean Oil Ltd. In June 1981, Adelaide gave Pan D'Or a put option to acquire the shares—that is, a written agreement that, on notice from Pan D'Or, Adelaide would buy the number of shares, up to 100 000 specified in the notice at $1.90 per share. Notice was to be given in the week from 28 December 1981 to 1 January 1982 if the option was to be exercised and the purchase was to be completed on the day of receipt of the notice or the following business day. Pan D'Or gave notice, but Adelaide refused to complete, arguing that changes to the law prevented it from doing so. Thus the agreement was unenforceable.

At the time the put option was given, Adelaide already held more than 20 per cent and less than 90 per cent of shares in Archean Oil. In addition, Adelaide had issued similar put options to other companies and, if all were accepted, it would have acquired 500 000 shares, or just over 30 per cent of Archean Oil. The argument was that, through the acquisition, Adelaide would acquire over 30 per cent of shares (in a situation where it held over 20 per cent and less than 90 per cent), and so the acquisition was contrary to the Code. Adelaide's argument did not succeed. The option gave Adelaide a 'relevant interest'. The shares that a person is prohibited

---

41 (1989) 14 ACLR 739 (Wallace J) and 15 ACLR 530 (Commissioner Murray QC).

42 See *TVW Enterprises Ltd v. Queensland Press Ltd (No. 2)* (1983) 7 ACLR 821 and Corporations Law, s. 30(5).

43 [1982] 1 NSWLR 167.

by s. 11 from acquiring are not the same shares as those that he or she is entitled to at the time of acquisition.[44]

A 'relevant interest' is, in turn, distinguished from an 'entitlement'. Under s. 615, a person must not acquire shares where the effect is to take that person's *entitlement* over 20 per cent of the voting shares in the company. A person's entitlement is the sum of his or her relevant interest plus the relevant interest of his or her associates (s. 609). Division 2 of pt 1.2 (ss. 10–17) outlines the concept of an 'associate'. Some relationships automatically make one party an associate of the other. A company's automatic associates are its directors and secretaries, any related bodies corporate, and the directors and secretaries of related bodies corporate (s. 11).[45] Associations can also occur as a result of two or more parties entering into, or proposing to enter into, one of the types of 'relevant agreements' specified by s. 12(d)–(g).[46]

Perhaps not surprisingly, the primary thrust of the recent proposals for simplification of the takeover provisions involves a restructuring of s. 615. The Corporations Law Simplification Task Force seeks to restructure the provision so as to achieve the same results, but in a clearer and more direct way. The Task Force observed that s. 615 relied on a number of 'artificial and complex concepts', such as 'acquisition', 'entitlement', 'relevant interest', and 'associate'. The Task Force proposes to use the concept of an 'acquisition' directly, bypassing the notions of 'entitlement' and 'associate'. It sees two advantages in this. First, '[f]raming the prohibition in terms of acquisitions of relevant interests which result in increasing someone's relevant interest in the 20% to 90% range provides a simpler and more certain rule'. Second, this approach would close some of the loopholes in the present s. 615:

> The section currently applies only where an acquisition of shares coincides with an increase in entitlement. At least in theory, the section can be avoided by separating the acquisition and the increase in entitlement. For example, a person could create an association (thus becoming entitled to the shares of the associate) and then acquire those shares without breaching the prohibition.[47]

A further change is to shift the focus of the prohibition from the number of voting shares to the overall voting power attached to a particular parcel of shares. This is to overcome the possibility of a situation where 'a person holds 20% of shares which carry full voting rights and the other 80% of the voting shares carry only fractional voting rights (because they are partly paid), [meaning that] the person can control a percentage of votes substantially above the 20% level (in theory up to 100%).[48] This shift in focus is to be supplemented by amending s. 51 so that a

---

44 This analysis of an option was followed in *Chew v. Hamilton* (1985) 3 ACLR 205; *Yaramin Pty Ltd v. Augold NL* (1987) 5 ACLR 783. See M. G. Hains, 'Options Revisited' [1989] 5 BCLB 53 at para. 67.

45 See also *Zytan Nominees Pty Ltd v. Laverton Gold NL* (1988) 14 ACLR 524.

46 'Relevant agreement' is defined in s. 9. The definition provided is very broad.

47 Corporations Law Simplification Task Force at 803 600.

48 M. Kollar, 'Takeover Rules to be Made Simpler' (1996) 3 ACN 33.

person will be taken to acquire a share whenever the person acquires power to vote in respect of the share, even if the person already has a relevant interest in the share.

A number of changes will also be made to the idea of a 'relevant interest':

- Power to substantially influence the exercise of voting power attached to voting shares as a result of an agreement, arrangement, or understanding will be included in the concept of a relevant interest.
- Every body corporate in a group will be regarded as having a relevant interest in shares controlled by any other body corporate in the group to allow transfers of significant parcels of shares within company groups.
- Pre-emptive rights in a company's articles will not give shareholders a relevant interest in each other's shares (thus overcoming the holding in *North Sydney Brick and Tile Co. Ltd v. Darvall*).
- Section 33 will be redrafted to clarify that the rule contained in it—that a person controlling 20 per cent of voting shares in a body corporate is deemed to control all shares controlled by the body and its associates—cannot be applied more than once, thus allowing tracing through a chain of 20 per cent holdings.
- Relevant interests will not be traced from relevant interests that are themselves disregarded under ss. 38–43.
- Section 34 will be redrafted to ensure that in situations where there are exchange-traded options or futures contracts over shares, a relevant interest should be attributed to the 'buyer' only when they become obliged to take delivery of the underlying share.
- A relevant interest arising from an agreement that is conditional upon approval by target shareholders under s. 623, or by the ASC under its exemption or modification powers, will be disregarded until the approval has been given if the agreement does not give the potential purchaser control over voting and does not restrict disposal of the subject shares for more than 3 months.

In addition, changes will be made to the content requirements of s. 750:

> [The existing] rules have been criticised mainly for requiring specific information in cases where it may be irrelevant for the purpose of target shareholders making an informed decision. For example, it has been argued that the source of finance or details of capital restructurings of the bidder for the past five years are usually of no interest to the target shareholders. Moreover, if a specific matter is relevant, then it is arguably covered by the general requirement. The counter argument is that even if a specific matter is covered by the existing general requirement, the relevant specific requirement goes further, because it is not limited to the information known to the person making the statement and [his or her] advisers.[49]

The Task Force's answer to this is to replace the current content rules for takeover documents with a general content rule extending to information that could be obtained by making reasonable enquiries:

---

49 Kollar at 33.

Although corporate advisers have lived with the general disclosure test in relation to prospectuses since 1991, some might argue that the general test is bound to become a source of litigation. The counter argument is that a general test is already in sec 750 and that there is therefore no reason to expect any increase in litigation. The pragmatic view on this is that hostile takeovers will continue to be contested, irrespective of the particular disclosure test required.[50]

Through the maze

Outside ch. 6, there are a number of other forms of corporate regulation that impact, directly or indirectly, on the takeover battle. These include:

- Corporations Law, s. 205, which makes it unlawful for a company to give financial assistance for the purpose of, or in connection with, an acquisition of its shares[51]
- Corporations Law, s. 227, which is the statutory right to dismiss directors. In the context of takeovers, s. 227 guarantees to the offeror the opportunity to replace the directors of the target's board by convening a special meeting of shareholders as soon as control is obtained. Because this right exists, the directors of the target will frequently resign voluntarily once it is clear that control has passed without the need for the exercise of the right. In some jurisdictions, where there is no right to remove directors without cause, the new controlling shareholder may have to wait for some considerable period before being able to exercise control at the board level.[52]
- Corporations Law, s. 709, which provides for disclosure of substantial shareholdings
- Corporations Law, ss. 717–27, which set up a procedure to allow the ASC, a listed public company, or a member of the public entitled to not less than 5 per cent of total voting rights in the company to trace the beneficial ownership of that company's shares, whether or not the beneficial owner has reached the 5 per cent threshold for mandatory disclosure[53]
- Australian Stock Exchange (ASX) listing rules, such as 3D, which limits the circumstances in which the company can limit the transfer of shares in public companies[54]
- securities legislation, particularly provisions relating to insider trading. A bidder is not permitted to bid if it possesses material, price-sensitive, non-public information, unless the information is disclosed in the market (Corporations Law, s. 750)[55]

---

50   Kollar at 33.

51   See *Darvall v. North Sydney Brick and Tile Ltd (No. 2)* (1988) 6 ACLC 184.

52   Baxt, in Farrar, p. 153.

53   *Crosley v. Nth Broken Hill Holdings Ltd* (1986) 4 ACLR 432; *ASC v. Bank Leumi Le-Israel (Switzerland) & Ors* (1995) 134 ALR 101; (1996) 14 ACLC 1576.

54   *FAI Insurances Ltd v. Pioneer Concrete Services Ltd* (1986) 4 ACLR 698.

55   The difficulties that arise when the offeror is subject to a duty of confidentiality in respect of information that is material to the value of the target were considered, though not resolved, in *Austen & Butta Ltd v. Shell Australia Ltd* (1992) 10 ACLR 610.

- liability for misstatements and omissions, under the TPA, s. 52 or the Corporations Law, ss. 995, 999, 1000, 1001, and 1005[56]
- TPA, s. 50, which may influence particular takeovers, either by barring them from proceeding or by allowing them to proceed only after modification. Where the legislation is restrictive, it can be used as a tactical tool. The substantive question under this provision is this: will the acquisition result in the offeror and its associates being in a position to dominate a market for goods or services?
- directors' duties, both at common law and under the Corporations Law
- foreign takeovers legislation.

Although a detailed consideration of all these forms of regulation is beyond the scope of this text, it is necessary to briefly discuss the last two.

REVIEW QUESTIONS

1 Takeovers raise a specific difficulty with respect to insider-trading law. The Corporations Law defines 'information' in wide terms for the regulation of insider trading (s. 1002A(1)). The fact that the bidder intends to make a takeover bid is itself information for this purpose, and will normally be material, price-sensitive, non-public information of a kind to which the insider-trading prohibitions will apply (s. 1002G). Is a bidder then constrained from proceeding with its bid as soon as it forms the intention to do so?

2 What form did the TPA, s. 50 take in the years 1974–77? Do you think that s. 50 in this form was more readily available for tactical purposes, or less so? What is the present test? In what other ways has the section been changed?

It's all done with mirrors: Directors' duties

The chief general law constraint operating in the takeover context is that of the fiduciary duties of directors. Directors are, of course, under duties to act honestly, and with good faith due care, and skill, both under the Corporations Law and under the general law. How do these duties function in the takeover context? Action to prevent a takeover may be motivated by self-interest or by a genuine concern for the company. Participating in a takeover may lead to secret profits for the directors.

---

56 In *Bond Corp. Holdings Ltd v. Grace Bros Holdings Ltd* (1983) 8 ACLR 61, the chairman of the target, Grace Bros, sent a telex to the financial press stating that the company had advice that, on redemption of redeemable preference shares offered as consideration by Bond Corporation, a premium element would be part of the recipient's assessable income for taxation purposes. In proceedings by Bond Corporation under the predecessor of s. 705, it was held that the telex was misleading because it was in positive terms, whereas Grace Bros actually had some reservations. Among the orders made by the court was one requiring Grace Bros to make a correcting statement. Directors of a target company are subject to a general law duty to shareholders not to mislead them when making a recommendation (see *Gething v. Kilner* [1972] 1 WLR 337).

Consider, for a moment, the BHP takeover battle. From 1983, Bell Resources threatened to gain control of BHP. By February 1986, Bell Resources acquired a relevant interest in approximately 19 per cent of BHP's issued capital. It then announced a partial takeover bid, which was opposed by the BHP board. The chairman of Bell Resources asked to be appointed as a director of BHP. BHP also opposed this and challenged the registration of the Bell Resources Part A statement, which was withdrawn on 24 March. A new offer, made in April, saw Bell Resources increase its entitlement in BHP to 28 per cent.

BHP, seeking to diversify its areas of interest, considered an association with Elders in 1985. Elders, in the process of rapid expansion, announced a bid for a British company, Allied-Lyons, in October 1985. This was strongly opposed, and Elders's means of financing the bid was criticised. Elders approached BHP to underwrite a $500 million equity issue to facilitate its bid, but BHP refused.

On 10 April 1986, Elders acquired 18 per cent of BHP's share capital in a sharemarket raid. On the same day, Bell Resources bought large parcels of Elders shares, suggesting a 'back-door' takeover of BHP through Elders. That evening BHP purchased Elders convertible bonds from European investors with the cooperation of Elders associates. Over the next three days, Elders issued preference shares and options, convertible into ordinary shares, to BHP, thereby raising $1000 million (which was paid in full the next day). Effectively, Elders was protected from a hostile takeover, and BHP gained a large shareholder as a counterbalance to Bell Resources.

During the NCSC investigation of these investments, one issue of concern was whether directors of either Elders or BHP had breached their fiduciary duties. Bell Resources alleged that the directors of BHP acquired Elders's bonds and preference shares to prevent Bell from proceeding with its takeover bid for BHP, but the Commission found that, with regard to the purchase of convertible bonds, although the transactions were completed with alacrity, BHP may have believed that the bonds were a good investment. The Commission also found that the directors of Elders allotted the preference shares to the value of $1000 million partly to prevent an unwanted takeover, as the immediate capital needs for the Allied-Lyons takeover was only $500 million. However, the Commission concluded that proceedings against Elders directors for breach of duty were inappropriate.

The obvious problem then, in the takeover context, is where to draw the line between directorial self-interest and the interests of the company. A wide variety of defensive tactics are available to directors. The NCSC, in its 1986 discussion paper 'Defensive Schemes and the Duties of Directors' divided defensive schemes into two categories: defensive strategies (involving long-term planning) and defensive tactics (a response to an actual or apprehended bid).

Defensive strategies included inter-company shareholdings between associated companies, inter-company shareholdings between non-associated companies, obtaining a foreign shareholder, share placements, employee share plans, superannuation funds, restructuring of capital, redeployment of assets, and the amendment of articles.

Defensive tactics included branding the bid inadequate, criticising the offeror, releasing favourable information, announcing higher dividends or a bonus issue, placements and 'friendly' purchases, agreed takeovers, appeal to suppliers or employees, appeal to courts and other regulators, asset redeployment and the institution of legal proceedings to challenge Part A statements and offers, often on the basis of inadequate disclosure.

A good deal of litigation surrounds the duty to act for a proper purpose. Often this involves directors issuing further shares in the target company to parties who will not accept the takeover offer. A fairly typical example is *Howard Smith Ltd v. Ampol Petroleum Ltd.*[57] In this case, the directors of R. W. Miller (Holdings) Ltd issued shares to Howard Smith Ltd. The Court found that they had done so for the improper purpose of reducing the majority shareholdings of Ampol Petroleum Ltd and Bulkships Ltd in Millers to a minority interest, thus facilitating a takeover by Howard Smiths. Their Lordships held that the power to issue shares must be exercised for the purpose for which it was granted; it must involve considerations of management within the proper sphere of the directors' powers; and a share issue purely for the purpose of creating voting power is improper. The court also found that, although self-interest is the most common instance of improper motive, mere absence of self-interest in the directors is not enough to validate an issue. Exercise of directors' powers to defeat a takeover is not validated by evidence that the directors genuinely believed that their continued management is in the company's best interests; that is a matter for their members to determine.[58]

Although the duty to act for a proper purpose is commonly seen to arise from the directors' duty to act bona fide in the interests of the company as a whole, Tony Steele argues that the duty actually arises from the evidentiary difficulties of proving a director's lack of bona fides, particularly in the takeover context.[59] Lack of bona fides, he argues, may be proved by showing that there were no sound commercial reasons for a share issue, through statements of improper motives made by directors in the board minutes and in answers to interrogatories, or through evidence given by the directors in court. All of these forms of evidence can be manipulated. Thus plaintiffs allege improper purpose, rather than a lack of bona fides.

The distinction between improper purpose and a lack of bona fides is clearly illustrated by *Advance Bank of Australia Ltd v. FAI Insurances Australia Ltd.*[60] The directors in that case embarked upon a series of single-minded and misleading actions to ensure their candidate's election to the board. Their antics included outright misrepresentation. An exceedingly charitable court held that, while they had acted bona fide, their single-minded attempt to ensure that their candidate was elected constituted a collateral purpose. In this case, Kirby P gave some indication of the extent of this duty in the context of elections of the board. The directors' exercise of the use of company funds in a board election must be bona fide in the inter-

---

57 [1974] AC 821.

58 *Ashburton Oil NL v. Alpha Minerals NL* (1971) 123 CLR 614.

59 T. Steele, 'Defensive Tactics in Company Takeovers' (1986) 4 CSLJ 30 at 36.

60 (1987) 5 ACLC 725.

ests of the company as a whole, and for a proper corporate purpose. In determining the latter, the court should look at the real purpose behind the directors' actions. This did not fall to be determined wholly by the directors' statements about their subjective intentions. Even where a director has acted bona fide and for the proper company purposes, their conduct may still be illegitimate if they exceed or abuse their powers. In the context of elections, this may occur where an unreasonable amount of company money has been spent, where the money is spent on material relevant to personality and not to corporate policy, or where the directors have otherwise acted in a manner excessive or unfair in the circumstances.[61]

Nevertheless, part of the difficulty in defining the parameters of the duty stems from the ambiguity of the expression 'the interests of the company as a whole'. Particularly apposite in the context of company takeovers is the question of whether directors should exercise their powers in the interests of the company as an ongoing corporate entity (the 'commercial entity' doctrine) or whether they should exercise their powers in the interests of the body of shareholders (the 'body of corporators' doctrine).

The duty to act for a proper corporate purpose in its 'commercial entity' formulation means that directors would be justified in exercising their powers to resist a takeover where, for instance, it can be shown objectively that a raider intends to transform the business so that it no longer reflects the goals of the corporators,[62] or where the changed control would be disadvantageous to the conduct of company business.[63] This view is supported by the Canadian decision in *Teck Corp. Ltd v. Millar*. In adopting this approach, Berger J applied a subjective test: 'I think that the directors are entitled to consider the reputation, experience and policies of anyone seeking to take over the company. If they decide, on reasonable grounds, a takeover will cause substantial damage to the company's interests, they are entitled to use their powers to protect the company'.[64]

Similarly, in *Darvall v. North Sydney Brick and Tile Co. Ltd and Others (No. 2)*,[65] a shareholder made a takeover bid for the company. The directors caused the company to enter into a joint venture with a third party to develop some real estate owned by the company. They hoped thereby to secure an alternative (and more lucrative) takeover bid. The shareholder alleged that this was an improper purpose. The majority[66] of the court dismissed the action. Mahoney J said:

---

61 See *Hannes and Ors v. MJH Pty Ltd and Ors* (1992) 10 ACLR 400.

62 As in *Re Tivoli Freeholds Ltd* [1972] VR 445. For support for the 'corporate entity' interpretation, see B. H. McPherson, 'Duties of Directors and the Powers of Shareholders' (1977) 51 ALJ 364 at 368; G. F. K. Santow, 'Defensive Measures against Company Takeovers' (1979) 53 ALJ 374 at 375; J. D. Heydon, 'Directors' Duties and the Company's Interests', in P. D. Finn (ed.), *Equity and Commercial Relationships*, Law Book Company, Sydney, 1987, p. 134.

63 As in *Rossfield Group Operations Pty Ltd v. Austral Group Ltd* [1981] Qd R 279; *Teck Corp. Ltd v. Millar* (1973) 33 DLR (3d) 288.

64 (1973) 33 DLR (3d) 288 at 337. See also *Cayne v. Global Natural Resource PLC*, unreported, 12 August 1982, Chancery Division; *Alberta Ltd v. Producers' Pipeline Inc.* (1991) 80 DLR (4d) 359.

65 (1989) 7 ACLC 659.

66 Mahoney and Clarke JJA.

It is not correct that ... a company has no legitimate interest in who are its shareholders or the price paid for its shares. In some circumstances, it will be proper for a company to concern itself with those who take its shares on transfer. Thus, a company may lose a government licence or a customer may refuse to do business with a company if a particular person takes a transfer of shares. It may then be 'in the interest of the company as a whole' for action to be taken. What a company may do in the circumstances will depend upon the circumstances.[67]

Critics of this 'corporate entity' doctrine argue that such an interpretation, on one hand, authorises directors to frustrate a bid and deny the shareholders the opportunity to make large returns on their investment and, on the other, prevents directors from taking action designed to increase the share price or maximise shareholder benefits.[68] There is thus authority for the 'body of corporators' view—that is, that the 'proper purpose' for which a power is exercised is that of ensuring the commercial well-being of corporators as individuals.[69] For instance, in *Greenhalgh v. Aderne Cinemas Ltd*, the test was stated this way by Evershed MR:

[T]he phrase, 'the company as a whole', does not (at any rate in such a case as the present) mean the company as a commercial entity, distinct from the corporators: it means the corporators as a general body. That is to say, the case may be taken of an individual hypothetical member and it may be asked whether what is proposed is, in the honest opinion of those who voted in its favour, for that person's benefit.[70]

On the basis of this view, directors can legitimately exercise their powers so as to maximise shareholder share prices. In the takeover context, however, it can be argued that higher share prices will seldom benefit all the shareholders. After all, raiders are often substantial shareholders who will be unlikely to see acceptance of a higher price as being in their interests.

REVIEW QUESTION

In the 1980s, there was a scheme called the 'Australia 2000 Club'. It was set up by a large brokerage house, and participants were large Australian companies. The broker provided an investment company for each participating client. Considerable funds were subscribed by each client to its investment company by way of redeemable preference shares. The broker invested those

---

67   (1989) 7 ACLC 659 at 704. There are, of course, some limits to how far the directors can go in protecting company interests. See, for instance, *Bailey v. Mandala Private Hospital Pty Ltd* (1988) ACLR 43, where a share allotment undertaken to place company assets beyond the reach of potential litigators was held to be an improper purpose.

68   See, for instance, Steele at 32.

69   See, for example, *Rossfield Group Operations Pty Ltd v. Austral Group Ltd*; *Ngurli Ltd v. McCann* (1953) 90 CLR 425; *Greenhalgh v. Aderne Cinemas Ltd* [1951] 1 Ch 286.

70   *Greenhalgh v. Aderne Cinemas Ltd* [1951] 1 Ch 286 at 291. In some situations, of course, it may also be necessary to have regard to the interests of creditors. See *Kinsela v. Russell Kinsela Pty Ltd (in liq.)* (1986) 4 ACLC 215.

funds at its discretion. The broker retained voting control. Was this a scheme that discouraged hostile takeovers or merely a scheme for facilitating long-term investment in Australian companies?

Not in *my* garden: Foreign takeovers legislation

In its essentials, the Foreign Acquisitions and Takeovers Act provides that a foreign interest seeking to acquire more than 15 per cent of the shares of an Australian company must obtain the federal treasurer's consent.[71] The Foreign Acquisitions and Takeovers Act empowers the treasurer to prohibit acquisitions of Australian businesses or assets by a foreign interest where that foreign interest would acquire or increase a holding of 15 per cent or more of the ownership or control of the Australian businesses or assets (or where two or more foreign interests would acquire an aggregate of 40 per cent or more of such ownership or control). The Act also enables the 'unscrambling' of acquisitions that were completed without the treasurer's notification. The actual examination of proposed acquisitions is carried out by the Foreign Investment Review Board, which then advises the treasurer.

To further complicate the maze, the relevant criteria for prohibition by the treasurer are not defined in the Act, and policy effected under it has changed considerably over time. In the past, individual industries and companies have been targeted for specific policies that aim to exclude foreign investors.[72] The substantive provisions of the Act are ss. 18 and 19, which deal with acquisitions of shares and assets, and ss. 20 and 21, which deal with arrangements relating to the directorates of corporations and control of Australian businesses. Section 26 makes it an offence for a person who proposes to acquire a 'substantial shareholding' in an Australian corporation to agree to do so unless she or he first notifies the treasurer of this intention and either 40 days expires or she or he receives notification that the Commonwealth does not object to the transaction.

Like ch. 6 of the Corporations Law, the legislation is heavily dependent upon definitions. The target 'corporations' referred to in ss. 18 and 20 are limited to 'prescribed corporations' carrying on an 'Australian business' and their 'holding corporations'. 'Prescribed corporations' are defined in s. 13, by reference to ss. 51(xx) and 122 of the Australian Constitution, as trading or financial corporations within s. 51(xx), as corporations incorporated in a territory, and as some categories of foreign corporation. An 'Australian business' is a business carried on wholly or partly in Australia in anticipation of profit or gain, although businesses carried on by Commonwealth, state, or local governments (or their instrumentalities) are excluded (Corporations Law, s. 7).

---

71 See *Equiticorp Industries Ltd v. Act International Ltd* [1987] VR 385.

72 See, for example, the *Banks (Shareholding) Act 1972* (Cth), the *Parliamentary Committees (Takeover Offers) Act 1972* (Vic.), and the *Gas Supplies (Shareholding) Act 1972* (Qld). Other legislation, such as the *Broadcasting and Television Act 1942* (Cth) and the *Income Tax Assessment Act 1936* (Cth), may also indirectly regulate foreign takeovers.

The treasurer exercises the power of prohibition when she or he is satisfied that:

1 where a corporation or Australian business is not yet foreign controlled, it would become so controlled, and that this would be 'contrary to the national interest'

2 where the corporation or business is already so controlled, the acquisition would involve some change in the identity of the foreign persons concerned, and that this result would be 'contrary to the national interest'.

'Control', in the case of one foreign person and 'associates' (s. 6), is shown by establishing that they have 15 per cent of the issued shares, voting power in general meetings, or assets of an Australian business (a 'controlling interest'); in the case of two or more foreign persons and their associates, 40 per cent is the benchmark (an 'aggregate controlling interest').[73] 'Foreign person' is defined by s. 5(1). A 'foreign corporation' is basically a foreign corporation within the meaning of s. 51(xx) of the Constitution. Sections 20 and 21 attempt to deal with the even more elusive 'arrangements' by which directors are obliged to act in accordance with the directions, wishes, or instructions of foreign persons holding a substantial interest in the corporation, and with licensing arrangements that would give foreign persons control over businesses carried on by prescribed corporations.

Out of the maze: No exit?

A maze of legislation, a maze of drafting, a maze of duties. The regulation of takeovers is confounding. John Farrar argues that takeover law is inherently anti-modern. He identifies three principles of modernity: incompatibility, flexibility (or user-friendliness), and a presumption of freedom of contract (that is, a need for a rational justification of mandatory laws that interfere with freedom of contract). In his discussion of 'incompatibility', he quotes Professor Zadeh:

> The closer one looks at a 'real world' problem, the fuzzier becomes its solution. Stated informally, the essence of this principle is that as the complexity of a system increases, our ability to make precise and yet significant statements about its behaviour diminishes until the threshold is reached beyond which precision and significance (or relevance) become almost mutually exclusive characteristics.[74]

Applied to law, this means that '[t]he more complex the legal structures and the phenomena to which they are applied, the more there is a need to resort to vague and loose concepts like the duty of care, fairness and fiduciary duties, in order to deal with the matter'.[75]

Applying these three principles of modernity—incompatibility, flexibility and presumption of freedom of contract—to corporate law, he argues: 'Judged by the

---

73 Corporations Law, s. 9.
74 As quoted in Farrar, p. 2.
75 Farrar, p. 2.

criteria of modernity identified … one arrives at a paradoxical conclusion. Traditional corporate law was more modern than much recent corporate legislation in the sense that it was simpler and more flexible and facilitated freedom of contract, subject to minimal restraints.[76]

But is the answer a deregulated 'freedom of contract' approach? Do we adopt, as Farrar suggests, a 'fuzzy law' approach to takeovers regulation? Should we adopt a system akin to the British system of a self-regulatory code? Should we adopt a new legislative scheme? Or should we be satisfied with attempts to 'band-aid' the existing scheme?

> The problem is that we constantly start in the middle when what we need to do is go back to first principles. If there is one weakness of legal education in British Commonwealth jurisdictions it is an unwillingness, and possibly an inability, to transcend the black letter law and to think conceptually about the subject and the underlying policies, and for this we pay the price of high cost and intellectual incoherence.[77]

REVIEW QUESTION

What is 'fuzzy law'? What would a 'fuzzy law' regulatory approach to takeovers look like? What are the problems of a 'fuzzy law' approach? What are its advantages?

---

76 Farrar, p. 11.
77 Farrar, p. 11.

PART 5

PROBLEMS OF POWER

14

THE MINORITY
SHAREHOLDER
AND INTEREST
GROUP POLITICS

Introduction

When an individual becomes a member of a company, they are generally entitled to two different types of rights. The first category involves rights that arise by virtue of membership. The second category involves rights conferred by law to protect the individual shareholder from abuse by the company's controllers (the directors and/or the majority of shareholders). As we have seen in chapter 9, day-to-day decisions within the company are made by the board of directors, while more structural decision-making falls to the general meeting. In company law, the minority shareholder is deemed to consent to the will of the majority, provided that will is legitimate. But if, as is often the case, the directors control management, and the directors are the majority shareholders, what controls are placed upon them to prevent them from abusing their positions? At what point does an exercise of majoritarian power cease to be legitimate? And where an exercise of power is found to be illegitimate, what mechanisms are available to a minority in seeking redress for such abuse?

The potential for the abuse of majoritarian power is always present within any association that is based upon essentially democratic principles. In such an association, be it a company or a nation state, there is likely to be a conflict of interests, and hence, disagreement among the association's members. Many nation states attempt to address this problem through reliance upon 'bills of rights' and other legislative vehicles. Companies generally do not incorporate anything like bills of rights in their constitutive documents. Instead, the protection of minority rights is conventionally imposed upon corporate structures from without, by the legislative regimes that make them possible and that regulate inter-corporate relationships. With regard to company law, therefore, the question is this: at what point does a disagreement between the majority and the minority become so serious that the court should intervene? On the one hand, you have the *commercial* truth that the investment of the majority is larger than that of the minority, and therefore it may seem that majority will should prevail. There is always a danger that a particularly difficult minority shareholder will block company action by vexatious litigation, brought on the basis of personal, as opposed to commercial, disagreement with the majority. On the other hand, you have the *moral* truth that a majority is capable of oppressing, or acting unfairly towards, a minority member. The majority can attempt to squeeze a dissident minority member out—by altering the articles, for instance, or by withholding information about company affairs. Sometimes, a particularly determined majority faction will seek to dilute the minority's shareholding by allotting additional share capital. The company structure, as we pointed out in chapter 1, creates a complex 'web' of relationships and interests. The aim of minority remedies is to control situations where there is a significant divergence of interests between the majority and the minority.

At common law, this control was ordinarily exercised in such a way that the majority view would prevail wherever possible. Minority rights were limited doctrinally by the rule that individuals could vote in company matters on the basis of self-interest, and by the policy of non-interference in internal company matters. Minority remedies, in turn, were limited by the application of the separate entity doctrine. These ideas are encapsulated in the so-called 'rule in *Foss v. Harbottle*'. This rule had two aspects. The first insists that, where a wrong is done to the company, it is the company and not the individual shareholder who is the proper plaintiff. The second aspect is the so-called 'internal management rule', which insists that courts should not intervene in internal company matters. In *Burland v. Earle*, Lord Davey restated the rule: '[it is] an elementary principle of the law relating to joint stock companies that the court will not interfere with the internal management of companies acting within their powers, and in fact has no jurisdiction to do so'.[1] In the leading Australian case on *Foss v. Harbottle*, *Hawkesbury Development Co. Ltd v. Landmark Finance Pty Ltd*,[2] the court, in turn, recited the rule laid down in *Burland v. Earle*[3] and continued:

> Again, it is clear law that in order to redress a wrong done to the company, the action should prima facie be brought by the company itself … But an exception is made to the second rule where the persons against whom the relief is sought, themselves hold and control the majority of the shares in the company, and will not permit an action to be brought in the name of the company … The cases in which the minority can maintain such an action are, therefore, confined to those in which the acts complained of are of a fraudulent character or beyond the powers of the company.[4]

Similarly, Macnaghten LJ in *Dovey v. Corey* said, 'I do not think it desirable for any tribunal … to formulate precise rules for the guidance or embarrassment of business men in the conduct of business affairs'.[5]

---

1   [1902] AC 83 at 93.
2   [1969] 2 NSWLR 782.
3   [1902] AC 83 at 93–4.
4   [1969] 2 NSWLR 782 at 788.
5   [1901] AC 477.

This reluctance to provide effective safeguards and avenues for redress against a delinquent majority has posed particular difficulties in the case of small, private companies, where minority shareholders may have no market for their shares or where the company constitution places restrictions upon the transferability of shares or confers pre-emptive rights over shareholdings. Shareholders in such companies are often more vulnerable to oppressive conduct, such as the withholding of dividends, the diversion of corporate assets to majority interests, or the alteration of the corporation so as to devalue their shareholding.

Although the statutory remedies have been instituted in an effort to overcome some of the deficiencies in the common law, there is an uncomfortable overlap between the common law and the legislation in this area. In addition, even though the legislation attempts to fill in many of the gaps left by the common law, some of its effectiveness has been limited by a narrow judicial interpretation of the relevant statutory provisions. The court's traditional reluctance to interfere in so-called 'internal' company matters can still be seen. Thus, regardless of parliamentary intention, minority shareholders have continued to have difficulties bringing actions to restrain an illegitimate majoritarian act.

REVIEW QUESTIONS

1 In addition to minority remedies, what other ways are there of controlling divergent interests that may arise between the majority and the minority within a company?
2 Do the existence of legal remedies for the minority effectively constrain illegitimate management practices? Give reasons for your answer.
3 Are companies democratic structures? Should they be? Give reasons for your answer.

A little fraud...

In discussing minority rights and remedies, it is important to realise that the duties of majority shareholders are not the same as the duties of directors. Directors, as we have seen, are in a fiduciary relationship with the company and are supposed to give the company's interests priority over their own. Shareholders, on the other hand, have no fiduciary duty and can vote in their own interests: 'The shareholders are not trustees for one another, and unlike directors, they occupy no fiduciary position and are under no fiduciary duties. They vote in respect of their shares, which are property, and the right to vote is attached to the share itself as an incident of property to be enjoyed and exercised for the owner's personal advantage'.[6] Similarly, in *Pender v. Lushington*, Jessel MR said, 'There is ... no obligation on a shareholder of

---

6   *Peters' American Delicacy Co. Ltd v. Heath* (1939) 61 CLR 457 at 504 per Dixon J.

a company to give his vote merely with a view to what other persons may consider the interests of the company at large. He has a right, if he thinks fit, to give his vote from motives or promptings of what he considers his own individual interest'.[7]

This principle means that a director who is also a shareholder could potentially vote, for instance, to ratify his or her own breach of duty.[8] In certain circumstances, however, such as alteration of the articles or ratification of a director's breach of duty, the courts have held that this voting right must be exercised 'bona fide for the benefit of the company as a whole'. For instance,

> a director of a company is precluded from dealing, on behalf of the company, with himself, and from entering into engagements in which he has a personal interest conflicting, or which possibly may conflict, with the interests of those whom he is bound by fiduciary duty to protect ... Any such dealing or engagement may, however, be affirmed or adopted by the company, provided such affirmance or adoption is not brought about by unfair or improper means, and is not illegal or fraudulent or oppressive towards those shareholders who oppose it.[9]

If the powers of the majority are not exercised 'bona fide for the benefit of the company as a whole', then the impugned act or resolution may constitute a 'fraud on the minority' and thus be actionable by the minority shareholder. The 'fraud' referred to is not common-law fraud (meeting the requirements of *Derry v. Peek*[10]) but equitable fraud (that is, 'fraud on a power'). As such, it may encompass unconscionable conduct, the use of majority power in an unfair or unconscionable manner, the imposition of financial loss, unfair treatment, and the misuse of a fiduciary position or position of trust:

> The term fraud in connection with frauds on a power does not necessarily denote any conduct on the part of the appointer amounting to fraud in the common law meaning of the term or any conduct which could be termed dishonest or immoral. It merely means that the power has been exercised for a purpose, or with an intention, beyond the scope of or not justified by the instrument creating the power.[11]

Estmanco (Kilner House) Ltd v. Greater London Council[12] provides an apt illustration of the idea of equitable fraud. In *Estmanco*, the Greater London Council formed a company, which owned a block of flats. The council decided to sell long leases to the flats. On each sale, the purchaser would acquire a share in the company, but until all the flats were sold, the council retained sole voting rights. After it sold twelve leases and shares, the council changed its policy and decided to rent the remaining flats with no transfer of shares. The existing owners were not to be

---

7   (1877) 6 Ch D 70 at 75–6.

8   *Mills v. Mills* (1938) 60 CLR 150.

9   *Northwest Transportation v. Beatty* (1887) 12 AC 589.

10 (1889) 14 AC 337.

11 *Vatcher v. Paul* [1915] AC 372 at 378.

12 [1982] 1 WLR 2 at 12 per Sir Robert Megarry VC.

granted voting rights in respect of their shares. In an action brought by one of the twelve shareholders, the court said:

> Plainly, there must be some limit to the power of the majority to pass resolutions which they believe to be in the best interests of the company and yet remain immune from interference by the courts. It may be in the best interests of the company to deprive the minority of some of their rights or some of their property, yet I do not think that this gives the majority an unrestrained right to do this, however unjust it may be, and however much it may harm shareholders whose rights as a class differ from those of the majority. If a case falls within one of the exceptions from *Foss v. Harbottle*, I cannot see why the right of the minority to sue under that exception should be taken away from them merely because the majority of the company reasonably believe it to be in the best interest of the company that this should be done. This is particularly so if the exception from the rule falls under the rubric of 'fraud on a minority'.[13]

Abuse of voting power by the majority is often divided into three categories:
1 majority voting for alteration of the constitution or variation of rights of members
2 majority unwilling to bring proceedings where a wrong has been committed against the company[14]
3 majority voting in other cases, such as election of directors[15] or resolutions approving the establishment of a trust fund for employees.[16]

A number of important practical and theoretical questions focus on the nature and scope of the voting rights of shareholders. The issues involved are extremely complex. A share, as you know, is a proprietary right. It follows that the attached vote is also a proprietary right, and theoretically shareholders ought to be free to make use of their votes in any way they see fit, subject to the limits of the general law. Nonetheless, the courts have, from time to time, suggested that the right is more limited, both generally and with regard to the question of class rights. In an early case, *Allen v. Gold Reefs of West Africa Ltd*,[17] the court held that the power possessed by the shareholders to alter the articles must be exercised bona fide for the benefit of the company as a whole. This test raises a difficult point. The use of the term 'bona fide' suggests that the test is subjective and demands examination of the motives for which the votes were cast, but the phrase 'for the benefit of the company as a whole' has been interpreted as objective. The case law in this area has conventionally been mixed. *Shuttleworth v. Cox Bros & Co. (Maidenhead) Ltd* [18] opted for a variant on the familiar reasonable person test (an objective test), while *Greenhalgh v.*

---

13 [1982] 1 WLR 2 at 12.
14 See, for instance, *Biala Pty Ltd v. Mallina Holdings Ltd (No. 2)* (1993) 11 ACSR 785; 11 ACLC 1082; *Dutton v. Gorton* (1917) 23 CLR 362.
15 *Theseus Exploration NL v. Mining and Associated Industries Ltd* [1973] Qd R 81.
16 *Clemens v. Clemens Bros Ltd* [1976] 2 All ER 268.
17 [1900] 1 Ch 656 at 671.
18 [1927] 2 KB 9.

Arderne Cinemas Ltd[19] opted for a subjective test. The latter case held that the test concerned the fairness of the resolution as between the members, and asserted that, if the resolution was fair as between the members, then each member was entitled to vote his or her own interests.

It is frequently suggested that voting rights cannot be exercised outside appropriate parameters—that they cannot be used as a fraud on a power. Where there is a collateral purpose in voting, and the interests of the shareholders as a whole do not enter calculations, the vote is improper. While shareholders are not expected to be wholly altruistic, neither are they permitted to exercise their votes purely for self-interested private purposes. Reliance upon the notion of the 'interests of the company as a whole' adds a further layer of complexity. Sometimes the phrase appears to refer to the corporators as a collective body. Other uses of the phrase clearly refer to the company as a commercial entity. The parameters of the phrase vary according to the circumstances in which it is used, and care is needed in its interpretation. Perhaps the best explanation of the nature of the test is that given by Jacobs J:

> The truth is that the courts in each generation ... have set a line up to which shareholders have been allowed to go on affecting the rights of other shareholders ... and beyond which they have not been allowed to go. It seems to me that no amount of legal analysis or analytical reasoning can conceal the fact that the decisions have turned ... on a value judgment ... formed not by any strict process of reasoning or bare principle of law, but upon the view taken of the conduct.[20]

The High Court recently considered the duties of controlling shareholders in the context of the power of the general meeting to alter the articles. In particular, it revisited this idea of the 'benefit of the company as a whole'. In *Gambotto v. WCP Ltd*,[21] 99.7 per cent of WPC's shares were held by Industrial Equity Ltd. WPC proposed to amend its articles so as to require its minority shareholders to sell their shares to the majority. The alteration would allow any member who was entitled, for the purposes of the *Corporations Law 1990*, to 90 per cent or more of the issued shares to compulsorily acquire all the issued shares at a price of $1.80 per share. The notice of the meeting was accompanied by a valuation of the shares at $1.36 per share.

The effect of this alteration was that WPC would become a wholly owned subsidiary of Industrial Equity Ltd. This would have produced substantial tax and administrative benefits for WPC. Despite the fact that the price to be offered for the shares was above market value, two minority shareholders brought an action, arguing that WCP's statutory power to alter the articles did not extend to the expropriation of shares in the manner contemplated by the articles.

The High Court upheld this view. It rejected the previously accepted view of Lindley MR in *Allen v. Gold Reefs of West Africa Ltd* that the power of the majority of the general meeting to alter the company's articles must be exercised 'bona fide for the benefit of the company as a whole'. The court limited that require-

---

19 [1951] 1 Ch 286.

20 *Crumpton v. Morrine Hall Pty Ltd* [1965] NSWLR 240 at 244.

21 (1995) 13 ACLC 342; 16 ACSR 1.

ment to the exercise of powers by directors and adopted a two-fold test. If the alteration of articles does not involve an actual or effective expropriation of shares or 'valuable proprietary rights attaching to shares', then it will be valid and binding on the minority unless it is '*ultra vires*, beyond any purpose contemplated by the articles' or oppressive. If the alteration is for the purpose of expropriation, then there is an additional requirement that it be fair. Fairness had two aspects. The first is procedural (that is, the process of alteration, of itself, has to be fair). The second is substantive (that is, as in the case before the court, the buyout price has to be fair). Such fairness was not to be assessed solely by reference to market price, but account should also be taken of assets, dividends, the nature of the company, and its likely future. The onus is on the majority to prove that the alteration is made for a proper purpose. In this case, the perceived taxation and administrative benefits were insufficient to prove that the alteration was for a proper purpose. On the other hand, where an alteration would save the company from significant harm or detriment, the High Court considered that it would constitute a proper purpose. Thus, 'an expropriation may be justified where it is reasonably apprehended that the continued shareholding of the minority is detrimental to the company, its undertaking or the conduct of its affairs—resulting in detriment to the interests of the existing shareholding generally—and expropriation is a reasonable means of eliminating or mitigating that detriment'.[22]

To a large extent, the idea of 'fraud on the minority' has now been encapsulated within the statutory doctrines of oppressive or unfair conduct. The duties (if any) of the majority in general meeting—outside the alteration of articles situation—remain uncertain. Although the actions of the majority may be binding on the minority, these actions may still give rise to (or form part of) a claim by a minority shareholder under either s. 260 (oppression) or s. 461 (winding-up) of the Corporations Law.[23]

REVIEW QUESTION

Is the minority obliged to exercise their powers for a proper purpose?[24]

Majority rules OK! The rule in *Foss v. Harbottle*

We have seen that the ability of shareholders to vote in their own interests at common law was constrained by ideas of equitable fraud. This idea was expressed doctrinally in the decision in *Foss v. Harbottle*.[25] In this case, promoters of a company, who were also its directors, sold the company plots of land at allegedly exorbitant prices. The court refused to allow two minority shareholders to bring an action on

---

22   (1995) 16 ACSR 1 at 9.

23   See *Northwest Transportation v. Beatty* (1887) 12 AC 589, where a director of a company, who was also a majority shareholder, approved actions executed in his capacity as director.

24   See *Humes Ltd v. Unity APA Ltd (No. 1)* (1987) 11 ACLR 641; 5 ACLC 15; [1987] VR 467.

25   (1843) 2 Hare 461; 67 ER 189.

the company's behalf, holding that the company itself was the proper plaintiff in the action. It was for the company (in practical terms, the majority) to determine whether proceedings should be brought. It was not the place of the court to interfere in this decision. Together, these two aspects of the *Foss v. Harbottle* decision—the 'proper plaintiff' rule and the 'internal management' rule—operated to uphold majority will despite minority opposition.

Because the court recognised that this rule could cause injustice, it made a number of exceptions to it. But to ensure that a disgruntled minority did not bring a vexatious action, the exceptions to the rule were circumscribed. The rule in *Foss v. Harbottle* deals with the enforcement of intra-corporate duties. While legislation is playing an increasingly important role in this area, it is essential to understand the common-law position fully, both because it remains important and because the nature and application of the legislation cannot be understood in isolation from the common law. The situation within a company should be contrasted with that which obtains in a partnership. If a major dispute arises in a partnership, or one partner acts outside the scope of allowable conduct, that partner may be readily called to account by his or her fellow partners. In a company, matters are nowhere near as simple. Because companies possess independent legal personality, only the company can call directors to account if they act in derogation of duty. The matter is further complicated by the fact that the directors frequently control voting power in the general meeting, either directly, through personal shareholdings, or indirectly, through the proxy mechanism. This provides them with a mechanism which they can use to advance private interests in preference to corporate interests. The area we are about to consider deals with the common-law remedy where there has been a fraud on the minority—that is, where the directors act in derogation of the interests of the company as a whole.

The rule in *Foss v. Harbottle* may be simply stated. In essence, it states that, where a wrong is done to the company, the company is the proper plaintiff. Thus, where there has been a wrong against the company, or where there is an irregularity in internal management that is capable of being remedied by a simple majority, no legal action by minority shareholders is allowable. Under such circumstances, any legal action must be brought by the company itself. The rule serves a number of useful purposes. First, it prevents multiple or duplicate litigation. Second, it preserves majority rule. Third, it shields the courts from involvement in commercial matters. Internal management is traditionally deemed to be a matter of commercial convenience. If, however, the rule were strictly enforced, it would tend to stifle litigation and leave the minority defenceless. A minority shareholder could seek redress:

1   where the act complained of was *ultra vires* [26]

---

26   Since the 1984 amendments to s. 67 (now s. 161) of the Corporations Law, the first exception is of little practical importance in Australia, although *FAI Insurances Ltd v. Urquart* (1986) 11 ACLR 114 suggests that it may still have some role to play in resolving disputes within the company. See also the relatively new concept of *ultra vires* in cases such as *Advance Bank of Australia Ltd v. FAI Insurances Australia Ltd* (1987) 5 ACLC 725, which arguably may also fall within the parameters of *ultra vires* as an exception to the rule in *Foss v. Harbottle*.

2 where the act complained of could only be effective if supported by more than a simple majority (for example, by a special resolution) that had not been obtained[27]

3 where the personal rights of the shareholder were infringed as a result of wrongful conduct by the company which could not be rectified by ordinary resolution[28]

4 where those in control of the company perpetrated a fraud on the minority, or

5 somewhat ambiguously, where the interests of justice so required.

While all of these are generally grouped together as exceptions to the rule in *Foss v. Harbottle*, only the fourth and fifth represent true exceptions. The others may be accounted for by quite independent areas of company law. Let us look at these exceptions in more detail.

Fraud on the minority

We have considered, above, the idea of a 'fraud on the minority', noting that this is equitable fraud (that is, abuse of power). In order to bring an action for fraud on the minority, a plaintiff must establish two things. First, the plaintiff must establish that the fraud is of such a serious nature that the controllers would be delinquent in allowing the company's cause of action to lapse by default. Ordinarily, complaints of fraud on the minority brought by a minority shareholder relate to the expropriation of company property, ratification of a director's abuse of power, and expropriation of members' property.[29] We will look at these categories in more detail below. Second, a plaintiff who wishes to bring an action alleging a fraud on the minority must establish that the wrongdoers have control of the company. In Australia, it would seem that the 'control' that needs to be established is that the wrongdoers 'command a majority of the votes at an ordinary general meeting of the company'.[30]

Expropriation of company property

Where controllers of the company expropriate company property for themselves, they effectively steal from the company. Such an act justifies a minority action on the company's behalf. *Menier v. Hooper's Telegraph Works*[31] provides an illustration of the application of the fraud on the minority exception to *Foss v. Harbottle* in regard to expropriation of company property. In this case, the majority procured the sale of a company concession to a rival concern and later passed a resolution to wind up the company to foreclose legal action. It was held that a minority

---

27 *Baillie v. Oriental Telephone and Electrical Co. Ltd* [1915] 1 Ch 503.

28 *Edwards v. Halliwell* [1950] 2 All ER 1064; *Kaye v. Croydon Tramways Co.* [1898] 1 Ch 358; *Pender v. Lushington*; *Grant v. John Grant and Sons Pty Ltd* (1950) 82 CLR 1; *Kraus v. J. G. Lloyd Pty Ltd* [1965] VR 232; *MacDougall v. Gardiner* (1875) 1 Ch D 13; *James v. Buena Ventrua Syndicate Ltd* [1896] 1 Ch 456.

29 *Re Overton Holdings Pty Ltd* (1985) 9 ACLR 255.

30 *Eromanga Hydrocarbons NL v. Australis Mining NL* (1988) 14 ACLR 486 at 489 per Malcolm CJ, applied in *Biala Pty Ltd v. Mallina Holdings Ltd (No. 2)*. Unfortunately it is not altogether clear that 'command' is any more susceptible to precise definition than was 'control'.

31 [1874] LR 9 Ch 350.

shareholder was entitled to bring an action on behalf of the company, as there was clear evidence of fraud and collusion.

Directors cannot ratify their own expropriation of company property. In *Cook v. Deeks*,[32] the allegations concerned the improper conduct of directors who took advantage of their position to obtain contracts privately and in competition with the company. A resolution was passed affirming that the company had no interest in the contracts. The court held that the contracts were held on trust for the company and that the resolution was invalid. Rights and benefits under a contract are proprietary rights and thus are part of company property. In taking for themselves the benefits of contracts, property belonging to the company, the directors in this situation effectively stole property belonging to the company. This rule applies irrespective of the bona fides of the directors and the nature of the purpose. Thus, in *Parke v. Daily News Ltd*,[33] the general meeting could not ratify the directors' decision to make gratuitous payments to the company's employees. The money belonged to the shareholders and could not be given away.

Improper ratification of directors' breach of duty

While the general meeting has the power to excuse a director's breach of duty to the company,[34] this power is not without its proper limits. Where the alleged breach of duty consists of using powers for an improper purpose, the majority must be careful not to commit a fraud on the minority when using its voting strength to ratify the breach in question.[35] In *Winthrop Investments Ltd v. Winns Ltd*,[36] Mahoney JA considered that a resolution of the general meeting to affirm a transaction voidable by reason of a breach of the directors' duties could be ineffective because it was passed for an improper purpose.[37]

Expropriation of members' property

Shares in a company have always been subject to a proprietary analysis. Where majority shareholders use their voting power so as to deprive members of their shares or 'valuable proprietary rights attaching to those shares', such as the power to vote, it may constitute a fraud on the minority. As you will recall, *Gambotto* held that an alteration of articles involving an actual or effective expropriation of shares,

---

32 [1916] 1 AC 554.

33 [1962] Ch 927. It is worth noting that the position differs in the USA and that the decision in *Parke*—disallowing the director's decision to provide substantive termination payments to long-standing employees who had been put out of work by the sale of the *Daily News*—led to legislative change in the United Kingdom permitting this kind of payment.

34 Early cases spoke poetically of 'forgiving the directors their sins'.

35 See the case of *Ngurli Ltd v. McCann* (1953) 90 CLR 425; *Bamford v. Bamford* [1970] Ch 212; *Winthrop Investments Ltd v. Winns Ltd* [1975] 2 NSWLR 666. The *Winthrop* case indicates that the general meeting cannot approve a breach of duty by directors where the approval itself is not bona fide for the benefit of the company as a whole.

36 [1975] 2 NSWLR 666 at 701.

37 See also *Advance Bank of Australia Ltd v. FAI Insurances Australia Ltd.*

or rights attaching to those shares, was distinguished from other types of alterations to the articles.[38] Because of this effective expropriation, the alteration was made subject to an additional requirement of fairness, both procedural and substantive.

Infringement of personal rights

Personal rights may be conferred by express contract, by the company's articles, or by law.

Express contract

A member can make a special contract with a company—a 'shareholder agreement'—to ensure that the company's affairs are conducted to a certain standard. A member can be liable to the company on an express contract, separate from the constitution,[39] or may have a cause of action for breach of contract if the terms of the contract are not abided by.

An example of the operation of an express contract may be seen in *Bailey v. New South Wales Medical Defence Union Ltd*, where the art. 6 of a company limited by guarantee provided that:

> [an applicant for membership] shall be deemed to have agreed to become a member of the union on receipt by the Secretary of an application for membership … Any such applicant (upon payment of the prescribed entrance fee and subscription) shall be entitled to the benefits of indemnity and assistance conferred by Articles 57–67 inclusive from the date of such payment until the date of his becoming a member or notification of refusal of his application for membership as the case may be.[40]

The purpose of the company was to provide professional indemnity insurance and assistance to medical practitioners. Article 57 provided that all financial members who required indemnity were indemnified by the Union. Bailey became a member and was later sued by C for professional malpractice. However, in the meantime, the company altered its articles so as to reduce members' entitlements to an indemnity. The issue was whether Bailey's entitlement had been effectively reduced. This issue turned on whether the indemnity arose under the articles, or from an express contract between Bailey and the Union.

The High Court found that the entitlement arose from the express contract as opposed to the deemed statutory contract. The cover was conferred when Bailey applied to become a member and continued for as long as he was a financial member, as provided in art. 6, which conferred rights to applicants for membership *before* they became members. Thus, the alteration of the articles could not reduce Bailey's entitlement to an indemnity.

---

38 Some express provisions of the Corporations Law allow for companies to compulsorily acquire minority shareholdings. See, for instance, s. 701 and s.195.

39 *Theseus Exploration NL v. Foyster* (1972) 126 CLR 507; 46 ALJR 448.

40 (1995) 132 ALR 1 at 15; 18 ACSR 521 at 535; 13 ACLC 1698 at1708.

Cause of action conferred by the Corporations Law or general law

When individuals join a company, they acquire certain rights and obligations as members. These rights and obligations are created both by the companies legislation and by case law. If one of these rights is infringed, the member does not have to show the existence of a contract. It is enough that legislation or case law has given the member that right. Examples of this kind of right are:

- the right to inspect the register of members[41]
- the right to vote at general meetings, unless denied by the constitution[42]
- the right to truly informative notice of meetings[43]
- rights attaching to classes of shares.[44]

The statutory contract

We have seen that, under the Corporations Law, a company's constitution is statutorily deemed to have the effect of a contract under seal between the company and each member; between the company and each eligible officer; and between a member and each other member (s. 180). Under this 'deemed contract', each of the parties agrees to observe and perform the provisions of the constitution as in force for the time being, so far as those provisions are applicable to that person. Because the articles are deemed to be equivalent to a contract under seal, it is settled law that s. 180 entitles members to enforce those terms of the articles that set out their rights as members.[45] Thus, if the majority breaches an article that confers personal rights on members, the majority can be restrained from so doing.[46]

King CJ suggested in *Residues Treatment & Trading Co. Ltd v. Southern Resources Ltd (No. 4)*[47] that shareholders have a personal right to protect the voting power of their shares against the improper actions of directors:

> A member's voting rights and the rights of participation which they provide for the decision making of the company are a fundamental attribute of membership and are rights which the member should be able to protect by legal action against improper diminution. The rule in *Foss v. Harbottle* has no application where individual membership rights as opposed to corporate rights are involved.[48]

REVIEW QUESTIONS

1   How does a court decide whether a breach is only an internal irregularity capable of being ratified, or whether it is a serious infringement of a personal right?[49]

---

41   *Mutter v. Eastern and Midlands Railway Co.* (1888) 38 Ch D 92 at 104.
42   *Pender v. Lushington* at 81.
43   *Kaye v. Croydon Tramways Co.* [1898] 1 Ch 358.
44   The area of variation of class rights has been discussed in chapters 8 and 13.
45   *Hickman v. Kent or Romney Marsh Sheepbreeders Association* [1915] 1 Ch 881.
46   See *Pender v. Lushington*.
47   (1988) 14 ACLR 569.
48   (1988) 14 ACLR 569 at 574.
49   See *MacDougall v. Gardiner*; *Pender v. Lushington*; *Bamford v. Bamford*.

2 Consider the facts of *Bailey v. New South Wales Medical Defence Union*, discussed above. If the articles had confined the benefit of an indemnity to members, would the express contract have still protected Bailey's entitlements?

Ultra vires *acts*

Ultra vires is no longer a true exception to the rule in *Foss v. Harbottle* because, under s. 162 of the Corporations Law, proceedings cannot be taken against the company, only against company officers. However, *ultra vires* is a ground for arguing oppression under s. 260 (see s. 162(7)(e)) and also for applying for an injunction under s. 1324 (see s. 162(7)(f)).[50]

Where a special majority is required

Where a special majority is required by the legislation or the articles (for example, s. 176) and that requirement is disregarded, members can bring an action to have the impugned resolution declared invalid. In *Edwards v. Halliwell*,[51] the rules of a trade union required that regular contributions be made by its members in accordance with certain tables. Any alteration to these rules had to be sanctioned by a two-thirds majority. A meeting of the union resolved to increase the contributions without a ballot of members. Two union members brought an action seeking a declaration that the alteration was invalid. It was argued that the rule in *Foss v. Harbottle* prevented the action. This was rejected. Jenkins LJ said that the reason for the exception was clear:

> [O]therwise, if the rule were applied in its full rigour, a company which, by its directors, had broken its own regulations by doing something without a special resolution which could only be done validly by a special resolution could assert that it alone was the proper plaintiff in any consequent action and the effect would be to allow a company acting in breach of its articles to do de facto by ordinary resolution that which according to its own regulations could only be done by special resolution.[52]

Where the 'interests of justice' require

The interests of justice exception is controversial. It was discussed in early cases, including *Foss v. Harbottle* and *Edwards v. Halliwell*. The substance of these early references was that the claims of justice should take priority over the technical rules of procedure. Procedure should not be allowed to thwart the demands of justice.

The case of *Hodgson v. NALGO*[53] affirmed the interests of justice exception as an independent ground of relief. This case did not concern a commercial company but a trade union, which lacked the capacity to sue in its own name, being unincorporated. Thus, the court considered that *Foss v. Harbottle* had no application because

---

50 Note that the exposure draft of the Second Corporations Law Simplification Bill repeals s. 162.
51 [1950] 2 All ER 1064.
52 [1950] 2 All ER 1064 at 1067.
53 [1972] 1 All ER 15.

the trade union was unincorporated and its remarks on the interests of justice exception could be interpreted as merely obiter.[54]

In *Prudential Assurance Co. Ltd v. Newman Industries Ltd*,[55] Vinelott J, at first instance, accepted the principle, regarding it as the real exception to the rule in *Foss v. Harbottle*, fraud being merely an example of the kind of injustice that would attract the assistance of equity. This approach was strongly disapproved of by the Court of Appeal. On the other hand, in *Estmanco (Kilner House) Ltd v. Greater London Council*, Megarry J (at 438) accepted that matters such as fraud and abuse or misuse of power were the 'real' exceptions, but added that, 'although injustice is not the test, it is a reason and a very important reason for making exceptions'.

In Australia, the exception has been recognised in *Hawkesbury Development Co. Ltd v. Landmark Finance Pty Ltd*,[56] although Street J considered that the alleged exception was extremely vague and ill-defined:

> There are to be found amongst discussions of the rule in *Foss v. Harbottle* some expressions of doubt as to whether there is in truth any room for any further extension of the exceptions under this broad heading. It is, perhaps, a useful door to be left open lest in some extremely unusual circumstances injustice would result from applying the rule. No exhaustive or even descriptive statement of such circumstances has been propounded. Nor have I been referred to any case constituting an example of the rule being disregarded solely because the justice of the case so required, nor being a case falling within one of the other recognised exceptions. It is the absence of definition or example of such exception that, no doubt, underlies such observations as are to be found to the effect that there is in truth no admissible ground for further exceptions. It would, however, be regrettable if the difficulty of foreseeing a possible need for allowing any further exceptions were to be elevated to an anticipatory refusal to recognise any future case as being justly treated as an exception.
>
> For the purposes of the present judgment I am prepared to accept the existence of a further exception to the rule in *Foss v. Harbottle* where justice so requires ... But I am unable to conclude that either of the two particular matters put forward is sufficient to render the present case within such an exception.[57]

More recently, in *Biala Pty Ltd v. Mallina Holdings Ltd (No. 2)*, Ipp J recognised the interests of justice exception, saying that equity 'is concerned with substance and not form, and it seems to me to be contrary to principle to require wronged minority shareholders to bring themselves within the boundaries of the well-recognised exceptions and deny jurisdiction to a court of equity even where an unjust or unconscionable result may otherwise ensue'.[58] Despite his willingness to entertain claims under the interest of justice exception, he was not prepared to find that the

54   Other references to this exception include *Hawkesbury Development Co.* and *Heyting v Dupont* [1964] 1 WLR 843.
55   [1981] Ch 229.
56   [1969] 2 NSWLR 782.
57   [1969] 2 NSWLR 782 at 790 per Street J.
58   (1993) 11 ACSR 785 at 848; 11 ACLC 1082 at 1102.

plaintiffs had made out a case establishing fraud on the minority, holding that they had not established the necessary degree of control.

REVIEW QUESTIONS

1 Are the 'exceptions' to the proper plaintiff rule better seen as cases where the general meeting cannot by ordinary resolution condone a wrong done to the company? What advantages would this view have?

2 Why do courts seem prepared to recognise the interests of justice exception, but seem reluctant to find the exception to be made out on the facts? In this context, you will find it helpful to think about the courts' more general reluctance to allow 'justice talk'.

Standing and the nature of the action

It is important that you understand the different nature of the potential actions under the exceptions to the rule in *Foss v. Harbottle* and why many commentators regard only the fraud on a minority exception and the interests of justice exception as 'true exceptions', the others having independent foundations that are not impugned by the rule in *Foss v. Harbottle*. Members can bring either a personal or a derivative action, depending upon the nature of their grievance.

A member has a personal action in cases where the wrongdoing affects a member's personal rights. As we have seen, a member may have a personal right of action in the following circumstances:

- under an express contract. Such a contract may exist as between the member and other members, or as between the member and the company
- under s. 180, to enforce the company constitution as a statutory contract
- on the basis of a personal cause of action accorded either by statute or the general law
- to check acts that are done in disregard of constraints that may be contained in the corporate constitution.

In such instances, the proper plaintiff is the member (under the personal rights exception to the rule in *Foss v. Harbottle*). Where the member is enforcing a personal right that is also enjoyed by other members, the matter may, for reasons of procedural convenience and cost savings, be brought by one member on behalf of the group or class affected—that is, the action is representative.[59] Despite its representative character, it remains within the personal rights exception to the rule in *Foss v. Harbottle*.

---

59 See, for example, *Pender v. Lushington*.

In this context it is interesting to return to the Court of Appeal decision in *Prudential Assurance Co. Ltd v. Newman Industries Ltd (No. 2).*[60] In addition to its action under the fraud on a minority exception, Prudential Assurance brought a personal action. The Court of Appeal was scathing in its treatment of the attempt to join a personal action and one under the fraud on a minority exception. It held that the attempt to bring a personal action was misconceived and, indeed, took the view that the personal action represented a blatant attempt to circumvent the rule. The court indicated that the plaintiff was not entitled to damages merely because the company was damaged and there had been a consequential diminution in share value. The shares were merely rights of participation on agreed terms and were not referable to any fixed quantum of corporate interests. The court observed:

> The plaintiffs in this action were never concerned to recover in the personal action. The plaintiffs were only interested in the personal action as a means of circumventing the rule in Foss v. Harbottle. The plaintiffs succeeded. A personal action would subvert the rule in Foss v. Harbottle and that rule is not merely a tiresome procedural obstacle placed in the path of a shareholder by a legalistic judiciary. The rule is the consequence of the fact that the company is a separate legal entity.[61]

The court emphasised that when individual shareholders accept shares they accepts that their fortunes follow those of the company and that their sole control is through their votes in general meeting. If the shareholder's position fails to command majority support, that is a risk inherent in democratic processes.

A derivative action, as its name suggests, is very different from a personal action. A derivative action arises when a wrong is done to the company as such, rather than to an individual member, in circumstances where the company cannot sue because the wrongdoers are in control. In a derivative action, a member (or group of members) takes the action on behalf of the company. The suit is prosecuted, not on the member's own behalf, but to secure redress for the company. Their right to bring the action is derived from that of the company. In a derivative action, paradoxically, the company is joined as a defendant. Because the wrongdoers control the company, the company cannot assume the role of plaintiff. Nonetheless, because the company is entitled to any damages that may be awarded, rather than the individual shareholder, it is essential that it be a party to the action. While the member or members initiating the action need not have been members at the date of the alleged wrong, the company must be in existence both at the date of the action and at the time at which judgment is given. The action is hedged about with procedural safeguards intended by the courts to minimise the possibility of vexatious litigation.

Clean hands

The first of the procedural hurdles that we will consider is the requirement that the plaintiff come before the court with 'clean hands'. The English decision in

---

60 [1982] Ch 204.
61 [1982] Ch 204 at 267.

Nurcombe v. Nurcombe[62] provides an excellent introduction to the ramifications of *Foss v. Harbottle*. For this reason, it provides a useful starting point. It is one of only two cases in the Commonwealth dealing with the requirement that a *Foss v. Harbottle* plaintiff must approach the court with clean hands. This requirement reflects the equitable roots of company law and emphasises the fact that the plaintiff in a *Foss v. Harbottle* action is presumed to be acting altruistically[63]—that is, on behalf of the company—rather than out of self-interest. Fundamentally, the allegation of the plaintiff is that those entrusted with the management of the company have failed to carry out their role and have failed to act in the interests of the company as a whole. As a consequence, the plaintiff has been compelled to act.

The facts of *Nurcombe v. Nurcombe* involve the classic ingredients of a private family company and a matrimonial dispute. The former husband held 66 per cent of the shares; the former wife held 34 per cent. The company was engaged in property speculation. During earlier divorce proceedings and thereafter, the plaintiff (the defendant's first wife) had been unaware of the details of her former husband's financial position. She learnt from a magazine article that, before the divorce, the defendant had been involved in the purchase of a particular parcel of land and that he had apparently profited to the extent of £128 000 from resale of the land. During the hearings for financial support, it emerged that the company had held contracts concerning this land and that the defendant had been actively engaged in the negotiations. These contracts gave the company an option over the subject land, which had been allowed to lapse. Immediately thereafter, another company controlled by the former husband, Maidsfield, had purchased a portion of the land, which it resold at a substantial profit. A substantial proportion of this profit reached the defendant. As a consequence of the evidence led in the matrimonial proceedings, the plaintiff received a lump sum settlement of £25 000 together with periodic payments of £1500 per annum.

Subsequently, the plaintiff sought standing to exercise her right as a minority shareholder in the company, which (as is required in an action under *Foss v. Harbottle*) had been joined as second defendant. Vinelott J, at first instance, held that the plaintiff had elected to abandon her right as minority shareholder when she chose to prosecute the settlement under the matrimonial cause. She appealed on the basis that she was unaware of the material facts until after the conclusion of the first proceedings and that, as she was suing on behalf of the company, her personal interest was, in any case, irrelevant.

On appeal it was held that the doctrine of election (in the common-law sense) was not involved. The plaintiff could not be said to have suffered any personal loss as a consequence of the defendant's defalcations. While the pecuniary value of her shares had diminished as a result of the defalcations, the shares themselves

---

62 [1985] 1 WLR 370.

63 The altruistic position of the plaintiff in a derivative action distinguishes the requirements for a successful action under the rule in *Foss v. Harbottle* from those under the Corporations Law, ss. 260 and 462, where the pleadings typically lack this altruistic element.

remained unaffected by the wrongdoing.[64] The Court of Appeal held that, because an action under an exception to *Foss v. Harbottle* is a procedural device to enable shareholders to do justice to a company controlled by miscreants, the plaintiff must bring the action for the benefit of the company and not for some other purpose. Thus, the plaintiff must be a proper person and must come before the court with clean hands. Here the plaintiff had taken the chance of success in the matrimonial cause before Rees J and had already received the sum of £25 000, which represented a part of the profits obtained by the defendant at the company's expense. Thus the plaintiff could not be granted standing to raise the issue. She sought not to act in the company's interests, but to enhance the monetary value of her shareholding with the hope of eventual pecuniary gain. Effectively, the company was irrelevant to the battle for assets between former husband and wife. Indeed, the fact that a wrong had been done to the company and the fact of its separate legal personality appeared to be wholly irrelevant. In essence, the court tacitly recognised that the company was no more and no less than the former husband and wife; it had neither identity nor interests that could be meaningfully separated from the interests of its principals. Lawton LJ noted:

> A minority shareholder's action in form is nothing more than a procedural device for enabling the court to do justice to a company controlled by miscreant directors or shareholders. Since the procedural device has evolved so that justice can be done for the benefit of the company, *whoever comes forward to start the proceedings must be doing so for the benefit of the company and not for some other purpose.* It follows that the court has to satisfy itself that the person coming forward is a proper person to do so ... A particular plaintiff may not be a proper person because his conduct is tainted in some way which under the rules of equity may bar relief. He may not have come with 'clean hands' or he may have been guilty of delay.[65]

Locus standi: *Two trials or one?*

The most significant hurdle that a potential plaintiff under an exception to the rule in *Foss v. Harbottle* is likely to confront is that of standing. In order to bring the substantive issues before the court, the plaintiff must obtain standing. Assuming that the threshold requirement for clean hands is met, there are two tests. The first is control. The plaintiff must prove that those perpetrating the wrong have control of the company. The second requirement, as noted, is a prima facie case that a fraud has been perpetrated against the company. Application is made to the court sitting in its equitable jurisdiction, and all the rules of equity apply. In *Prudential Assurance Co. Ltd v. Newman Industries Ltd*, the Court of Appeal took the view that the judge in a derivative action should determine the question of the plaintiff's standing as a

---

64   This is, of course, a classic formulation of the doctrine of separate legal personality. Over the years, the former husband had stripped the company of all the assets to which it had been entitled, but because the former wife retained her shares in the company, she had lost nothing. The rights and obligations pertaining to those shares remained intact; only the money had vanished.

65   [1985] 1 WLR 370 at 377 per Lawton LJ (emphasis added).

preliminary issue, before hearing the main case on its merits. This meant that, before the merits could be reached, it would be necessary for the plaintiff to make out a prima facie case that the company was entitled to the relief claimed and that the action fell within one of the accepted exceptions to the rule in *Foss v. Harbottle*.

The Court of Appeal reasoned as follows. If the plaintiff can require that the court must assume that every allegation in the claim is factual, the plaintiff will be able to out-manoeuvre the rule. Equally, if the plaintiff is required to prove both fraud and control at the outset, a full trial may be necessary to ascertain if the action is legitimate. Either way, the role of the rule in foreclosing unnecessary litigation is demolished. If fraud is not proved, there is no issue. If fraud is proved, the delinquent has been held accountable. As a consequence, the Court of Appeal concluded that the issue of standing must be settled at the outset of litigation. They thought it unjust to subject the parties to a full trial to ascertain if a full trial was appropriate. They held, therefore, that the plaintiff must establish at the outset a prima facie case that the company was entitled to relief, and that the action fell within the boundaries of the rule and the exceptions thereto. Only then could a trial on the merits commence. As their Lordships noted:

> It cannot have been right to have subjected the company to a 30 day action (as it was then estimated to be) in order to enable him to decide whether the plaintiffs were entitled in law to subject the company to a thirty day action. Such an approach defeats the whole purpose of the rule in *Foss v. Harbottle* and sanctions the very mischief that the rule is designed to prevent … In the present case a board, of which all the directors save one were disinterested … had reached the conclusion before the start of the action that the prosecution of the action was likely to do more harm than good. That might prove a sound or unsound assessment, but it was the commercial assessment of an apparently independent board … [T]he board clearly doubted whether there were sufficient reasons for supposing that the company would at the end of the day be in a position to be able to count its blessings; and clearly feared, as counsel said, that it might be killed by kindness.[66]

In Australia, the position would appear to be less hard and fast, and a healthy pragmatism prevails. In *Hurley v. BGH Nominees*,[67] King CJ, after considering the approach to standing taken in *Prudential Assurance Co. Ltd*, concluded that a preliminary hearing to determine if a prima facie case existed might run as long as a full trial and prove less satisfactory. Thus, standing should be determined in the circumstances of each case on the basis of what appeared to be just and convenient in the circumstances before the court.[68]

---

66 [1981] Ch 204 at 221. While the approach of their Lordships seems harsh, it must be remembered that litigation of this kind is formidably expensive; very often it requires a fine degree of judgment to determine whether, after the dust has settled, the damages gained (even with the costs rule) outweigh the expense and distraction of litigation and the potential for bad publicity.

67 (1982) 1 ACLC 387.

68 (1982) ACLC 387 at 390–1. This view was upheld in *Dempster v. Biala Pty Ltd* (1989) 15 ACLR 191; 1 WAR 266; 7 ACLC 552. It goes without saying that this approach maximises the discretion available to the judge.

Despite the concern of the English Court of Appeal with the potential for vexatious litigation, the structure of the action in itself would appear sufficient to minimise vexatious litigation. One of the critical features of a derivative action, and a powerful disincentive to bringing such an action, is the ambiguous position of the minority shareholder. While the minority shareholder necessarily has carriage of the action, and bears the costs if the action is unsuccessful, she or he has little if anything to gain even from a successful action. Undoubtedly the cost structure is one of the most powerful deterrents to its use for vexatious litigation.[69]

For this reason, if for no other, where a minority member brings a derivative action, and that action is upheld, it would seem appropriate that the company should pay those costs of the plaintiff that are not recovered from the defendant. In England it has been held that a minority shareholder who brings a derivative action can apply by summons in the action for directions as to whether to proceed.[70] If the court finds that an independent board of directors would have authorised an action by the company, it may order the company to indemnify the plaintiff.[71] It can do this even if the action fails, provided that the action was 'a reasonable and prudent course to take in the interests of the company'. However, any damages awarded go back to the company and not to the member(s) who initiated the action.

Under s. 50 of the *Australian Securities Commission Act 1989* (Cth), the Australian Securities Commission (ASC) can bring a 'class action' on behalf of members or investors to recover damages for fraud, negligence, breach of duty, or other misconduct. The action must be in the public interest and result from an ASC investigation. In *Deloitte Touche Tohmatsu v. ASC*,[72] it was held that, before litigating on behalf of a company, the ASC should take into account the rule in *Foss v. Harbottle*. Thus, in general, the only circumstances in which it would be appropriate for the ASC to bring proceedings in the company's name without the directors' consent would be where the directors participated in the impugned conduct. On appeal, however, the court found that there is nothing in the statutory context or in the purpose of s. 50 that compels the conclusion that *Foss v. Harbottle* principles should be taken into account in forming a public interest judgment under s. 50.[73]

The Second Corporate Law Simplification Bill 1995 proposes the introduction of a statutory derivative action.[74] On enactment, derivative rights arising from the exceptions to the rule in *Foss v. Harbottle* will be abolished. Under the proposed leg-

---

69 The authors are aware, of course, that the issue of costs is likely to be less telling where the 'minority shareholder' is itself a major corporation, as was the case in *Prudential*. In such circumstances, the plaintiff has the 'deep pocket' essential to fund the action.

70 *Wallersteiner v. Moir (No. 2)* [1975] QB 373. The judgment of Lord Denning is excellent on this point.

71 In *Parker v. NRMA* (1993) 11 ACSR 370; 11 ACLC 866, the New South Wales Court of Appeal refused to grant such an indemnity, based upon the trial judge's finding, at first instance, that no improper conduct had occurred.

72 (1996) 14 ACLC 604 at 613 per Lindgren J.

73 (1996) 14 ACLC 1486.

74 A number of reports have recommended the introduction of such an action. See, for instance, Companies and Securities Law Review Committee, *Enforcement of the Duties of Directors and Officers of a Company by Means of a Statutory Derivative Action*, CSLRC, Melbourne, 1990. Such an action has been available for some time in overseas jurisdictions (Ontario being an excellent example).

islation, the leave of the court must be obtained before 'proceedings on behalf of the company' can be brought. Both members and former members of the company or a related company will be eligible to apply for such leave, as will directors and officers of the company and the ASC. The relevant proceedings are those that the company has against a director for breach of duties owed to the company or a third party, either for a breach of a contract or for a tort committed by that third party. Four criteria must be satisfied before the court can grant leave:

1   There must be a failure to act on the part of the company
2   The applicant must be bringing the action in good faith
3   The action must appear to be in the best interests of the company
4   The matter must involve the determination of a serious question.

Any ratification that has taken place will not necessarily prevent the court from granting leave to proceed, although ratification may be taken into account. The court must be satisfied that any ratification that took place was by fully informed, independent members. The court will have a broad discretion regarding orders for costs.

REVIEW QUESTIONS

1   Is a new statutory derivative action necessary when the legislation already provides remedies under ss. 260 and 1324?
2   Is a member precluded from suing as a plaintiff in a derivative action on behalf of the company because he or she has a personal remedy on the same facts?[75]
3   What is the effect of liquidation on a derivative action?[76]

Statutory rights and remedies

So far we have examined the common-law position with regard to minority remedies brought about by the rule in *Foss v. Harbottle*. It is important to note the shortcomings of the *Foss v. Harbottle* rule, including the fact that exceptions to the rule are ambiguous; their scope is uncertain; they focus upon single acts or transactions rather than providing redress for conduct that occurs over a period of time; and the element of control, for the purposes of the fraud on the minority exception, is often difficult to make out.[77]

---

75   See *Hurley v. BGH Nominees Pty Ltd*.
76   See *Farrow v. Registrar of Building Societies* [1991] 2 VR 589.
77   For discussion of the shortcomings of the general law and minority actions, see K. Yeung, 'Disentangling the Tangled Skein: The Ratification of Directors Actions' (1992) 66 ALJ 343; J. Hill, 'Protecting Minority Shareholders and Reasonable Expectations' (1992) 10 CSLJ 86; D. Wishart, 'A Conceptual Analysis of the Control of Companies' (1984) 14 MULR 601; S. Fridman, 'Ratification of Directors' Breaches' (1992) 10 CSLJ 10; S. M. Beck, 'An Analysis of Foss v Harbottle', in J. S. Ziegal (ed.), *Studies in Canadian Company Law*, Butterworths, Toronto, 1967, pp. 556–7.

Minority rights and remedies have been considerably strengthened by legislation. Under the Corporations Law, the potential rights and remedies of the aggrieved minority shareholder include:

- application under ss. 197, 198, and 414 to object to reductions of capital, infringements of class rights, and compulsory acquisition (although note the potential effects of the Second Corporate Simplification Bill)
- application under s. 205 to oppose the company giving financial assistance in connection with shares
- application under s. 212 to seek rectification of the share register
- application under ss. 246 and 247 to requisition a general meeting of the company
- application under s. 260 for remedy in cases of oppression or injustice in the conduct of the company's affairs
- application under s. 319 to obtain court approval to inspect company records[78]
- application under ss. 460–1 for an order for the winding-up of the company
- complaint under s. 536 about the conduct of the liquidator
- application under s. 597 for an order to examine persons concerned with the corporation
- application under s. 598 for an order against persons concerned with the corporation
- application under ss. 705, 737, 739, or 740 to seek damages or other relief where the takeovers provisions of the legislation have been breached
- application under s. 777 for an order to enforce the listing rules
- application under ss. 995 and 1005 seeking the remedy for misleading and deceptive conduct with regard to a prospectus
- application under ss. 1005 and 1013–15 to seek compensation where a shareholder is a victim of market rigging and/or insider trading
- application under s. 1322 (2) to correct a procedural irregularity, such as lack of notice or failure to call a poll, where that procedural irregularity has caused substantial injustice[79]
- application under s. 1324 for an injunction or other order in respect of conduct in contravention of the legislation.[80]

These statutory provisions help aggrieved minority shareholders in a number of ways. For example, one way in which company controllers can frustrate attempts by a minority member to take action for wrongdoing is to withhold relevant information. To ensure that minority shareholders have access to essential information, legislation provides that shareholders can gain information by utilising s. 319 and

---

78 There are a number of conditions that must be satisfied in order to satisfy the court that an inspection should be granted. In particular, the inspection must be for a proper purpose: see *Re Humes Ltd* (1987) 5 ACLC 64.

79 *Mamouney v. Soliman* (1992) 10 ACLC 1674.

80 For instances of injunctions, see *Broken Hill Pty Co. Ltd v. Bell Resources Ltd* (1984) 2 ACLC 157.

applying to the court for permission to inspect the company's books.[81] This is a positive right, although it is subject to the court granting permission.

Apart from this positive right, the statutory rights of the minority shareholder are largely negative in character. That is, they establish boundaries of behaviour over which the majority or the board should not step. Of these rights and remedies, those that have attracted the most significant comment have been the oppression remedy (s. 260) and the just and equitable winding-up (s. 461). The just and equitable winding-up was discussed in chapter 10. In this chapter, we will consider the scope of the remedies available under s. 260.

The oppression remedy

Section 260 of the Corporations Law is as follows:

> 260(1)   An application to the Court for an order under this section in relation to a company may be made:
>
> (a)   by a member who believes:
>
> (i)   That affairs of the company are being conducted in a manner that is oppressive or unfairly prejudicial to, or unfairly discriminatory against, a member or members, or in a manner *that is contrary to the interests of the members as a whole*; or
>
> (ii)   That an act or omission, or a proposed act or omission, by or on behalf of the company, or a resolution, or a proposed resolution, of a class of members, was or would be oppressive or unfairly prejudicial to, or unfairly discriminatory against, a member or members or *was or would be contrary to the interests of the members as a whole*.[82]

Section 260 is based on s. 210 of the *Companies Act 1948* (UK), which empowered the court to give relief for oppressive conduct other than an order for winding-up (which was considered to be a drastic remedy), although it has been progressively expanded in recent years. One of the most notable areas of expansion has been the dropping of the original requirement for a continuing course of conduct and the availability of the remedy for an isolated act or omission. This expansion, it was thought, largely provided a statutory alternative to an exception under the rule in *Foss v. Harbottle*.

The oppression remedy is available in many of the cases where the facts would allow relief on the basis of one of the exceptions to the rule in *Foss v. Harbottle*, such as abuse of the voting power of the majority in altering the constitution or improperly ratifying a wrong done to the company, or an abuse of power by the directors. It is irrelevant whether the impugned conduct infringes an individual membership right or would give rise to a derivative action.

---

81   This is not an unqualified right: The tests applied by the court are that the application must be made in good faith and for a proper purpose (not, for example, to obtain information to assist a takeover bid). See *Re Humes Ltd*; *Cescastle Pty Ltd v. Renak Holdings Ltd* (1991) 9 ACLC 1333.

82   Emphasis added.

A matter of interpretation

The potential scope of the oppression remedy, as you can see from its wording, is very great and should provide relief for an aggrieved minority shareholder in a range of circumstances. The section has, however, generally been subject to a narrow interpretation. There are a number of reasons for this. First, it is significant that, to the extent that a 'typical' s. 260 plaintiff exists, he or she is an 'involuntary' member in a closely held company. The substantive ground for the action very often is the inability of such a shareholder to sell his or her shares at anything like the asset backing of the company.[83]

Oppression is not defined in the Corporations Law. Consequently, courts must refer to the ordinary meaning of the word and the context in which it is used.[84] The legislature originally intended 'oppression' to mean a departure from a standard of fair dealing and fair play, but it has been read restrictively by some courts to specify that conduct was 'burdensome, harsh or wrongful'[85] and 'lacking in probity'.[86] 'Wrongful' in this context has been interpreted as requiring actual illegality or invasion of legal rights.[87] This restrictive interpretation was, on one level, an attempt by the courts to limit shareholder actions by distinguishing between 'mere' minority disagreement and cases of abuse of power, in the absence of unambiguous standards.[88] It is clear that the cause of action requires substantially more than a mere disagreement between the minority and the majority. Lord Cooper stated that oppressive conduct should be equated with

> unfair abuse of powers and an impairment of confidence in the probity with which the company's affairs are being conducted, as distinguished from mere resentment on the part of a minority at being outvoted on some issue of domestic policy … The essence of the matter seems to be that the conduct complained of should at the lowest involve a visible departure from the standards of fair play on which every shareholder who entrusts his money to the company is entitled to rely.[89]

The restrictive interpretation also reflects the court's traditional reluctance to judge the merits of a board's decisions where those decisions are essentially commercial in nature:[90] 'Prima facie, it is for the directors and not for the court to decide whether the furthering of a corporate object which is inimical to a

---

83 It is interesting that typical plaintiffs are acting in pursuit of their individual interests, not in pursuit of corporate interests.

84 See *Re H. R. Harmer Ltd* [1958] 3 All ER 689 at 698 per Jenkings LJ. Inevitably, because the legislative provision did not exclude the common law, recourse was had to judicial definitions of oppression under previous provisions.

85 *Scottish Co-operative Wholesale Society Ltd v. Meyer* [1959] AC 324.

86 *Re Jermyn Street Turkish Baths Ltd* [1971] 1 WLR 1042.

87 *Re Broadcasting Station 2GB* [1964–65] NSWR 1648; *Re Bright Pine Mills Pty Ltd* [1969] VR 1002 at 1012.

88 For a general discussion of the oppression remedy, see G. P. Stapledon, 'Use of the Oppression Provision in Listed Companies in Australia and New Zealand' (1993) 67 ALJ 575, and for a discussion of the non-interventionist stance in this area, see D. Wishart, 'A Fresh Approach to s. 320' (1987) 17 UWALR 94.

89 *Elder v. Elder and Watson Ltd* [1959] SC 49.

90 Support for the traditional non-interventionist stance can be seen in *Re G. Jeffrey (Men's Store) Pty Ltd* (1984) 9 ACLR 193 at 198; *Zephyr Holdings Pty Ltd v. Jack Chia (Australia) Ltd* (1988) 14 ACLR 30.

member's interests should prevail over those interests or whether some balance should be struck between them'.[91]

The policy is seen by some not only as outdated but also as somewhat illogical. The courts ritualistically defer to directors' judgment, despite the fact that the common law does not require that a director have particular qualifications or expertise.[92] On the other hand, does a court have the necessary commercial expertise to interfere with a board's decisions?

In 1983, the oppression remedy in Australia was amended to extend the application of that remedy to behaviour that was unfairly prejudicial, behaviour that was unfairly discriminatory or contrary to the interests of members as a whole, conduct that continued over time, and past conduct, and to allow members to redress wrongs done to other companies of which they were members. But despite these amendments, decisions still tended to uphold the narrow view.

REVIEW QUESTION

To what extent should judges interfere with the business decisions of directors? For instance, if the board were to make a decision that was in good faith and made for a proper purpose, but unfair to a particular member, could the court intervene on the basis of oppression?[93]

One principle or four categories?

As a consequence of the 1983 amendments, s. 260 refers to conduct that is 'oppressive or unfairly prejudicial or unfairly discriminatory … or contrary to the interests of the members'. Section 260 now contains four grounds that justify intervention by the courts. There is some question whether the grounds in s. 260 are examples of some broader principle or whether the individual grounds can stand alone. An example of the first approach may be found in the judgment of Young J in *Morgan v. 45 Flers Avenue Pty Ltd*: 'In my view a court now looks at subs 2(a) as a composite whole and the individual elements mentioned in the section should be considered merely as different aspects of the essential criterion, namely commercial unfairness'.[94]

In *Thomas v. H. W. Thomas Ltd*,[95] Richardson J held that the grounds in s. 260 were not alternatives that should be considered as distinct categories. Rather each should be interpreted in the context provided by the others. The legislature intended to provide minority shareholders with a remedy where there were instances or courses of conduct that amounted to unjust detriment:

---

91 *Wayde v. New South Wales Rugby League Ltd* (1985) 3 ACLC 799 at 806 per Brennan J.

92 Hill at 88, fn. 21.

93 See *Wayde v. New South Wales Rugby League Ltd* (1985) 61 ALR 225 at 234 per Brennan J.

94 (1986) 10 ACLR 692 at 704. The term 'commercial unfairness', like its cousin 'commercial morality', is not susceptible to precise definition.

95 [1984] 1 NZLR 686; (1984) 2 ACLC 610

In employing the words 'oppressive, unfairly discriminatory or unfairly prejudicial' parliament has afforded petitioners a wider base on which to found a complaint. Taking the ordinary dictionary definition of the words from *The Shorter Oxford English Dictionary*: oppressive is 'unjustly burdensome'; unfair is 'not fair or equitable; unjust'; discriminate is 'to make or constitute a difference in or between; to differentiate'; and prejudicial, 'causing prejudice, detrimental, damaging to rights, interests etc.' I do not read the subsection as referring to three distinct alternatives which are to be considered separately in watertight compartments. The three expressions overlap, each in a sense helps to explain the other, and read together they reflect the underlying concern of the subsection that conduct of the company which is unjustly detrimental to any member of the company whatever form it takes and whether it adversely affects all members alike or discriminates against some only is a legitimate foundation for a complaint.[96]

Other judges, however, have treated these grounds as distinct, rather than reading them as a composite whole. In *Re Spargos Mining NL*,[97] Murray J held that the fourth ground (conduct contrary to the interests of the members of the company as a whole) was a discrete ground for relief. An order was made granting a remedy under the oppression remedy where the directors had acted with an 'endemic incapacity' to deal with the company's affairs. The impugned transactions were almost completely lacking in any commercial benefit to the company and showed clear cases of conflict of interest that disadvantaged the company.[98] Similarly, in *Re Norvabron Pty Ltd*, the court held that it was not necessary for a member to demonstrate both oppression and unfair prejudice, as it is sufficient (where relevant) for only one of those grounds to be made out.[99]

It's so unfair!

It is easy to see how the interplay of the four grounds affects interpretation. It has been held that the minimum content of the expression 'oppression' in s. 260 is unfairness.[100] For instance, in *Re Spargos Mining NL*, Murray J said, 'I conclude that unfairness may lie in the harm suffered as a result of the conduct of management, the prejudice caused, the lack of reasonable commercial justification for the court taken or simply in the decision-making process within the company'.[101] The concept of discrimination in s. 260 implies either that a burden is unfairly distributed between members or that a benefit is conferred on some members to the exclusion of others, with no rational ground for the unequal treatment. But mere prejudice is not necessarily unfair. According to Brennan J, '[i]t is not necessarily unfair for directors in good faith to advance one of the objects of the company to the prejudice of a member where the advancement of the object necessarily entails prejudice to that member or discrimination against him'.[102]

---

96   [1984] 1 NZWLR 686 at 693; (1984) 2 ACLC 610 at 616–17.
97   (1990) 3 ACSR 1.
98   (1990) 3 ACSR 1 at 42.
99   (1987) 11 ACLR 279. See also *Edwards v. Idaville Pty Ltd* (1996) 19 ACSR 556.
100 *Wayde v. New South Wales Rugby League Ltd* (1985) 10 ACLR 87 at 95.
101 (1990) 3 ACLR 1 at 44.

In *Wayde*, the High Court argued that the term 'unfairly' qualified 'prejudice' in s. 260. It followed that mere prejudice, even severe prejudice, was insufficient. The additional element of unfairness was essential to the possibility of a remedy. It is easy to see how this reasoning arose, given the facts of *Wayde*. The directors of the New South Wales Rugby League Ltd determined that it was in the interests of the league to exclude one football club from premiership competition. Because exclusion meant that the club could not survive, the directors of the club brought an action under s. 260. The High Court declined to intervene to provide a remedy to the football club, as the articles allowed the directors to discriminate by excluding it. In other words, the operation of the article, although prejudicial to the football club, was not *unfairly* prejudicial. On the reasoning used by the High Court, it appears unlikely that unfair prejudice really adds anything to the concept of oppression. Both concepts originate in unfairness. On the other hand, it is worth noting just how far removed from the usual commercial case the facts of *Wayde* really are. Once the league decided it was essential to reduce the number of clubs in the premiership competition—an action that the league believed to be in the interests of the game and the league—it could not carry out this resolve without acting prejudicially towards at least one of the clubs. Unfortunately for the plaintiff club, it was the weakest club in the competition. In the more usual setting of a closely held commercial company, the facts are unlikely to be as clear cut.

The fact that, in contrast to *Wayde*, all members are treated in a uniform manner does not mean that conduct is fair. In *Scottish Co-operative Wholesale Society Ltd v. Meyer*,[103] yarn was, at the time of the case, subject to licensing control. Two licensees joined the Scottish Co-operative Wholesale Society to form a company. The aim of the company was to buy yarn and deal in rayon cloth. Of the £7900 issued capital, 4000 £1 shares were held by the society, and 3900 by individuals. The company's board was composed of five directors, two of whom were individual members, the other three being nominee directors nominated by the society.

The company was successful, and when the value of a £1 share had reached £6, the society sought to acquire more shares at par value. This was opposed by individual members. After cotton regulation ended, the society was able to buy yarn without a licence. It then adopted a policy of refusing supplies of rayon cloth to the company, on the basis that the company had served its purpose. The society's board refused an offer made by the individual members to sell their shares at £4, 16 s per share. The nominee directors let the company's business languish while the society entered into competition with the company. When the minority members brought an action for oppression, the society was ordered to purchase the shares of individual members at £3, 15 s each. Thus, although everyone was treated equally, the conduct was still unfair. As Lord Denning put the matter:

> So long as the interests of all concerned were in harmony, there was no difficulty ... But, so soon as the interests of the two companies were in conflict, the nominee directors were

102   *Wayde v. New South Wales Rugby League Ltd* (1985) 10 ACLR 87 at 95.
103   [1959] AC 324.

placed in an impossible position. Thus, when the realignment of shareholding was under discussion, the duty of the three directors to the company was to get the best possible price for any new issue of its shares ... whereas their duty to the society was to obtain the new shares at the lowest possible price—at par, if they could. Again, when the society determined to set up its own rayon department, competing with the business of the company, the duty of the three directors to the company was to do their best to promote its business and to act with complete good faith towards it ... It is plain that, in the circumstances, these three gentlemen could not do their duty by both companies and they did not do so ... By subordinating the interests of the company to those of the society, they conducted the affairs of the company in a manner oppressive to the other shareholders.[104]

The court's jurisdiction under s. 260 can be activated by a completed or proposed act or omission (or the general conduct of the affairs of a company) that is or would be contrary to the interests of the members as a whole. This ground does not seem to flow directly from the concept of unfairness in the same way that the first three grounds do. In *Zephyr Holdings Pty Ltd v. Jack Chia (Australia) Ltd*,[105] Brooking J considered that those words meant something different from the expression 'oppressed member or members' used earlier in s. 260. He also said that 'anything that is oppressive or unfairly prejudicial to the members as a whole would seem necessarily to be also contrary to their interests'. The fourth ground allows the court to take into account the *combined* effect of the conduct complained of, in order to determine whether it is contrary to the interests of the members as a whole.

An objective test

In commercial companies, oppression will be assessed as a question of commercial fairness, judged objectively (as by a commercial bystander). In the *Wayde* case, it was held that, where the conduct complained of is that of the directors, the commercial bystander is taken to be a director. Who are 'reasonable directors'? According to Brennan J in the *Wayde* case, they are those 'possessing any special skill, knowledge or acumen possessed by the directors and having in mind the importance of furthering the corporate object on the one hand and the disadvantage, disability or burden which their decision will impose on a member on the other'.[106]

So, what will constitute 'oppression' for this provision? Obviously an actual (as opposed to threatened) financial detriment to a member will be sufficient.[107] Other circumstances may constitute oppression, although there must be more than mere allegations of mismanagement.[108] Oppression has been found where directors forgo an opportunity for the company, and direct business to another entity of which they are members, as in the *Scottish Wholesale* case outlined above.[109] Similarly, where (in a family company) a governing director has continued to ignore the other directors

---

104   [1959] AC 324 at 367.
105   (1988) 14 ACLR 30 at 37.
106   (1985) 10 ACLR 87 at 95.
107   *Re Broadcasting Station 2GB Pty Ltd.*
108   *Re Five Minute Car Wash Service Ltd* [1966] 1 WLR 745.
109   See also *Re Bright Pine Mills Pty Ltd.*

and the board's resolutions, the conduct has been held to be oppressive.[110] Oppression has also been found where:

- a company unfairly restricts dividends[111]
- excessive remuneration has been supplied to a controller or associate of the company[112]
- share issues are made with the dominant purpose of diluting a minority shareholding[113]
- where there is an alteration of articles in circumstances where a shareholder's shares are compulsorily acquired without consent.[114]

Additional instances of oppression include situations in which access is denied to company information;[115] board meetings are conducted oppressively;[116] or decisions are made for the benefit of related companies, rather than for the shareholders of the company.[117] Perhaps most remarkably, using company funds to defend oppression proceedings has been regarded as oppressive.[118]

Superficially, these circumstances may appear to have little in common. To the extent that a common thread exists, it may be stated in these terms. Where conduct targets minority shareholders and is conduct that, from the perspective of a reasonable director, appears to be devoid of corporate advantage, it will be deemed oppressive. Where, on the other hand, conduct is commercially reasonable (even if it is disadvantageous to particular shareholders), it will be allowed to stand. The courts have not been willing to extend the oppression remedy sufficiently to allow it to provide relief to locked-in minority shareholders in family companies unless there has been an invalid exercise of powers or an improper removal from management. Where either of these criteria is present, however, the partnership analogy will come into play and redress may be possible.

Standing

Under s. 260, members, legal representatives of members, and the ASC have standing to bring an oppression action, although it has been held that unregistered purchasers[119] and applicants with collateral purposes lack standing.[120]

A question arises as to whether a minority shareholder is limited by the same equitable considerations that govern the common-law 'fraud on the minority' exception to *Foss v. Harbottle*. Although it has been argued on a number of occasions that an applicant must come to court with clean hands, it would seem that this is

---

110   *Re H. R. Harmer Ltd*; *Shannon v. Reid* (1993) 11 ACLC 1.
111   *Re City Meat Co. Pty Ltd* (1983) 8 ACLR 673; *Re Bagot Well Pastoral Company* (1992) 9 ACSR 129.
112   *Sanford v. Sanford Courier Service Pty Ltd* (1986) 10 ACLR 549; 5 ACLC 394.
113   *Re Dalkeith Investments Pty Ltd* (1984) 9 ACLR 247; (1985) 3 ACLC 74.
114   *WCP Ltd v. Gambotto* (1993) 11 ACLC 457.
115   *Re Back 2 Bay 6 Pty Ltd* (1994) 12 ACSR 614; 12 ACLC 253.
116   *John J. Starr (Real Estate) Pty Ltd v. Robert R. Andrew (Australasia) Pty Ltd* (1991) 6 ACSR 63; 9 ACLC 1372.
117   *Re Spargos Mining NL.*
118   *Re D. G. Brims and Sons Pty Ltd* (1995) 16 ACSR 559.
119   *Niord Pty Ltd v. Adelaide Petroleum NL* (1990) 2 ACSR 347; 54 SASR 87.
120   *Re Bellador Silk Ltd* [1965] 1 All ER 667.

not the case.[121] On the other hand, although clean hands are not essential, the conduct of the applicant cannot be entirely disregarded. Nourse J asserted in *Re London School of Electronics Limited*:

> The combined effect of sub-ss. (1) and (3) is to empower the court to make such order as it thinks fit for giving relief, it is first satisfied that the affairs of the company are being or have been conducted in a manner which is unfairly prejudicial to the interests of some part of the members. The conduct of the petitioner may be material in a number of ways of which the two most obvious are these. First, it may render the conduct on the other side, even if it is prejudicial, not unfair … Secondly, even if the conduct on the other side is both prejudicial and unfair, the petitioner's conduct may nevertheless affect the relief which the court thinks fit to grant under sub-section (3). In my view there is no independent or overriding requirement that it should be just and equitable to grant relief or that the petitioner should come to the court with clean hands.[122]

At the same time, an action under s. 260 must be genuine: 'A petition which is launched not with the genuine object of obtaining the relief claimed, but with the object of exerting pressure in order to achieve a collateral purpose is, in my judgment, an abuse of the process of the court, and it is primarily on that ground that I would dismiss this petition'.[123]

Unlike an action for fraud on the minority under common law, an application for indemnity cannot be brought for the oppression action, as the applicant is taken to be seeking protection of the rights of members rather than corporate rights.[124]

REVIEW QUESTIONS

1 What possible orders can the court make if it finds that an action for oppression under s. 260 of the Corporations Law is made out?

2 In assessing a s. 260 action, is the court concerned with the motives of the wrongdoers or with the effect of the conduct on the minority shareholder?

3 Section 1324 of the Corporations Law provides that the ASC and 'a person whose interests have been, are or would be affected by' conduct in contravention of the Corporations Law can apply to the court for an injunction. This section has been given a broad interpretation.[125] To what extent does s. 1324 represent an exception to *Foss v. Harbottle*?[126]

---

121 *Morgan v. 45 Flers Avenue Pty Ltd* (1986) 10 ACLR 692 at 706. See also (albeit in respect of s. 461) *Pizem v. Malek* (1985) 3 ACLC 612.

122 [1985] 3 WLR 474 at 482.

123 *Re Bellador Silk Limited* [1965] 1 All ER 667 at 672 per Plowman J.

124 *Re Sherborne Park Residents Co. Ltd* (1986) 2 BCC 528.

125 See *Broken Hill Proprietary Co. Ltd v. Bell Resources Ltd*, where a target company gained standing to apply for an injunction to restrain the circulation (among members) of documents that did not comply with the prospectus requirements of the companies legislation.

126 See *Mesenberg v. Cord Industrial Recruiters Pty Ltd* (1996) 19 ACSR 483; 14 ACLC 519; *Premier Gold NL v. Ocean Resources NL* (1994) 14 ACSR 695; 12 ACLC 931.

4   Carter Pty Ltd transfers assets at a considerable undervalue to Grabbit Pty Ltd. The two companies have a common board of directors. Carter is then placed in liquidation. A creditor of Carter Pty Ltd seeks an order under s. 1324 to have the assets transferred back. Does the creditor have standing under s. 1324? Can damages be obtained under s. 1324, even though no injunction has been sought?[127]

5   Where the court finds oppression in a particular case, and determines that the company or the member whose conduct is oppressive should be ordered to compulsorily acquire the minority's shares, what factors are taken into account in determining the value of the shares?[128] Will an expectation on the part of the applicant that he or she was to take part in management be a relevant factor in valuing the applicant's shares?[129]

6   In *Thomas v. H. W. Thomas Ltd*, the court said:

> Fairness cannot be assessed in a vacuum or simply from one member's point of view. It will often depend on weighing conflicting interests of different groups within the company. It is a matter of balancing all the interests involved in terms of the policies underlying the companies legislation in general and [the equivalent of s. 260] in particular: thus to have regard to the principles governing the duties of a director in the conduct of the affairs of a company and the rights and duties of a majority shareholder in relation to the minority; but to recognise that [s. 260] is a remedial provision designed to allow the court to intervene where there is a visible departure from the standards of fair dealing; and in the light of the history and structure of the particular company and the reasonable expectations of the members to determine whether the detriment occasioned to the complaining member's interests arising from the acts or conduct of the company in that way is justifiable.[130]

Compare the oppression remedy with the common-law doctrine of unconscionability in contract law. What standards of fair dealing do these doctrines impose? What factors justify court intervention?

Conclusion

Traditionally, the rights and remedies of the minority shareholder were restricted by the rule in *Foss v. Harbottle*, which only allowed a minority shareholder to maintain an action in limited circumstances—most notably, where the controllers of the company commit a fraud on the minority. The minority shareholder today has a variety of rights and remedies available under the Corporations Law. Judges are still concerned, however, to ensure that a minority shareholder's action is warranted.

---

127   See *Dempster v. Biala Pty Ltd*.
128   See *ES Gordon Pty Ltd; AT Browning Pty Ltd v. Idameneo (No 123) Pty Ltd* (1995) 15 ACSR 536; *Re D. G. Brims and Sons Pty Ltd* (1995) 16 ACSR 559; *Re Quest Exploration Pty Ltd* (1992) 6 ACSR 659.
129   See *Re Bird Precision Bellows Ltd* [1984] Ch 419.
130   (1984) 2 ACLC 610 at 617–18.

There is thus a judicial tendency to take at least a suspicious, if not at times restrictive, view of minority actions. The particular approach taken often depends on the political and commercial climate.[131]

---

131   See *Mesenberg v. Cord Industrial Recruiters Pty Ltd* (1996) 19 ACSR 483 at 488–9 per Young J, in reference to s. 1324 of the Corporations Law.

15

FROM BEDROOM TO BOARDROOM: WOMEN AND COMPANIES[1]

Introduction

We have entitled this chapter 'From Bedroom to Boardroom' to stress the changing nature of the relationship between companies and women. Traditionally, women have been excluded from the control of companies. As a generalisation, it is safe to say that most women have related to companies from a position of relative powerlessness: many women have been employees of companies, or consumers of goods and services supplied by companies. Few women have sat on the boards of public companies, and although a number of women have been directors of private companies, they have been primarily passive directors of companies that 'belonged' to their male spouses. As women reach out from the so-called 'private' sphere of society into the 'public' sphere of life, the relationships between women and corporations are changing. Many more women today own small companies. More women are appearing on the boards of public companies. But change is very, very slow. Studies continue to show that women are largely excluded from the boardroom, and many women continue to find themselves disadvantaged in their roles as 'passive' directors in small proprietary companies.

As we consider these issues in this chapter, it is important to note that there are two factors that will inevitably complicate any discussion of women and companies. The first is a problem that has appeared elsewhere in our discussion of the corporate form: the company creates a web of interests. Thus, to suggest that there is 'a' relationship between women and companies is a gross oversimplification. Which women? Which companies? Even a relationship between a single company and a single woman may have different facets. For example, Helen might be a shareholder in X Co. as well as a consumer of X Co.'s products. Kate might be a director of a small family company, as well as an employee of a large public company.

The second complicating factor is that there is a dearth of feminist analysis of the corporation, despite the fact that there has been considerable feminist analysis of the

---

1   This chapter is essentially an expanded version of the discussion of women and companies that appeared in S. Berns, P. Baron, & M. Neave, *Gender and Citizenship: Materials for Australian Law Schools*, Department of Employment, Education and Training, Canberra, 1996.

economy, and of law in general. It is difficult to state conclusively why this should be so, although some analysts have speculated:

> This discussion of modern market organization has paid little particularized attention to accompanying legal structures. This, too, seems a natural choice of emphasis; to the extent that feminist analysis of market economics to date has been profoundly critical and has called for clean-sweeping change, attempts to rehabilitate individual legal constructs may appear premature.
>
> Are there, however, additional reasons that feminist agendas have ignored corporate and related topics? Is it arguable, for instance, that our present market economy is so dominated by historically male values that feminist inquiry simply has no immediate response other than generalized invocation of the concept of 'oppression'? Or that feminists simply have realized that addressing a corporate law audience on feminist concerns would be, for the speaker, a sublime waste of time and for the most indulgent in the audience, an exercise akin to observing an embroidery demonstration at a board meeting? ... [T]he answer, as to so many multiple choice questions, is both all and none of the above.[2]

In this chapter, we will begin by outlining the idea of the public/private divide. From this point, we will consider the way in which the public/private dichotomy has affected women's participation in, and experiences of, the corporate form. Finally, we will make some general remarks about the ways in which those experiences are connected with the problem of power and the uneasy interpellation of public and private in corporate law.

The bedroom and the boardroom

The bedroom and boardroom form an analogy of the private/public divide, a theme that characterises much feminist literature. The public/private dichotomy is, in its most simple form, the concept that some areas of social life are private (that is, beyond the scope of government regulation), while others are public (that is, rightly within the scope of government regulation).[3]

---

2   T. A. Gabaldon, 'The Lemonade Stand: Feminist and Other Reflections on the Limited Liability of Corporate Shareholders' (1992) 45 Vand LR 1387 at 1415. The answer, in Australia at least, may be simpler still. Women have only recently begun to infiltrate legal academia in substantial numbers. Very often, particularly in 'traditional' high profile law schools, corporate law has been a prestigious speciality, and one that until recently was either taught by high profile senior (male) academics or by practitioners. Women, being clustered in the less elevated realms of the law schools, to the extent they were present at all, tended not to teach (and therefore research) in areas such as corporate law. In practice, they were more likely to be found clustered in the Family Court or, perhaps, representing legal aid clients in magistrates' courts. They were neither corporate law professors nor corporate counsel.

3   At the outset, we want to emphasise that the concepts of public and private are relative, not absolute. Something can be public (or private) only in relation to something else. As you have learnt, the *Corporations Law 1990* provides for private companies and public companies. The distinction turns upon whether the company can make an offer to the public. The requirements in respect of, *inter alios*, directors are stricter for public companies than for private companies. On the other hand, in Australia in the 1980s, it was not unusual for the holding company in a corporate group that controlled millions of dollars of investors funds to be the family company (a private or proprietary company) of an entrepreneur.

This classification is a particular instance of a more pervasive dualistic thinking common to Western philosophy in general. So, although the proposition that some areas are within, and some outside, government intervention seems simple enough (even though you may disagree with it), the public/private dichotomy is far more complex than it would first appear. This is, first, because the boundaries between the 'public' and the 'private' are not static. Second, it is because the public/private distinction is not, at any particular point in time, necessarily consistently defined, either in judicial decision-making or political rhetoric: 'There is no "public/private distinction". What does exist is a series of ways of thinking about public and private that are now constantly undergoing revision, reformulation, and refinement. The law contains a set of imageries and metaphors, more or less coherent, more or less prone to conscious manipulation, designed to organise judicial thinking according to recurrent, value-laden patterns'.[4]

This complexity is illustrated by Anne Jennings, who suggests that you may draw one list of social distinctions as follows:[5]
- public/private
- (market) economy/family
- man/woman
- rational/emotional
- mind/body
- historical/natural
- objective/subjective
- science/humanities
- economics/sociology
- competitive/nurturant
- independent/dependent.

Culturally, we have traditionally associated the first term in each dualism with 'masculine' values, while we have associated the second term with 'feminine' values. Many people in our society tend to privilege the 'masculine' values over the feminine; that is, there is a hierarchy inherent in these dualisms. Society tends to value competitive behaviour over nurturant behaviour, independence over dependence, and so on. The 'opposites' are far from equal. Thus, 'woman' is not just defined as different from man; woman is 'not man', just as the family is 'not the economy'. On the other hand, 'man' is not defined as 'not woman' but as a universal category, parallel to and informed by the economy.[6]

---

4   K. E. Klare, 'The Public/Private Distinction in Labor Law' (1982) 130 *University of Pennsylvania Law Review* 1358 at 1361, as quoted in M. Thornton, 'The Cartography of Public and Private', in M. Thornton (ed.), *Public and Private: Feminist Legal Debates*, Oxford University Press, Melbourne, 1995, p. 2.

5   A. L. Jennings, 'Public or Private? Institutional Economics and Feminism', in M. A. Ferber & J. A. Nelson, *Beyond Economic Man*, University of Chicago Press, Chicago, 1993, p. 124.

6   In this part of the chapter we are tracing some of the common themes in feminist legal scholarship to assist readers who are unfamiliar with them. In this context we note that reference to feminine and/or masculine values is not intended to denote any unchallengeable, natural divide; it is simply a shorthand way of characterising sets of attitudes that are often thought to be gendered.

In this list of dualisms, you would probably place 'company' in the first column, therefore associating it with the public, the economy, masculinity, and so on, and in opposition to women and the family. It follows that, being part of the public sphere, the company should be subject to government regulation and control. Jennings goes on, however, to observe that you could draw another list of social distinctions as follows:

- private/public
- (market) economy/state
- individual/social
- amoral/moral
- freedom/regulation
- enterprise/constraint
- efficiency/inefficiency
- objective/subjective
- science/politics.

In this second list of distinctions, corporations would be associated with the *private*—identified with the market, the individual, freedom and enterprise—whereas in the previous list, we suggested that corporations would naturally be associated with the public. According to this schema, the company is an inherently private affair and should not be subject to government regulation. We can see the operation of this idea in contractarian theories of corporate governance. The company is a matter of private contract among the corporators; its affairs are no business of government. The 'private' nature of the company is also manifested in cases where judges are reluctant to pass judgment on the business decisions of directors. The public/private divide, then, is something far more complex than the word 'dichotomy' would suggest:

> A tripartite configuration of family/economic-social/polity then emerges to take cognisance of the particular character of the market. However, recent feminist writing on the reclamation of the public social sphere agrees with Habermas that it should be separated from the sphere of government. Thus, for the purposes of analysis, one might be more inclined to accept a quadripartite schema than a dichotomy or trichotomy. The fourth category of social organisation is a reclaimed sphere of civil society, or what Habermas calls 'the bourgeois public' which is distinguishable from both the market and the state qua government. In this sphere of civil society, private people come together to form a quasi-public, as can be seen by the example of unions, as well as by religious, academic, and community groups. Nevertheless, refined schemata do not necessarily lead to greater precision because of what Habermas refers to as 'the blurred blueprint': the disintegration of the bourgeois public resulting from the mutual infiltration of public (polity) and private (market) spheres.[7]

---

7   Thornton, p. 7. One might speculate that the corporation began as a 'quasi-public' in the sense used by Jurgen Habermas. As the notion of the corporation as a 'body of corporators' gave way to the notion of the company as largely comprised of 'passive investors', this quasi-public status was gradually eroded and ultimately abandoned.

The public/private dichotomy and its complexity are themes taken up by Fran Olsen.[8] In particular, she notes that the State's so-called 'neutrality'—that is, the refusal of the State to intervene in so-called 'private' matters, such as the reluctance of authorities to intervene in domestic violence situations, or the reluctance to regulate the internal workings of companies—is not neutrality at all. Instead, the State's position reinforces existing power relations, such as the power of the male over the family, or the power of the company over the employee. As Margaret Thornton notes, '[t]he temporally permeable nature of the "dichotomy" enables it to operate as an ideological device: "private" being effectively invoked if the state espouses non-intervention; "public" to the contrary'.[9] The public/private dichotomy, then, can be seen as a complex idea; yet one that simultaneously seeks to deny complexity:

> Human activities regularly have transgressed the nineteenth-century boundaries between spheres. Ironically, those transgressions often have been pursued in the name of laissez-faire or separate gender spheres. For example, both the creation of 'social homemaking' professions for woman and the suffrage movement often relied on an idea of women's special moral and maternal nature to gain access for women to public spheres ... These struggles exploited the ambiguity of social meanings that results from the basic multidimensionality of human thought and activities. Such multidimensionality, which challenges the facile compartmentalization of activities and roles, must be denied by conservative interests seeking to sustain existing categorizations and distinctions.[10]

The law reinforces the traditional dichotomy between the public and private in various ways. For instance, in relation to women, the law may act positively, as it has in the past, by excluding them from the market economy. Similarly, with respect to companies, the law has denied companies the right to shield their affairs from the scrutiny of the public, although individual entrepreneurs and partnerships are entitled to do so. The boundaries of the private are thus, from the perspective of the company, circumscribed, while the boundaries of the public are greatly enlarged.

The law may also reinforce the public/private distinction by inaction. In company law, a classic form of inaction may be found in the law's reluctance to grant a remedy for injustice within the company.[11] In this respect, a parallel may be drawn between intra-corporate relationships and intra-familial relationships. Just as the company is represented in the public sphere by its (male) directors, and relationships within the company are properly 'veiled', so too the family is represented in the public sphere by its (male) head, and relationships within the family are also veiled (even where violence is involved). In both cases, only where the internal dysfunction is so severe as to impair the functioning of the entity in the public sphere is this reluctance likely to dissipate.

---

8   F. Olsen, 'The Family and the Market: A Study of Ideology and Legal Reform' (1985) 96 Harv LR 1497.

9   Thornton, p. 11.

10 Jennings, p. 124.

11 See chapter 14 for a comprehensive discussion of minority remedies and their selective appearance or disappearance. Also, with respect to women, consigning an issue to the private sphere frequently ensures that a remedy is unavailable. The reluctance of the law to provide redress to victims of domestic violence is a classic example.

Yet the public and private spheres are not in any way fixed or given. They expand and contract, appearing in different guises in different circumstances. Given the inconsistency between identification of public and private, and between the ideas of 'intervention' and 'neutrality', it is little wonder that our ideas of corporate regulation often seem inconsistent.

This tension between public and private spheres shapes (perhaps the better word is 'distorts') the relationship between women and companies. On the one hand, women were historically excluded from participation in commercial life and, hence, *inter alia*, from participation in the management of public companies. On the other hand, where women have traditionally participated in the corporate form (that is, within small family companies as second directors), the court has refused to intervene in the 'privateness' of those companies to relieve injustice. We will consider these problems in more detail in the next section.

REVIEW QUESTION

In considering the idea of 'dualistic' thinking, you may wish to consider the prioritisation of economics within our current political and social discourses. One economist is scathing of the priority given to economics:

> 'Economism', the social prioritizing of market processes as the desiderata of social well-being and a basic principle of mainstream economic theory, is a cultural myth with quasi-religious status that perpetuates itself by exclusion and invidious distinction. It is also a Procrustean bed that accommodates the historical record only by dismissing its own origins, along with other inconvenient information. In part because our compartmentalized notions are falsely universalized, we are blinded to alternative interpretations; we see distinctions between social spheres as functionally necessary and fail to note how dualistic interpretations are central to our traditional views of knowledge itself. The recognition that knowledge is culturally determined leads to an understanding of cultural continuity that challenges dualistic constructions and compartmentalizations, and prompts the suspicion that our myths do not describe the historical record very well.[12]

Do you agree? What are the implications of this prioritisation for the relationship between women and companies?

Exclusion: Business is a man's world (or 'Don't you worry your pretty head ... ')

The boards of the majority of public companies have traditionally been male. Despite the considerable increase in women's participation in business in recent

---

12 H. E. Longin, 'Economics for Whom?', in M. A. Ferber & J. A. Nelson, *Beyond Economic Man*, University of Chicago Press, Chicago, 1993, p. 160.

years, this is still the case, as we will discuss below. Historically, this exclusion is relatively easy to explain. Traditionally, at law, women were themselves 'property', either that of a husband or of a father. Through such male kin, a woman attained status, social classification, and any economic power that she might have. Wealth was traditionally created by inheritance and/or contract; and women, as 'property' rather than as 'persons', were largely denied direct access to either.

This was not always the case, however. Sandra Berns observes that, before the Norman conquest, 'relative economic independence of husband and wife appears to have been the norm, each retaining the personal status of birth, with individual rights of inheritance and control of separate property, including its transmission by will'.[13]

Throughout the medieval period, women had independent standing in some craft guilds and dominated such trades as baking and brewing.[14] The feudal system allowed them to hold land in their own right where tenure was by free and common socage. But by around 1534, women could no longer hold property, and men acquired the right to physical custody of their wives and the right to administer moderate corporal punishment.[15] Despite the decline of women's independent status, aristocratic women in the seventeenth century still actively managed the family household and estate. In the eighteenth century, many women engaged in a variety of commercial pursuits, such as fan-making or catering, or continued in their husband's trade or business in a variety of other commercial pursuits.[16]

Women's exclusion from commerce was largely a result of the industrial revolution in general, and of two factors in particular. The first was the increased separation of business premises from the home. The second was the impact of the rise of the middle class. By the beginning of the nineteenth century, the ideal of 'refinement', to which the majority of the middle class aspired, dictated that women outside the working class should not seek employment unless it was absolutely necessary to do so. In essence, this mimicked the domestic situation of the aristocracy. The maintenance of an economically unproductive family was a powerful status symbol.[17]

> It is difficult to assess whether, and if so, in what way business ethics may have developed differently if women had participated in commerce in the nineteenth century. What can be suggested, however, is that this dichotomy between 'work' and 'home' and between commercial life and family life ... lead to the development of a 'moral polarity': if commercial man was expected to be essentially self-regarding, family woman was expected to be other-regarding; if commercial man was legitimately egoistic, family woman was

---

13   S. Berns, 'Women in English Legal History: Subject (Almost), Object (Irrevocably), Person (Not Quite)' (1993) 12 *University of Tasmania Law Review* 1 at 32.

14   Berns at 16.

15   Berns at 4.

16   P. Baron, 'Shells of Steel and Bodies of Pulp: Commercial Man, Commercial Morality' (1993) 11 Law in Context 3.

17   Berns at 19.

rightly altruistic. Ethically, man's world, the commercial world, was one of utility; women's world, one of uselessness. It was believed that commerce was an activity which women were incapable of partaking in or which they had no business in participating. Commercial morality, then, may be seen as a morality developed by and for men. Of course, to state that women were excluded from commerce is not to imply that women were excluded from the workforce. Much as commercial man may have placed his own family upon a pedestal, he had few scruples about working another man's wife and children long and hard in factories, mines or within his own home as servants.[18]

We will examine the legacies of this 'moral polarity' below. But it is worth noting that commerce and, correspondingly, commercial and company law developed largely devoid of female control or influence:[19]

To the extent that the themes of [the nineteenth century] reverberate in present day organizational law, they will continue to incur feminist criticism. The totemism of 'will', the rigidity of on-off answers to participant liability questions, and any notion that individuals regularly may be severed from the nonbeneficial consequences of acts from which they themselves were intended to benefit are in any guise objectionable to feminists.

Also deplorable to feminist analysis would be the ritual segregation of various social and legal structures. In other words, the existence of separate spheres for the various tasks of life is disquieting. Compartmentalization requires abstraction, and abstraction values order over context, thus precluding care.[20]

Still on the sidelines

Despite the fact that women no longer are regarded as 'property', they continue to be excluded from the management of public companies (as we shall see below) or disadvantaged in their participation in private companies. Why should this be so? Part of the answer could lie in direct discrimination against women. Much of the answer is far more subtle and far more complex than this, and can be traced to the 'moral polarity' identified above.

We have seen in the previous chapters that economics is the dominant discourse in our society, and contract is the dominant paradigm of that discourse. Both economics and contract, however, stress ideas of competition and participation in the market. Both are based on a 'male' model of individualism. In order to contract, the free and independent individual requires certain elements. Essentially, these are

---

18 Baron at 9.

19 Even where women did exert some influence, their impact received no recognition. 'In the early 1900's [*sic*] women were among the leaders in the newly-developing field of business management science. Lillian Gilbreth, among other women innovators in the area of behavioural management science, made substantial contributions. She co-authored "The Primer of Scientific Management". But only her husband's name appears on the book because the publisher did not want a woman listed as collaborator': Internet <http://www.feminist.org> December 1995.

20 Gabaldon at 1445.

information and/or knowledge, property, and opportunity. The image bequeathed to us by economic theory is that of a free and equal individual possessed of perfect knowledge satisfying his or her desires in competition with other similarly situated individuals. The characteristics of 'perfect knowledge', freedom, and equality are essential to the model.[21]

Many women, however, find it difficult, even impossible, to conform to this model. They may lack these contractual 'necessities', for any one of a number of reasons. Women are generally socialised to take fewer risks than men. Women may be excluded from participation in public life because of sexual harassment. They may be denied credit by lending institutions (because it is assumed that they should be partnered) or denied independent advice in financial transactions because they are considered to be one 'unit' with their male partners.

Ultimately, of course, many of these reasons can be related to the societal expectation that women are the primary care-givers within our society. This assumption has a number of implications: It may exclude women from, or disadvantage women within, the paid workforce. Exclusion is self-evident. Many women are unable to take on full-time work because of their obligation to care for the elderly or for children. Disadvantage is likely to manifest itself in a number of different ways. The care-giver role may force women into part-time work, which often has less opportunity for promotion, and is poorly remunerated. It may perpetuate job segregation, whereby women are overrepresented in service areas, such as teaching or nursing, often because these forms of employment are perceived to be appropriate and are often compatible with other roles. Women may be forced to work a 'double shift'— that is, retain primary responsibility for domestic duties, despite full-time employment.[22] The disadvantage is compounded by the fact that women's income is often considered to be 'secondary' to that of men, and areas in which women predominate may not be as well paid as so-called 'masculine' areas. In addition, as this income is 'secondary', it is more likely to be spent on consumables (children's clothing, schooling, holidays, homewares) rather than being invested in assets. Further, women's careers may then be subordinated to those of their male partners, restricting women's mobility in the market. A woman may not be able to take advantage of employment opportunities because her partner (who is likely to earn more money) is tied to a job in a particular place.

As we shall see, a significant consequence of the idea of 'woman as carer' is that society often expects women to give what property they do have, rather than sell it in the market-place:

> Patriarchy demands altruism of its women and two centuries of capitalist development ensure that this translates into financial insecurity. It is not only that a woman's capacity

---

21 Access to resources is, of course, also essential, but is not generally mentioned when the model is discussed.

22 See M. Bittman, *Juggling Time: How Australian Families Use Time, A Report on the Secondary Analysis of the 1987 Pilot Survey of Time Use, Prepared for the Office of the Status of Women, Department of the Prime Minister and Cabinet, May 1991*, AGPS, Canberra, 1992.

to earn an independent wage gets 'elbowed out' by the demands of her family and her other social responsibilities. It is also that in a society dominated by market values, by the language of exchange, the voice of 'altruism' has little or no power ... Furthermore, women who use the language of the market and demand a better deal for themselves, whether as mothers, volunteers or paid workers in the welfare industry, are seen to undercut the very essence of their obligations to others, to 'hang their conscience' on the picket line with the pegs of self-interest and to bargain with the fortunes of the weak and vulnerable.[23]

So far, we have argued that women's inability to participate meaningfully in commercial life in general, and thus in the control or ownership of companies in particular, is largely the result of historical factors, but that the legacy of gender stereotypes lives on:

Many families and male–female relationships are still patriarchal and reflect the 'separate spheres' doctrine to varying degrees ... The authority, dominance and control of males, both interpersonally and institutionally, is legitimated and approved by both familial and religious cultures, workplace structures, educational agencies, advertising and the media. [Women] continue to depend on males to mediate for them. There is widespread deference by women to male authority and expertise in matters of the public sphere, including business, commerce and legal transactions.[24]

These stereotypes are, in addition, self-perpetuating. Because women traditionally lacked power and authority, they are perceived to be incapable of effectively exercising power and authority. 'Woman', then, as a category, is problematic when placed in the context of a hierarchical, bureaucratic structure, such as a public company.

Earlier we discussed the idea that so-called 'state neutrality' can simply serve to perpetuate existing power relations. Similarly, stereotypes are often internalised and so perpetuated by the law, often (ironically) in its attempts to ensure 'gender neutrality':

Despite the formal achievement of full legal capacity and control over separate property, in substance, the law does not ensure that a woman shares the prosperity of her close male associates; on the other hand, it frequently permits access by the male's creditors to a woman's separate property in circumstances of insolvency. It also encourages or promotes business structures which facilitate the exclusion of woman from substantive control. Thus, apparently gender neutral legal forms and doctrines frequently interact with the reality of women's commercial, economic and emotional dependence, their subordinate position in family structures and relationships, their exclusion from commercial positions and experience, their inferior position in the workplace and their relative lack of access to

---

23 P. Harris, 'Penny Pinching Activities: Managing Poverty under the Eye of Welfare', in K. Saunders & R. Evans (eds), *Gender Relations in Australia: Domination and Negotiation*, Harcourt Brace Jovanovich, Sydney, 1992, p. 299.

24 J. Dodds Streeton, 'Feminist Perspectives on the Law of Insolvency' (1994) 6 *Adelaide Law Review* (Research Paper no. 1) 11–12.

information, to ensure that a woman's property is made available to the creditors of a business enterprise conducted by a male in circumstances where she was guaranteed neither a share of control nor possible prosperity. Thus, the law of insolvency, while it appears largely gender neutral on the surface, in fact masks a partial perpetuation of the situation which existed prior to the Married Women's Property Acts; viz, exclusion from the control and entitlement to profits of a business venture, ironically accompanied by full liability for its potential failure.[25]

The perpetuation of traditional stereotypes and expectations has two primary implications for the purposes of this discussion. First, in any dealings of a contractual nature with the company, any ideas that we may have of 'equality of bargaining power' between women and the corporation are going to be, in many cases, very much a fiction. This can be seen particularly in cases where women's relationships with the company are those of consumers or employees. Second, companies are effectively 'boys' toys', and corporate exclusion or oppression of women with regard to their participation in the company continues to exist. We will consider each of these implications in turn.

REVIEW QUESTION

Read the following:

> The changes that have occurred have been fought for by women, but the greatest gains have been made where these are consonant with the demands of the economic system or where they serve state purposes. There has been far less evidence of change in evaluation of the worth of women's traditional activities, there is little change where male power is directly challenged, and there is little change where women have been seeking cultural change, for instance, in attitudes relating to violence, and in the achievement of more cooperative, less hierarchical forms of group interaction and management.[26]

Do you agree? Justify your answer. You may wish to consider the different ideas of 'rightful' ethical and moral conduct in commercial matters. If women are rightly altruistic and companies have a primary duty to make a profit, where does that leave women and companies in commercial dealings?

The possession of knowledge and the existence of relationship are both potential sources of duty, and therefore of culpable dereliction of duty, in the contractual contexts of misunderstanding, disclosure, and mistake. The central question here is when and why one contractual party should be responsible for protecting the other from ignorance, whether by searching out the other party's interpretation of the agreement or by sharing information with the other party. The central difficulty is

---

25 Dodds Streeton at 34.
26 C. Dalton, 'An Essay in the Deconstruction of Contract Doctrine' (1985) 94 Yale LJ 997 at 1035 and 1061.

that the law contains contradictory impulses without providing determinative guidelines for the relevant scope of application of each principle. The law suggests that each party to a contract must look out for his or her own interest without concern for that of the other party, while simultaneously suggesting that this self-interest must have limits.

Whiter than white? Corporations and women as consumers

We have said that, because of the disadvantages that many women suffer, not least because of the societal expectation of altruism, the assumption that women and companies are on 'equal terms' in the bargaining process is largely a nonsense. The rise of the corporation has had significant implications for the consumer. In particular, an imbalance of power and the potential for abuse has been caused by the separation of buyer and seller, both geographically and emotionally. In many jurisdictions, such as Australia, legislation has been introduced to try to redress this imbalance. But large companies often have the luxury of mobility and can locate themselves in countries that offer them advantages in terms of tax liability, or cheap labour markets. Consider, for a moment, the ability of Australian clothing manufacturers to produce clothing more cheaply in Asian countries. While corporations have increased mobility, they also have access, in many cases, to world markets. Corporations can often utilise their power and mobility to successfully evade liability for defective products or unsafe work practices.

A very good example of this was the worldwide marketing of the Dalkon Shield, a contraceptive device that was developed in the early 1960s. The Dalkon Shield Corporation was incorporated in 1968 and the product became a considerable commercial success. Women were particularly attracted by the company's claims that the device was a safe and efficient alternative to the contraceptive pill (as a considerable number of women suffered side effects from the contraceptive pill). Because of its success and the media attention, the product was purchased by the A. H. Robins Company, a pharmaceutical company, in 1970. Robins began marketing the product in 1970, and more than 4 million devices were sold. Between 100 000 and 160 000 devices were distributed in Australia.

Unfortunately, the Shield had numerous 'side effects' for women, including perforated uteri, pelvic inflammatory disease, spontaneous septic abortions, ectopic pregnancies, and in some cases, death. It was alleged that the device caused 17–18 deaths in the USA. However, even after the device was withdrawn from the United States market, it continued to be sold in other countries, including Australia. In 1974 the company stopped marketing the Shield in the face of mounting law suits. More than 7000 women in Australia alone eventually sued the company for their injuries.

Robins's response to the threat of law suits was to mobilise its considerable legal resources to delay litigation. It subjected female plaintiffs to extensive and often humiliating investigations of their sexual history. In early proceedings, Robins alleged that significant documents had been lost. In point of fact, these documents had been destroyed by a company lawyer.

The onus of publicising the deadline for the filing of claims in the USA was placed on the company. The majority of advertising was confined to the USA. After the deadline expired, 90 per cent of claimants were United States residents, even though only 60 per cent of the products were distributed in the USA. Not surprisingly, the majority of claims that were settled before bankruptcy proceedings were instituted involved American women.[27]

After it had lost a number of court proceedings, Robins declared itself bankrupt. Falling stock prices made it an attractive takeover prospect, and American Home Products agreed to buy it. The agreement established a $2.5 billion trust fund for Dalkon Shield victims. The settlement also precluded further suits against Robins's officers and insulated them from punitive damages awards. In addition, $700 million was to be paid to Robins's stockholders, most of that to Robins family members, who had been obliged to contribute to the trust fund but who nevertheless stood to gain many more millions than their respective trust fund contributions.

The story of the Dalkon Shield illustrates a number of problems inherent in the female consumer–corporation relationship. The first of these is the imbalance of power and information that can exist between the consumer and the corporation. Given the 'feminisation of poverty' and women's traditional exclusion from business information and education, women are often in an even more unequal relationship with the corporation than are many men. Robins knew that the Shield was unsafe; but nevertheless proceeded to market the device.[28] In the face of litigation, Robins could pay for legal assistance to fend off potential suits. The defects in the device were not readily understood by the consumer, nor were they evident on a casual inspection. The fact that the company was physically situated in the USA but could market its product all over the world posed problems for both regulation and redress. Consider the plight of women in Third World countries who were also harmed by the device:

> [T]o date almost all legal claims have been by white women from English-speaking common law countries (the United Kingdom, Canada, the US, Australia and New Zealand). The product was of course distributed on a large scale in 80 countries, including many third world countries through international aid organizations. Large numbers of the devices, many sold at a discount without sterilisation, were dumped abroad after the product was taken off the market in the United States. Whatever one may think of the plight of women claimants in their struggle with the company and the legal system, one

---

27 P. Cashman, 'The Dalkon Shield', in P. Grabosky & A. Sutton (eds), *Stains on a White Collar*, Hutchinsons, Sydney, 1989, pp. 105, 112.

28 As we pointed out in chapter 4, some commentators have also pointed to the 'risky shift' that occurs in groups. That is, business people in role plays will make 'riskier' decisions when acting in a small group than when acting alone (see p. 104).

should not lose sight of the fact that unknown numbers of women are still wearing the device and untold others have suffered illness and injury without ever becoming aware of the fact that legal redress is available. It is a long way from the villages of Bangladesh to the courtrooms of the United States.[29]

This problem means that the national governance of companies—although a topic of considerable attention within a number of countries, including Australia—is in some ways irrelevant:

[I]nventing this thing called a company or a corporation and allowing limited liability was a way of allowing capital to aggregate and a way of rewarding enterprise, [and] this meant, several hundred years ago, that the West basically exploited the East. But I wonder if those exploitations aren't still facilitated by company law allowing companies to operate in so-called third world countries. So that although we are asking for reforms at the small end of company law … to say that we need to distinguish big companies from the small companies is in fact ignoring the global connection, and the connection between exploited workers here and exploited workers in other countries. So that for example big companies can go and do their exploiting somewhere else and we don't have to live with the consequences, we don't see them, we are not embarrassed by them. Women might be set against each other in other countries, but we don't know about it and it doesn't impact on our consciences all that much.[30]

The Dalkon Shield is hardly an isolated example of the problems faced by female consumers. Consider the recent controversy surrounding silicon implants, and complications arising from fertility treatments.

She works hard for a living: Women as employees

It is not only as consumers that women feel the inequality of power between themselves and the corporation. Many companies have exploited their powerful position in labour relations.

Example 1
Consider the following case history, which occurred in the USA in the late 1970s.[31] Mercer, an officer of American Cyanamic Company's Willow Island plant in West Virginia, held meetings with groups of the plant's female employees. The topic for discussion was the presence in the plant of a number of chemicals that were known to be hazardous to the health of foetuses. Mr Mercer announced a new corporate

---

29 Cashman, p. 114.

30 A. Rhodes-Little, J. Gillard, & S. Cerepinko, 'In Search of the Ethics of Company Law' (1994) 2 A Fem LJ 180 at 190–1.

31 J. R. Desjardings & J. J. McCall, *Contemporary Issues in Business Ethics*, 2nd edn, Wadsworth Publishing Company, Belmont, Calif., 1990, p. 216.

policy that would exclude women of child-bearing age from those areas of the plant where these chemicals were present. This exclusion would apply to every woman between the ages of 16 and 50 years unless the individual employee could present documents that proved that she had been sterilised. In addition, the female employees were given information at these meetings about the ease of sterilisation procedures and about the local availability of such procedures. Initially, this exclusionary policy was to apply to all but seven of the jobs in the plant. Mercer told the approximately thirty women who would be subject to the policy that those who were not sterilised or were not awarded the remaining non-hazardous jobs would face dismissal. After some months, American Cyanamid altered this policy so that it applied to only one department. Of the seven women in that department, five were sterilised and two were assigned to other jobs with reduced remuneration.

The final exclusionary policy applied to a department where there was environmental exposure to airborne lead. American Cyanamid maintained that it was unable to reduce the lead levels in the air so as to comply with the Occupational Safety and Health Administration (OSHA) standards, which OSHA believed were safe even for foetuses. When American Cyanamid did not reduce lead levels, OSHA proposed a fine of US$10 000 on the ground that the policy of sterilisation or reassignment/termination was, in itself, a hazard to the women's health. On appeal, an administrative law judge exempted the plant from the standards in question, on the basis that compliance was not 'economically feasible'.

The Oil, Chemical and Atomic Workers' Union represented the female employees. It brought two suits against the company. One alleged that the administrative law judge erred in his decision that the exclusionary policy was not itself a health hazard. The other suit alleged that the exclusionary policy was a form of discrimination prohibited by law.

In the first case, Judge Robert Bork, sitting on the District of Columbia Court of Appeals, wrote a decision upholding the original decision of the administrative law judge. Bork held that precedent from previous court cases and the legislative history of the *Occupational Safety and Health Act 1970* both indicated that the term 'hazard' in that Act refers only to the physical or environmental conditions in the workplace. Accordingly, the exclusionary policy was not a hazard according to the Act. Since the sex discrimination suit was settled out of court by American Cyanamid, there was no clear precedent establishing legal principles for such exclusionary policies.

The case is a good example of the law's apparent inability to deal with the female subject. Ngaire Naffine points out:

If we think about the techniques still being deployed by sex discrimination laws to have women recognised as full subjects of public life, it becomes even clearer that our legislators have seen no need to refigure the meaning of law's subject with the explicit inclusion of women in new legislation. For the standard move of anti-discrimination laws is to demand that women be treated the same (that is, as well) as men, but only if we can demonstrate that they are similarly situated to a man. There has been no endeavour to ensure that women, as women, living the cultural and biological lives of women (that is, our female specificity) should be afforded the protections of such laws. In other words, women in their difference are explicitly excluded from the benefits of legislation designed to prohibit discrimination against women for being women.[32]

It is not only large companies, however, that are guilty of exploitative labour practices. Consider the plight of the employee faced by an employer that is a '$2' company.

Example 2

The following is an extract from an interview that appeared in the *Australian Feminist Law Journal* Praxis Notes (AR-L is Andrea Rhodes-Little, the author. JG is Julia Gillard, partner at Slater and Gordon, Melbourne):

AR-L: What happened?

JG: At Jeanswear in Geelong for two years … running in December people who have worked in a clothing factory doing machining work which is relatively poorly paid. The employers said on the last working day before Christmas 'Your employment is finished, I don't have any money to pay you for holiday pay, I don't have any money to pay you for pay in lieu of notice or redundancy money'.

             Kilmarnock Clothing Pty Ltd traded for four or five years ending in December 1992. Its two directors were George Train and his wife, or then wife, Norma Train and the supervisor in the factory was a woman called Vivian Howell. That company closed down in circumstances where workers didn't get paid anything. The next January, January 1993, George Train rings round some of the people who used to work for him, not all of them, and says 'I'm opening up a new business, I'd like you to come and work for me again' and given the employment circumstances in Geelong and the clothing industry generally, people took up that offer and they commenced working for a company called Jeanswear Pty Ltd. The directors of which are Vivian Howell, the former supervisor and the accountant of the company, Kilmarnock. George Train continued to be the effective day to day boss but wasn't one of the directors and again in December 1993 business shut down in circumstances where people don't get paid.

             [Julia Gillard proceeded to discuss the concept of limited liability, and the fact that most business people will understand that a $2 company is something of a credit hazard and will accordingly demand a personal guarantee.] The employees are basically the only

---

32 N. Naffine, 'Sexing the Subject (of Law)', in M. Thornton (ed.), *Public and Private: Feminist Legal Debates*, Oxford University Press, Melbourne, 1995, p. 31.

people who don't come along and get a personal guarantee. They are just employees of the company. Something like 80% of small businesses fail in their first two years. It is the employees who are looking solely to the company for the money that they are owed, not to the individuals[,] and the company, by definition, won't have it …

AR-L: It strikes me that migrant women, being employees who are aggregated at the bottom of the whole employment structure in the sense that they do 60 per cent or more of factory work are more vulnerable than anyone else.

JG: It is quite an aged workforce. The newer end of the industry, the workforce is different, but in the sort of historic clothing factories the workforce is predominantly migrant women and these days predominantly older migrant women. And they are particularly vulnerable.

Some of the things which should alert them that there is trouble they don't pick up on because of language difficulties or not understanding the sort of system. For example I will meet with migrant women in the clothing industry who have worked in the same factory on the same machine for the same boss for ten years and when they show you their group certificates, every group certificate will have a different company on it as the employer. So the effective employer, the boss, has basically incorporated and collapsed companies a number of times to avoid payment of creditors and probably to assist with some argument about not paying long service leave. Not reading and writing English, they give their tax arrangements to their accountant who basically takes care of it for them and there is nothing that has alerted them to problems with the business …

I think that as a general proposition it is true to say that women are more fearful of complaining and more fearful of insisting upon their rights than male workers. And they tend to be in settings where it is more difficult to do those things. In less unionised workplaces, in workplaces where there isn't that kind of culture of complaint and having grievances dealt with as there may be in the more predominantly male industries, like, say, the building industry where there is a culture of getting issues dealt with on the job. It's not the same.[33]

In our earlier discussions we have seen that many companies have little compunction about treating their male employees in a less than ideal way. And, indeed, in Example 1, exposure to lead would also have had detrimental effects upon male employees. In addition, in earlier chapters, we explored the problems relating to corporate social responsibility, accountability, and morality. There is little doubt that these problems are influential in the relationship between female consumers or

---

33 Rhodes-Little at 183–5.

female employees and the company. But there are two factors that make women's position in relation to the corporation worse than that of men. In the first place, as we have pointed out, there is a power imbalance resulting from societal expectations of female altruism and 'rightful' female conduct. The second factor is that very few companies have, in the past, been managed or controlled by women. Is it any wonder, then, that the company fails to consider female interests (other, of course, than those that generate profit)? We turn now to consider the problems posed by companies as 'boys' toys'.

Boys' toys? Male management

By virtue of the private/public dichotomy, as we have seen, women have been largely excluded from commercial life, and correspondingly, from the management of corporations. Despite the fact that, in the 1990s, women's roles in public life are expanding, they remain, for the most part, securely locked outside the boardroom. This is an aspect of public life that remains elusive:

> For women, neither the polity nor the market have been realms of freedom or self-realisation, but realms of hostility. Women have been largely confined to sex-segregated jobs reflective of their designated private sphere work, involving caring for others, cleaning, or acting as handmaidens to important men. Although no longer formally excluded from participation in the professions or the polity, women are still thought to be lacking in authority. A paradox is therefore immediately obvious in that the feminist reform movement has been compelled to rely upon the good graces of a masculinist public qua polity that has been antipathetic to the feminine.[34]

The fact that women are still marginalised in corporate public life is reflected in the figures relating to women's participation in the management of companies. Figures from the USA show the following:
- 4.5 per cent of the 'Fortune 500' industrial directorships are held by women
- 5.6 per cent of the directors of the 'Fortune 500' service companies are women, and the rate of increase is so slow that it will take 125 years for parity with men to be achieved.
- In corporate senior management, women comprise 40 per cent of all executive, management, and administrative positions, but they are confined primarily to the middle and lower ranks. A 1990 study showed that of the top 'Fortune 500' companies, only 2.6 per cent of corporate officers were women, and in service companies, where women compose the majority of workers, only 4.3 per cent of corporate officers were women. At the current rate of increase, this report estimated that it will be 475 years before women reach parity with men in this regard.[35]

---

34 Thornton, p. 7.
35 'Executive Suites Lack Women', *Empowering Women in Business*, Internet <http://www.feminist.org> December 1995.

Similarly, a study into Australian boards notes that '[t]he representation of women on boards has been virtually static over the last few years, and remains low. Women now constitute four percent of all board members; one percent of executive directors (no change from last year) and five percent of non-executive directors. The latter represents a relative increase of 25 percent, but obviously from a very small base'.[36] Of 101 listed public companies, this study showed that some 69 per cent had no women directors. Of 111 unlisted public companies, 59 per cent did not have a woman director.[37] Similar studies in the United Kingdom show that the changes to women's participation on company boards have been relatively minimal:

[S]omething that remains unchanged since the earlier survey in 1989 is that women continue to be more likely to be non-executive: just over 80% of women directors are non-executives. A continuing trend that is as important as it is worrying. Some commentators question whether it indicates tokenism.

[It] must be said that however valued non-executive directors may be, most are out-siders invited to join the board. It is executive directors who hold the key role as decision makers inside the organisation. Whilst so few women are among the group of executive directors it is difficult to say that substantial progress is being made for women.[38]

So, despite the change to women's status within society, their increasing numbers in the workforce, and the effects of anti-discrimination and affirmative action legislation, women seem to have made only a little progress in terms of their position:

Women and 'she merchants' were approximately 2% of the merchants in colonial New York City. According to Jean Jordan, 'merchants were at the summit of the colonial economy … positions of comparable power and prestige today would be those of president or chairman of the board of major business corporations'. In other words, women are only slightly more successful in reaching the highest levels of business today than they were in colonial times.[39]

Studies continue to show that, just as the labour market in general remains sharply segregated by sex, women executives are concentrated into certain types of jobs—generally staff and support jobs—that offer little opportunity for advancement. A 1986 *Wall Street Journal* survey found that the highest ranking women in most industries are in non-operating areas such as personnel, public relations, or, occasionally, finance specialties, which seldom lead to the most powerful top-management posts. But even when women do enter job areas that have the

---

36   Korn/Ferry International and Australian Institute of Company Directors, *Fourteenth Study of Boards of Directors*, as quoted in P. Spender, 'Corporations Law' in R. Graycar & J. Morgan (eds), *Materials on Gender, Work and Violence*, Department of Employment, Education and Training, Canberra, 1995, p. 24.

37   Of 458 proprietary companies studied, however, only 33 per cent did not have a woman director. But this last figure does not necessarily reflect an increasing gender equality; as we shall see, women in small proprietary companies may be the victims of a gendered form of exploitation.

38   V. Holton, 'Corporate Governance Report: Surveying the Situation for Women Directors in the UK' (1995) 3 *Corporate Governance Reports* 102 at 103.

39   'The Feminist Difference', *Empowering Women in Business*, Internet <http://www.feminist.org> December 1995.

prospect of significant advancement, it is not likely to be 'in a crucial part of the business' or the type of job that can 'mark them as leaders.' The 'old boys network' has been cited as a significant barrier to the advancement of 'corporate woman'. The dictates of 'homosocial reproduction' are such that, when deciding who to promote into management, male corporate leaders tend to select people as much like themselves as possible:

> Women executives are frequently excluded from social activities and often describe the 'clubbiness' among the men that exists at the top. The corporate executive suites are 'the ultimate boys' clubs.'
>
> Even on a more formal level, women report there are 'certain kinds of meetings' they don't get invited to because they are not seen as policy makers. Corporate women don't travel on business as frequently as men, according to surveys by Korn/Ferry International (1982) and *Wall Street Journal* Gallup (1984).[40]

Even the authority given to women is different from that given to men. One study found that, among executives at the same level, men 'managed greater numbers of people, had more freedom to hire and fire, and had more direct control of the company's assets' than women. The *Wall Street Journal* Gallup Poll showed that more than 80 per cent of the executive women polled said that there were disadvantages to being a woman in the business world. These disadvantages included men not taking women seriously. Sixty-one per cent of the women said that they had been mistaken for a secretary at a business meeting; 25 per cent said that they had been hindered on their way up the ladder by male attitudes towards women; and 70 per cent believed that they are paid less than men of equal ability.[41]

These studies suggest that, even if she can overcome the barriers posed by discrimination, a woman must become a 'pseudo man' to succeed in the corporate hierarchy. The company is intolerant of the feminine. The more general issue of the company as 'male' is discussed in greater detail below. For now, it is worth thinking about the ways in which a corporation can be problematic for female managers:

> [L]iberal feminist analysis of the corporation has tended to focus upon the constraints that the corporate structure generates for women employees (particularly female managers). It has called upon women to accept their gender difference and to change themselves in order to fit into male dominated organisations (such as the corporation) where gender based roles exist. In the process, however, women have been required to adopt traditionally masculine characteristics in order to succeed and to subordinate or fragment their own feminine identities.[42]

Similarly, Theresa Gabaldon notes:

In the words of one commentator, the uniting feminist task is to 'name, expose, and eliminate the unequal position of women in society.' To the casual reader, this suggests that

---

40 'The Glass Ceiling', *Empowering Women in Business*, Internet <http://www.feminist.org> December 1995.

41 'The Glass Ceiling'.

42 K. Hall, 'Starting from Silence: The Future of Feminist Analysis of Corporate Law' (1995) 7 (2) Corp & Bus LJ 157.

feminist corporate law analysis should be at an end if women are admitted to board rooms and corporate offices. In fact, to such a reader, feminist corporate law analysis need never have started, because employment discrimination law—a different subject—is both adequate to, and more appropriate for, the task.

[I]nequality also inheres in 'one size fits all' social and legal institutions. Thus, an actor may experience unequal treatment—and personal discomfort—if required to function in a setting that is adapted to the values, abilities, and needs of others dissimilar to that actor and that therefore fails to accommodate, much less reflect, the actor's own values, abilities and needs.[43]

REVIEW QUESTION

Thornton writes:

> The public sphere, mediated through law, has enabled benchmark men to construct normativity, like God, in their own image. The seeds of invidiousness associated with the domestic sphere attach to women, who have been marked as its indigenous inhabitants. The stigmata of affectivity continue to detract from the rationality and authority of women and others in public office. Conventionally, a 'public woman' was a prostitute, a figure of derision, in contrast to a 'public man', a figure of approbation who acted in and for the universal good. This signification helps us to understand why benchmark men continue to dominate the most powerful institutions of the public sphere, including parliaments, courts, and universities. It also helps to explain why some women and 'others' seek to enhance their authority by assuming the characteristics associated with benchmark men.[44]

What difficulties do women who wish to assume a role in the management of public corporations face? Can you offer suggestions of ways in which these problems can be overcome?

Boys' toys? Male ownership

Public companies, then, have traditionally been managed by male boards. In private companies, women have often been directors, but this does not mean that they have power or control. Small, private companies, as we have seen, often function as a vehicle for the business activities of small traders. In such cases, there is often an intersection of 'family law' with 'commercial law', an uncomfortable meeting of the liberal public and private spheres:

> One very common way in which women who are employed at home operate as independent contractors is in business with their spouses. The increase in the numbers of persons in the paid workforce who work from home includes a majority, of both men

---

43 Gabaldon at 1415–16.
44 Thornton, p. 13.

and women, who describe themselves as self-employed. With the present restructuring of the public work relationships and the increased activity of employment agencies, this mode of organisation of work is likely to become more popular, especially in many male-dominated industries. For the male 'breadwinner', part of the attraction of this way of organising work relationships in the paid workplace is the opportunity it offers for increasing the financial reward for the work via the corporate law and taxation system and the mechanism of incorporating other family members (notably the wife, but also the children) into their business.

The prevalence of this practice is suggested by the high proportion of women among those employed at home in traditional 'male' areas, such as the construction industry. The occupational breakdown by sex of the work performed by women employed at home suggests that women (wives) are brought in the paid workforce as an appendage to the work of the man (their husband), to perform the clerical and administrative work that supports the main or primary work of the man. Available evidence suggests that, in such relationships, women are often in a position of powerlessness and dependence in contrast to men, who actively control the business.[45]

In many cases, a male sole trader satisfies the requirement for a second director in the *Corporations Law 1990* by nominating his wife or de facto spouse as second director. He may, however, refuse, or neglect, to provide her with any control over, or information in regard to, company activities. Yet, she attracts full legal liability as a second director and may be required, for the sake of the business, to provide personal guarantees for the company's debts. This is one aspect of a phenomenon known as 'sexually (or, more accurately, emotionally) transmitted debt', which has been defined as '[t]he transfer of responsibility for a debt incurred by a party to his/her partner in circumstances in which the fact of the relationship, as distinct from an appreciation of the reality of responsibility for the debt, is the predominant factor in the partner accepting liability'.[46]

A woman may undertake such liability in two ways. She may become liable as a primary debtor. This occurs where she is the second director in a company that is the vehicle for her partner's trading. She may also accept secondary liability. This occurs where she guarantees the debts of her partner's company.

The Corporations Law, until late 1995, provided in s. 221(1) that a 'public company shall have at least 3 directors and a proprietary company shall have at least 2 directors'. Thus, in many companies, women became directors so that their male spouses could operate what was, in essence, a sole-trader business as a company. Many women in such a situation faced considerable problems They lacked both control and information. In a general sense, this deficiency can be the result of traditional gender stereotypes. The female director may be a home-maker, and may have had little opportunity to acquire business experience or knowledge. She may

---

45   R. Owens, 'The Peripheral Worker', in M. Thornton (ed.), *Public and Private: Feminist Legal Debates*, Oxford University Press, Melbourne, 1995, p. 56.

46   R. Jukic, *Til Debt Us Do Part*, Consumer Credit Legal Service, Melbourne, 1994, pp. 21–2.

take no interest at all in the business. Sometimes her ignorance is by 'conscious design', where her partner declines (or refuses) to provide the information. Where her ignorance is by design rather than accident, her lack of control and of information can be attributed to the male spouse's conduct. Her partner may guard the business jealously, regarding it as 'his' business. He may not allow her access to business records or allow her to read relevant documentation. Sometimes he may actually misinform her about the state of the business, the extent of the company's debts, or the use to which loan money will be put. She may benefit if the company prospers, but often only indirectly.

The problems that this situation can pose for many women can be illustrated by the case of *Metal Manufacturers Pty Ltd v. Lewis*.[47] In this case, an action was brought by a company creditor against Mrs Lewis, who was a director of the company. The company sought recovery of the debt on the basis that, when the debt was incurred, there were reasonable grounds to believe that it would not be paid. Mrs Lewis's husband had complete control over the company, and Mrs Lewis took no active role in company affairs at all. Mrs Lewis defended the action on the basis that the debt had been incurred without her express or implied consent, and that she did not have reasonable cause to suspect that the company would not be able to meet its debts as and when they became due.

Mrs Lewis gave evidence that she did not realise that she was a director of the company and did not know when the company had commenced to trade. She also stated in evidence that she signed documents at her husband's request without reading them. Despite her evidence, the court found that Mrs Lewis could not rely on the defence that she had no reasonable cause to suspect that the company was insolvent or nearly insolvent. In relation to conduct such as that of Mrs Lewis, Julie Dodds Streeton argues:

> It is not 'unreasonable' for a woman in a patriarchal family structure or relationship to be ignorant of duties entailed by her formal status as a director, or ignorant of circumstances which would have been discovered had she been aware of and fulfilled those duties. Far from being unreasonable, such ignorance is a natural consequence of conformity to a socially and legally endorsed stereotype of passivity, dependent and derivative participation in commercial activity. In some cases, an aggressive or violent male associate might insist that the woman refrain from inquiry or participation. In extreme cases, her acquiescence in an inactive and ignorant role may be the price of physical safety. The reasons for remaining ignorant may range across a broad spectrum, from compliance with the traditional stereotype of femininity to threats of physical violence.[48]

At first instance, Hodgson J found that Mrs Lewis did not expressly or impliedly authorise or consent to the incurring of the debt in question. On appeal, the majority found that Mrs Lewis had no knowledge of the debt and did

---

47 (1986) 4 ACLC 739.

48 Dodds Streeton at 40.

not know of the company's insolvency. There was, however, a dissent. Kirby P (as he then was) argued:

> The time has passed when directors can simply surrender their duties to the public and those with whom the corporation deals by washing their hands with impunity, leaving it to one director or a cadre of directors or to a general manager to discharge their responsibilities for them …
>
> The fact that the managing director arrogated authority to himself is, as it seems to me, irrelevant to the question whether the respondent expressly or by implication authorised or consented to the company's activities being conducted through him. Clearly she did. Equally clearly, she must have known (or must be taken by the statute to have known) that opting out of concern in the company's affairs would mean, in effect, that the company, as a continuing trading entity, would have to incur debts which would thereupon be incurred by her husband, as managing director, on behalf of the company and with her implicit acquiescence, authority and consent. No other inference is available from the course which she adopted, being a director with the responsibilities which the Code imposes upon her, being sufficiently concerned about the company's liquidity to ask about it, and being prepared to be brushed off by the generalities of her husband, the managing director.[49]
>
> …
>
> It might be said that, given the true nature of the relationship between the respondent and her husband, her reaction was entirely understandable. Perhaps it was. But it was not a reaction which the Code permitted her to take. And if the consequence is that a creditor can attack assets which have been acquired or placed in her name, the answer comes back that this is so because Parliament has so provided. People should not become (relevantly) directors of companies, if they wish to avoid exposing themselves and their assets to the liabilities now imposed by s. 556. If they are directors, they should exercise the reasonable care and diligence which the Code now requires of them. They cannot surround themselves with a shield of immunity from the operation of s. 556, by the simple expedient of washing their hands of the company's affairs and leaving it to a co-director to attend to those affairs and to incur the debts with third parties which it is the very purpose of s. 556 to control.[50]

His Honour's view heralded a return to a stricter view of women's liability in these situations.

In a later case, *Statewide Tobacco Services v. Morley*,[51] Mrs Morley, a widow, did not participate in the family tobacco business during her husband's lifetime. She was then discouraged from participation after her husband's death because her son was reluctant to provide her with information. Ormiston J accepted that Mrs Morley

> knew nothing about her responsibilities as a director and that nobody informed her that they involved doing something more than signing a few documents from time to time

---

49 (1988) 13 NSWLR 315 at 319.

50 (1988) 13 NSWLR 315 at 321.

51 (1990) 8 ACLC 827.

upon the say-so of her son, or possibly of the company's accountants. Those patterns unfortunately for her, do not excuse her failure to perform her duties. [I]f people choose to use a corporate vehicle to carry on their business activities, then they must accept the consequential responsibility.[52]

It would seem, then, that the courts interpret the Corporations Law as imposing the following minimum obligations upon directors:

- to take a 'diligent and intelligent interest' in the information provided to them
- to demand any other information that they believe is necessary or that, in the circumstances of each case, should be provided
- to pay particular attention to keeping up to date with the company's financial position and, when they lack the appropriate expertise, to seek independent expert advice.[53]

For many women who are second directors in small private companies, these standards may be very difficult to attain:

> Many of these women are primarily concerned with raising their children and with home duties: their ability to access commercial information is necessarily curtailed. In many circumstances, as noted above, a man may deliberately deny his partner access to such information, and this may be done on a number of bases: he may not wish 'to worry her'; or he may simply believe that her role is purely a formality. In some cases, she may wish to become informed and he may resent what he sees as her 'interference'. Even seeking truly independent legal advice may be difficult for women in this situation.[54]

Of course, there is a problem here if you believe that directors should be accountable for wrongdoing. Why should we excuse female non-participating directors? At the same time, many women who are acting as directors do so at a real disadvantage. The alternative to relieving women of responsibility for breach of directors' duties is to prevent them from becoming passive directors in the first place. Recent amendments to the Corporations Law have tried to overcome the problems faced by female passive directors by allowing companies to have only one director:

> I should highlight the importance of the provisions in the Bill which enable sole traders to incorporate without the need to involve a second shareholder or director in the business. This amendment will alleviate a number of problems which have a particular impact on women who are involved in business. Reports over recent years suggest that women are heavily involved in small business and, in fact, are setting up their own businesses at a much faster rate than men.
>
> The current requirement for a minimum of two directors and shareholders for a company has presented significant practical difficulties for many women.
>
> First, businesswomen may find it difficult to find another person willing to act as a director of their companies. They may be unwilling to have their husbands or partners as

---

52 (1990) 8 ACLC 827 at 843.

53 S. Woodward, 'Directors: Be Informed or Beware' (1993) *Law Institute Journal* 274 at 275.

54 Berns, Baron, & Neave, p. 109.

directors or shareholders out of a desire to retain a degree of independence within the family unit.

Secondly, the minimum number requirement often leads to women becoming directors of companies controlled by their spouse in which they do not play any meaningful role. This can expose these women to the legal liabilities of a company director, without them having any influence over the operation of the company. As recent cases have shown, people acting as directors without being involved in the company's affairs can be responsible for the company's debts on insolvency. The outcome is similar to the problem which results from 'sexually transmitted debt' when a person acts as a guarantor for the debts of their spouse.

The bill will address these problems, and help women to establish themselves in business in their own terms.[55]

However, given that banks still demand personal guarantees for company debts, there is some doubt about whether these amendments will solve the problem of women's assumption of the debt of the businesses of those close to them. And the Bill will not redress the vulnerability of many women:

The fundamental problem of women's vulnerable position in personal and family relationships with men, and their relative exclusion from commercial experience and control cannot be solved by law. The dominance of a male associate in many relationships may be such that women would be influenced to risk their property without any ostensible external pressure. If the law attempted to address the problem of the pervasive vulnerability of women as a group by absolutely precluding creditors from access to their assets, it would effectively destroy their legal capacity, restrict their access to credit, and totally undercut the achievement of equal and independent status.[56]

REVIEW QUESTIONS

1   How real a 'choice' did Mrs Morley have in the use of the corporate form?
2   Dodds Streeton argues that the ostensibly gender-neutral test used in *3M Australia Ltd v. Kemish*[57] for the purposes of directors' liability for insolvent trading is, in fact, far from gender neutral in reality:

[J]ust as criminal law issues predicated upon the standard of the 'reasonable man' have been imposed upon women in a gender biased way, it is likely that the standard of 'a director or manager of ordinary competence' imposed a male standard to which women directors or managers must conform. While the stated test seems objective and fair, it in fact masks an inherent gender bias. The reality is that many women occupy directorships in a merely formal role, are dominated both person-

55   M. Lavarch, First Corporate Law Simplification Bill 1994, Second Reading Speech, Commonwealth of Australia, *Hansard*, House of Representatives, 8 February 1995, pp. 707–8.

56   Dodds Streeton at 16.

57   (1986) 4 ACLC 185.

ally and professionally by male associates and are excluded from information and the decision-making process. Although there may be reasonable grounds to expect insolvency in one sense, such women directors have no access to or capacity to appreciate those grounds, by reason of their dependency. The objective standard of liability, when applied to their situation, is a blunt instrument which will ensure that prima facie accountability pursuant to the term of the section.

Do you agree?

3 A further issue in so-called 'sexually transmitted debt' cases is the relationship between the woman and the credit provider, ordinarily a company. A number of judges in these cases have been concerned about the resulting 'inconvenience' to lending institutions if the contract is struck down.[58] For some time, the provision of independent advice to women in sexually transmitted debt situations has meant that these women are less likely to succeed in having a contract set aside. Recently, however, in the decision of *Gough v. Commonwealth Bank of Australia*,[59] the majority of the New South Wales Court of Appeal held that the responsibility upon lending institutions to ensure that advice is provided was circumscribed. What responsibility should credit providers have to ensure that women in these situations receive independent legal advice?

4 Similarly, in *Barclays Bank v. O'Brien*, it was said:

> It is easy to allow sympathy for the wife who is threatened with the loss of her home at the suit of a rich bank to obscure an important public interest, viz, the need to ensure that the wealth currently tied up in the matrimonial home does not become economically sterile. If the rights secured to wives by the law renders vulnerable loans granted on the security of matrimonial homes, institutions will be unwilling to accept such security, thereby reducing the flow of loan capital to business enterprises. It is therefore essential that a law designed to protect the vulnerable does not render the matrimonial home unacceptable as security to financial institutions.[60]

Is this statement valid?

Sexing the company

If the company, whether private or public, large or small, has traditionally been subject to male ownership and management, is it any wonder that the company has been criticised for being inherently 'masculinist' in nature?

> Corporate law…is dominated by men—whether as judges, lawyers, academics or politicians. This results in certain questions being asked, certain issues being valued and certain methods being used. It means that women's perspectives are omitted and marginalised, and it 'universalises' an essentially male point of view.

---

58 See, for instance, *Peters v. Commonwealth Bank Australia* [1992] Aus Con Rep 90-012 at 89 322 per Brownie J.

59 [1994] ASC 56-270.

60 [1993] 4 All ER 417 at 422.

Secondly, corporate law reflects the masculinist values of capitalism, patriarchy and dominance. For example, it promotes capitalism through the development of free enterprise and the exploitation of business opportunities. This results in disparities of wealth which reinforce the broad class and gender divisions in society. Capitalism is masculinist because it is about power and dominance, and because the group with overriding power in our society (namely white, 'middle class' men) consider it a universal value appropriate for all.

Finally, corporate law operates through gender neutral 'objective' concepts and rules which mask the effect of the law upon women. As women do not have equal access to information, education and opportunity, gender neutral rules can impose injustices upon women. They hide the reality of inequality in society and ignore the different effect of the law upon women.[61]

Andrew Wicks and colleagues[62] share Hall's view of the masculinist values of corporations. They acknowledge that it would be 'absurdly complex and reductive' to isolate the myriad images and structures that are distinctively masculine in our everyday environment. But they also expose what they consider to be the 'most egregious' examples of masculine metaphors within the corporation, such as the idea that the corporation is an autonomous entity that is fundamentally separate from its environment, and that firms confront an external environment that they should seek to control. Wicks and colleagues argue that feminist insights can offer 'a new vocabulary, with its own distinct set of concepts and metaphors, that enables us to envision an innovative and enriching context within which to think about the firm'.[63]

In a similar vein, John Dobson and Judith White ask whether the 'masculine' firm is optimal or desirable, and they suggest that it is the 'masculine' value characteristics of the firm that give rise to inefficiencies.[64] But is it not possible that this view of the value of 'feminine' characteristics is simply being used to further the traditional views of economic corporate efficiency, while simultaneously rejecting corporate social responsibility? And is it possible to say that some characteristics are inherently male, while others are inherently female? Perhaps we are skirting the edge of an essentialist trap, one that may rely on the traditional stereotypical assumptions that much feminist theory and practice has taken pains to reject: 'Do the social, cultural, and economic conditions that generated [a predominantly female perspective on moral reasoning] place intrinsic limits on the normative value of that perspective? We must ask whether our conception of "the feminine" remains too entangled in a complex array of insufficiently disinterested assumptions to be a useful category for reflection'.[65]

---

61 Hall at 149.

62 A. C. Wicks, D. R. Gilbert, & R. E. Freeman, 'A Feminist Reinterpretation of the Stakeholder Concept' (1994) 4 (4) *Business Ethics Quarterly* 475 at 479–83.

63 Wicks et al. at 482.

64 J. Dobson & J. White, 'Towards the Feminine Firm: An Extension to Thomas White' (1995) 5 (3) *Business Ethics Quarterly* 463 at 469.

65 M. M. Moody-Adams, 'Gender and the Complexity of Moral Voices', in C. Card (ed.), *Feminist Ethics*, University of Kansas Press, Kansas, 1991, p. 201.

Perhaps, in order to escape this essentialist trap, we should take the feminist argument at its most minimal point—that is, that more women should manage or own companies.[66] But, as discussed above, simply placing women in management positions may not change the corporate ethos. In order to attain those positions, it is often essential for women to adopt the values and ethics of the corporation itself. Neither will sex discrimination necessarily decrease as the proportion of women in business increases. Studies suggest that as women increase their numbers and get closer to the top in corporations, the resistance from men hardens, and discrimination becomes more open.[67] Kathleen Lahey and Sarah Salter suggest that even those who supposedly hold power in the corporation are, effectively, powerless. Is the 'masculinist' corporation perhaps beyond control?

> [T]he business corporation is a perfection of the masculinist version of self—existence as property, separation of accountability and enjoyment, abstract rules as justice, domination as ownership. The only irony in this scenario is the fact that the corporation so perfects and depoliticises domination that even the human 'managers' ... have become the instruments and agents of the corporation, rather than the title-holders of its immense powers, which they had initially set out to be.[68]

Where do we go from here?

The corporate form as we know it is not some sort of inevitability. Its values and principles are a matter of choice:

> Company law is about capitalism. It provides the formal legal structure necessary to the operation of the capitalist system. The capitalist invests shares in a company set up and managed by an entrepreneur, who employs on his behalf as many workers, or machines, as are necessary to the profitable operation of the business. The shareholders provide the finance, the managers the ideas, the drive and the organization, and the employees do the work. The managers and the other employees are paid a salary or wage out of the takings of the business. The remaining profit goes exclusively to the shareholders who own and control the business and who also bear the risk of any loss which may be incurred ...
>
> Even if there is very little historical truth in such a pure model of capitalism, it none the less provides the theoretical justification for the basic organization of industry and commerce throughout most of the western world. There is nothing necessary or natural

---

66　This is, of course, a classic 'liberal feminist' stance, but given the intensely problematical nature of the corporation itself, it is difficult to see how installing women in management positions will of itself help us with the larger project of finding ways to live with the corporations among us. We need to find ways of acting directly upon corporations, installing the essential moral circuitry, if we are to ensoul the corporation. We cannot simply 'add woman' and get, as if by magic, 'the moral corporation'.

67　'Myths', *Empowering Women in Business*, Internet <http://www.feminist.org> December 1995.

68　K. A. Lahey & S. W. Salter, 'Corporate Law in Legal Theory and Legal Scholarship: From Classicism to Feminism' (1985) 23 OHLJ 543 at 555.

about this. The ownership and control of business enterprises, and the distribution of profits arising in them, can be structured in any number of ways.[69]

Could corporations, then, be structured in ways that are more responsive to women? Ideas for reform tend to be inherently conservative, at least to the extent that they imply acceptance of the received corporate form. Gabaldon, for instance, argues that what is needed is a complete restructuring of the corporate form in order to accommodate the interests of women. In this regard, she writes that corporations should be less hierarchically managed, smaller, and more flexible. Their decision-makers should contextualise the consequences of their decisions in terms of their impact upon others, such as employees and consumers.[70] A recent proposal for a Business Feminist Agenda, based on a plan formulated at the National Women's Conference in 1977, makes, *inter alia*, the following recommendations:

- Ensure equal representation for women on corporate boards, in senior management, in professional organizations and associations, and in all decision-making positions in business;
- Implement a comprehensive plan to increase the percentage of women and minorities at all levels and in all positions with specific sanctions against those who violate its tenets;
- Adopt effective policies that ensure women are given the same advancement and promotion opportunities that men receive;
- Create internal mechanisms designed to identify and develop potential women managers, and to accelerate their development through 'fast track' programs until gender-balance in senior management is achieved;
- Develop a workplace conducive to the growth of women and men;
- Adopt a comprehensive policy for the positive portrayal of women in diverse roles in corporate sponsored media, advertising, and communications.[71]

But if more women manage and own companies, will we see any difference in the ways in which companies function? Or are our expectations of corporations fundamentally determined by the way corporations are now? Do these proposed reforms go far enough? There is little doubt that what is needed is more feminist analysis of corporations and business culture. As one analyst has put it, 'what feminists had initially thought was just a silly (male) fancy of the corporate world might well turn out to be a truly dreadful reality which women ignore at their peril'.[72]

---

69 T. Hadden, *Company Law and Capitalism*, Weidenfeld & Nicolson, London, 1972, pp. 3–4.

70 Gabaldron at 1429.

71 As quoted in 'A Feminist Agenda', *Empowering Women in Business*, Internet <http://www.feminist.org> December 1995.

72 Lahey & Salter at 571.

REVIEW QUESTION

Gabaldon writes:

> According to this Frankensteinian view [of the corporation], irresponsible corporate impresarios regularly dispatch inhuman corporate entities to roam the countryside in search of profits. Lacking both conscience and capital, these entities will inflict injuries for which they cannot, and their heedless inventors need not, pay. In an uncharitable, but not necessarily unrealistic, permutation, the corporate scientist quite deliberately may design the creature to generate short-run gains for the creator, while surreptitiously imposing tremendous costs on third parties.[73]

Is this view valid?

---

73 Gabaldon at 1387.

16

THE IMPERIAL COMPANY

Introduction

In chapter 7 we first encountered the paradox of the corporate group. While the law, more-or-less consistently, treats the corporate group as 'fiction' and the individual company as 'fact',[1] those in the business and financial world who deal with corporate groups understand them in a very different way. For many of them, as we saw in chapter 7, the 'reality' of the group all but obliterates the individual entities within it.[2] Financial decisions, including the decision to extend substantial lines of credit, are routinely made on the basis of the assumed financial stability of the group. Within law, on the other hand, group reality is at best granted a grudging acceptance, as, for example, where the directors of companies within such a group find themselves unwilling or unable to sustain a distinction between the welfare of the individual company and the welfare of the group. This matter was discussed by Pennycuick J in one such case:

> *As I have already found the directors of Castleford looked to the benefit of the group as a whole and did not give separate consideration to the benefit of Castleford* ... Each company in the groups is a separate legal entity and the directors of a particular company are not entitled to sacrifice the interest of that company ... The proper test, in the absence of actual separate consideration, must be whether an intelligent and honest man in the position of a

---

1 A limited exception is the requirement for the presentation of consolidated accounts. While the directors of a group holding company, often called a parent company, have for some time been required by law to prepare consolidated accounts in respect of the holding company and its subsidiaries, the law in this area was widely regarded as ineffective. Its reliance on the language of subsidiary and holding company significantly limited its effectiveness. In 1991 the law was amended to adopt the discourse of 'entity' and 'control' recommended by the Australian Accounting Research Foundation (AASB 1024). The *Corporations Law 1990*, s. 323A requires the disclosure of 'entities'—including companies, partnerships, and trustees (s. 294A(4) and (5))—where they are part of the 'economic entity' formed by the 'chief entity' and its controlled entities. For balance-sheet purposes, control is determined at the end of the appropriate accounting period. While the reporting requirements are being tightened for corporate groups, the 'fiction' of separate identity is otherwise maintained. Creditors are not entitled to recourse against the group if one of its members becomes insolvent.

2 See particularly the discussion of the financial perception of the Skase operation (p. 173).

director of the company concerned, could, in the whole of the existing circumstances, have reasonably believed that the transactions were for the benefit of the company.[3]

There are two levels of reality then: legal reality and commercial reality. Legally, each company is an independent entity. Practically, though, a director in the position of the directors of Castleford who disregarded the welfare of the group and focused exclusively on the welfare of the individual corporate cell within that group would be incompetent or mad or both. The art lies in the balance, and very often that balance dictates that priority be given to the welfare of the group, perhaps because, from the perspective of the corporate group, the role of that particular entity is to serve the interests of the group.

On the other hand, at least in circumstances where the subsidiaries are not wholly owned (and sometimes even where they are), drawing the line between the reasonable belief required in *Charterbridge* and the somewhat different scenario in *Reid Murray Holdings Ltd (in liq.) v. David Murray Holdings Pty Ltd*[4] is problematical enough to cause concern.[5] In *Charterbridge*, Pennycuick J was prepared to accept that an honest and reasonable person in the position of the director could have believed that the transactions were for the benefit of Castleford, given the services that were provided to Castleford by the group. However, the facts in *Reid Murray Holdings* were just different enough to suggest that the arrangements did not provide any benefit whatever to David Murray that might counterbalance the liabilities it undertook as a consequence of the guarantees given. David Murray was a wholly owned subsidiary of Reid Murray. It executed a guarantee to Reid Murray for all advances, present and future, to other (insolvent) subsidiaries of Reid Murray. The consideration stated was known by all concerned to be void. Although Mitchell J accepted the *Charterbridge* test, he did

> not believe that the directors could have had a belief that the transaction as it was set forth in the guarantee was for the benefit of David Murray had they applied their minds to the whole of the circumstances … [He continued by quoting from *Charterbridge* and noted that] where one company is a member of a group with common shareholding 'each company in the group is a separate legal entity and the directors of a particular company are not entitled to sacrifice the interests of that company.'[6]

---

3   *Charterbridge Corp. Ltd v. Lloyd's Bank Ltd* [1970] 1 Ch D 62 at 74 (emphasis added). In *Charterbridge* the transactions were essential to the welfare of the group and did not directly impugn the well-being of the individual company.

4   (1972) 5 SASR 386.

5   The acceptance of cross guarantees by the Australian Securities Commission (ASC) Class Orders provisions highlights the problematical nature of this line-drawing exercise: Class Order 95/1530 (1991) 2 *Australian Securities Commission Releases* 119 654 (issued on 10 November 1995; updated 28 May 1996).

6   (1972) 5 SASR 386 at 402. More precisely, given the level of integration in the corporate group, the directors should not be entitled to act in ways that defeat the interests of the creditors of the company. In these circumstances, given the company's wholly owned status and the level of cross-shareholding, the economic interests of the members were probably best served by disregarding the separate entity doctrine, although their interests as members of David Murray were not best served. Given that shareholders are entitled to vote in their own private interests, they undoubtedly could, and probably would, have ratified the board's decision had the question been put.

The question that was not asked, or answered, of course, was whether David Murray had any interests apart from the group. The answer to that question—a very difficult question within the context of our legal and political structures—depends entirely upon whether one gives priority to the individual entity[7] or to the economic and enterprise unit constituted by the group. The present difficulty, which is the principle concern of this chapter, is that the legal order and the economic and commercial order tend to answer questions like this very differently.

By the early 1990s, as Australian courts worked their way through the detritus of the 1980s, the *Charterbridge* test was still being applied, but concern about whether it provided an appropriate standard or guide for conduct was increasing. This concern was perhaps compelled by the fact that, during the 1980s, the interests of the group had clearly been given primacy. In *Equiticorp Finance Ltd v. Bank of New Zealand*,[8] two members of the New South Wales Court of Appeal, Clarke and Cripps JJA, expressed their reservations concerning its appropriateness in these terms:

> A preferable view may be that where the directors have failed to consider the interests of the relevant company they should be found to have committed a breach of duty. If, however, the transaction was, objectively viewed, in the interests of the company, then no consequences would flow from the breach. Such an inquiry would not require the court to consider how the hypothetical honest and intelligent director would have acted. On the contrary it would accept that a finding of breach of duty flows from a failure to consider the interests of the company and would then direct attention at the consequences of the breach.[9]

The question thus elided is whether, given the reality of the corporate group, it is possible for directors (who may well have no choice but to pursue the interests of the group) to fulfil their obligations if the standard is set in these terms. If the law in these circumstances sets an unrealistic (perhaps unattainable) standard, suggesting that breach is inevitable (although no consequences will flow from it where the company is not harmed), it does the law no credit.[10] Neither does it assist directors in determining the extent to which they may look to the interests of the group in making decisions.

The present dichotomy between legal reality and commercial reality would be of less concern were it not for the opportunities it presents for the avoidance of legal constraints and for the expenses it occasions for those who are compelled to deal with the 'corporate jellyfish'.[11] According to Tom Hadden,

---

7   Very often, the law regards the individual entity as a 'nexus of contracts', and the interests with which the law is concerned are those of the contracting parties, strictly read and defined by privity of contract.

8   [1993] 32 NSWLR 50.

9   [1993] 32 NSWLR 50 at 148. It is a cause for concern that some members of the judiciary continue to have difficulty accepting the impossibility of the entity model, given the realty of modern corporate structures.

10   It may, in fact, encourage litigation by minority shareholders and others keen to test the notion of whether, objectively viewed, the transaction could be said to have been for the benefit of the company.

11   See the discussion of this analogy in chapter 5, fn. 8 (p. 111).

[s]ix broad categories of manipulation and abuse, whether of the techniques of group control and integrated financing or of group structures in themselves, may be identified:

(i)   the techniques of group control, notably those involving interlocking shareholdings and directorships, may be used to entrench the positions of incumbent managers against any possible threat from external shareholders;

(ii) the techniques of integrated financing, notably the freedom to pass assets and liabilities from company to company within the group, and the creation of complex groups structures may be used to conceal the true financial position of individual companies or of the group as a whole from their shareholders or creditors;

(iii) both techniques may be used to ensure that the interests of shareholders and directors of the group are preferred to those of minority shareholders in subsidiaries and to conceal that this has been done;

(iv) the techniques of integrated financing may be used to avoid taxation by ensuring that maximum profit is generated in forms or in jurisdictions which attract low levels of tax;

(v)   the creation of separate companies for particular operations, supplemented by the techniques of integrated financing, may be used to avoid liability to external creditors by relying on the limited liability of each constituent company within the group;

(vi) more or less complex group structures may be used to avoid the impact of regulatory measures on a wide range of matters, such as monopolies and mergers legislation, health and safety provisions, employee participation and planning requirements.[12]

Hadden notes that all of these features were particularly noticeable in the structure of Australian corporate empires in the 1980s. He cites the Adelaide Steamship/David Jones group and the corporate empires of Christopher Skase and Alan Bond as examples of this level of corporate integration.

The law in this area confronts a conundrum of its own making. The doctrinal structures that began to ossify with *Salomon v. Salomon & Co. Ltd*[13] insist that the only reality that the law can acknowledge is that of the individual company. It, not the corporate group of which it is a part, is the law's reality. There is, however, another reality. In the fully integrated corporate group, which has become the rule rather than the exception in the closing years of the twentieth century, commercial reality ever more closely approaches the level of integration of the colonial jellyfish. Although they are all legally discrete and independent entities, more and more often the subsidiaries within such a group are not only functionally inseparable from the group in their commercial activities but also fully integrated in their financial arrangements. The fiction is that of independence; the reality is one

---

12 T. Hadden, 'Regulation of Corporate Groups in Australia' (1992) 15 UNSWLJ 61 at 65. We touched on some of these issues in earlier chapters. In this chapter we will be largely concerned the ways in which the law's seeming inability to come to terms with the 'corporate jellyfish' allows it to escape the general law and to effectively establish its own ground rules, both with respect to municipal law and with respect to international law.

13 [1897] AC 22.

of total integration.[14] In a further paradox, but one that is somehow not surprising, Melvin Eisenberg tells us:

> With few if any exceptions, wholly owned groups exist only as a response to legal rules. It is very difficult to find economic reasons for wholly owned groups, because almost any economic goal that can be achieved by the creation of a wholly owned subsidiary can be equally well achieved by the creation of a division … In fact, a corporation that puts some of its business units into subsidiary form is likely to treat those units in exactly the same way that it treats other businesses that are divisions *with the limited exception that a lawyer in a small office may spend an hour or so each year writing up fictitious minutes for fictitious meetings of the subsidiaries' fictitious boards.*[15]

Eisenberg goes on to describe a curious process of corporate generation in the USA. Noting that a significant factor in the formation of wholly owned subsidiaries is the desire to avoid legal rules that restrict the conduct of businesses such as banks and insurance companies, he adds:

> In other cases, wholly owned subsidiaries are created for the purpose of limiting or circumventing the rights of corporate creditors or shareholders. In some cases, the purpose of the wholly owned subsidiary is to insulate the parent corporation, as well as the parent's shareholders, from liability arising out of business activity that the parent economically conducts. In these cases the function of the subsidiary is to deny to third parties claims they would have if the subsidiary had not been formed. In other cases, the purpose of the wholly owned subsidiary is to circumvent rights that the parent's shareholders would otherwise have.[16]

The transition from the relatively small entrepreneurial enterprise of the nineteenth century to the giant corporation of the late twentieth century is not an accident. Rather, it is a legal artefact; it is a product of law's disciplinary gaze, not at its wonderful new toy, the limited liability company, but at the explosion of transport, production, and wealth generation that followed the industrial revolution. Existing within a legal environment, companies and their lawyers sought to develop structures that would enable them to maximise their ability to operate within that environment while minimising their exposure to the new forms of legal liability and patterns of regulation thrown up by the twentieth century. They were very successful indeed.

The doctrine of separate legal personality—the hallmark of the common law's enduring attachment to the idea of the entity as the fundamental unit of corporate

---

14 British courts have been marginally more willing to come to terms with this reality than have those in Australia, at least where this does not compromise limited liability. See *Smith, Stone, & Knight Ltd v. Birmingham Corporation* [1939] 4 All ER 116; *DHN Food Distributors Ltd v. Tower Hamlets London Borough Council* [1976] 1 WLR 852. Compare these cases with the much less progressive attitude in *Pioneer Concrete Services Ltd v. Yelnah Pty Ltd* (1986) 11 ACLR 108.

15 M. A. Eisenberg, 'Corporate Groups', in M. Gillooly (ed.), *The Law Relating to Corporate Groups*, Federation Press, Sydney, 1993, pp. 1, 4–5 (emphasis added).

16 Eisenberg, pp. 5-6.

law—became, in the hands of companies and their lawyers, a truly marvellous tool. Despite belated recognition that, in its exclusive attention to the entity at the expense of the enterprise, the law perpetuates the abuses that it seeks to constrain, the doctrine retains its attraction in Anglo-Australian law. It and the corporate veil that it flaunts are the subjects of this chapter. In this way we come again to a topic we canvassed briefly in chapter 7. In that chapter, however, it was the corporate veil itself that concerned us. Here our concern is with the law's apparent inability to address the reality of corporate groups and with the role that doctrines such as separate legal personality play in maintaining the fiction that the law ought to be concerned with the entity and not the corporate group.

We begin with a question that we will return to on a number of occasions: why does the law continue to insist upon the fiction of separate legal personality, even when that fiction enables a controlling parent company to insulate itself from the debts of its wholly owned subsidiary? What is its magic? Templeman LJ noted:

> A parent company may spawn a number of subsidiary companies, all controlled directly or indirectly by the shareholders of the parent company. If one of the subsidiary companies, to change the metaphor, turns out to be the runt of the litter and declines into insolvency to the dismay of its creditors, the parent company and the other subsidiary companies may prosper to the joy of shareholders without any liability for the debts of the insolvent subsidiary.[17]

Those who deal with the 'imperial company', also known as the enterprise, may find it illusive. It is not only creditors who are likely to be dismayed, even disbelieving, when they find that they are dealing with the 'runt of the litter' rather than the enterprise itself. Sometimes the runt is just small enough to enable the company to avoid the effort and expense of complying with legislation proscribing discrimination or requiring enterprises of a particular size to take measures to eradicate the effects of structural discrimination. At other times, the runt may be an ideal sacrificial offering. If it is too small or too inefficient to comply with occupational health and safety requirements, it can be left to confront the costs of its failure 'on its own'. It may be underinsured and unable to meet claims for defective products. After all, it is not always economically feasible to maintain full product liability insurance for a high-risk subsidiary. (From the perspective of the enterprise, the subsidiary is the 'insurance'.) Often, a 'runt' can 'insulate' a healthy parent or sibling company from the threat of litigation, either by its existence (or its disappearance) or by providing a local target. Sometimes, the imperial company may, as has happened in the United Kingdom, provide a trap for the trade union movement, structurally creating the illusion of a secondary boycott although the reality is of a single enterprise operated by multiple entities. Regularly, perhaps even as a matter of normal practice, creditors and minority shareholders in such entities are put at risk. Hadden notes that, in practice,

---

17   *Re Southard & Co. Ltd* [1979] 1 WLR 1198 at 1208.

it will often be difficult for minority shareholders in a subsidiary—and virtually impossible for its creditors—to establish that their interests have been subordinated to those of the group. The directors of the subsidiary will normally owe their primary loyalty, not least in terms of job security and prospects of promotion, to the group and will rarely be willing to assert the interests of the subsidiary or to disclose the details of detrimental transactions undertaken in the interests of the group. In the absence of specific procedural measures to require the directors at least of non-wholly-owned subsidiaries to account for and report on potentially detrimental transactions with other group companies, oppression remedies are unlikely to work … The best protection for minority shareholders in a subsidiary within an integrated corporate group, however, would be a general right to require the holding company to buy them out at a fair price. This principle has been adopted in the context of take-over bids in most jurisdictions. There is no reason in principle why it should not be extended on a more general basis.[18]

In the next section, we will look (from various perspectives) at some of the by-products of corporate structure and of the law's failure to come to terms with the reality of the corporate jellyfish. Hugh Collins identifies

two competing paradigms of analysis of the problem of power in the corporation. On one side, the contractual model informs the analysis of the arrangements of a productive enterprise, and provides the starting-point for debates about the proper scope and aims of legal regulation. On the other side, an organizational model, one which draws on notions of bureaucracy, governance, and public responsibility offers a radically different paradigm for analysis and intervention. Each paradigm offers valuable insights, yet seems incomplete on its own …

The questions raised by groups of companies can be examined from these two perspectives. The contractual perspective sees the relation between parent and subsidiary as a contractual relation of investment; whereas the organizational framework insists upon the effective unity of the two companies within one organization. The contractual perspective advocates the distinction between corporate entities; the organizational perspective insists that at least for certain purposes the group of companies should be treated as one unit for issues of responsibility and accountability …

[T]he organizational perspective is at once more challenging to existing legal arrangements and more obscure. There is good reason for both these features of this paradigm. The organizational discourses fit uneasily into the private law framework out of which the law of corporations has been forged by imaginative legal draughtsmen. It contests the public/private divide which absolves the company from social responsibilities. At the same time it refuses to conceive the corporation as composed of the traditional building blocks of private law in its concepts of contract and trusts.[19]

---

18 Hadden at 77. If there are no minority shareholders in the subsidiaries in such a group, it would perhaps make more sense for the law to treat the group as the entity and allow creditors redress against the collectivity rather than the individual entity.

19 H. Collins, 'Organizational Regulation and the Limits of Contract' in J. McCahery, S. Picciotto, & C. Scott, *Corporate Control and Accountability*, Clarendon Press, Oxford, 1993, pp. 91, 93–4.

REVIEW QUESTIONS

1 Consider the decision in *Charterbridge* with great care. Many companies involved in the 1980s collapses in Australia structured their affairs in a similar way. Do you believe that the decision was reasonable on the facts of that case, particularly considering that the entire issue of separate legal personality appears to have been disregarded?

2 Law reform bodies have regularly considered the problems posed by nominee directors and interlocking directorates. More recently they have attempted to address the reality of wholly integrated corporate financial structures, at least as far as financial reporting is concerned. To date, while acknowledging the urgent need for reform, they have been unable to generate concrete proposals capable of balancing commercial realities, separate legal personality, and the potential for conflict of interest between the nominating group and the company. Might it be reasonable to enact legislation that, at least for certain purposes, treated an interlocking group of companies as a legal entity and that enabled the creditors of any company within the group to have recourse against the entire group?

3 Complex structures frequently arise because management believes it to be rational (and legally acceptable) to isolate risky ventures to ensure that they will not adversely affect the group as a whole if they fail. Should this sort of strategy be permitted to succeed?

4 Can you identify any downside risks to Hadden's proposal that minority shareholders in subsidiaries of integrated corporate groups be entitled to require the parent to buy them out at a fair price?

The imperial company and the worker

The evolution of avoidance

Corporations develop complex structures for many reasons. Collins describes one such set of reasons:

> [T]he decision with respect to firm size also has a profound bearing on the potential liabilities of the company as a result of the limitation of legal responsibility to the firm's own actions and omissions. The capital boundary problem which arises consists of this: because the firm determines its own size, it also chooses the limits of its legal responsibilities which in turn provides an open invitation for the evasion of mandatory legal duties.
>
> The effects of the acceptance of such an invitation are noticeable in all branches of the law concerned with productive activities. In connection with employment protection rights, for example, many legal systems relieve small employers from some or all obligations towards employees, such as maternity rights or compensation for dismissal. By keeping firms small and securing production through a series of contractual relations

between independent firms, employers can avoid or reduce their legal obligations towards employees. Here we see a combination of the group responsibility principle and a statutory limit being exploited through the freedom to determine firm size in order to deprive workers of elementary rights.[20]

For instance, a large enterprise[21] can be required to comply with the reporting requirements of the *Affirmative Action (Equal Employment Opportunity for Women) Act 1986* (Cth) in respect of the steps it is taking to implement equal employment opportunity principles. But if an identical enterprise had elected to channel its operations into discrete legal entities, each of which was responsible for one aspect of the activities of the enterprise, and none of which exceed the statutory threshold, it would escape these reporting requirements (which are triggered by size) altogether.[22] This does not seem to be a reality of which the law should be particularly proud.

As Collins notes, 'the common law lacks a more general principle which might enable the courts to defeat the power of capital to organise itself in ways which reduce or eliminate liabilities from productive activities'.[23] The image of personality, even in the shadow form of legal personality, is one that consistently defeats the search for an organising principle able to deal with the corporate jellyfish in a manner that is efficient and that imposes the minimum costs upon those caught up in the debris that often attends the activities of corporate groups. As a consequence, piecemeal remedies accumulate, and the detritus of their failures continues to build up.

Walling off the damage: The Baryulgil story

In chapter 7, we encountered one attempt at such a 'piecemeal remedy' in *Briggs v. James Hardie & Co. Pty Ltd*.[24] Now we will look a little more carefully at the social and regulatory failures behind that case. To understand the relationship between those failures and what Collins describes as the 'capital boundary problem', we need to examine the facts more carefully. Rogers AJA tells us that in 1946 the plaintiff, Mr Briggs, 'moved to Baryulgil and obtained employment at the asbestos mine and mill. When he commenced this employment he was healthy.

---

20 H. Collins, 'Ascription of Legal Responsibility to Groups in Complex Patterns of Economic Integration' (1990) 53 MLR 731 at 737.

21 The threshold is 100 employees.

22 Section 9.1 of the First Corporate Law Simplification Bill 1994 makes a distinction between 'small' proprietary companies (ones with at least two of the following three characteristics: fewer than fifty employees, gross operating revenue of less than $10 million, gross assets of less than $5 million) and a 'large' proprietary company. The account and audit regime for small proprietary companies is significantly less onerous. It is puzzling that an entity could be small for one regulatory purpose and large for another.

23 Collins, 'Ascription of Legal Responsibility' at 738. Collins is particularly interesting on the interaction of this aspect of corporate law with the various laws regulating employment. See also S. Baughen, 'Multinationals and the Export of Hazard' (1995) 58 MLR 54 at 57, where the author suggests that, through the medium of the limited liability company, 'economic units enjoy great freedom to define their identity or identities … Consequently, the key question in tort—'which person committed this wrong?'—is likely to receive an artificial answer when the wrongdoer has made use of the doctrine of separate corporate personality to redefine itself'.

24 (1989) 7 ACLC 841.

He worked at the mine altogether for about six years, between 1946 and 1966. All the time he worked at the mine, he was in contact with asbestos dust and fibre'.[25] At the time, and for all material times thereafter, the mine was operated by Asbestos Mines Pty Ltd (AMPL). We also learn that, for some 'unexplained' reason, the plaintiff sought permission to proceed against Hardies and Wunderlich, rather than against the subsidiary, AMPL, which had formerly employed him.[26] The context within which these events played themselves out becomes clearer still when we learn a little of the history of the Baryulgil deposit and of the plant. Neil Gunningham recounts the story:

> The existence of an asbestos deposit at Baryulgil in northern New South Wales was known as long ago as 1918, but it was only in the early 1940s that any serious attempt was made to mine it. In 1940, Wunderlich Ltd (later a subsidiary of CSR) began the development and the mining plant was installed in 1943 and 1944. In 1944 Asbestos Mines Pty Ltd (AMPL) was formed to operate the mine with 50 per cent of shares being held by Wunderlich and the other 50 per cent by the James Hardie Group of Companies (hereafter Hardies). In 1953, Hardies bought Wunderlich's share and from that time until 1976 the operating company, AMPL, was a wholly owned subsidiary of Hardies. The mine was sold to Woodsreef Mines Ltd in 1976, and finally closed in April 1979.
>
> Throughout the period 1953 to 1976, AMPL operated the mine through a mine manager employed by that company. The workforce engaged in the quarry and mill varied between 15 and 40 at any one time, the greater number being occupied in the quarry. Of that workforce, a small number, usually four or five, were engaged in the milling process—separating the asbestos from the host rock. The workforce consisted mostly of people of Aboriginal descent drawn from the local community.[27]

After the Aboriginal Legal Service attempted to obtain compensation for both workers and residents, conditions at Baryulgil became the subject of a parliamentary inquiry. According to the 1984 Baryulgil Report:

> Nowhere in any of the internal company documents to which the committee had access, was there any reference to the need to educate or inform the workforce or the Baryulgil community about the hazards of asbestos ... It is an indictment of Hardies that although they were aware of the asbestosis hazard by the 1950s, neither then nor at any subsequent time did they attempt to communicate their knowledge to the workforce or to warn them of the dangers.[28]

---

25 (1989) 7 ACLC 841 at 847.

26 That the reason had to do with AMPL's impecunious state should not surprise us. Neither should it be surprising that AMPL was created to work the mine at Baryulgil.

27 N. Gunningham, 'Asbestos Mining at Baryulgil: A Case of Corporate Neglect', in P. Grabosky & A. Sutton, *Stains on a White Collar*, Federation Press, Sydney, 1989, p. 208. Gunningham also tells us that Baryulgil did not comply with the relevant Occupational Health and Safety provisions until 1978. It was a 'marginal mine' and compliance was expensive. See Gunningham, pp. 218–23.

28 House of Representatives Standing Committee on Aboriginal Affairs, 'The Effects of Asbestos Mining on the Baryulgil Community', AGPS, Canberra, 1984. The hazards posed by asbestos were well known by the early 1930s. See chapter 6, pp. 114–15.

Gunningham comments:

> Symptomatic of Hardies' attitude towards Baryulgil was the low ranking it had in the Hardie Group's industrial hygiene programme, introduced during the 1960s. Baryulgil, by all accounts, had a worse dust problem than Hardies' other operations, yet it was among the last to benefit from an industrial hygiene survey or the internal medical surveillance scheme. *The explanation may well lie in the fact that the mine was a small and economically marginal operation, that it was tucked away in a relatively obscure corner of New South Wales, lacking any effective union organisation, and that it had a compliant and unsophisticated Aboriginal workforce.*[29]

The efforts of the Aboriginal Legal Service to secure Commonwealth compensation for workers and community members at Baryulgil ultimately failed, although some assistance was obtained in cleaning up the site to protect the health of those who continued to live there. While the Baryulgil Report accepted that workers and residents would experience substantial difficulty in obtaining compensation,

> [t]he Committee concluded that any such inadequacies result from *features of the general law* and affect all claimants. Members of the Baryulgil community suffer no particular disadvantage in this regard. For example, the principal disadvantage which prospective Baryulgil claimants would suffer is that the company against which the claim would be brought is a subsidiary company with no funds to meet any award of damages that may be made.[30]

To describe the barriers to compensation confronting Baryulgil claimants as 'features of the general law' is akin to describing them as somehow natural and resistant to change, in the same way that mountains, rivers, or canyons are natural and resistant to change. More accurately and precisely, these features are an integral part of the way in which the law has constructed corporate identity. They presently reward corporate persons for structuring their enterprises in particular ways, and thus (albeit by indirection) make it likely that change will be resisted by those who profit from present arrangements.

Lest it be thought that the situation that arose in *Briggs v. James Hardie* was somehow unique (or even unique to Australia[31]), in *Adams v. Cape Industries plc*[32] the situation was almost identical. Here the English Court of Appeal explicitly

---

29 Gunningham, p. 217 (emphasis added). The approach taken by Hardies seems to be typical of that adopted by the mining industry more generally in this period. Multinational corporations that have successfully negotiated with indigenous peoples in other parts of the world continue to resist negotiation with indigenous communities in Australia. For a sample of the relevant literature, see 'Aboriginals and Mining: To Die for Uranium' (1978) *Economist* 85; G. Stokes, 'Mining Corporations and Aboriginal Land Rights in Australia: A Critique and Proposal' (Winter 1987) *The Australian Quarterly* 182; A. Walton, 'Cocktail Exploitation: Uranium, Aboriginal Land Rights, Gold, Diamonds and National Parks' (1987) 26 ALB 6.

30 Gunningham, p. 229 (emphasis added).

31 Similar issues were litigated in another of the 'asbestos cases', *Barrow and Heys v. Colonial Sugar Refinery Ltd*, unreported, Supreme Court WA, 4 August 1988, Library no. 7231.

32 [1991] 1 All ER 929.

acknowledged that corporate groups could structure their affairs to ensure that any legal liability that might arise in respect of particular activities would fall upon a particular legal person within that group.[33] Should such liability eventuate, it would, of course, be unfortunate if that particular entity was without the resources (as was the case in *Briggs*) to compensate the victims, even if (as was also the case in *Adams*) that consequence was one that the corporate structure was designed to ensure. According to the Court of Appeal, '[o]ur law, for better or worse, recognises the creation of subsidiary companies, which, although in one sense the creatures of their parent companies, will nevertheless under the general law be treated as separate legal entities with all the rights and liabilities which would normally attach to separate legal entities'.[34]

In a potent warning of the difficulties that multinational corporations pose for legal understandings that are firmly wed to notions of entity (and nationality), Simon Baughen goes on to discuss the relevant principles of private international law and their implications for a potential plaintiff:

> For any foreign judgment to be enforceable under the general principles of private international law, the English company would have had to have submitted to the jurisdiction of the foreign court. Alternatively it would have had to have been 'present' in the jurisdiction at the time the proceedings were started. In *Adams v. Cape Industries plc*, the Court of Appeal confirmed that such 'presence' will not be established merely through the presence in the foreign jurisdiction of either a subsidiary company or a company which is in reality entirely controlled by the defendant corporation.

Submission and presence are potentially inaccessible alternatives for a plaintiff without the resources to commence action in England, and potentially useful shields for a parent company seeking to deflect liability. Baughen goes on: 'The foreign plaintiff, therefore, *has* to sue in England if intending to obtain an enforceable judgment'. As if this 'must' were not a sufficient barrier in and of itself, he continues:

> *The Albaforth* suggests that the *locus* of the tort is the natural forum. It is therefore necessary to establish where the cause of action in tort arose. This procedural question is inextricably linked with the substantive issue of the likely ultimate basis of the English company's liability in tort, if any. If it is found vicariously liable for the acts and omissions

---

33 [1991] 1 All ER 929 at 1026.

34 [1991] 1 All ER 929 at 1019. Academic commentators have, for some time, expressed concern regarding the doctrine and its effects. See B. Baxt, 'Tensions between Commercial Reality and Legal Principle—Should the Concept of the Corporate Entity be Re-examined' (1991) ALJ 352. United States Courts have not allowed the principle of independent legal personality to hamstring decision-making to the same extent as British and Australian courts. See *US v. Milwaukee Refrigerator Transit Co.* (1905) 142 Fed 247 at 255 per Sanborn J. It is worth noting that, in England, not only are the courts more likely to lift the corporate veil, but also the Parliament has in a number of areas legislated to overcome the difficulties involved. For a detailed discussion of the particular issues involved, see R. Carroll, 'Corporate Parents and Tort Liability', in M. Gillooly (ed.), *The Law Relating to Corporate Groups*, Federation Press, Sydney, 1993, p. 91.

of the foreign company, then the cause of action will arise in the country in which the foreign company broke its duty of care …

However, with primary liability it is less clear where the cause of action in tort will arise. In *Distillers Co. (Biochemicals) Ltd v. Thompson*, one of the Thalidomide cases, the Privy Council had to consider whether the tort had been committed in England where the drugs were made or in New South Wales where they were marketed and then used by the plaintiff. It was held that there is no tort merely in making a dangerous drug. It only became dangerous when it was put into circulation without adequate warning being given to those who marketed it. The failure to warn the Australian distributors of the hazards of the drug was the tortious act and this act, which founded the cause of action, took place in New South Wales.[35]

Without principles of enterprise liability firmly in place, and without procedures for lifting the corporate veil and for facilitating inter-jurisdictional suits, a new public/private distinction is emerging. Before the law, the parent company remains publicly known, but untouchable. Its subsidiaries are, in the eyes of the law, equally independent, equally publicly known. Their relationship, however, becomes a matter of private contract, an agreement between two separate individuals that is not relevant to third parties. Because it is private, its absence becomes the absence of a remedy, a wrong that is invisible to the law.

The fragmented master: A case of multiple legal personality

We have seen that corporate structures have the potential to frustrate claims such as those discussed in the last section, but we have only skimmed the surface of the potential pitfalls in the area of employment law. The complexities, and the potential pitfalls, are aptly illustrated by the facts of *McDermid v. Nash Dredging & Reclamation Co. Ltd*.[36] The plaintiff seaman worked as a deckhand on a tugboat—a self-contained stand-alone enterprise (it might seem) if ever there was one. When the plaintiff deckhand was injured through the negligence of the captain, the matter appeared simple enough on the surface: a straightforward case in which the employer would be liable at common law for an injury to its servant in the course of employment.[37] It is simple enough, at least, until we attempt to untangle the actual organisational structure. Within the micro-environment of the tugboat, we find not one employer, but several employers. While these different employers are parts of the same corporate group, they are nonetheless independent. The plaintiff deckhand is employed by one of these companies, the negligent captain by another. The deckhand's employer is, in turn, a (wholly owned) subsidiary of the Dutch company that employed the captain. Only the device of non-delegable duties—a tort doctrine

---

35 Baughen, at 55–6.

36 [1987] 1 AC 906.

37 Alternatively, of course, an employee in this situation would be entitled to claim under the relevant compensation legislation. This would avoid the inconvenience of multiple legal personalities, but the amount of compensation will be substantially less in the case of serious injury.

that insists that performance can be delegated, but not responsibility[38]—permits the common law to circumvent the inconvenience that would otherwise be caused by this elaborate structure. Because of the operation of this doctrine, the subsidiary (as employer) is liable for the negligence of the captain.

The chain of delegation works this way. The deckhand's employer owes to all of its employees a common-law duty of care and safety. In ordinary circumstances, where the employer is a sole trader, this obligation falls on the individual employer. Where the employer is a company, it falls on the company. Here the matter is a little more complicated. More likely than not, the Dutch parent company 'caused' its subsidiary to provide deckhands for its tugboat operations. The parent company in turn provided the captain. Thus, two discrete 'entities' collaborated in staffing the tugboat. The boat, in all likelihood, was owned or leased either by one of those entities or by yet another member of the corporate group. From a common-law perspective, the deckhand's employer is responsible for doing everything that is required to meet its duty of care and safety. If, from a common-law perspective, the master has arranged for some aspect of this global obligation to be performed by another—in this case the parent company (which selected the captain)—it retains legal responsibility for ensuring that the obligation is duly performed. If logically this seems a somewhat inelegant result, at least it is one that entitles the plaintiff deckhand to compensation for his injuries.

What is important here is the degree to which such structures are at odds with logic. If the ordinary rules of the sea apply, the deckhand was under the command of the captain, bound to carry out any commands that he was given. It seems reasonable to assume that the captain is either the deckhand's employer or an agent of his employer. Despite this, common sense proves problematical. Not only is the captain not the deckhand's employer, but they do not even work for the same entity. They have simply been placed, by virtue of corporate structures, in a particular kind of relationship to one another—a relationship that gives the captain de facto and *de jure* authority over the deckhand.

If, in *McDermid*, common-law resources enabled ascription of responsibility (as has been the situation in cases dealing with similar issues in Australia[39]), resolution is likely to prove more difficult in other areas. A particularly graphic illustration of the kinds of problems that can arise occurs as a consequence of the interaction between corporate structures and laws designed to regulate trade union activity, in particular, strike activity. One characteristic group of laws, which was recently reintroduced into Australia, prohibits forms of industrial activity that are characterised

---

38 This doctrine was originally devised to circumvent another legal doctrine with unpalatable consequences: the doctrine of common employment, which allowed the master to escape liability altogether where the negligence was that of a fellow servant.

39 *Kondis v. State Transport Authority* (1984) 55 ALR 225. *Kondis* is actually substantially more straightforward, in that part of the operation was carried out by an independent contractor. There was not, therefore, the potential confusion entailed by a structure that made the idea of an identifiable employer illusory.

as 'secondary boycotts'.[40] In a secondary boycott, a trade union seeking to apply negotiating pressure on one firm takes industrial action against another firm. A classic example is where a trade union threatens strike action against one firm if it continues to supply goods or services to another firm against which the union is already taking industrial action.

Consider again the factual situation in *McDermid*, where different categories of employees engaged in a common enterprise were, in fact, employed by different employers. Where this type of corporate structure prevails, if industrial action is taken by one group of employees, that industrial action inevitably (and unavoidably) targets at least one additional 'firm', and perhaps more than one. If such action were to be held to violate the legal proscriptions against secondary boycotts (and on the face of it, all industrial action in these circumstances necessarily constitutes a secondary boycott), the effect (intentional or otherwise) would be to prohibit all forms of industrial action against businesses that adopted this structure. This would be a reasonably draconian outcome from the point of view of the union, but one that might provide a substantial incentive for some businesses to structure their operations in this way. As Donaldson MR observed:

> It may strike some people as odd that the liability of the union should depend upon what they may reasonably regard as almost being a matter of chance, namely, whether the directors of the TBF group decided to arrange that one subsidiary should employ journalists and another undertake printing as contrasted with deciding that one subsidiary should undertake both printing and journalism. Whether or not the union would be right to so regard the position, that appears without doubt to be the law.[41]

Although, as we suggested above, there are those who might find this outcome highly desirable, most ordinary people would probably be surprised by it, and even more surprised by the logic of a legal regime that prefers an invisible set of boundaries drawn for economic (and legal) convenience to the reality of particular enterprises and their commercial activities. Such logic seems particularly absurd when those invisible boundaries enable enterprises to modulate their interaction with the law.

REVIEW QUESTIONS

1 If the evidence strongly suggests that a particular corporate structure has been adopted because, *inter alia*, it confined risk (as was the case in *Briggs v. James Hardie*), should this be a factor in the court's decision-making?

---

40 *Trade Practices Act 1974* (TPA), s. 45D–E prohibits 'secondary boycotts'. The provision has had a chequered history. It was part of the trade practices legislation at its inception, but sat uneasily with Labor Party ideas and was ultimately repealed under the Labor government. It has since been re-enacted as part of the Liberal government's industrial relations reform legislation.

41 *Dimbleby & Sons Ltd v. National Union of Journalists* [1984] ICR 386 at 402, appeal dismissed.

2 Think about the idea of a non-delegable duty. In *McDermid v. Nash Dredging*, the plaintiff was able to recover because it was held that the employer company delegated performance of its non-delegable duty to the captain (and thus to the company that employed him under the principles of vicarious liability). Why was this doctrine not available in *Briggs v. James Hardie*?

Consolidated accounts and other marvels: The birth of enterprise liability

The statutory regime

Consolidated accounts

While the corporate group has thrown up a number of regulatory challenges to 'entity' theory (as the doctrine of strict enforcement of separate legal liability is known), efforts to address these challenges are still in their infancy in Australia. One area where some progress is being made is that of group accounts. Some of these regulatory mechanisms have occasioned fear, and there is still concern that they will defeat limited liability altogether, but as we learned in chapter 7, the *Corporations Law 1990* contains a number of special rules that govern the presentation of a company's accounts and those of any 'entities' that it happens to 'control'.[42] According to Hadden,

> [t]he legislation now requires consolidated accounts of all controlled entities to be produced by a 'parent entity' in any case where it is itself or where it controls a reporting entity. The clarification of what is meant both by an entity and by control is then in effect delegated to the Australian Accounting Standards Board ('AASB') in the formulation of the relevant accounting standard. The definition eventually adopted under AASB 1024 ... is based on broad economic rather than traditional legal criteria for both 'entity' and 'control':
>
> entity: any legal, administrative, or fiduciary arrangement, organisational structure or other party (including a person) having the capacity to deploy scarce resources in order to achieve objectives
>
> control: the capacity of an entity to dominate decision-making, directly or indirectly, in relation to the financial and operating policies of another entity so as to enable that other entity to operate with it in achieving the objectives of the controlling entity.[43]

---

42 Corporations Law, s. 294A provides that 'entity', 'parent entity', 'economic entity', and 'reporting entity' shall have the meaning ascribed to them by the accounting standards. Section 294A(4) states that each of the following is an 'entity': a company, a recognised company, any other corporation, a partnership, an unincorporated body, and a person in a capacity of a trust that has only one trustee.

43 Hadden at 72. It seems to us that this set of working criteria might well be useful in other circumstances—for example, in determining whether a parent company ought to be liable in tort in circumstances such as those in *Briggs v. James Hardie*.

Section 290 requires that the directors of a company 'do whatever is necessary to ensure that the financial year of each entity that the company controls coincides with the financial year of the company'. Two further provisions spell out the reporting requirements in some detail:

295A(1)   The company's directors must cause to be made out, before the deadline after that accounting period, a consolidated profit and loss account that gives a true and fair view of the profit or loss, for that accounting period, of the economic entity constituted by the company and the entities it controlled from time to time during that accounting period (even if the company did not control the same entities throughout the accounting period).

295A(2)   To avoid doubt, if the company did not control a particular entity throughout that accounting period, the consolidated profit and loss account must relate to the entity's profit or loss for each part of that accounting period throughout which the company controlled the entity, but not to the entity's profit or loss for any other part.

295B   The company's directors must cause to be made out, before the deadline after that accounting period, a consolidated balance-sheet, as at the period's end, that gives a true and fair view of the state of affairs, as at the period's end, of the economic entity constituted by the company and the entities that it controls at the period's end.[44]

As Hadden notes, these provisions have their genesis in economics (and organisational theory) rather than legal traditions. As a consequence, they are predisposed towards acknowledgment of the reality of the enterprise and its operation. They are concerned with establishing objective economic reporting requirements for corporate groups.

Despite this (tentative) statutory recognition that the economic health of the group and of the individual companies within it may well be inseparable, the approach of the courts would appear to remain hamstrung, if we are to go by the High Court decisions in *Industrial Equity Ltd v. Blackburn*[45] and *Walker v. Wimborne*.[46] The position adopted by Mason CJ (with whom the court agreed) in *Industrial Equity Ltd v. Blackburn* could hardly be clearer or more straightforward: 'it can scarcely be contended that the provisions of the Act operate to deny the separate legal personality of each company in the group. Thus, in the absence of contract creating some additional right, the creditors of company A, a subsidiary company

---

44 While these provision do not unseat the common-law presumption that companies are financially independent, they do recognise the reality of the situation—in particular, the fact that it is impossible to determine the economic well-being of individual companies in a corporate group without knowing the well-being of the group as a whole. They do not provide creditors with redress against solvent group members except in extraordinary circumstances.

45 (1977) 137 CLR 567.

46 (1976) 137 CLR 1.

within a group, can only look to that company for payment of their debts'.[47] We are left with a legal reality at variance with commercial reality, and (at least in the case of wholly owned subsidiaries) at variance with common sense. The nexus between corporate identity and legal personality remains strong. While, as we saw in *Briggs*, the courts are becoming uncomfortable with some of the consequences of this nexus, they remain reluctant to take any steps that might expose individual shareholders to liability for corporate wrongs and corporate debts.[48]

The approach suggested by Rogers ACJ in *Qintex Australia Finance Ltd v. Schroders Australia Ltd* [49] makes some progress in this direction and is vastly more appealing. In attempting to untangle the financial arrangements surrounding a forward exchange contract, His Honour said:

> Again, according to Mr Hunt, the manager of futures of the defendant when, in mid December 1988, he said to Mr Pratt, that 'We are looking at the establishment of credit limits for other treasury products for you, we will need to know which company we are looking at', the response was 'It does not matter to us. Choose whichever company you feel the most comfortable with' … This attitude may have been more extreme than was the norm, but it is none the less a reflection of general commercial attitudes …
>
> It may be desirable for Parliament to consider whether this distinction between the law and commercial practice should be maintained. This is especially the case today when the many collapses of conglomerates occasion many disputes. Regularly, liquidators of subsidiaries, or of the holding company, come to court to argue as to which of their charges bears the liability … As well, creditors of failed companies encounter difficulty when they have to select from among the moving targets the company with which they consider they concluded a contract. The result has been unproductive expenditure on legal costs, a reduction in the amount available to creditors, a windfall for some, and an unfair loss to others. This may be illustrated by the argument in the present case. The plaintiff had received the proceeds of the sale of ¥1.2bn into its account. Its submission was that the liability for the forward contract for ¥1.2bn fell on QTL, which it said was the contracting party and that accordingly, the defendant was not entitled to make the set off against moneys standing to the plaintiff's credit in the books of the defendant. Attractively as the plaintiff's case was presented, its intrinsic merits were not readily apparent. If I may venture the observation, *there is a great deal to be said for the suggestion advanced by those in charge of the demised Hooker group of companies that assets and liabilities of the parent and the subsidiaries should be aggregated. It may be argued that there is justification for preserving the same attitude in relation to the demised companies as was displayed during their active commercial life.* [50]

---

47 (1977) 137 CLR 567 at 577.

48 It would be possible, however, to construct a limited exception to this principle where, to use the language of the Corporations Law, the relevant level of control exists. We would suggest that an exception could be crafted in these terms: where an entity controls another entity and is its sole shareholder, the parent entity (as entity) shall be responsible for the debts of its subsidiary.

49 (1990) 3 ACSR 267.

50 (1990) 3 ACSR 267 at 269 (emphasis added).

As things stand, we are left with a legal reality that positively rewards such structures (by its reluctance to ignore the 'company of convenience'[51]) and drives liability home as commercial reality suggests is appropriate.[52]

The 'Class Orders' regime

Given the difficulties posed by such structures and the lack of economic justification for them, it is hardly surprising that various attempts have been made to circumvent these fictions and install practices that more closely track commercial reality. The Australian Securities Commission (ASC) under the Corporations Law, s. 313 has the power to issue Class Orders. According to Jennifer Hill, '[t]he effect of these Class Orders is to grant relief from separate accounting and audit requirements of the Corporations Law to wholly-owned subsidiaries, on certain preconditions. The preconditions include that the subsidiary must have entered into a prescribed deed of cross guarantee with its holding company and that consolidated accounts are prepared'.[53] The present regime replaces an earlier attempt to grant wholly owned subsidiaries relief from separate accounting and audit requirements,[54] which did not provide adequate protection for creditors and, in particular, failed to incorporate any mechanism for enforcement. According to Hill,

> [t]he structure of the new deed is in the form of a guarantee whereby each group company guarantees payment in full to each creditor of any debt in accordance with the deed. Of the two kinds of guarantee referred to by Mason CJ in *Sunbird Plaza Pty Ltd v. Mahoney*, this would appear to be in the form of a conditional agreement to pay a liquidated sum, as opposed to any undertaking by the guarantor that the debtor will perform its obligations to the creditor, sounding in damages only. However the matter is not entirely free from doubt. Under the deed of cross guarantee, no creditor is under an obligation to give notice to any group company of breach of an agreement giving rise to the debt, a matter which historically has been significant in characterising the guarantor's obligations as falling within the second class ...
>
> The Class Orders clearly regard the cross guarantee as dissolving the boundaries between group companies for the purposes of liability to creditors. For example, one of the preconditions to the operation of Class Orders is that the directors ensure that a statement is made as to whether there are reasonable grounds to believe that the companies

---

51 English courts have occasionally recognised the 'company of convenience' for what it is. In *Re FG (Films) Ltd* [1953] 1 WLR 483, the English court acknowledged that a British subsidiary of a United States film company was simply a corporate shell established to facilitate the registering of films made by the United States company as 'British films', thus obtaining financial advantage.

52 For further discussion of this and related issues, see P. I. Blumberg, 'Limited Liability and Corporate Groups' [1986] 11 J Corp Law 623; R. Corroll, 'Corporate Parents and Tort Liability', in M. Gillooly (ed.), *The Law Relating to Corporate Groups*, Federation Press, Sydney, 1993. There is, of course, a very important ethical question underlying these issues. We question whether it ought to be possible for an enterprise to structure its affairs so as to avoid liability for wrongs while it and its shareholders profit from those wrongs.

53 J. Hill, 'Cross Guarantees in Corporate Groups' (1992) 10 CSLJ 311.

54 ASC Class Order 95/1530 (1991) 2 *Australian Securities Commission Releases* 119 654.

which are parties to the deed can 'as an economic entity' satisfy any current or potential liability thereunder.

Other provisions of the Corporations Law, which are structured upon entity assumptions, may create havoc with the operation of such a cross guarantee. Take for example s. 592. Personal liability may be imposed upon a director pursuant to this section where a debt was incurred by the company at a time when

> there were reasonable grounds to expect that, if the company incur[red] the debt, it would not be able to pay all its debts as and when they became due.

In … *Bank of China v. Hawkins*, Rogers CJ … held that the execution of a guarantee by Equiticorp International Plc, in respect of liabilities to the bank of two other companies in the group, constituted the incurring of a debt for the purposes of s. 592.[55]

Whether or not the ASC's most recent Class Orders regime will be able to alleviate the inconvenience caused by the separate entity doctrine without shattering it remains to be seen. The mischief caused by the doctrine is amply evidenced by the torturous mechanisms necessary to circumvent it. Doctrines such as the separate entity doctrine are not problems thrown up by a recalcitrant reality, in which corporate legal personality surfaces as an immovable object upon which the law works, or fails to work, its way. Corporate personality is a fiction, a myth of our own making, a Frankensteinian monster in whose creation we have colluded. That this fiction should itself become an (autonomous) actor in dramas that the law tardily endeavours to control should not surprise us any more than does its ability to escape those efforts.

REVIEW QUESTIONS

1 If, as Eisenberg suggests, there is no 'economic' justification for the development of corporate groups comprised of a parent company and its wholly owned subsidiaries, we need to think carefully about the reasons such entities have grown up and flourished. What do you think Eisenberg means by 'no economic justifications'?

2 If the only justifications are 'legal justifications', and if many of these 'legal justifications' represent avoidance strategies, can you think of any good reasons why Australian law should not aggregate the assets and liabilities of such companies in certain circumstances?[56]

3 It may also be appropriate for the law to treat all such entities as 'enterprises' in areas such as anti-discrimination law and employment law, as well as for the purposes of ascertaining compliance with other regulatory regimes and assuring compliance. Can you foresee any problems with such an approach?

---

55 Hill at 315–16.

56 Appropriate circumstances might include those in which it is necessary to permit recovery for various classes of creditors, whether commercial creditors or those who have been granted an award of damages by the courts.

Recognising enterprise principles

The open reliance upon economic principles and forms of evaluation in the new consolidated accounts regime—together with increasingly outspoken judicial voices calling for reform, at least in some areas—should encourage us to consider how mechanisms for assigning intra-group liability and for regulating the corporate group (rather than the individual entity) can be developed, given our present legal traditions. Phillip Blumberg, an American scholar who has written extensively on corporate groups, suggests that:

> [t]he jurisprudential significance of the law of corporate groups may be best understood as another manifestation of the increasing emergence of relational law. In this case, it rests on the economic interrelationship between the parent and subsidiary corporations. The affiliated corporations are collectively conducting a common business. In the areas recognized by the law of corporate groups, the attribution of rights and the imposition of liabilities may be as the law, unconfined by traditional notions of entity, following the business and allocating legal consequences to the business.

> [T]he law of corporate groups rests on two unifying factors that lead, in appropriate cases, to the application of enterprise principles to impose intragroup liability or other legal consequences in place of traditional entity law. These primary unifying factors are 'control,' typically arising from ownership or control of voting stock, and economic interrelationship. Economic interrelationship comprises not only vertical and horizontal integration of processes of production, distribution, or supply of services, but also such additional elements as administrative and financial interdependence of the affiliated corporations, integration of employee relationships, and use of a common group persona. In sum, these factors are the hallmark of a unitary enterprise that has been fragmented among the affiliated corporations as a matter of legal form, with the companies continuing in the collective conduct of the business under a central, coordinated control. In imposing liability or otherwise attributing legal consequences in the light of the symbiotic interrelationships, the law is being molded to match the economic reality.

> Where a group does not meet these sharply defined conceptual boundaries, enterprise law does not apply. Thus, enterprise principles recognize and respond to the reality that the general class of corporate groups embraces a wide variety of operational and structural patterns … Enterprise law takes these differences into account. Thus while enterprise law is often directed at hierarchical groups resting on ownership of a majority or other percentage of voting shares, the concepts of de facto 'control,' controlling influence over the management or policies, 'participating interest' and 'dominant influence' are flexible enough to respond not only to hierarchical groups, but also to newer forms of groups such as networks or other interrelationships.[57]

Blumberg argues that 'enterprise law' is the 'conceptual solution being developed by courts and legislatures to respond to the inadequacies of anachronistic entity law inherited from the small-business world of the nineteenth century'.[58] One wonders

---

57 P. I. Blumberg, *The Multinational Challenge to Corporation Law: The Search for a New Corporate Personality*, Oxford University Press, New York, 1993, pp. 245–6.

58 Blumberg, p. 253.

whether this challenge to the ghost of Aron Salomon and his company, and to the model of entity law bequeathed to us by the House of Lords decision in *Salomon's* case, is ultimately too little and comes too late. The answer to this question will turn upon whether Anglo-Australian jurisprudence has the intellectual resources to eschew the contract model that lies at the root of conventional approaches to corporate regulation and move towards a more fluid and open model.

The need for enhanced flexibility and for a conceptually fresh approach to corporate groups is clear. While, understandably (given recent Australian corporate history), much of the current debate has focused on various aspects of the financial affairs of corporate groups,[59] we believe that there are at least three distinct constellations of issues that warrant consideration.

The first of these constellations circles the idea of internal corporate governance. Its central concern is with the conduct of directors in corporate groups and the position of minority shareholders in such groups. In most cases, the logic and dynamic of corporate structures encourage, even compel, directors to 'think globally'. In wholly owned subsidiaries, this tendency is unproblematical from the perspective of the internal governance of the corporate entity. Where there are minority shareholders, of course, this tendency becomes intensely problematical. Here, under the present legal regime, it is difficult, sometimes even impossible, for minority shareholders to secure any form of meaningful redress for decision-making that tends to sacrifice the interests of the individual entity to those of the group.[60] The literature suggests a variety of possible solutions. Robert Austin suggests that it might be appropriate for Australian law to treat a controlling shareholder as fiduciary for interests otherwise likely to be disregarded in group decision-making.[61] Then there is the reasonably straightforward suggestion that, in such circumstances, minority shareholders should be entitled to be bought out at a fair price.[62]

A very different perspective is that put forward by Michael Gillooly, who argues that our legal treatment of corporate groups requires a fundamental change of emphasis. He suggests that we have been asking the wrong question. According to

---

59 For a representative sample of recent literature on this topic, see 'Corporate Regulation and the New Corporations Law' (1992) 15 UNSWLJ (a special issue of the *University of New South Wales Law Journal*) and M. Gillooly (ed.), *The Law Relating to Corporate Groups*, Federation Press, Sydney, 1993.

60 See S. Bottomley, 'Shareholder Derivative Actions and Public Interest Suits: Two Versions of the Same Story?' (1992) 15 UNSWLJ 127; I. Ramsay, 'Corporate Governance, Shareholder Litigation and the Prospects for a Statutory Derivative Action' (1992) 15 UNSWLJ 149; P. Redmond, 'Problems for Insiders', in M. Gillooly (ed.), *The Law Relating to Corporate Groups*, Federation Press, Sydney, 1993, p. 208; R. P. Austin, 'Problems for Directors within Corporate Groups' in Gillooly (ed.), p. 123; M. Gillooly, 'Outside Shareholders in Corporate Groups', in Gillooly (ed.), p. 159. The problems in this area are of two distinct kinds. First, litigation (whether under an exception to the rule in *Foss v. Harbottle* or under Corporations Law, s. 260) is expensive and often has limited prospects of success for technical reasons. Second, individual shareholders have little reason to bring such actions. They are unlikely to gain directly (because, by definition it is the company that has been wronged), so any ultimate gain will only come indirectly by way of an increase in share prices. There is, therefore, little if any financial incentive to commence litigation, and substantial financial disadvantage is involved.

61 Austin, p. 158. This approach draws upon United States law. See Eisenberg, pp. 20–1.

62 Hadden at 77.

Gillooly, it simply is not possible to regulate the activities of corporate groups adequately,[63] and perhaps more significantly, we have no good reason to do so. He, therefore, suggests a 'modest reform':

> As far as intra-group decision-making goes, here is a fundamental conflict between how things are done and how the law says they ought to be done. In reality, the normal criterion for management decisions within a group is the group interest. If the group interest happens to coincide with the interests of the individual company in question there is no legal problem. However, if those interests do not coincide, the decision-makers in that company may find themselves subject to liability. I submit that there is nothing inherently wrong with taking decisions in the group interest and that decision-making on this basis should be lawful provided the interests of outside shareholders and persons outside the group structure are adequately protected.
>
> I therefore suggest the following legislative change. Directors and shareholders in general meeting should be able to exercise their powers in the group interest rather than in the interests of their individual company, where a resolution to become part of a group has been passed by a 90 per cent majority at general meetings of all the companies concerned. Copies of the resolutions would need to be lodged at the ASC. Any dissenting shareholders would be entitled to have their shares purchased by their company. In order to protect creditors, such resolutions could only have effect whilst the company was solvent.[64]

This is modest indeed, perhaps too modest. It relieves the directors of the 'inconvenience' of being legally required to comply with an unrealistic paradigm for decision-making, like the proposals mentioned in the paragraph above, but it does nothing to eliminate the ability of the corporate group to deflect liability for wrongs and to evade the disciplinary regimes of the State more or less at will. This is, of course, hardly surprising. Neither is it surprising that the modest proposals we have considered thus far do not even begin to address many of the abuses that corporate groups facilitate. Of the recognised abuses—manipulation of control holdings so as to ensure continued control by an incumbent board, misleading accounts (and, in particular, reliance upon the various forms of off-balance sheet accounting discussed earlier), oppression of minority interests, avoidance of liability, avoidance of taxation, and avoidance of antitrust, monopoly, or other regulations[65]—they confront two at most. One of the blessings of a relatively myopic gaze, of course, is that other issues and difficulties recede from view. If such proposals have the capacity to simplify the internal corporate structures and minimise the incidence of abuse (and this is by no means certain), the extent to which they also enhance our capacity to address wider issues is less clear. We will discuss these wider issues next.

---

63 This is undeniably true so far as multinational corporations are concerned.

64 Gillooly, p. 159.

65 The listing is Tom Hadden's. See Hadden, 'Regulating Corporate Groups: An International Perspective', in J. McCahery, S. Picciotto, & C. Scott (eds), *Corporate Control and Accountability*, Clarendon Press, Oxford, 1993, pp. 359–60.

The second constellation of issues that we must address is, of course, implicit in both of the proposals above. If, as these proposals suggest, directors are to be allowed to act in the interests of the group and not simply the individual company, some form of expanded redress for creditors becomes essential. We are particularly concerned with appropriate protection for the interests of 'outside creditors'—that is, those who are not members of the company or of any of its affiliated companies. The interests of outside creditors can be protected (at least to an extent that allows the maintenance of some form of limited liability) in a number of different ways. The simplest measure, of course, would be to give 'outside' creditors[66] recourse to the resources of the entire group to the extent needed, although we believe that it would be reasonable to allow this benefit to be waived contractually should an individual creditor so elect. To the extent that enterprise liability is imposed, it ought to be pro-rata rather than joint and several.[67]

It is imperative that corporate law shift away from an entity approach to the regulation of corporate groups and towards adopting an 'enterprise' approach. As discussed earlier in this chapter, traces of a shift to an enterprise approach are already evident in the consolidated accounts provisions and in some judges' willingness to concede that it is not inappropriate for the directors of group members to take the interests of the group into account in making corporate decisions. Further, albeit marginal, evidence of some realignment may be found in the Australian approach to the obligations of nominee directors.[68] We would argue that to the extent it is acceptable for nominee directors to represent 'outside' interests on corporate boards, it is also acceptable for 'group interests' to be represented. Certainly an acceptance of this general principle must have been implicit in the decision in *Re Broadcasting Station 2GB Pty*.[69] In the context of a transfer of control in respect of 2GB from Broadcasting Associates to the John Fairfax group of companies (50 per cent of shares being held by the Fairfax group), Jacobs J said:

> It may well be, and I am inclined to regard it as the fact, that the newly appointed directors were prepared to accept the position that they would follow the wishes of the Fairfax interests without a close personal analysis of the issues. I think that at the board meetings … that is what they did, but I see no evidence of a lack in them of a bona fide belief that the interests of the Fairfax company were identical with the interests of the company as a whole. I realize that, upon this approach, I deny any right in the company as a whole to

---

66 We propose to deal with the protection of tort creditors separately, not least because, unlike ordinary commercial creditors, tort creditors are involuntary creditors.

67 This avoids the inequities of the partnership model, while still providing a broader base for redress. While such liability is relatively unusual in the common-law world, California apparently had such a regime between 1849 and 1931. This is particularly important in the case of tort creditors. Unlike other creditors, tort victims are not able to make an informed judgment in advance. Still more attractive is Bruce Wellings's proposal for a tort of undercapitalisation of a corporation as a form of negligently caused economic loss. See B. Wellings, *Corporate Law in Canada: The Governing Principles*, 2nd edn, Butterworths, Toronto, 1991, pp. 144–9.

68 See *Levin v. Clark* [1962] NSWR 686; *Re Broadcasting Station 2GB* [1964–65] NSWR 1648.

69 [1964–65] NSWR 1648.

have each director approach each company problem with a completely open mind, but I think that to require this of each director of a company is to ignore the realities of company organisation. Also, such a requirement would, in effect, make the position of a nominee or representative director an impossibility.[70]

Re Broadcasting Station 2GB dealt not with the 'normal' dynamic of the relationships within a corporate group, but with the negotiations that were attendant upon a partial takeover and a reconstitution of the board to ensure that decision-making was in accord with Fairfax interests. However, if this case is correctly decided, it explicitly authorises enterprise decision-making rather than countenancing only entity decision-making as being in accord with the fiduciary role of the director. While this decision, like *Levin v. Clark*,[71] runs very much against the grain of conventional understandings of the fiduciary principle,[72] we also believe that it represents the only sensible understanding of the role of the board in a corporate group. While, undeniably, this approach places minority shareholders in an unenviable position, that position arises simply as a consequence of their minority status, rather than as a consequence of any mala fides on the part of the directors. As is the case with a 'locked-in' shareholder in a closely held company,[73] the problem is a consequence of corporate structure, rather than of impropriety.

In a somewhat different context, the High Court's response to the factual situation in *Wayde v. New South Wales Rugby League Ltd*[74] makes much the same point. While the decision of the Rugby League signed a death warrant for one constituent club, that decision was taken in good faith and in the interests of the League as a whole. As the court pointed out, once the board (in good faith) decided that it was necessary to reduce the number of clubs in the league, any decision it could make would have extremely prejudicial consequences for at least one of the constituent clubs. Ostensibly, decisions such as these are made within the entity paradigm and reflect a traditional understanding of corporate law as a blend of contract and trust. However they also reflect a wider awareness of the settings within which corporate law is called upon to resolve disputes, and they make it clear that particular forms of conduct fall to be evaluated within particular contexts, not in the abstract.

The final constellation of issues that the law must address are those that arise in the context of the general law. A representative issue in this category concerns the

---

70　[1964–65] NSWR 1648 at 1663.

71　[1962] NSWR 686.

72　For a more orthodox approach to the role of the nominee director, see *Bennetts v. Board of Fire Commissioners of New South Wales* (1967) 87 WN (NSW) 307; *Scottish Co-operative Wholesale Society Ltd v. Meyer* [1959] AC 324; *Lindgren v. L & P Estates Ltd* [1968] Ch 572. A distinction needs to be drawn between two different uses made of the nominee structure. In *Re Broadcasting 2GB*, the shift in composition of the board marked a change in control, as Fairfax moved from minority shareholder status to a position of control. This position of control was, not surprisingly, reflected on the board. In such circumstances, we believe that it is appropriate for the minority interest to be bought out at a fair price (providing other regulations so permit). In *Bennetts* the position was very different. The role of the nominee director was to represent the interests of a particular outside body in the deliberations of the board.

73　See *Re G. Jeffrey (Men's Store) Pty Ltd* (1984) 9 ACLR 193.

74　(1985) 61 ALR 225.

legitimacy of avoiding tort liability through corporate structure, as occurred in *Briggs v. James Hardie*. Similar issues arise where corporate form is used to circumvent laws designed to confer particular sorts of benefits upon employees as a class[75] or to frustrate the pursuit of wider social objectives, as in the case of anti-discrimination law. Issues in this group are classical issues in a number of respects. First, they exemplify the use of the corporate group to manipulate or evade legal rules. Second, they cannot be successfully addressed by relatively simple mechanisms, such as altering the parameters of directors' duties. Successfully dealing with issues of this sort would seem to require wholehearted adoption of an enterprise approach rather than an entity approach. It is necessary, therefore, to ask whether there are any substantial disadvantages to an enterprise-based approach to corporate groups, and if there are, whether they can be overcome or whether they are fundamental. That will be part of our task as we examine multinational corporations.

The multinational corporation and the nation state

> Politically, we live in a world of nation-states. Economically we live in a world of multinational corporations ('MNCs'). The nation-state is sovereign within its borders; beyond them it has little authority except over its own subjects. The MNC seeks to maximize profit and efficiency on a world-wide basis; its ultimate goal is not the well-being of a particular country but the success of its global operations.[76]

As readers who have consulted the footnotes will be aware, this is hardly news. That progress in controlling these beasts has been remarkably slow is also well known. The problems and issues identified by Steven Chance in 1978—which included expropriation and restrictive business practices, tax-avoidance schemes, labour-management issues, currency movement, and improper or illegal payments[77]—are still with us. Further problems have emerged as, increasingly, we try to come to terms with the global market-place. Among the issues that have attracted a good deal of attention in recent years are those associated with environmental concerns and with the sale of potentially hazardous products.[78]

We will begin with the latter, and with a well-known story: that of the Dalkon Shield. While a great deal has been written about the marketing of the Dalkon Shield, and about the unfinished struggle for compensation on the part of many of those injured by it,[79] the multinational character of the defendants has been an incidental feature rather than the focus. Here we want to focus specifically on the structural aspects of the story rather than upon the issues, such as causation and

---

75 Collins cites as an example the practice of requiring only firms above a threshold size to provide maternity leave.

76 S. K. Chance, 'Codes of Conduct for Multinational Corporations' (1978) 33 *The Business Lawyer* 1799 at 1799.

77 Chance at 1801.

78 See, for example, Baughen at 54. Baughen discusses the issues that would arise if a foreign national attempted to bring suit against an English parent company for the tort of a foreign subsidiary.

79 See the discussion in chapter 15, pp. 434–6.

limitation problems, which more properly belong to the law of torts. Peter Cashman tells the structural story in these terms:

> The Australian assets of A H Robins Pty Ltd are limited. The assets of the parent American company are under siege from hundreds of thousands of American and foreign plaintiffs and, at this stage, protected pursuant to bankruptcy proceedings.
>
> Moreover, the insurance cover of the American corporation has been largely exhausted and there are a large number of unanswered questions concerning the insurance cover for its Australian subsidiary. The product was manufactured by the United States parent and the local activities of the Australian subsidiary were carefully controlled from the United States. Moreover, most of the shares in the Australian company are held by members of the parent company.
>
> Given that the claims of Australian (and other) women were being frustrated by the United States bankruptcy proceedings (while the parent company and its foreign subsidiaries continue to trade profitably) some important policy questions arise as to:
>
> (a)   Whether multinational corporations should be allowed to trade in Australia only if they can demonstrate sufficient assets to meet claims against them by injured consumers;
>
> (b)   Whether some form of financial bond should be required;
>
> (c)   Whether separate product liability insurance should be compulsory;
>
> (d)   Whether product liability insurers should be able to avoid paying claims under the policy on the basis of non-disclosure by the company.[80]

These are interesting and important questions indeed, but they must be tested against the reality of the multinational corporation and its capacity to escape regulation. In many cases, these same questions are relevant in the case of corporate groups that are wholly Australian. Regardless of whether the company is A. H. Robins Pty Ltd (an Australian subsidiary of an United States multinational) or AMPL (an Australian subsidiary of an Australian company), and regardless of whether the potential claimants are former employees and the victims of corporate neglect or consumers and the victims of corporate opportunism, the central question is identical: to what extent should the law permit corporate arrangements that allow entities to engage in potentially hazardous conduct while minimising the risk that compensation claims regarding that conduct will cause financial difficulties for the group (or, more precisely, for its parent corporation)? If that question is difficult in the case of a 'wholly Australian' corporate group (and it has proved almost intractable), it is ten times more difficult in the case of a multinational. Profit and demand are opposite sides of the same coin.

A. H. Robins Pty Ltd was profitable because it had a product that Australian consumers either wanted or could be encouraged to want. While the product could have been imported directly from the parent or a sibling company in the

---

80 P. Cashman, 'The Dalkon Shield', in P. Grabosky & A. Sutton, *Stains on a White Collar,* Federation Press, Sydney, 1989, pp. 105–6.

USA, the legal milieu in which Robins operated made incorporation in Australia advantageous. The A. H. Robins saga throws one aspect of the issues that we have been discussing into stark relief. If we adopt an 'entity' approach, we focus on an Australian proprietary company. While, admittedly, this company is a subsidiary of a United States parent company, and while one assumes that the United States parent owned that proportion of the shares in its Australian subsidiary that the foreign ownership rules of Australia allowed, those factors are relatively unimportant from an entity perspective.

If, on the other hand, we focus on the enterprise, the picture is very different and, in some ways, very much more complex. Even in the simplest case, where the enterprise is a fully integrated group, the practical absence of any semblance of a world legal order[81] and the ramifications of the extraterritorial application of enterprise law are concerning. Initial skirmishes seem likely to revolve around jurisdictional questions. However, it seems reasonable to suppose that the nationality of the parent is the nationality of the enterprise. Having said this, an initial problem emerges. It is likely that any current attempt by a host country to impose liability on a foreign parent for the obligations of a local subsidiary would be received with hostility by the home country of the parent. Even in a best case scenario, a likely counter to such a move would be a threat of withdrawal and retreat to a more hospitable jurisdiction. To date, the only reasonably successful model for multinational regulation is that represented by the various international taxation treaties.[82]

If we reflect on some of the issues concerning corporate social responsibility and corporate morality raised in chapters 5 and 6, it is disheartening to note that legal developments that appear essential to resolve basic problems of corporate governance and accountability often create further problems for apparently promising models such as stakeholder theory or dual investor theory. First, the shift of emphasis from the individual entity to the enterprise as a whole may weaken the connection between the company and the community within which it operates. The difficulty is that the enterprise—that fabulously wealthy investment club of which we spoke in chapter 5—often lacks that connection in any sort of meaningful way. While the individual entities that are its international subsidiaries depend on the communities in which they operate for workers, infrastructure, raw material, and markets, the enterprise as a whole is global, rather than local, in character. Upon what does it depend, and what patterns of obligations may be constructed upon the foundation of these dependencies?

If we look at the multinational corporation from the perspective of municipal law and the municipal legal order, we find 'visible', legally knowable entities—

---

81 To the extent that there is a world legal order, full legal personality within that order is available only to sovereign states.

82 Even here, where transnational regulation is well established, an unwanted by-product of such regulation has been the development of a number of 'tax havens'—small, frequently less-developed, jurisdictions that rely on their ability to provide relief from the imposition of taxation to attract enterprise to their shores. See also Baughen at 54 for a discussion of transnational efforts to regulate the export of hazard by multinationals.

subsidiaries incorporated within a jurisdiction such as Australia to conduct business under the laws of that jurisdiction. To the extent that the entity is, for example, a wholly owned subsidiary controlled by a foreign parent—one based perhaps in London or New York—the entity itself is visible. The parent is, from the perspective of the municipal law, a series of entries in the corporate accounts, a shadowy 'other' beyond the reach of the municipal legal order. From the perspective of international law we also find 'visible' entities. Fleur Johns suggests that the transnational company's (TNC's)

> role in international law is generally defined by reference to its alleged ties to a particular state. The juristic personality of the TNC was confirmed in the *Barcelona Traction, Light and Power Co. Case* as analogous to that of individuals, that is, as a national of a state. This personality gives rise to a right of diplomatic protection which may be exercised by the relevant state on a TNC's behalf. It may also give rise to state responsibility for conduct of a TNC in the state's own territory that impacts adversely upon another state so as to constitute a breach of international law.[83]

Again, to the extent international law 'knows' the multinational, it knows it as its component entities, and those entities exist only within the context of their 'corporate citizenship', their nationality. In this way, we return to the paradox we confronted in chapters 6 and 7: that of the 'citizen' that, being soulless, is incapable of loyalty. The matter is further complicated by the fact that,

> [f]or a corporation operating across many states' territories and through many legal systems, selection of a state of incorporation may be a matter of mere convenience—a decision made at a particular time for tax or other reasons. The fact that this decision may have lasting significance at international law seems therefore ludicrous. Equally, states of incorporation and national states of shareholders may have neither the capacity nor the inclination to exercise the powers which international law confers upon them.[84]

And therein, of course, is the rub. To the extent that international control over TNCs depends, ultimately, on the willingness and the ability of nation states to exercise control over those parent entities that international law treats as its 'nationals', it is unlikely that any meaningful control exists. Western liberal governments are, for the most part, both unwilling and unable to exercise any meaningful control over the activities of their corporate 'citizens'. Even should they attempt to do so, it is difficult to see how, given traditional legal conventions, it would be possible to hold a parent company responsible for the activities of its offshore subsidiaries for as long as corporate law remains wedded to the notion of entity rather than enterprise liability.[85]

---

83 F. Johns, 'The Invisibility of the Transnational Corporation: An Analysis of International Law and Legal Theory' (1994) 19 MULR 893 at 894–5.

84 Johns at 896.

85 Even more difficult problems arise where the activity is one that violates legal norms in the jurisdiction of the parent company but that is much more laxly regulated (if, indeed, it is regulated at all) in the jurisdiction where the subsidiary carries on business. The use of child labour and the maintenance of discriminatory practices are obvious examples.

Increasingly, it is recognised that '[m]any multinational corporations have become at least as powerful as some of the states in which they function ... [I]n 1989, the combined profits of the 17 largest TNCs exceeded the combined Gross National Product of the world's 41 poorest nations. In 1993, TNCs allegedly controlled 70% of world trade'.[86] What is truly problematical is the way in which the legal regime has positioned the multinational corporation. In effect, only the entity is visible to the law at the municipal level, and so, at the international level, the entity becomes the citizen and the enterprise slips from view. As Johns reminds us, the TNC 'does not have a concrete presence in international law. Rather it is an apparition, reappearing in many different forms and contexts—its actuality sifted through the grid of state sovereignty into an assortment of secondary rights and contingent liabilities'.[87]

Neither does the multinational corporation have a concrete presence in municipal law. Rather, its constituent parts become—in international law as in municipal law—the 'nationals' of modern nation states, private citizens engaged in 'private' activities. The multinational corporation itself does not exist, except in economic terms. Because it does not exist, it is beyond the disciplinary gaze of the law, which grants 'those men performing ostensibly "public" roles of great influence worldwide an international anonymity that allows for their continued exercise of power without international accountability'.[88] They, and their activities, are shrouded by the corporate veil, and by the interlocking legal fictions that accord reality to the individual entity, but deny reality to the enterprise and to those who direct its activities.

REVIEW QUESTION

The corporation has 'no soul to damn and no body to kick', and perhaps no true 'nationality'. If this is the modern multinational corporation, the appropriate question may be not how, but whether, we can regulate it. If the multinational is truly beyond the reach of the law, should individual nation states continue to provide a statutory framework within which such entities can be created?

---

86 Johns at 904.
87 Johns at 893.
88 Johns at 918.

17

CONCLUSION

Introduction

If there is a single key to the pitfalls that corporate regulators encounter, and to the general law's apparent inability to bring corporations to account for wrongdoing, it is to be found in the dynamics of power. Imbalances in power permeate almost every aspect of company law. Sometimes these imbalances occur simply because the size and wealth of the modern multinational corporation exceed the size and wealth of some nation states, and this alone is sufficient to give it enormous power when dealing with smaller entities and with governments. More frequently, they are a product of our legal understandings of the corporation and of the relationships within it. Questions of power permeate most of the areas of corporate law that we have examined in this book. In this, the concluding chapter, we will link some of these issues and ideas together using power as the connecting thread. We will be concerned with the ways in which the familiar elements of two paradigms—those of neo-classical economics and those of the modern democratic state—are subtly refigured by the law's understanding of the corporate person and, in particular, by the doctrine of corporate legal personality. We will also be concerned, following Albert Hirschman,[1] with questions of 'exit' and 'voice', and with the explanatory power of these ideas both in the area of minority rights and more generally.

Figurings of power: From the moment of conception to the dying of the light

A question of disclosure: Corporate multiple personality

Much of the case law concerning promoters and their duties is arcane—redolent of the purchase of dubious (and substantially overvalued assets) for subsequent resale

---

1 A. O. Hirschman, *Exit, Voice and Loyalty: Responses to Decline in Firms, Organizations and States,* Harvard University Press, Cambridge, Mass., 1970. See also A. O. Hirschman, 'Exit and Voice: An Expanding Sphere of Influence', in A. O. Hirschman (ed.), *Rival Views of Market Society and Other Recent Essays,* Viking, New York, 1986, p. 96.

to a company newly formed to acquire them. So arcane is much of this case law that it has been characterised as of little relevance to anyone other than private companies. We live, after all, in a modern world in which 'full disclosure' is statutorily demanded, new issues are typically underwritten by brokerage houses, and common-law redress for defective disclosure in, *inter alia*, prospectuses is available.[2] Despite this, and because it provides a useful starting point for our tracings of the lineaments of power, we have chosen to begin with one of the most colourful of these passages. According to Lord Macnaghten in *Gluckstein v. Barnes*,[3]

> [t]hese gentlemen set about forming a company to pay them a handsome sum for taking off their hands a property which they had contracted to buy with that end in view. They bring the company into existence by means of the usual machinery. They appoint themselves sole guardians and protectors of this creature of theirs, half-fledged and just struggling into life, bound hand and foot while yet unborn by contracts tending to their private advantage, and so fashioned by its makers that it could only act by their hands and only see through their eyes. They issue a prospectus representing that they had agreed to purchase the property for a sum largely in excess of the amount which they had, in fact, to pay. On the faith of this prospectus they collect subscriptions from a confiding and credulous public. And then comes the last act. Secretly, and therefore dishonestly, they put into their own pockets the difference between the real and the intended price.

On the question of whether a proper disclosure was made his Lordship continued:

> *'Disclosure' is not the most appropriate word to use when a person who plays many parts announces to himself in one character what he has done and is doing in another.* To talk of disclosure to the thing called the company, when as yet there were no shareholders, is a mere farce.[4]

And yet, despite his Lordship's disquiet, and as he undoubtedly well knew, much (perhaps most) of company law is precisely about a person playing many parts and solemnly 'disclosing' to one 'persona' what has been done by another. For all of the colourful language of the late Victorian era, the issues of power are set out clearly and concisely, and all of them are inherent in law's understanding of the corporate person. From the moment of the company's conception, it is at the mercy of those who control it, be they promoters (before its legal birth) or directors (from birth until the funeral rites commence and the liquidator steps solemnly on stage). Because the company can only see through the eyes of those who control it and act through their hands, it is at their mercy. To the extent that the corporation 'knows' anything, it knows only what they allow it to know. To the extent that it possesses will, it wills only that which its controllers allow it to will. While the law maintains the fiction of 'shareholder control', in reality this

---

2   P. Redmond, 'Problems for Insiders', in M. Gillooly (ed.), *The Law Relating to Corporate Groups*, Federation Press, Sydney, 1993, pp. 145–6.

3   [1900] AC 240.

4   [1900] AC 240 at 248–9 (emphasis added).

control is increasingly circumscribed,[5] and in large companies, it is often limited in practice to the (largely theoretical) power to appoint new directors and to remove the existing directors if the shareholders are displeased with their performance.[6] This, at any rate, is the 'legal story'.

Exit and voice in corporate structures: A dilemma for participatory models

In this context, work done by Hirschman on the complex relationship between the degree to which individuals are able to make their voices heard within a relationship, and on the feasibility of exit from that relationship, is acutely relevant. It forms a valuable conceptual backdrop for much of what we want to say in the context of the associative model of the company and of the conceptual framework provided by the fiction of shareholder democracy. According to Hirschman, active participation within any relationship,[7] irrespective of size and of other characteristics, depends on the balance between two potential capabilities: the ability of the individual to abandon that relationship more or less without cost, which he terms 'exit', and the ability of that individual to make herself or himself heard within that relationship and to actively participate in decision-making, which he terms 'voice'. Hirschman makes the point that, where exit is readily available, the art of voice is unlikely to develop. It can be both difficult and risky to develop voice, and so, where exit is readily available at little cost, it is cheaper and easier to opt for exit. Similarly, where the exit option is restricted or limited in feasibility, voice is unlikely to be effective, since the ability to threaten exit seriously is a powerful way of commanding attention and making one's voice heard.[8]

In those two opposing paradigms (both of which effectively negate the development of a participatory, as opposed to hierarchical and authoritarian, organisational model) we have the story of much of modern company law. The large public company whose shares are traded on the open market exemplifies the circumstance in which exit is so readily available as to make the development of voice improbable (at least as far as ordinary shareholders are concerned). To make oneself heard in an environment that encourages silence and acquiescence (through the proxy mechanism, for example) requires effort and commitment. Even more to the point, it requires an effort and a commitment for which there is likely to be little reward.[9] Only indirectly, and to a limited extent, does the law recognise the barriers to being

---

5   *Automatic Self-Cleansing Filter Syndicate Co. Ltd v. Cunninghame* [1906] 2 Ch 34 emphasised that the directors were in the position of managing partners.

6   In practice, of course, even this power is often ceded to the board. If the articles entitle the board to fill 'casual vacancies', it is a simple enough matter to arrange for all new vacancies to be 'casual' and only reappointments to be submitted to the membership.

7   Hirschman explicitly spoke of these phenomena in the context of complex associations such as firms, other organisations, and states.

8   Hirschman, *Exit, Voice and Loyalty*, pp. 43, 55, 83. See also Hirschman, 'Exit and Voice'.

9   Despite the persistent concern of the courts that relaxing the barriers to standing under the exceptions to the rule in *Foss v. Harbottle* might flood the courts with vexatious litigation by disgruntled shareholders, the entire structure of the action is designed to stifle, rather than encourage, voice. It exemplifies the situation in which, to make themselves heard, minority shareholders potentially incur enormous costs and, even if they are successful, gain no reward.

heard inherent in the corporate structure. Perhaps the clearest example (and we believe it is significant that it is a statutory development without any common-law parallel) is to be found in the provisions of the Corporations Law, ch. 6. In particular, the gradual shift from equality of opportunity to formal equality in the takeover context can be interpreted as legislative recognition of the need to protect voice within the takeover context. Because of the magnitude of the differentials of power (particularly in the form of knowledge) in this context, unless voice is protected, exit is likely to be costly and disadvantageous.[10]

The picture in the closely held private company is very different. Here, both because of corporate articles restricting the transfer of shares and because no real market exists for such shares, exit is unlikely to be a realistic option, at least if those shareholders desiring exit also seek to realise anything like a fair price for their shares. Where exit is effectively unavailable, voice can be stifled at little cost.[11] In these cases, 'locked-in' minority shareholders have recourse to the courts, only to be told (typically) that the 'oppression remedy' has not been enacted to enable locked-in minority shareholders to compel the company to buy them out at a price that reflects the asset backing of their shares.[12] Only where it becomes clear that the parties will not be able to co-exist within the corporate form (that is, where voice is clearly present but counterproductive, and exit is not feasible) is the court willing to adopt an alternative approach. Such cases typically involve potential deadlock and the likelihood of ongoing battles if the court does not intervene. In a recent case of this type, *Pizem v. Malek*,[13] Hodgson J made the following remarks, which are directly relevant to the need, in closely held companies, to ensure that voice is fostered:

> I have stated my view that a person in the position of Mrs Malek may be subject to 'expectations' or 'equities' arising out of Mr Pizim's dealings with the late Mr Malek. That is not to say that those expectations or equities would be precisely the same as those to which Mr Malek was subject … What I think was required on both sides was reasonable conduct with a view to establishing a relationship appropriate to the satisfactory conduct of the business of the companies, with a reasonable degree of mutual trust and confidence and a reasonable approach to the roles the parties were to take.[14]

Despite the continuing prosperity of the business, the court ordered that the company be wound up on the just and equitable ground, there being no reasonable prospect that the parties would be able to develop a mutually satisfactory working

---

10 See chapter 13 for a discussion of the takeover provisions.

11 The most explicit acknowledgment of this in recent Australian law may be found in the judgment of Crockett J in *Re G. Jeffrey (Men's Store) Pty Ltd* (1984) 2 ACLC 421 at 421–3 .

12 *Re A Company Pty Ltd* [1983] Ch 178 per Lord Grantchester. See also *Thomas v. H. W. Thomas Ltd* (1984) 2 ACLC 610; *Re G. Jeffrey (Men's Store) Pty Ltd*.

13 (1985) 3 ACLC 612.

14 (1985) 3 ACLC 612 at 618. However, on the facts, the mutual relationship of trust and confidence that had obtained between Messrs Pizem and Malek was held to impose certain obligations upon Mrs Malek after she succeeded to her late husband's position. Her 'voice' was unacceptable. What the court required was a voice that more closely approximated that of her late husband, and that was not forthcoming.

relationship. The denial of voice, in circumstances where that denial is clearly 'commercially improper', has also provided a sub-text in other successful cases, notably *Re H. R. Harmer Ltd* [15] and *Re City Meat Co. Pty Ltd*. [16] In both these cases, the active and capricious denial of voice by the controlling director and majority shareholder, when coupled with the unavailability of exit, induced the court to provide a remedy. Denial of voice, on its own, however, appears not to be enough. [17]

The contrast between the legal fiction of 'shareholder control' and the practical reality (in which corporate knowledge, understanding, vision, and action are the knowledge, understanding, vision, and action of the company's controllers) has set the stage for many of the ongoing debates in corporate law. At the deepest level many of these debates are about exit and voice. The legal debates surrounding the exceptions to the rule in *Foss v. Harbottle* are, at a fundamental level, debates concerning the appropriate parameters of voice within the company and the conditions under which voice is possible. The question of control (which, as we have seen, is the key element in the battle for standing) is also, and fundamentally, a question about voice. In particular, it is about the degree to which it is appropriate to allow the voices of minority shareholders to be heard. In cases such as *Prudential Assurance Co. Ltd v. Newman Industries Ltd (No. 2)*, [18] while exit was clearly feasible for Prudential, it was (one assumes) not feasible at a favourable price, and in those circumstances, the battle for voice appeared worth fighting. Here, it is worth quoting at length from the Court of Appeal judgment in *Prudential* to highlight the issues involved:

> It is commonly said that an exception to the rule in *Foss v. Harbottle* arises if the corporation is 'controlled' by persons implicated in the fraud complained of, who will not permit the name of the company to be used as plaintiffs in the suit … But this proposition leaves two questions at large, first, what is meant by 'control,' which embraces a broad spectrum extending from an overall absolute majority of votes at one end, to a majority of votes at the other end made up of those likely to be cast by the delinquent himself plus those voting with him as a result of influence or apathy. Secondly, what course is to be taken by the court if … the court is confronted by a motion on the part of the delinquent or by the company, seeking to strike out the action? For at the time of the application the existence of the fraud is unproved. It is at this point that a dilemma emerges. If, upon such an application, the plaintiff can require the court to assume as a fact every allegation in the statement of claim, as in a true demurrer, the plaintiff will frequently be able to outmanoeuvre the primary purpose of the rule in *Foss v. Harbottle* by alleging fraud and 'control' by the fraudster. If on the other hand the plaintiff has to prove fraud and 'control' before he can establish his title to prosecute his

---

15 [1958] 3 All ER 689.

16 (1983) 8 ACLR 673.

17 *Re A Company Pty Ltd* per Lord Grantchester. See also *Thomas v. H.W. Thomas Ltd*; *Re G. Jeffrey (Men's Store) Pty Ltd*.

18 [1982] Ch 204.

action, then the action may need to be fought to a conclusion before the court can decide whether or not the plaintiff should be permitted to prosecute it ...

In the present case a board, of which all the directors save one were disinterested ... had reached the conclusion before the start of the action that the prosecution of the action was likely to do more harm than good. That might prove a sound or unsound assessment, but it was the commercial assessment of an apparently independent board.[19]

Despite Lord Macnaghten's insistence that shareholders will be able to hold errant promoters and directors in check even after the company's 'birth',[20] in reality there is little reason to hope that the shareholders will be able to maintain any real control over corporate affairs.[21] About these issues, D. A. V. Boyle comments:

'The issue for corporate governance is how to strengthen the accountability of boards of directors to shareholders.'

In considering this issue it is important to differentiate *role* from *power* ...

In practice, the position of individual shareholders is very weak. First, it is likely that they own shares only in a financial vehicle of the investment trust or unit trust variety. Secondly, even if they own shares directly in the 'underlying' companies, they probably do so only as beneficiaries, their legal rights being held by the nominee company controlled by their discretionary fund manager. Thirdly, as the success of fund managers is determined entirely by the overall financial performance of the portfolios under management, weak or poorly performing shares will be replaced in preference to any attempt being made to repair a company's fortunes.[22]

The author goes on to point out that it is unlikely today that shareholders will even be aware that they are 'failing in their stewardship',[23] given that corporate financial documents are often 'economical with the truth' and shareholders are unlikely to have anything like the information needed to make an informed decision in respect of the performance of the directors or the calibre of proposed new directors. In Australia, where levels of individual share-ownership have traditionally been low, and where the great majority of corporate shareholders are institutional, it

---

19 [1982] Ch 204 at 219, 221.

20 *Gluckstein v. Barnes* [1900] AC 240 at 248–9.

21 It is not even altogether clear that this would be desirable. To the extent that one of the major advantages of the corporate form is its ability to segregate investment from management, it is clear that a tacit choice has been made to facilitate exit at the expense of voice.

22 D. A. V. Boyle, 'The Unitary Board and the One Man Band' (1993) 3 AJCL 252 at 263. It is not altogether clear exactly what merit might lie in having greater oversight by shareholders who serve the interests of yet another corporate person (since, in the case of institutional shareholders, that is precisely what would be involved in any attempt, through the guise of the general meeting, to 'repair a company's fortunes'). In Australia, we hasten to add, it is probable that a substantial institutional shareholder would have board representation in the guise of a nominee director and would be content for its 'stewardship' to be confined to that mechanism in all but extraordinary circumstances. In such circumstances, it is clear that ensuring exit on an equitable basis is essential, voice being unattainable except in the stories the law tells about company structure.

23 Committee on the Financial Aspects of Corporate Governance, *Report*, GCC, London, December 1992 (the Cadbury Report), p. 49, para. 6.6.

seems likely that actual levels of shareholder control are even lower than might be the case in the United Kingdom.[24]

Whatever the law may assume concerning 'shareholder stewardship', we believe that it is clear that shareholders possess little if any real power and are generally unlikely to be moved to exercise what little they do possess.[25] The law's fantasy remains that stated by Wigram VC: 'I attribute to the proprietors no power which the Act does not give them: they have the power, without the consent and against the will of the directors, of calling a meeting and of controlling their acts.'[26]

However, the law's reality is very different. Collins MR put the matter in these terms:

> It is by the consensus of all the individuals in the company that these directors become agents and hold their rights as agents. It is not fair to say that a majority at a meeting is for the purposes of this case the principal so as to alter the mandate of the agent … If the mandate of the directors is to be altered, it can only be under the machinery of the memorandum and articles themselves.[27]

Cozens-Hardy LJ was even blunter:

> I cannot see anything in principle to justify the contention that the directors are bound to comply with the votes or the resolutions of a simple majority in an ordinary meeting of the shareholders. I do not think it true to say that the directors are agents. It think it is more nearly true to say that they are in the position of managing partners appointed to fill that post by a mutual arrangement between all the shareholders.[28]

Given that corporate structures, both in large publicly held companies and in small privately held companies, militate against the development of voice by ordinary shareholders (particularly minority shareholders), the question for those seeking a revised model for corporate governance is how to call the company to account. When we add to the reality of the shareholder as passive investor a trend towards decision-taking rather than decision-making by directors (at least in the context of the large public company), it becomes clear that existing legal models are ill-suited to the task of making the company accountable.

In the case of the large company, the actual decision-making power lies, all too often, not in the official organs of the company, but in the layers of management beneath the board. The shareholders are well advised to exercise the exit option if difficulties arise, and the law seems, in general, to be unable to reach those who make the actual decisions.

---

24 There are, of course, well-publicised exceptions, such as the furore over the Arnotts takeover.

25 These matters were discussed in detail in chapter 9. If studies in the USA and in the United Kingdom (discussed below) are accurate, the legal debate about whether the general meeting or the board is the 'real' or 'ultimate' decision-making mechanism is almost laughable. The real power, in large companies at least, lies in the levels of corporate management beneath the board. See also chapters 5 and 6.

26 *Foss v. Harbottle* (1843) Hare 461 at 497.

27 *Automatic Self-Cleansing Filter Syndicate Co. Ltd v. Cunninghame* [1906] 2 Ch 34 at 43.

28 [1906] 2 Ch 34 at 45.

In the case of the closely held private company, existing legal models are equally inconsistent with actual decision-making patterns and the power relations within them. In such companies, our existing legal model is problematical precisely because the expectations of the individuals concerned are deeply and profoundly at odds with the corporate structure. In closely held companies, the power, as we have seen, lies with the directors (or, more usually, with one of them); the problem for the law is how best to constrain that power and to ensure, first, that it is devoted to corporate ends rather than private ends and, second, that those corporate ends are also ends that are acceptable to the law.[29]

REVIEW QUESTIONS

1 How does neo-classical economics describe the perfect market? (It may be helpful to re-read chapter 14.) How is the operation of economic markets altered by the presence of multinational corporations?

2 You may wish to think about the impact of the multinational corporation on the balance between exit and voice in modern nation states. Do you think that the presence of such corporations and their relative power (and therefore relative capacity to be heard)—particularly when coupled with their capacity to relocate a substantial part of their enterprise offshore—alters the balance between exit and voice for ordinary members of the community?

3 If, indeed, the passive shareholder is the reality, and the activist shareholder the anomaly, how should the law be altered to ensure management accountability? And to whom should management be accountable?

Calling the errant director to account

Self-interest or commercial judgment

A critical feature of the recurring dilemmas of corporate governance lies in their inconsistency with some of the central legal understandings of the nature of the corporation and of the appropriate role of law with respect to corporate affairs. As we have seen, three themes have recurred again and again in the history of corporate regulation. The first, and perhaps the most familiar, of these themes lies in the tension between two very different policy stances. On the one hand, it is argued that it is improper for directors to pursue their own self-interest at the expense of the company. On the other hand, and specifically to encourage entrepreneurship and wealth creation, it is argued that the courts should not second-guess directors on matters

---

29 At some point, we believe, it will be essential for Parliament to consider the position of the 'involuntary shareholder' in closely held companies and to determine how best to deal with the position of the locked-in 'involuntary shareholder'. The present position is unsatisfactory. It fails to provide consistent redress for individual shareholders. It also occasions expensive and wasteful litigation.

that can be plausibly characterised as ones of commercial judgment. This tension has been recognised in a variety of ways by different courts. As Latham CJ put the matter in the Australian High Court decision in *Mills v. Mills*:

> Very many actions of directors who are shareholders, perhaps all of them, have a direct or indirect relation to their own interests. It would be ignoring realities and creating impossibilities in the administration of companies to require that directors should not advert to or consider in any way the effect of a particular decision upon their own interests as shareholders. A rule which laid down such a principle would paralyse the management of companies in many directions … A director … is not, in my opinion, required by the law to live in an unreal region of detached altruism and to act in a vague mood of ideal abstraction from obvious facts which must be present to the mind of any honest and intelligent man when he exercises his powers as a director.[30]

While it has been suggested that the approach of Latham CJ comes close to offering *carte blanche* to directors, the tension it reveals between a policy of non-interference in commercial judgment and a strict view of fiduciary duties is palpable. More recently in *Kinsela Pty Ltd v. Kinsela*, Powell J said:

> I have come to the conclusion that, given its origin in the analogy between directors and trustees, and given the general principle applied to fiduciary powers, the true duty of directors is to refrain from exercising any of the powers vested in them in order to obtain for themselves or any of them some private advantage or in order to achieve some other object other than that for which the power was vested in them, and that everything else which the authorities seem to add by way of gloss is, in reality, no more than an embellishment dictated, or suggested by the particular power the exercise of which is in issue in each case. If this be correct, then, so it seems to me, the two questions ultimately to be answered in such a case are:
>
> (a) For what purpose or purposes was this power conferred upon the company and/or the directors?
> (b) Was the purpose, or were the purposes, for which the power was exercised within the permitted purpose or range of purposes, and were the matters to which the directors had regard when determining to exercise the power relevant to such permitted purpose or purposes?[31]

Always, the inherent tension between, on one hand, the fiduciary principles derived from partnership law and from the role of the trustee, and, on the other hand, the pragmatic and inherently self-interested decision-making expected of commercial men operating in a commercial setting remains unmistakably close to the surface of the judgment.

A part, although surely not all, of the difficulty lies in the insistent universalisation of the law, the attempt to apply one more-or-less uniform 'corporations law' to

---

30 (1938) 60 CLR 150 at 163–4.
31 (1983) 8 ACLR 384 at 404. See further *Jeffree v. NCSC* (1989) 7 ACLC 556.

very different structures. If these differences were restricted to the simplistic—for example, the distinction between the closely held family company[32] and the public company—they might be easy to address. But they are not restricted in this way, and indeed, the structural permutations today seem almost limitless.

Private (parents) and public (puppets)

As we saw earlier,[33] in Australia during the 1980s a number of high-profile entrepreneurs formed tightly integrated corporate structures, which they ultimately governed through the mechanism provided by their 'private', closely held family companies. This enabled them to maximise their control of the empires that they had created while attempting to minimise the associated financial risks. Therefore, even when we turn our attention to public companies, and beyond them to corporate groups, we find a multiplicity of corporate structures, which we believe pose very different questions of governance.

At one end of the spectrum we find an Anglo-American conglomerate, the structure of which has many features in common with the Australian groups discussed in chapter 7. The entrepreneur was Robert Maxwell; the group was Pergamon Press:

> Pergamon Press Inc (PPI) … is a 70% owned subsidiary of Pergamon which is responsible for your company's book sales and for collecting journal subscriptions in the western hemisphere. Repeated attempts have been made by your Board to obtain the orderly transfer of the supervision of PPI from the Board under Mr Maxwell's chairmanship to a Board to be designed by your company. Attempts in the New York Courts to call an extraordinary meeting of shareholders with the idea of changing the composition of the Board were defeated. Furthermore, your Board's action in the High Court to re-enfranchise the Pergamon Press Ltd Shareholders in PPI also failed. A change of the Articles of PPI in June, 1969 resulted in Pergamon being debarred from calling an extraordinary general meeting although the directors of PPI have consistently claimed that this was not the purpose of the change …
>
> [Y]our board is continuing to press vigorously with every means at its disposal to obtain control for Pergamon over PPI. Such control is an essential ingredient in the continuing fiscal health of your Company.[34]

Underlying these internecine power struggles were corporate decisions in which Robert Maxwell, as executive director of Pergamon Ltd, caused substantial credit to be provided to his sister's private company (PPI) and for all sales from parent to subsidiary to be made on a 'sale or return basis'. During the course of an investigation into these transactions, it was noted that

> this was the most far reaching agreement that Pergamon … ever entered into. It involved Pergamon in a huge contingent liability … Yet not a single director of Pergamon ever saw

---

32 The companies in both *Mills v. Mills* and *Kinsela Pty Ltd v. Kinsela* were closely held family companies. Similar issues arose in *Bailey v. Mandala Private Hospital Pty Ltd* (1988) ACLC 43.

33 See chapter 7 for a discussion of the public/private interface in the structure of Australian corporate groups.

34 Pergamon Press Ltd, *Annual Report 1970*, as quoted in Boyle at 253–4.

this document apart from Mr Maxwell who wrote it, or was aware of its existence until some time in 1969, with the possible exception of Mr Clark. It would not be an exaggeration to say that Mr Maxwell by this agreement handed over an important part of Pergamon's future to an American private company set up for the benefit of his sister and her children ... a company over which Maxwell had considerable influence.[35]

When such power struggles erupt, whether within an individual company or between subsidiary and parent, the 'stewardship' of the shareholders is, and is likely to remain, altogether illusory.[36] While Boyle advocates a range of legal changes to 'empower' shareholders,[37] he does not consider how, or even if, these could be effective without first building into corporate and legal structures substantial disincentives to the role of passive investor. In large, publicly traded companies, as we saw above, the ready availability of the exit option makes an active monitoring role on the part of shareholders both unattractive and excessively costly.

A question of formalities: Decision-taking or decision-making by directors?

More recently, and more disturbingly from a legal perspective, studies in the USA and the United Kingdom have suggested that the stewardship of the board of directors is also a matter of form, rather than substance, in many large public companies. Here we confront yet another permutation of corporate form, and another way of delineating the lines of power. If, in the last section, we saw how power might be ceded by board members to a single director,[38] the board thereby becoming a mere rubber stamp for the decisions of the individual entrepreneur, here we explore a very different mechanism for rendering the board effectively nugatory. While the names of the leading Australian entrepreneurs of the 1980s still dominate Australian corporate folklore, a very different pattern is emerging in the case of many large publicly held corporations. In this pattern, while the board apparently continues to exercise the formal legal powers prescribed by law, the real decision-making occurs elsewhere, in the layered tiers of management beneath the board. One study in the USA found that, in large public companies,

the board commonly performed three functions. First, it provided a source of advice and counsel to management in such matters as the negotiation of finance, review of pension plans or decisions on plant location and concomitant capital appropriation. However, the directors' contribution to management decision making in such matters

---

35   Department of Trade and Industry (UK), *Report on Maxwell Scientific International (Distribution Services) Ltd, Robert Maxwell & Co. Ltd, and Final Report on Pergamon Press Ltd*, HMSO, London, 1973, para. 774, as quoted in Boyle at 254.

36   So too, for all practical purposes, is the actual (as opposed to formal) leadership of the board.

37   Boyle at 266–7.

38   Table A, art. 67(1) of the Corporations Law enables the directors, by power of attorney, to appoint any person an attorney of the company with such powers (being powers of the board) that they see fit. Article 76(1) provides that they may delegate any of their powers to a committee or committees consisting of such numbers as they see fit. Articles 79 and 80 enable the directors to appoint a managing director and confer upon that managing director any or all of the powers exercisable by them.

usually derived not from their status as members of the board but from their commercial backgrounds, experience and connections. Only rarely did their advice lead to reversal of a management decision. Secondly, the discipline of periodic appearances before the board, even without the anticipation of penetrating and challenging questioning, was found to exert a more rigorous standard of internal management reporting and served to protect, through a corporate conscience function, against unconscionable management compensation policies. Finally, the directors served as a decision making body in certain crisis situations, principally the sudden death or incapacity of, or unsatisfactory performance by, the chief executive officer.

Significantly, the roles which directors performed did not include three functions classically assigned to company boards in management and legal literature. Directors did not establish basic objectives, strategies and policies for the company; non-executive directors simply did not have the time to make the studies necessary for these judgments. Secondly, they did not ask discerning questions of senior executives; board meetings were considered an inappropriate forum for such questioning, the more so since outside directors were largely selected by the chief executive. Thirdly, directors did not select the company's chief executive except in crisis situations; in practice it fell to the chief executive to determine her or his successor.[39]

Sociologists have characterised the role of the board in this type of corporate authority structure as that of a 'legitimating institution':

> To be sure, the final yea or nay at a board meeting may be seen as the decision point, and may so appear in corporate histories ... But the board actions we have observed are better interpreted we feel, merely as ratifications of decisions made earlier and elsewhere, sometimes by much more junior men, about which the board had no practical alternative. The distinction between 'making' and 'taking' decisions is relevant. Boards of directors are, we feel, best conceived as decision-taking institutions, that is, as legitimating institutions, rather than as decision-making ones.[40]

Corporate culpability: Will the 'reasonable corporation' please stand up?

Not infrequently, most particularly where the question is of corporate culpability for wrongs, the tension between the 'legal' fiction that the board is the ultimate decision-making body and the management reality that, at most, the board is a 'legitimating institution' can be profoundly problematical. In chapter 4 and again in chapter 15 we looked at some of the difficulties encountered when society attempts

---

39 Redmond, pp. 293–4, citing a study by M. L. Mace, *Directors: Myth and Reality*, Division of Research, Graduate School of Business Administration, Harvard University, Boston, 1971.

40 Committee of Inquiry on Industrial Democracy, Department of Trade (UK), *Report*, Cmnd 6706, HMSO, London, 1977, as quoted in Redmond, pp. 294, 295.

to make corporate persons legally accountable for wrongdoing. In companies where the board serves a legitimating role, to the extent that the law seeks for a 'legally knowable' directing mind and will, that 'mind and will' may best be seen as a diffuse neural network distributed throughout management ranks.

A law designed with individual human actors in mind demands a 'guilty mind' or a reckless attitude as an ingredient in an offence, or asks whether a reasonable (corporate) person in the position of the company would have been aware of the potential risk. But locating that mental element within a diffuse neural network, which is likely to be capable of coordination but not of 'focused intention', may (and often does) prove impossible. If, on the other hand—resigned to the impossibility of treating a complex social organism as an individual—recourse is had to older notions of individual culpability, the structure that frustrated attempts to assign culpability to a 'group' will prove an equally effective barrier to attempts to assign responsibility to any individual or group within the corporation, whatever its formal legal status. The decision-taking board is as devoid of mental element as is the social organism.[41]

In many cases, individual decisions are taken to avoid bad publicity;[42] to isolate the potential costs of production in plants using outdated and poorly maintained equipment, and employing a less than ideally skilled labour force;[43] or to dispose of supplies of excess widgets to cover the costs of production and maintain profitability.[44] These decisions have come together to produce an 'effect' that the law labels 'harm' of a particular type. At neither the individual nor the collective level can there be found any discernible mental element of the type required. Such intentions as do exist are likely to involve 'burnishing' the corporate image and ensuring that it is not compromised by bad publicity, maintaining production in an environment chosen explicitly because costs were comparatively low, and avoiding the need to 'write off' widgets with the consequential downside impact on corporate profits. All of these intentions are, within the existing legal framework, entirely proper (and, indeed, even laudable) corporate purposes.

Interpreted from a different perspective, however, they herald yet another shift that is worth mentioning in this context. Writing in the USA against the background of anti-corporate litigation in cases involving 'mass toxic torts',[45] Jonathan Simon alerts us to the rise of the 'actuarial subject':

---

41 Therefore, in much modern consumer legislation, as we saw in chapter 14, consumers have recourse to strict liability, but the situations covered are by no means exhaustive.

42 The international campaign to conceal the hazards posed by asbestos fibres is a clear example of decisions driven by the desire to manage information, to avoid undesirable publicity, and to minimise the costs potentially involved in upgrading dated and inefficient plants. See chapters 5–7, 15.

43 All of these factors appear to have been involved in the Bopal disaster.

44 The aggressive campaign to market the Dalkon Shield in Australia and, subsequently, in the Third World after it had been banned in the USA because of undesirable side effects (including death) is a good example, as is the current of litigation concerning silicon implants.

45 The specific example discussed is the 'Agent Orange' litigation. See. P. Schuck, *Agent Orange on Trial: Mass Toxic Tort Disasters in the Courts,* Harvard University Press, Cambridge, Mass., 1986, p. 4.

[I]ndividuals, once understood as moral or rational actors, are increasingly understood as locations in actuarial tables of variations. This shift from moral agent to actuarial subject marks a change in the way power is exercised on individuals by … large organisations. Where power once sought to manipulate the choices of rational actors, it now seeks to predict behavior and situate subjects according to the risk they pose …

Rather than make people up, actuarial practices unmake them.[46]

It is precisely the 'actuarial subject' to which decisions like those discussed above are addressed. According to the dominant model for decision-making, it is rational for corporations to make decisions about publicity, production costs, product distribution, and even plant relocation and/or closure on an actuarial basis. Given this, it may be that the sorts of considerations to which the law has repairs in determining, for example, the knowledge that a 'reasonable corporation' ought to have had in taking a decision simply were irrelevant to a corporate actor.

In the USA, the evidence points to decision-taking boards and to the emergence of complex neural networks within corporate structures. But to complicate matters further, in England, the 1997 report of the Committee of Inquiry on Industrial Democracy found the scene to be one of almost infinite variability:

The Industrial Participation Association distinguished at least nine different company structures: from the small company with a board of executive managers closely involved in every aspect of a company's affairs, to the decentralised group with a holding company board appointing senior managers and allocating resources, but leaving operating policy to its subsidiary boards. We heard of companies where equally there was little delegation of authority to subsidiary boards, so that though they were boards of separately incorporated companies they were no more than legal entities which had no power and rarely met. We also heard of companies which had boards of directors, who were not directors at all in the strict legal sense but who nevertheless exercised considerable powers. A clear example of this is where a company is organised into divisions, each one controlled by a committee or board of senior executives who are referred to in the company as 'divisional directors'. Such a divisional board … may look and act very much like the board of a separately incorporated subsidiary: it may indeed have more power. But in legal terms its directors may have no legal standing as such and, if so, may not be subject to the requirements of company law concerning directors.[47]

In a further twist, the boards of many large companies are drawn from the ranks of senior management, so that it becomes impossible to pinpoint any actual chain of decision-making and to offer anything approximating a general model. Our concern is not with how and where decisions are actually taken. Neither does it stem from any predilection for any particular model of corporate governance. Rather, we

---

46 J. Simon, 'The Ideological Effects of Actuarial Practices' (1988) 22 *Law and Society Review* 771, as quoted in G. E. Marcus, 'Mass Toxic Torts and the End of Everyday Life', in A. Sarat & T. R. Kearns (eds), *Law in Everyday Life*, The Amherst Series in Law, Jurisprudence, and Social Thought, University of Michigan Press, Ann Arbor, 1995, pp. 237, 254.

47 Committee of Inquiry on Industrial Democracy, as quoted in Redmond, p. 294.

believe the question to be one of accountability, both in the sense of accountability for corporate wrongdoing[48] and in the sense of accountability to wider institutions for decisions that affect those institutions, sometimes fundamentally.[49] The multiplicity of possible models for corporate decision-making itself imposes significant social costs. When an individual commits a tort or a crime (or breaches a statute imposing strict liability), issues of responsibility turn on conventional legal assumptions. Over time, the law has developed a range of mechanisms for allocating individual responsibility in a variety of circumstances.

The same cannot be said, at least in respect of the common law, about the mechanisms available for allocating collective or group responsibility. When a corporate person commits a tort or a crime, the question of responsibility immediately becomes entangled in the reality of corporate governance. Whose mind, it is sometimes asked, is the corporate mind? Whose will is the corporate will? Where the board is decision-taking, rather than decision-making, under what circumstances is it legally possible to say that a particular decision or course of action reflects the corporate will? If the corporate will is to be found in the 'accepted channels of communication', as recent Australian authority[50] suggests, this also suggests that a wholly particularised investigation into corporate channels of communication will be essential. It also suggests that—particularly where the individual company is a member of a corporate group—it may be difficult, even impossible, and that bringing the responsible entity to account will be even more unlikely.[51]

Corporate 'bonding': Formal and informal corporate groups

Earlier we spoke of three major themes in corporate regulation. The first of these themes involved the division of power between the general meeting and the board, and the inadequacy of current mechanisms for accountability. We now turn to the second of these themes: the way in which these internal struggles have been immeasurably magnified by the development of complex corporate groups.

The second major theme in corporate governance, then, involves the common law's failure to develop the legal principles necessary if it is to deal with corporate groups in a consistent and coherent way. Here law's failure to develop coherent principles of collective responsibility is magnified many times over by the sheer magnitude of the groups that it seeks to regulate. The fault lines left by this failure have not gone unnoticed by those who chart the structures and activities of those same groups:

> The principle of group responsibility normally functions by the recognition of a legal person or entity as a representative of the group, and then by the doctrines of agency and

---

48   See chapter 4 for a detailed discussion of the issues involved.
49   These themes were analysed in some detail in chapters 5 and 6.
50   *Re Chisum Services Pty Ltd* (1981) ACLC 292.
51   And here all of the trans-jurisdictional issues canvassed in the last chapter reappear.

vicarious liability, the group becomes liable for the acts of its members. It follows that the application of the principle of group responsibility is contingent upon the recognition of a single legal personality for the group.[52]

In our discussion of the difficulties inherent in ascribing responsibility to single corporate entities, a difficulty that is most acute where the law requires a mental element, we examined the difference between the stories law tells about the responsibilities of various corporate organs and the ways in which those organs appear to function as a matter of commercial reality. These problems become even more acute when we turn our attention to corporate groups. Here, because the law fails to recognise the corporate group as a distinct entity, calling the group to account for wrongdoing becomes, as we saw in our earlier analysis of the issues in *Briggs v. James Hardie & Co. Pty Ltd*,[53] profoundly difficult.

Hugh Collins identifies three distinct forms of bonding within complex productive organisations and argues that principles of group responsibility ought to be developed to enable the law to hold groups of all three configurations responsible in some circumstances.[54] These three forms of bonding he terms 'ownership', 'contract', and 'authority'. In this context, we shall primarily be concerned with the first of these, although we shall touch on the third in the context of conglomerates, where control is maintained through complex patterns of cross-shareholding.

Vertical integration: The parent–subsidiary relationship

In chapters 4 and 5, and again in Chapter 16, we touched upon a number of the legal and social issues involved with the most straightforward of these avenues of corporate 'bonding': ownership. As Collins notes, '[g]roup management steers the conglomerate according to the latest principles of financial accounting, but the law regards each company within the group as a distinct legal entity'.[55]

In such circumstances, the dynamics of power are hardly straightforward. From a corporate perspective, there is little doubt that the group is 'real', while the individual entities are bookkeeping mechanisms or historical relics. The law oscillates between recognition of the reality of the group, as with the provisions for group accounts discussed in chapter 15,[56] and its bondage to the separate entity doctrine entrenched by *Salomon v. Salomon & Co. Ltd*.[57]

Corporate groups are as various as the circumstances of their development. Sometimes they arise simply as a consequence of merger or takeover activity. Where this is the case, the individual entities may remain largely independent, although this is by no means always the case. At other times, the group is much more tightly integrated. Tightly integrated conglomerates may arise as a consequence of merger

---

52 H. Collins, 'Ascription of Legal Responsibility to Groups in Complex Patterns of Economic Integration' (1990) 53 MLR 731 at 733.

53 (1989) 7 ACLC 841. See Chapters 7 and 15 for a more detailed discussion of these issues.

54 Collins at 733.

55 Collins at 733. This is, of course, only one model of the corporate conglomerate.

56 Corporations Law, ss. 290, 295A–D and 213 (covering Australian Securities Commission Class Orders).

57 [1897] AC 22.

or takeover activity (or through the acquisition of ventures formerly operated as partnerships or by sole traders). It goes without saying that the subsidiaries acquired in these ways may be wholly owned or partially owned. While this may not affect the degree of control exercised, it may raise questions of oppression if decisions are taken in the interests of the group rather than the individual entities within it.

Corporate groups may also develop because management has determined that it is appropriate for different aspects of corporate activities to be undertaken by independent entities and has, therefore, caused those entities to be formed. In the last chapter we termed the companies that emerged as a consequence of these sorts of decisions, 'companies of convenience'. As a consequence of some of these decisions, subsidiary companies may even give 'birth' to their own 'parents' in a curious form of reverse corporate biology, so that the parent company becomes the 'company of convenience'.[58]

In the case of tightly integrated conglomerates in which the subsidiaries are wholly owned, the central regulatory issue is the extent to which the law should (and, perhaps, has the capacity to) ratify and enforce the commercial decision already taken by corporate management. If a conglomerate is run according to the 'latest principles of financial accounting' and no real distinction is made between the interests of the whole and the interests of the individual entity, to what extent should the law recognise this? The circumstances in which recognition may become critical are varied. Insolvency and corporate wrongdoing (whether tortious or criminal) come readily to mind.[59] So too do questions of compliance with various statutory regimes: consumer protection legislation, occupational health and safety,[60] anti-discrimination legislation,[61] the regulation of trade union activity,[62] and so forth. In all of these areas, legal outcomes are likely to be very different if the law accepts the reality of the group rather than focusing on the individual entity.

There is, of course, a price. In a tightly integrated corporate group, and particularly in a multinational group, developing a legal model that can impose collective responsibility upon a corporate form with emanations in a multitude of jurisdictions with wholly different legal systems may be a task beyond the capability of any national legal system. Even the effort to do so may be in direct conflict with other national agendas, such as the legal requirement that a multinational company wishing to do business in a particular jurisdiction must form a local subsidiary (and, perhaps, allow a degree of local ownership). Unless the attempt is made, however, such groups and their activities will largely escape regulation, and this has undesirable consequences for the community as a whole.

---

58 As we saw in chapter 15, this sometimes enables companies to elude regulatory regimes aimed at particular industries.

59 *Briggs v. James Hardie & Co. Pty Ltd* is a compelling illustration of the issues that arise in the case of corporate wrongdoing. See also *Tate v. Freecorns* [1972] WAR 204; *Adams v. Cape Industries plc* [1991] 1 All ER 929 at 1026; *McDermid v. Nash Dredging & Reclamation Co. Ltd* [1987] 1 AC 906; *Qintex Australia Finance Ltd v. Schroders Australia Ltd* (1990) 3 ACSR 267 (dealing with that ultimate form of corporate wrongdoing: insolvency).

60 *Briggs v. James Hardie & Co. Pty Ltd*; *McDermid v. Nash Dredging & Reclamation Co. Ltd*; *Adams v. Cape Industries plc*.

61 See chapter 15.

62 *Dimbleby & Sons Ltd v. National Union of Journalists* [1984] ICR 386 at 402.

Horizontal integration: Complex patterns of interlocking shareholdings

Where the group is less obviously tightly structured, matters of governance become even more complex and intractable. Often, in such a group, formal parent subsidiary relationships do not exist. Despite this, interlocking patterns of cross-shareholdings frequently provide a foundation upon which tight and effective management can be built. The capacity of such a group to evade the disclosure requirements of the Corporations Law has already been noted.[63] John Spalvin's Adelaide Steamship group was the Australian exemplar of such a group. Despite the total absence of formal parent–subsidiary relationships, the group functioned as a tight and effective whole, and was for some years held out as a prime example of effective group management.

Where a substantial control is exercised by a single entrepreneur, as was the case with the Adsteam group, it is tempting to liken the group to a single entity, despite the presence of other interests and the apparent independence of the various boards. The development of this kind of authority pattern is greatly facilitated by a corporate environment (both legal and commercial) that accepts the reality of passive shareholders and decision-taking by boards rather than decision-making. It is also, obviously, intimately linked with a management style based upon what we shall, if only for convenience, term the 'cult of personality'.[64] The characteristic feature of cult-of-personality groups is the dominance of a single entrepreneur—a dominance that sometimes effectively overwhelms the legal structure and renders it largely irrelevant, except as a matter of formality.[65] In other corporate groups with apparently similar structures, a substantial degree of independence in decision-making may be the norm. Even where it is acknowledged that the relationship between the various entities comprising the group is not of a kind that makes it appropriate to regard the group as functionally (and perhaps legally) a single entity, such a group has a substantial capacity to deflect the impact of the regulatory regimes that impinge upon it.

Needless to say, informal control can extend well beyond the formal manifestations of corporate groups with interlocking directorates. A degree of informal control is also likely where a substantial creditor, frequently a major bank, extracts a nominee directorship as a condition of making loan funds available, whether by way of overdraft (perhaps secured by a floating charge) or other credit arrangement.[66]

---

63 See chapters 4 and 15.

64 'Cult-of-personality' groups have been, in the recent past, common both in Australia and overseas. Among the household names are Fairfax, Spalvin, Bond, Skase, Murdoch, Maxwell, and, perhaps, Gates.

65 See, for example, *Alan Bond & Ors v. Australian Broadcasting Tribunal* (1989) 89 ALR 185 (discussed in chapter 7).

66 See, for example, *Levin v. Clark* [1962] NSWR 686 and *Re Broadcasting Station 2GB* [1964–65] NSWR 1648. The latter case involved nominee directors appointed by the Fairfax interests that had taken over the station. The court held it was appropriate for them to act in the interests of the Fairfax group unless there was evidence to suggest that they would thereby disadvantage the company. More recently, the attempt by FAI Insurances, which held a 10 per cent holding in the Advance Bank, to elect representatives to the board of the bank provided the catalyst for a campaign of 'dirty tricks' by some members of the incumbent board. See *Advance Bank of Australia Ltd v. FAI Insurances Ltd* (1989) 12 ACLR 118.

Collins suggests that, in some cases, the informal control achieved in this way can be sufficient to alter behaviour.

The integrated company and the nominee director

A common thread in the various forms of horizontal and vertical integration that have emerged is the fostering of high levels of coordination and integration through the judicious placement of nominee directors. As Roman Tomasic and Stephen Bottomley[67] ascertained in the course of an empirical study of the duties of directors in Australian public companies, in highly integrated corporate groups it is the norm, not the exception, for nominee directors on the boards of the various subsidiaries to see themselves as part of a unified management team, and not as directors of independent companies. In realistic terms, it is almost certainly essential to the well-being of the group that they do so, at least where the group operates as a tightly integrated whole. It is also a position that is extremely difficult, perhaps impossible, to reconcile with conventional understandings of the fiduciary obligations to which all directors are legally subject.

Legal reality and commercial reality currently remain at loggerheads. Directors remain legally bound to act in the interests of the individual companies and not the corporate group, and these interests extend to ensuring that the interests of creditors are taken into account.[68] Commercially, however, a director who gave priority to the interests of the individual entity above those of the group would be unlikely to survive.

The issues are clearly illustrated by the facts and the split decision in *Equiticorp Finance Ltd (in liq.) v. Bank of New Zealand*.[69] The Bank of New Zealand (BNZ) provided finance to a member of the Equiticorp group. At the time when the loan was granted, Hawkins was the executive chairman of the group and a member of the boards of many of the constituent companies. After BNZ reviewed its exposure to Equiticorp, Hawkins agreed that there would be an early repayment of this particular liability. When the subsidiary was unable to retire the debt, Hawkins applied a liquidity reserve established by two other group subsidiaries to satisfy the debt. At first instance, the 'Charterbridge test' was applied and the trial judge held that, faced with the impact of a default on the group's relationship with BNZ, Hawkins could have believed he was acting in the interests of the relevant companies. On appeal, the decision at first instance was upheld, although the majority preferred to suggest that, while there had been a breach, the companies suffered no adverse consequences and therefore no remedy was required. Kirby P, in dissent, took a very different, and strongly formalist approach. He insisted that

---

67   R. Tomasic & S. Bottomley, *The Fiduciary Duties of Directors in Listed Public Companies: An Empirical Study of Directors' Duties and the Law in Corporate Australia*, Centre for National Corporate Law Research, University of Canberra, Canberra, 1991, p. 10.

68   *Walker v. Wimborne* (1976) 137 CLR 1 at 6–7; *Nicholson v. Permakraft (NZ) Ltd* (1985) ACLC 453. For more recent applications of the strict approach, see *Spedley Securities Ltd v. Greater Pacific Investments Pty Ltd (in liq.)* (1992) ACSR 155; *Linter Group Ltd v. Goldberg* (1992) 11 ASCR 642.

69   (1993) 11 ACSR 642.

in recognising the 'realpolitik of corporate control' the court 'debase[d] the integrity of company law'.[70]

So long as the law fails to develop principles to address the reality of integrated corporate groups, cases like Equiticorp will continue to come before the courts. Both vertically and horizontally integrated groups are likely to be a permanent feature of the commercial landscape. We believe that the development of appropriate principles for addressing the issues that flow from interlocking directorates and nominee directors who sit on the boards of many or all of the companies in such groups is of the highest importance. Whether one thinks, with Kirby P (as he then was), that recognising the reality of corporate control debases the integrity of company law, or whether one takes the view that a law that is so far out of step with contemporary reality as to be unrealistic does the legal system no credit (a view to which the present authors incline), it is clear that these issues are not likely to vanish from the corporate stage.

The corporation and the law: Citizen, subject, or ... ?

The final dilemma of corporate governance, and the most significant as we approach the twenty-first century, lies in the law's relation to the multinational corporation. Here, we believe, the law must necessarily enter uncharted territory. Inevitably, the dilemmas discussed earlier in this chapter, particularly those discussed in the last section, bear directly upon this question. Here too, we hesitate to offer even a tentative solution. The most salient features of the multinational corporation are its ability to extricate itself from regulation that appears to be contrary to its interests, and to shift operations almost at will from jurisdiction to jurisdiction. Neither the multinational corporation nor the men (and, even today, those who control multinational corporations generally remain male) who manage them seem capable of being called to account by any nation state. They, and the economic system whose health or otherwise their performance is taken to signal, are increasingly global rather than local phenomena.

Our legal systems, on the other hand, are largely municipal. Attempts at the extra-territorial application of municipal laws have largely failed in this as in other contexts, and are widely decried. International law has yet to develop any effective forms of regulation for corporate entities. As we saw in chapter 16, international law has, to date, treated multinational corporations as emanations of national states (thus collapsing them into the entities of which they are comprised) and not as international legal persons in their own right. Until this is altered, and this does not seem likely in the near future—for this, given the structure of international law, would liken them to nation states, the regulation of such entities will fall back to nation states.

---

70 (1993) 11 ACSR 642 at 677.

Law's inability to come to terms with the reality of the multinational corporation is sobering. The success or failure of corporate regulation in the twenty-first century is likely to be determined by whether it proves possible to develop appropriate principles for the regulation of corporate groups and, ultimately, of multinational corporations.

ACKNOWLEDGMENTS

The authors and publisher are grateful to the following copyright holders for granting permission to reproduce textual material in this book:

Adelaide Law Review for extracts from J. Dodds Streeton, 'Feminist Perspectives on the Law of Insolvency'; C. Sampford, 'Rethinking the Core Curriculum'

American Law Institute for extracts from its Principles of Corporation Governance and Structure, © 1994 by the American Law Institute

Attorney General's Department (NSW) for extracts from *Crumpton v. Morrine Hall Pty Ltd*; *Equiticorp Finance Ltd v. Bank of New Zealand*; *Hawkesbury Development Co. Ltd v. Landmark Finance Pty Ltd*; *Metal Manufacturers Ltd v. Lewis*; *North Sydney Brick and Tile Co. Ltd v. Darvall*; *Re Allebart Pty Ltd*; *Re Broadcasting Station 2GB*; Unreported 1989, no. CA 40598, 1992 NSW Lexis 7510, BC9203017 (Full Court NSW SC) (cases are subject to Crown copyright)

Australian Government Publishing Service for extracts from the Australian Law Reform Commission, *General Insolvency Inquiry*, vol. 1, report no. 45; the Company Law Advisory Committee to the Standing Committee of Attorneys-General, *Second Interim Report*; the *Corporations Law 1990*, © Commonwealth of Australia (1990); the *Explanatory Memorandum to the Corporate Law Reform Bill*; the second reading speech of the First Corporate Law Simplification Bill 1994

Blackwell Publishers for extracts from W. Twining (ed.), *Legal Theory and Common Law*

Butterworths for extracts from *Coleman v. Myers* in the New Zealand Law Reports; J. H. Farrar & L. G. S. Trotman, *Australian Corporation Law*; H. A. J. Ford & R. P. Austin, *Principles of Corporation Law*, 7th edn; J. Gooley, *Corporations and Associations Law*, 3rd edn; R. Tomasic, J. Jackson, & R. Woellner, *Corporations Law: Principles, Policy and Process*, 2nd edn

Cambridge University Press (Australia) for extracts from I. Shapiro, *The Evolution of Rights in Liberal Theory*

Corporate and Business Law Journal and K. Hall for extract from K. Hall, 'Starting from Silence: The Future of Feminist Analysis of Corporate Law'

Creighton Law Review for extract from R. C. Mangrum, 'In Search of a Paradigm of Corporate Responsibility'

Department of Justice, Victoria, and the Council of Law Reporting in Victoria for extracts from various cases in the Victorian Reports

Elsevier Science Ltd, The Boulevard, Langford Lane, Kidlington OX5 1GB, UK, for extract from Pergamon Press Ltd, *Annual Report 1970*

Federation Press for extracts from P. Cashman, 'The Dalkon Shield' and N. Gunningham, 'Asbestos Mining in Baryulgil: A Case Study of Corporate Neglect', both in P. Grabosky & A. Sutton (eds), *Stains on a White Collar*; M. A. Eisenburg, 'Corporate Groups' and M. Gillooly, 'Outside Shareholders in Corporate Groups', in M. Gillooly (ed.), *The Law Relating to Corporate Groups*

Greenwood Publishing Group, Inc., Westport, CT for extracts from W. J. Samuels & A. S. Miller (eds), *Corporations and Society*, copyright © 1987 by W. J. Samuels and A. S. Miller

Harcourt Brace & Company, Australia for extract from K. Saunders & R. Evans (eds), *Gender Relations in Australia*, copyright © 1992 by Harcourt Brace & Company, Australia

Harvard Law Review for extract from E. M. Dodd, 'For Whom are Corporate Managers Trustees?', copyright © by the Harvard Law Review Association

Her Majesty's Stationary Office for extracts from Committee of Inquiry on Industrial Democracy, Department of Trade (UK), *Report*, Cmnd 6706; Company Law Amendment Committee, *Report 1925–26*, Cmnd 2657; Department of Trade and Industry (UK), *Report on Maxwell Scientific International (Distribution Services) Ltd, Robert Maxwell & Co. Ltd, and Final Report on Pergamon Press Ltd*; various cases reported in All England Reports, Appeal Cases, Chancery, Chancery Division, King's Bench, Queen's Bench, Weekly Law Reports

International Monetary Fund for extract from Professor Zadeh, 'International Monetary Fund'

Journal of Law and Society, Cardiff Law School, for extract from P. Ireland, I. Grigg-Spall, & D. Kelly, 'The Conceptual Foundations of Modern Company Law'

K. L. Kelly for extract from *Reid Murray Holdings Ltd v. David Murray Holdings Pty Ltd*

Law and Society Association for extract from J. Simon, 'The Ideological Effects of Actuarial Practices'

LBC Information Services for extracts from J. Hill, 'Cross Guarantees in Corporate Groups', *Company and Securities Law Journal*; Sir D. Menzies, 'Company Directors', *Australian Law Journal*; E. I. Sykes & S.Walker, *The Law of Securities*; K. E. Lindgren, H. H. Mason, & B. L. J. Gordon, *The Corporation and Australian Society*; P. Redmond, *Companies and Security Law*

Osgoode Hall Law Journal for extract from K. A. Lahey & S. W. Salter, 'Corporate Law in Legal Theory and Legal Scholarship: From Classicism to Feminism'

Oxford University Press, Australia and New Zealand, for extracts from J. Farrar (ed.), *Takeovers: Institutional Investors and the Modernization of Corporate Laws*; M. Thornton (ed.), *Public and Private: Feminist Legal Debates*; D. Wishart, *Company Law in Context*

R. Tomasic and the National Centre for Corporate Law and Policy Research for extract from R. Tomasic & S. Bottomly, 'The Fiduciary Duties of Directors in Listed Public Companies: An Empirical Study of Directors' Duties and the Law in Corporate Australia'

Sage Publications for extract from L. J. Moral, 'Corporate Criminal Capacity: Nostalgia for Representation', *Social and Legal Studies*

Sweet and Maxwell for extract from R. R. Formoy, *The Historical Foundations of Modern Company Law*

Sydney Law Review for extracts from Lim Wen Ts'ai, 'Corporations and the Devil's Dictionary: The Problem of Individual Responsibility for Corporate Crimes'

Vanderbilt Law Review for extract from T. A. Gabaldon, 'The Lemonade Stand: Feminist and Other Reflections on the Limited Liability of Corporate Shareholders'

Victorian Council of Law Reporting for extracts from *Commissioner of Corporate Affairs v. Harvey*; *Re Fowler's Vacola Manufacturing Co. Ltd*; *Re Tivoli Freeholds*; Victorian Law Reform Commission, *Report*, 1979

Wadsworth Publishing Company for extracts from W. H. Shaw & V. Barry, *Moral Issues in Business*, 6th edn, copyright © 1995 by Wadsworth Publishing Company

Washington Law Review for extract from H. N. Butler & L. E. Ribstein, 'Opting out of Fiduciary Duties: A Response to the Anti-Contractarians'

West Group for extract from *People v. Hotchkiss*, New York Supplement

Wright Books for extract from N. E. Renton, *Company Directors: Masters or Servants?*

All legislation herein is reproduced by permission but does not purport to be the official or authorised version. It is subject to Commonwealth of Australia copyright. The *Copyright Act 1968* permits certain reproduction and publication of Commonwealth legislation. In particular, s. 182A of the Act enables a complete copy to be made by or on behalf of a particular person. For reproduction or publication beyond that permitted by the Act, permission should be sought in writing from the Australian Government Publishing Service. Requests in the first instance should be addressed to the Manager, Commonwealth Information Services, Australian Government Publishing Service, GPO Box 84, Canberra ACT 2601.

Every effort has been made to trace the original source of all material reproduced in this book. Where the attempt has been unsuccessful, the authors and publisher would be pleased to hear from the copyright holder concerned to rectify any omission.

INDEX